STATISTICS FOR SOCIAL DATA ANALYSIS

Statistics for Social Data Analysis

Fourth Edition

David Knoke
University of Minnesota

George W. Bohrnstedt
American Institutes for Research

Alisa Potter Mee
Concordia University

F. E. Peacock Publishers
Itasca, Illinois 60143

For our teachers, Edgar F. Borgatta and David R. Segal

Cover illustration: Erich Lessing/Art Resource, NY/ARS, NY
© 2002 Artists Rights Society (ARS), New York/ADAGP, Paris

Copyright © 2002

F. E. Peacock Publishers, Inc.

Library of Congress Catalog Card No. 2002102712

ISBN 0-87581-448-4

10   9   8   7   6   5   4   3   2   1

07   06   05   04   03   02

ABBREVIATED CONTENTS

CONTENTS

PREFACE

The fourth edition of *Statistics for Social Data Analysis* blends continuity and change. Structurally, the book preserves the chapter organization of the third edition. At the same time, it benefits from the contributions of a new co-author, Alisa Potter Mee, who brings the freshness and enthusiasm of a new generation of social researchers who grew up on previous editions of this text.

As in previous editions, we continue to emphasize how analysts apply statistical methods to answer research questions in a variety of substantive fields. Hence, we constantly underscore the importance of formulating substantive hypotheses as the essential prelude to undertaking quantitative data analyses. We also stress the desirability of estimating intervals within which population parameters may occur, and of measuring the magnitudes of associations between variables. We believe this approach offers students superior insights into the ways that social scientists are actually conducting research today, as opposed to older conventions involving hypothesis tests about point estimates.

At least four distinctive features characterize this book. First, we focus on the *continuous-discrete distinction* when considering the level at which a variable is measured. Second, we emphasize the importance of establishing whether meaningful *substantive relationships* exist between and among variables. Third, we use *real data in examples* whenever possible. Finally, we provide students with the *opportunity to analyze a real survey dataset*, the 1998 General Social Survey, using the Statistical Package for the Social Sciences (SPSS).[1]

---

[1]SPSS is a trademark of SPSS Inc. of Chicago, IL, for its proprietary computer software. No materials describing such software may be produced or distributed without the written permission of SPSS Inc.

We abstain from the four conventional levels-of-measurement distinctions (nominal, ordinal, interval, and ratio) that continue to prevail in many other texts. Instead, we discuss statistics for analyzing continuous and discrete variables separately and in combination. Although debates continue in the social science methodology journals about the best choices among statistical techniques, even a cursory examination of the leading journals indicates that the continuous-discrete distinction is widely applied by current practitioners. Most researchers use either covariational techniques (variations of the general linear model) or analyses of crosstabulated categoric variables. The fundamentals of both approaches are well represented in this volume.

Many statistics texts begin with univariate statistics, followed by chapters on inference and hypothesis testing, before finally examining bivariate and multivariate relationships. As a result, for most of a semester the student may not realize that scientists are rarely, if ever, interested in describing and making inferences about a single variable. For this reason we make special efforts to explain to the student that social scientists seek to establish relationships between and among variables. We begin this emphasis in the first chapter, in which we describe the research process in general, and reiterate it throughout the book. Even chapter 2, which involves frequency distributions and their description, explains that social scientists are rarely interested in a single frequency distribution and its description (e.g., its mean and standard deviation).

We use real datasets for most examples. Our purpose is to show how the substance of social science is tied to statistics in the research cycle, rather than focusing solely on techniques. By studying propositions and hypotheses, together with methods for evaluating them, the student learns to appreciate the entire research process.

Our hands-on approach emphasizes analyzing realistic examples. We designed many of the end-of-chapter problems to require only pencil and paper or a hand-held calculator to find a solution, while other problems allow students to analyze the substantively diverse 1998 General Social Survey with computers. This combination permits the student to learn the step-by-step computations needed for calculating each statistic, and also to experience the excitement and frustration of testing hunches and hypotheses with real data.

We extracted the 1998 General Social Survey as a stand-alone SPSS file for use in a personal computer. A portable version of this file can be downloaded from Knoke's homepage at <http://www.soc.umn.edu/~knoke/>. Click "COURSES" and then "BASIC SOCIAL STATISTICS (SOC3811)" to find its location. After downloading the "GSS1998.zip" file to your PC, open it using WinZip. Our *Instructor's Manual*, available from the publisher at <http://www.fepeacock.com/>, describes how to import the file with your SPSS program and save the dataset for further analyses. The manual provides basic instruction in using SPSS data manipulation and analysis programs. It also includes SPSS commands for all chapter problems, as well as a bank of examination questions for each chapter.

Other special features of the book should facilitate student mastery of social statistics. We avoid excessive proofs and theorems, relegating many to boxes set off from the main text. All key concepts introduced in the text are also defined in the margins. This feature not only underscores key concepts but enables students to review them quickly. A list of key concepts and statistical symbols appears at the end of each chapter, in order of presentation in the text, to indicate the material the student should have mastered while studying the chapter. A glossary at the end of the book contains an alphabetical list of all key terms and their definitions. Thus, students can easily find key concept definitions or statistical symbols without having to hunt for their original locations.

Implicit in this book is our enduring conviction that successful social statistics teaching must foster cooperative learning. We do not believe that cooperation precludes constructive criticism, however. Over the years, we have been gratified to receive numerous comments and suggestions from instructors and students who have identified errors and problems, and who have proposed remedies and alternatives that have enhanced the text's accessibility and usefulness. We are hopeful that users of the current edition will help us continue this tradition. Please e-mail your suggestions to David Knoke at <knoke@atlas.socsci.umn.edu >.

We are indebted to A. Hald for permission to reprint the Area Under the Normal Curve and E. S. Pearson and H. O. Hartley for the *F*-Distribution Table. We are also grateful to the literary executor of the late Ronald A. Fisher, F. R. S., to Dr. Frank Yates, F. R. S., and to the Longman Group Ltd. of London, for permission to reprint Tables III and IV from the sixth edition of their book *Statistical Tables for Biological, Agricultural and Medical Research*, published in 1974.

We acknowledge permission from SPSS Inc. to use their software package SPSS™ throughout the book to illustrate how to analyze survey data with the help of a computer. We also acknowledge the National Opinion Research Center and the Inter-University Consortium for Political and Social Research for collecting and distributing the General Social Surveys.

We are grateful for the fine editorial and production help provided by F. E. Peacock Publishers. We also thank Karl Krohn for assistance with data preparation. We thank our publisher, Ted Peacock, and our editor, Richard Welna, for their steadfast encouragement over the years.

Finally, we thank our spouses and children for their continuing support.

David Knoke
George W. Bohrnstedt
Alisa Potter Mee

I. Basic Concepts and Measures

1

STATISTICS IN THE RESEARCH PROCESS

Our emphasis throughout this book is on how to use statistics as a tool to analyze social data. Statistical methods assist us to answer substantive questions about social relations, whether the primary motivation comes from theoretical issues or from practical concerns. Our central interest is in reducing uncertainty, or put more positively, increasing knowledge about how humans behave in a variety of social situations. As a general principle, we believe that explaining variation is the central task shared by all social scientists: How do people, groups, communities, or nations differ from one another, and what are the consequences of such variation? The particular behaviors to be explained may differ from discipline to discipline and from researcher to researcher, but the general approach remains universal. All social and behavioral scientists seek to account for the differences they observe among people, groups, and organizations by examining the patterns of variation in their characteristics, activities, and attitudes.

For example, can we explain differences in the annual incomes that people earn by measuring their differences in years of education, work experience, supervisory responsibilities, and work ethics? Or should we also take into consideration their companies' market positions, union bargaining contracts, and racial and sex discrimination practices? As another example, can we understand why some people vote for the Republican presidential candidate, others for the Democrat, and others stay home on Election Day? Are different electoral behaviors attributable to variation in voters' attitudes towards the candidates, the political parties, and the election issues, as well as to their own social group memberships? If so, which factors are most important in shaping voters' decisions? The large and sophisticated body of statistical techniques available to social researchers offers a variety of ways to answer such questions. Properly and cautiously applied, social statistics can permit researchers to reach tentative conclusions about the existence and strength of social relationships.

Our approach to statistics stems directly from a conviction that adequately explaining any human behavior is equivalent to showing how variations in that behavior are related to multiple, measured causes. As a tool, statistical analysis occupies a key position within the larger set of activities that make up the social research process. Although every research project follows a unique course, there are enough similarities to let us describe this process as a succession of steps from initial design through final conclusion.

1. Researchers formulate what are often initially vague ideas into more concrete, researchable problems.

2. The relations among abstract concepts are translated into rigorous hypotheses containing variables that can be measured.

3. Instruments are created, borrowed, or adapted that measure the variables specified by the research hypotheses.

4. Observations on a representatively selected sample of social units (e.g., persons, organizations, communities) are systematically recorded.

5. Observational data are reduced to a set of numbers and entered into a storage device, typically a personal computer, for later analysis.

6. Appropriate statistical methods are applied to key variables in the data set to determine whether evidence can be garnered in support of the hypothesized relations.

7. The researcher reaches a conclusion about the relative importance of the sources of variation initially believed to explain the social phenomena of interest. The typical result is an incremental improvement in our collective understanding of the social worlds in which we live.

This chapter fills in some details of the social research process. Because social statistics is an integral part of that process, the subject cannot be studied in isolation from the larger issues of hypothesis formation, operationalization, sampling, and measurement. These issues will rise again and again as you proceed through this book and learn the variety of statistical techniques available to the modern social researcher. Nothing can substitute for a thorough grasp of the larger research enterprise in which statistical methods play a central role. To help you acquire a feel for the research experience, we illustrate statistical procedures with many examples taken from the 1998 General Social Survey, described in Box 1.1. Moreover, at the end of every chapter, we provide problems that ask you to apply your newly gained knowledge of social statistics. Ultimately, our desire is for students to acquire sufficient statistical skill to design and carry out their own projects. The most rewarding (although sometimes frustrating!) way to comprehend the beauty of social research is to grapple directly with the numerous dilemmas and decisions that researchers must confront and resolve at every step in the research cycle.

1.1 Ideas into Research Projects

Scientific research is the effort to reduce uncertainty about some aspect of the world by systematically examining the relationships among its parts. Every research project builds on the current state of knowledge while seeking to extend understanding into previously unknown areas. If inquiry were simply confined to demonstrating again what is already known, it could not be called research. Scientific activity differs from other types of scholarship—such as philosophy, theology, literature, and even pure mathematics—by insisting that its explanations be limited to the real world of observable objects. The existence of the soul, the number of angels that can dance on a pinhead, and the essence of the good are all questions of faith and assumption, irrelevant to the conduct of scientific inquiry. In other words, research restricts itself to aspects of the empirical world whose properties can be verified through observation and manipulation. In the sense that the state of reality ultimately defines what information a researcher can learn, the laboratory experiment of a chemist differs little from the consumer attitude survey of a market analyst.

Given that all science continually seeks to improve its explanations of observable phenomena, where do the ideas for research projects come from? At any time, disciplinary specialists stake out particular topics as ripe for debate and analysis. For example, some recent vogues in sociology include organizational births and deaths, the origins of the welfare state, the ecological concentration of the urban underclass, the role of biological maturation in shaping the life course, and the relationship of age

scientific research—the effort to reduce uncertainty about some aspect of the world by systematically examining the relationships among its parts

Box 1.1   General Social Survey Samples

The GSS (General Social Survey) is a regular, ongoing omnibus personal interview survey of U.S. households, conducted by the National Opinion Research Center (NORC) with James A. Davis, Tom W. Smith, and Peter V. Marsden serving as Principal Investigators and advice provided by a Board of Overseers. The basic purposes of the GSS are to gather data on contemporary American society in order to monitor and explain trends and constants in attitudes, behaviors, and attributes; to examine the structure and functioning of society in general as well as the role played by relevant subgroups; to compare the United States to other societies in order to place American society in comparative perspective and develop cross-national models of human society; and to make high-quality data easily accessible to scholars, students, policy makers, and others, with minimal cost and waiting.

The first GSS took place in 1972, and since then 38,000 respondents have answered more than 3,260 different questions in 23 independent cross-sectional surveys of the adult household population of the United States. Previously an annual survey, the program switched to biennial with double GSSs in 1994. The GSS is the largest sociology project funded by the National Science Foundation (NSF) and has frequently been described as a national resource. Its use by sociologists is second only to the U.S. Census. NORC has documented the publication of thousands of journal articles and books analyzing the data.

The GSS pools all surveys into one cumulative database, facilitating the analysis of time trends and the examination of subgroups. The questionnaires contain a standard core of demographic and attitudinal variables, plus certain topics of special interest selected for rotation (called "topical modules"). The exact wording of many GSS items is retained to facilitate time trend studies as well as replications of earlier findings. Replicated topics include national spending priorities, drinking behavior, marijuana use, crime and punishment, race relations, quality of life, confidence in institutions, and membership in voluntary associations.

(continued)

On-line information about the GSS, including searchable files of all questions and a bibliography of previous publications, is available at the General Social Survey Data and Information Retrieval System (GSSDIRS) web site: http://www.icpsr.umich.edu/GSS/

The 1998 GSS analyzed in this book has 2,832 cases, a double sample size; in effect, the 1998 GSS was fielded as two GSSs administered simultaneously. Both samples were further divided into three "ballots," each using a slightly different version of the questionnaire, containing "modules" of special topics. For example, in addition to core items asked of all respondents, one subset of respondents was asked about medical ethics, while another subset was asked about religious beliefs and activities. No GSSs were conducted in 1999 and 2001, but the 2000 and 2002 surveys were also double GSSs.

Although the GSS uses a complex sampling procedure that violates simple random sampling assumptions, the principal investigators advise applying statistical tests in the conventional manner. Because our main use of the 1998 GSS is to illustrate how social statistics can be applied to large data sets, we apply the various statistical tests without modification.

---

to criminal activity. Within each topical specialty, an active community of research scholars (which may be scattered across international boundaries) communicates its current findings, new ideas, and proposals for new research projects through a variety of media: journal publications, conferences, working papers, guest lectures, retreats, electronic bulletin boards, list servers, and foundation review panels. From this constant flood of information, both established and novice researchers can extract suggestions for further investigations that could lead to new insights about phenomena of interest.

Some research projects are generated by practical concerns about the impact or effectiveness of specific social programs and public policies. **Applied research** attempts to explain social phenomena with immediate public policy implications. For example, does the Head Start preschool program increase the scholastic performance of children living in poverty? How can drug addicts be persuaded to stop sharing needles that spread

applied research— research that attempts to explain social phenomena with immediate public policy implications

AIDS? Can the error rates of airline pilots be reduced by redesigning instrumental panel layouts? Do work-release experiences and halfway houses lower recidivism among former prisoners? Policymakers and administrators who grapple daily with serious social problems urgently need answers to such questions. They demand practical solutions based on the application of social science knowledge. Many applied research projects are initiated by state and federal funding agencies through "requests for proposals" (RFPs) that strictly specify the design and analysis requirements that must be met by the applicants. Whether the project findings have relevance beyond the confines of a particular study generally has little importance for funders and principal investigators.

Other research projects arise primarily from investigators' theoretical interests, without concern for immediate applications of the results. Rather, **basic research** examines the validity of general statements about relationships involving fundamental social processes. Basic researchers develop knowledge about general principles of social behavior that may account for a wide range of specific activities. For example, is the division of household labor between husbands and wives best conceptualized as an exchange process or as a symbolic interaction involving self-conceptualizations? Do neo-Marxist ideas of capitalist exploitation of labor better predict corporate job-training practices than neoclassical economists' notions of human capital formation? Are voters' presidential choices influenced mainly by mass media messages or by their local social networks? In answering these questions, researchers mainly strive to verify or disprove assertions embedded in general theories of human behavior, even if the practical policy implications are not obvious. Indeed, the ability to illustrate abstract analytic relations is typically the project's primary aim. Basic research projects are usually initiated by academic investigators who have devoted a substantial portion of their careers to mastering a specific theoretical background. The National Science Foundation, a federal agency whose mission is to support all sciences, is a major funding source for basic social science research in the United States. It seldom solicits proposals but relies on investigator-initiated proposals for research grants, which are then evaluated and approved by "peer review" panels of senior scientists who consider each proposal's basic scientific merits. Other federal agencies that fund basic social research, in specific areas, include the National Institute of Mental Health, National Institute for Drug Abuse, and the National Institute on Aging.

Whether applied or basic research motivations drive a project, a researcher's primary goal is to account accurately for the observed variation in the phenomena under investigation. In practice, reaching this goal requires the researcher to identify the major factors creating differences

basic research—research that examines the validity of general statements about relationships involving fundamental social processes among the persons, objects, or events of interest. For example, in an applied study of why some elderly people require nursing home care and others are able to remain in their own homes, an investigator would want to include factors such as the individual's physical health and mobility, mental alertness, retirement income and savings, care-providing relatives, availability of a personal automobile or mass transit, and vacancy rates in nursing homes. Or, to explain participation in social movement protests, a basic researcher ought to consider factors such as potential participants' benefit-harm calculations, distributive justice and equity norms, public good valuations, solidarity of social attachments, perceptions of probable state repression, and so forth. The key point is that almost all social behaviors are caused by many factors with differing impacts. (Basic features of causal analysis are discussed in detail in chapter 11.) These diverse causes must be explicitly included in the analysis if we are to produce an accurate account of the sources of variation. The process of examining the causes of social behaviors begins with specifying testable hypotheses, as described in the following section.

1.2   Concepts into Propositions

The core component of a social research project is a formal **proposition**, a statement about the relationship between abstract concepts. Many propositions take an implied "If …, then …" format, where the element in the first clause is usually assumed to be a cause of the element in the second clause. For example, a common proposition in organizational research, numbered here for reference, is

proposition—a statement about the relationship between abstract concepts

P1:   The more centralized the decision making, the lower the employee commitment to the organization.

Based on personal experience, many employees feel that this proposition states a plausible causal relationship between these two concepts, at least in modern industrial societies. Certainly, we would doubt the truth of a statement relating centralized decision making to higher commitment to the organization. But what, exactly, do the concepts "decision making" and "employee commitment" represent? A **concept** entails a precisely defined object, behavior, perception (of self or others), or phenomenon that is relevant to the particular theoretical concerns at hand. Thus, the full meaning of proposition P1 requires definitions of these two abstract concepts, which are not to be confused with their meanings in everyday language.

concept—a precisely defined object, behavior, perception (of self or others), or phenomenon that is relevant to the particular theoretical concerns at hand

Concepts are usually defined according to meanings of the term that are already widely accepted by the scientific audience with whom one wishes to communicate. Definitions generally consist of lists of attributes or characteristics that are necessary and sufficient for a particular real entity to qualify unambiguously as an instance of the concept. Thus, an organizational researcher might define "centralized decision making" as "the ratio of supervisors to workers choosing among alternative actions affecting organizational performance." The concept of "employee commitment" could be defined as "expressed intentions to continue as an employee of an organization." Other definitions may offer narrower and more precise criteria that are better suited to a particular research project. Much of the debate in social theory centers on the most appropriate way to define abstract concepts.

social theory—a set of two or more propositions in which concepts referring to certain social phenomena are assumed to be causally related

When a sequence of propositions is connected through common concepts, the resulting set may compose a social theory for research purposes. More formally, a **social theory** is a set of two or more propositions in which concepts referring to certain social phenomena are assumed to be causally related. To continue the organizational example, a second proposition may be stated as follows:

P2: The lower the employee commitment to the organization, the higher the rate of job turnover.

To make P2 fully comprehensible, we would need a formal definition of the "job turnover" concept, presumably one emphasizing vacancies due to employee decisions rather than actions by the firm (i.e., quitting a job rather than being laid off or fired). To produce a minimal social theory, P1 can be linked to P2 through the common concept of "employee commitment." The following logical deduction brings together the unique concepts of both propositions:

P3: The more centralized the decision making, the higher the rate of job turnover.

Again, our commonsense notions of these terms suggest that this relationship can be supported by personal experiences. A more elaborate theory of alienation in formal organizations might be constructed by adding propositions that causally link the three concepts to others, such as employee earnings and organizational values.

linearity—the amount of change (increase or decrease) in one concept caused by a change in another concept is constant across its range

These three propositions stated did not state the explicit forms of their relationships. In the absence of contrary assertions, **linearity** is typically assumed. That is, the amount of change (increase or decrease) in one concept caused by a change in another concept is constant across its range. The linearity assumption is widespread in the social sciences, where nonlinear conceptualization (e.g., exponential, power, and logarithmic curves) have not penetrated into theoretical thinking. An extended discussion of the plausibility of linear relations and their application to statistical techniques is provided in section 1.7.

Very few theoretical propositions claim to be true at all times and places without exception. Most are created to explain observed variations in fairly restricted circumstances, although subsequent research may show them to have broader applications. Nevertheless, during their initial stages of development and testing, theories should identify the **scope** or **boundary conditions**—the times, places, or activities—under which their propositions are expected to be valid. For example, a theoretical proposition about fathers' roles in socializing their male children may be irrelevant to societies in which the mother's brother takes over many of these functions. In another example, the importance of social network ties for occupational mobility may differ greatly in market, state socialist, and pre-capitalist economies. By specifying the apparent limits of their propositions, theorists can help researchers to avoid unsuitable tests as well as to probe the boundaries of situations to which theories may apply.

scope/boundary conditions—the times, places, or activities under which the propositions of a social theory are expected to be valid

1.3 Variables into Hypotheses

The term **variable** refers to any characteristic or attribute of persons, objects, or events that can take on different numerical values. Thus, the number of people quitting their jobs in a given month may range from zero to the entire workforce. As we will demonstrate, variables can be classified in several ways. One of the most important ways is to distinguish between latent and manifest variables. **Latent variables** are not observable and can be measured only indirectly. Examples of latent variables include concepts such as the degree of centralization in decision making and the degree of employee commitment—concepts used in the propositions discussed in section 1.2. **Manifest variables**, logically enough, can be observed. Examples of manifest variables include the ratio of supervisors to line workers and the number of absences an organization has per month, i.e., phenomena that can be directly observed and counted.

variable—any characteristic or attribute of persons, objects, or events that can take on different numerical values

latent variable—a variable that cannot be observed and can only be measured indirectly

manifest variable—a variable that can be observed

Theoretical propositions are necessarily stated in abstract terms, using concepts that cannot be directly observed. This analytic abstraction makes it possible for theories to apply to a wide range of empirical occurrences. To be useful for scientific research, therefore, the concepts must be restated in terms that allow measurement and testing of relationships. In

operational hypothesis— a proposition restated with observable, concrete referents or terms replacing abstract concepts

effect, propositions are translated into **operational hypotheses** by replacing the abstract concepts with observable, concrete referents or terms (operationalizing the concepts). For example, P1 can be turned into H1 by substituting for both concepts:

> H1: The larger the number of task assignments made only by supervisors, the lower the percentage of workers expressing desires to continue working for the organization.

Centralization is operationalized by the number of task assignments made exclusively by supervisors, and employee commitment is operationalized by verbal expressions of desires to continue their employment. Similarly, if we substitute "voluntary job quits per month" for the abstract concept "rate of job turnover," P2 can be rewritten as H2:

> H2: The lower the percentage of workers expressing desires to continue working for the organization, the greater the number of voluntary job quits per month.

In each instance, a concept was replaced by an indicator that, in principle, can be observed for a set of social units—in this example, work organizations. That is, latent concepts or variables are replaced with manifest variables.

constant—a value that does not change

A variable can be contrasted to a **constant** that has an unchanging value. "State of residence" is a variable because it differs across the U.S. population, but "Minnesota" is a constant that is invariant for all persons living there. Note that constants may be the values composing a variable: "male" and "female" are constants for individuals that constitute the variable *gender*.

independent variable— a variable that has an antecedent or causal role, usually appearing first in the hypothesis

dependent variable— a variable that has a consequent, or affected, role in relation to the independent variable

Variables can also be classified by the roles they play in a hypothesis that states or implies a causal relationship. An **independent variable** has an antecedent or causal role, usually appearing first in the hypothesis. The **dependent variable** plays a consequent, or affected, role in relation to the independent variable. That is, its values depend on the values taken by the independent variable. It usually comes second in the hypothesis. No ambiguity is present in a statement such as "An increase in unemployment causes a decrease in consumer confidence." Note that some variables may be both independent and dependent variables, even within the same theory. Workers' expressed desires to continue working for the organization is a dependent variable in H1 and an independent variable in H2. The distinguishing criterion is whether changes in a variable produce changes in the values of other variables or whether changes in a variable are produced by changes in other variables.

Some variables cannot be manipulated; they are called **status variables**. Examples include race, gender, and, for most people, religious affiliation. Even though status variables cannot be manipulated, they nevertheless are often treated as independent variables in researchers' propositions and hypotheses. The outcomes associated with status variables are not usually believed to occur through causal processes. Instead, they are assumed to be noncausal associations that must be explained by other variables. Observed associations involving status variables are very important in social and behavioral research because they stimulate researchers to search for causal processes that can explain these relationships. For example, the observation that African Americans and Latinos on average have lower incomes than Asian Americans and Caucasians is a noncausal association, but this observation should stimulate researchers to identify causal variables that explain racial differences in incomes (e.g., education, values, family structures, discrimination in hiring and promotions).

status variable—a variable whose outcomes cannot be manipulated

When researchers translate theoretical propositions into operational hypotheses, care must be taken to preserve a fairly rigorous correspondence between the latent and observed variables. Too loose a fit between both systems can result in empirical tests using indicators that have little relevance to the ideas motivating the research project. A variable's **validity** refers to the degree to which its operationalization accurately reflects the concept it is intended to measure. For example, the abstract concept *attitude towards sexual permissiveness* would appear much better operationalized by asking people whether they agree that "the only moral standard of sexual conduct is found in the Bible" than by inquiring, "How many different sex partners did you have in the past year?" The former measure is attitudinal, but the latter is behavioral. Researchers should strive to create the strongest possible **epistemic relationship** connecting abstract concepts to operational variables, so that results of empirical tests will permit meaningful conclusions about the theoretical propositions. Weak linkages between concepts and variables render the empirical findings ambiguous as a test of the theory. More detailed discussions of how to establish validity can be found in various research methodology textbooks.

validity—the degree to which a variable's operationalization accurately reflects the concept it is intended to measure

epistemic relationship—the relationship between abstract, theoretical (unobserved) concepts and their corresponding operational (observed) measurements

A closely related consideration in selecting appropriate variables for operational hypotheses is whether they are reliable indicators of the intended concepts. **Reliability** refers to the extent to which different operationalizations of the same concept produce consistent results. High

reliability—the extent to which different operationalizations of the same concept produce consistent results

reliability means that two procedures yield the same outcome, or the same procedure reapplied over time shows high agreement. For example, we could alternatively operationalize the concept *industrialization* with variables at the national level such as "kilowatt hours of electricity per capita" and "proportion of gross national product in manufacturing." These two measures tend to rank the same countries as high or low and can thus be judged highly reliable measures of industrialization. By contrast, few social scientists would argue that "frequency of church attendance" and "tons of wheat harvested" are reliable indicators of industrialization. Most methodology texts also extensively discuss ways to assess measurement reliability.

Recent years have seen the rapid development of statistical techniques that combine both unobserved concepts and observed variables into a unified framework. These methods permit simultaneous estimation of both the causal relationships among concepts and the epistemic relationships connecting variables to concepts. We will examine some of these procedures in chapter 12.

1.4 Observations into Records

After researchers have translated their theoretical propositions into research hypotheses involving variables, they next apply procedures to make the observations necessary for determining how well the data fit the hypotheses. The general term **data collection** applies to all manner of activities by which researchers construct a project's primary data records. Although some projects actually involve prolonged periods in natural settings (such as participant observation in communities or household personal interviews), for many researchers the data collection period consists of short, intense bursts of work in confined settings: experimental manipulations in human subjects laboratories, telephone interviews, mail questionnaires, computer simulations, content analyses of historical documents, and transcriptions of verbal exchanges. Each data collection method involves complex routines with unique requirements and limitations. These issues can be fully addressed only in texts devoted to examining the nuances of various research methodologies.

A common concern for all researchers is the selection of objects for observation, or **units of analysis**. Depending on how the research hypotheses are stated, the level of social phenomena from which data are to be collected may range from nations to communities to groups to individuals and on down to highly specific actions such as conversational greetings. The entire set of persons, objects, or events that has at least one

data collection—the activity of constructing primary data records for a given sample or population of observations

unit of analysis—an object for observation

common characteristic of interest to a researcher constitutes the **population** under investigation. Except for censuses that attempt to collect data from every unit in a population, observations can usually be made only on a **sample**—a subset of cases or elements selected from the population. Time and money constraints typically prevent researchers from enumerating and investigating the entire population. Properly conducted sampling procedures can, however, ensure cost-efficient conclusions that correctly reflect what is going on in the population.

The key to drawing a good sample is **representativeness**—choosing units of analysis whose characteristics accurately reflect the larger population from which the sample was selected. A representative sample is critical for statistical data analysis because many tests allow a researcher to generalize findings about samples to the parent population only if the probability of a unit's selection is known. The only way to guarantee representativeness is to draw a **random sample** of units from a list that completely enumerates all members of the population. Each population unit has an equal chance of being included in the sample. The actual choices are made either by a "simple random selection" of every sample element (typically using a table of random numbers or a "random number generator" computer routine) or by a "systematic random selection" that takes every kth case from the list beginning with a randomly chosen start. When k is small, the sample will be larger, and vice versa. For example, in a state university of 30,000 students, selecting every 50th case produces a sample of 600 students, while setting $k = 200$ yields a sample of only 150 cases. An investigator can choose a sample size—the number of cases to be selected (which also determines the **systematic sampling interval** width, k)—according to the required accuracy of statistical estimates, as discussed in chapter 3.

When complete population listings are either not available or too costly to create, more complicated sampling procedures can be used to try to ensure representativeness. Details of these methods are available in specialized textbooks. Because the statistics discussed in this book assume simple random samples, we will not bother to describe these other sampling designs. Instead, we will simply assume that the distortions created by treating complex samples as though they were generated by simple random sampling are minimal, as noted in Box 1.1.

Whenever living human beings are the subjects of social and medical research, questions of ethical treatment must be answered before proceeding with data collection. Research funding agencies usually require prior approval of investigators' plans for protecting their subjects' integrity before they will release grants. Most universities maintain internal human subjects committees, composed of diverse faculty members who certify

population—the entire set of persons, objects, or events that has at least one common characteristic of interest to a researcher

sample—a subset of cases or elements selected from a population

representativeness—the selection of units of analysis whose characteristics accurately stand for the larger population from which the sample was drawn

random sample—a sample whose cases or elements are selected at random from a population

systematic sampling interval—the number of cases between sample elements in a list used for a systematic random sample

that proposals pass muster. Many professional societies also have formal codes of research ethics to which they encourage their members to adhere. These criteria typically include no risk of harm to subjects (physical or psychological); informed consent to participate, especially from underage or mentally impaired subjects; confidential protection of subjects' identities from parties outside the project; and responsible representation of research findings. Social researchers have an obligation to put the well-being of those whom they study ahead of whatever personal or disciplinary benefits the project may produce. Abuse and fraud in social research can destroy the fragile trust and credibility that scientists must preserve with the society that supports their activities.

1.5   Data into Numbers

measurement—the process of assigning numbers to observations according to a set of rules

The process of assigning numbers to observations according to a set of rules is **measurement**. Often the numerical codes for each variable have been set up long before the first interview or content analyses begin. For example, a Gallup poll question—"How well is the President doing his job?"—has used a standard four-category response for sixty years: 1 = Poor, 2 = Fair, 3 = Good, and 4 = Excellent. For such forced-response items, coding merely requires transferring the number on the interview schedule into a storage device, typically directly onto a computer file. Other types of field records, particularly historical documents and verbal transcripts but also open-ended survey questions, require more elaborate coding procedures to extract information and reduce it to numerical values. Sometimes the coding categories can be anticipated in advance of data collection, but more often the codes are inductively generated in the process of examining each case. New categories are created and assigned unique numbers as different responses are encountered. Some variables may have dozens or hundreds of categories, depending on how varied the sample's responses are and how much detail the investigator wishes to preserve.

missing data—no meaningful information for a given observation on a particular variable

A special problem experienced in every data collection is **missing data**. With few exceptions, all projects encounter cases from which no meaningful information for a particular variable is forthcoming. Some items are skipped because they do not apply to a given subject, such as asking a single person how happy she is with her marriage. Sometimes a subject refuses to answer a very personal question, such as his annual income or whether she has ever had an abortion. Another subject simply may not know the answer to a difficult question, such as her maternal grandfather's occupation when her mother was 16 years old. Occasionally, a field worker fails to record information properly and a call-back proves impossible. To cover such instances, special codes must be designated to indicate the data values that are missing. Sometimes several missing values should be created for a given variable; for example, one might use 8 = Doesn't Know, 9 = No Answer, –1 = Refused to Answer, 0 = Inappropriate Question (Skipped). Missing data codes enable analysts to omit these cases from later statistical analyses.

The end result of coding is to assign a unique value to every case for each variable. In other words, good coding schemes must be **mutually exclusive** (each observation receives one and only one code on a given variable) and **exhaustive** (every case must receive a code for each variable, even if only a missing value can be assigned). Coding instructions that allow more than one numerical value to be assigned to a particular case for a given variable violate the mutual exclusivity criterion. For example, when ethnic origins are measured, a code of "1" for "Chinese" and "2" for "Asian" is clearly flawed; the analyst must decide whether countries or continents are desired. Note that if greater detail is initially recorded, variables may be later **recoded** to produce grosser classifications. Thus, Chinese, Japanese, Korean, Indian, Vietnamese and other nationalities could be collapsed into a single "Asian origin" category. By contrast, if only the broader measure "Asian" is initially recorded, recovering the finer detail will be impossible.

The coding process produces two products: the **codebook**, a complete record of all coding decisions, and a **data file** containing the entire set of numerical values for each variable for every case. A codebook should report information about the sampling and field operations, including interviewer and coder instructions; verbatim question wording for every variable; numerical codes of all valid responses and missing data; column locations of each item in the data file; and other miscellaneous information likely to be useful to future users. A codebook usually exists physically on printed pages and often is also stored as a machine-readable file on a computer diskette or tape that can be distributed together with the data file. The data file itself initially consists of a rectangular array of numbers. Each line (row) in the array contains all the information for a particular case. For example, a survey with $N = 2,832$ respondents will have a data file with 2,832 lines. Each column in the array contains the numerical codes of a specific variable for the N cases. (Such formats are still sometimes called "card image records," in reference to a bygone era when data were physically stored as holes punched into 80-column cards.)

Most data files are stored today as **system files** created by computer software packages such as SPSS, SAS, or STATA. A system file contains

mutually exclusive—each observation must receive one and only one code on a given variable

exhaustive—every case must receive a code for each variable, even if only a missing value can be assigned

recode—the process of changing the codes established for a variable

codebook—a complete record of all coding decisions

data file—the entire set of numerical values for each variable for every case

system file—a data file created by a computer software statistics package

not only the numerical records but also the names of every variable, their value labels, and the missing data codes. Such files can be accessed directly by the statistical and data management programs in the package, saving substantial time when the data are analyzed repeatedly. For our use in writing this book, we extracted and stored the 1998 General Social Survey file as SPSS exportable system files for the personal computer. As Box 1.1 indicates, these data are available for your use if you have access to the SPSS package either on personal or mainframe computer. Box 1.2 provides more information about the SPSS package.

A final task in data set preparation is dissemination to the wider community. Most federally funded projects require that data collected with taxpayer funds ultimately become publicly available. Various archiving services, such as the Interuniversity Consortium for Political and Social Research (ICPSR) at Ann Arbor, MI, and the Roper Center at Storrs, CT, receive numerous data files from projects around the world. These files are archived and cataloged for eventual redistribution to secondary users. We obtained the 1998 GSS from one of these archives.

1.6 Statistical Analysis

With a data set in hand, the researcher can now begin statistical analyses to test the operational hypotheses. How do we choose the most appropriate statistical procedures for particular measures and hypotheses? We will cover this topic extensively throughout the remainder of this book. The basic principle is to select procedures that retain the maximum amount of information available in the data. An important consideration is

discrete variable— a variable that classifies persons, objects, or events according to the kind or quality of their attributes

nonorderable discrete variable— a discrete measure in which the sequence of categories cannot be meaningfully ordered

orderable discrete variable— a discrete measure that can be meaningfully arranged into an ascending or descending sequence

whether the variables to be analyzed are discrete or continuous measures, because certain types of analyses are suitable only to particular kinds of variables. Thus, log-linear models (chapter 10) require discrete variables, regression analysis (chapter 6) uses primarily continuous measures, and analysis of covariance (chapter 8) combines both types.

A **discrete variable** classifies persons, objects, or events according to the kind or quality of their attributes. A small number of distinct categories contain all the cases, including a separate category for the cases with missing values. For example, U.S. citizens could be classified into four regions, "North," "South," "East," and "West," with a fifth category "Other" for persons living in the territories and overseas. No intrinsic order from high to low can be imposed on these labels, so the variable is **nonorderable discrete**. If the categories can be meaningfully arranged into an ascending or descending sequence, however, then it is an **orderable discrete variable**. Many attitude variables take such

---

Box 1.2   SPSS—Statistical Package for the Social Sciences

Over the past four decades, SPSS computer software programs have become some of the most comprehensive and widely available data management and analysis packages. All statistical tests described in this book can be done on the personal computer using such SPSS routines as FREQUENCIES, MEANS, CROSSTABS, ANOVA, CORRELATION, REGRESSION, and LOGISTIC REGRESSION. Because of its simplified syntax in a Windows version, SPSS is easy to learn and apply, requiring about two hours of classroom instruction using the brief expository materials in the *Instructors' Manual* for this text. Consequently, we have built the examples and computer exercises in each chapter around SPSS analyses of the 1998 General Social Survey. This dataset is available as a zipped SPSS exportable file [GSS98.POR] that can be downloaded from Knoke's home page <http://www.soc.umn.edu/~knoke/>. It can be unzipped and imported as an SPSS save file [GSS98.SAV], and then stored as a mainframe or personal computer file for students to use in homework and laboratory assignments.

---

form: for example, recording responses to statements in Likert-type scales such as "strongly agree," "agree," "neither agree nor disagree," "disagree," and "strongly disagree." Similarly, asking respondents for their self-placements as "upper, middle, working, or lower class" produces an ordered discrete measure. A special type of discrete variable is the **dichotomous variable**, which may either be ordered or not. A dichotomy (literally "two-cut") classifies cases into two mutually exclusive categories (exhaustiveness is assured by providing codes for missing values). Gender is a fundamentally nonorderable dichotomous variable: female and male are the only meaningful categories (assuming that hermaphrodites do not occur). An ordered dichotomy is exemplified by a supervisor-subordinate classification of employees.

dichotomous variable— a discrete measure with two categories that may or may not be ordered

In contrast to discrete measures, **continuous variables** can, at least in theory, take on all possible numerical values in a given interval. Social science measures lack the precision of natural sciences' instruments that can record time, weight, and length to millionths and billionths of a unit.

continuous variable— a variable that, in theory, can take on all possible numerical values in a given interval

Still, many variables contain large numbers of ordered categories that in principle represent points along an intended continuum. Most importantly, they can be treated as though they were continuous variables, for use in statistical analyses that require continuous measures. Age is a continuous variable, even though most projects record only the year of the respondent's last birthday. However, a child development study might record ages to the nearest month or even day. Other variables commonly treated as continuous are the number of years people attended school, the number of children ever born, occupational prestige, and annual earned income. If the units of analysis are not individuals but collectivities such as organizations, cities, or nations, many measures will have continuous properties: the number of employees, the average annual burglaries per 100,000 population, the percentage of substandard dwellings, and so forth.

You should be alert to a common practice by social scientists of treating many ordered discrete variables as continuous measures. Although agreement with attitude items offering five or seven response categories is technically a discrete ordered variable, an analyst can make use of very powerful statistical techniques by assuming that these categories have continuous properties. The rationale behind this assumption is that "strength of attitude" is fundamentally a continuous property that our measuring devices only crudely tap. Our major concern should be whether treating ordered categories as continuous will produce distorted conclusions from statistical analyses. So far, most evidence suggests that statistical techniques are fairly "robust" under such circumstances. The one clearly inappropriate treatment is the use of nonorderable discrete measures in analyses that require continuous variables. In no meaningful way can the code numbers for respondents' religious affiliations, states of residence, or preferred leisure activities be analyzed and interpreted as though they formed continuous measures.

scale construction—the creation of new variables from multiple items

In addition to analyzing single measures taken directly from data sets, new variables may be created using multiple items. **Scale construction** is often performed with attitude items that were designed to capture beliefs and opinions about a certain domain—for example, political alienation, marital happiness, or interracial tolerance. Interviewers typically present respondents with a "battery" of items tapping related facets of some unobserved attitude. The responses can be analyzed using techniques such as factor analysis, latent structure analysis, or Guttman scaling to determine whether they form a single-dimensional multi-item scale with high reliability. Most of these methods are beyond the scope of this book. However, the increasing importance of models combining measurement and structural relations requires that you learn some basics of the factor analytic approach. Chapter 12 provides a general introduction to these issues.

Statistical analysis consists of two broad branches with divergent aims. **Descriptive statistics** are concerned with summarizing the properties of a sample of observations. Chapter 2 presents many basic sample statistics for describing the typical values and the amount of variation in a variable's values. These summary statistics do not directly reveal much about the population from which the sample was drawn. For that purpose, **inferential statistics** apply the mathematical theory of probability to make decisions about the likely properties of populations based on sample evidence. An **inference** is a generalization or conclusion about some attribute of a population based on the data in a sample. If a sample is highly representative of the population, as random sampling assures, then inferences about the parent population can be made with a high level of confidence (although not with complete certainty). **Statistical significance tests** thus allow us to make statements about the probability that hypothesized relationships actually occur. We can decide to minimize the risk of being incorrect when making statements about a population on the basis of a particular sample's results. Further, as investigators in charge of the analysis, we can control the level of risk or error that we wish to incur when making such inferences from sample to population. Inferential statistics comprise the major portion of this text, beginning with chapter 3.

We view statistical significance testing as an adjunct to the most essential goal of social data analysis: estimating the strength of relationships among variables. A variable whose relationship with another is weak may be statistically significant only because a large sample size enables us to detect this marginal connection. For example, during the presidential elections of the 1980s, several analysts argued that a "gender gap" in voting existed, with men more likely than women to vote for Republican candidates. However, while a statistically significant difference did occur in some political opinion polls, the difference rarely amounted to more than 5%—certainly a very weak effect although perhaps enough to swing a tight race. To assess the magnitude of relations among variables, various statistical **measures of association** have been developed. In this book we will devote considerable attention to methods for measuring the size, direction, and strength of independent variables' effects on the variation in dependent measures.

By the end of statistical analysis, an investigator is usually in a good position to reach a conclusion about the propositions or informed hunches that originally motivated the project. Both the probabilistic decisions

descriptive statistics—statistics concerned with summarizing the properties of a sample of observations

inferential statistics—statistics that apply the mathematical theory of probability to make decisions about the likely properties of populations based on sample evidence

inference—a generalization or conclusion about some attribute of a population based on the data in a sample

statistical significance test—a test of inference that conclusions based on a sample of observations also hold true for the population from which the sample was selected

measures of association—statistics that show the direction and/or magnitude of a relationship between variables

regarding the operational hypotheses and the measures of strengths of relationships among causal variables should reveal whether the results challenge or support previous knowledge about some social phenomenon. The conventional strategy is to assume that the current state of knowledge is correct unless compelling evidence indicates the falsity of those claims. This requirement of disproof is a conservative stance that places the burden on challengers to show where and how prior beliefs are incorrect. A theory whose propositions have withstood many attempts to refute them holds a strong position in any science. It is never "proven" to be true, however; it is just "not disproven." Future research may uncover evidence, perhaps under specialized conditions, that casts doubt on the truth value of the theory. By testing hypotheses capable of being rejected, we enable social knowledge to grow incrementally as the limits of its relevance are probed. Thus, any outcome from a well-designed and carefully conducted research project is potentially useful. Results will either reinforce existing knowledge, thereby giving greater confidence that we understand the way the world operates. Or they will cast doubt on what we think we already know, and thus force us to revise our understanding of social reality. In either event, the stage is set for the next cycle through the never-ending research process.

1.7 The General Linear Model

general linear model— a model that assumes the relationships among independent and dependent measures basically vary according to straight-line patterns

In learning about the diverse statistical methods in the following chapters, you may become bewildered by the apparent dissimilarities among them. Be reassured that substantially greater unity exists than is first apparent. For example, several statistical techniques are special instances of an approach known in mathematical statistics as the **general linear model**. Without going into technical details, the general linear model assumes that the relationships among independent and dependent measures basically vary according to straight-line patterns. You are likely to be familiar with such lines from high school algebra, where a plot of the general equation $Y = a + bX$ produces a straight line with positive or negative slope depending on the sign of b. All that is required are numerical values for a and b to fix the line precisely on a set of Cartesian coordinates (i.e., horizontal and vertical axes on graph paper).

An assumption of linear relationships among variables is generally compatible with the research hypotheses that typically abound in the social sciences: "The greater the X, the greater (or lesser) the Y." The implication is that a measured change in X creates a predictable change in Y, a linear expectation. Social scientists seldom express hypotheses about the numerical values of the slope (*b*) and intercept (*a*), preferring to leave these values to be estimated from observational data. Indeed, many empirical patterns of joint variations among pairs of variables suggest reasonably linear approximations: for example, the U.S. states' per capita personal income and percentage of adults with college degrees in 1999, as shown in Figure 1.1.

Statistical methods based on linearity assumptions among variables offer a powerful way to analyze social data consistent with the way most social scientists conceptualize and interpret these relations. The general linear model is a highly flexible tool that can be modified to suit specific combinations of discrete and continuous measures available for testing hypotheses. Thus, where all variables are continuous, regression

FIGURE **1.1**
Graph of Per Capita Income and Percent with College Degree, U.S. States

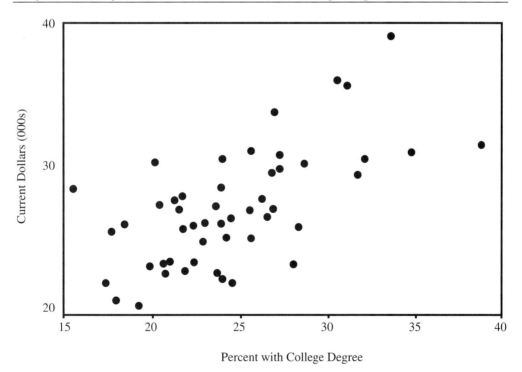

Percent with College Degree

Source: Statistical Abstract of the U.S. (2000).

analysis is appropriate (chapters 6 and 8). If the dependent variable is continuous but the independent variables are discrete, the analysis of variance is the appropriate technique (chapter 4). A dichotomous dependent variable with continuous independent variables points to logistic regression (chapter 9). A combination of continuous and discrete independent variables suggests the analysis of covariance (chapter 8). And the integrated-measurement—structural-equation models in chapter 12 presume linearity among observed and unobserved variables. These convergences among seemingly disparate techniques through the underlying general linear model mean that statistical analysis is really not as complicated it appears. We hope to demonstrate this assertion in the following chapters.

Review of Key Concepts

These key concepts are listed in the order of appearance in this chapter. Combined with the definitions in the margins, they will help you to review the material and can serve as a self-test for mastery of the concepts.

scientific research
applied research
basic research
proposition
concept
social theory
linearity
scope/boundary conditions
variable
latent variable
manifest variable
operational hypothesis
constant
independent variable
dependent variable
status variable
validity
epistemic relationship
reliability
data collection

unit of analysis
population
sample
representativeness
random sample
systematic sampling interval
measurement
missing data
mutually exclusive
exhaustive
recode
codebook
data file
system file
discrete variable
nonorderable discrete variable
orderable discrete variable
dichotomous variable
continuous variable
scale construction

descriptive statistics

inferential statistics

inference

statistical significance test

measures of association

general linear model

PROBLEMS

General Problems

1. Give a formal definition of the concept *age strata* that could be used in a theory of aging.

2. Use the following concepts to form two bivariate propositions: television viewing; parental supervision; school achievement; delinquent behavior.

3. What theoretical scope condition(s) is/are implied by the following statement: "The rate at which contraceptive technology diffused increased with the social workers' ability to win support from social leaders among the village women."

4. Translate the following proposition into an operational hypothesis: "Acceptance of egalitarian sex roles by marital partners is positively related to a more equitable household division of labor."

5. Identify the independent and dependent variables in the following propositions:

    a. Hourly wages of black men are significantly lower than hourly wages of white men.

    b. The more vulnerable a corporation's business is to overseas competition, the more likely it is to form a strategic alliance with a foreign partner.

    c. The growing popularity of new religious cults is a consequence of increased psychological insecurities among young people.

6. Which of the following are variables and which are constants?

    a. brunette

    b. bureacratization

    c. residential segregation

    d. Great Depression

    e. political mobilization

    f. Mount Rushmore

7. MegaCorp has a work force of 4,376 non-executive employees. Business Trends, Inc. wants to draw a sample of 300 workers to interview about their job satisfaction. Assuming the company will provide a list of all employees, how large should the systematic sampling interval, k, be in order to assure a sufficient sample (assuming no employees refuse to be interviewed)?

8. a. What measurement criteria are violated if only the following categories are used to record U.S. respondents' national origins?

   (1) England   (4) South America

   (2) Brazil   (5) Africa

   (3) Italy   (6) Tokyo

   b. What changes in the preceding categories would you suggest?

9. Indicate whether the following variables are nonorderable discrete, orderable discrete, dichotomous, or continuous.

   a. murder rate: annual frequency

   b. job performance rating: poor, average, very good, outstanding

   c. annual income: to nearest $100

   d. grade point average (1–4 scale)

   e. labor force status: employed or unemployed

   f. service club memberships: Kiwanis, Elks, Lions

   g. liking of movie stars: 7-point scale from "strongly like" to "strongly dislike"

   h. yard work: average amount of time spent per week

10. Fill in the blanks to complete the following statements.

    a. A _____ is a set of two or more propositions in which the concepts are assumed to be causally related.

    b. _____ examine the validity of general statements about relationships involving fundamental social processes.

    c. A variable is _____ to the extent that different operationalizations of the same concept produce consistent results.

    d. While the _____ variable has the consequent or affected role, the _____ variable has an antecedent or causal role in a hypothesis.

e. _____ constructs the primary records for a given set of observations.

f. A _____ is the entire set of persons, objects, or events having at least one characteristic of interest to a researcher.

g. _____ occur when no meaningful information is available for a given observation of a particular variable.

2

DESCRIBING VARIABLES

In this chapter we will introduce methods for describing the distributions of discrete and continuous variables for a set of observations. As noted in chapter 1, discrete variables classify persons, objects, or events according to the *quality* of their attributes, while continuous variables classify them according to their *quantities*. We will first show how to represent compactly the full distribution of a single variable for a given set of observations. Next, we will show how to summarize a variable's distribution using just two values—its average or central tendency and its dispersion or variance. These statistics describe a distribution's basic features and provide a foundation for inquiries into the joint distributions of two or more variables, a topic that will be discussed in later chapters.

2.1 Frequency Distributions for Discrete and Continuous Variables

The first step in constructing a distribution is to determine how many observations occur in each response category of the variable. Suppose we want to find out how satisfied American workers are with their jobs. The 1998 General Social Survey (GSS, described in Box 1.1) asked a sample

tally—a count of the frequency of outcomes observed for a variable or the frequency of joint outcomes of several variables

frequency distribution—a table of the outcomes, or response categories, of a variable and the number of times each outcome is observed

outcome—a response category of a variable

relative frequency distribution—a distribution of outcomes of a variable in which the number of times each outcome is observed has been divided by the total number of cases

percentage distribution—a distribution of relative frequencies or proportions in which each entry has been multiplied by 100

relative frequency/proportion—the number of cases in an outcome divided by the total number of cases

percentage—a number created by multiplying a proportion by 100

rounding—expressing digits in more convenient and interpretable units, such as tens, hundreds, or thousands, by applying an explicit rule

of 2,832 American adults, "On the whole, how satisfied are you with the work you do—would you say you are very satisfied, moderately satisfied, a little dissatisfied, or very dissatisfied?" By offering respondents only four choices, this item forms a distribution with four orderable categories. However, 616 people either were not working, didn't know, or would not answer the question about their job satisfaction. We combine the last three types of nonresponse into a "not appropriate" category. Next, we make a **tally** of the number of GSS respondents recorded in each of these five categories. (We used a personal computer to tally the data stored in a permanent file and to print out the number of observations or cases in each category.) From the tally results we construct a **frequency distribution, which is a table of the outcomes, or response categories, of a variable and the number of times each outcome is observed.** The first column of Table 2.1 shows there are 1,067 very satisfied respondents, 851 moderately satisfied, 223 a little dissatisfied, and 75 very dissatisfied, while 616 people either weren't working, didn't know, or gave no answer. We conclude that most Americans are satisfied with their jobs.

These counts can be transformed into **relative frequency distributions** and **percentage distributions**, as shown in the second and third columns of Table 2.1. To form **relative frequencies**, or **proportions**, we divide the number of cases in each outcome by the total number of cases. In the 1998 GSS, the proportion of very satisfied workers is 1067/2832 = 0.377; of moderately satisfied is 851/2832 = 0.300; of a little dissatisfied is 223/2832 = 0.079; and so on. We again conclude that a majority of Americans are satisfied with their jobs, but comparisons to other frequency distributions based on different total numbers of cases are now easier to make and more meaningful with relative proportions. Proportions are transformed into **percentages** by multiplying by 100. For example, in the third column in Table 2.1, the percentage of workers who are very dissatisfied is (.026)(100) = 2.6%. Percentages *standardize* for sample size by indicating the number of observations that would fall into each outcome of a variable if the total number of cases were 100.

Percentages are usually presented to the nearest tenth. Because speaking about tenths of a person is awkward, we could round our results up or down to the nearest whole percent. Generally values of 0.1 to 0.4 are rounded down to the next whole number, and values of 0.5 to 0.9 are rounded up. (Rules for **rounding** appear in Box 2.1.) Thus, we conclude that 38 of every 100 persons in the GSS are very satisfied with their jobs. Alternatively, we could multiply each percentage by 10 and say that if we were to observe 1,000 persons, we would expect 377 to be very satisfied, 851 moderately satisfied, and so forth. Either procedure makes an important point clear: *Whenever data are summarized, some distortion*

TABLE 2.1
Job Satisfaction of Working Respondents

Job Satisfaction	Frequency (f)	Proportion (p)	Percent (%)	Cumulative frequency (cf)	Cumulative percent (c%)
Very Satisfied	1,067	.377	37.7	1,067	37.7
Moderately Satisfied	851	.300	30.0	1,918	67.7
A Little Dissatisfied	223	.079	7.9	2,141	75.6
Very Dissatisfied	75	.026	2.6	2,216	78.2
Not Appropriate	616	.218	21.8	2,832	100.0
Total	2,832	1.000	100.0	2,832	100.0

Source: 1998 General Social Survey.

almost always occurs. The trade-off in comprehension and interpretation usually makes small distortions worthwhile. For this reason, social researchers who use percentages become accustomed to dealing with fractions of cases.

We use a shorthand notation for frequencies and relative frequencies. N denotes the total sample size (in the 1998 GSS, $N = 2,832$). f_i denotes the frequency associated with the ith outcome (category) of a variable. The subscript i can take values from 1 to the number of response categories (K) into which the variable is coded. For Table 2.1, $K = 5$. If we code very satisfied = 1, moderately satisfied = 2, a little dissatisfied = 3, very dissatisfied = 4, and not appropriate = 5, then $f_1 = 1,067$ (there are 1,067 very satisfied in the distribution), $f_2 = 851$, $f_3 = 223$, $f_4 = 75$, and $f_5 = 616$. The first column of Table 2.1, labeled f, gives the number of cases in each job-satisfaction category. The sum of the frequencies for each outcome equals the total sample size:

$$f_1 + f_2 + f_3 + \cdots + f_K = N$$

In the 1998 GSS,

$$1,067 + 851 + 223 + 75 + 616 = 2,832$$

The *proportion* of cases in the ith outcome of a variable is p_i. Its formula is

$$p_i = \frac{f_i}{N}$$

BOX 2.1   Rules for Recoding and Rounding

Recoding Rules
1. The more measurement precision, the better.
2. Choose an interval width that is narrow enough not to distort the original distribution of observations, but wide enough to avoid too many categories concealing the underlying distribution shape.
3. The number of intervals should be somewhere between 6 and 20. A larger number of categories generally cannot be easily grasped by the reader.

Rounding Rules
1. Round digits 1 to 4 down by leaving the digit to the left unchanged.
2. Round digits 6 to 9 up by increasing the digit to the left by 1.
3. Numbers ending in 5 are rounded alternately; the first number ending in 5 is rounded down, the second is rounded up, the third is rounded down, and so forth.
4. Never round past the original measurement interval.

Here are several examples of rounding for data originally recorded to the nearest tenth of a year:

Unit of Measurement	Original Number (in years)	Rounded Number
Years	22.6	23
Years	648.3	648
Decades	22.6	2
Decades	648.3	65
Centuries	22.6	0
Centuries	648.3	6

As shown in the second column of Table 2.1, the proportion of Americans who were very satisfied with their jobs in the GSS data is $p_1 = f_1/N$ = 1,067/2,832 = 0.377.

The sum of all the proportions in a frequency distribution always equals 1.00 (except for any rounding error). In the case where $K = 5$,

$$p_1 + p_2 + p_3 + p_4 + p_5 = \frac{f_1}{N} + \frac{f_2}{N} + \frac{f_3}{N} + \frac{f_4}{N} + \frac{f_5}{N}$$
$$= \frac{(f_1 + f_2 + f_3 + f_4 + f_5)}{N}$$
$$= \frac{N}{N} = 1.00$$

Because a percentage is simply a proportion multiplied by 100, the sum of the percentages associated with all the categories in a frequency distribution always equals 100.0%. The total of the third column in Table 2.1 verifies this summation.

Table 2.2 shows the relative frequency distributions for three other *discrete variables*. The genders of the 2,832 GSS respondents were determined visually by the interviewer at the beginning of the interview. Region of residence uses the Census Bureau's classification of states into nine categories. To measure the number of children ever born to respondents, interviewers asked, "How many children have you ever had? Please count all that were born alive at any time (including any you had from a previous marriage)." Nine categories of increasing frequency were offered for their responses (the GSS combined eight or more children into

TABLE 2.2
Percentage Distributions of Gender, Region of Residence, and Number of Children

Gender		Region of Residence		Number of Children	
Male	43.5%	New England	5.0%	None	28.3%
Female	56.5	Middle Atlantic	15.1	One	16.7
Total	100.0%	E. North Central	17.4	Two	26.2
(N = 2,832)		W. North Central	7.2	Three	14.5
		South Atlantic	18.8	Four	7.4
		E. South Central	6.7	Five	3.0
		W. South Central	10.6	Six	1.7
		Mountain	6.6	Seven	0.7
		Pacific	12.6	Eight or More	1.2
		Total	100.0%	No Answer	0.2
		(N = 2,832)		Total	99.9%*
				(N = 2,832)	

Source: 1998 General Social Survey.
*Does not total to 100.0% due to rounding.

a single category). Respondents were not explicitly offered "no answer" as a choice: The interviewer recorded that response only when a respondent did not give a number.

The response categories associated with gender and region of residence clearly are *not* continuous variables, because they do not classify respondents according to magnitude or *quantity* of the response. Instead, they are *nonorderable discrete variables*, because the sequence of their categories has no intrinsic order. However, number of children is an *orderable discrete variable*, because only one sequence of categories is meaningful. (It is not a continuous variable, because fractional numbers of children are not possible.) A variable having only two categories is a **dichotomous variable**, or **dichotomy** (literally, "cut in two"). Gender—male or female—is an example of a dichotomy.

dichotomous variable/dichotomy—a variable having only two categories

2.2 Grouped and Cumulative Distributions

Building frequency distributions for discrete variables is easy. Tallying the numbers of men and women poses little difficulty, as does counting the numbers of children ever born. However, constructing a frequency distribution for a *continuous* variable first requires **grouped data**. That is, a researcher must decide how to collapse together observations having different values.

grouped data—data that have been collapsed into a smaller number of categories

In principle, any two coded values of a continuous variable can be subdivided infinitely. For example, suppose someone's weight is recorded with a pointer on a bathroom scale, as in the illustration.

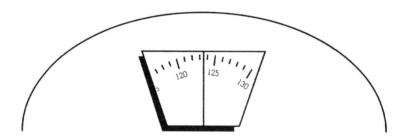

This person's weight is 123.4625 pounds, to be very precise, but usually we do not require this much precision. In everyday conversation we would round to the nearest whole number and say that the person weighs 123 pounds. For some scientific work, that value may be too imprecise.

A scientist may decide that measurement in tenths of a pound is precise enough, in which case the person's weight would be recorded as 123-and-a-half pounds, or 123.5 pounds.

For continuous variables, measurement precision can be as accurate as the measuring instrument will allow. Ultimately, however, a researcher must decide how to group observations having different values. In other words, a **measurement interval** or **measurement class** must be selected within which observations will be treated as having equal value. For some variables the measurement interval is obvious. The year of birth is probably sufficiently accurate in a study of adult voters. For a study of infants' social learning, age to the nearest month is essential, because many important changes occur within very short time spans. For many social analyses, measurement units are less clear since standard, well-investigated scales have not been developed. Most attitude scales, which typically record responses to statements in orderable sequences from "strongly disagree" to "strongly agree," have this characteristic. Clearly, continuous variables require researchers to decide in detail the degree of measurement precision.

measurement interval/ measurement class—a grouping of observations that is treated equally

The process of grouping continuous variables from many initial values into fewer categories is called **recoding**. For example, an age distribution for the U.S. population cannot easily display the hundred or more reported values. Instead, we might recode annual ages into nine decade-wide categories:

recoding—the process of grouping continuous variables from many initial values into fewer categories

   10 years or less
   11–19 years
   20–29 years
   30–39 years
   40–49 years
   50–59 years
   60–69 years
   70–79 years
   80 years or more

The preceding intervals do not overlap the categories' endpoints as in the following list:

   10 years or less
   10–20 years
   20–30 years
   30–40 years
   and so on

Such overlapping violates the mutual exclusiveness principle discussed in section 1.5. Persons aged 10, 20, 30, 40, 50, 60, 70, or 80 years could be placed in two categories rather than in a single measurement class. Box 2.1 summarizes some basic principles for grouping or recoding measures.

How wide should measurement intervals be for continuous variables? The measurement intervals should be narrow enough not to distort the original distribution but wide enough to avoid too many categories that conceal the underlying distribution. Generally, between 6 and 20 intervals should be used to present data in a frequency distribution. Sometimes fewer than six intervals will not seriously distort the shape of the distribution. Readers often find that more than 20 categories are difficult to interpret. Common sense indicates that eight 10-year intervals may be practical for a study of all Americans' ages but would not be satisfactory for a survey of elementary school students because only the first two categories would apply.

Researchers often need to know a specific outcome's *relative* position in a distribution of continuous scores. If 2.5% of Minnesota's labor force is unemployed, is that rate high or low relative to other states? This question can be answered by a cumulative frequency distribution or cumulative percentage distribution. The **cumulative frequency** at a given score is the total number of observations at or below that score. Every GSS asks respondents, "What is the highest grade in elementary school or high school that you finished and got credit for?" High school graduates are also asked, "Did you complete one or more years of college for credit?" and "Do you have any college degrees?" These responses are used to determine the numbers of years of formal education (from 0 to 20). Table 2.3 reports four distributions for these data. In the third column, the **cumulative frequency distribution** (denoted *cf*) is the distribution of responses at or below each year of education. The cumulative frequency to 8 years (grade school graduate) is 160, to 12 years (high school graduate) is 1,337, to 16 years (college graduate) is 2,515, and so on. To produce each *cf*, simply start with the frequency in the lowest category (f_1), add to it the frequency in the next highest category (f_2), then add to that sum the frequency in the third highest category (f_3), and so forth.

Easier to interpret is a **cumulative percentage** of responses, denoted *c%* in the fourth column of Table 2.3. To form this **cumulative percentage distribution**, divide the cumulative frequencies in column four by the total *N*. That is, instead of cumulating the frequencies, cumulate the percentages at each category. Both the percentage distribution and the cumulative percentage distribution make clear the standing of a given observation *relative* to others. For example, almost 75 percent of the GSS respondents had less than a college education (16 years).

cumulative frequency—for a given score or outcome of a variable, the total number of cases in a distribution at or below that value

cumulative frequency distribution—a distribution of scores showing the number of cases at or below each outcome of the variable being displayed in the distribution

cumulative percentage—for a given score or outcome of a variable, the percentage of cases in a distribution at or below that value

cumulative percentage distribution—a distribution of scores showing the percentage of cases at or below each outcome of the variable being displayed in the distribution

TABLE 2.3
Cumulative Distributions of Respondent Education in Years

Education	f	%	cf	c%
None	2	0.07	2	0.07
1	0	0.00	2	0.07
2	5	0.18	7	0.24
3	10	0.35	17	0.60
4	9	0.32	26	0.92
5	8	0.28	34	1.21
6	23	0.82	57	2.02
7	21	0.74	78	2.77
8	82	2.91	160	5.67
9	75	2.66	235	8.33
10	113	4.01	348	12.34
11	138	4.89	486	17.23
12	851	30.18	1,337	47.41
13	270	9.57	1,607	56.99
14	350	12.41	1,957	69.40
15	146	5.18	2,103	74.57
16	412	14.61	2,515	89.18
17	86	3.05	2,601	92.23
18	109	3.86	2,710	96.10
19	41	1.45	2,751	97.55
20	69	2.45	2,820	100.00

No Answer, Don't Know = 12.
Source: 1998 General Social Survey.

Cumulative percentage distributions are commonly used in calculating percentiles—for example, in showing the relative achievement test scores of students. The calculation of percentiles is presented in section 2.6.

2.3 Graphing Frequency Distributions

Frequency distribution tables are one way to communicate quantitative information in a clear, precise manner. We give some principles of **statistical table** construction in Box 2.2. Other ways to display single variable distributions are **diagrams** or **graphs**, such as bar charts and

statistical table— a numerical display that either summarizes data or presents the results of a data analysis

diagram/graph—a visual representation of a set of data

BOX 2.2   Statistical Tables

Statistical tables are basic tools of the social researcher's trade. The arts of constructing, reading, and interpreting tables can best be learned, as are all crafts, by much practice. Some basic principles of tabular display are summarized here. Authors should consult recent issues of a journal to which they expect to submit papers for examples of that journal's table style.

Tables come in two basic forms: those that display "raw data" and those that present analyses. Raw-data tables contain frequencies or counts of observations classified in various ways, such as the number of robberies reported in each of 32 neighborhoods last year, or the number of homicides classified according to familiarity between murderer and victim in each of four regions of the United States. Analytic tables display the consequences of some manipulation of the data by a researcher that claims to give an interpretation of the process producing the raw data. Such tables are highly varied and may range from a simple percentagizing of raw data all the way to systems of nonlinear simultaneous equations for complex mathematical models.

Each table begins with a heading, usually the word *Table*, an identifying number, and a short phrase describing its central contents. Examples from a recent issue of the *American Sociological Review* include

Table 1. Estimated Percentage Change in Men's Nominal Income Following Separation, by Share of Pre-Disruption Household Income: Panel Study of Income Dynamics, 1982 to 1992

Table 2. Estimated Annual Probabilities of Marital Dissolution, by Wife's Employment Status and Marital Duration

Table 3. Findings on the Association between Parents' Sexual Orientations, Other Attributes of Parents, and Parent-Child Relationships: 21 Studies, 1981 to 1998

Under the heading, usually below a rule, are subheadings that label the various columns in the main body of the table.

(continued)

These subheadings most often are either variable names and categories or summary statistics such as column marginals (*N*s). To save space, short labels are preferred. If further clarification is required, subheadings can be footnoted, with the expanded explanations appearing at the bottom of the table.

Additional information, as in a crosstabulation between two or more variables, appears in the column farthest to the left (sometimes called the *stub*). Each entry in this column describes the content of one of the rows forming the body of the table. For example, if attitude responses appear in the rows, the labels or response categories in the first column, from top to bottom, might be: "Strongly Agree," "Agree," "Neither Agree Nor Disagree," "Disagree," and "Strongly Disagree."

The main body of the table consists of the intersections of the entries under column and row headings. It displays the appropriate data in either raw or analyzed form. If the table contents are percentages, the preferable way to arrange them is so that they total to 100% down each column. A percentage total is usually the next to last row entry. The last row, labeled Total at the left, gives the base frequencies on which the percentages were calculated. An example of a percentage table in this chapter is Table 2.2. Note that no vertical lines are used in tables.

The number of cases with missing data (observations that could not be used in the main body of the table due to lack of information) may be reported directly below the body of the table. Any additional information about the data (such as its source) or about the analyses performed should be included in notes below the table.

histograms. In this section we will describe some elementary features of data graphs, whose choice depends on whether the variables are discrete or continuous.

For nonorderable discrete variables, a **bar chart** offers effective visual images. First, categories of the discrete variable are arrayed along a horizontal axis. Then, equally spaced vertical bars are erected above each category label to heights proportional to the frequency of the observations in each category (either the actual case counts or the percentages). The frequencies or the percentages are sometimes printed above each bar.

bar chart—a type of diagram for discrete variables in which the numbers or percentages of cases in each outcome are displayed

Figure 2.1 is a bar chart illustrating the nine regions of residence in the 1998 GSS, using the data in Table 2.2. Importantly, whenever discrete variable categories have no inherent order, the bars should not touch one another but should stand apart. A bar chart adds no information beyond that found in a table displaying the same data. In fact, it communicates less information if the sample sizes on which categories are based are omitted and only the percentages are shown. Diagrams can be constructed only after the information for a table has been assembled.

histogram—a type of diagram that uses bars to represent the frequency, proportion, or percentage of cases associated with each outcome or interval of outcomes of a variable

For orderable discrete and grouped continuous variables, **histograms** can display the distributions. The vertical bars of a histogram touch one another, indicating an underlying order among categories that is absent from the nonorderable variables in bar charts. Figure 2.2 shows a histogram for the number of children ever born to GSS respondents, using the data in Table 2.2. If the midpoints of the categories are connected by lines, rather than depicting the categories as vertical bars, the resulting diagram is a **polygon**. Figure 2.3 shows a polygon for the "children ever born" variable. As with bar charts, constructing histograms or polygons requires frequency or percentage distributions of a variable.

polygon—a diagram constructed by connecting the midpoints of a histogram with a straight line.

For an elegant discussion of principles of graphic display for social science data, with many stunning examples of both good and bad usage, see Edward Tufte's classic *The Visual Display of Quantitative Information* (1983).

2.4 Measures of Central Tendency

Two broad purposes are served by two descriptive statistics that summarize a frequency distribution. First, a single number summarizes the **central tendency** or average value of a set of scores (e.g., "The median income of people with masters' degrees is…"; "The modal political party preference in Canada is…"). Second, a single number summarizes the amount of **variation** or dispersion in a distribution, because a central tendency statistic does not reveal how typical that number is of the other sample observations. For example, most scores may be close to the central tendency score or spread widely away from it. If most scores are near the average value, that statistic describes the distribution much more accurately than if the scores are widely dispersed.

central tendency—average value of a set of scores

variation—the spread or dispersion of a set of scores around some central value

The mode, the median, and the mean are the commonly used central tendency statistics. We illustrate their calculation with two frequency distributions. Table 2.3 displays the GSS respondents' years of education. Table 2.4 shows the numerical grades for a test taken by 20 sophomores in an American high school, where A = 8, B+ = 7, B = 6, C+ = 5, C = 4,

Figure 2.1
Bar Chart Showing Region of Residence

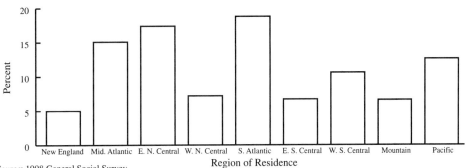

Source: 1998 General Social Survey.

Figure 2.2
Histogram Showing Number of Children Ever Born

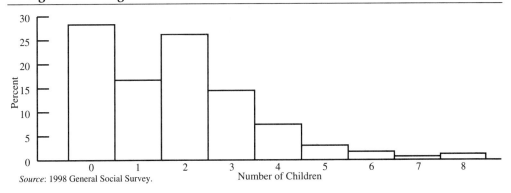

Source: 1998 General Social Survey.

Figure 2.3
Polygon Showing Number of Children Ever Born

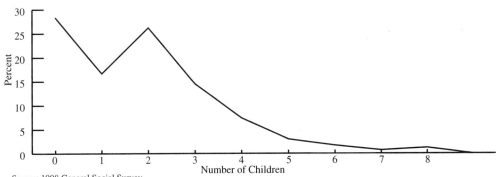

Source: 1998 General Social Survey.

TABLE 2.4
Grades of Sophomores in an American High School

Student No.	Grade	Score
1	B	6
2	D	2
3	C	4
4	C	4
5	A	8
6	B	6
7	D+	3
8	C+	5
9	C	4
10	C+	5
11	C+	5
12	B	6
13	C+	5
14	C	4
15	C	4
16	B+	7
17	B	6
18	B+	7
19	C+	5
20	B+	7

Source: James S. Coleman and Lingxin Hao. 1989. "Linear systems analysis: Macrolevel analysis with microlevel data." *Sociological Methodology 19*: 395–422.

D+ = 3, and D = 2. These two variables exemplify how to calculate descriptive statistics for both grouped and ungrouped distributions, respectively.

2.4.1 Mode

mode—the single category among the *K* categories in a distribution with the largest number (or highest percentage) of observations

The **mode** is that single *category* among the *K* categories in a distribution with the largest number (or highest percentage) of observations. For example, if 43 people say that their favorite snack is pretzels, 57 say potato chips, and 36 say popcorn, then the modal category is "potato chips."

Do not confuse the *modal frequency* (number of cases) with the *modal category*. A modal category is not required to contain a majority of the cases, but simply *more than* any other category. Some distributions are *bimodal* (i.e., they have *two* modes). Strictly speaking, in a bimodal distribution the largest two categories must each have exactly the same number of observations. In practice this equality very rarely occurs, however, and scientists use the term "bimodal" to describe any distribution where two categories are roughly equal and contain substantially more cases than the remaining categories.

The modal category of the 1998 GSS respondents is twelve years of education, since the 851 high school graduates compose 30% of the sample. The distribution of student grades shows that two sets of five sophomores have identical grades (numbers 3, 4, 9, 14, and 15 with C and numbers 8, 10, 11, 13, and 19 with C+), so the two modal categories are "C" and "C+," or "4" and "5" on the numeric scale.

Any statistic describing discrete measures can also describe continuous measures. Thus, the mode is a central tendency statistic applicable to both types of variables.

2.4.2 Median

The **median** (Mdn) applies only to variables whose categories can be ordered in a sequence from lowest to highest. The median is the outcome that divides an orderable distribution exactly into halves. That is, half the cases will have scores above the median value and half will have scores below the median. Whether any case exists that has the median value depends on whether the number of observations is odd or even. Consider three example distributions:

median—the outcome that divides an ordered distribution exactly into halves

    Distribution X: 1, 4, 6, 8, 9, 10, 13
    Distribution Y: 1, 4, 6, 8, 9, 10, 13, 17
    Distribution Z: 4, 7, 8, 8, 9, 13

Distribution X has an odd number of cases (seven). Its median is the score of the fourth observation, or 8. Distribution Y has an even number of cases (8), so its median falls halfway between the scores of the fourth and fifth cases. Its value is the average of the values of these two cases, $(8 + 9)/2 = 8.5$. Although the values surrounding the median case in distribution Z are both 8, the rule still applies that the median is either the score of the middle case (for an odd number of observations) or the average of the scores for two cases (for an even number of cases). Hence, the median value of Z is $(8 + 8)/2 = 8$. The median is easy to calculate in distributions with small numbers of observations.

For grouped frequency distributions, many statistics textbooks recommend the complex formula on page 55 in section 2.6 to calculate the median value as the 50th percentile. We offer a simpler and more accurate approach to finding the median: For any grouped frequency distribution, the median is the value of that category at which the cumulative percentage reaches 50.0%. In such instances, median values calculated using ungrouped data will not precisely equal medians when the same data are grouped. The grouping process loses information about the individual scores. However, researchers often have only the grouped data displays, for example, from published census tables and newspaper charts. Seldom does one category exactly cumulate to 50.0%. In such instances, the median value is the first category in the cumulative distribution to exceed 50.0%. (The SPSS FREQUENCIES program also calculates medians in this way.) The modal education category of GSS respondents can be calculated from the data displayed in Table 2.3. Given 2,820 responses, the median value must fall between cases 1,410 and 1,411. As shown by the *cf* and *c%* in the third and fourth columns, both cases fall into the response category "13 years," and hence, this value (one year past high school graduation) is the median of that distribution.

2.4.3 Mean

mean—the arithmetic average of a set of data in which the values of all observations are added together and divided by the number of observations

The arithmetic **mean**, often called the *average*, is the most common measure of central tendency. It can be calculated only for continuous distributions. The values of all observations are added together and divided by the total number of observations. The formula for the mean statistic is

$$\bar{Y} = \sum_{i=1}^{N} \frac{Y_i}{N}$$

The Greek capital letter sigma (Σ) symbolizes the summation operation. Appendix A, "The Use of Summations," gives basic rules on its use. The formula for the mean tells us to add all the scores in the Y distribution from the first to the Nth observation and then divide that sum by the number of cases, N. Because a constant can be moved from inside to outside a summation sign, an equivalent formula for the mean is

$$\bar{Y} = \left(\frac{1}{N}\right) \sum Y_i = \frac{\sum Y_i}{N}$$

The incompletely labeled sum sign is understood to indicate that summation occurs over all observations of Y from the first to the Nth case.

To illustrate computation of the mean, apply the formula to the student grades in Table 2.4:

$$\bar{Y} = (6 + 2 + 4 + \cdots + 7 + 5 + 7)/20 = (103)/20 = 5.15$$

The formula given at the beginning of this section cannot be used to calculate the mean of a grouped frequency distribution. A slightly more complex formula for the mean of grouped data is

$$\ast \quad \bar{Y} = \sum_{i=1}^{K} \frac{(f_i Y_i)}{N}$$

where

f_i = The frequency of cases with score Y_i

K = The number of categories in the distribution

Each score is "weighted" by the number of times it appears in the distribution, and then the K weighted products are added together and divided by the total number of cases in the distribution.

Applied to the group education data in Table 2.3, the mean is

$$\begin{aligned}
\bar{Y} = \ & [0(2) + 1(0) + 2(5) + 3(10) + 4(9) + 5(8) + 6(23) + 7(21) + 8(82) \\
& + 9(75) + 10(113) + 11(138) + 12(851) + 13(270) + 14(350) \\
& + 15(146) + 16(412) + 17(86) + 18(109) + 19(41) + 20(69)]/2{,}820 \\
= \ & 13.25 \text{ years of schooling}
\end{aligned}$$

The formula for grouped data should be used only in situations where the raw data are not available.

The mean of a dichotomous variable is a special case of the grouped frequency mean. Coding the first category "0" and the second category "1," a dichotomous variable's mean is simply the proportion of cases with the score "1." The formula becomes

$$\begin{aligned}
\bar{Y} &= \frac{\sum f_i Y_i}{N} \\
&= \frac{(f_0)(0) + (f_1)(1)}{N} = \frac{(f_1)(1)}{N} = \frac{f_1}{N} \\
&= p_1
\end{aligned}$$

where

f_0 = The number of cases coded 0

f_1 = The number of cases coded 1

p_1 = The proportion of cases coded 1

The gender distribution in Table 2.2 has 1,600 women and 1,232 men. If women are coded 1 and men coded 0, the mean score is $[((1,232)(0) + (1,600)(1))/2,832] = 0.565$, which is the proportion of women in the sample. (Although the proportion of women in the U.S. adult population was about 0.525 according to the 1990 Census, every GSS has a higher female proportion because men tend to be less available for interviews [e.g., in the armed forces, in prison, on business trips] and because women are more likely than men to grant interviews.)

2.5 Measures of Dispersion

The choice of a measure to describe the dispersion among a set of scores depends on whether the variable is discrete or continuous. In this section we will discuss the indices of diversity and qualitative variation, range, average absolute deviation, variance, and standard deviation. We will also describe how to measure skewness, another aspect of a frequency distribution's shape.

2.5.1 Indices of Diversity and Qualitative Variation

index of diversity—measures whether two observations selected randomly from a population are likely to fall into the same or into different categories

Statistics describing discrete variable variation can be applied to orderable and to nonorderable measures. The **index of diversity**, *D*, measures whether two observations selected randomly from a population are likely to fall into the same or different categories. To calculate *D*, we simply square the proportion of cases in each of the *K* discrete categories, sum these squares, and subtract from 1.

$$D = 1 - \sum_{i=1}^{K} p_i^2$$

where

p_i = The proportion of observations in the *i*th category

The higher the value of *D*, the more equally dispersed are the cases among the variable's *K* categories. The minimum possible value of *D* is 0, when all cases fall into a single category. The maximum value of *D* occurs when the proportions in every category are equal. However, the number of categories limits the maximum possible value. The more categories a discrete variable has, the larger the maximum value *D* can attain. For example, *D* for a four-category variable (each $p_i = .25$) cannot be larger than 0.75, while *D* for a 10-category variable (each $p_i = .10$) can attain a maximum value of 0.90. *Thus, values of D for discrete variables with different numbers of categories cannot be compared directly*

Instead, a second dispersion statistic describing discrete variables, the **index of qualitative variation** (IQV), standardizes the diversity index for the number of categories.

index of qualitative variation—a measure of variation for discrete variables; a standardized version of the index of diversity

$$IQV = \frac{1 - \sum_{i=1}^{K} p_i^2}{(K-1)/K}$$

$$= \frac{K}{K-1}(D)$$

The maximum IQV value is always 1.0 whenever cases are equally spread over all K categories, that is, when $p_i = 1/K$ for every p_i. Thus, it is possible to make direct comparisons of the dispersion among discrete variables with differing numbers of categories.

For example, consider both the region of residence and number of children in Table 2.2 as discrete variables. The values of D for these measures are

$$
\begin{aligned}
D_{residence} &= 1 - (0.050^2 + 0.151^2 + 0.174^2 + 0.072^2 + 0.188^2 \\
&\quad + 0.067^2 + 0.106^2 + 0.066^2 + 0.126^2) \\
&= 0.868
\end{aligned}
$$

and

$$
\begin{aligned}
D_{children} &= 1 - (0.283^2 + 0.167^2 + 0.262^2 + 0.145^2 + 0.074^2 \\
&\quad + 0.030^2 + 0.017^2 + 0.007^2 + 0.012^2 + 0.002^2) \\
&= 0.795
\end{aligned}
$$

When adjusted for the differing numbers of categories (nine and ten), their IQV values are

$$IQV_{residence} = \frac{0.868}{8/9} = 0.977$$

and

$$IQV_{children} = \frac{0.795}{9/10} = 0.883$$

suggesting a more equal distribution for the regional measure than for the "children ever born" variable.

2.5.2 Range

The simplest statistic for describing dispersions of both orderable discrete and continuous variables is the **range.** A distribution's range is defined as the difference between the largest and smallest scores. The range of education shown in Table 2.3 is from 0 to 20 years, or $20 - 0 = 20$. Because it uses only the two extreme scores, the range provides almost no information about the other $N - 2$ observations in the sample. It cannot reveal how spread out or clustered these cases are between the highest and lowest scores. Only small proportions of respondents in Table 2.3 have fewer than 9 years or more than 18 years of schooling, indicating that most cases are bunched around the center of the distribution. Other dispersion statistics better summarize the spread among *all* the scores.

2.5.3 Average Absolute Deviation

As a measure of central tendency, the mean uses information about every observation in a continuous variable's distribution. A good measure of variation should also summarize how much each observation deviates from central tendency—that is, the difference between it and the mean. The deviation, or distance, of a score, Y_i, from the mean, $\overline{Y}$, is commonly calculated as

$$d_i = Y_i - \overline{Y}$$

In any distribution where the scores are not all identical, some deviations are positive (above the mean) and some are negative (below the mean). However, the mean of all N deviations is always 0, because the arithmetic mean equalizes the sum of deviations in both positive and negative directions. (Try this exercise on Table 2.4.) Therefore, the average deviation is an unsuitable measure of dispersion because its value is always zero.

One solution is to remove negative signs by taking absolute values of the deviations before averaging them. The formula for the **average absolute deviation** (AAD) uses vertical bars to indicate the absolute values of d_i:

$$AAD = \frac{\Sigma \ |d_i|}{N}$$

AAD is larger than zero, except when all N observations have exactly the same score.

Unfortunately, the AAD cannot fulfill an important requirement for a measure of dispersion—the spread of scores around the mean is a minimum. If the median is used as the central tendency measure when computing deviations (that is, if $d_i = Y_i -$ Mdn), then the formula for AAD gives a smaller numerical value than when deviations are computed using the mean. To illustrate the problem, consider the education data in Table 2.3, which has a mean of 13.25 years and a median of 13 years (i.e., the cumulation to 50.0% falls into this category). The average absolute deviation about the median (2.23) is smaller than the average absolute deviation about the mean (2.26), which is always the case. The AAD fails to meet an important criterion for an acceptable dispersion statistic; therefore, it is never used in social data analysis.

2.5.4 Variance and Standard Deviation

Another procedure for eliminating the negative signs from a distribution of deviations is squaring. The arithmetic mean, defined in section 2.4.3, minimizes the average squared deviation of all scores in a distribution. That is, no other number (including the median) produces a smaller value when we calculate the deviations from the mean, square them, and average them over all observations. This desirable feature of the mean is built into a very important dispersion statistic for a continuous distribution: the **variance**. The formula for the variance—the mean squared deviation, s_Y^2 —can be expressed in two equivalent ways:

variance—the mean squared deviation of a continuous distribution

$$s_Y^2 = \frac{\sum_{i=1}^{N} d_i^2}{N - 1}$$

$$s_Y^2 = \frac{\sum_{i=1}^{N} (Y_i - \bar{Y})^2}{N - 1}$$

If the mean, $\bar{Y}$, is replaced in these formulas by any other number (such as Mdn), a larger value for s_Y^2 will always result. Unlike the mean formula, which has N in the denominator, both variance formulas divide the numerator by $(N - 1)$. This divisor produces an *unbiased* estimate of the population variance, a highly desirable property for any statistic (see section 3.10).

Table 2.5 shows the step-by-step calculation of the variance for the student grades in Table 2.4, using a mean of 5.15. Because of the squaring, the variance is always a nonnegative number and sometimes larger than any of the original scores. The grades variable s_Y^2 is equal to 2.2395.

TABLE 2.5
Calculation of Variance for Student Grades in Table 2.4

$(Y_i - \bar{Y})$		$2d_i$	d_i^2
6 – 5.15	=	0.85	0.7225
2 – 5.15	=	–3.15	9.9225
4 – 5.15	=	–1.15	1.3225
4 – 5.15	=	–1.15	1.3225
8 – 5.15	=	2.85	8.1225
6 – 5.15	=	0.85	0.7225
3 – 5.15	=	–2.15	4.6225
5 – 5.15	=	–0.15	0.0225
4 – 5.15	=	–1.15	1.3225
5 – 5.15	=	–0.15	0.0225
5 – 5.15	=	–0.15	0.0225
6 – 5.15	=	0.85	0.7225
5 – 5.15	=	–0.15	0.0225
4 – 5.15	=	–1.15	1.3225
4 – 5.15	=	–1.15	1.3225
7 – 5.15	=	1.85	3.4225
6 – 5.15	=	0.85	0.7225
7 – 5.15	=	1.85	3.4225
5 – 5.15	=	–0.15	0.0225
7 – 5.15	=	1.85	3.4225

$$\sum_{i=1}^{N} d_i^2 = 42.55$$

$$s_Y^2 = \frac{\sum_{i=1}^{N} d_i^2}{N-1}$$

$$= \frac{42.55}{19} = 2.2395$$

$$\text{and } s_Y = \sqrt{2.2395} = 1.4965$$

The unit of measure for this variance is not a grade point but a "squared grade," which makes an intuitively meaningful interpretation practically impossible.

To restore the original measurement intervals, we take the positive square root of the variance, called the **standard deviation**. Its formula is simply

$$s_Y = \sqrt{s_Y^2}$$

For the student data, the standard deviation of the grade point distribution is

$$\sqrt{2.2395} = 1.4965$$

Looked at in isolation, the standard deviation lacks intuitive meaning. However, some valuable applications of the standard deviation will be presented in chapter 3.

For grouped data, such as Table 2.3, the variance formula requires weighting by the relative frequency in each category:

$$s_Y^2 = \frac{\sum_{i=1}^{K} d_i^2 f_i}{N-1} = \frac{\sum (Y_i - \bar{Y})^2 f_i}{N-1}$$

Each deviation is first squared and then multiplied by the number of cases having score Y_i. Then, the weighted squared deviations for the K outcomes of Y are summed and divided by $(N-1)$, which removes bias in the sample variance. Table 2.6 shows the calculations for the education data, yielding a variance of 8.57 and a standard deviation of 2.93 years of schooling.

Dichotomous grouped frequency distributions are a special case. The formula for the variance of a 1-0 dichotomy reduces to

$$s_Y^2 = (p_0)(p_1)$$

where

p_0 = The proportion of cases coded 0

p_1 = The proportion of cases coded 1

Thus, 1,600 women and 1,232 men in the 1998 GSS give a gender variance of $(1,600/2,832)(1,232/2,832) = (.565)(.435) = 0.246$ and a standard deviation of 0.496. A dichotomy's variance always has a smaller numerical value than its standard deviation, because the product of two proportions is less than 1.00 and the square root of a number less than 1.00 is always a larger value. To demonstrate that the variance formula for a

TABLE 2.6
Calculation of Variance for Education in Table 2.3

$(Y_i - \bar{Y})$	d_i	d_i^2	f_i	$d_i^2 f_i$
$(0 - 13.25)$	-13.25	175.5625	2	351.1250
$(2 - 13.25)$	-11.25	126.5625	5	632.8125
$(3 - 13.25)$	-10.25	105.0625	10	1050.6250
$(4 - 13.25)$	-9.25	85.5625	9	770.0625
$(5 - 13.25)$	-8.25	68.0625	8	544.5000
$(6 - 13.25)$	-7.25	52.5625	23	1,208.9375
$(7 - 13.25)$	-6.25	39.0625	21	820.3125
$(8 - 13.25)$	-5.25	27.5625	82	2,260.1250
$(9 - 13.25)$	-4.25	18.0625	75	1,354.6875
$(10 - 13.25)$	-3.25	10.5625	113	1,193.5625
$(11 - 13.25)$	-2.25	5.0625	138	698.6250
$(12 - 13.25)$	-1.25	1.5625	851	1,329.6875
$(13 - 13.25)$	-0.25	0.0625	270	16.8750
$(14 - 13.25)$	0.75	0.5625	350	196.8750
$(15 - 13.25)$	1.75	3.0625	146	447.1250
$(16 - 13.25)$	2.75	7.5625	412	3,115.7500
$(17 - 13.25)$	3.75	14.0625	86	1,209.3750
$(18 - 13.25)$	4.75	22.5625	109	2,459.3125
$(19 - 13.25)$	5.75	33.0625	41	1,355.5625
$(20 - 13.25)$	6.75	45.5625	69	3,143.8125

$$\sum d_i^2 f_i = 24,159.75$$

$$s_Y^2 = \frac{\sum d_i^2 f_i}{N - 1} = \frac{24,159.75}{2,819} = 8.5703$$

$$s_Y = \sqrt{8.5703} = 2.9275$$

dichotomy equals the variance of any grouped frequency distribution, you should also calculate the gender variance using the standard formula for the variance.

2.5.5 Skewness

When the distribution of a continuous variable is graphed, the plot may be nonsymmetric about its median value. That is, there may be more categories with small numbers of observations on one side of the median than on the other side. Whenever this condition occurs, and one end of the distribution has a long "tail" (i.e., there are many categories with small frequencies), the result is said to be a **skewed distribution**. Thus, the distribution of education, using data from Table 2.3, is skewed. When distributions are skewed, the mean and the median differ, as they do in this example (mean = 13.25, Mdn = 13). When the long tail is to the right of the median (toward the high-valued categories), the distribution is said to have **positive skew**; when the tail is to the left of the median (toward the low-valued categories), the distribution has **negative skew**. (Put another way, a positively skewed distribution has a mean that is higher than its median, while a negatively skewed distribution has a median that is higher than its mean.) Years of schooling in Table 2.3 has a positive skew.

One measure of skewness in a distribution is

$$\text{Skewness} = \frac{3(\overline{Y} - \text{Mdn})}{s_Y}$$

If the mean and median are identical, skewness equals zero, but as the mean and median differ by large amounts relative to the distribution's standard deviation, skewness takes on either large positive or negative values. The skewness for education is $[(3)(13.25 - 13)]/2.93 = 0.26$, indicating a very slightly positive skew.

When a distribution is relatively symmetric, its mean and median will be very close to one another, as they are in the education example. When a distribution is highly skewed, however, these two central tendency measures can differ rather sharply. As the skewness formula shows, the mean is higher than the median for distributions with a positive skew. The opposite ordering holds for distributions with a negative skew. The mean and median differ because the mean is a weighted average—extreme values affect it—whereas the median is not. Consequently, many social scientists favor using the median as a central tendency measure for distributions that are highly skewed, such as distributions of personal income. For example, the U.S. Census Bureau's analyses of earnings by Americans of different races, genders, ages, or regions typically report median values for people in these categories, to avoid distortions that would result from using means.

2.6 Percentiles and Quantiles

A useful statistic that can be derived from cumulative distributions is the **percentile**, which is the outcome or score below which a given percent-

skewed distribution—a distribution that is nonsymmetric about its median value, having many categories with small frequencies at one end

positive skew—the tail of a skewed distribution is to the right of the median (mean greater than median)

negative skew—the tail of a skewed distribution is to the left of the median (median greater than mean)

percentile—the outcome or score below which a given percentage of the observations in a distribution falls

age of the observations falls. For example, in Table 2.3, 11 years of education is at the 17th percentile. That is, 17% of the respondents have 11 or fewer years of education. The median is the 50th percentile. The median is the outcome that divides the distribution in two halves. In Table 2.3 the median is 13 years of education; the 97th percentile is 19 years of education.

When data are grouped in categories of more than one unit width, calculating percentiles can be quite tedious. Their computation requires a knowledge of true limits and midpoints, topics to which we turn now.

2.6.1 True Limits and Midpoints

Grouping data into measurement classes raises the problem of determining the true limits and midpoints of intervals. For the purpose of instruction only, the education data in Table 2.3 have been recoded into the wider intervals shown in Table 2.7. The widths of most intervals are 4 years, as you can see in the first column of the table. The interval limits are defined by whole numbers—such as 9–12 years—but the **true limits** of that interval are 8.5 to 12.5. These numbers are the exact lower and upper bounds of numerical values that could be rounded into the category. (Here we ignore the rounding rule that decimals ending in 0.5 should be alternately rounded up or down to a whole integer.) Note that true limits cover the entire interval so as to ensure that no gaps or holes appear in the distribution. The second column of Table 2.7 shows the true limits for the five measurement intervals created for this example.

The **midpoint** of an interval is calculated by adding the true limits of each measured category and dividing by 2. For example, the midpoint of the interval 12.5–16.5 years is (12.5 + 16.5)/2 = 29/2 = 14.5. The midpoints for all the other intervals are shown in the third column of Table

true limits—the exact lower and upper bounds of numerical values that could be rounded into the category

midpoint—a number exactly halfway between the true upper and lower limits of a measurement class or interval, obtained by adding the upper to the lower limits and dividing by 2

TABLE 2.7
Distribution of Grouped Education Data

Years	True Limits	Midpoint	f	p	cf
0–4	−0.5–4.5	2.0	26	.009	26
5–8	4.5–8.5	6.5	134	.048	160
9–12	8.5–12.5	10.5	1,177	.417	1,337
13–16	12.5–16.5	14.5	1,178	.418	2,515
17–20	16.5–20.5	18.5	305	.108	2,820

Source: Table 2.3.

2.7. *The midpoint is the single number that best represents the entire measurement interval.*

Once we have selected the measurement interval, we tally the frequency (*f*), or the number of cases, in each interval, as shown in the fourth column of Table 2.7. These frequencies are next converted to proportions and cumulative frequencies as shown in the last two columns of the table.

2.6.2 Computing Percentiles

When the data are grouped such as they are in Table 2.7, percentiles are computed using the formula

$$P_i = L_p + \left(\frac{(p_i)(N - cf_p)}{f_p} \right)(W_i)$$

where

P_i = The score of the *i*th percentile

L_p = The true lower limit of the interval containing the *i*th percentile

p_i = The *i*th percentile written as a proportion (e.g., the 75th percentile becomes 0.75 in the formula)

N = The total number of observations

cf_p = The cumulative frequency up to *but not including* the interval containing P_i

f_p = The frequency in the interval containing the *i*th percentile

W_i = The width of the interval containing P_i; $W_i = U_p - L_p$

where U_p and L_p are the upper and lower true limits of the interval containing P_i.

From the grouped data in Table 2.7, we see that the 90th percentile must fall into the 17–20 year interval. The value of the 90th percentile is calculated as

$$P_{90} = 16.5 + \left(\frac{(.90)(2,820) - 2,515}{305} \right)(4) = 16.80 \text{ years}$$

since $i = 90$, $L_p = 16.5$, $N = 2,820$, $cf_p = 2,515$, $f_p = 305$, and $W_i = 4$.

The median years of education for the ungrouped data in Table 2.3 is 13, the value between cases 1,410 and 1,411 in the distribution. By contrast, the median number of years for the grouped data in Table 2.7, where the data have been more coarsely grouped, is the 50th percentile, estimated as

$$P_{50} = 12.50 + \left(\frac{(.50)(2,820) - 1,337}{270} \right)(1) = 12.77 \text{ years}$$

As this example makes clear, grouping a data distribution can create nontrivial errors in its description, especially if the ungrouped distribution is highly skewed. When computing descriptive statistics such as the mean, median, or variance, it is always preferable to use the data in their most disaggregated form.

2.6.3 Quantiles

quantile—a division of observations into groups with known proportions in each group

quartiles—the values of a number scale that divide a set of observations into four groups of equal size

quintiles—the values of a number scale that divide a set of observations into five groups of equal size

deciles—the values of a number scale that divide a set of observations into 10 groups of equal size

Percentiles are special cases of **quantiles**, which divide a set of observations into groups with known proportions in each group. Other special cases of quantiles are quartiles, quintiles, and deciles.

Quartiles are the values of a number scale that divide the observations into *four equal groups of equal size*. Q_1 is that point below which one-fourth of the observations lie, Q_2 is the point below which one-half of the observations lie, and so on. **Quintiles** divide the observations into *5 equal groups*, and **deciles** into *10 equal groups*. As we saw previously, *percentiles* divide observations into *100 equal groups*.

P_i is used to designate the *i*th percentile, D_i the *i*th decile, K_i the *i*th quintile, and Q_i the *i*th quartile. In this notation, $Q_1 = P_{25}$—the first quartile is exactly the same as the 25th percentile. Similarly, $K_1 = D_2$—the first quintile is the same as the second decile. Box 2.3 shows the relationship of the various quantiles to percentiles in tabular form.

To find quantile values, simply apply the appropriate percentile formula. For example, to obtain the third quartile (Q_3) for years of education in Table 2.3, calculate the 75th percentile (P_{75}). We see that this value must fall into the category of 16 years, which has true limits of 15.5–16.5 and an interval width of 1.00. The values are $P_{75} = Q_3 = 15.53$ years of education. That is, 75% of respondents have 15.53 or fewer years of education; alternatively, just 25% of the sample have 15.53 or more years of education.

2.7 Standardized Scores (Z Scores)

Researchers often compare scores across two or more distributions with different means and standard deviations, but an identical score can mean something quite different in each sample. For example, an annual income

Box 2.3 **Relationships of Quartiles, Quintiles, and Deciles to Percentiles**

Of all the quantiles, the percentile provides the largest number of equal-sized groups—100 of them. The relationships of quartiles, quintiles, and deciles to percentiles is therefore easily shown, as in the following table:

Quartile	Percentile	Quintile	Percentile	Decile	Percentile
Q_1	P_{25}	K_1	P_{20}	D_1	P_{10}
Q_2	P_{50}	K_2	P_{40}	D_2	P_{20}
Q_3	P_{75}	K_3	P_{60}	D_3	P_{30}
		K_4	P_{80}	D_4	P_{40}
				D_5	P_{50}
				D_6	P_{60}
				D_7	P_{70}
				D_8	P_{80}
				D_9	P_{90}

of \$150,000 would be quite unusual in a sample of school teachers, but not for a sample of physicians. To compare scores across distributions, taking their different means and standard deviations into account, we can transform the original distribution to *standardized scores* (**Z scores**, as they are more commonly called). Using a distribution's mean and standard deviation, the Z transformation puts all the scores in each distribution onto the same scale, one where the unit of measurement is the standard deviation. The Z score formula for the ith case in a distribution is

Z scores—a transformation of the scores of a continuous frequency distribution by subtracting the mean from each outcome and dividing by the standard deviation

$$Z_i = \frac{d_i}{s_Y} = \frac{(Y_i - \bar{Y})}{s_Y}$$

The Z_i score corresponding to a given Y_i score is the number of standard deviations that case i lies above or below the mean of its distribution. The larger the Z score in the positive or negative direction, the farther away that case lies from the sample mean. A Z score of 0 occurs when an observation falls exactly at the distribution's mean.

Table 2.8 shows the calculation of Z scores for the student grades. For example, the Z score for student #5 (+1.90) is almost as many standard deviation units above the mean percentage as student #2's Z score

TABLE 2.8
Z Scores for Student Grades

Student	Y_i	$\dfrac{(Y_i - \bar{Y})}{s_Y}$	Z_i
1	6	(6 − 5.15) / 1.50	+0.57
2	2	(2 − 5.15) / 1.50	−2.10
3	4	(4 − 5.15) / 1.50	−0.77
4	4	(4 − 5.15) / 1.50	−0.77
5	8	(8 − 5.15) / 1.50	+1.90
6	6	(6 − 5.15) / 1.50	+0.57
7	3	(3 − 5.15) / 1.50	−1.43
8	5	(5 − 5.15) / 1.50	−0.10
9	4	(4 − 5.15) / 1.50	−0.77
10	5	(5 − 5.15) / 1.50	−0.10
11	5	(5 − 5.15) / 1.50	−0.10
12	6	(6 − 5.15) / 1.50	+0.57
13	5	(5 − 5.15) / 1.50	−0.10
14	4	(4 − 5.15) / 1.50	−0.77
15	4	(4 − 5.15) / 1.50	−0.77
16	7	(7 − 5.15) / 1.50	+1.23
17	6	(6 − 5.15) / 1.50	+0.57
18	7	(7 − 5.15) / 1.50	+1.23
19	5	(5 − 5.15) / 1.50	−0.10
20	7	(7 − 5.15) / 1.50	+1.23

Source: Table 2.4.

(−2.10) is below the mean. All but six students' Z scores fall within ±1.00 standard deviations of the mean. Four of these five noteworthy Z scores all occur at the upper end of the range, reflecting the distribution's positive skew. Those students each have B+ or higher grades.

Because the Z transformation standardizes a distribution of scores, not surprisingly every distribution of Z scores has the *same* mean, variance, and standard deviation. Specifically, the mean of a Z score distribution is always zero, and its variance and standard deviation always equal 1. Box 2.4 gives proofs of the mean and variance for a standardized distribution. Z scores are easy to compute for ungrouped data, as shown in Table 2.8. If you transform the grouped education data in Table 2.3 to Z scores, using that distribution's mean and standard deviation, and apply the mean and variance formulas for grouped data, you will also see

---

Box 2.4 The Mean and Variance of a Z-Score Distribution

Any numerical distribution that is transformed to Z scores remains a distribution having a specific mean and variance. Hence, using the formula for the mean, we can calculate the mean of a Z-score distribution by substituting Z in place of Y:

$$\bar{Z} = \sum_{i=1}^{N} \frac{Z_i}{N}$$

But the numerator ($\sum Z_i$) is equal to $\sum (Y_i - \bar{Y})$, which is always zero (see section 2.5.3). Hence, $\bar{Z} = 0$.

A Z score's variance is

$$s_z^2 = \frac{\sum (Z_i - \bar{Z})^2}{N - 1}$$

However, because the mean of Z scores is 0, the variance reduces to

$$s_z^2 = \frac{\sum (Z_i - 0)^2}{N - 1} = \frac{\sum Z_i^2}{N - 1}$$

To find the numerical value of the Z-score distribution's variance, we must convert from the standard score back into the original Y values. The Z score in its original Y-score form is $Z_i = (Y_i - \bar{Y})/s_Y$. Substitute this quantity in the equation for the variance of Z:

$$s_z^2 = \frac{\sum Z_i^2}{N - 1} = \frac{\sum [(Y_i - \bar{Y})/s_Y]^2}{N - 1}$$

Simplify the right-hand side by squaring the fraction in the numerator and dividing both the top and bottom by $(N-1)$:

$$s_z^2 = \frac{\sum (Y_i - \bar{Y})^2}{(s_Y^2)(N - 1)}$$

$$= s_Y^2/s_Y^2 = 1.00$$

since in the second-to-last step, the term $\dfrac{\sum (Y_i - \bar{Y})^2}{N - 1}$ is the definition of s_Y^2.

that the *Z* score mean is 0 and the variance is 1 (within rounding error limits). Because we use *Z* scores *very* often in this text, you should be sure that you thoroughly understand this section.

2.8   Exploratory Data Analysis Methods for Displaying Continuous Data

exploratory data analysis—the methods for displaying distributions of continuous variables

stem-and-leaf diagram— a type of graph that displays the observed values and frequency counts of a frequency distribution

In this section we provide a brief introduction to some techniques for displaying continuous data called **exploratory data analysis** (EDA). One EDA method for displaying frequency distributions of grouped continuous data is called a **stem-and-leaf diagram**. Figure 2.4 shows a stem-and-leaf diagram for voter turnout for 50 U.S. states in the 1998 congressional election. This variable is the percentage of eligible voters casting ballots in that election. To construct a stem-and-leaf display, take the following steps:

1. Order the data values from lowest to highest.

2. Decide on the *leading digit* and the *trailing digit* in the display. Ordinarily the number of leading digits should be no more than *N*/3 so that the display is interpretable.

3. For each observation, write down each leading digit from lowest to highest under a column labeled "stem," and adjacent to each stem write the relevant trailing digits, which are called "leaves."

In this example, the 50 states' congressional voting turnout values range from 10.0% to 59.2%. We chose the 10's place (the decile) as the leading digit and the 1's place as the trailing digit. Any digits after the decimal point were simply ignored by rounding to the nearest whole percent. For example, in Louisiana's turnout of 10.0%, the leading digit is "10" and its trailing digit is "0." For Minnesota, with the highest turnouts at 59.2%, the leading digit is "5" and the trailing digit is "9." Note that these data require only five leading digits (1–5), much fewer than the maximum under step 2 (50/3 = 17).

A stem-and-leaf diagram somewhat resembles a histogram turned on its side. The vertical stem of Figure 2.4 consists of the leading digits of the turnout data. To the right of each stem are its leaves, consisting of the trailing digits of the relevant data points. Thus, in the "1" stem, Louisiana's "0" and Florida's "1" appear as leaf values. In the "5" stem, representing observed turnouts of 50–59%, the "0", "1", "4", and "9" leaves represent the turnouts of Wyoming, Montana, Alaska, and Min-

FIGURE 2.4
Stem-and-Leaf Diagram for Voter Turnout in the 1998 Congressional Election

Stems	*Leaves*	*(N)*
1	01	(2)
2	2355889	(7)
3	00222334455667778899	(20)
4	00011333444456799	(17)
5	0149	(4)

Source: U.S. States Data Set.

nesota, respectively. *Importantly, each entry on the leaf stands for one observation*. Thus, each leaf's total can be written in parentheses at the extreme right of the diagram, as we have done to facilitate interpretation. The range below the median is a bit wider (38 – 10 = 28) than is the range above the median (59 – 38 = 21). However, with the mean (37.1%) almost identical to the median (37.5%), the state turnout distribution has only a slight negative skewness of –0.16 (see section 2.5.5). An advantage of a stem-and-leaf diagram over a histogram is the reader's ability to recover more precise information about the individual data points comprising the distribution. For example, how many states had turnouts of 37%?

A second EDA technique for displaying and interpreting orderable data is called a **box-and-whisker** diagram or more simply a **boxplot**. A box-and-whisker diagram shows the central tendency, dispersion, and general shape of a data distribution. To construct box-and-whisker diagrams you must know the range, the median, and the "hinges" of a distribution. We illustrate using the rounded voter turnout data in Figure 2.4.

The **lower hinge** is the value of the observation that divides the first quartile (Q_1) from the upper three-quarters of a distribution and is signified by H_L. The data in Figure 2.4 consist of 50 observations, making the 12th case in the distribution the lowest quartile. This observation is a state with a turnout of 32%. Hence, $H_L = 32$. The **upper hinge** is the value of the observation that divides the top quartile (Q_3) from the lower three-quarters of an orderable distribution and is signified by H_U. In Figure 2.4 the 38th case marks the upper quartile; this state had a 44% voter turnout. Therefore, $H_U = 44$.

To construct the boxplot, draw a rectangular box between the two hinges, H_L and H_U, as shown in Figure 2.5. The median is noted by a hor-

box-and-whisker/ boxplot—a type of graph for discrete and continuous variables in which boxes and lines represent central tendency, variability, and shape of a distribution of observed data

lower hinge—the value of the observation that divides the lower quartile from the upper three-quarters of an ordered distribution. Symbolized by H_L

upper hinge—the value of the observation that divides the upper quartile from the lower three-quarters of an ordered distribution. Symbolized by H_U

FIGURE 2.5
Box-and-Whisker Plot of 1988 Voter Turnout

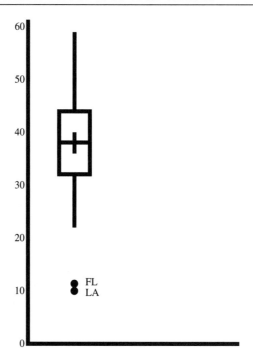

outlier—an observed value that is so extreme (either large or small) that it seems to stand apart from the rest of the distribution

izontal line inside the box (37.5%). Next determine whether the distribution contains any **outliers**. An outlier is any value that is so extreme (either large or small) that it seems to stand far apart from the rest of the distribution. One way to identify outliers is to calculate whether any observations lie below the **lower inner fence** (LIF) or above the **upper inner fence** (UIF). To compute the LIF and UIF, we must first determine the H-spread (short for **hinge spread**) of the distribution, which is merely the difference between the upper and lower hinges. That is,

lower inner fence—that part of an ordered distribution below which an observation is considered an outlier. Symbolized by LIF

upper inner fence—that part of an ordered distribution above which an observation is considered to be an outlier. Symbolized by UIF

$$HS = H_U - H_L$$

where HS is the hinge spread.

hinge spread/H-spread—the difference between the upper and lower hinges, i.e., $H_U - H_L$. Symbolized by HS

For voter turnout, HS = 44 − 32 = 12. With this information we can now determine the two inner fences and see whether the distribution contains any outliers.

$$\text{LIF} = H_L - (1.5)(\text{HS})$$

$$\text{UIF} = H_U + (1.5)(\text{HS})$$

For the turnout data in Figure 2.4, LIF = 32 – (1.5)(12) = 14% and UIF = 44 + (1.5)(12) = 62%. No outliers appear in the upper end of the distribution. However, Louisiana's 10% and Florida's 11% voter turnouts are clearly outliers at the lower end of the distribution. An outlier is given special attention in a box-and-whisker plot by identifying it as a point with a label, as shown in Figure 2.5.

The diagram is completed by drawing a whisker (vertical line) from H_U (the upper hinge) to the largest value in the distribution that is not an outlier: 59% in this example. The second whisker is drawn from H_L (the lower hinge) to the smallest value in the distribution that is not an outlier: 22% in this case.

The 1998 state voter turnout distribution's slight negative skew is not evident from identical distance in the box-and-whisker diagram from the median to both the upper hinge (H_U) and the lower hinge (H_L). However, the negative skew is indicated by the substantially greater distance of outliers Louisiana and Florida below the lower hinge and an absence of outliers at the upper end of the distribution.

In this section we have provided only a brief overview of how exploratory data analysis techniques can usefully describe distributions. In chapter 4 we will present a second example comparing two distributions using stem-and-leaf and boxplot diagrams.

Review of Key Concepts and Symbols

These key concepts and symbols are listed in the order of appearance in this chapter. Combined with the definitions in the margins, they will help you to review the material and can serve as a self-test for mastery of the concepts.

tally	rounding
frequency distribution	dichotomous variable (dichotomy)
outcome	grouped data
relative frequency distribution	measurement interval (measurement class)
percentage distribution	recoding
relative frequency	cumulative frequency
proportion	cumulative frequency distribution
percentage	cumulative percentage

cumulative percentage distribution
statistical table
diagram (graph)
bar chart
histogram
polygon
central tendency
variation
mode
median
mean
index of diversity
index of qualitative variation
range
average absolute deviation
variance
standard deviation
skewed distribution
positive skew
negative skew
percentile
true limits
midpoint
quantile
quartile
quintile
decile
Z score (standardized score)
exploratory data analysis (EDA)
stem-and-leaf diagram

box-and-whisker diagram (boxplot)
lower hinge
upper hinge
outlier
lower inner fence
upper inner fence
hinge spread (H-spread)
N
f_i
p_i
cf
$c\%$
Mdn
$\%$
$\bar{Y}$
D
IQV
d_i
AAD
s_Y^2
s_Y
P_i
D_i
K_i
Q_i
Z_i
H_i
LIF
UIF
HS

PROBLEMS

General Problems

1. Construct a frequency distribution for the following set of
   outcomes

12	6	7	5	6	8
9	7	8	10	6	7
11	7	8	9	7	6

2. Construct a table of relative frequencies and a percentage
   distribution for the following states of residence for a sample of
   college students, where M = Minnesota, W = Wisconsin, I = Iowa,
   N = North Dakota, and S = South Dakota:

   M W M I S S W N I M W M S N W M M I M

3. Construct cumulative frequency and cumulative percentage
   distributions for the following prices of personal computers, using
   the following measurement intervals: $999 and under;
   $1,000–1,499; $1,500–1,999; and $2,000 and over:

   $1,499.35 $1,999.27 $1,999.78 $1,499.56 $999.48

   $1,499.39 $1,999.11 $1,499.88 $999.10

4. Round the following numbers to the units of measurement shown:

Original	*Rounded Units*
a. $8.57	Dollars
b. $3.47	Dollars
c. $645.39	Hundreds
d. $1,256.01	Hundreds
e. $18,500.22	Thousands
f. $4,499.99	Thousands

5. Construct a histogram and a polygon for the following data on
   frequency of listening to classical music: Never = 40; Occasionally
   = 8; Regularly = 3.

6. For the following data, 8, 12, 14, 11, 13, compute the (a) range; (b)
   average absolute deviation; (c) variance; (d) standard deviation.

7. In 13 games, a basketball team scored the following number of
   points: 62, 70, 84, 51, 63, 78, 54, 63, 71, 63, 52, 60, 85. Compute
   the (a) mean; (b) median; (c) mode of this distribution.

8. According to United Nations figures, the populations of the world's ten largest nations in 2000 (rounded to the nearest million inhabitants) were as follows: China, 1,278; India, 1,014; United States, 278; Indonesia, 212; Brazil, 170; Pakistan, 156; Russia, 147; Bangladesh, 129; Japan, 127; and Nigeria, 112. Find the (a) mean; (b) mode; (c) median; (d) variance; (e) standard deviation.

9. The gender composition of the 7,483 members of the freshman class at Humongous State U is 52% female and 48% male. What is the variance of this distribution?

10. On an 8-point scale rating dormitory food services, a sample of 83 students has a mean of 5.3 and a standard deviation of 0.7. What are the Z scores for: (a) 7; (b) 3; (c) 4?

Problems Requiring the 1998 General Social Survey

11. Describe the frequency distribution of respondents' brothers and sisters (SIBS), using all the central tendency and dispersion statistics discussed in this chapter. Change the "Don't Know" and "No Answer" responses to missing values.

12. For the ideal number of children (CHLDIDEL) reported by respondents, give the (a) mode, (b) median, (c) range, (d) mean, (e) variance, (f) standard deviation, (g) skewness, and (h) calculate the Z score for someone choosing 4 children. Change the "As many as you want," "Don't Know," "No Answer," and "Question Not Asked" responses to missing values.

13. For the frequency of sexual activity in the past year (SEXFREQ), give the (a) mode, (b) median, (c) range, (d) mean, (e) variance, (f) standard deviation, (g) skewness, and (h) calculate the Z score for someone having sex "once or twice per year" (category = 1). Change the "Don't Know," "No Answer," and "Question Not Asked" responses to missing values.

14. Compare respondents' approval of abortion under conditions in which a woman isn't married (ABSINGLE) and where a woman's health is seriously endangered (ABHLTH). What are the modal categories of each variable? Change the "Don't Know," "No Answer," and "Not Applicable" responses to missing values.

15. Compare respondents' confidence in the American press (CONPRESS) with their confidence in medicine (CONMEDIC), using whatever statistics you think appropriate. Change the "Don't Know," "No Answer," and "Not Applicable" responses to missing values.

II. Statistical Inference

3

MAKING STATISTICAL INFERENCES

Social scientists seldom study a sample because they are only interested in describing that sample's central tendency and dispersion. Rather, they also wish to draw inferences about the population from which the sample was selected. Because assessing the entire population is often too costly, some method is required for *generalizing* from the sample results to the larger population. Reasonably accurate conclusions can be reached using elementary principles of probability theory. In this chapter we will introduce some basic concepts necessary for understanding the topic of statistical inference. We will explain estimation and hypothesis testing for single-sample estimates of population values from sample data and show how to apply some fundamental probability distributions.

3.1 Drawing Inferences About Populations from Samples

A statistical significance test permits one to make a reasonable **inference** that conclusions drawn from a sample of observations are true for the population from which that sample came. Absolute certainty is never possible, for by chance one might have selected an unusually deviant set of

inference—the process of making generalizations or drawing conclusions about the attributes of a population from evidence contained in a sample

sample cases. If the sample is drawn randomly, however, we can make an inference about the population situation with a calculable probability that the conclusion cannot be rejected.

random sampling—
a procedure for selecting a set of representative observations from a population, in which each observation has an equal chance of being selected for the sample

Random sampling, introduced in chapter 1, requires that each observation (i.e., a person, an object, or an event) in a population has an equal chance of being selected for the sample. That is, if the population consists of N units, each unit has a probability of exactly $1/N$ of being chosen for the sample. The 1998 General Social Survey sampled 2,832 American adults,[1] only a tiny fraction of the 200,344,000 people aged 18 and over.[2] Each person had approximately one chance in 70,743—or a probability smaller than .000014—of being interviewed. Furthermore, literally trillions of unique samples of 2,832 persons could have been drawn by the National Opinion Research Center. Given that only one of these possible samples was actually selected, how likely is it that these results accurately reflect some attribute of interest in the entire population? Probability theory and hypothesis-testing procedures help to ensure that the chances of mistaken conclusions are small.

3.2   Some Basic Probability Concepts

probability distribution—
a set of outcomes, each of which has an associated probability of occurrence

The observations in a population have an associated **probability distribution**. For example, in a randomly shuffled deck of 52 playing cards, the chance that the first card dealt is the ace of spades is 1/52. Similarly, the chance of randomly drawing a card from the heart suit is 13/52 or 1/4. Probabilities are usually expressed not as fractions but as proportions; thus, the probability of drawing the ace of spades is .019 and the probability of drawing a heart is .25. The probabilities for all observations in the population must add up to 1.00. Thus, the sum of the probabilities for the heart, diamond, club, and spade suits is .25 + .25 + .25 + .25 = 1.00. If an outcome cannot occur, such as a joker card excluded from the deck, it has a probability of .00.

---

[1]A U.S. national sample cannot be selected by simple random sampling, which requires a complete listing of every person in the population. Survey research organizations use more cost-efficient sampling techniques, which we will not describe here. We analyze the GSS data as though they had been drawn using simple random procedures, which causes only minor errors in statistical inference.

[2]Population figures are taken from "Residential Population Estimates of the U.S. by Age and Sex: April 1, 1990, to July 1, 1999, with Short-Term Projection to April 1, 2000," published May 24, 2000, by the Population Estimates Program, Population Division, U.S. Census Bureau, Washington, DC (http://www.census.gov/population/estimates/nation/intfile2-1.txt).

3.2.1 Continuous Probability Distributions

The preceding examples show how easy it is to calculate probabilities for a small population with discrete outcomes. They are simply relative frequencies or proportions (see section 2.1). As noted in chapter 1, many social measures are continuous, classifying observations by the quantity of an attribute: annual income, achievement test scores, rates of AIDS infection. In principle, a **continuous probability distribution** means that no interruptions occur between a variable's outcomes. Probabilities attached to various outcomes of a continuous variable can be connected by a single continuous line, as in the hypothetical example in Figure 3.1. A very precisely measured continuous variable (such as an income of $31,277.15) means that few cases will have identical outcomes; hence, the probability of observing any outcome approaches zero in a large sample with continuous measures. For this reason, probabilities for continuous variables are measured as the area between two outcomes, *a* and *b*. The probability of observing an outcome of variable *Y* lying between points *a* and *b* is labeled alpha (α); that is, $p(a \leq Y \leq b) = \alpha$. This expression is read, "The probability that outcome *Y* is greater than or equal to *a* and less than or equal to *b* is alpha," where alpha is a probability expressed as a decimal between .00 and 1.00. In general, the probability of a variable *Y* can simply be denoted as $p(Y)$.

continuous probability distribution—a probability distribution for a continuous variable, with no interruptions or spaces between the outcomes of the variable

3.2.2 Discrete Probability Distributions

In the same way that researchers can describe and summarize a sample with statistics such as the mean, they also can describe and summarize

FIGURE 3.1
A Continuous Probability Distribution

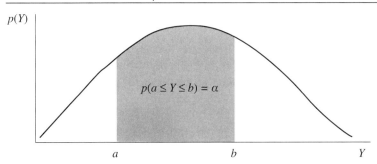

Source: David Knoke and George W. Bohrnstedt, *Basic Social Statistics* (Itasca, IL: F. E. Peacock Publishers, Inc., 1991), 153.

population distributions. The three major population descriptors are the mean, variance, and standard deviation. These descriptors are called **population parameters** because they are *constants* in the populations. By contrast, the sample mean, variance, and standard deviation are *variables*, because their numerical values vary from sample to sample. Because population parameters are often unknown, sample statistics are used as estimators of parameters.

population parameter— a descriptive characteristic of a population, such as a mean, standard deviation, or variance. Symbolized by θ

The single number that best describes a probability distribution of discrete scores is its **expected value**, labeled $E(Y)$ and given by

expected value—the single number that best describes a probability distribution of discrete scores

$$E(Y) = \sum_{i=1}^{K} Y_i p(Y_i)$$

In computing the expected value of a probability distribution, we simply weight each of the K outcomes by its probability of occurrence and add up the resulting terms. That is, the score of the observations in the ith category is multiplied by the probability of a case falling into that category, and then these products are summed across all K categories in the distribution.

mean of a probability distribution—the expected value of a population of scores

The **mean of a probability distribution**, labeled μ_Y (Greek letter *mu*), is defined the same way as the expected value; that is,

$$\mu_Y = \sum_{i=1}^{K} Y_i p(Y_i)$$

For example, the mean of the distribution of outcomes of a die toss is computed as the sum of the products of the die face value times the (equal) probability of that face value: $\mu_Y = 1(1/6) + 2(1/6) + 3(1/6) + 4(1/6) + 5(1/6) + 6(1/6) = (1 + 2 + 3 + 4 + 5 + 6)(1/6) = 21/6 = 3.5$.

We can also compute the expected value of other functions of Y, which are represented by a very general function, call it $g(Y)$. In this case,

$$E\left[g(Y)\right] = \sum_{i=1}^{K} g(Y_i) p(Y_i)$$

variance of a probability distribution—the expected spread or dispersion of a population of scores

One application of this general formulation for expected values is provided by the definition of the **variance of a probability distribution**, which is labeled σ_Y^2 (Greek letter *sigma*). First, let $g(Y) = (Y - \mu_Y)^2$. Then it follows that

$$\sigma_Y^2 = E(Y - \mu_Y)^2$$
$$= \sum_{i=1}^{K} (Y_i - \mu_Y)^2 p(Y_i)$$

As in a sample, the variance of a probability distribution measures the spread or dispersion in the population.

The square root of the population variance is called the standard deviation, as it is with sample statistics (see chapter 2). For a population, it is symbolized σ_Y and is given by

$$\sigma_Y = \sqrt{\sigma_Y^2}$$

Using die tosses as an example (recall that $\mu_Y = 3.5$), we can calculate that $\sigma_Y^2 = (1 - 3.5)^2(1/6) + (2 - 3.5)^2(1/6) + (3 - 3.5)^2(1/6) + (4 - 3.5)^2(1/6) + (5 - 3.5)^2(1/6) + (6 - 3.5)^2(1/6) = (17.5)/6 = 2.92$ and $\sigma_Y = \sqrt{2.92} = 1.71$.

Because researchers ordinarily cannot observe entire populations, the parameters μ_Y and σ_Y^2 are of largely theoretical interest. You need to understand the concept of expected value, however, in order to understand the discussion of inference in the sections and chapters that follow.[3] Box 3.1 provides a summary of symbols used for the sample statistics introduced in chapter 2 and the population parameters used thus far in this chapter.

In the following sections we will introduce some theorems that can be used to estimate the probability of observing a given outcome in a distribution having a known mean and standard deviation. These preliminaries will illustrate the rarity of a given sample mean occurring in a population of sample means generated by taking all possible samples of size N. In drawing an inference we first hypothesize that a population has a mean equal to some value μ_Y. If the discrepancy between the *observed* sample mean and the *hypothesized* population mean is too large—that is, if it is too "deviant" to have come from a population with a mean of μ_Y—we reject the hypothesis about the value of the population mean, μ_Y.

3.3 Chebycheff's Inequality Theorem   Nope

A close connection exists between the distance of an observation from the mean of a distribution and the probability of that observation: on average, observations far from the mean occur less often than those close to the mean. Thus, a score that is one-half standard deviation above the

---

[3]We have not discussed the expected value, mean, and variance for continuous probability distributions because integral calculus is required. However, the meanings of the mean and variance for continuous probability distributions are identical to those used for discrete probability distributions.

Box 3.1   Population Parameter and Sample Statistic Symbols

Statistical formulas may apply either to an entire population of observations or to a sample drawn from a population. While the formulas are often the same or similar, the symbolic notation differs. Roman letters are used for *sample statistics* calculated on sample data, while Greek letters stand for the *population parameters*. For some basic statistics and parameters, the symbols are listed below.

Name	*Sample Statistic*	*Population Parameter*
Mean	$\overline{Y}$	μ_Y (mu)
Variance	s_Y^2	σ_Y^2 (sigma squared)
Standard Deviation	s_Y	σ_Y (sigma)

---

mean ($Z = +.50$; see chapter 2) has a higher probability of occurring than a score that is two standard deviations below the mean ($Z = -2.00$). In general, the more distant an outcome is from its mean, the lower the probability of observing it.

The Russian mathematician Pafnuty Chebycheff (a.k.a. Pavnutii Tchebycheff) was the first to prove a theorem about the relationship between the size of a deviation and the probability of observing the associated outcome. His result refers to the outcomes in a population, not in a sample, and it holds for any shape of distribution, no matter how skewed. **Chebycheff's inequality theorem** states that the probability of a variable differing absolutely from the mean by k or more standard deviations is *always* less than or equal to the ratio of 1 to k^2 (for all k greater than 1.0):

$$p(\,|Z| \geq k) \leq \frac{1}{k^2}$$

This equation says that the probability that the absolute value of an observation's Z score is k or more standard deviations from the mean is equal to or less than 1 divided by the square of k standard deviations. Clearly, as k gets larger in the positive or negative direction, the proba-

Chebycheff's inequality theorem—the probability a variable differs absolutely from the mean by k or more standard deviations is *always* less than or equal to the ratio of 1 to k^2 (for all k greater than 1.0)

bility decreases; hence, according to Chebycheff, extreme scores are unlikely.

For example, consider a student scoring two standard deviations above the class mean on a midterm exam. The theorem states that the probability of observing a score this far above or below the mean is $1/(2^2)$ or less (i.e., $p \leq .25$). Also, an observed $Z = \pm 3$ or greater has a probability of $1/(3^2) = .11$ or less. Chebycheff's inequality theorem applies regardless of the underlying shape of a population distribution. Importantly, the theorem is a claim about *probability*, not about certainty. It does not guarantee that any given outcome will be rarer than another outcome that is closer to the mean. It only asserts that, without information about the shape of a distribution, the probability of an observation decreases the farther it lies from the mean.

More precise probability statements can be made if we have some knowledge of the distribution's shape. If a population distribution is unimodal (has one mode) and is symmetric about its mean, a derivation of Chebycheff's inequality theorem states

$$p(\,|Z| \geq k) \leq \left(\frac{4}{9}\right)\left(\frac{1}{k^2}\right)$$

Thus, in a unimodal symmetric distribution, outcomes that are two or more standard deviations from the mean will be observed with probability $(.444)(1/2^2) = (.444)(.25) = .111$ or less. Compare this probability to .25 when no assumptions can be made about the shape of the distribution. Chebycheff's inequality shows how knowledge about a distribution's shape affects the probability of observing deviant cases, a point relevant to the next section.

3.4 The Normal Distribution

A very important family of unimodal, symmetric distributions in inferential statistics is the family of Gaussian distributions, named after the German mathematician Carl Friedrich Gauss. Unfortunately, today they are exclusively called **normal distributions**, because they were originally believed to be useful in establishing social norms for many kinds of variables. Although we now know that almost no social data take such shapes, the term continues to be widely used today. All normal distributions are described by a rather formidable equation:

normal distribution—a smooth, bell-shaped theoretical probability distribution for continuous variables that can be generated from a formula

$$p(Y) = \frac{e^{-(Y - \mu_Y)^2/2\sigma_Y^2}}{\sqrt{2\pi\sigma_Y^2}}$$

FIGURE 3.2
Two Examples of Normal Distributions

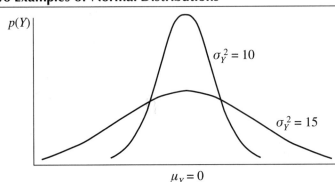

Source: David Knoke and George W. Bohrnstedt, *Basic Social Statistics* (Itasca, IL: F. E. Peacock Publishers, Inc., 1991), 157.

A particular normal curve's shape is determined by only two values: the population mean, μ_Y, and its variance, σ_Y^2. Figure 3.2 show two normal curves, one with $\sigma_Y^2 = 10$ and the other with $\sigma_Y^2 = 15$, and both with $\mu_Y = 0$. The smaller the population variance, the closer on average are its observations to the mean, and hence the "thinner" the tails of that normal distribution. Although the tails of the normal seem to touch the horizontal axis, the theoretical distribution of values actually ranges from $-\infty$ to $+\infty$. Thus, the tails approach but never actually reach the horizontal axis in each direction.

Calculating probabilities of outcomes for normal distributions with differing means and variances would be tedious and time-consuming. However, every distribution of scores can easily be converted to standardized (Z) scores (see section 2.7 in chapter 2). The Z-score formula for populations is $Z_i = (Y_i - \mu_Y)/\sigma_Y$. Thus, only one table of probabilities associated with distributions is necessary—the standardized normal distribution table in Appendix C, "Area Under the Normal Curve." A schematic appears in Figure 3.3.

The total area under a normal curve is unity (1.00). We noted above that the probabilities of all the cases in a distribution must sum to 1.00. Half the area in a normal curve lies to the right of the mean (which is .00, because the mean of Z scores is always zero; see Box 2.4 in chapter 2). All the Z scores in this portion are positive numbers. The other half of the area under the normal curve lies to the left of the mean, corresponding to

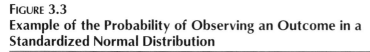

FIGURE 3.3
Example of the Probability of Observing an Outcome in a Standardized Normal Distribution

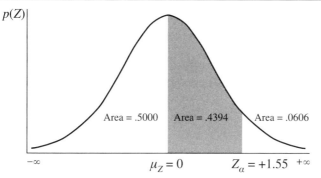

Source: David Knoke and George W. Bohrnstedt, *Basic Social Statistics* (Itasca, IL: F. E. Peacock Publishers, Inc., 1991), 159.

negative Z scores. In Figure 3.3, Z_α refers to a specific Z score whose probability of occurrence we seek. The shaded area refers to the probability of a value between $Z = 0$ and Z_α.

For example, suppose that we want to determine the probability that an outcome is at least 1.55 standard deviations above the mean of a normal distribution. Then $Z_\alpha = (+1.55)(\sigma_Z) = +1.55$, because the standard deviation of Z scores (σ_Z) is always 1 (see Box 2.4 in chapter 2). Turn to Appendix C to find the probability that this particular value occurs. First, look *down* the left column of the table until you find 1.55. Then look *across* that row to the second column. The number in this cell is .4394, the probability of an outcome lying *between* $Z = 0$ and $Z_\alpha = 1.55$. Now look in the third column, where the number .0606 appears. This value is the probability that $Z_\alpha \geq +1.55$, which is the area in the right tail of the normal distribution. Because a normal distribution is symmetric, it should be clear that the probability of an observation –1.55 or more standard deviations (i.e., to the left of the mean) also equals .0606. Probabilities from both halves of the normal curve can be added. Thus, .8788 of the area lies between $Z_\alpha = -1.55$ and $Z_\alpha = +1.55$ (i.e., $p(\,|Z_\alpha|\leq 1.55)$ = .4394 + .4394 = .8788; while only .1212 of the area lies in the two tails beyond Z_α scores of –1.55 and +1.55 (i.e., $p(\,|Z_\alpha|\geq 1.55)$ = .0606 + .0606 = .1212).

3.4.1 The Alpha Area

The area in the tail of a normal distribution that is cut off by a given Z_α is called the **alpha area**, or simply α. It is defined as

alpha area—the area in the tail of a normal distribution that is cut off by a given Z_α

$$p(\,|Z| \geq |Z_\alpha|\,) = \alpha$$

This expression is read, "The probability that the absolute value of an observed Z score is equal to or greater than Z_α absolute standard deviations equals alpha." Because an α area might also be located in the left tail, the formula above uses absolute values of Z and Z_α. Z_α is called a **critical value** because it is the minimum value of Z necessary to designate an alpha area.

critical value—the minimum value of Z necessary to designate an alpha area

We illustrate an α area in Figure 3.4, where the portion of the normal distribution between Z_α and $+\infty$ is labeled α. When we discuss hypothesis testing in section 3.8, in some cases we will split α equally between the left and right tails of the normal distribution. In such instances, the probability located in the right tail is $\alpha/2$, and the probability in the left tail is also $\alpha/2$. The two critical Z scores cutting off these areas are labeled $Z_{\alpha/2}$ and $-Z_{\alpha/2}$, respectively. Figure 3.5 illustrates these critical values, as do the following examples.

Assume that using the normal curve is appropriate and that we choose to concentrate $\alpha = .05$ entirely in the right tail, as in Figure 3.4.

FIGURE 3.4
Probability Distribution for a Type I Error in the Right Tail

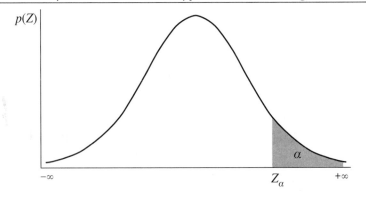

Source: David Knoke and George W. Bohrnstedt, *Basic Social Statistics* (Itasca, IL: F. E. Peacock Publishers, Inc., 1991), 160.

FIGURE 3.5
Areas Under the Normal Curve for Various *Z* Scores

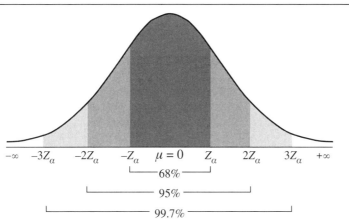

Source: David Knoke and George W. Bohrnstedt, *Basic Social Statistics* (Itasca, IL: F. E. Peacock Publishers, Inc., 1991), 161.

What value of Z_α will exactly cut off the upper 5% of the normal curve? We look up .4500 in the body of Appendix C, because .5000 − .4500 = .0500. The two tabled entries closest to .4500 are .4495 and .4505, corresponding respectively to $Z = 1.64$ and $Z = 1.65$. Averaging these two values, we conclude that Z scores that are +1.645 standard deviations or larger occur for only 5% of the observations in a normally distributed population. Therefore, $Z_\alpha = +1.645$ for this problem. What value of Z_α cuts off .01 in the left tail of a normal distribution?

Suppose we decide to split α between both tails, as in Figure 3.5. If we set $\alpha = .05$, then $\alpha/2 = .025$. To determine the pair of $Z_{\alpha/2}$ values that will put 2.5% of the area into each tail, we first calculate that .5000 − .0250 = .4750. Next, using Appendix C, we determine that the $+Z_{\alpha/2}$ associated with .4750 is +1.96. Because a normal curve is symmetric, $-Z_{\alpha/2}$ = −1.96. Thus, 95% of the area under the standardized normal distribution lies between $-Z_{\alpha/2} = -1.96$ and $+Z_{\alpha/2} = +1.96$. A total of 5% of the scores are located even farther from the mean in the two tails. You should be able to demonstrate that about 68% of the outcomes in a normal curve fall between standard deviations of −1 and +1. What proportion of the scores fall outside the range from −3 to +3 standard deviations? Assuming a normal distribution, any observation that is three or more standard deviations from the mean is rare indeed. Figure 3.5 graphically summarizes this information.

3.5 The Central Limit Theorem

central limit theorem—
if all possible random
samples of N observations
are drawn from any
population with mean μ_Y
and variance σ_Y^2, then as N
grows larger, these sample
means approach a normal
distribution, with mean μ_Y
and variance σ_Y^2/N

A very important use of the normal curve depends on the **central limit theorem**, which states:

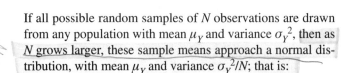

> If all possible random samples of N observations are drawn from any population with mean μ_Y and variance σ_Y^2, then as N grows larger, these sample means approach a normal distribution, with mean μ_Y and variance σ_Y^2/N; that is:

$$\mu_{\bar{Y}} = \mu_Y$$

$$\sigma_{\bar{Y}}^2 = \sigma_Y^2/N$$

The central limit theorem says that, for samples of the same size N, the mean of all sample means equals the mean of the population from which these samples were randomly drawn. Furthermore, the variance of this new hypothetical distribution is smaller than the original population variance by a factor of $1/N$. No assumptions need to be made about the shape of the population.

The hypothetical distribution of all possible means for samples of size N is called the **sampling distribution of sample means**. A sampling distribution for means involves the mean of every sample of size N that could be formed from a given population. Because any large population contains billions and trillions of unique samples, no one can actually compute the means making up a sampling distribution. It remains a purely theoretical construct. Yet, because the central limit theorem relates two population parameters (μ_Y and σ_Y^2) to the sampling distribution's mean and variance, its shape is completely determined by just these two parameters. The central limit theorem guarantees that a sample mean comes closer to the population mean as the sample size (N) increases, because the sampling distribution's variance becomes smaller as N increases. The standard deviation of a sampling distribution is called the **standard error**. Its formula is the square root of the sampling distribution variance:

$$\sigma_{\bar{Y}} = \frac{\sigma_Y}{\sqrt{N}}$$

sampling distribution of sample means—a distribution consisting of the means of all samples of size N that could be formed from a given population

standard error—the standard deviation of a sampling distribution

Knowing that sample means are normally distributed, regardless of the population from which the samples were drawn, and assuming that N is large, we can reach some important conclusions. Suppose we draw a random sample of $N = 400$ observations from a population with $\mu_Y = 100$ and $\sigma_Y = 15$. Using the formula immediately above, the standard error of the sampling distribution of means for samples of size 400 is

$$\sigma_{\bar{Y}} = \frac{15}{\sqrt{400}} = 0.75$$

From our understanding of the normal curve, we know that 95% of all sample means fall within ±1.96 standard errors of the population mean. Therefore, in this example 95% of the sample means fall in the interval between 98.53 and 101.47—that is, 100 ± (1.96)(.75). The central limit theorem assures us, first, that the mean of a random sample should equal the population mean (100), and second, that only 5% of these samples have means that lie outside the interval from 98.53 to 101.47. Suppose we increase the sample size from 400 to 1,000. The standard error now becomes even smaller; specifically,

$$\sigma_{\bar{Y}} = \frac{15}{\sqrt{1000}} = .47$$

Thus, 95% of this sampling distribution's means occur between 99.08 and 100.92, that is, inside the interval bounded by 100 ± (1.96)(.47). Thus, on average, one sample mean in 20 will fall outside this interval. We can have considerable confidence that *any* random sample of size 1,000 would give us a very accurate estimate of the mean of the population from which it was drawn.

Although the central limit theorem requires a large N to be applicable, we cannot pinpoint precisely how large a sample must be. Some textbooks recommend 30 observations; others suggest 100. On the basis of experience, we suggest that when the sample size is 100 or more the sampling distribution of means closely approximates a normal distribution. For samples with 30 or fewer cases, however, we would hesitate to assume a normal sampling distribution. For sample sizes between 30 and 100 cases, one may cautiously assume the central limit theorem applies unless the underlying population has an extremely odd shape.

3.6 Sample Point Estimates and Confidence Intervals

The central limit theorem has an important corollary: the mean of a random sample ($\bar{Y}$) is the best single estimate of the mean of the population, μ_Y, from which the sample was drawn. The sample mean is a **point estimate** of the population mean, because only a single value is estimated. We can also construct a **confidence interval** around this estimate, allowing us to express the degree to which we believe this interval contains the true population mean. (An interval either does or does not contain the population parameter, but because we do not know with certainty what

point estimate—a sample statistic used to estimate a population parameter

confidence interval— a range of values constructed around a point estimate that makes it possible to state the probability that an interval contains the population parameter between its upper and lower confidence limits

that value is, we can only form a judgment regarding our best guess as to where the parameter occurs.)

Again, the central limit theorem allows us to use the normal curve to construct a confidence interval having a specific probability, α. The formula for calculating the upper and lower limits of an α level confidence interval is

$$\bar{Y} \pm (Z_{\alpha/2})(\sigma_{\bar{Y}})$$

upper confidence limit— the highest value of a confidence interval

lower confidence limit— the lowest value of a confidence interval

To find the **upper confidence limit** (or **UCL**), add the product of the critical value ($Z_{\alpha/2}$) and the standard error to the sample mean. To get the **lower confidence limit** (or **LCL**), subtract this product from the sample mean. For example, if we choose $\alpha = .05$, the critical values of $Z_{\alpha/2}$ which put .025 of the area into each tail of the normal distribution are -1.96 and $+1.96$. We can expect that 95% of the intervals bounded by 1.96 standard errors above and below the sample mean will contain the population mean, μ_Y. For a 95% confidence interval, the LCL is $\bar{Y} - 1.96\sigma_{\bar{Y}}$ and the UCL is $\bar{Y} + 1.96\sigma_{\bar{Y}}$. Similarly, for a 68.26% confidence interval, the LCL is $\bar{Y} - \sigma_{\bar{Y}}$ and the UCL is $\bar{Y} + \sigma_{\bar{Y}}$. For a 99% confidence interval, the LCL is $\bar{Y} - 2.58\sigma_{\bar{Y}}$ and the UCL is $\bar{Y} + 2.58\sigma_{\bar{Y}}$. The smaller the α, the wider is the confidence interval.

The symbol $Z_{\alpha/2}$, introduced previously, can now be more precisely defined. In Appendix C, $Z_{\alpha/2}$ is the value that cuts off an area on the right tail of the normal curve equal to $\alpha/2$. To be 95% confident that a given interval contains μ_Y, $\alpha = .05$ by implication, and $\alpha/2 = .025$. As shown in section 3.5, $Z_{\alpha/2} = \pm1.96$ gives the correct interval for a specific $\sigma_{\bar{Y}}$.

Caution is in order when interpreting confidence intervals. It is tempting to conclude that one can be 95% confident that a given interval contains the population mean. In fact, after an interval has been constructed, the probability that it contains the population mean is either 1.00 or 0.00, depending on whether the population mean is actually inside or outside the interval. We *can* conclude that with repeated construction of confidence intervals, 95% of such intervals will contain the population mean.

Figure 3.6 illustrates the concept of a confidence interval. The solid vertical line represents the true population mean, a constant ($\mu_Y = 50.5$ in this example). The horizontal lines represent the confidence intervals constructed around the means of 15 different random samples. All but two (the 5th and 14th intervals from the top) contain the population mean, $\mu_Y = 50.5$. The point estimates (i.e., the sample means) appear next to each interval. If we were able to construct confidence intervals for every pos-

FIGURE 3.6
Example Illustrating the Concept of a Confidence Interval

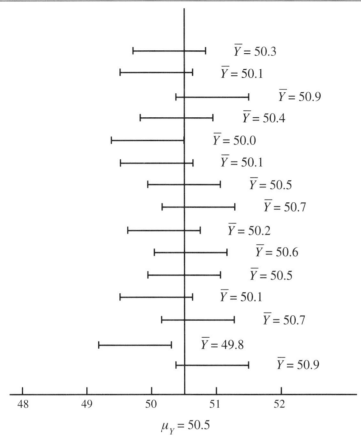

Source: David Knoke and George W. Bohrnstedt, *Basic Social Statistics* (Itasca, IL: F. E. Peacock Publishers, Inc., 1991), 167.

sible sample of size N, we would find that $100 - \alpha$ of them contain the population mean and only α of them do not.

In general, for a given confidence interval, larger sample sizes produce smaller intervals around the sample mean. Suppose we know that $\sigma_Y = 15$ and we observe $\bar{Y} = 51.0$ for a random sample of $N = 100$. To be 95% confident that a particular interval contains the population mean, the interval is bounded by $LCL = 51.0 - 1.96 \, (15/\sqrt{100}) = 48.06$ and $UCL = 51.0 + 1.96 \, (15/\sqrt{100}) = 53.94$. Suppose we observe $\bar{Y} = 51.0$

for a random sample of $N = 500$. The 95% interval for such samples is bounded by LCL = $51.0 - 1.96$ $(15/\sqrt{500}) = 49.69$ and UCL = $51.0 + 1.96$ $(15/\sqrt{500}) = 52.31$. Thus, for a given α, increasing the sample size decreases the confidence interval's width.

To construct a confidence interval around a sample mean, three assumptions are necessary: (1) that the sample for estimating μ_Y is drawn randomly; (2) that N is "large" (at least > 30); and (3) that we know the population variance (σ_Y^2), so that the standard error ($\sigma_{\bar{Y}}$) can be computed. Most often the third assumption is violated. Clearly, if we knew σ_Y^2, we would not need to analyze sample data. Most of the time we do not know the population parameters and thus must estimate their probable values from sample evidence. When N is large, a good estimate of the standard error of the sampling distribution can be made by using the sample standard deviation, s_Y. Putting a caret (^) above $\sigma_{\bar{Y}}$ signifies that it is an estimated value:

$$\hat{\sigma}_{\bar{Y}} = \frac{s_Y}{\sqrt{N}}$$

The GSS sample data in Table 2.3 in chapter 2 provided a sample estimate of mean education = 13.25 years, with a standard deviation = 2.93. The sample size on which these statistics were calculated was 2,820 respondents. Applying these sample statistics to the formula above yields an estimated standard error of $\hat{\sigma}_{\bar{Y}} = 2.93/\sqrt{2820} = 2.93/53.10 = 0.055$. The interval defined by $13.25 \pm (1.96)(.055)$ has a 95% probability of containing the population mean. This computes to an LCL of 13.14 years and a UCL of 13.36 years. What are the limits defining the 99% confidence interval? This very large sample produced a confidence interval that is small relative to the size of the sample standard deviation, underscoring the importance of N in making inferences. To increase your confidence that your interval contains the population parameter, all you can realistically do is increase the interval width by setting a smaller α-level.

Another important application of the central limit theorem is to determine the size of a sample necessary for attaining a particular level of accuracy in estimating the population mean. For a large sample, assuming a normally distributed population,

$$p\left(\left|\frac{\bar{Y} - \mu_Y}{\sigma_{\bar{Y}}}\right| \leq Z_{\alpha/2}\right) = p\left(\left|\frac{k\sigma_Y}{\sigma_{\bar{Y}}}\right| \leq Z_{\alpha/2}\right) = 1 - \alpha$$

This expression states that the probability is approximately $1 - \alpha$ that the difference between the sample mean and the population mean falls within k standard deviations. Suppose we desire an accuracy of no more than

.25 standard deviation at $\alpha = .05$ (hence, $Z_{\alpha/2} = \pm 1.96$). Solving the formula above for N yields the following results:

$$\frac{k\sigma_Y}{\sigma_{\bar{Y}}} = Z_{\alpha/2}$$

$$\frac{.25\sigma_Y}{\sigma_Y/\sqrt{N}} = 1.96$$

$$.25\sqrt{N} = 1.96$$

$$N = \left(\frac{1.96}{.25}\right)^2 = 61.47 \text{ cases}$$

That is, at least 62 cases are required. To improve accuracy to within .10 standard deviation, N must be increased to at least 385 observations.

3.7 The *t* Distribution

The previous examples assume that the standard error of the sampling distribution ($\sigma_{\bar{Y}}$) is known. Fortunately, another family of theoretical distributions, the *t* **distributions**, does not require us to know the standard error. They are sometimes called "Student's *t*" because W. S. Gossett, who first applied them to an important problem, signed his 1908 article "Student." (To protect its trade secrets, Gossett's employer, a brewery, prevented him from openly publishing his discovery.) The formula for a *t* **variable**, or *t* **score**, is

$$t = \frac{Y - \mu_Y}{s_Y/\sqrt{N}}$$

where $s_Y/\sqrt{N}$ uses the sample standard deviation and sample size to estimate the sampling distribution's standard error.

t **distribution**—one of a family of test statistics used with small samples selected from a normally distributed population or, for large samples, drawn from a population with any shape

t **variable/*t* score**—a transformation of the scores of a continuous frequency distribution derived by subtracting the mean and dividing by the estimated standard error

The similarity of *t* scores to *Z* scores for drawing inferences is evident. The only difference is that *t* involves the sample standard deviation (s_Y), whereas *Z* assumes a knowledge of the population standard deviation (σ_Y), which, as we noted previously, is usually not available.

The shape of each *t* distribution varies with sample size and sample standard deviation. As with *Z*-transformed normal distributions, all *t* distributions are symmetrical and bell-shaped and have a mean of zero, yet a normal distribution and a *t* distribution differ in two important ways. First, using a *t* distribution to test hypotheses requires that the sample be drawn from a normally distributed population. However, violating this assumption has only minor effects on *t* score computation. Therefore, unless we are certain that the underlying population from which the sample is drawn is grossly nonnormal (does not approximate a normal distribution), we can use a *t* distribution even if *N* is small.

Second, a *t* distribution for a given sample size has a larger variance than a normal *Z* distribution. Thus, the standard errors of the family of *t* distributions are all larger than the standard error of a standardized normal distribution or *Z* curve (see Figure 3.7). This assumption also must be qualified. As the sample *N* grows larger (i.e., in the range of 30 to 100 cases or more), *t* distributions increasingly approach the normalized *Z* distribution in shape. For a very large *N*, the probabilities associated with outcomes in both distributions are almost identical. You can verify their convergence by comparing probabilities for *Z* values in Appendix C with *t* values for $N = \infty$ in Appendix D. But for a small sample *N*, more cases fall into the extreme sections of the tails of a *t* compared to a *Z* distribution, as Figure 3.7 makes clear. In other words, *t* distributions have "thicker" tails than the *Z* distribution. Thus, at given values of α such as .01, t_α will always be larger than Z_α (or $t_{\alpha/2}$ will be greater than $Z_{\alpha/2}$).

As noted in Section 2.5.4, the denominator of the sample variance (s_Y^2) involves the constant $N - 1$. This numerical value is therefore a parameter in each *t* distribution. It is called the **degrees of freedom**, and it is symbolized by *df* and also by ν (lower case Greek *nu*). The concept of

degrees of freedom—the number of values free to vary when computing a statistic

FIGURE 3.7
Comparing a *t* Distribution with Four Degrees of Freedom with the Standardized Normal Distribution

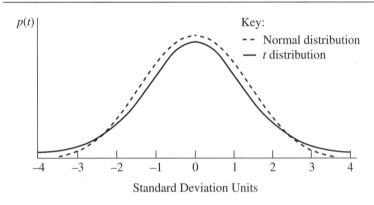

Key:
- - Normal distribution
—— *t* distribution

Standard Deviation Units

Source: David Knoke and George W. Bohrnstedt, *Basic Social Statistics* (Itasca, IL: F. E. Peacock Publishers, Inc., 1991), 169.

degrees of freedom comes from the restriction that the sum of all deviations about the mean must equal zero (see section 2.5.3 in chapter 2). Although you could arbitrarily assign values to $N - 1$ of the deviations, the
value of the last deviation would be completely determined by your other
choices; that is, this final score is *not* free to vary. For example, if you
know that the mean of four observations is 8 and three of these scores are
4, 7, and 9, then the fourth value must be 12. Once the mean and
$N - 1$ values are fixed, the Nth value is completely constrained. In a given
set of N deviations from the mean, $N - 1$ of them may assume any values, but the Nth score has no freedom to vary for a given mean. Hence,
there are $N - 1$ *df* in a *t* distribution for a sample of N observations.

All *t* distributions are bell-shaped, symmetric curves having zero
means and standard errors that vary with both the population standard deviation and the degrees of freedom. The smaller the *df*, the flatter the
curve. Figure 3.7 compares a *t* distribution with 4 degrees of freedom to
a standard normal distribution. Because *t* distribution values are nearly
identical to Z-normal values when N is very large (well over 100 cases),
they can always be used to make inferences from a sample mean to a
population mean. Inferences about means reported in published research
are almost always made using a *t* distribution. If N is small, applying a *t*
distribution requires that a normal population be randomly sampled. However, unless the population is grossly nonnormal, violating this assumption
does not cause serious inferential problems.

A confidence interval around the sample mean point estimate can be
constructed with confidence $1 - \alpha$ by applying the formula

$$\bar{Y} \pm (t_{\alpha/2})(s_Y/\sqrt{N})$$

Begin by choosing a desired degree of confidence, which specifies α. For
example, for a 99% confidence interval $\alpha = .01$. Next, find the entry in
the row in Appendix D labeled "Two-Tailed Test" that contains the specified α level (in this example, .01 above the sixth column). Go down this
column until it intersects the row listing the correct *df* for your sample;
the entry is the critical value of *t* that defines the α-level confidence interval. Insert this critical value, sample standard deviation, and sample
size into the confidence interval formula above; then calculate both the
upper and lower confidence limits. Suppose that the sample point estimate of the mean $\bar{Y} = 46$; the sample standard deviation $s_Y = 12$; the sample size $N = 23$; and you choose $\alpha = .05$. For $df = 23 - 1 = 22$, Appendix
D gives the critical value of *t* as 2.074. The UCL $= 46 + (2.074)(12/\sqrt{23})$
$= 51.2$ and the LCL $= 46 - (2.074)(12/\sqrt{23}) = 40.8$.

3.8 Hypothesis Testing

3.8.1 Null Hypotheses

Suppose we draw a sample of observations and find that two variables are related. We want to know whether we are justified in concluding that this relationship also occurs in the population from which the sample data came. The basic question of statistical inference is this: What is the probability that the relationship observed in the sample data could come from a population in which there is *no* relationship between the two variables? If we can show that this probability is very high, then even though a relationship occurs in the sample, we would be extremely hesitant to conclude that the two variables are related in the population. If the chance were small (perhaps less than 1 in 20 or less than 1 in 100) that the sample relationship could have been created by randomly sampling observations from a population in which no relationship exists, we would decide that the hypothesis should be accepted.

When samples are small, the probability of observing a relationship in the sample where none exists in the population is higher than when samples are large. For example, suppose that in a population of 1,000 no relationship exists between a pair of variables. If we choose a sample of 900 observations, the probability that we would find sample results indicating a relationship among two variables is much smaller than if we were to draw a sample of only 50 observations. Conversely, if a relationship *does* exist in a population, the probability is much greater in a larger sample than in a smaller sample that we would observe a sample outcome that indicates a relationship.

Suppose we have a hypothesis that two variables (for example, voting and years of education) are related in a population of interest (e.g., adult Americans). One way to determine whether two variables are related in the population is to test the hypothesis that they are *unrelated* using the sample observations (as noted in chapter 1). The way to make this test is to state a **null hypothesis** that *no* relationship between the variables exists in the population. This statement is contrary to the research hypothesis stating an expected relationship between variables, either based on theory or past research. Although as social scientists we firmly believe that the research hypothesis is correct, we actually perform the statistical inference test on the null hypothesis, because we hope to show that it is a false statement about the situation. In other words, we expect to "nullify" that hypothesis. The basic question of inference arises: What is the probability that the relationship found in the sample data could have come from a population in which there is no relationship between the two vari-

null hypothesis—
a statistical hypothesis that one usually expects to reject. Symbolized H_0

research hypothesis—
a substantive hypothesis that one usually does not expect to reject

ables? The research hypothesis can be restated as a null hypothesis, using the symbol H_0 (where the subscript zero stands for "null"):

H_0: Voting is not related to years of education.

We really expect to show that this null hypothesis is an untrue statement about the population of adult Americans. If the probability is small—less than .05 (that is, less than 1 chance in 20)—that the sample evidence could have arisen as the outcome of a random sampling from such a population, then we reject this null hypothesis. In concluding that H_0 is false, we accept its alternative—the research hypothesis H_1 stating that the two variables do in fact covary in the population:

H_1: Voting is related to years of education.

From a scientific point of view, the acceptance of an **alternative hypothesis** is conditional, because the truth about social relationships can only be assessed indirectly, through the rejection of false hypotheses.

alternative hypothesis—a secondary hypothesis about the value of a population parameter that often mirrors the research or operational hypothesis. Symbolized H_1

As another example of a null hypothesis, consider research on the relationship between social class and alienation. If you suspect that a relationship exists between these two variables—for example, that working-class people are more alienated than middle-class people—then you might formulate a research hypothesis in these terms:

H_1: The higher the social class, the lower the alienation.

However, in testing this relationship with a random sample of observations drawn from some population, you would restate the research hypothesis as a null relationship in which the two variables do not covary:

H_0: Social class is unrelated to alienation.

Notice that the research and null hypotheses are consistent with your real expectation of finding evidence that social classes differ in their levels of alienation. You hope to reject the null hypothesis, thus lending weight to the original social relationship that you believe exists between class and alienation.

If the research hypothesis is correct, then you should find evidence in the sample that will allow you to reject the null hypothesis. On the other hand, if social class and alienation really *are* unrelated, as some studies indicate, then your sample data should turn up insufficient evidence to reject this H_0. You would then conclude that your original research hypothesis is probably not true. That conclusion, however, always carries a probability of being incorrect. We turn next to procedures for deciding the level of probability of reaching a false conclusion.

3.8.2 Type I and Type II Errors

Whenever we deal with probabilities, we run the risk of making an incorrect decision. Otherwise we would be dealing with certainties, which is never the case. A **probability** (a, or **alpha**) **level** for rejection of a null hypothesis is usually set at .05 (that is, one chance in 20) or lower. By setting this a level before beginning to examine the data, we deliberately choose to run a given risk of incorrect inference from a sample relationship to a population relationship.

In making inferences, we might make two different types of judgment error. First, based on the significance test results, we might reject a null hypothesis that in fact is true; that is, we might reject the hypothesis that the two variables are unrelated, based on the sample results, when in the population they are in fact unrelated. In other words, if we had known the truth about the population, we would not have rejected H_0, but unfortunately we did reject H_0 and thus made an error. Such an error occurs when, simply by chance, the sample we draw contains many of the most deviant observations in the population from which it was selected. Even when sampling is done randomly, there is always some chance that one will select a sample whose variables show a relationship that is quite different from the population relationship. Concluding that H_0 is false when in the population it is really true leads to a **Type I error**, or **false rejection error**. The chance of making this mistake is the same as the probability level that we set for rejection of the null hypothesis (a). Thus, Type I error is also called a-*error*, or *alpha error*.

The second type of error, **Type II error**, may also be called a **false acceptance error**. This error occurs in the opposite fashion: Although the null hypothesis is actually false, we fail to reject it on the basis of the sample data. This type of decision-making error is also called β-*error*, or *beta error*. Box 3.2 offers some help in distinguishing between the two types of error.

The probability of making a Type II error is not simply 1.0 minus the probability of a Type I error; that is, if a is .05, β is *not* just $1.00 - .05 = .95$. It is more complicated than that. A complete account of how to find the probability of a Type II error would take us into a long discussion of the "power" of statistical tests and lead us away from our immediate goal, which is to present the basis of significance tests.

---

probability/alpha level— the probability selected for rejection of a null hypothesis, which is the likelihood of making a Type I error

Type I error/false rejection error— a statistical decision error that occurs when a true null hypothesis is rejected; its probability is alpha

Type II error/false acceptance error— a statistical decision error that occurs when a false null hypothesis is not rejected; its probability is beta

---

Box 3.2   Remembering Type I and Type II Errors

Type I and Type II errors are often confused. One way to distinguish between them is to memorize this table.

		Based on the sample results, the decision made is	
		Reject null hypothesis	*Do not reject null hypothesis*
In the population from which the sample is drawn, the null hypothesis is	*True*	Type I or false rejection error (α)	Correct decision
	False	Correct decision	Type II or false acceptance error (β)

Although no simple mathematical relationship exists between Type I and Type II errors, it is important to note that they are related to one another. Reducing the potential probability of making a false rejection error—setting α at a very low level, such as .001—tends to increase the risk of making a false acceptance error. Standard methods for offsetting false acceptance error are (1) to increase the sample size, thus reducing sampling error in making inferences about population relationships from sample data; or (2) to repeat the study using another, independently drawn sample, so that consistent results strengthen our belief in the findings.

3.9   Testing Hypotheses About Single Means

3.9.1 An Example of a Hypothesis Test About a Single Mean with Exact Hypotheses

We use a rather contrived example to show hypothesis testing about a single mean. The example is contrived because social science theory is ordinarily not precise enough to suggest two exact alternatives. However, the example helps make clear some of the important features about hypothesis testing that would otherwise be difficult to show. Suppose we have two competing hypotheses based on two previous surveys, suggesting somewhat different estimates of the number of hours that Americans watch television each day. Suppose that the results of one poll suggest that Americans spend 2.7 hours per day and a second, unrelated poll suggests that the daily average is 2.9 hours. The null hypothesis and its alternative can then be stated as follows:

$$H_0: \mu_Y = 2.7$$

$$H_1: \mu_Y = 2.9$$

(The decision regarding which result is the null and which is the alternative hypothesis is clearly arbitrary in this example.) We now use the 1998 GSS data to determine whether H_0 can be rejected. We will use a t test to evaluate H_0.

Suppose we set $\alpha = .05$. Using Appendix D and employing a one-tailed test, the observed t must be about 1.645 or larger to reject H_0. We can use this information to see how large the observed mean would have to be in order to reject H_0. In general, to test a hypothesis about a single mean we use the formula

$$t = \frac{\bar{Y} - \mu_{Y_0}}{s_Y / \sqrt{N}}$$

where μ_{Y_0} is the hypothesized mean under H_0.

Using the 1998 GSS data, we find that $s_Y = 2.25$ for $N = 2{,}337$. Therefore, the estimated standard error of the sampling distribution of means is $s_Y / \sqrt{N} = 0.047$. To determine how large $\bar{Y}$ would have to be in order to reject H_0 at $\alpha = .05$, we can substitute these numbers in the formula above as follows:

$$1.645 = \frac{\bar{Y} - 2.7}{0.047}$$

Solving for $\bar{Y}$, we obtain $\bar{Y} = 2.78$, which is the critical value (c.v.) for the null hypothesis test. That is, if $\bar{Y} \geq 2.78$, we will reject H_0 in favor of H_1. This situation is depicted in Figure 3.8.

Note that there are two separate sampling distributions, the left one under the assumption that H_0 is true and the right one under the assumption that H_1 is true. The shaded area in the tail of the distribution under H_0 is $\alpha = .05$, or the probability of falsely rejecting the null hypothesis (see Box 3.2). But there is also a probability of making a Type II, or false

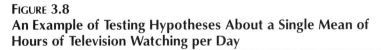

FIGURE 3.8
An Example of Testing Hypotheses About a Single Mean of Hours of Television Watching per Day

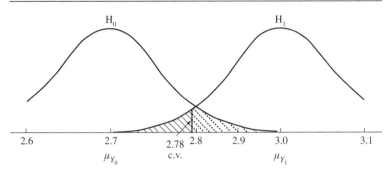

acceptance, error that can now be calculated. It is the cross-hatched area in the left tail of the sampling distribution under the assumption that H_1 is true. This is the probability of falsely accepting H_0 when H_1 is true. The formula for calculating this probability is as follows:

$$t = \frac{\text{c.v.} - \mu_{Y_I}}{s_Y/\sqrt{N}}$$

where μ_{Y_1} is the hypothesized mean under H_1.

To compute β in this example, we insert the c.v. = 2.78, μ_{Y_1} = 2.90, and the estimated standard error, 0.047, into the formula for t:

$$t = \frac{2.78 - 2.90}{0.047} = -2.55$$

We next consult Appendix D for one-tailed tests (using the row for ∞ *df*), which shows that the probability from −∞ to −2.55 = .005. That is, roughly 5 times in 1,000 one would fail to reject the null hypothesis, H_0, when in fact the alternative hypothesis, H_1, is true. The probability $1 - \beta$ is called the **power of the test**. It is the probability of correctly rejecting H_0 when H_0 is false. In our example, the power of the test is $1 - .005$ = .995. That is, if H_1 is true, we would correctly reject H_0 more than 99.5% of the time.

We will not hold you in suspense any longer. The 2,337 respondents in the 1998 GSS reported watching an average of 2.86 hours of television per day. Therefore, since the c.v. is 2.78, we reject the null hypothesis that the mean television watching is 2.7 hours per day. Instead, we

power of the test—the probability of correctly rejecting H_0 when H_0 is false

accept the alternative hypothesis that Americans watch 2.9 hours of television per day.

As stated above, this example is somewhat contrived in that it assumes either the null or the alternative hypothesis is true. In all likelihood, of course, neither one is true. Indeed, another option is that of **suspending judgment** pending further research. The example does demonstrate, however, that one can compute the probability of a Type II error and the power of the test if one is able to specify two exact alternative hypotheses. Box 3.3 summarizes the steps for testing a single mean with two exact hypotheses.

Our example can also be used to illustrate another important point—the power of the test can be increased or decreased simply by increasing or decreasing the sample size. For example, suppose that $N = 40$ instead of 2,337. Then the standard error increases from 0.047 to $2.25/\sqrt{40} = 0.356$. You can easily demonstrate for yourself that in this case the critical value for the observed mean $\bar{Y} = 3.29$. Under H_1, this generates a t value of 1.10 for which the value of β is calculated using Appendix D (using the row for ∞ df), which shows that the probability from ∞ to 1.282 $= .10$. Hence, by decreasing the sample size from 2,337 to 40, the power

---

Box 3.3   Summary of Steps in Testing Between Two Exact Hypotheses About Means

Step 1. Choose an α level (probability of a Type I or false rejection error) for the null hypothesis.

Step 2. Examine Appendix D to determine how large the t value must be under H_0 in order to reject the null hypothesis.

Step 3. Estimate the standard error of the sampling distribution from the data using $s_Y/\sqrt{N}$, and use μ_0 in the formula for the t statistic to determine the critical value (c.v.) for rejecting H_0.

Step 4. Calculate β (the probability of a Type II or false acceptance error) using the estimated standard error and the mean hypothesized to be true under H_1 in the formula for the test statistic.

Step 5. Compare the observed sample mean with the critical value, and decide either to reject or not to reject H_0.

of the test, $1 - \beta$, decreases from .995 to .900. That is, in a sample of 40 one would correctly reject the null hypothesis when it is false only 90 times out of 100. Furthermore, if the alternative is true, one would fail to reject the null hypothesis about 10 times out of 100 (Type II error). This example should make it very clear that using a large sample size substantially improves the power of the test and reduces the likelihood of making a false acceptance error.

3.9.2 One-Tailed Test About a Single Mean

Suppose we are interested in knowing how often American adults read the newspaper. In particular, we are curious about the newspaper-reading habits of men as compared to women. The 1998 GSS asked respondents how often they read the newspaper, recording their responses on a five-point scale: "every day" (coded 1), "a few times a week" (coded 2), "once a week" (coded 3), "less than once a week" (coded 4), and "never" (coded 5). The mean response in the 1998 GSS for women ($N = 1,059$) is 2.26, suggesting that women read the newspaper somewhere between a few times a week and less than once a week. Because we surmise that men are more likely to be employed outside of the home than women, we hypothesize that men are also likely to read the newspaper more often than women, due to work-related reasons. Consequently, our null and alternative hypotheses are

$$H_0: \ \mu_Y \geq 2.26$$

$$H_1: \ \mu_Y < 2.26$$

We can test the null hypothesis with the 1998 GSS to determine whether H_0 can be rejected in favor of H_1. First we select the 811 males who answered the question on the frequency of newspaper reading. Then we evaluate H_0 with a *t* **test**. The degrees of freedom for this test are $N - 1 = 811 - 1 = 810$. Because the alternative hypothesis is inexact in one direction, the only grounds for rejecting the null hypothesis is when the sample mean is less than the hypothesized parameter of 2.26 (remember that lower values on this variable indicate more frequent newspaper reading). This alternative concentrates the entire region of rejection (alpha) into one tail of the sampling distribution. Hence, a test with this form of H_1 is called a **one-tailed hypothesis test**.

Suppose we set $\alpha = .05$. With α located entirely in the sampling distribution's left tail, the critical value of *t* for 810 *df* is –1.645 (using the row for ∞ *df* in Appendix D as an approximation). The test statistic cal-

t **test**—a test of significance for continuous variables where the population variance is unknown and the sample is assumed to have been drawn from a normally distributed population

one-tailed hypothesis test—a hypothesis test in which the alternative is stated in such a way that the probability of making a Type I error is entirely in one tail of a probability distribution

culated from sample data must be smaller than -1.645 (i.e., greater in the negative direction) in order to reject H_0. The general formula to test a hypothesis about a single mean is

$$t = \frac{\bar{Y} - \mu_{Y_0}}{s_Y/\sqrt{N}}$$

where $\bar{Y}$ is the sample mean;
μ_{Y_0} is the hypothesized mean under H_0;
and $s_Y/\sqrt{N}$ is the estimated standard error of the sampling distribution.

In the 1998 GSS, the mean frequency of newspaper reading for men is $\bar{Y} = 2.08$ with $s_Y = 1.27$. Therefore, the t for the test is

$$t_{810} = \frac{2.08 - 2.26}{1.27/\sqrt{811}} = -4.04$$

We have subscripted the t with its degrees of freedom. Because $t = -4.04$, it is clearly smaller than -1.645, and the difference between the newspaper-reading habits of women and men is sufficiently large to reject the null hypothesis in favor of the alternative. Hence we conclude that men do read the newspaper more frequently than women. Box 3.4 shows the steps in performing a statistical test of a null hypothesis about a single mean with an inexact directional alternative. The procedures for testing statistical significance are basically similar for all the statistics employed in this text. *Thus, you should memorize the steps in this box.*

As mentioned in section 3.9.1, exact hypotheses can rarely be stated as compelling tests of theory in the social sciences. Therefore, hypothesis testing usually offers only a weak analysis of one's substantive hypotheses. By choosing a very large N (as in the previous example), a researcher can reduce the estimated standard error of the sampling distribution to a very small size (recall that $\hat{\sigma}_{\bar{Y}} = s_Y/\sqrt{N}$). Thus, almost any null hypothesis can be rejected—hardly an encouraging foundation for erecting a sophisticated science. Given the weakness of statistical significance tests, we emphasize the importance of *estimation* in making inferences from sample statistics to population parameters. After testing a hypothesis, we recommend using the sample mean as a point estimate around which to construct a confidence interval. In the example, given $\bar{Y} = 2.08$ and $s_Y = 1.27$ for $N = 811$, the 99% confidence interval is

$$2.08 \pm (2.576)(1.27/\sqrt{811})$$

or LCL = 1.96 and UCL = 2.20. On average, 99 out of 100 samples with confidence limits so derived will contain the parameter for the frequency of men's newspaper reading.

Box 3.4   Statistical Significance Testing Steps

Step 1. State the research hypothesis believed to be true in the form of a statistical alternative hypothesis (H_1).

Step 2. State the statistical null hypothesis (H_0) that you expect to reject.

Step 3. Choose an α level (probability of a Type I or false rejection error) for the null hypothesis.

Step 4. Examine the tabled values of the test statistic to see how large it must be in order to reject the null hypothesis at α. This is the critical value, or c.v., for that test statistic.

Step 5. Calculate the test statistic, entering the sample descriptive statistics into the appropriate formula.

Step 6. Compare the test statistic to the critical value. If the test statistic is as large as, or larger than, the c.v., then reject the null hypothesis, with an α-probability of a Type I (false rejection) error. If it is smaller than the c.v., then do not reject the null hypothesis, with a β-probability of a Type II (false acceptance) error.

3.9.3 Two-Tailed Test About a Single Mean

Often social researchers have only vague ideas about their alternative hypotheses. Although the null hypothesis is clearly stated, H_0 might be rejected by either a larger *or* a smaller sample mean. In this situation, a **two-tailed hypothesis test** is a suitable procedure. In two-tailed tests, the alternative hypothesis is inexact and without a specific direction. This form of H_1 admits that one does not know whether the population parameter is smaller or larger than the exact value in H_0.

Suppose we are uncertain about how people perceive their standard of living as compared to that of their parents. The 1998 GSS recorded responses to such a question on a five-point scale, from "much worse" (coded 5) to "much better" (coded 1). Without prior knowledge, we might guess that respondents tend to choose the scale midpoint, "about the same" (coded 3), but we do not know whether the population response is more likely to be higher or lower. Hence, our best alternative is simply

two-tailed hypothesis test—a hypothesis test in which the region of rejection falls equally within both tails of the sampling distribution

to hypothesize that the mean population parameter is something other than 3.00. Stated more formally, these two statistical hypotheses are as follows:

H_0: $\mu_Y = 3.00$

H_1: $\mu_Y \neq 3.00$

The statistical test is two-tailed because the probability of a Type I error must be equally distributed between the upper and lower tails of the sampling distribution. In this sense, a two-tailed test parallels constructing a confidence interval around the mean hypothesized under H_0. (Of course, a confidence interval is built around a sample mean, *not* a population parameter.)

As in all significance testing, one first chooses an α level, say .001 in this case. Then the critical value of the test statistic is located in the appropriate appendix table. Two c.v.s exist for two-tailed hypothesis tests: one in the negative tail and the other in the positive tail of the sampling distribution. Figure 3.9 shows this relationship for the general case. For our test of mean living standard, $N = 1,879$, and thus $df = 1,878$. The

FIGURE 3.9
The *t* Distribution for Two-Tailed Hypothesis Tests About a Single Mean

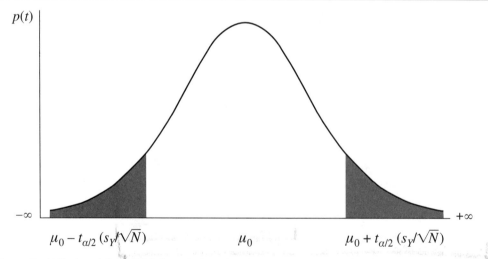

Source: David Knoke and George W. Bohrnstedt, *Basic Social Statistics* (Itasca, IL: F. E. Peacock Publishers, Inc., 1991), 184.

sample standard deviation is 1.10, so the estimated standard error is $1.10/\sqrt{1879} = .025$. Appendix D shows that the c.v. necessary to reject the null hypothesis in favor of the two-tailed alternative is ±3.291. (Box 3.5 explains how Appendix D is used for both one- and two-tailed hypothesis tests.) Because H_0 specifies that $\mu_Y = 3.00$, the two critical values defining the regions of rejection are LCL = 3.00 – (3.291)(.025) and UCL = 3.00 + (3.291)(.025), or 2.92 and 3.08, respectively. That is, if the observed sample mean is either less than 2.92 or greater than 3.08, H_0 must be rejected in favor of H_1. Because the 1998 GSS sample mean is 2.19, the null hypothesis that perceived standard of living falls at the scale midpoint must be rejected. Instead, the most likely population parameter is the same as the sample value, 2.19, which is close to a "somewhat better" standard of living compared to parents.

Box 3.5   Using Appendix D for One- or Two-Tailed Hypothesis Testing

Appendix D can be used to place the probability of a Type I error (α) all in one tail or to divide it between the left and the right tails of a t distribution. To place the probability entirely into the right tail, look along the row labeled "One-tailed" until you reach the value you chose for α. Then look down the column under that α level to find the critical value (c.v.) corresponding to the df in the stub on the left. For example, for $\alpha = .05$ and $N = 31$, the critical value of t is found by looking across the row labeled "One-tailed test" until you come to .05, and then looking down that column until you come to the row for $df = 31 - 1 = 30$. Thus, the c.v. of $t = 1.697$. Recall that for $\alpha = .05$, c.v. $Z = 1.645$. This difference in critical values illustrates that when N is small, a larger c.v. is necessary to be able to reject the null hypothesis than when N is very large.

Appendix D can also be used to divide the probability of a Type I error equally into both tails of a t distribution. This division is especially useful for computing confidence intervals, as well as computing two-tailed hypothesis tests. For example, for $\alpha = .05$ and $df = 30$, look across the row labeled "Two-tailed test" until you come to .05. Then look down this column until you come to the row labeled 30. In this example, c.v. = 2.042.

Although hypothesis testing has a long tradition in the social sciences, we strongly believe that *estimation is much more useful and important than hypothesis testing*, because virtually any statistical hypothesis can be rejected by simply choosing a large enough sample size. For this reason, even though hypothesis testing is very common, we urge that confidence intervals always be estimated.

The 99.9% confidence interval around the GSS sample mean of 2.19 for perceived standard of living is bounded by LCL = 2.19 – (3.291)(.025) = 2.11 and UCL = 2.19 + (3.291)(.025) = 2.27. We hope you agree that knowing with 99.9% confidence that the true population mean probably lies between 2.11 and 2.27 is more informative than the outcome of the hypothesis test—i.e., knowing only that we must reject our initial hypothesis that the population mean is 3.00.

3.9.4 One-Tailed Versus Two-Tailed Tests

If current knowledge allows a directional alternative hypothesis, then a one-tailed significance test should be used. A one-tailed H_1 permits a more powerful statistical test than does a two-tailed alternative, except when the observed sample mean falls into the tail of the test statistic opposite from that predicted. A one-tailed hypothesis test rewards you with powerful tests for correctly anticipating into which tail of the t distribution the mean falls, but you are penalized if your expectation turns out to be wrong. Nevertheless, if you have a directional alternative, then a one-tailed test should be used. Many researchers and applied statisticians would contest this principle because one-tailed tests require a smaller c.v. to reject H_0, thus stacking the deck in favor of rejection. If previous research results were mixed, the research is purely exploratory, or good notions about the population parameter are absent, then a two-tailed test is preferable. Most importantly, however, population parameters should always be estimated along with hypothesis testing when making inferences about population parameters from sample data.

The hypothesis tests discussed in this chapter involve single means. Most social researchers wish to compare statistics across several groups. For example, do liberal arts, engineering, or agricultural graduates earn higher starting salaries? Are rates of AIDS infection lower for persons using condoms, other prophylactic methods, or no method at all? Such questions require comparing *two or more* sample values and asking whether they are likely to differ significantly from one another in the populations. Evaluating this type of question is the topic of the following chapters.

3.10   Properties of Estimators

Chance factors operate even in random sampling to ensure that a particular sample's point estimates of means and variances will not be identical to the population values. The basic goal of inferential statistics is to use the sample values as *estimators* of corresponding population parameters. To be a good estimator of population parameter θ, a sample statistic $\hat{\theta}$ should be unbiased, consistent, efficient, and sufficient.

An **unbiased estimator** equals, on average, the population parameter. That is,

$$E(\theta) = \theta$$

The expected value (i.e., the mean) of the estimator for all possible samples of size N from the same population equals the population parameter. For example, the central limit theorem in section 3.5 indicates that $E(\bar{Y}) = \mu_Y$. Thus, the sample mean, $\bar{Y}$, is an unbiased estimator of the population mean, μ_Y. Similarly, if we take all possible random samples of size N from a population and compute each sample's variance,

$$s_Y^2 = \frac{\Sigma(Y_i - \bar{Y})^2}{N - 1}$$

then the mean of this sampling distribution will equal the population variance; that is,

$$E(s_Y^2) = \frac{\Sigma(Y_i - \bar{Y})^2}{N} = \sigma_Y^2$$

The difference in the denominators of the sample statistic ($N - 1$) and the population parameter (N) is required to produce an unbiased estimate. Because $E(s_Y^2) = \sigma_Y^2$, we conclude that the sample variance is an unbiased estimator of the population variance.

A **consistent estimator** approximates the population parameter more closely as N gets larger. A sample statistic θ is a consistent estimator if, as $N \to \infty$, $E(\hat{\theta} - \theta)^2 \to 0$. That is, as N approaches infinity, the expected variance of the difference between a sample statistic and a population parameter gets closer to zero. Both the sample mean and the median are consistent estimators of the population mean, μ_Y; as N increases, the variance of each sampling distribution gets smaller.

An **efficient estimator** has a sampling distribution whose standard error, at a given N, is smaller than any other estimator. That is, the variance of the difference between a sample statistic and a population parameter, $E(\hat{\theta} - \theta)^2$, is as small as possible. We previously showed that the

unbiased estimator—an estimator of a population parameter whose expected value equals the parameter

consistent estimator—an estimator of a population parameter that approximates the parameter more closely as N gets larger

efficient estimator—the estimator of a population parameter among all possible estimators that has the smallest sampling variance

variance of the sampling distribution for the mean is σ_Y^2/N. The sampling distribution variance for the median is $(\pi/2)(\sigma_Y^2/N)$ for a large N. Thus, the mean is roughly $\pi/2$ more efficient than the median as an estimator of μ_Y, and hence, it is preferred as the more efficient estimator of μ_Y.

sufficient estimator—an estimator of a population parameter that cannot be improved by adding information

Finally, an estimator is **sufficient** if it cannot be improved by adding information. The sample value contains all the information available about the population parameter. For a normally distributed variable, the sample mean is sufficient to estimate the population mean.

The sample mean $(\bar{Y})$ and sample variance (s_Y^2) are unbiased, consistent, efficient, and sufficient estimators, respectively, of the population mean (μ_Y) and variance (σ_Y^2). These properties make them indispensable statistics in inferential analysis.

3.11 The Chi-Square and *F* Distributions

With knowledge of the standardized normal distribution learned in section 3.4, we can now introduce two theoretical probability distributions that are very valuable for the statistical significance tests to be presented in the following chapters. Both make use of the normal distribution in their construction.

chi-square distribution— a family of distributions, each of which has different degrees of freedom, on which the chi-square test statistic is based

Like the normal curve, the **chi-square distribution** (χ^2) is actually a family of distributions. Each family member varies in the number of degrees of freedom used in its creation. To construct a χ^2 variable, begin with a normally distributed population of observations, having mean μ_Y and standard deviation σ_Y^2. Then take a random sample of N cases, transform every observation into standardized (Z score) form, and square it. For the ith case:

$$Z_i^2 = \frac{(Y_i - \mu_Y)^2}{\sigma_Y^2}$$

The distribution of the sum of these squared Z scores is called a chi-square distribution with N degrees of freedom. To form a χ^2 with one degree of freedom, cases are sampled from the normal distribution one at a time. A χ^2 with one *df* is shown in Figure 3.10. As a result of the squaring, a χ^2 distribution has no negative values but is very skewed, ranging between 0 and positive infinity. Because most of the values in the standardized normal distribution lie between -1.00 and $+1.00$, most of the values for χ^2 with one degree of freedom fall below 1.00.

To find the chi-square distribution for two degrees of freedom (χ_ν^2, where the subscript ν indicates two *df*), two observations (Y_1 and Y_2) are independently and randomly drawn from the normal distribution. Again,

FIGURE **3.10**
χ^2 **Distributions with 1, 2, 8, and 22 Degrees of Freedom**

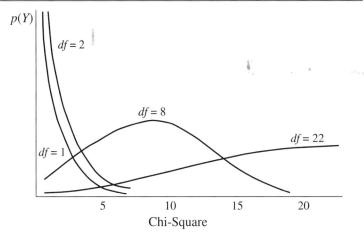

they are transformed to Z scores, squared, and then added together. Thus, the score of the first plus the second case is

$$\frac{(Y_1 - \mu_Y)^2}{\sigma_Y^2} + \frac{(Y_2 - \mu_Y)^2}{\sigma_Y^2} = Z_1^2 + Z_2^2$$

As shown in Figure 3.10, this chi-square distribution is somewhat less skewed, with a lower probability that values fall between zero and 1.00.

Suppose we continue to generate chi-square distributions with ν degrees of freedom by adding ν independently sampled, squared Z scores. As these new probability distributions are created, they become progressively less skewed and more bell-shaped, as shown in Figure 3.10 for χ^2 distributions with 8 and 22 *df*. The exact shape and location of each member of this family of distributions depend only on the degrees of freedom involved in creating it from an underlying standardized normal distribution. The mean of each chi-square distribution is the product of its degrees of freedom and the variance of Z (which is always 1; see Box 2.4 in chapter 2). In other words, the mean of a chi-square for a distribution based on ν independent observations is ν, its *df*. Further, the variance of a chi-square distribution with ν *df* is always 2ν. Thus, knowledge of the degrees of freedom is sufficient to specify completely a given chi-square distribution. Chapter 5 shows how to use tabled values of chi-square to reach conclusions about the probable independence of variables in a population from which a sample has been randomly drawn.

F distribution—
a theoretical probability distribution for one of a family of F ratios having v_1 and v_2 df in the numerator and denominator, respectively

The second very important theoretical distribution is the **F distribution**, named after Sir Ronald Fisher, who developed many important applications. Research hypotheses often involve inferences from sample data about the equality of the variances of two populations. The F distribution provides a suitable test statistic for such questions. It requires that random, independent samples be drawn from two normal populations that have the same variance (i.e., $\sigma_{Y_1}^2 = \sigma_{Y_2}^2$). Then the F variable is formed as the ratio of two chi-squares, each divided by its degrees of freedom, v_1 and v_2:

$$F = \frac{(\chi_{v_1}^2 / v_1)}{(\chi_{v_2}^2 / v_2)}$$

The F ratio distribution is nonsymmetric and ranges across the nonnegative numbers (because of the two squared chi-squares), and its shape depends on the degrees of freedom associated with the numerator (v_1) and denominator (v_2). In chapter 4 we will demonstrate how to use the tabled values of F to make decisions regarding the probable equality of population variances, based on sample estimates.

Review of Key Concepts and Symbols

These key concepts and symbols are listed in the order of appearance in this chapter. Combined with the definitions in the margins, these will help you review the material and can serve as a self-test for mastery of the concepts.

inference
random sampling
probability distribution
continuous probability distribution
population parameter
expected value
mean of a probability distribution
variance of a probability distribution
Chebycheff's inequality theorem
normal distribution
alpha area

critical value
central limit theorem
sampling distribution of sample means
standard error
point estimate
confidence interval
upper confidence limit (UCL)
lower confidence limit (LCL)
t distribution
t variable (t score)
degrees of freedom

null hypothesis Z_α

alternative hypothesis $Z_{\alpha/2}$

probability (alpha) level

Type I error; false rejection error $\mu_{\bar{Y}}$

Type II error; false acceptance error $\sigma_{\bar{Y}}^2$

power of the test $\hat{\sigma}_{\bar{Y}}$

suspending judgment t

t test

one-tailed hypothesis test ν

two-tailed hypothesis test df

unbiased estimator $t_{\alpha/2}$

consistent estimator H_0

efficient estimator H_1

sufficient estimator

chi-square distribution α

F distribution β

N t_β

$p(Y_i)$ $1 - \beta$

$E(Y)$ θ

μ_Y $\hat{\theta}$

$g(Y)$ χ^2

σ_Y^2 F

σ_Y ν_1

α ν_2

$\alpha/2$

PROBLEMS

General Problems

1. Find the expected values of the following probability distributions:

a. Y_i	$p(Y_i)$	b. Y_i	$p(Y_i)$
5	.15	5	.20
10	.25	10	.30
15	.05	15	.15
20	.20	20	.30
25	.35	25	.05

2. In a population of test scores not known to be normally distributed, the mean is 50 and the standard deviation is 5. What proportion of the observations will fall in the interval from 40 to 60?

3. What is the standard error in a population with $\sigma_Y = 150$ and (a) $N = 25$; (b) $N = 36$; (c) $N = 225$?

4. Find the Z scores for the normal distribution that corresponds to the following alphas:

   a. $\alpha = .05$, one-tailed   d. $\alpha = .05$, two-tailed

   b. $\alpha = .10$, one-tailed   e. $\alpha = .08$, two-tailed

   c. $\alpha = .01$, one-tailed   f. $\alpha = .15$, two-tailed

5. Using the central limit theorem, find the means and standard errors of sampling distributions with the following characteristics:

	μ_Y	σ_Y^2	N
a.	10.5	50	25
b.	50	115	115
c.	25	75	250
d.	12	70	35
e.	100	100	200

6. For $\mu_Y = 75$, $\sigma_Y = 10$, and $N = 25$, find the critical values for (a) $\alpha = .05$, one-tailed; and (b) $\alpha = .01$, two-tailed.

7. For a sample of $N = 16$ with $\sigma_Y = 6$ and $\bar{Y} = 18$, find (a) the LCL and UCL for the 95% confidence interval; and (b) the LCL and UCL for the 99% confidence interval.

8. Test the null hypothesis that $\mu_Y = 75$ for a sample of 25 subjects in which $\bar{Y} = 81$ and $s_Y = 10$ for a one-tailed test in which $\alpha = .01$. State (a) critical value; (b) degrees of freedom; (c) test statistic; and (d) your decision.

9. Test the null hypothesis that $\mu_Y = 50$ for a sample where $N = 36$, $\bar{Y} = 47.5$, and $s_Y = 12$ using a two-tailed test in which $\alpha = .001$. State (a) critical value; (b) degrees of freedom; (c) test statistic; and (d) your decision.

10. After six months in office, a U.S. senator evaluates her public approval rating by surveying 50 citizens. Their responses indicate that the senator has a 63% mean approval rating, with a variance of 16. If 60% is the minimum approval rating the senator will accept in order to continue her current agenda, can she conclude that her approval rating is significantly above the minimum? Set $\alpha = .01$.

Problems Requiring the 1998 General Social Survey

11. Find the empirical probability distribution for GSS respondents' ages when their first children were born (AGEKDBRN), and determine the probability that a respondent was 28 years old or older when his/her child was born. Is this probability greater or less than the probability that a respondent was 21 years old or younger when his/her child was born? Change the "Don't Know," "No Answer," and "Not Applicable" responses to missing values.

12. Test the hypothesis that respondents were drawn from a population in which the mean preference for spending a social evening with neighbors (SOCOMMUN) is 4.00 or lower on a seven-point scale. Set $\alpha = .01$. Change the "Don't Know," "No Answer," and "Not Applicable" responses to missing values.

13. Using the SPSS selection procedures to select only female respondents (SEX = 2), test the null hypothesis that the mean is agreement with the statement "Family life suffers if Mom works full time" (FAMSUFFR = 2). Set $\alpha = .05$. Change the "Can't Choose," "No Answer," and "Not Applicable" responses to missing values.

14. Selecting only men (SEX = 1) whose labor status is working full-time (WRKSTAT = 1), test the null hypothesis that the mean number of times they volunteered for a charitable organization in the last 12 months (VOLWKCHR) is 2.00 or higher. Set $\alpha = .01$.

Change the "Can't Choose," "No Answer," and "Not Applicable" responses to missing values.

15. A director of educational and community programming for an art museum has a hunch that older people do not think that modern painting reflects talent, because anyone could just "slap paint on a canvas." Evaluate this hunch by selecting respondents aged 75 and older (AGE GE 75) and testing the null hypothesis that the mean response to MODPAINT is greater than 2.00. Set $\alpha = .01$. Change the "Don't Know," "No Answer," and "Not Applicable" responses to missing values.

III. Analyzing Bivariate Relationships

4

ANALYSIS OF VARIANCE

In this chapter we will consider a special version of the general linear model, in which the independent variable is a set of discrete categories and the dependent variable is a continuous measure. This technique is called the **analysis of variance**, or ANOVA for short. We will show how to test a hypothesis that the sample means of several groups—*J* groups in general—come from the same, rather than different, populations. We will also present a special case of ANOVA in which differences in the means of only two groups are analyzed. We will consider only ANOVA models in which a single variable classifies observations into groups; hence, they are sometimes called *one-way* analyses of variance. More advanced ANOVA techniques that simultaneously categorize observations according to two or more variables are too complex for treatment here.

analysis of variance— a statistical test of the difference of means for two or more groups

4.1 The Logic of ANOVA

4.1.1 An Example of Attendance at Religious Services

An example illustrates the logic of the analysis of variance. We are interested in the question of whether adults living in different regions of the country vary in terms of how often they attend religious services. Specifically, we wondered whether adults living in the South and Midwest attend more often than those living in the Northeast and West, allegedly due to more traditional values in the former two regions. To test this hypothesis, we used the 1998 GSS data set and recoded its eight region categories into the four U.S. Bureau of the Census classifications: South (South Atlantic, South Central, and West South Central), Midwest (East North Central and West North Central), Northeast (New England and Mid-Atlantic), and West (Mountain and Pacific). Respondents were asked to indicate how often they attended religious services, on a scale ranging from "never" (coded 0) to "more than once a week" (coded 8).

Our initial research hypothesis is that religious service attendance is highest in the South (S), followed in order by the Midwest (M), the Northeast (N), and the West (W). The null hypothesis is that these four population means—labeled μ_S, μ_M, μ_N, and μ_W—equal one another. Hence, the four regional means also equal the overall mean, or the **grand mean**, of all respondents in the population, μ. However, if the alternative hypothesis is true and the null hypothesis rejected, we then expect to find that $\mu_S > \mu_M > \mu_N > \mu_W$.

grand mean—in analysis of variance, the mean of all observations

An ANOVA model offers techniques to test the null hypothesis that all J sample means come from the same population and, therefore, all equal one another. Formally, the null hypothesis for every ANOVA is

$$H_0: \ \mu_1 = \mu_2 = \cdots = \mu_J$$

The alternative hypothesis is that at least one sample mean comes from a population whose mean differs from the other population means. Rejecting the null hypothesis implies one of several alternative possibilities:

1. Each population mean differs from every other mean, i.e.,

$$H_1: \ \mu_1 \neq \mu_2 \neq \cdots \neq \mu_J$$

2. Some subsets among the population means differ from one another (e.g., μ_1 differs from μ_2 but equals μ_3 and μ_4).

3. Some combinations of means differ either from a single mean or from another combination of means (e.g., μ_2 differs from the average of μ_3 and μ_4).

ANOVA is a test of the null hypothesis about equal population means. If the results compel rejection of the null, we still must determine which observed means differ from the others.

4.1.2 Effects of Variables

To examine the impact of a group classification on a continuous dependent variable in an ANOVA, consider a single population having mean μ for the dependent measure. As H_0 states,

> If the J group means all equal one another, then they also all equal this population's grand mean, μ.

We used this fact to measure the **effects** of the classification variable on the dependent variable. The effect of the jth group, labeled α_j, is defined as the difference between that group's mean and the grand mean:[1]

$$\alpha_j = \mu_j - \mu$$

effect—the impact of the classification variable on the dependent variable

If group j has no effect on the dependent variable, then $\alpha_j = 0$; that is, $\mu_j = \mu$. Whenever a group effect occurs, however, α_j will be either positive or negative, depending on whether that group's mean is above or below the grand mean, μ.

In the 1998 GSS data, the mean religious service attendance score for 2,788 respondents is 3.64. The regional rates are South, $\mu_S = 4.00$; Midwest, $\mu_M = 3.69$; Northeast, $\mu_N = 3.39$; and West, $\mu_W = 3.16$. Thus, the effects for each region are $\alpha_S = +0.36$; $\alpha_M = +0.05$; $\alpha_N = -0.25$; and $\alpha_W = -0.48$. We can see already that the South and Midwest have higher rates of attendance at religious services than the other two regions. We still need to determine whether these differences are statistically significant in the sense that the observed 1998 data reflect a relationship probably occurring in the population of repeated observations of religious service attendance.

4.1.3 The ANOVA Model

An ANOVA asks what proportion of the total variation in dependent variable Y can be attributed to individual i's membership in the jth group classification. The general model for an ANOVA with one independent variable decomposes an observed score into three components:

---

[1] The use of alpha with a subscript (α_j) is not to be confused with α without a subscript, which refers to the probability of a Type I error (see section 3.8.2).

$$Y_{ij} = \mu + a_j + e_{ij}$$

where

Y_{ij} = The score of the ith observation in the jth group.

μ = The grand mean, common to all cases in the population.

a_j = The effect of group j, common to every case in that group.

e_{ij} = The error score, unique to the ith case in the jth group.

error term—in ANOVA, that part of an observed score that cannot be attributed to either the common component or the group component

By rearranging the formula above, we see that the **error term**, or residual, is that part of an observed score that cannot be attributed to either the common component or the group component:

$$e_{ij} = Y_{ij} - \mu - a_j$$

The error terms in ANOVA can be viewed as discrepancies between observed scores and those predicted by membership in a group. ANOVA error terms take into account the fact that every case i in group j does not have the identical observed Y_j score. For example, every adult in the South does not have a religious service attendance score of 4.00; some people have higher scores, while others have lower. The error term, e_{ij}, reflects this fact.

4.2   ANOVA Tables: Sums of Squares, Mean Squares, *F* Ratio

4.2.1   Sums of Squares

To determine the proportion of variance in Y_{ij} attributable to the group effects (the a_j) and the proportion due to error (e_{ij}), begin with the numerator of the sample variance:

$$\sum_{i=1}^{N} (Y_i - \bar{Y})^2$$

Each of the N observations in a sample is a member of one of the J groups. If n_j is the number of cases in the jth group, then $n_1 + n_2 + \cdots + n_J = N$. That is, the sum of observations across the J subgroups equals the total sample size, N. Thus, by attaching to each case both an individual (i) and group (j) subscript, the variance numerator can also be written using a double summation operator (see Appendix A):

$$\sum_{i=1}^{N} (Y_i - \bar{Y})^2 = \sum_{j=1}^{J} \sum_{i=1}^{n_j} (Y_{ij} - \bar{Y})^2$$

The term $\sum_{j=1}^{J} \sum_{i=1}^{n_j} (Y_{ij} - \bar{Y})^2$ is the **total sum of squares**, or SS_{TOTAL}. It shows the sum of squared deviations of each score from the grand mean of all groups, ($\bar{Y}$).

total sum of squares— a number obtained by subtracting the scores of a distribution from their mean, squaring, and summing these values

For example, suppose there are $N = 5$ observations, each belonging either to group 1 or group 2 (i.e., $J = 2$), with the number of observations in each group $n_1 = 3$ and $n_2 = 2$. Then, expanding the terms on the right

$$\sum_{j=1}^{J} \sum_{i=1}^{n_j} (Y_{ij} - \bar{Y})^2 = [(Y_{11} - \bar{Y})^2 + (Y_{21} - \bar{Y})^2 + (Y_{31} - \bar{Y})^2]$$
$$+ [(Y_{12} - \bar{Y})^2 + (Y_{22} - \bar{Y})^2]$$

The first line contains the sum for group $j = 1$, and the second line contains the sum for group $j = 2$.

A one-way ANOVA partitions the total sum of squares into two components: (1) the sum of squares lying between the means of the group categories, the **between sum of squares**, or SS_{BETWEEN}; and (2) the sum of squared deviations from the group means, the **within sum of squares**, or SS_{WITHIN}. In forming this partition, the same value can be simultaneously added to and subtracted from any expression without changing its value. Therefore, subtract and add $\bar{Y}_j$ (the mean of the jth group to which case i belongs) to that case's deviation from the grand mean:

between sum of squares— a value obtained by subtracting the grand mean from each group mean, squaring these differences for all individuals, and summing them

$$Y_{ij} - \bar{Y} = Y_{ij} + (\bar{Y}_j - \bar{Y}_j) - \bar{Y}$$

within sum of squares— a value obtained by subtracting each subgroup mean from each observed score, squaring, and summing

Rearrange the four terms on the right to create two deviations:

$$Y_{ij} - \bar{Y} = (Y_{ij} - \bar{Y}_j) + (\bar{Y}_j - \bar{Y})$$

The first term on the right, $(Y_{ij} - \bar{Y}_j)$, is the deviation of the ith individual's score from the mean of the jth group, to which it belongs. It is the sample estimate of the error term, e_{ij}. The second term on the right, $(\bar{Y}_j - \bar{Y})$, is the deviation of the jth group's mean from the grand mean of all groups. It is the sample estimate of the jth group's effect, $\alpha_j = \mu_j - \mu$. Squaring both sides of this equation and summing across all scores yields

$$\sum_{j=1}^{J} \sum_{i=1}^{n_j} (Y_{ij} - \bar{Y})^2 = \sum_{j=1}^{J} \sum_{i=1}^{n_j} (Y_{ij} - \bar{Y}_j)^2 + \sum_{j=1}^{J} n_j (\bar{Y}_j - \bar{Y})^2$$

This equality demonstrates that the total sum of squares can always be partitioned into

$$SS_{\text{WITHIN}} = \sum_{j=1}^{J} \sum_{i=1}^{n_j} (Y_{ij} - \bar{Y}_j)^2$$

and

$$SS_{\text{BETWEEN}} = \sum_{j=1}^{J} n_j (\bar{Y}_j - \bar{Y})^2$$

Therefore,

$$SS_{\text{TOTAL}} = SS_{\text{WITHIN}} + SS_{\text{BETWEEN}}$$

Except where all observations in a sample have identical scores, their variance is greater than zero. Some proportion of this variation may be attributable to the effects of the groups to which the observations belong. In other words, the *between*-group sum of squares summarizes the effects of the independent classification variable under study. Within a specific group, cases may still differ among themselves because of random factors such as sampling variation or from the effects of unobserved causal variables. Thus, the *within*-group sum of squares reflects the operation of unmeasured factors. To treat every group member as having the same score would result in errors.

4.2.2 Sums of Squares in the Attendance at Religious Services Example

If the null hypothesis about regional differences in religious service attendance were true, then we would observe equal means in all groups; that is, $\mu_S = \mu_M = \mu_N = \mu_W$. The SS_{BETWEEN} would equal zero, and hence $SS_{\text{TOTAL}} = SS_{\text{WITHIN}}$. That is, all the observed variation in religious service attendance would be random error variance. In instances where the independent variable has no effect, the general ANOVA model for sample data reduces to

$$Y_{ij} = \bar{Y} + e_{ij}$$

Suppose, however, that region was related to religious service attendance, that is, $\mu_S > \mu_M > \mu_N > \mu_W$. Assume, further, that each respondent *within* a particular region attends the same number of religious services; that is, no deviations occur around each group mean. Then, for sample data, religious service attendance for the four regions would equal

$$Y_{i,S} = \bar{Y} + a_S$$
$$Y_{i,M} = \bar{Y} + a_M$$
$$Y_{i,N} = \bar{Y} + a_N$$
$$Y_{i,W} = \bar{Y} + a_W$$

where these four a_j sample effects estimate the α_j population effects.

In this case $SS_{TOTAL} = SS_{BETWEEN}$, meaning that *all* the variation in religious service attendance is attributable to the region in which a respondent lives. In reality, of course, one discrete variable can never explain *all* the variation in a dependent variable. First, unmeasured *systematic* factors might affect the dependent variable. For example, denominational variation or ethnic composition might affect a particular region's rate of religious service attendance. These factors are not controlled in a one-way ANOVA. Second, *random* factors, such as media coverage of particularly admirable behavior by religious leaders, could also affect a region's rate of religious service attendance. Because variation in the dependent variable may arise from both unmeasured systematic and random factors, the set of equations for sample data must include both effects and error terms:

$$Y_{i,S} = \bar{Y} + a_S + e_{i,S}$$
$$Y_{i,M} = \bar{Y} + a_M + e_{i,M}$$
$$Y_{i,N} = \bar{Y} + a_N + e_{i,N}$$
$$Y_{i,W} = \bar{Y} + a_W + e_{i,W}$$

Because, for each region, the respondents' attendance scores range from 0 to 8, some within-group variation (error) occurs among respondents in all four regions. Moreover, the fact that the four regional means are not exactly equal suggests that between-group variation also occurs. Thus, the variation in religious service attendance (SS_{TOTAL}) seems to be attributable to both $SS_{BETWEEN}$ and SS_{WITHIN}. To determine whether these apparent differences are statistically significant requires calculating several ANOVA quantities, including the sums of squares, the mean squares, and an *F* test.

To compute SS_{TOTAL}, subtract each observation from the grand mean, square it, and sum, as in the following example for five GSS respondents' hypothetical religious service attendance scores (3.00, 2.00, 5.00, 4.00, 3.00), with a grand mean of 3.64: $(3.00 - 3.64)^2 + (2.00 - 3.64)^2 + (5.00 - 3.64)^2 + (4.00 - 3.64)^2 + (3.00 - 3.64)^2$. The actual 1998 GSS data set contains too many cases to allow for hand calculation of SS_{TOTAL} here. The SS_{TOTAL} for the GSS example is 21,395.00. $SS_{BETWEEN}$ is directly calculated by subtracting the grand mean from each group mean, squaring each difference, multiplying by group size, and summing, according to the formula

$$SS_{BETWEEN} = \sum_{j=1}^{J} n_j(\bar{Y}_j - \bar{Y})^2$$

which, in this example, is simply $(1{,}003)(4.00 - 3.64)^2 + (688)(3.69 - 3.64)^2 + (558)(3.39 - 3.64)^2 + (539)(3.16 - 3.64)^2 = 290.77$.

Finally, SS_{WITHIN} can be computed by direct calculation, where the *group* mean is subtracted from each observation, each difference is squared, and then the results are added:

$$SS_{\text{WITHIN}} = \sum_{j=1}^{J} \sum_{i=1}^{n_j} (Y_{ij} - \bar{Y}_j)^2$$

An alternative procedure uses the fact that $SS_{\text{TOTAL}} = SS_{\text{BETWEEN}} + SS_{\text{WITHIN}}$ to compute by simple subtraction from the two previous quantities:

$$SS_{\text{WITHIN}} = SS_{\text{TOTAL}} - SS_{\text{BETWEEN}}$$

Thus, $SS_{\text{WITHIN}} = 21{,}395.00 - 290.77 = 21{,}104.23$.

4.2.3 Mean Squares

The next step in an ANOVA is to compute the mean squares corresponding to SS_{BETWEEN} and SS_{WITHIN}. The two **mean squares** each estimate a variance—the first due to group effects and the second due to error. If no group effects exist, the two estimates should be identical. If a significant group effect exists, the between-group variance, called the **mean square between** (MS_{BETWEEN}), will be larger than the within-group variance, called the **mean square within** (MS_{WITHIN}). Mean squares are averages computed by dividing each sum of squares by its appropriate degrees of freedom (df). (See section 3.7 for a discussion of degrees of freedom.) The degrees of freedom associated with the between-group variance are simply $J - 1$, because once we know the grand mean ($\bar{Y}$) and the means of $J - 1$ of the groups ($\bar{Y}_j$), the mean of the Jth group is automatically determined. Thus, to compute MS_{BETWEEN}, simply divide SS_{BETWEEN} by $J - 1$:

$$MS_{\text{BETWEEN}} = \frac{\sum_{j=1}^{J} n_j (\bar{Y}_j - \bar{Y})^2}{J - 1}$$

$$= \frac{SS_{\text{BETWEEN}}}{J - 1}$$

mean square—estimate of variance used in the analysis of variance

mean square between—a value in ANOVA obtained by dividing the between sum of squares by its degrees of freedom

mean square within—a value in ANOVA obtained by dividing the within sum of squares by its degrees of freedom

Therefore, in the religious service attendance example,

$$MS_{\text{BETWEEN}} = 290.77/(4 - 1) = 96.92$$

The degrees of freedom associated with the within-group variance is $N - J$. Each group has $n_j - 1$ degrees of freedom, so adding across all J groups gives

$$(n_1 - 1) + (n_2 - 1) + \cdots + (n_J - 1) = \underbrace{(n_1 + n_2 + \cdots + n_J)}_{N \text{ cases}} - \underbrace{(1 + 1 + \cdots + 1)}_{J \text{ of these}}$$

$$= N - J$$

Therefore, to compute MS_{WITHIN}, divide SS_{WITHIN} by $N - J$:

$$MS_{\text{WITHIN}} = \frac{\sum\limits_{j=1}^{J} \sum\limits_{i=1}^{n_j} (Y_{ij} - \bar{Y}_j)^2}{N - J} = \frac{SS_{\text{WITHIN}}}{N - J}$$

For the religious service attendance example,

$$MS_{\text{WITHIN}} = 21{,}104.23/(2788 - 4) = 7.58.$$

The estimated variance due to group membership is much larger than the estimated variance due to error (96.92 vs. 7.58). Such a difference would occur if a regional effect on religious service attendance exists. The next step in ANOVA is to determine how much larger MS_{BETWEEN} must be relative to MS_{WITHIN} before the null hypothesis of no group effect can be rejected.

4.2.4 The *F* Ratio

We introduced the family of F distributions in section 3.11. In ANOVA, an F test statistic is computed simply as the ratio of the two mean squares. Its two degrees of freedom, ν_1 and ν_2, are the *df* for these two *MS*:

$$F_{J-1,\, N-J} = \frac{MS_{\text{BETWEEN}}}{MS_{\text{WITHIN}}}$$

The sampling distribution of F can be used to test the null hypothesis that none of the variance in the dependent variable is due to group effects. Two assumptions are required:

1. The J groups are independently drawn from a normally distributed population.

2. The population variance is identical to the variances of the J groups.

This latter assumption is called **homoscedasticity**. When the J population variances differ, they are *heteroscedastic*.

    If both assumptions hold, the computed F ratio statistic is distributed according to a theoretical F distribution with $J - 1$ *df* in the numerator and $N - J$ *df* in the denominator. Because the alternative hypothesis in ANOVA typically expects the between-group estimate of the variance to

homoscedasticity— a condition in which the variances of two or more population distributions are equal

be larger than the within-group variance estimate *in the population*, the significance test requires only one tail of the distribution. (Recall from chapter 3 that each F distribution is formed as a ratio of two chi-square distributions.) If the computed F ratio is larger than the critical value associated with a chosen α level, we reject the null hypothesis and conclude that group effects occur.

For $\alpha = .05$, .01, and .001, Appendix E provides three tables of critical values for many F distributions. The numerator *dfs* (v_1) run across the column headings of each table, while the denominator *dfs* (v_2) appear in the rows. The entry in the intersection of a row and column is the c.v. of F necessary to reject the null hypothesis at the α level for that table.

We can apply the F test to the religious service attendance data. Given $MS_{\text{BETWEEN}} = 96.92$ and $MS_{\text{WITHIN}} = 7.58$,

$$F_{3,2784} = \frac{96.92}{7.58} = 12.79$$

Because $J = 4$ and $N = 2{,}788$ in this example, this F ratio has $4 - 1 = 3$ degrees of freedom in the numerator and $2{,}788 - 4 = 2784$ *df* in the denominator. Choose $\alpha = .01$, and turn to the second F table in Appendix E to find the entry where $v_1 = 3$ and $v_2 = \infty$ (the closest approximation for 2,784). The critical value for F is 3.78. Because the computed F ratio is 12.79, we can reject the null hypothesis of no group effects with only a .01 chance of making a false rejection or Type I error. We conclude that religious service attendance in 1998 differed significantly among the four regions. Exactly where the differences occur remains to be determined. Section 4.5 provides some procedures for testing some hypotheses about differences among means.

The results of a one-way analysis of variance are commonly presented in an **ANOVA summary table**, as illustrated by Table 4.1. It provides easy access to all the relevant information needed to interpret the

ANOVA summary table— a tabular display summarizing the results of an analysis of variance

TABLE 4.1
Summary of ANOVA for Attendance at Religious Services

Source	SS	df	MS	F
Between group	290.77	3	96.92	12.79*
Within group	21,104.23	2,784	7.58	
Total	21,395.00	2,787		

*Significant at $\alpha = .01$.

hypothesis test—the sums of squares, degrees of freedom, mean squares, *F* ratio, and probability level.

4.3 Tests for Two Means

Analyses of variance are usually performed when a classification results in three or more groups. However, ANOVA is equally possible with just two groups. The *Z* and the *t* distributions (both discussed in chapter 3) are also available to test the statistical significance of differences in two population means. After presenting these tests, we show that they are special cases of the more general ANOVA and thus give the same results. We apply these tests to an example from the 1998 GSS in which the null hypothesis is that the political views of men and women do not differ significantly. This variable is operationalized by asking survey respondents to rate themselves on a seven-point scale from "extremely liberal" (1) to "extremely conservative" (7), with "moderate" as the scale midpoint (4). Our alternative hypothesis is that men and women hold different political views, but we do not have compelling grounds to assert which gender is more conservative. Hence, a two-tailed alternative hypothesis is plausible:

$$H_0: \; \mu_F = \mu_M$$

$$H_1: \; \mu_F \neq \mu_M$$

4.3.1 *Z* Test Procedures

The central limit theorem (see section 3.5) guarantees that for large samples the distribution of all sample means (i.e., the sampling distribution) will be normal, and its mean is an unbiased estimate of the mean of the population from which the samples were selected. To test the difference between the means of two populations, a corollary of the central limit theorem is relevant:

The distribution of the difference between two sample means, from random samples of N_1 and N_2 with population means μ_1 and μ_2 and variances σ_1^2 and σ_2^2, follows a normal distribution that has mean $\mu_1 - \mu_2$ and standard deviation (standard error) $\sqrt{\sigma_1^2/N_1 + \sigma_2^2/N_2}$. No assumptions are required about the shape of the original population distributions.

When the population parameters are unknown, the sampling distribution's values can be computed as

$$\mu_{(\bar{Y}_1 - \bar{Y}_2)} = \mu_1 - \mu_2$$

$$\sigma_{(\bar{Y}_1 - \bar{Y}_2)} = \sqrt{\sigma_1^2/N_1 + \sigma_2^2/N_2}$$

mean difference hypothesis test—
a statistical test of a hypothesis about the difference between two population means

The table of probabilities associated with the normal distribution allows us to perform a **mean difference hypothesis test** about two population means. It only requires that N_1 and N_2 are large (that is, $N_1 + N_2$ should be *at least* 60 and preferably 100 or more) and that the variances of both populations (σ_1^2 and σ_2^2) are known. Because these population parameters are seldom known, they are usually estimated from the sample statistics. If $N_1 + N_2$ is large, the known sample variances, s_1^2 and s_2^2, can be substituted for the unknown population variances, σ_1^2 and σ_2^2, to estimate the standard error:

$$\hat{\sigma}_{(\bar{Y}_1 - \bar{Y}_2)} = \sqrt{s_1^2/N_1 + s_2^2/N_2}$$

To test the null hypothesis that $\mu_1 = \mu_2$, which implies that $\mu_1 - \mu_2 = 0$, refer to the summary of steps in Box 3.4. Choose an α level (the probability of making a Type I error) and calculate the test statistic. Next, determine the critical value and compare it to the observed test statistic. Finally, decide whether to reject the null hypothesis in favor of the alternative.

For our analysis of male-female political views in the 1998 GSS, we choose $\alpha = .01$. Given the large number of cases in each gender ($N_1 = 1,187$ men; $N_2 = 1,600$ women), the standardized normal or Z score is the appropriate theoretical distribution. The Z test statistic for the difference in means has $(\bar{Y}_1 - \bar{Y}_2) - (\mu_1 - \mu_2)$ in the numerator and $\sigma_{(\bar{Y}_1 - \bar{Y}_2)}$ in the denominator. Appendix C shows that the critical values for a two-tailed test at $\alpha = .01$ are $-Z_{\alpha/2} = -2.58$ and $+Z_{\alpha/2} = +2.58$.

Under the null hypothesis, H_0: $\mu_1 - \mu_2 = 0$, the mean of the first population equals the mean of the second population. We test whether the observed difference in the two sample means ($\bar{Y}_1 - \bar{Y}_2$) could have occurred if the true difference in population means were exactly zero; that is, $(\mu_1 - \mu_2) = 0$. Thus, this term drops out of the numerator of the Z score used to test H_0:

$$Z_{(\bar{Y}_1 - \bar{Y}_2)} = \frac{(\bar{Y}_1 - \bar{Y}_2) - (\mu_1 - \mu_2)}{\sigma_{(\bar{Y}_1 - \bar{Y}_2)}}$$

$$= \frac{\overline{Y}_1 - \overline{Y}_2}{\sqrt{\sigma_1^2/N_1 + \sigma_2^2/N_2}}$$

Or, using our large sample estimate for $\sigma_{(\overline{Y}_1 - \overline{Y}_2)}$:

$$Z_{(\overline{Y}_1 - \overline{Y}_2)} = \frac{\overline{Y}_1 - \overline{Y}_2}{\hat{\sigma}_{(\overline{Y}_1 - \overline{Y})}}$$

$$= \frac{\overline{Y}_1 - \overline{Y}_2}{\sqrt{s_1^2/N_1 + s_2^2/N_2}}$$

Figure 4.1 diagrams two situations for a sampling distribution where $H_0: \mu_2 - \mu_1 = 0$ is true. In the top diagram, the difference in sample means

FIGURE 4.1
Two Examples of Outcomes When the Null Hypothesis About Mean Differences Is True

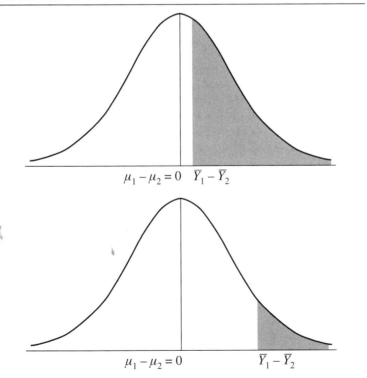

Source: David Knoke and George W. Bohrnstedt, *Basic Social Statistics* (Itasca, IL: F. E. Peacock Publishers, Inc., 1991), 202.

$(\bar{Y}_1 - \bar{Y}_2)$ is a small positive value lying close to the hypothesized population difference of zero. We would not reject the null hypothesis at conventional levels of α because this small difference is highly probable in a population where $\mu_1 - \mu_2 = 0$. The observed sample difference in the bottom diagram is substantial. We most probably would reject the null hypothesis that the two samples came from populations where $\mu_1 - \mu_2 = 0$, as this outcome is very unlikely in the sampling distribution (it occurs in the far right tail). These two sample means probably came from populations where $\mu_1 > \mu_2$.

The mean of political views for the 1,187 men is 4.19, while the mean for the 1,504 women is 4.02. The two sample variances are 1.89 and 1.96, respectively. Hence, the test statistic is computed as

$$Z_{(\bar{Y}_1 - \bar{Y}_2)} = \frac{4.19 - 4.02}{\sqrt{\dfrac{1.89}{1,187} + \dfrac{1.96}{1,504}}} = \frac{0.170}{0.054} = +3.15$$

Because this computed Z value exceeds the c.v. (+2.58), we can reject the null hypothesis in favor of the alternative that men and women differ in their political views.

4.3.2 Hypothesis Testing with Proportions

In chapter 2 we defined a proportion as the frequency of cases of a specific type, divided by the total number of cases. The sample mean is given by $\bar{Y} = \sum Y_i / N$. But when Y_i has only values of 1 and 0, the numerator term, $\sum Y_i$, equals f_1. Thus, as section 2.4.3 showed, the mean of a dichotomous variable is the proportion of cases having the value 1, that is, p_1. For example, 1,906 of 2,599 1998 GSS respondents agreed that they were "in favor of the death penalty for persons convicted of murder." Hence, $p_1 = 1,906/2,599 = 0.733$, or 73.3%.

The same formulas used in section 4.3.1 to test hypotheses about mean differences can be applied to dichotomous dependent variables, to perform **significance testing with proportions**. The variance of a dichotomy is simply pq, where $q = 1 - p$. Thus, in the capital punishment example, the sample variance is $s_Y^2 = (0.733)(1 - 0.733) = (0.733)(0.267) = 0.196$. And the standard error of a sampling distribution of proportions, s_p, is

significance testing with proportions—using statistical tests to determine whether the observed difference between sample proportions could occur by chance in the populations from which the samples were selected

$$s_p = \sqrt{pq/N}$$

In this example, $s_p = \sqrt{(0.733)(0.267)/2,599} = 0.009$.

Suppose we hypothesize that Republicans, who are conventionally considered more conservative, favor the death penalty more strongly than do Democrats. Then the two hypotheses are

$$H_0: p_R \leq p_D$$

$$H_1: p_R > p_D$$

where p_R is the proportion of Republicans favoring the death penalty and p_D is the proportion of Democrats. In the 1998 GSS, of the 902 Republicans (including Independents leaning towards the Republican Party) with opinions, 80.9% supported capital punishment, while only 66.9% of the 1,218 Democrats (including Democrat-leaning Independents) favored the death penalty. Hence, $p_R = .809$ and $p_D = .669$. Setting $\alpha = .05$, we can calculate the test statistic for the difference between two means:

$$Z_{(p_R - p_D)} = \frac{0.809 - 0.669}{\sqrt{\dfrac{(0.809)(0.191)}{902} + \dfrac{(0.669)(0.331)}{1,218}}}$$

$$= \frac{0.140}{0.019} = +7.37$$

Because the critical value of Z_α for a one-tailed alternative is $+1.645$, we reject the null hypothesis. We conclude that Republicans support the death penalty at a higher level than do Democrats.

The formula above for the standard error used in the test statistic clearly shows that, as N_1 and N_2 get large, the standard error grows smaller. If N_1 and N_2 are sufficiently large, almost *any* difference in $\bar{Y}_1$ and $\bar{Y}_2$ will become significant. For this reason, more cautious strategies of hypothesis testing should be adopted. For example, unless the mean difference is at least one-quarter standard deviation, it could be considered unimportant regardless of statistical significance. An even better approach would be to estimate the strength of a relationship among variables. How large a relationship should be depends on the specific research problem, so a general principle is impossible to state. Most importantly, mere statistical significance cannot reveal the entire story.

4.3.3 *t* Test Procedures

When data consist of two small samples—usually where $N_1 + N_2 < 100$ and certainly where fewer than 60 cases are available—the assumptions necessary for the Z test of mean differences are untenable. However, the family of t distributions may be used instead, if two key assumptions can be made: (1) both samples are drawn randomly from two independent, normally distributed populations; and (2) the two population variances are homoscedastic; that is, $\sigma_1^2 = \sigma_2^2 = \sigma^2$. Unlike the Z test discussed previously, the shapes of the population distributions are important when using the t test. In practice, however, violating this assumption may have only a small impact on the results.

To make a single estimate of the population variance, the two sample variances are pooled, using

$$s^2 = \frac{(N_1 - 1)(s_1^2) + (N_2 - 1)(s_2^2)}{N_1 + N_2 - 2}$$

where
$N_1 + N_2 - 2$ is the df associated with the pooled estimate.

The degrees of freedom equal the sum of the dfs associated with s_1^2 and s_2^2. Specifically, $df_1 + df_2 = (N_1 - 1) + (N_2 - 1) = N_1 + N_2 - 2$.

For small samples, the test statistic for the difference between two means is

$$t_{(N_1 + N_2 - 2)} = \frac{(\bar{Y}_1 - \bar{Y}_2) - (\mu_1 - \mu_2)}{s_{(\bar{Y}_1 - \bar{Y}_2)}}$$

$$= \frac{\bar{Y}_1 - \bar{Y}_2}{\sqrt{s^2/N_1 + s^2/N_2}}$$

$$= \frac{\bar{Y}_1 - \bar{Y}_2}{s\sqrt{1/N_1 + 1/N_2}}$$

where $s_{(\bar{Y}_1 - \bar{Y}_2)}$ is the estimated standard error of the mean difference.

To illustrate this procedure, we examine whether older women are more likely than older men to believe that doctors are not as thorough in working with patients as they should be. Specifically, the 1998 GSS asked respondents to indicate the extent to which they agreed with the statement "Doctors are not as thorough as they should be in dealing with patients." Response options ranged on a scale from "strongly agree" (coded 1) to "strongly disagree" (coded 5), with "uncertain" coded 3. A total of 47 adults age 82 or older answered the question, 19 males and 28 females. Table 4.2 shows the data. Because the two groups are small, a t test is appropriate for comparing men's and women's responses, if we assume that the data are independent samples drawn randomly from two normally distributed populations.

TABLE **4.2**
Attitude Towards the Thoroughness of Doctors' Work for Older Women and Men (Age 82 or Older)

	OLDER WOMEN			OLDER MEN	
Case	*Attitude Score*		*Case*	*Attitude Score*	
1	4.0		1	2.0	
2	2.0		2	4.0	
3	2.0		3	4.0	
4	4.0		4	5.0	
5	2.0		5	4.0	
6	2.0		6	2.0	
7	3.0		7	2.0	
8	3.0		8	4.0	
9	2.0		9	2.0	
10	2.0		10	1.0	
11	2.0		11	1.0	
12	4.0		12	4.0	
13	4.0		13	2.0	
14	2.0		14	4.0	
15	3.0		15	4.0	
16	2.0		16	5.0	
17	2.0		17	1.0	
18	4.0		18	4.0	
19	4.0		19	4.0	
20	2.0				
21	2.0				
22	1.0				
23	4.0				
24	2.0				
25	4.0				
26	2.0				
27	2.0				
28	3.0				

$N_1 = 28$ $N_2 = 19$

$\overline{Y}_1 = 2.68$ $\overline{Y}_2 = 3.11$

$s_1 = 0.94$ $s_2 = 1.37$

Source: 1998 General Social Survey.

The null and alternative hypotheses, where group 1 is older women and group 2 is older men, are

$$H_0: \mu_1 - \mu_2 = 0$$

$$H_1: \mu_1 - \mu_2 < 0$$

Setting $\alpha = .01$ for $df = 28 + 19 - 2 = 45$ gives a critical value in Appendix D of -2.423 for a one-tailed test to reject the null. Calculating s^2 and taking its square root to obtain s, we find

$$s = \sqrt{\frac{(28-1)(0.94)^2 + (19-1)(1.37)^2}{28 + 19 - 2}} = 1.13$$

Thus, t is calculated as

$$t_{45} = \frac{2.68 - 3.11}{(1.13)\sqrt{1/28 + 1/19}} = \frac{-0.43}{0.34} = -1.26$$

Therefore, the sample data do not support the alternative hypothesis that older women are more likely than older men to believe that doctors are not as thorough as they should be.

Researchers almost exclusively use t tests rather than Z tests for analyzing differences in two means. As N increases, the t and Z distributions converge to the latter's critical values. In Appendix D (the t distribution), look across the row where df equals infinity (∞) to the t entry under the column headed by a given α. Compare it to the Z value in Appendix C for the same α; and you will find that they are identical. Also, as N increases (beyond 100 or more), the central limit theorem renders the assumption that the samples come from normally distributed populations increasingly unimportant (see section 3.5). Finally, because researchers almost never know the standard error of the population, a t test is preferable. Although you should know the difference between a Z and a t distribution, in practice one always uses t tests.

4.3.4 Comparing Two Distributions with Stem-and-Leaf Diagrams and Boxplots

In section 2.8 we showed how to construct stem-and-leaf diagrams and box-and-whisker plots for a single distribution. In this section we show how these same tools can be used to compare two distributions.

FIGURE **4.2**
Stem-and-Leaf Diagrams for Attitudes Towards the Thoroughness of Doctors' Work

Stems	Leaves	(N)
Women Aged 82 and Older		
1	0	(1)
2	000000000000000	(15)
3	0000	(4)
4	00000000	(8)
5		(0)
Men Aged 82 and Older		
1	000	(3)
2	00000	(5)
3		(0)
4	000000000	(9)
5	00	(2)

Source: 1998 General Social Survey.

Using the data from Table 4.2, Figure 4.2 shows two stem-and-leaf diagrams of attitudes regarding doctors' thoroughness for older women and men. Figure 4.3 shows the boxplots for the older women and older men separately. The median for the older women is between the 14th and 15th observations and has the value $Mdn_W = 2.0$. The lower hinge is the 7th observation. Hence, $H_1 = 2.0$. Similarly, the upper hinge is the 21st observation, or $H_2 = 4.0$. And the hinge spread, $HS_W = H_2 - H_1 = 2.0$. To check for outliers, we compute the lower and upper inner fences

$$LIF_W = 2.0 - (1.5)(2.0) = -1.0$$

and

$$UIF_W = 4.0 + (1.5)(2.0) = 7.0$$

Since no value is smaller than -1.0 or larger than 7.0, we conclude that there are no outliers in the older women's data. The boxplot for these data is shown in the right side of Figure 4.3.

Because the older men's data have 19 observations, the median, Mdn_M, is the 10th observation and has the value of 4.0. Verify for yourself

FIGURE 4.3
Box-and-Whisker Plots for Attitudes of Older Women and Men Towards the Thoroughness of Doctors' Work

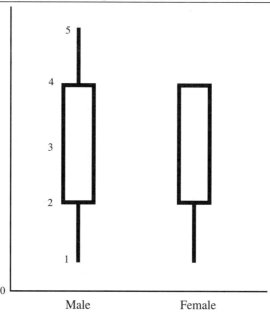

that $H_1 = 2.0$, $H_2 = 4.0$, and $HS_M = 2.0$. Hence, $\text{LIF}_M = -1.0$ and $\text{UIF}_M = 7.0$, the same as for the women. Because no observation is smaller than -1.0 or larger than 7.0, there are also no outliers in the older men's data.

Figure 4.3 visually confirms that older women and men hold similar attitudes regarding the thoroughness of doctors' work.

4.3.5 Confidence Intervals and Point Estimates

confidence interval for mean differences—an interval constructed around the point estimate of the difference between two means

point estimate for mean differences—the difference between the sample means used to estimate the difference between two population means

A **confidence interval for mean differences** can be constructed around the point estimate of the difference between two means, just as we showed for a single mean in section 3.6. For any desired level of confidence, such as $1 - \alpha$, the formula is

$$(\bar{Y}_1 - \bar{Y}_2) \pm t_{\alpha/2} s_{(\bar{Y}_1 - \bar{Y}_2)}$$

To compute a 95% confidence interval around the sample estimate of difference scores between older women's and men's attitudes towards doctors' thoroughness, start with the **point estimate for mean differences**,

$\bar{Y}_1 - \bar{Y}_2 = .43\%$. The estimated standard error is $s_{(\bar{Y}_1 - \bar{Y}_2)} = 1.13$. Appendix D shows that for a 95% confidence level with $N_1 + N_2 - 2 = 45$ *df*, $t_{\alpha/2}$ is approximately 2.021. Therefore, the upper confidence limit (UCL) is $-0.43 + (2.021)(1.13) = 1.85$, and the lower confidence limit (LCL) is $-0.43 - (2.021)(1.13) = -2.71$. In other words, we can be 95% confident that the interval bounded by -2.71 and 1.85 contains the true population difference between older women and older men in attitudes towards doctors' thoroughness. Importantly, the interval includes 0, no difference in population means.

A confidence interval around the difference in proportions is given by

$$(p_1 - p_2) \pm t_{\alpha/2} s_{(p_1 - p_2)}$$

The data in section 4.3.2 on Republican and Democratic support of the death penalty were $p_R - p_D = .140$ and $s_{p_R - p_D} = .019$. Sample sizes were $N_R = 902$ and $N_R = 1{,}218$, for $df = 902 + 1{,}218 - 2 = 2{,}118$. From Appendix D, a 99% confidence interval requires $t_{\alpha/2} = \pm 2.58$. Thus, the LCL is $0.140 - (2.58)(0.019) = 0.091$ and the UCL is $0.140 + (2.58)(0.019) = 0.189$. We can be 99% confident that the true population difference in proportions of Republicans and Democrats favoring capital punishment lies within the interval 0.091 and 0.189. Furthermore, our best estimate of the true population difference is the point estimate, $p_R - p_D = .140$. In other words, on the death penalty question, the difference between Republicans and Democrats is greater than zero.

4.3.6 Relationship of *t* to *F*

The *t* test and the *F* test for testing the differences in means are intimately related. When only two groups are compared, that is, when $J = 2$, both ANOVA and the *t* test give identical results. In fact, applied to the same data, the square root of an *F* ratio with 1 and v_2 degrees of freedom equals a *t* value with v_2 degrees of freedom. Hence,

$$t_{v_2} = \sqrt{F_{1,v_2}}$$

Usually when $J = 2$ the researcher reports only a *t* test, while when $J > 2$, the results of an ANOVA are always reported.

4.4   The Correlation Ratio: Eta-Squared

If a *Z* test, *t* test, or an analysis of variance allows the null hypothesis to be rejected, the next question is: How strong is the relationship between the variables? Because a sufficiently large *N* allows almost any difference among means to be significant, the results of a statistical test are no guide to the importance of a relationship. Therefore, after rejecting a null hypothesis, the strength of the relationship should be assessed by computing the **correlation ratio** or **eta-squared**, or η^2 (Greek letter *eta*).

correlation ratio/ eta-squared—a measure of nonlinear covariation between a discrete and a continuous variable, the ratio of $SS_{BETWEEN}$ to SS_{TOTAL}

In section 4.2.1 we showed that $SS_{TOTAL} = SS_{BETWEEN} + SS_{WITHIN}$. Dividing both sides of that equation by SS_{TOTAL}, it becomes

$$1.00 = \frac{SS_{BETWEEN}}{SS_{TOTAL}} + \frac{SS_{WITHIN}}{SS_{TOTAL}}$$

$$= \text{"Explained SS"} + \text{"Unexplained SS"}$$

The ratio of $SS_{BETWEEN}$ to SS_{TOTAL} represents the proportion of the total sum of squares that is explained (in a statistical sense) by the independent or group variable. Similarly, the ratio of SS_{WITHIN} to SS_{TOTAL} can be considered the unexplained proportion of the total sum of squares. These two components add up to 1.00. Therefore, the proportion of variance in the dependent variable attributable to the group variable is defined as

$$\eta^2 = \frac{SS_{BETWEEN}}{SS_{TOTAL}}$$

Because η^2 is a population parameter notation, its sample estimate is designated with a caret (i.e., $\hat{\eta}^2$). Eta-squared always ranges between zero and 1.00. The more that the sample means differ from one another and the smaller the sample variances, the relatively larger the $SS_{BETWEEN}$, and thus the closer $\hat{\eta}^2$ comes to 1.00.

Using the statistics from the ANOVA in Table 4.1,

$$\hat{\eta}^2 = \frac{290.77}{21,395.00} = 0.014$$

That is, 1.4% of the variation in adults' religious service attendance can be explained statistically by the region in which they live. As social science analyses go, this is a minimal proportion of variance explained. Typically, a single independent variable in social research seldom accounts for more than 25% to 30% of the variance in a dependent variable, and often for as little as 2% to 5%.

4.5 Testing Differences Among Means (Post Hoc)

The alternative hypothesis for an ANOVA can take several forms, as noted in section 4.1. Three possibilities are as follows:

1. All the population means differ from one another.

2. Some subsets of the population means differ from one another.

3. Some combination of the means differs from some single mean or from some other combination of means.

The *F* value itself is uninformative about which of these alternatives is true in a given situation. Using a series of *t* tests to examine all possible pairs of means is not legitimate, because not all $J^2 - J$ comparisons among the *J* group means are independent of one another. A method is required that is guided by the researcher's ideas about where differences among the groups may occur.

There are two basic approaches for comparing means. The first, called *a priori* or **planned comparison**, unfortunately requires more mathematical treatment than we can assume for this book. The second approach, called *a posteriori* or **post hoc comparison**, is less statistically powerful but still useful in social science research. In this section we will briefly introduce one form of post hoc comparison, the **Scheffé test**.

To make multiple comparisons among *J* means, a contrast can be formed. A **contrast**, labeled Ψ (Greek letter *psi*), among *J* population means is defined as

$$\Psi = c_1\mu_1 + c_2\mu_2 + \cdots + c_j\mu_j$$

where the c_j are weights under the constraint that $c_1 + c_2 + \cdots + c_J = 0$; that is, the c_j sum to zero.

planned comparison— hypothesis test of differences between and among population means carried out before doing an analysis of variance

post hoc comparison— hypothesis test of the differences among population means carried out following an analysis of variance

Scheffé test—one form of post hoc comparison of differences in group means

contrast—a set of weighted population means that sum to zero, used in making post hoc comparisons of treatment groups

Using the religious service attendance example, we hypothesize that the South and Midwest regions have higher attendance rates than the Northeast and West. Thus, we must form contrasts between the two former regions and the two latter regions, as follows: $c_S = c_M = -1/2$ and $c_N = c_W = 1/2$. By using these plus and minus signs, the c_js add to zero: $c_S + c_M + c_N + c_W = -1/2 - 1/2 + 1/2 + 1/2 = 0$. The contrast for this hypothesis—call it Ψ_1—is given by

$$\Psi_1 = \left(\frac{1}{2}\right)\mu_S + \left(\frac{1}{2}\right)\mu_M + \left(-\frac{1}{2}\right)\mu_N + \left(-\frac{1}{2}\right)\mu_W$$

$$= \frac{\mu_S + \mu_W}{2} + \frac{-\mu_N - \mu_W}{2}$$

The *average* of the South and Midwest is contrasted to the *average* of the Northeast and West. Other contrasts consistent with the hypothesis are possible. For example, we could have let $c_S = 1$, $c_M = 1$, $c_N = -1$, and $c_W = -1$, which also sum to zero.[2] Once we form a contrast using sample means, we must compare its size to its standard error, much as a t test does. If the ratio is sufficiently large, we conclude that the comparison between the means is significant. If not, we cannot reject the null hypothesis that the true difference among means is zero. An unbiased estimate of a contrast using sample data is given by

$$\hat{\Psi} = c_1 \overline{Y}_1 + c_2 \overline{Y}_2 + \cdots + c_j \overline{Y}_j$$

and the estimated variance of a contrast is given by

$$\hat{\sigma}_{\hat{\psi}}^2 = MS_{\text{WITHIN}} \left(\frac{c_1^2}{n_1} + \frac{c_2^2}{n_2} + \cdots + \frac{c_J^2}{n_J} \right)$$

where

MS_{WITHIN} = The mean square within obtained from the ANOVA.
n_j = The number of observations in the jth group.

The test statistic for a post hoc comparison is formed by the ratio of the absolute value of $\hat{\Psi}$ to its standard error:

$$t = \frac{|\hat{\Psi}|}{\hat{\sigma}_{\hat{\psi}}}$$

The critical value against which to evaluate this test statistic is given by

$$\text{c.v.} = \sqrt{(J-1)(F_{J-1, N-J})}$$

where

$F_{J-1,N-J}$ = The critical value for the α-level chosen to test the null hypothesis in the ANOVA.

Therefore, whenever $|\hat{\Psi}|/\hat{\sigma}_{\hat{\psi}} \geq \sqrt{(J-1)(F_{J-1, N-J})}$, we reject the null hypothesis. There are $N - J$ degrees of freedom associated with this t test.

The religious service attendance example illustrates how to perform a multiple mean comparison. The hypothesized contrast is

$$\hat{\Psi}_1 = \frac{(4.00 + 3.69)}{2} + \frac{(-3.39 + -3.16)}{2} = 0.57$$

---

[2]Many ANOVA computer packages, such as SPSS, require either integer contrasts or single decimal-place contrasts. Thus, 0.5 and –0.5 are permissible, but contrasts such as 0.25 would be rounded incorrectly to 0.3.

and

$$\hat{\sigma}^2_{\hat{\psi}_1} = (7.58)\left[\frac{(1/2)^2}{1,003} + \frac{(1/2)^2}{688} + \frac{(-1/2)^2}{558} + \frac{(-1/2)^2}{539}\right] = 0.012$$

Taking the square root,

$$\hat{\sigma}_{\hat{\psi}_1} = \sqrt{0.012} = 0.11$$

Therefore, the test statistic is $t = |-0.57|/.11 = 5.18$. The critical value for $\alpha = .01$ is $\sqrt{(4-1)(3.78)} = 3.37$. Because 5.18 is larger than 3.37, we conclude that the hypothesized paired regional differences cannot be rejected. Since we know from the ANOVA that the four means are not equal, the next plausible contrast is the Western states versus the other three regions. What weights should be assigned to form this contrast?

At this point, you should know how to do an ANOVA for multiple groups, to perform a t test for two groups, and to make post hoc comparisons among means. Thus, you should be able to undertake meaningful tests of hypotheses involving two or more means.

Review of Key Concepts and Symbols

These key concepts and symbols are listed in the order of appearance in this chapter. Combined with the definitions in the margins, they will help you to review the material and can serve as a self-test for mastery of the concepts.

analysis of variance (ANOVA)
grand mean
effect
error term
total sum of squares
between sum of squares
within sum of squares
mean squares
mean square between
mean square within
homoscedasticity
ANOVA summary table
mean difference hypothesis test

significance testing with proportions
confidence interval for mean differences
point estimate for mean differences
correlation ratio (eta-squared)
planned comparison
post hoc comparison
Scheffé test
contrast
α_j
e_{ij}
SS_{TOTAL}
SS_{BETWEEN}
SS_{WITHIN}

MS_{BETWEEN}	$\hat{\sigma}_{(\bar{Y}_1 - \bar{Y}_2)}$	$\hat{\eta}^2$
MS_{WITHIN}	s_p	ψ
$\mu_{(\bar{Y}_1 - \bar{Y}_2)}$	s^2	c_j
$\sigma_{(\bar{Y}_1 - \bar{Y}_2)}$	η^2	$\hat{\sigma}^2_\psi$

PROBLEMS
General Problems

1. A voting analyst hypothesizes that support for campaign finance reform is highest among self-identified Democrats, next strongest among Independents, and lowest among Republicans. Write the null and alternative forms of the hypothesis in symbolic form.

2. A sociologist studying volunteerism finds for a random sample of adults that the overall mean number of hours spent volunteering per month is 11.2. If the mean score for adults aged 65 and older is 18.7, for adults aged 55–64 is 11.8, and for adults aged 45–54 is 3.1, what are the effects of being in each age group?

3. A human resources administrator at an engineering firm administers an employee satisfaction instrument to a sample of 50 employees. He obtains means of 91.5 from 18 engineers, 83.0 from 12 technicians, and 74.6 from 20 administrative support staff. What are the effects (α_j) for each type of employee, using the weighted sample mean as an estimate of the population mean?

4. Find the degrees of freedom and critical values of F for the following:
   a. $\alpha = .05$, 3 groups, 20 subjects.
   b. $\alpha = .01$, 2 groups, 125 subjects.
   c. $\alpha = .001$, 6 groups, 36 subjects.
   d. $\alpha = .001$, 25 groups, 65 subjects.

5. Find the degrees of freedom and critical values of F for the following:
   a. $\alpha = .05$, $n_1 = 17$, $n_2 = 10$.
   b. $\alpha = .01$, $n_1 = 20$, $n_2 = 13$, $n_3 = 10$.

   c. $\alpha = .001$, $n_1 = 5$, $n_2 = 10$, $n_3 = 5$.

   d. $\alpha = .001$, $n_1 = 24$, $n_2 = 20$, $n_3 = 10$, $n_4 = 10$.

6. An experimenter divides 100 subjects into three groups, two of which have the same size and the third of which is as large as the other two combined. If the mean ages of the two smaller groups are 21 years and 29 years, what is the mean age of the third group, if the grand mean is 33 years?

7. A total of 75 subjects, divided equally into three groups, yields a total sum of squares = 324.61 and a within sum of squares = 293.50. What is the $MS_{BETWEEN}$?

8. A researcher draws random samples of voters from four counties in California, with sample sizes of 27, 38, 34, and 25. On a 10-point scale measuring attitudes towards the current governor, the $SS_{TOTAL} = 297.33$ and the $SS_{BETWEEN} = 38.22$. What is the value of eta-squared? Is the probability less than $\alpha = .05$ that the population means differ significantly across the four counties? Report the observed F ratio and critical value.

9. Listed below are the reading quiz scores from a class of 15 first graders who were assigned to three different reading groups: (1) reading aloud with an adult; (2) reading aloud with an older student; and (3) reading aloud with a classmate:

With Adult	With Older Student	With Classmate
7	8	4
6	7	6
8	8	7
9	6	7
10	8	9

Compute the effect parameters (α_j) for each treatment condition. Then calculate the total sum of squares, the between sum of squares, and the within sum of squares. Determine the mean squares and the F ratio, and evaluate it against the null hypothesis that the three population means are equal, setting $\alpha = .05$. Display these results in an ANOVA summary table. Finally, compute $\hat{\eta}^2$ and interpret the results.

10. Test the post hoc hypothesis in Problem 9 that reading with an adult is superior to the other two methods. Set $\alpha = .05$. Report $\hat{\Psi}$ and $\hat{\sigma}^2_{\hat{\Psi}}$.

Problems Requiring the 1998 General Social Survey

11. Test the hypothesis that approval of "pro athletes giving thanks to God" (GODSPORT) is related to region of residence (REGION), by performing an analysis of variance. Set $\alpha = .001$. Compute $\hat{\eta}^2$ and interpret the results. Change the "Don't Know," "No Answer," and "Not Applicable" responses to missing values.

12. What is the relationship between a person's age and attitude toward divorce law (DIVLAW)? Recode AGE into six roughly decade-wide categories [i.e., RECODE AGE (LO THRU 29=1)(30 thru 39=2) ... (70 THRU 89=6)]. Then recode DIVLAW [RECODE DIVLAW (1=1)(3=2)(2=3)], and change the value labels for DIVLAW [VALUE LABELS DIVLAW 1 'Easier' 2 'Stay the Same' 3 'More Difficult']. Finally, perform an ANOVA with DIVLAW as the dependent variable. Set $\alpha = .001$. Compute $\hat{\eta}^2$ and interpret the results.

13. Does the attitude that Blacks can work their way up and "can overcome prejudice without favors" vary by race? Perform an ANOVA with WRKWAYUP and RACE. Set $\alpha = .001$. Compute $\hat{\eta}^2$ and interpret the results. Change the "Don't Know," "No Answer," and "Not Applicable" responses to missing values.

14. Do people who approve of the Supreme Court's ruling against reading the Lord's Prayer or Bible verses in public schools (PRAYER) consider themselves to be less politically conservative (POLVIEWS) than those who disapprove of the Court's decision? To answer this question, run a *t* test. Set $\alpha = .05$. Change the "Don't Know," "No Answer," and "Not Applicable" responses to missing values.

15. What is the relationship between a person's age and his/her attitude towards premarital sex? Recode AGE into six roughly decade-wide categories [i.e., RECODE AGE (LO THRU 29=1)(30 thru 39=2), ... , (70 THRU 89=6)]. Then perform an ANOVA with PREMARSX as the dependent variable. Set $\alpha = .001$. Change the "Don't Know," "No Answer," and "Not Applicable" responses to missing values.

5

ANALYZING CATEGORIC DATA

5.1 Bivariate Crosstabulation

5.2 Using Chi-Square to Test Significance

5.3 Measuring Association: Q, Phi, Gamma, Tau c, Somers's d_{yx}

5.4 Odds and Odds Ratios

Analysis of variance reveals the relationship between two variables by examining means on a continuous dependent variable for the categories of a discrete independent variable. There are additional techniques for finding how two variables are related. One is crosstabulation, described in this chapter; another is bivariate regression, introduced in chapter 7. In this chapter, we will explain the logic of bivariate crosstabulation, a method for detecting statistical significance. We will also describe ways to estimate the strength of the relationships between two discrete variables.

5.1 Bivariate Crosstabulation

The **bivariate crosstabulation** or *joint contingency table* displays the simultaneous outcomes of observations on two discrete variables. The categories of either variable may be orderable or nonorderable. The inferential and descriptive statistics discussed in this chapter can be applied to crosstabulations (or "crosstabs," as they are often called) of either type, although some measures of association can be meaningfully interpreted only when the variables' categories are orderable in a sequence from lowest to highest.

bivariate crosstabulation/ joint contingency table— a tabular display of the simultaneous outcomes of observations on two discrete variables

Suppose we are interested in the relationship between level of education and attitude towards women's roles outside the home, taking sex-role attitude as the dependent variable. Respondents in the 1998 GSS were asked whether they strongly agreed, agreed, disagreed, or strongly disagreed with the statement: "It is better for everyone involved if the man is the achiever outside the home and the woman takes care of the home and family." Respondents' highest degree earned in school was coded into one of five ordered categories: less than high school, high school diploma, junior college (associate's degree), bachelor's degree, graduate degree. Crossing the four sex-role categories with the five degree categories results in 20 combinations. Because we treat sex-role attitude as a dependent variable with education as a predictor, we display their joint distribution as a four-row, five-column crosstabulation (or a 4 × 5 table—read as "four by five"—for short). As shown in the frequency crosstab in Table 5.1, the column values increase from left to right, and the row values go from disagreement at the bottom to agreement at the top. Hence, even though many computer programs print their crosstabs with the lowest categories in the top row, you should reorder pairs of jointly tables variables in this sequence. When presented in this manner, the categories of orderable variables conform to an $X \times Y$ coordinate system such as those used for graphing two continuous variables (see chapter 6).

The **cells** making up the body of a crosstab contain the number of cases having particular joint values of the two variables. The **marginal distributions** (or as they are more simply called, the *marginals*) are the row totals (**row marginals**) shown on the right and the column totals (**column marginals**) shown at the bottom of the table. The grand total of all

cell—the intersection of a row and a column in a crosstabulation of two or more variables. Numerical values contained within cells may be cell frequencies, cell proportions, or cell percentages

marginal distributions—the frequency distribution of each of two crosstabulated variables

row marginals—the frequency distribution of the variable shown across the rows of a crosstabulation

column marginals—the frequency distribution of the variable shown down the columns of a crosstabulation

TABLE 5.1
Frequency Crosstabulation of Sex Roles by Degree

Man Achieves Outside Home, Woman Takes Care of Home & Family	HIGHEST LEVEL OF EDUCATION COMPLETED					
	Less Than High School	High School	Junior College	B.A. Degree	Graduate Degree	Total
Strongly Agree	34	73	6	11	5	129
Agree	110	273	24	77	25	509
Disagree	90	471	67	142	63	833
Strongly Disagree	21	157	30	85	47	340
Total	255	974	127	315	140	1,811

Missing data: 1,021 cases.
Source: 1998 General Social Survey.

cases, *N*, appears in the lower right cell (1,811 persons). The missing data frequency, reflecting cases with no information on one or both variables, is reported in a footnote to the table (1,021 cases in this example, because not all of the GSS respondents were asked the sex-role item).

A frequency crosstabulation is seldom useful for deciding whether two variables covary and, if so, how. When a frequency distribution has unequal marginals, direct comparisons of cell frequencies are difficult to make. We need some way to standardize the joint frequency table to a common denominator, so that the pattern of covariation is more apparent. A *percentage crosstabulation* allows such a pattern to emerge. *Percentages should always be calculated within categories of the independent variable.* For our example, we chose formal educational degree as the independent variable, on the assumption that such a condition is lifelong, while sex-role attitude is more likely to undergo change. To calculate percentages within each of the five degree categories, we first locate the column total for "less than high school" (255), in the last row of Table 5.1. We then divide this total into each of the four cell frequencies in that column and multiply by 100 to change those proportions to percentages. Thus, among respondents with less than a high school degree, the percentage strongly agreeing that men should achieve outside the home while women take care of home and family is $(34/255)(100) = 13.3\%$; the percentage agreeing is $(110/255)(100) = 43.1\%$; 35.3% disagree and 8.2% strongly disagree. Similar computations were performed on the other columns, including the total column, as shown in Table 5.2.

TABLE 5.2
Percentage Crosstabulation of Sex Roles by Degree

Man Achieves Outside Home, Woman Takes Care of Home & Family	*HIGHEST LEVEL OF EDUCATION COMPLETED*					
	Less Than High School	*High School*	*Junior College*	*B.A. Degree*	*Graduate Degree*	*Total*
Strongly Agree	13.33	7.49	4.72	3.49	3.57	7.12
Agree	43.14	28.03	18.90	24.44	17.86	28.11
Disagree	35.29	48.36	52.76	45.08	45.00	46.00
Strongly Disagree	8.24	16.12	23.62	26.98	33.57	18.77
Total	100.0%	100.0%	100.0%	99.99%*	100.0%	100.0%
(*N*)	(255)	(974)	(127)	(315)	(140)	(1,811)

Missing data: 1,021 cases.
*Does not total to 100.0% due to rounding.
Source: 1998 General Social Survey and Table 5.1.

Now we can quite clearly see that a gradient of increasing disagreement with the sex-role statement occurs from the less-educated to the more-educated. The percentage strongly disagreeing is more than 25% higher among those respondents with graduate degrees than among those without a high school diploma. Persons with intermediate degrees have percentages that fall in between. The opposite pattern appears across the columns within the "strongly agree" row: the percentage of respondents without a high school diploma is nearly 10% larger than the percentage of strongly agreeing graduates. Later, we will discuss some descriptive statistics that summarize how strongly two variables are related in a crosstabulation. But first we will show how to test whether a pattern observed in sample data is likely to reflect covariation in the population from which the sample was drawn.

5.2 Using Chi-Square to Test Significance

chi-square test—a test of statistical significance based on a comparison of the observed cell frequencies of a joint contingency table with frequencies that would be expected under the null hypothesis of no relationship

In section 3.11, we discussed some properties of the chi-square (χ^2) family of sampling distributions, which is based on the normal curve. When the sample N of a bivariate crosstabulation is large (e.g., 100 or more observations), a **chi-square test** of statistical significance can be used to determine the probability that the two variables are unrelated in the population. That is, the null hypothesis is that no covariation exists between the two variables in the population. The alternative hypothesis is that the two variables are related in the population and in the same manner as in the sample crosstab. The chi-square test compares the observed cell frequencies of the sample crosstabulation table with the frequencies that one would expect to observe *if* the null hypothesis were true. Determining these expected frequencies holds the key to calculating the value of chi-square for a crosstab.

statistically independent—a condition of no relationship between variables in a population

If no relationship exists between two crossed variables, we say that they are **statistically independent**. This condition implies that, for the population, identical percentages of the dependent variable will be found within each category of the independent variable. Similarly, within each category of the dependent variable, the same percentages of the independent responses would occur. For example, if the GSS respondents' sex-role attitudes were unrelated to their education, except for sampling error, we would expect to find the percentages within the five columns of Table 5.2 to equal one another and thus to equal the percentages in the row marginals. That is, because 7.1% of all 1,811 respondents strongly agreed, we would expect that 7.1% in each of the five degree groups would also strongly agree. Similarly, 28.1% would agree, 46.0% would disagree, and 18.8% would strongly disagree within each column. Only one of the five columns ("high school") comes close to this distribution, suggesting that statistical independence does not occur.

We can calculate what the bivariate crosstab frequencies would be *if* the two variables were statistically independent, that is, if the H_0 of no relationship were true. Panel A of Table 5.3 displays an independence relationship for the sex-role attitude and degree crosstab in Table 5.1. These cell entries, carried out to two decimal places for accuracy, are the **expected frequencies** under the null hypothesis of independence. Panel B reveals that the percentages within each column of these expected frequencies are identical, while panel C discloses that the percentages within each row are also identical. Calculated either way, these percentage distributions are identical to either the row marginals (last column in panel B) or the column marginals (bottom row in panel C).

expected frequency—in a chi-square test, the value that cell frequencies are expected to take, given the hypothesis under study (ordinarily, the null hypothesis)

The row and column marginal frequencies in Table 5.1 were used to calculate the 20 expected frequencies in the cells of Panel A in Table 5.3. If the two variables in any crosstabulation are independent, the formula for the expected frequency in row *i* and column *j* is

$$\hat{f}_{ij} = \frac{(f_{i\bullet})(f_{\bullet j})}{N}$$

where

$\hat{f}_{ij}$ = The expected frequency of the cell in the *i*th row and the *j*th column.

$f_{i\bullet}$ = The total in the *i*th row marginal.

$f_{\bullet j}$ = The total in the *j*th column marginal.

N = The grand total, or sample size for the entire table.

For example, the expected frequency under the null hypothesis of independence for strongly disagreeing persons with graduate degrees (row 4, column 5) is

$$\hat{f}_{45} = \frac{f_{4\bullet}f_{\bullet 5}}{N} = \frac{(340)(140)}{1,811} = 26.3$$

The χ^2 test statistic summarizes the differences across the 20 pairs of cells between the observed frequencies in Table 5.1 and the expected frequencies in Table 5.3. (Because the row and column marginals of both tables are identical, these values are not used.) If $\hat{f}_{ij}$ is the expected frequency under the null hypothesis and f_{ij} is the observed frequency for the same cell, then the chi-square for the table is calculated by the formula

TABLE 5.3

Expected Frequencies for Crosstabulation of Sex Roles by Degree, Under Null Hypothesis of Independence

Man Achieves Outside Home, Woman Takes Care of Home and Family	HIGHEST LEVEL OF EDUCATION COMPLETED						
	Less Than High School	High School	Junior College	B.A. Degree	Graduate Degree	Total	(N)
A. Expected Frequencies							
Strongly Agree	18.16	69.38	9.05	22.44	9.97	129	
Agree	71.67	273.75	35.69	88.53	39.35	509	
Disagree	117.29	448.01	58.42	144.89	64.40	833	
Strongly Disagree	47.87	182.86	23.84	59.14	26.28	340	
Total	254.99*	974.00	127.00	315.00	140.00	1,811	
B. Column Percentages							
Strongly Agree	7.12	7.12	7.12	7.12	7.12	7.12	
Agree	28.11	28.11	28.11	28.11	28.11	28.11	
Disagree	46.00	46.00	46.00	46.00	46.00	46.00	
Strongly Disagree	18.77	18.77	18.77	18.77	18.77	18.77	
Total	100.00%	100.00%	100.00%	100.00%	100.00%	100.00%	
(N)	(255)	(974)	(127)	(315)	(140)	(1,811)	
C. Row Percentages							
Strongly Agree	14.08	53.78	7.02	17.40	7.73	100.1%[†]	(129)
Agree	14.08	53.78	7.02	17.40	7.73	100.1%	(509)
Disagree	14.08	53.78	7.02	17.40	7.73	100.1%	(833)
Strongly Disagree	14.08	53.78	7.02	17.40	7.73	100.1%	(340)
Total	14.08	53.78	7.02	17.40	7.73	100.1%	(1,811)

*Totals do not add up to whole integers due to rounding.
[†]Percentages do not total to 100.0% due to rounding.
Source: 1998 General Social Survey.

$$\chi^2 = \sum_{i=1}^{R} \sum_{j=1}^{C} \frac{(\hat{f}_{ij} - f_{ij})^2}{\hat{f}_{ij}}$$

where

$\hat{f}_{ij}$ = The expected frequency of the cell in the ith row and the jth column.

f_{ij} = The observed frequency in the corresponding cell.

C = The number of columns in the crosstabulation.

R = The number of rows in the crosstabulation.

The following version of the formula may be easier to remember:

$$\chi^2 = \sum_{i=1}^{R} \sum_{j=1}^{C} \frac{(E_{ij} - O_{ij})^2}{E_{ij}}$$

where

E_{ij} = The expected frequency in the ith row, jth column under independence.

O_{ij} = The observed frequency in the corresponding cell.

The difference between an observed and expected frequency in a given cell is first squared (to remove plus and minus signs) and then divided by the expected frequency for that cell. The 20 chi-square components in our example are arranged in the cells of Table 5.4. The larger the value, the greater the relative difference between observed and expected frequencies for that cell. The 10 largest differences in Table 5.4 are underscored to highlight where the major deviations from the null hypothesis of independence occur. Both Tables 5.1 and 5.3 must be inspected to determine where the excesses and deficits occur, because the squaring masks the directions of these differences. The discrepancies are generally small within the junior college and bachelor's degree columns, but the independence model greatly overestimates the observed frequencies in three cells (respondents without high school diplomas who disagree and strongly disagree and high school graduates who strongly disagree). The independence model also greatly underestimates the observed frequencies in five cells (respondents without high school diplomas who agree, respondents with bachelor's degrees who strongly disagree, high school graduates who disagree, graduates who strongly disagree, and respondents without high school diplomas who strongly agree). In other words, the independence hypotheses fail to capture the tendencies for the least-educated to endorse the sex-role item and for those with bachelor's degrees and graduate degrees to reject it.

TABLE 5.4
Chi-Square Components for Crosstabulation of Sex Roles by Degree

Man Achieves Outside Home, Woman Takes Care of Home and Family	HIGHEST LEVEL OF EDUCATION COMPLETED				
	Less Than High School	*High School*	*Junior College*	*B.A. Degree*	*Graduate Degree*
Strongly Agree	<u>13.82</u>	0.19	1.03	<u>5.83</u>	2.48
Agree	<u>20.50</u>	0.002	<u>3.83</u>	1.50	<u>5.23</u>
Disagree	<u>6.35</u>	1.18	1.26	0.06	0.03
Strongly Disagree	<u>15.08</u>	<u>3.66</u>	1.59	<u>11.31</u>	<u>16.34</u>

Source: 1998 General Social Survey.

The sum of the 20 components in Table 5.4 is 111.27. Thus, we say that $\chi^2 = 111.27$ for the independence (null) hypothesis in this crosstabulation. To understand the meaning of this number in making a decision about whether or not to reject the null hypothesis, we must compare it to the critical value for the chi-square under the null hypothesis. The chi-square test statistic for a large N follows a chi-square distribution for specific degrees of freedom, as discussed in section 3.11. For a bivariate crosstabulation, the degrees of freedom depend on the number of rows and columns. For a frequency crosstabulation with R rows, if we know the total in a given column and the frequencies within $R - 1$ cells of that column, then the frequency in the Rth row of that column is determined by subtraction. Hence, each column has only $R - 1$ degrees of freedom. Similarly, within a given row, there are only $C - 1$ degrees of freedom because the row marginals are fixed. For *every* bivariate crosstab, the total degrees of freedom equal the product of the number of rows less 1, times the number of columns less 1:

$$df = (R - 1)(C - 1)$$

Table 5.1 has $(4 - 1)(5 - 1) = 12$ *df*. Thus, the sampling distribution appropriate to evaluating the chi-square of 111.27 obtained for Table 5.4 is a χ^2 sampling distribution with 12 degrees of freedom. Using the tabled values of chi-square distributions in Appendix B, we find that the critical value for rejecting H_0 at $\alpha = .001$ is 32.909 for $df = 12$. Clearly, the covariation in Table 5.1 is unlikely to be observed in a population in which the sex-role attitude and education variables are unrelated. We therefore reject the null hypothesis of independence with only a very small probability of making a Type I or false rejection error and conclude that not only are attitude and educational attainment related in the 1998 GSS sample, but this relationship is statistically significant; that is, these two variables are likely to be related in the population as well.

One reason why the χ^2 test statistic was so large is that chi-square values are directly proportional to the sample size. For example, tripling every cell frequency in a crosstab will triple the calculated value of chi-square but leave its *df* unchanged. This sensitivity of χ^2 to sample size in a crosstab underscores the important difference between statistical significance and substantive importance. A large sample size provides a good basis for drawing an inference about the population from which the sample came. But the magnitude of the population relationship may not have much substantive importance; that is, it may exhibit little covariation. Thus, although a large sample N allows us more easily to reject the null hypothesis, that decision fails to give us much information about the strength, or magnitude, of the population relationship. Statistical significance is only the first part of an answer to the question, "How are two social variables related?" If a statistical significance test reveals that the variables are probably related in the population, we can then turn to the second part of the answer, which requires us to find out how strongly the variables are related. In the next section we will discuss suitable measures of the magnitude of association.

5.3 Measuring Association: *Q*, Phi, Gamma, Tau *c*, Somers's d_{yx}

In this section we will examine five **measures of association**, statistics that describe the strength of the covariation between pairs of discrete variables. All good measures of association use a *proportionate reduction in error (PRE)* approach. The PRE family of statistics is based on comparing the errors made in predicting the dependent variable with knowledge of the independent variable, to the errors made without information about the independent variable. Thus, every PRE statistic reflects how well knowledge of one variable improves prediction of the second variable. The general formula for any PRE statistic is given in terms of decision rules about expected values of one variable, *Y*, conditioned on the values of a second variable, *X*. A general PRE formula involves the ratio between two decision rules:

measures of association— statistics that show the direction and/or magnitude of a relationship between pairs of discrete variables

$$\text{PRE statistic} = \frac{\text{Error without decision rule} - \text{Error with decision rule}}{\text{Error without decision rule}}$$

TABLE 5.5
Frequency and Proportion Crosstabulations of Fear of Walking at Night by Gender

| | GENDER | | |
Afraid?	Male	Female	Total
Frequency Crosstabulation			
Yes	203	569	772
No	583	496	1,079
Total	786	1,065	1,851
Percentage Crosstabulation			
Yes	25.8	53.4	41.7
No	74.2	46.6	58.3
Total	100.0%	100.0%	100.0%
(*N*)	(786)	(1,065)	(1,851)

Missing data: 981 cases.
Source: 1998 General Social Survey.

When variables X and Y are unrelated, we are unable to use any of our knowledge about the first variable to reduce errors when we try to estimate values of the second variable. Thus, the PRE statistic's value is zero. In the opposite case, when a perfect prediction from one variable to the other is possible, we make no errors, and the PRE statistic takes its maximum value of 1.00. Intermediate values of the PRE statistic show that we have greater or lesser degrees of predictability.

2 × 2 table—
a crosstabulation of a pair of dichotomies

To illustrate measures of association, we use a **2 × 2 table** ("two by two"), crosstabulating a pair of dichotomies. Table 5.5 displays both the frequency and percentage crosstabs for two nonorderable dichotomies—fear of walking at night by gender—among 1,851 GSS respondents. Women are more than twice as likely as men to say that they are afraid to walk at night in their neighborhoods.

The first four italic letters designate the four cells of a 2 × 2 table, as follows:

Variable X

	1	2	Total
2	a	b	$a + b$
1	c	d	$c + d$
Total	$a + c$	$b + d$	$a + b + c + d$

Variable Y (label on left, rows 2 and 1)

By definition, the categories of nonorderable dichotomies have no intrinsic sequence, so their sequence in a tabular display is arbitrary. We chose to arrange Table 5.5 with the "male" heading the left column and "female" in the right column, thus treating women as the higher gender. Hence, measures of association calculated on these data must be interpreted consistently with this arbitrary category sequence. Had we instead organized the table so that "male" appeared in the right column, then any measure of association would have had the reverse interpretation.

Using the conventional cell notation, an approximate formula for χ^2 in a 2×2 table is

$$\chi^2 = \frac{N(bc - ad)^2}{(a + b)(a + c)(b + d)(c + d)}$$

A 2×2 table has only 1 degree of freedom, because $(R - 1)(C - 1) = (2 - 1)(2 - 1) = 1$. Cells b and c are called the *main diagonal* cells, while a and d are the *off-diagonal* cells. Thus, the numerator of χ^2 involves the *cross-product differences* between the main and off-diagonal cells. These values reappear below in the formulas for several measures of association. For the fear of walking at night by gender crosstab in Table 5.5,

$$\chi^2 = \frac{1{,}851((569)(583) - (203)(496))^2}{(772)(786)(1{,}065)(1{,}079)} = 141.70$$

Because the c.v. for χ^2 at $\alpha = .01$ with $df = 1$ is 6.63, the calculated value of χ^2 is significant at $p < .01$. We reject the null hypothesis that no gender difference in fear of walking at night exists in the population, with less than one chance in 100 of making a Type I error.

5.3.1 Yule's Q

Yule's Q is a measure of association that uses the cross-product difference of a 2×2 table; that is,

Yule's Q—a symmetric measure of association for 2×2 crosstabulations

$$Q = \frac{bc - ad}{bc + ad}$$

Yule's Q ranges between -1.00 and $+1.00$, with $Q = 0.0$ indicating no relationship between the dichotomies. A positive value means that the two high categories are associated, as are the two low categories. A negative sign indicates an inverse relationship, meaning that the high category on one variable is associated with the low category on the other variable. For Table 5.5, where "female" and "yes" are considered the high categories, the value of Q is

$$Q = \frac{(569)(583) - (203)(496)}{(569)(583) + (203)(496)} = \frac{231,039}{432,415} = +0.53$$

Thus, the positive sign means that women are *more* likely than men to be afraid to walk at night, a direction that is evident in the percentage differences between the two gender columns.

Interpreting the magnitudes of Yule's Q is somewhat arbitrary. We suggest the following verbal labels be applied to *absolute values* of Q that fall into these intervals:

.00 to .24   "virtually no relationship"
.25 to .49   "weak relationship"
.50 to .74   "moderate relationship"
.75 to 1.00   "strong relationship"

Thus, the Q of $+0.53$ represents a moderate relationship between gender and fear of walking at night, with a significant chi-square. Note that this finding is both statistically significant and substantively important.

Yule's Q gives misleading information when one of the four cells has a zero frequency. In such cases, Q is either -1.00 or $+1.00$ (convince yourself of this by computing a simple example). Yet less than a "perfect" relationship may exist between the two dichotomies. By *perfect*, we mean that all cases fall into either the two main diagonal cells or the two off-diagonal cells. The cells of a 2×2 table should always be examined for the presence of zero frequencies. If a zero cell is present, then some alternative measure of association should be chosen.

5.3.2 Phi

phi—a symmetric measure of association for 2×2 crosstabulations

Phi (φ) also measures association in a 2×2 table. As with Yule's Q, phi ranges between -1.00 and $+1.00$, with 0.00 indicating no relationship.

The value of phi is sensitive to the row and column marginals of the table, as shown by the denominator of its formula:

$$\varphi = \frac{bc - ad}{\sqrt{(a + b)(c + d)(a + c)(b + d)}}$$

For any 2×2 table with a given set of row and column totals, phi can attain a maximum or minimum value that may be considerably short of the hypothetical range between -1.00 and $+1.00$. Some researchers prefer to adjust phi to remove this limitation. The value of **phi adjusted** (φ_{adj}) involves dividing the observed value of phi by the maximum absolute value, **phi maximum** (φ_{max}):

$$\varphi_{adj} = \frac{\varphi}{|\varphi_{max}|}$$

The parallel bars around phi maximum indicate "absolute value."

To calculate φ_{max} for a given set of 2×2 table marginals, you must first find the proportions in the row and column marginals—that is, divide the four row and column totals by the sample N. Next, identify the row and the column with the smallest proportions (if one or both marginal proportions exactly equal 0.50, either may be chosen). Compare these two proportions, calling the smaller of the two p_j and the larger of the two p_i (this step finds the proportion of cases having the rarest occurrence, sometimes called "item difficulty" in attitude research). Then estimate φ_{max} for the table as

$$\varphi_{max} = \frac{\sqrt{p_j - p_j p_i}}{\sqrt{p_i - p_i p_j}}$$

Table 5.6 illustrates this procedure for the crosstab for being afraid to walk at night and gender. The value of phi calculated from the observed frequencies in the top panel is $+0.277$. The proportions in the bottom panel show that the smallest row marginal is 0.417 (for people who are afraid) and the smallest column marginal is 0.425 (for men). Hence, $p_j = .417$ and $p_i = .425$. The estimated value of φ_{max} is

$$\sqrt{(.417 - (.417)(.425))} / \sqrt{(.425 - (.425)(.417))} = 0.984.$$

Finally, the adjusted value is $\varphi_{adj} = (+0.277)/|.984| = +0.282$. This adjustment indicates a slightly stronger inverse relationship than suggested in the observed data. Although φ_{adj} is sometimes reported in analyses of a 2×2 table, we recommend reporting both the actual and

phi adjusted— a symmetric measure of association for a 2×2 crosstabulation in which phi is divided by phi maximum to take into account the largest covariation possible, given the marginals

phi maximum—the largest value that phi can attain for a given 2×2 crosstabulation; used in adjusting phi for its marginals

TABLE 5.6
Calculation of Phi Adjusted for Fear of Walking at Night by Gender Crosstabulation

Afraid?	GENDER		Total
	Male	*Female*	*Total*
Observed Values			
Yes	203	569	772
No	583	496	1,079
Total	786	1,065	1,851

$$\varphi = 0.277$$

	Male	*Female*	*Total*
Proportions			
Yes	.110	.307	.417
No	.315	.268	.583
Total	.425	.575	1.000

$$\varphi_{max} = 0.984, \; \varphi_{adj} = 0.298$$

Sources: 1998 General Social Survey and Table 5.5.

the adjusted values. However, φ_{adj} is preferable to reporting only the actual values of φ.

5.3.3 Gamma

gamma—a symmetric measure of association suitable not only to crosstabs of two dichotomies, but also to tables whose variables are both ordered discrete measures with more than two categories

The **gamma** (*G*) measure of association is suitable not only to crosstabs of two dichotomies but also to tables whose variables are both ordered discrete measures with more than two categories. Gamma is a *symmetric PRE measure of association; that is, the same gamma value is obtained whether the first variable predicts the second variable or vice versa.* Gamma ranges between −1.00 and +1.00, with zero indicating no relationship. Unlike φ, it is a "margin-free" measure of association, meaning that its value does not depend on the row or column marginals.

The crosstab in Table 5.7 shows a 3 × 3 joint frequency distribution of two ordered variables. GSS respondents were presented with a list of nine national institutions and asked, "As far as the people running these institutions are concerned, would you say you have a great deal of confidence, only some confidence, or hardly any confidence at all?" Among

TABLE 5.7

Frequency and Percentage Crosstabulations of Confidence in Business by Confidence in Labor

Confidence in Major Companies	*CONFIDENCE IN ORGANIZED LABOR*			
	Hardly Any	*Only Some*	*A Great Deal*	*Total*
Frequency Crosstabulation				
A Great Deal	134	257	76	467
Only Some	294	602	108	1,004
Hardly Any	111	98	21	230
Total	539	957	205	1,701
Percentage Crosstabulation				
A Great Deal	24.9	26.9	37.1	27.5
Only Some	54.5	62.9	52.7	59.0
Hardly Any	20.6	10.2	10.2	13.5
Total	100.0%	100.0%	100.0%	100.0%
(*N*)	(539)	(957)	(205)	(1,701)

Missing data: 1,131 cases.
Source: 1998 General Social Survey.

those institutions were "major companies" and "organized labor." If respondents' support for one institution were unrelated to their support for the other, the percentage distributions within columns would be identical (save for sampling error). As the bottom panel in Table 5.7 shows, 37.1% of persons with great confidence in organized labor also have a great deal of confidence in major companies, while those with some or hardly any confidence in labor have smaller percentages expressing a great deal of confidence in business (26.9% and 24.9%, respectively). This modest positive covariation in the sample is sufficient to reject the null hypothesis that the two measures are unrelated in the population ($\chi^2 = 43.2$, $df = 4$, $p < .001$). However, the relationship is far from one of perfect predictability, since some respondents with great confidence in one institution have hardly any confidence in the other.

Gamma measures the strength of association between pairs of ordered variables such as those displayed in Table 5.7. Its calculation

untied pair—one in which both cases have different values on two variables

concordant pair—in a crosstabulation of two orderable discrete variables, one observation has a higher rank on both variables than does the other member of the pair

discordant pair—in a crosstabulation of two orderable discrete variables, one member of a pair of observations ranks higher than the other member on one variable but ranks lower on the second variable

requires systematically evaluating *all* pairs of observations in a cross-tabulation, counting the total number that are **untied** concordant pairs and the total number that are untied discordant pairs. (An untied pair is one in which both cases have different values on two variables.) In a **concordant pair**, one observation has a higher rank on both variables than does the other member of the pair. For example, a person who has great confidence in both business and labor has higher rank that someone with hardly any confidence in both institutions. In a **discordant pair**, one member of a pair of observations ranks higher than the other member on one variable but ranks lower on the other variable. For example, compare one respondent with great confidence in labor and hardly any confidence in business to a second person who has some confidence in both institutions. In this pair, the first respondent ranks higher than the second in labor confidence and lower in business confidence.

To find the total number of concordant pairs (n_c) in a crosstab, we must systematically count pairs of observations having consistent rank orderings in the table. The observations in a given cell form concordant pairs with the sum of cases in all the cells in rows below it and to the left. For example, in Table 5.7, the 76 observations in the *upper-right* cell (top row and right column) form concordant pairs with the 1,105 (= 294 + 602 + 111 + 98) respondents in the four cells below it and to its left. That is, (76)(1,105) = 83,980 concordant pairs involve the upper-right cell. Still within the top row, proceed to the 257 observations in the middle column. These cases rank consistently higher on both variables than the 405 cases (= 294 + 111) in the two cells below it and to the left. Thus, another (257)(405) = 104,085 concordant pairs are added to the cumulative total. Within the second row of the table, the 108 observations in the right column have higher ranks than the 209 (= 98 + 111) cases below it and to its left, for (108)(209) = 22,572 concordant pairs. Finally, in the second row, middle column, 602 cases ranking higher than 111 below it and to the left contribute (602)(111) = 66,822. Summing, Table 5.7 contains 83,980 + 104,085 + 22,572 + 66,822 = 277,459 concordant pairs.

To calculate the total number of untied discordant pairs (n_d), proceed across the crosstab in the opposite direction. Observations in a given cell form discordant pairs with the sum of cases in all cells in rows below it and to the right. In Table 5.7, the 134 observations in the *upper-left* cell have higher rank on the row variable (confidence in major companies) but lower rank on the column variable (confidence in organized labor) compared to the 829 cases (= 602 + 108 + 98 + 21) in the four cells below it and to its right. Thus, (134)(829) = 111,086 discordant pairs involve the upper-left cell. Still within the top row, the 257 cases in the middle column form discordant pairs with the 129 (= 108 + 21) observations in the two cells below it and to the right, for an additional $(257)(129) =$ 33,153 discordant pairs. Switching to the second row, we find $(294)(119)$ $= 34,986$ and $(602)(21) = 12,642$ discordant pairs. Thus, Table 5.7 contains 191,867 discordant pairs.

The formula for gamma uses the total number of untied pairs of both types:

$$G = \frac{n_c - n_d}{n_c + n_d}$$

The formula clearly shows gamma's PRE character. If we randomly draw any pair of observations from a crosstab and try to predict whether they have consistent ranks or inconsistent ranks, the chances of a correct prediction depend on the numbers of concordant and discordant pairs in the table. When $n_c = n_d$, prediction is no better than chance and gamma equals zero. But if n_c is far larger than n_d, gamma will be positive, and we will be more successful in predicting that the respondent with the higher value on one variable will also have the higher value on the second variable, compared to the second member of the pair. Note especially that when $n_d = 0$ (i.e., there are no discordant pairs), $G = 1.00$. Prediction error is also reduced when n_d is substantially larger than n_c. In this case gamma is negative, meaning that we predict that when one member of a pair ranks higher than the other member on one variable, reverse rank order occurs for that pair on the other variable. The maximum negative value, $G = -1.00$, occurs whenever $n_c = 0$ (i.e., there are no concordant pairs).

Applying the formula for gamma to the data in Table 5.7, the association between confidence in major companies and in organized labor is

$$G = \frac{277,459 - 191,867}{277,459 + 191,867} = \frac{85,592}{469,326} = +0.18$$

Given that gamma's maximum positive value is +1.00, this value suggests virtually no relationship between the two confidence measures.

The population parameter that G estimates is labeled γ (Greek lowercase gamma). If we have a simple random sample of cases, the sampling distribution of G approaches normality as N becomes large (50 or more). The test statistic is approximated by

$$Z = (G - \gamma) = \sqrt{\frac{n_c + n_d}{N(1 - G^2)}}$$

where
γ = The population value of gamma under the null hypothesis.

Because the formula gives a rather conservative estimate of Z, there may be circumstances where the absolute value of Z is larger than the result computed this way. The exact calculations are given elsewhere.[1]

In this example, the null and alternative hypotheses are H_0: $\gamma \leq 0$ and H1: $\gamma > 0$. To test the null hypothesis, we choose $\alpha = .01$. Appendix C shows that the critical value is $Z = +2.33$. Now, using the sample value of G calculated previously, the standard score (that is, the test statistic) is

$$Z = (0.18 - 0) \sqrt{\frac{277,459 + 191,867}{1,701 \ (1 - 0.18^2)}} = 3.04$$

Because 3.04 exceeds +2.33, we reject the null hypothesis and instead conclude that confidence in major companies and confidence in organized labor probably have a weak positive association in the population.

When the formula for G is applied to a 2×2 table, its value is identical to Yule's Q, showing that Yule's Q is a special case of the more general gamma measure of association.

5.3.4 Tau *c*

tau *c*—a non-PRE-type measure of association that uses information about the number of concordant and discordant unified pairs in a crosstab of two discrete ordered variables

tied pair—a pair in which both cases have the same value on at least one of the variables

Although it is not a PRE-type measure of association, **tau *c*** (τ_c) uses information about the number of concordant and discordant untied pairs in a crosstab of two discrete ordered variables. It also counts the number of **tied pairs** of observations in the table. A tied pair is one in which both cases have the same value on at least one of the two variables. For example, if one case has hardly any confidence in labor and some confidence in business while the second case has some confidence in both institutions, they form a tied pair. The number of rows and columns in a table do not have to be the same (i.e., a nonsquare table can be analyzed). Tau *c* ranges in value from –1.00 to +1.00 and equals zero when the two variables are unrelated. The formula for tau *c* is as follows:

$$\tau_c = \frac{2m(n_c - n_d)}{N^2(m - 1)}$$

where
m = The smaller of R rows or C columns.

Unlike gamma, whose denominator counts only the number of concordant and discordant pairs, τ_c's denominator counts *all* pairs, including the pairs of tied observations. Thus, tau *c* for a given table always has a

---

[1]See H. T. Reynolds, *The Analysis of Cross-Classification* (New York: Free Press, 1977), pp. 85–88.

smaller value than gamma. If many tied pairs occur in a crosstab, gamma's value will be much larger than tau c's value. Neither statistic is preferred to the other. They simply conceptualize the meaning of an association between two discrete ordered variables in different terms.

Applied to the square crosstab in Table 5.7 and based on the knowledge from computing G that $n_c = 277{,}459$ and $n_d = 191{,}867$, the positive association between confidence in major companies and confidence in organized labor appears again:

$$\tau_c = \frac{(2)(3)(277{,}459 - 191{,}867)}{(1{,}701)^2(3 - 1)} = \frac{513{,}552}{5{,}786{,}802} = +0.089$$

The standard error of the sampling distribution for tau c is very complex and will not be presented here. However, Somers developed a quick and not-too-dirty estimate:[2]

$$\hat{\sigma}_{\tau_c} = \sqrt{\frac{4(R + 1)(C + 1)}{9NRC}}$$

This formula can be used as an approximation only when there is simple random sampling and the null hypothesis states that $\tau_c = 0$ in the population.

To test whether $\tau_c = 0.089$ differs significantly from zero, we choose $\alpha = .01$. The critical value is then $+2.33$ for a one-tailed test (see Appendix C). The test statistic is

$$Z = \frac{\tau_c}{\hat{\sigma}_{\tau_c}}$$

In this example, the test statistic is calculated as follows:

$$Z = \frac{0.089}{\sqrt{\dfrac{4(3 + 1)(3 + 1)}{9(1{,}701)(3)(3)}}}$$

$$= \frac{0.089}{0.022}$$

$$= 4.05$$

Because this value is greater than $+2.33$, we reject the null hypothesis and again conclude that confidence in organizations and confidence in organized labor are weakly related in the population.

---

[2]Somers, R. (1980). "Simple Approximations to Null Sampling Variances: Goodman and Kruskal's Gamma, Kendall's Tau, and Somers's d_{yx}." *Sociological Methods and Research,* 9, pp. 115–26.

5.3.5 Somers's d_{yx}

Somers's d_{yx} is an *asymmetric* PRE measure of association for discrete ordered variables that counts not only the number of concordant and discordant untied pairs, but also the number of tied pairs of a certain type. Unlike gamma and tau c, the value of Somers's d_{yx} depends on which variable is considered independent and which dependent. In trying to predict variable Y from knowledge of variable X, we take into account only the pairs of observations that are tied on variable Y, the dependent variable. We ignore any pairs on which both observations are tied on the independent variable, X. Somers's d_{yx} for predicting variable Y from variable X (assuming that Y is the row variable and X is the column variable) is given by the formula

$$d_{yx} = \frac{n_c - n_d}{n_c + n_d + T_r}$$

where

T_r = The number of ties associated with the row variable.

To count the number of ties associated with the row variable in Table 5.7, simply begin at the upper-left cell, where the first row and first column join. Multiply the frequency of cases (134) in that cell by the sum of the cases in the cells to the right within that row (257 + 76 = 333). The product is (134)(333) = 44,622. Next, move to the cell to the right in that row and multiply its frequency by the total observations in cells to the right; i.e., (257)(76) = 19,532. Because no observations are found to the right of the final column in the first row (the row marginals are ignored), the process continues by moving to the next row. Again, multiply a given cell's frequency by the sum of frequencies in cells to the right within that row. For the second row in Table 5.7, these products are (294)(710) = 208,740 and (602)(108) = 65,016. For the third row, the two products are (111)(119) = 13,209 and (98)(21) = 2,058. Adding together all these terms gives T_r = 44,622 + 19,532 + 208,740 + 65,016 + 13,209 + 2,058 = 353,177, which is entered into the denominator of Somers's d_{yx} as

$$d_{yx} = \frac{277,459 - 191,867}{277,459 + 191,867 + 353,177} = \frac{85,592}{822,503} = +0.104$$

The presence of numerous tied pairs means the value of Somers's d_{yx} will be much smaller than the value of gamma for the same crosstab.

Somers presents an approximation to the standard error of the sampling distribution that can be used to test for the significance of $\hat{d}_{yx}$:[3]

---

[3]Somers, "Simple Approximations to Null Sampling Variances."

$$\hat{\sigma}_{d_{yx}} = \frac{2}{3R} \sqrt{\frac{(R^2 - 1)(C + 1)}{N(C - 1)}}$$

The test statistic for $\hat{d}_{yx}$ is

$$Z = \frac{\hat{d}_{yx}}{\hat{\sigma}_{d_{yx}}}$$

If we again choose $\alpha = .01$, the critical value is +2.33 for a one-tailed test. We compute

$$Z = \frac{0.104}{\frac{2}{(3)(3)} \sqrt{\frac{(3^2 - 1)(3 + 1)}{1,701(3 - 1)}}}$$

$$= 4.83$$

Since 4.83 is larger than +2.33, we must reject the null hypothesis that confidence in major companies and confidence in organized labor are unrelated.

The asymmetric nature of Somers's d_{yx} means that two different values are likely to be found in any table larger than 2 × 2. For d_{xy}, the T_r is replaced in the denominator by T_c, the number of ties associated with the column variable. A procedure identical to that described above is used to calculate T_c. Verify that Somers's d_{xy} for Table 5.7 is +0.11, treating confidence in labor as the dependent variable. Although the two statistics have very similar values in this example, you should always clearly state the dependent variable when reporting this measure of association, since they will not always have similar magnitudes.

As the reader has most certainly discerned, the calculation of concordant and discordant pairs can be quite tedious, especially in larger tables. Although a more general algorithm for the computations could be presented, computers carry out such calculations with great ease, allowing the analyst to concentrate on other tasks.

5.4 Odds and Odds Ratios

In current statistical practice, the most important measure of association for crosstabulations is the odds ratio, which is the foundation for the techniques presented in chapter 10. Games of chance have familiarized most people with the concept of odds. **Odds** express the frequency of being in

odds—the frequency of being in one category relative to the frequency of not being in that category

one category relative to the frequency of not being in that category. For example, in poker the odds that the first card dealt is the Queen of Hearts are 1/51 (pronounced "one to fifty-one"). The odds, expressed as a decimal, are equal to .01961. Contrast odds with a probability, which is the ratio between a category of interest and all categories. The probability of drawing the Queen of Hearts is 1/52 (pronounced "one fifty-second"). This ratio expressed as a decimal is .01923, a lower value than the equivalent odds. The contrast between odds and probability is even sharper when relatively larger proportions of cases per category are involved. For example, in poker the odds that a first card dealt is a club are 13/39 (which reduces to 1/3), whereas the probability of a club is 13/52 (which reduces to 1/4). Expressed as decimals, the odds (.333) are a much higher value than the probability (.250). Another important difference in these descriptive statistics is their ranges. Probabilities are constrained within the range between .00 (i.e., a zero chance of occurrence) and 1.00 (i.e., certainty of occurrence). But because odds are the ratio between occurrence and nonoccurrence, the values range between zero and positive infinity. That is, whenever the chance of a category occurring is greater than the chance it will not occur, the odds exceed 1.00. For example, the odds that the Queen of Hearts will *not* be drawn are 51/1, or 51.00 as a decimal. Note that when an outcome is as likely to occur as not to occur, the odds reduce to 1/1, or 1.00 as a decimal. In probability terms, however, equally likely outcomes have a probability of .50.

Probabilities are easily translated to odds by dividing the proportion corresponding to a category of interest (p_i) by the proportion obtained after subtracting it from 1.00:

$$\text{odds}_i = \frac{p_i}{1 - p_i}$$

The odds for empirical events can easily be computed from the numbers and percentages reported in various media. For example, in 1997 among Americans aged 25–34 who died, cancer was the principal cause of death for 10.1%. Therefore, the odds of a death by cancer were 0.101/0.899 = 0.112, or one to nine.

conditional odds—the chance of being in one category of a variable relative to the remaining categories of that variable, within a specific category of a second variable

The concept of simple odds can be extended to the **conditional odds** within the cells of a crosstabulation, analogous to the percentages discussed earlier in section 5.1. Conditional odds represent the chance of being in one category of a variable relative to the remaining categories of that variable, within a specific category of a second variable. Thus, separate conditional odds may be calculated for the different categories of the second measure. Consider again the 2 × 2 crosstab of gender and being afraid to walk at night in Table 5.5. In the total column at the right, the simple odds of being afraid are the ratio of that row's total (772 observations) to the total in the second row (1,079). Thus, the odds that a respondent is afraid are 772/1,079 = .72. However, these simple odds are not the same as the conditional odds found within columns for the second variable, gender. Among women, the conditional odds of being afraid are 569/496 = 1.15, while men yield a lower conditional odds of 203/583 = .35. In other words, the respondents' gender *conditions* their fear. The more information we have about a person's gender, the more accurately we can predict that person's chances of being afraid to walk at night.

When variables in a crosstab are related (as shown by both a chi-square significance test and a descriptive measure of association), their conditional odds are not equal. To compare two conditional odds directly, a single descriptive statistic called the **odds ratio** (OR) can be formed by dividing one conditional odds by another. In terms of the standard symbols designating the cell frequencies of a 2×2 table, the formula for the odds ratio of variables *X* and *Y* is

$$OR^{XY} = \frac{b/d}{a/c} = \frac{bc}{ad}$$

odds ratio/cross-product ratio—the ratio formed by dividing one conditional odds by another conditional odds

Note that the simplified OR formula on the right multiplies the main diagonal cell frequencies and divides this product by the product of the off-diagonal cell frequencies. The odds ratio is thus sometimes called the **cross-product ratio**. The odds ratio for being afraid (F) by gender (G) in Table 5.5 is $OR^{FG} = (569)(583)/(203)(496) = 3.29$, which indicates that the odds of being afraid for women are over three times greater than the odds of being afraid for men. If the gender columns had been switched while the row order remained the same, we appear to find a different OR^{FG}: (203)(496)/(569)(583) = .30. However, this apparent inconsistency is resolved by recognizing that our substantive interpretation of the relationship between the two variables must also be reversed: the odds of being afraid for men are only about one-third the odds of being afraid for women. If either of these ORs is inverted, the other value is revealed: 1/0.30 = 3.30 and 1/3.30 = .30. Thus, each combination of four cells yields odds ratios having a consistent interpretation, as long as we keep track of the reference categories.

If two variables are unrelated, their conditional odds are identical and, therefore, the OR = 1.00. Odds ratios greater than 1.00 indicate a positive covariation of the variables (i.e., a tendency for the "high" categories of both variables to be associated), while ORs lower than 1.00 indicate a negative or inverse covariation (i.e., a tendency for the "high" category of one variable to be associated with the "low" category of the other variable). Because an odds is undefined when its denominator is zero, an OR cannot be calculated whenever a zero cell occurs. This problem exists as well with Yule's Q for 2×2 tables. Note that Yule's Q is a simple function of the odds ratio:

$$Q = \frac{\text{odds ratio} - 1}{\text{odds ratio} + 1} = \frac{bc/ad - 1}{bc/ad + 1} = \frac{bc - ad}{bc + ad}$$

In other words, Q is simply an OR that has been "normed" to be symmetrical with a range constrained between −1.00 and +1.00. Note that when OR = 1 (no relationship), Q = 0.00 (also no relationship).

Odds ratios can also be computed for large crosstabulations. All we need are four cells identified by two columns and two rows. Table 5.8 is a 2×7 crosstab of 1996 presidential vote (P) by political views (V). This relationship is highly significant, as indicated by χ^2 = 344.70 for df = 6, $p < .001$ (gamma = +0.66, tau c = +0.52, and Somers's d_{yx} = +0.41 with vote as the dependent variable). Many ORs can be calculated with the frequencies in this crosstab. For example, the OR of having voted for Dole versus Clinton among extreme conservatives relative to conservatives is $(66)(41)/(14)(198) = 0.98$. Similarly, the OR of having voted for Dole among conservatives versus slight conservatives is $(198)(104)/(133)(66) = 2.35$. In this table, 21 such odds ratios can be computed involving pairs of categories of the independent variable (political views).

TABLE 5.8
Frequency and Percentage Crosstabulations of 1996 Presidential Vote by Political Views

Presidential Vote in 1996	POLITICAL VIEWS							
	Extremely Liberal	Liberal	Slightly Liberal	Moderate	Slightly Conservative	Conservative	Extremely Conservative	Total
Frequency Crosstabulation								
Voted for Dole	3	18	31	154	133	198	41	578
Voted for Clinton	34	179	157	346	104	66	14	900
Total	37	197	188	500	237	264	55	1,478
Percentage Crosstabulation								
Voted for Dole	8.1	9.1	16.5	30.8	56.1	75.0	74.5	39.1
Voted for Clinton	91.9	90.9	83.5	69.2	43.9	25.0	25.5	60.9
Total	100.0	100.0	100.0	100.0	100.0	100.0	100.0	100.0
(N)	(37)	(197)	(188)	(500)	(237)	(264)	(55)	(1,478)

Missing data: 1,354 cases.
Source: 1998 General Social Survey.

Obviously, not all of these relations are independent. Indeed, given that only six degrees of freedom are available in this table, we can have only six unique odds ratios. Once these six ORs have been determined, the remaining ORs are constrained to particular values. In chapter 10, you will learn about log-linear models, methods based on the odds ratio measure of association, which permit very elaborate hypotheses about relationships among tabulated variables to be tested for statistical significance.

Review of Key Concepts and Symbols

These key concepts and symbols are listed in the order of appearance in this chapter. Combined with the definitions in the margins, they will help you to review the material and can serve as a self-test for mastery of the concepts.

bivariate crosstabulation (joint contingency table)	discordant pair	γ
	tau c	n_c
cell	tied pair	
marginal distribution	Somers's d_{yx}	n_d
row marginals	odds	τ_c
column marginals	conditional odds	
chi-square test	odds ratio (cross-product	m
statistical independence	ratio)	t_c
expected frequency		
measures of association	f_{ij}	$\hat{\sigma}_{\tau_c}$
2×2 table	PRE	d_{yx}
Yule's Q	Q	T_r
phi		
phi adjusted	φ	$\hat{\sigma}_{d_{yx}}$
phi maximum	φ_{adj}	OR^{XY}
gamma		
untied pair	φ_{max}	
concordant pair	G	

PROBLEMS

General Problems

1. A public health researcher theorizes that men are more likely to smoke than women are. The researcher gathers the following information from 25 subjects (M=Male; F=Female; S=Smoker; N=Non-smoker). Construct a bivariate cross-tabulation for these data, including marginals.

F S	M S	M S
F N	M N	M N
F N	M N	M S
M S	F N	F N
M N	M S	F S
M S	F S	M S
M S	F N	M N
F N	F N	
F S	F N	

2. In several presidential elections, researchers have observed a "gender gap" in which men and women vote for candidates in different proportions. Test this hypothesis by calculating χ^2 and Yule's Q for these frequencies from the 1998 General Social Survey:

Vote by Gender

Did You Vote for Clinton or Dole?	Gender	
	Men	Women
Clinton	351	572
Dole	283	306

Missing data = 1,320.
Source: 1998 General Social Survey.

3. A poll of 80 state legislators finds that 30 Republicans favor an income tax rebate, while 5 Republicans do not favor it. Similarly, among 45 Democrats, 20 favor the tax rebate and 25 do not. Calculate phi for these data.

4. Calculate phi adjusted for the data in question number 3. Compare phi adjusted to phi. What can you conclude?

5. Suppose you collect the following data on the political attitudes and views on public funding for private schools held by 60 adults. Calculate gamma. What do you conclude?

Attitude Towards Public Funding of Private Schools	Political Attitude		
	Liberal	Moderate	Conservative
For	2	6	12
For in some situations, against in others	4	10	4
Against	14	5	3

6. For the data in problem 5, calculate tau c and its approximate standard error. Does τ_c differ significantly from zero? Set $\alpha = .01$.

7. For the data in problem 5, calculate Somers's d_{yx} and its approximate standard error. Does Somers's d_{yx} differ significantly from zero? Set $\alpha = .01$.

8. The 1998 GSS states, "There are always some people whose ideas are considered bad or dangerous by other people. For instance, somebody who is against all churches and religion… If such a person wanted to make a speech in your (city/town/community) against churches and religion, should he/she be allowed to speak, or not?" Among the male GSS respondents, 631 said they would allow the speech and 154 would not allow it. Among the female respondents, 762 would allow and 303 would not allow the speech. What are the conditional odds in favor of allowing an atheist to speak, and what is the odds ratio?

9. Now consider whether tolerance for civil liberties is a function of education. For this table from the 1998 GSS, calculate the conditional odds in favor of allowing an atheist to speak in public for the stated levels of education, and the odds ratio for the table.

Atheist Speech by Education

If such a person wanted to make a speech... against churches and religion, should he/she be allowed to speak, or not?	Education	
	Less Than College	Some College +
Yes	865	525
No	372	83

Missing data = 987.
Source: 1998 General Social Survey.

10. Does exposure to television weaken or strengthen one's confidence in the press? Calculate gamma for this crosstabulation from the 1998 GSS.

Confidence in the Press by Television Viewing

As far as the people running the press, would you say you have...	Hours of TV Watching on an Average Day		
	0–1 Hour	2–4 Hours	5 or More
A great deal of confidence	26	71	28
Only some confidence	170	400	90
Hardly any confidence	162	351	95

Missing data = 1,439.
Source: 1998 General Social Survey.

Problems Requiring the 1998 General Social Survey

11. Which race—black or white—is more tolerant of allowing a racist to speak in public? Crosstabulate SPKRAC by RACE, after omitting "other" race, and compute chi-square and phi. Change the "Don't Know," "No Answer," and "Not Applicable" responses to missing values. What do you conclude?

12. Are less-educated people more or less likely than better-educated people to tolerate a communist speaker in public? Find this relationship by crosstabulating SPKCOM with EDUC recoded into three categories (0–11 years, 12–15 years, 16 or more years). Calculate chi-square, gamma, tau c, and Somers's d_{yx}. Change the "Don't Know," "No Answer," and "Not Applicable" responses to missing values. What do you conclude?

13. Does the three-category education measure in Problem 12 have the same pattern with SPRAC? Calculate chi-square, gamma, tau c, and Somers's d_{yx}. Change the "Don't Know," "No Answer," and "Not Applicable" responses to missing values. What do you conclude?

14. How strongly related are traditional sex role attitudes and sexual morality? Test this relationship in the 1998 GSS data set by crosstabulating FEHOME ("It is better for the man to work and the woman to tend the home") by attitude towards premarital sex (PREMARSX), treating PREMARSX as the dependent variable. Change the "Don't Know," "No Answer," and "Not Applicable" responses to missing values. Interpret chi-square and Somers's d_{yx} for this relationship. What do you conclude?

15. Are more-educated people more tolerant of homosexuality? Interpret chi-square and Somers's d_{yx} for the relationship between DEGREE and HOMOSEX, treating homosexuality as the dependent variable. Change the "Don't Know," "No Answer," and "Not Applicable" responses to missing values.

6

BIVARIATE REGRESSION AND CORRELATION

6.1 Scatterplots and Regression Lines
6.2 Estimating a Linear Regression
Equation
6.3 *R*-Square and Correlation

6.4 Significance Tests for Regression
Parameters
6.5 Standardizing Regression Coefficients
6.6 Comparing Two Regression Equations

The crosstabulations discussed in chapter 5 reveal the covariation between pairs of discrete variables in a sample of observations. In this chapter we will examine relationships among pairs of continuous variables. The bivariate regression and correlation procedures assume that the *form* of the relationship between *Y* and *X* is *linear* and that the dependent variable is distributed normally at every level of the independent variable. Even when data violate these assumptions, however, the methods may still be quite **robust**; that is, we will seldom be wrong when making a conclusion about statistically significant or insignificant results.

robust—methods used in which violating assumptions will seldom produce wrong conclusions

6.1 Scatterplots and Regression Lines

Displaying the relationship between pairs of continuous measures requires different graphic display techniques than previously described. The **scatterplot** is a useful method for visualizing how two continuous variables covary. To construct a scatterplot, begin with a set of Cartesian coordinates, such as you used in high school algebra. Values of the independent variable (*X*) are located on the horizontal axis, while values of the dependent variable (*Y*) are situated on the vertical axis. Then the

scatterplot—a type of diagram that displays the covariation of two continuous variables as a set of points on a Cartesian coordinate system

position of the *i*th observation is plotted as a data point on the graph at its *X, Y* coordinates. The scatterplot of all points reveals how the pair of variables covaries. Figure 6.1 graphs four idealized patterns of bivariate relationships.

FIGURE 6.1
Scatterplots of Four Idealized Bivariate Relationships

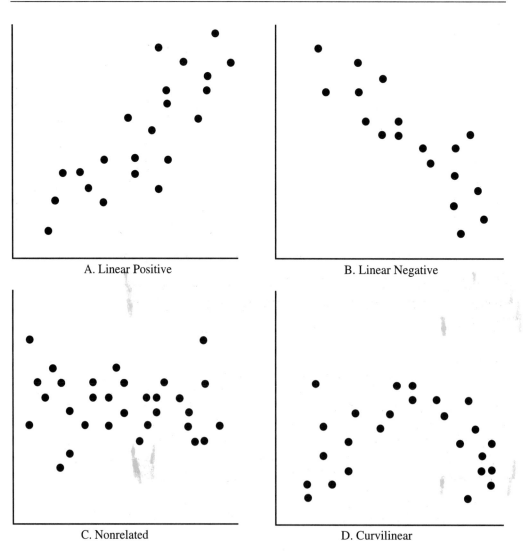

A. Linear Positive

B. Linear Negative

C. Nonrelated

D. Curvilinear

Suppose we hypothesize that occupational prestige in the U.S. co-varies with citizens' educational levels:

H$_1$: The greater the number of years of education, the higher the occupational prestige.

Figure 6.2 plots a random subsample of fifty 1998 GSS respondents' occupational prestige scores against the respondents' numbers of years of education completed. Positive covariation is evident in the scatter of points from the lower left to the upper right. Low values of one variable tend to be found with low values of the other, and high values of both tend to be associated. This figure provides visual evidence supporting our hypothesis.

FIGURE 6.2
Scatterplot of Occupational Prestige by Years of Schooling for a Sample of *N* = 50

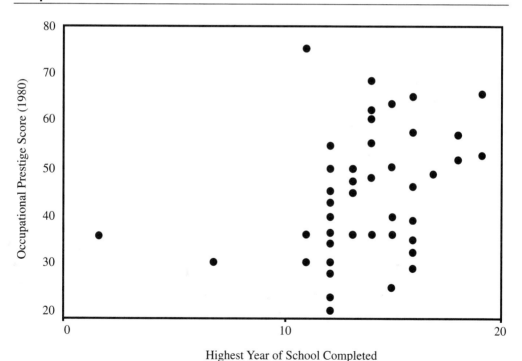

Source: 1998 General Social Survey.

Expressing a hypothesized relationship in statistical form requires a specific notation system to designate both variables and observations. Consistent with the scatterplot notation, a dependent variable in a regression analysis is designated Y, while the independent variable (sometimes called the **predictor variable**) is X. To indicate a specific individual observation—such as a person, city, or state—a subscript represents the case number (from 1 to N, the sample size). In general, X_i stands for the score of the ith observation on variable X. By replacing the general subscript with a specific number, we indicate the score of a specific observation. In the education and occupational prestige example, X_{37} denotes the value of education for the 37th respondent on the ordered list, 14 years of education. Similarly, Y_{37} represents this respondent's occupational prestige score, 66 (on a scale ranging from 17 to 86, with higher values indicating higher prestige).

predictor variable— independent variable in a regression analysis

Estimating the **linear relationship** between a dependent variable (Y) and an independent variable (X), we "regress Y on X," producing a **bivariate linear relationship**, or more simply, bivariate regression. The general form of a linear equation in algebraic form is written as

linear relationship— covariation in which the value of the dependent variable is proportional to the value of the independent variable

bivariate linear relationship/bivariate regression—a regression of Y on X

$$Y = a + bX$$

The ordinate, or Y value, equals the sum of a constant, a (the point at which the line intercepts the Y-axis), plus the product of the slope, b, times the X value. The line's Y intercept, a, shows the Y value when $X = 0$. The line's slope, b, shows the amount of change in Y units for a one-unit change in X.

Social researchers typically assume that two variables are linearly related unless there are strong initial reasons to believe that a nonlinear form, such as an exponential or logarithmic function, is more accurate. A linear relationship is the most elementary form and hence a reasonable first approximation. Because *parsimony* (simplicity) is a major aim of all science, determining whether a linear function best describes the relationship between two variables makes sense as a first step. Only after a straight line is clearly found not to describe a relationship should more complex functional forms be explored. In chapter 9 we will look at several nonlinear forms, including logistic regression.

If the GSS respondents' occupational prestige scores had a perfect linear relationship with number of years of education, then all the data points would fall on a straight line, showing how each year of education leads to occupational prestige ranks. The scatterplot in Figure 6.2 obviously falls considerably short of such perfect linearity, but it is not so far away as to be a completely random pattern. The figure does *not* suggest that a curvilinear function would better describe the data. Therefore, we proceed to apply techniques that measure how well a straight line approximates the covariation of two continuous variables.

We begin with a **prediction equation** in which the *i*th observation's value on the dependent variable is an exact linear function of the value on its independent variable:

$$\hat{Y}_i = a + b_{YX}X_i$$

prediction equation— a regression equation without the error term, useful for predicting the score on the dependent from the independent variable(s)

The subscript of the *b* indicates the order of the regression, with the dependent variable followed by the independent variable. The caret or "hat" (ˆ) over the Y_i indicates it is a predicted (or "expected") value, which may or may not equal the observed value for that case (Y_i, without a hat). Actual social data never follow a perfect linear relationship, as we saw in Figure 6.2. Consequently, we must take deviations from the linear prediction into account, through the **linear regression model**:

$$Y_i = a + b_{YX}X_i + e_i$$

linear regression model— a model that takes into account deviations from the linear prediction by showing the linear relationship between a continuous dependent variable and one or more independent variables, plus an error term

The absence of the caret over the dependent variable means that it is the observed rather than the predicted score of *Y*. The **error term** (e_i) represents that portion of the *i*th observation's score on variable *Y* that is not predicted from its linear relation to *X*. Thus, e_i measures the discrepancy in making a prediction by using a linear regression equation. Across *N* observations, some prediction errors will be positive (> 0); some will be negative (< 0); and some may be exactly zero (i.e., when the predicted score exactly equals the observed score). Just as with deviations from the mean of a distribution, the sum of the errors (Σe_i) equals zero because the positive and negative values exactly cancel one another.

error term—the difference between an observed score and a score predicted by the model

A regression error term is also called a **residual**, because it is the amount that remains after subtracting the prediction equation from the linear regression model:

$$
\begin{aligned}
Y_i - \hat{Y}_i &= [a + b_{YX}X_i + e_i] - [a + b_{YX}X_i] \\
&= e_i
\end{aligned}
$$

residual—the amount that remains after subtracting the prediction equation from the linear regression model

A basic task of regression analysis is to estimate the values for the two regression coefficients based on the observed data. The estimates *a* and b_{YX} must minimize the residuals—that is, make the prediction errors using that equation smaller than the errors made with any other linear relationship.

A **regression line** can be superimposed on the scatterplot of data points. This line has the useful property that, for each value of X_i, a pre-

regression line—a line that is the best fit to the points in a scatterplot, computed by ordinary least squares regression

cise $\hat{Y}_i$ value is predicted on the assumption of that linear relationship. Then the location of the data points can be compared to their values predicted by the regression line to determine the errors for all observations. The next section presents a method for estimating the two parameters of the linear regression model from sample data, for fitting a regression line through the scatterplot, and for determining how closely the predicted scores approach the observed scores.

6.2 Estimating a Linear Regression Equation

6.2.1 The Least Squares Criterion

All N sample observations on two variables are used to estimate a bivariate regression equation. Estimators for the two coefficients (a and b_{YX}) comply with a minimum *least squares error sum* criterion. Because the sum of the residuals ($\sum e_i$) is always zero, squaring removes the negative signs so that the sum of these squared errors is greater than zero. Consequently, summing the squared differences between each observed score (Y_i) and its score predicted by the regression equation ($\hat{Y}_i$) produces a quantity smaller than that obtained by using any other straight-line equation. That is,

$$\sum_{i=1}^{N}(Y_i - \hat{Y}_i)^2 = \sum_{i=1}^{N} e_i^2$$

is a minimum.

ordinary least squares—a method for obtaining estimates of regression equation coefficients that minimizes the error sum of squares

Estimators having this minimum error property produce **ordinary least squares (OLS)** estimates of a and b_{YX}. OLS regression procedures resemble the calculation of the arithmetic mean. Section 2.5.4 showed that the mean has the desirable property of minimizing the sum of all the squared deviations for a set of scores. Similarly, the regression line minimizes the sum of squared prediction errors.

bivariate regression coefficient—a parameter estimate of a bivariate regression equation that measures the amount of increase or decrease in the dependent variable for a one-unit difference in the independent variable

The OLS estimator of the **bivariate regression coefficient**, or regression slope (b_{YX}), from the observed X and Y scores is as follows:

$$b_{YX} = \frac{\sum(Y_i - \bar{Y})(X_i - \bar{X})}{\sum(X_i - \bar{X})^2}$$

(Box 8.2 shows how this OLS estimate is derived for multivariate regression equations.) The numerator in the formula is the sum of the product of the deviations of the X and Y variables around their means. When this term is divided by $N - 1$, it is called the **covariance**, labeled s_{YX}. That is,

$$s_{YX} = \frac{\Sigma(Y_i - \bar{Y})(X_i - \bar{X})}{N - 1}$$

Its computing formula is

$$s_{YX} = \frac{N \Sigma X_i Y_i - \Sigma X_i \Sigma Y_i}{N(N - 1)}$$

The denominator of the formula for b_{YX} is the sum of squared deviations around the mean of the independent variable, $\bar{X}$. As shown in chapter 3, dividing this term by $N - 1$ forms the sample *variance*

$$s_X^2 = \frac{\sum_{i=1}^{N} (X_i - \bar{X})^2}{N - 1}$$

The computing formula for the variance is

$$s_X^2 = \frac{N(\Sigma X^2) - (\Sigma X)^2}{N(N - 1)}$$

Because $N - 1$ appears in both the denominator of the covariance and the sample variance, that term cancels out of their ratio. Therefore, the OLS estimator of the bivariate regression coefficient can be estimated by the ratio

$$b_{YX} = \frac{s_{YX}}{s_X^2}$$

Although the two formulas for b_{YX} given previously are conceptually accurate, they are difficult to calculate without a computer. The following **computing formula for b**, which requires no deviations, gives identical numerical results and can be done with only a hand calculator:

$$b_{YX} = \frac{N \Sigma Y_i X_i - \Sigma Y_i \Sigma X_i}{N \Sigma X_i^2 - (\Sigma X_i)^2}$$

The OLS estimator of the **intercept** (a) is simply

$$a = \bar{Y} - b\bar{X}$$

This formula assures that the coordinate pair $(\bar{X}, \bar{Y})$ always falls on the regression line, regardless of the specific values of a and b. Hence, to calculate the intercept, we compute the bivariate regression coefficient first and then enter it into the preceding formula along with the means of both variables.

conditional mean—the expected average score on the dependent variable, Y, for a given value of the independent variable, X

A linear regression equation estimates a **conditional mean** for Y— that is, one predicted value of the dependent variable ($\hat{Y}_i$) for each specific value (condition) of the independent value (X_i). If no linear relationship exists between Y and X, then the slope b_{YX} equals zero. As shown in Figure 6.3, in such a situation the regression line parallels the X-axis at a distance exactly $\bar{Y}$ units from the origin (recall that all regression lines pass through the means of both variables). All predicted values equal a, because $\hat{Y}_i = a + 0X_i$ implies that $\hat{Y}_i = a$ and thus $\hat{Y}_i = \bar{Y}$. When the regression slope is zero, knowledge of a specific X_i value does not produce a predicted value of Y that differs from the mean of all observations. However, when Y and X are indeed linearly related, the conditional mean of Y depends on the specific value of X_i. Furthermore, these

FIGURE 6.3
The Regression Line When b = 0

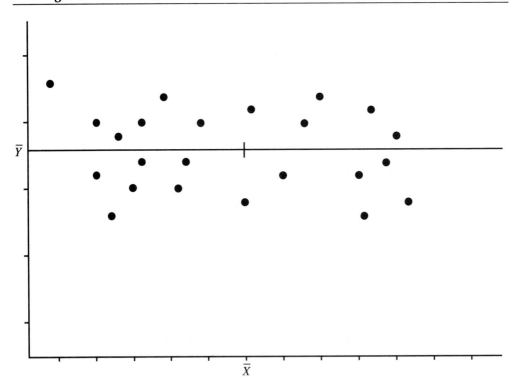

conditional means fall precisely on the straight line determined by the regression slope and intercept.

6.2.2 Linear Regression Applied to GSS Respondents' Occupational Prestige

To apply the OLS computing formulas for b_{YX} and a to the GSS example data, Table 6.1 displays the 50 individual respondents' values and their sums. Other relevant statistics appear at the bottom of the table. Given these values,

$$b_{YX} = \frac{(50)(30{,}317) - (2{,}191)(676)}{(50)(9{,}544) - 456{,}976} = 1.717$$

Or alternatively, $b_{YX} = s_{YX}/s_X^2 = 14.177/8.255 = 1.717$.

A bivariate regression coefficient measures the amount of change in a dependent variable for a one-unit difference in an independent variable. Thus, a one-year increase in a respondent's years of education is associated with an expected increase in occupational prestige of 1.717 points.

Given $\bar{X} = 13.52$, $\bar{Y} = 43.82$, and $b_{YX} = 1.717$, we easily compute $a = 43.82 - (1.717)(13.52) = 20.61$. Thus, the complete bivariate regression equation is

$$\hat{Y}_i = 20.61 + 1.72X_i$$

Figure 6.4 shows the regression line drawn through the scatterplot of the 50 data points. Notice that the line intercepts the Y-axis at 20.61. If a respondent had no education, the predicted occupational prestige score would be 20.61—the value of the intercept. The regression equation has a positive slope of 1.72. Although the line comes close to several observations, only one of the 50 data points falls on the line. A regression line always passes through the means of both Y and X. In this example, that point has coordinates 43.82 and 13.52.

Figure 6.5 illustrates the concept of residuals, or *errors in prediction*. As noted in section 6.1, a residual is simply the difference between an observed value and the value predicted using the regression equation—that is, $e_i = Y_i - \hat{Y}_i$. Figure 6.5 illustrates two errors in prediction, one positive (observation X_{46}, respondent #46) and one negative (observation X_6, respondent #6). Residuals provide a way to measure the magnitude of the linear relationship between two continuous variables, as the next section explains.

Table 6.1
Calculation of Means, Variances, and Correlation and Regression Coefficients for GSS Respondents' Occupational Prestige (Y) and Years of Education (X)

(1) Respondent	(2) Y	(3) X	(4) X^2	(5) YX	(6) Y^2
1	30	8	64	240	900
2	59	16	256	944	3,481
3	36	12	144	432	1,296
4	25	15	225	375	625
5	30	12	144	360	900
6	21	12	144	252	441
7	36	2	4	72	1,296
8	39	16	256	624	1,521
9	51	12	144	612	2,601
10	64	16	256	1,024	4,096
11	53	18	324	954	2,809
12	61	14	196	854	3,721
13	32	12	144	384	1,024
14	63	15	225	945	3,969
15	35	12	144	420	1,225
16	30	11	121	330	900
17	22	12	144	264	484
18	33	16	256	528	1,089
19	39	12	144	468	1,521
20	40	15	225	600	1,600
21	36	12	144	432	1,296
22	36	13	169	468	1,296
23	35	16	256	560	1,225
24	46	12	144	552	2,116
25	54	12	144	648	2,916
26	30	11	121	330	900
27	64	19	361	1,216	4,096
28	36	15	225	540	1,296
29	48	13	169	624	2,304
30	50	13	169	650	2,500
31	51	15	225	765	2,601
32	49	14	196	686	2,401
33	36	12	144	432	1,296
34	55	14	196	770	3,025

(continued)

TABLE 6.1 *(continued)*
Calculation of Means, Variances, and Correlation and Regression Coefficients for GSS Respondents' Occupational Prestige (*Y*) and Years of Education (*X*)

(1) Respondent	(2) Y	(3) X	(4) X^2	(5) YX	(6) Y^2
35	54	19	361	1,026	2,916
36	28	12	144	336	784
37	66	14	196	924	4,356
38	51	17	289	867	2,601
39	60	14	196	840	3,600
40	51	12	144	612	2,601
41	57	18	324	1,026	3,249
42	36	14	196	504	1,296
43	49	14	196	686	2,401
44	48	16	256	768	2,304
45	36	11	121	396	1,296
46	73	11	121	803	5,329
47	47	12	144	564	2,209
48	29	16	256	464	841
49	30	11	121	330	900
50	51	16	256	816	2,601
SUMS (Σs)	2,191	676	9,544	30,317	104,051

Source: 1998 General Social Survey.

$$\bar{Y} = \frac{2,191}{50} = 43.82$$

$$\bar{X} = \frac{676}{50} = 13.52$$

$$s_Y^2 = \frac{(50)(104,051) - (2,191)^2}{(50)(49)} = 164.110$$

$$s_X^2 = \frac{(50)(9,544) - (676)^2}{(50)(49)} = 8.255$$

$$s_{YX} = \frac{(50)(30,317) - (676)(2,191)}{(50)(49)} = 14.177$$

FIGURE 6.4
Scatterplot of Occupational Prestige by Years of Schooling with Regression Line for a Sample of $N = 50$

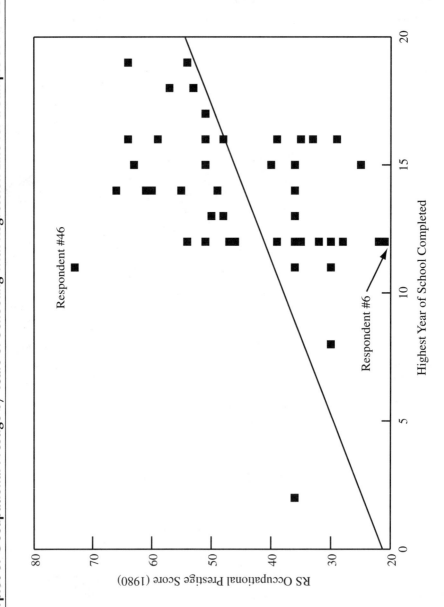

Source: 1998 General Social Survey.

FIGURE 6.5
Method of Accounting for an Observation by the Regression Line and an Error Component

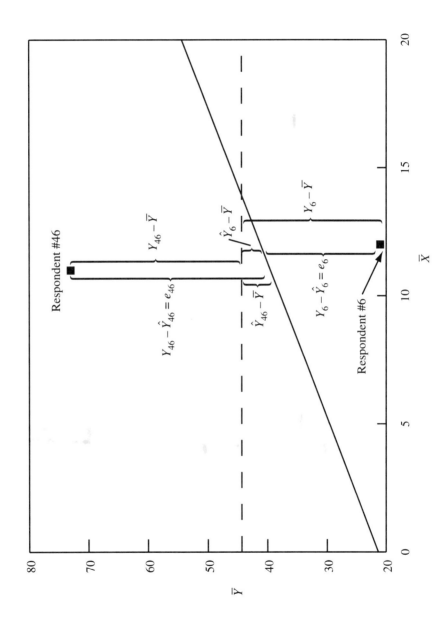

6.3 *R*-Square and Correlation

6.3.1 Partitioning the Sum of Squares

One way to determine how strongly two variables covary is to measure how closely the values of the observations approach the regression line. In the ideal situation where all observations fall exactly on the regression line, the N $\hat{Y}_i$ scores predicted from X_i would have no errors (i.e., $\hat{Y}_i - Y_i = 0$). But perfect prediction simply is not possible with actual social data. Greater or lesser amounts of error are always present in any regression. Our realistic goal is to determine the relative contributions of both prediction and error to the variation that we observe in the dependent variable. Because the variation in Y is attributable both to the effects of X and to random error, we can partition the total sum of squares in a distribution of scores into a systematic component and a random component.

Create a deviation by subtracting the mean from observation Y_i. Then both add and subtract the expected score (due to linear regression) from this deviation, producing the identity

$$(Y_i - \bar{Y}) = (Y_i - \hat{Y}_i) + (\hat{Y}_i - \bar{Y})$$

Every observation thus has two components:

1. $Y_i - \hat{Y}_i$ indicates the discrepancy between an observation and its predicted value; this discrepancy is the error term e_i.

2. $\hat{Y}_i - \bar{Y}$ indicates that portion of an observed score that is due to the linear relationship between Y and X.

regression sum of squares—a number obtained in linear regression by subtracting the mean of a set of scores from the value predicted by linear regression, squaring, and summing these values

Squaring both sides of the identity above and summing across all N sample observations results in the **regression sum of squares** and the **error sum of squares**. (This method works because the sum of the cross-multiplied components on the right side of the equation is zero.) If we rearrange these terms, it turns out that

$$\sum_{i=1}^{N}(Y_i - \bar{Y})^2 = \sum_{i=1}^{N}(\hat{Y}_i - \bar{Y})^2 + \sum_{i=1}^{N}(Y_i - \hat{Y}_i)^2$$

error sum of squares—a numerical value obtained in linear regression by subtracting the regression sum of squares from the total sum of squares

total sum of squares—the total of regression and error sums of squares

The term to the left of the equal sign is called the **total sum of squares**, or SS_{TOTAL}, and it is recognizable from section 2.5.4 as the numerator of the variance. The two terms to the right of the equal sign represent, respectively, the regression sum of squares and the error sum of squares. Thus, the simplified accounting identity is

$$SS_{\text{TOTAL}} = SS_{\text{REGRESSION}} + SS_{\text{ERROR}}$$

This accounting equation shows that, assuming Y and X are linearly related, all the variation observed in a dependent variable (SS_{TOTAL}) can be allocated to a portion due to its linear relationship with the independent variable and to a portion due to errors of prediction.

6.3.2 The Coefficient of Determination

How much prediction error could be eliminated by using a regression model? If we lacked all knowledge of how two variables are related, our best guess about Y_i for each X_i would be simply the sample mean, $\bar{Y}$ (see section 6.2.1 and Figure 6.3). That is, the sum of squared errors $\sum(Y_i - \hat{Y}_i)^2$ would be reduced to $\sum(Y_i - \bar{Y})^2$ because the mean would be substituted for the predicted value in every case. But then SS_{ERROR} would be identical to SS_{TOTAL}; hence, $SS_{REGRESSION}$ would equal zero. To the extent that we can use information about X_i to improve our prediction of Y_i, we eliminate errors up to but not exceeding the total sum of squares.

Because SS_{TOTAL} depends on sample size, a procedure to standardize the partitioned values is necessary in order to make comparisons across a variety of distributions. The sum of the squared errors for regression (SS_{ERROR}) and the sum of the squared errors about the mean (SS_{TOTAL}) contain the information necessary to construct a standardized *proportional reduction in error* (PRE) measure of the partitioning in linear regression. As discussed in section 5.3, all PRE measures have the following general form:

$$\text{PRE statistic} = \frac{\text{Error without decision rule} - \text{Error with decision rule}}{\text{Error without decision rule}}$$

If the application of a decision rule leaves an error as large as the one occurring when no decision rule is used, then the PRE value is 0. That is, none of the error is reduced by the decision rule. In contrast, if no error remains after applying the decision rule, then the PRE value reaches its maximum of 1.00, meaning that *all* of the error was eliminated by the decision rule. Hence, a PRE statistic standardizes a partition between 0 and 1.00, with higher values indicating the proportion of variation "explained" by the decision rule.

Thus, linear regression can be viewed as a decision rule about expected mean values $\hat{Y}_i$, conditional on observed X_i values. If any linear relation exists between Y and X, the regression equation produces a proportionally smaller prediction error than that which occurs when only the mean is used as the decision rule.

coefficient of
determination—a PRE
statistic for linear
regression that expresses
the amount of variation in
the dependent variable
explained or accounted for
by the independent
variable(s) in a regression
equation

The regression PRE statistic is called the **coefficient of determination** because it indicates the proportion of total variation in Y "determined" by its linear relationship to X. Its symbol, R^2_{YX} (read "R-square"), is derived by substituting two of the partition components into the general PRE formula

$$R^2_{YX} = \frac{\sum(Y_i - \bar{Y})^2 - \sum(Y_i - \hat{Y}_i)^2}{\sum(Y_i - \bar{Y})^2}$$

or

$$R^2_{YX} = \frac{SS_{TOTAL} - SS_{ERROR}}{SS_{TOTAL}}$$

$$= 1 - \frac{SS_{ERROR}}{SS_{TOTAL}}$$

Thus, R-square equals 1 minus the ratio of the error sum of squares to the total sum of squares. The squaring confines the range of R_{YX}^2 between 0.0 and 1.00. Whenever SS_{ERROR} is zero (perfect prediction occurs), $R^2_{YX} = 1.0$, and whenever $SS_{ERROR} = SS_{TOTAL}$ (i.e., all variation is due to error), $R^2_{YX} = 0.0$. Because $SS_{REGRESSION} = SS_{TOTAL} - SS_{ERROR}$, it follows that a fourth formula for R-square is

$$R^2_{YX} = \frac{SS_{REGRESSION}}{SS_{TOTAL}}$$

The coefficient of determination is clearly the proportion of the total sum of squares attributable to a least squares regression line fitted to the data.

A computing formula for the bivariate coefficient of determination involves the ratio of the square covariance to the product of both variances:

$$R^2_{YX} = \frac{s^2_{YX}}{s^2_X s^2_Y}$$

Applying the calculating formula for the covariance in section 6.2.1 to the sample GSS data in Table 6.1, we find

$$s_{YX} = \frac{(50)(30,317) - (676)(2,191)}{(50)(49)} = 14.177$$

Using the column sums in Table 6.1, we compute $s^2_X = 8.255$ and $s^2_Y = 164.110$. The R-square formula yields

$$R^2_{YX} = \frac{(14.177)^2}{(8.255)(164.110)} = 0.148$$

Thus, 14.8% of the variation in respondents' occupational prestige is "explained" (statistically) by years of education.

The quantity $1 - R_{YX}^2$ is the amount of variance in the variable Y that *cannot* be attributed to its linear relationship with X. Hence, it is called the **coefficient of nondetermination**. In our example its numerical value is $1 - 0.148 = 0.852$. That is, the linear relationship of Y to X cannot account for 85.2% of the variance in Y. In chapter 9 we discuss how adding predictors to create a multiple regression equation may further reduce the proportion of unexplained variation in a dependent variable.

coefficient of nondetermination— a statistic that expresses the amount of variation in a dependent variable that is left *un*explained by the independent variable(s) in a regression equation

6.3.3 The Correlation Coefficient

The square root of R_{YX}^2, which summarizes the linear relationship between two continuous variables, is called the Pearson product-moment **correlation coefficient**, after the statistician Karl Pearson. Its formula is

correlation coefficient— a measure of association between two continuous variables that estimates the direction and strength of linear relationship

$$r_{YX} = \sqrt{R_{YX}^2}$$

$$= \frac{s_{XY}}{s_Y s_X}$$

The correlation coefficient's usefulness lies in showing the direction of the relationship between X and Y. Whereas R_{YX}^2 conceals whether the two variables are directly or inversely related, a positive or a negative sign is attached to r_{YX} to indicate the direction of the covariation. This sign must agree with the sign of the regression coefficient (b_{YX}). In our example, the correlation between occupational prestige and years of education is $+0.385$. Unlike R_{YX}^2, which is confined between 0 and 1.00, r_{YX} can range between -1.00 for a perfect inverse association to $+1.00$ for a perfect direct association. If $r_{YX} = 0$, then Y and X are unrelated.

From the definition of R-square, it follows that the correlation coefficient is *symmetric*:

$$r_{YX} = \frac{s_{YX}}{s_Y s_X}$$

$$= \frac{\sum (Y_i - \bar{Y})(X_i - \bar{X})/(N-1)}{s_Y s_X}$$

$$= \frac{\sum (X_i - \bar{X})(Y_i - \bar{Y})/(N-1)}{s_X s_Y}$$

$$= \frac{s_{XY}}{s_X s_Y}$$

$$= r_{XY}$$

Although the correlation coefficient is symmetric, you should convince yourself that the bivariate coefficient b_{YX} from regressing Y on X does *not* equal the coefficient b_{XY} from regressing X on Y. In section 6.3.5 we discuss how the regression and correlation coefficients are related.

6.3.4 Correlating Z Scores

Standardizing two variables (that is, changing them from Y and X to Z_Y and Z_X) and then correlating them produce some interesting results. Recall from Box 2.4 that a distribution of Z scores always has variance and standard deviation = 1.00. Given that $r_{YX} = s_{YX}/(s_Y s_X)$, the formula for the correlation of two Z scores is

$$r_{Z_Y Z_X} = \frac{s_{Z_Y Z_X}}{s_{Z_Y} s_{Z_X}} = \frac{s_{Z_Y Z_X}}{(1)(1)} = s_{Z_Y Z_X}$$

Thus, the correlation of two Z scores equals their covariance! Furthermore, because the mean of a Z score is zero (i.e, $\bar{Z}_X = \bar{Z}_Y = 0$), and because $s_{Z_Y Z_X} = \Sigma(Z_{Y_i} - \bar{Z}_Y)(Z_{X_i} - \bar{Z}_X)/(N-1)$, the correlation coefficient can be expressed entirely in terms of Z scores:

$$r_{Z_Y Z_X} = s_{Z_Y Z_X} = \frac{\Sigma Z_Y Z_X}{N-1}$$

Furthermore, given the definition of both Z scores in terms of the original Y and X variables—$Z_{Y_i} = (Y_i - \bar{Y})/s_Y$ and $Z_{X_i} = (X_i - \bar{X})/s_X$—it follows that

$$
\begin{aligned}
r_{Z_Y Z_X} &= \frac{\Sigma Z_Y Z_X}{N-1} \\[2mm]
&= \frac{\Sigma[(Y_i - \bar{Y})/s_Y][(X_i - \bar{X})/s_X]}{N-1} \\[2mm]
&= \frac{\Sigma(Y_i - \bar{Y})(X_i - \bar{X})/(N-1)}{s_Y s_X} \\[2mm]
&= \frac{s_{YX}}{s_Y s_X} \\[2mm]
&= r_{YX}
\end{aligned}
$$

That is, the correlation of two Z-transformed variables, Z_Y and Z_X, equals the correlation of their original variables, Y and X. Importantly, the correlation coefficient remains unchanged whether the variables are measured in their original metrics or transformed to standardized scores.

6.3.5 The Relationship Between Regression and Correlation

The relationships between a bivariate correlation coefficient and a regression coefficient are functions of both variables' standard deviations. First, recall that b_{YX} can be expressed as the ratio of covariance to variance: $b_{YX} = s_{YX}/s_X^2$. Rearranging these terms to isolate the covariance gives $s_{YX} = b_{YX}s_X^2$. Next, substituting $(b_{YX})(s_X^2)$ for s_{YX} in the equation for the correlation $r_{YX} = s_{YX}/s_Y s_X$ yields $r_{YX} = (b_{YX})(s_X^2)/(s_Y s_X)$. Thus, a correlation coefficient can be expressed in terms of a bivariate regression coefficient

$$r_{YX} = b_{YX}\frac{s_X}{s_Y}$$

and conversely,

$$b_{YX} = r_{YX}\frac{s_Y}{s_X}$$

Knowing the values for b_{YX}, s_Y, and s_X allows the calculation of r_{YX}. Or knowing r_{YX}, s_Y, and s_X allows b_{YX} to be determined. In the GSS data example,

$$r_{YX} = b_{YX}\frac{s_X}{s_Y} = (1.717)\left(\frac{2.873}{12.811}\right) = +0.385$$

$$b_{YX} = r_{YX}\frac{s_Y}{s_X} = (0.385)\left(\frac{12.811}{2.873}\right) = 1.717$$

These relationships hold only in the bivariate regression case. The multiple regression coefficients discussed in chapter 8 do not have such simple relations to the correlation coefficients.

6.4 Significance Tests for Regression Parameters

As with other descriptive statistics, researchers typically use sample data to estimate bivariate regression and correlation coefficients. Corresponding to each statistic—b_{YX}, a, R_{YX}^2, and r_{YX}—are population parameters β_{YX}, α, ϱ_{YX}^2, and ϱ_{YX}. To draw inferences about these population parameters from sample data, we need test statistics having known probability distributions, as described in the following subsections.

6.4.1 Testing the Coefficient of Determination

For the coefficient of determination, the basic null hypothesis is that, in the population, none of the dependent variable's variance can be attributed to its linear relation with the independent variable:

$$H_0: \varrho_{YX}^2 = 0$$

where ϱ_{YX}^2 (Greek letter *rho*) refers to the population parameter.

The alternative hypothesis is that *R*-square in the population is greater than zero: $H_0: \varrho_{YX}^2 > 0$. The statistical significance test for the sample R_{YX}^2 uses the *F* distribution discussed in chapter 3. In a regression analysis the SS_{TOTAL} has $N - 1$ degrees of freedom associated with it. Because the $SS_{REGRESSION}$ (defined in section 6.3.1) is estimated from b_{YX} (which is a single function of the X_i's), it has only 1 degree of freedom. Just as the total sum of squares can be partitioned into two mutually exclusive components (see section 6.3.1), degrees of freedom can also be partitioned:

$$df_{TOTAL} = df_{REGRESSION} + df_{ERROR}$$
$$N - 1 = 1 + df_{ERROR}$$
$$N - 2 = df_{ERROR}$$

mean squares—estimates of variance in a linear regression

The next step is to compute the mean squares associated with $SS_{REGRESSION}$ and SS_{ERROR}. In computing **mean squares** we are calculating two variances, one due to the effect of the independent variable on the dependent variable and one due to error. If a nonzero regression effect exists, then the **mean square regression** ($MS_{REGRESSION}$) will be significantly larger than the **mean square error** (MS_{ERROR}). Both terms are calculated by dividing the appropriate sum of squares by its associated degrees of freedom:

mean square regression— a value in linear regression obtained by dividing the regression sum of squares by its degrees of freedom

mean square error— a value in linear regression obtained by dividing the error sum of squares by its degrees of freedom

$$MS_{REGRESSION} = \frac{SS_{REGRESSION}}{1}$$

$$MS_{ERROR} = \frac{SS_{ERROR}}{N - 2}$$

If the null hypothesis about the population coefficient of determination ($H_0: \varrho_{YX}^2 = 0$) is true, then both $MS_{REGRESSION}$ and MS_{ERROR} will be unbiased estimates of σ_e^2, the variance of prediction errors (i.e., the e_i). However, if the true population parameter is greater than zero ($H_1: \varrho_{YX}^2 > 0$), then we also expect $MS_{REGRESSION} > MS_{ERROR}$ in the sample.

Because F is simply the ratio of two estimates of the same σ_e^2, the null hypothesis can be tested by calculating

$$F_{1,N-2} = \frac{MS_{\text{REGRESSION}}}{MS_{\text{ERROR}}}$$

where the two degrees of freedom are $v_1 = 1$ and $v_2 = N - 2$, respectively.

If the calculated value of F is as large as, or larger than, the critical value for the chosen α probability level, then we reject the null hypothesis and conclude that ϱ_{YX}^2 is greater than zero (with an α chance of Type I or false rejection error). If the F ratio is less than the critical value, we cannot reject the null hypothesis that $\varrho_{YX}^2 = 0$ in the population.

The simplest way to compute $SS_{\text{REGRESSION}}$ follows from the fact that $R_{YX}^2 = SS_{\text{REGRESSION}}/SS_{\text{TOTAL}}$, as shown in section 6.3.2. Therefore,

$$SS_{\text{REGRESSION}} = (R_{YX}^2)(SS_{\text{TOTAL}})$$

Combining the definition of the variance in section 2.5.4,

$$s_Y^2 = \sum(Y_i - \bar{Y})^2/(N - 1)$$

with the expression $SS_{\text{TOTAL}} = \sum(Y_i - \bar{Y})^2$, the total sum of squares can be calculated:

$$SS_{\text{TOTAL}} = (s_Y^2)(N - 1)$$

Hence, calculate $SS_{\text{REGRESSION}} = (R_{YX}^2)(s_Y^2)(N - 1)$. Finally, from the accounting equation for partitioning sums of squares, we obtain the last component we need by subtraction:

$$SS_{\text{ERROR}} = SS_{\text{TOTAL}} - SS_{\text{REGRESSION}}$$

From the education-occupational prestige data in Table 6.1, $s_Y^2 = 164.110$, $R_{YX}^2 = 0.148$, and $N = 50$. Therefore, applying the formulas above, we have

$$SS_{\text{TOTAL}} = (164.110)(49) = 8,041.390$$

$$SS_{\text{REGRESSION}} = (0.148)(8,041.39) = 1,190.126$$

and

$$SS_{\text{ERROR}} = 8,041.390 - 1,190.126 = 6,851.264$$

Furthermore,

$$MS_{\text{REGRESSION}} = \frac{1,190.126}{1} = 1,190.126$$

and

$$MS_{\text{ERROR}} = \frac{6,851.264}{(50 - 2)} = 142.735$$

TABLE 6.2
Summary of GSS Respondents' Occupational Prestige Analysis

Source	SS	df	MS	F
Regression	1,190.126	1	1,190.126	8.34*
Error	6,851.264	48	142.735	
Total	8,041.390	49		

*Significant at $\alpha = .01$.

If we set $\alpha = .01$, we see from Appendix E that the critical value for an F with 1 and 40 degrees of freedom is 7.31. But our test statistic is $F_{1,48} = 1,190.126/142.735 = 8.34$. Hence, we can reject the null hypothesis that $\varrho_{YX}^2 = 0$ in the population in favor of the alternative that $\varrho_{YX}^2 > 0$. Table 6.2 summarizes these computations in a conventional format which, for reasons explained in chapter 5, is called an analysis of variance table.

6.4.2 Testing the Correlation Coefficient

Because the sample correlation coefficient, r_{XY}, is simply the square root of the coefficient of determination, R_{YX}^2, the significance test for the latter also serves for the former. However, a second statistical significance test exists for the correlation coefficient. The standardized normal distribution (Z) is used to find the probability of observing a given r_{XY} under the null hypothesis H_0: $\varrho_{YX} = 0$. The **r-to-Z transformation**, developed by the English statistician Ronald Fisher, uses the natural logarithm function

r-to-Z transformation—a natural logarithm transformation in the value of the correlation coefficient to a Z score, to test the probability of observing r under the null hypothesis

$$Z = \left(\frac{1}{2}\right) \ln\left(\frac{1 + r_{XY}}{1 - r_{XY}}\right)$$

For persons whose hand calculators lack a natural logarithm (ln) key, Fisher's r-to-Z table in Appendix F gives values for virtually all possible correlation coefficients (for negative correlations, just attach a negative sign to the tabled values, because the normal distribution is symmetrical).

This Z score's variance is inverse to sample size:

$$\hat{\sigma}_Z^2 = \frac{1}{N - 3}$$

The test statistic involves the difference between Z scores and is also distributed as a standardized normal variable:

$$Z = \frac{Z_r - Z_\varrho}{\hat{\sigma}_Z}$$

Under the null hypothesis that the population correlation is zero, $Z_\varrho = 0$.

For the GSS data, we already know that $r_{YX} = 0.385$ is significantly different from zero, so let us instead test a different null hypothesis. For example, what is the probability that $\varrho_{XY} = 0.50$, given that the sample correlation is 0.385 and $N = 50$? Suppose we set $\alpha = .05$ (i.e., the critical value for a one-tailed test is -1.645). The r-to-Z transformations in Appendix F for those two correlations are 0.549 and 0.406, respectively, while $\sigma_Z^2 = 1/(50 - 3) = 0.021$. Hence the test statistic, distributed approximately as a Z score following the normal distribution, is computed as

$$\frac{0.406 - 0.549}{\sqrt{0.021}} = -0.99$$

This Z value falls considerably short of the critical value necessary to reject the hypothesis. Therefore, we conclude that we cannot reject the hypothesis that the true population correlation is 0.50. Of course, many other values in the same vicinity as the sample point estimate of 0.385 also cannot be rejected as highly unlikely values for the parameter.

6.4.3 Testing *b* and *a*

Throughout this chapter, we have written the bivariate regression equation in Roman letters, implying that it is estimated with sample data:

$$\hat{Y}_i = a + b_{YX} X_i$$

The corresponding **population regression equation** is written using Greek letters for the parameters:

population regression equation—a regression equation for a population rather than a sample

$$\hat{Y}_i = \alpha + \beta_{YX} X_i$$

The population parameters α and β_{YX} are estimated by a and b_{YX} in the sample data. Do not confuse these a and β parameters with other uses of the same Greek symbols, such as the α probability level and the β probability of a Type II error. Unfortunately, modern statistics makes limited use of the Greek alphabet, with several symbols serving multiple purposes.

The typical null hypothesis about the population regression parameter is that it equals zero: H_0: $\beta_{YX} = 0$. Selecting an alternative hypothesis, hence choosing a one- or two-tailed test, depends on our knowledge of the relationship between X and Y. If we really have no idea whether X's effect is to increase or decrease Y, then the alternative H_1: $\beta_{YX} \neq 0$ implies a two-tailed region of rejection. But if we believe that only a positive effect is plausible, then the alternative H_1: $\beta_{YX} > 0$ puts the entire region of rejection in the right tail of the test statistic's sampling distribution.

Conversely, if only a negative relationship is credible, then the one-tailed alternative $H_1: \beta_{YX} < 0$ locates the entire region of rejection in the left tail.

To test whether the sample regression estimate, b_{YX}, differs significantly from the hypothesized population parameter, the t sampling distribution is used to estimate the probability of making a Type I error by falsely rejecting the null hypothesis. The t test for the null hypothesis that $\beta_{YX} = 0$ is as

$$t = \frac{b_{YX} - \beta_{YX}}{s_b}$$

$$= \frac{b_{YX} - 0}{s_b}$$

where s_b is the estimate of σ_b, the standard error of the regression coefficient.

Here the *standard error*, a concept introduced in section 3.5, is the standard deviation of the sampling distribution of the regression coefficient. To test the hypothesis that β_{YX} differs from zero, two assumptions are necessary:

1. Y is normally distributed for every outcome of X in the population.

2. The variances of the prediction errors are identical at every outcome of X, a condition known as **homoscedasticity**.

homoscedasticity—
a condition in which the variances of the prediction errors are equal at every outcome of the predictor variable

Then, according to the central limit theorem, the sampling distribution of b_{YX} will be normally distributed as N becomes large. The mean of this sampling distribution equals the population regression parameter β_{YX}, and its variance is

$$\sigma_b^2 = \frac{\sigma_e^2}{\Sigma(X_i - \bar{X})^2}$$

An estimate of the denominator can be obtained from the sample variance of the X_i's by $\Sigma(X_i - \bar{X})^2 = (s_X^2)(N - 1)$. An estimate of the numerator, σ_e^2 (the variance of the prediction errors) is the MS_{ERROR} from the R-square significance test

$$\hat{\sigma}_e^2 = MS_{ERROR}$$

Because the MS_{ERROR} has $N - 2$ degrees of freedom, the t test for the regression coefficient also has $N - 2$ df. Thus, its t ratio, with the df indicated in the subscript, is

$$t_{N-2} = \frac{b_{YX} - \beta_{YX}}{\sqrt{\dfrac{MS_{ERROR}}{\Sigma(X_i - \bar{X})^2}}}$$

$$= \frac{b_{YX} - 0}{\sqrt{\frac{MS_{\text{ERROR}}}{(s_X^2)(N-1)}}}$$

For the GSS education-occupational prestige data, a one-tailed alternative (H_1: $\beta_{YX} > 0$) is plausible, because we expect prestige to increase with education. For $\alpha = .01$ and $df = 48$, the critical value of t in Appendix D is less than 2.423 (using $df = 40$ as an approximation). We compute

$$t_{48} = \frac{1.717 - 0}{\sqrt{\frac{142.735}{(8.255)(49)}}} = \frac{1.717}{0.594} = 2.891$$

Because we will need this information in section 6.4, note that $s_b = 0.594$. Given that $t_{48} = 2.891$ exceeds the critical value of 2.423, we can reject the null hypothesis that $\beta_{YX} = 0$ in the population. With little chance of being wrong, we conclude that occupational prestige and the number of years of education significantly covary in a positive direction among the 50 respondents selected randomly from the 1998 GSS. Note that the t value of 2.89 when squared equals 8.35, the value of the F when the R_{YX}^2 was tested for significance. This correspondence is no coincidence. In the bivariate case there is an intimate relationship between r_{YX} (and hence R_{YX}^2) and b_{YX}, as was shown in section 6.3.5. When one is significant, the other also will be significant. Furthermore, $t_{v_2}^2 = F_{1,v_1}$ for the t and F involved in the two tests of significance. Hence, only one of these tests needs to be conducted.

A t test can also be applied to the significance of the population regression intercept, α. Its formula is

$$t_{N-2} = \frac{a - \alpha}{\sqrt{MS_{\text{ERROR}}} \ \sqrt{\frac{1}{N} + \frac{\overline{X}^2}{(N-1)s_X^2}}}$$

where $\overline{X}$ = mean of X and s_X^2 = variance of X.

In the education-occupational prestige example, where the sample $a = 20.61$ and $N = 50$, if we set the probability of rejection at $\alpha = .05$, a two-tailed test of the null hypothesis, H_0: $\alpha = 0$ yields

$$t_{48} = \frac{20.61 - 0}{\sqrt{142.735} \ \sqrt{\frac{1}{50} + \frac{(13.52)^2}{(49)(8.255)}}} = 2.51$$

Because the critical value is 2.021, the null hypothesis also can be rejected with a probability less than .05 of making a Type I error or false rejection error. As pointed out previously, the intercept in this example is the expected occupational prestige score for respondents with zero years of education. The unlikelihood of such a condition makes the intercept a relatively uninformative parameter estimate in this case. This result underscores the point that social researchers must think about their statistical analyses rather than just mechanically applying the formulas.

6.4.4 Confidence Intervals

As we stress throughout this book, confidence intervals built around point estimates are more important than tests designed to reject the hypothesis that a parameter is zero in the population. The estimated standard error of the regression coefficient, s_b, can be used to construct a confidence interval around the sample point estimate, b_{YX}. In general, the upper and lower confidence intervals for a given α level are $b_{YX} \pm (s_b)$(c.v.). First, decide on a probability level for a two-tailed test (because the interval must be symmetric around the sample point estimate of b_{YX}). For example, setting $\alpha = .05$ for $df = 48$ designates critical t values equal to ± 2.021. Therefore, the upper and lower limits of the 95% confidence interval are $b + s_b (2.021)$ and $b - s_b (2.021)$.

For large samples (with more than 100 cases), the critical values for t at $\alpha = .05$ are ± 1.96 (i.e., the Z scores for a two-tailed significance test). Because these values are very close to 2.00, a statistical approximation asserts that if a regression coefficient is twice its standard error in size, then b_{YX} is significant at the .05 level. Remember the correct interpretation is that across repeated samples of size N, the confidence interval on average will contain the β_{YX} population parameter only $(1 - \alpha)$ of the time. As pointed out in section 3.6, however, to say that the population parameter has a 95% chance of being inside a particular interval is *not correct*: it is either inside that specific interval or it is not.

In the education-occupational prestige equation, the confidence interval around the b_{YX} regression estimate is bounded by LCL = $1.717 - (0.594)(2.021) = 0.52$ and UCL = $1.717 + (0.594)(2.021) = 2.92$. Therefore, the confidence interval is from 0.52 to 2.92, a fairly wide range but one that still does not include zero. Does the confidence interval for $\alpha = .001$ include zero?

6.5 Standardizing Regression Coefficients

The meaning of a regression coefficient is clear when both independent and dependent variables have obvious units of measurement. Thus, a year of schooling or a dollar of income are well-understood scales whose units make intuitive sense. However, many social variables lack intrinsically interpretable scales. For example, religiosity might be measured by the frequency of agreement with seven statements such as "The Bible is God's word" and "There is a life after death," or workers may be asked to rate their job satisfaction on a 1 to 10 scale. Regression coefficients estimated for such arbitrary scales do not have an obvious meaning. Consequently, many researchers prefer to standardize their regression coefficients.

The symbol for a standardized bivariate regression coefficient, usually called a **beta coefficient**, or **beta weight**, is $\beta*$.[1] Standardization involves rescaling both the independent and dependent variables in terms of their standard deviations. A simple rescaling procedure involves first converting both the Y and X variables to Z scores and then estimating the regression equation as before. The same result is reached by first multiplying b_{YX} by the standard deviation of the independent variable and then dividing by the standard deviation of the dependent variable:

beta coefficient/beta weight—a standardized regression coefficient indicating the amount of net change, in standard deviation units, of the dependent variable for an independent variable change of one standard deviation

$$\beta^*_{YX} = (b_{YX})\left(\frac{s_X}{s_Y}\right)$$

In the preceding section we saw that this transformation is also the correlation between X and Y. Hence, in the bivariate case only, a standardized regression coefficient equals its correlation coefficient: $\beta^*_{YX} = r_{YX}$.

β^*_{YX} is interpreted in standard deviation units. For a difference of one standard deviation in X, the expected difference in Y is β^*_{YX} standard deviation units, either larger or smaller depending on the sign of the coefficient. In the education-occupational prestige example, the correlation coefficient of 0.38 indicates that each standard deviation increase in years of education predicts a +0.38 standard deviation increase in prestige.

Because the mean of a standardized variable equals zero, the intercept in a standardized regression equation is also zero. This result is demonstrated by inserting zeros for the means of X and Y in the formula for the intercept of the nonstandardized equation: $a = \overline{Y} - b_{YX}\overline{X}$, i.e., $a = 0 - b0 = 0$. Therefore, the prediction equation expressing the linear relation between two Z-score variables has no intercept term:

$$\hat{Z}_Y = \beta^*_{YX}Z_X$$
$$= r_{YX}Z_X$$

In our income-education example, the standardized prediction equation is $\hat{Z}_Y = 0.38Z_X$.

---

[1]Once again, we encounter the practice in statistics of using a few Greek symbols for many purposes. Here we star (*) the beta coefficient ($\beta*$) to distinguish it from the population parameter β, introduced in the preceding section.

Finally, we note that everything previously stated about the regression of Y on X could be restated for the regression of X on Y. Although it is always true that $r_{YX} = r_{XY}$ (i.e., the correlation coefficient is symmetric), it is *not* generally the case that the unstandardized $b_{YX} = b_{XY}$. (If this is not apparent to you, reread section 6.3.5.) However, the product of two standardized bivariate regression coefficients is the same as the product of their correlation coefficients: $(\beta^*_{YX})(\beta^*_{XY}) = (r_{YX})(r_{XY})$. But the right-hand side of the equation is the same as squaring the correlation coefficient, which is the coefficient of determination: $(r_{YX})(r_{XY}) = r^2_{YX} = R^2_{YX}$. Hence, multiplying the complementary bivariate regression parameters reveals the proportion of variance in either variable explained statistically by its linear association with the other variable, regardless of which one is assumed to be the independent and which the dependent variable. Examining R^2_{YX} to determine the proportion of variance explained is obviously much more straightforward.

6.5.1 Regression Toward the Mean

The standardized form of the prediction equation is useful for understanding how the term *regression* came to be applied to this form of analysis. Suppose we are interested in the relationship between mothers' and daughters' weights. We sample 500 mothers, match them to their oldest daughters, and weigh both members of each pair. We find that $\bar{X} = \bar{Y} = 135$, $s_Y = s_X = 15$, and $r_{XY} = 0.70$, where X and Y refer to mothers' and daughters' weights, respectively.

Now if we standardize the two variables, our prediction is

$$\hat{Z}_Y = 0.70 Z_X$$

Notice that mothers whose weight is one standard deviation above the mean (i.e., $Z_X = 1$) are predicted to have daughters whose weights on average are only +0.70 standard deviations above the mean. In contrast, mothers whose weights place them one standard deviation below the mean (i.e., $Z_X = -1$) are predicted to have daughters who are only –0.70 standard deviations below the mean. That is, a daughter's weight exhibits **regression toward the mean**; or, on average, daughters are predicted to be closer to the mean in weight than their mothers are.

This regression can be seen clearly by examining Table 6.3, which gives examples of observed and predicted values for mothers' and daughters' weights (both standardized and unstandardized). On average, mothers who are above the mean are predicted to have daughters who weigh less than they do, and mothers below the mean are predicted to have daughters who are heavier than they are. This seems to imply that the population of

regression toward the mean—a condition demonstrated when the predicted scores on the dependent variable show less variability about the mean than the observed scores do, due to the imperfect correlation between two variables

TABLE 6.3
Illustration of Regression Toward the Mean, Using the Prediction of Daughter's Weight from Mother's Weight

STANDARDIZED WEIGHT		UNSTANDARDIZED WEIGHT	
Observed Mother's Weight	Predicted Daughter's Weight	Observed Mother's Weight	Predicted Daughter's Weight
+3	+2.1	180	166.5
+2	+1.4	165	156.0
+1	+0.7	150	145.5
0	0.0	135	135.0
−1	−0.7	120	124.5
−2	−1.4	105	114.0
−3	−2.1	90	103.5

<table>
<tr><td align="center">Prediction Equation
$\hat{Z}_y = 0.7 Z_Y$</td><td align="center">Prediction Equation
$\hat{Y} = 40.5 + 0.7X$</td></tr>
</table>

women is becoming more homogeneous with respect to weight across time. Indeed, there is less variability in the *predicted* weight of the daughters (compare the second and fourth columns in Table 6.3). However, the fact that the predicted scores are closer to the mean and have less variance should *not* lead you to an erroneous conclusion. Because we found in our sample that s_X and s_Y were identical, as much variance exists in the daughters' *observed* weights as occurs in the mothers' observed weights.

Imperfect correlation is the source of regression towards the mean. Notice that when two variables are perfectly correlated, $\hat{Z}_Y = (1.00)Z_X$, no regression toward the mean will occur. But if $r_{XY} = 0.2$, the amount of regression will be substantial. These examples reaffirm that the weaker the relationship between two variables, the greater the regression towards the mean, or alternatively, the more the mean becomes the best predicted outcome for Y for any value of X. Furthermore, the smaller the correlation between X and Y, the smaller the variance of $\hat{Y}$ (the predicted dependent variable). We state without proof

$$s_{\hat{Z}_Y}^2 = r_{XY}^2$$

As the relationship between X and Y approaches zero, the variance of $\hat{Y}$ approaches zero as well, thereby accounting for the *apparent* homogenization of observations.

6.6   Comparing Two Regression Equations

Sometimes researchers are interested in whether the regression and correlation coefficients between a pair of variables, X and Y, are equal across two populations, 1 and 2. To find out, two statistical tests are available: a correlation difference test and a regression difference test. Whereas the regression difference test compares unstandardized coefficients (b_{YX}), the correlation difference test is equivalent to comparing standardized regression coefficients β^*_{YX}. Because standard deviations of variables may differ greatly across populations and thus differentially adjust these two types of regression coefficients, the two statistical tests may not always yield identical results. Researchers should consider performing both tests before drawing conclusions about two populations' similarities or differences.

Assuming that two independent random samples of size N_1 and N_2 are drawn from the two populations, the **correlation difference test** takes the null hypothesis that the correlations are equal across both populations, $H_0: \varrho_1 = \varrho_2$, and tests it against a two-tailed alternative, $H_1: \varrho_1 \neq \varrho_2$. The first step is to change both the *sample* correlations, r_1 and r_2, into Z scores using Fisher's r-to-Z transformation table in Appendix F. Then, choose an α level and compute the test statistic using the formula:

correlation difference test—a statistical test to determine whether two correlation coefficients differ in the population

$$Z = \frac{(Z_{r_1} - Z_{r_2}) - (Z_{\varrho_1} - Z_{\varrho_2})}{\sqrt{\dfrac{1}{N_1 - 3} + \dfrac{1}{N_2 - 3}}}$$

where

$Z_{r_1} - Z_{r_2}$ is the sample difference in Z-transformed correlation coefficients

$Z_{\varrho_1} - Z_{\varrho_2}$ is the hypothesized zero population difference

and $\sqrt{\dfrac{1}{N_1 - 3} + \dfrac{1}{N_2 - 3}}$ is the estimated standard error of the difference.

In the 1998 GSS, the correlation between years of education (X) and occupational prestige (Y) is $r_M = 0.474$ for 1,196 men, while the same pair of variables correlate $r_W = 0.538$ for 1,472 women. Appendix F indicates that $Z_{r_M} = 0.517$ and $Z_{r_W} = 0.604$. Therefore,

$$Z = \frac{(0.517 - 0.604) - 0}{\sqrt{\dfrac{1}{1{,}196 - 3} + \dfrac{1}{1{,}472 - 3}}} = -2.23$$

Because the critical value of Z at $\alpha = .05$ is ± 1.96, we reject the null hypothesis. That is, the education-occupational prestige correlation is probably stronger in the female population than in the male population. Our sample correlations reveal that education statistically explains $(0.538)^2 = 0.289$ of the variance in women's occupational prestige, but only $(0.474)^2 = 0.225$ of the men's variance.

The **regression difference test** takes the null hypothesis that the unstandardized regression coefficients are equal across the two populations, $H_0: \beta_1 = \beta_2$, and tests it against a two-tailed alternative, $H_0: \beta_1 \neq \beta_2$. In other words, it assesses the probability that the difference in population regression slopes is zero. Testing this hypothesis involves using the following t ratio:

regression difference test—a statistical test to determine whether two regression coefficients differ in the population

$$t = \frac{(b_1 - b_2) - (\beta_1 - \beta_2)}{\sqrt{s^2_{b_1} + s^2_{b_2}}}$$

In the two 1998 GSS subsamples, the coefficients for the bivariate regression of occupational prestige on education are $b_M = 2.15$ for men and $b_W = 2.59$ for women, and their respective standard errors are $s_{b_M} = 0.12$ and $s_{b_W} = 0.11$. Therefore,

$$t = \frac{(2.15 - 2.59) - (0)}{\sqrt{(0.12)^2 + (0.11)^2}} = -2.70$$

Because the critical value for a two-tailed t for these two large samples is ± 2.58 at $\alpha = .01$, we easily reject the null hypothesis that these regression coefficients are probably equal in the population. Instead, we conclude that each year of education produces a larger occupational prestige gain for women than for men, with less than one chance in a hundred of making a Type I or false rejection error.

Review of Key Concepts and Symbols

These key concepts and symbols are listed in the order of appearance in this chapter. Combined with the definitions in the margins, they will help you to review the material and can serve as a self-test for mastery of the concepts.

robust	a	σ_e^2
scatterplot	b_{YX}	$\hat{\sigma}_e^2$
predictor variable		
linear relationship	e_i	β^*_{YX}
bivariate linear relationship	$\hat{Y}_i$	$\hat{Z}_Y$
(bivariate regression)		
prediction equation	s_{YX}	$s^2_{\hat{Z}_Y}$
linear regression model	SS_{TOTAL}	
error term		
residual	$SS_{REGRESSION}$	
regression line	SS_{ERROR}	
ordinary least squares	R^2_{YX}	
bivariate regression coefficient		
covariance	r_{YX}	
computing formula for b	$r_{Z_Y Z_X}$	
intercept		
conditional mean	α	
regression sum of squares	β_{YX}	
error sum of squares		
total sum of squares	ϱ_{YX}	
coefficient of determination	ϱ^2_{YX}	
coefficient of nondetermination		
correlation coefficient	df_{TOTAL}	
mean squares	$df_{REGRESSION}$	
mean square regression	df_{ERROR}	
mean square error		
r-to-Z transformation	$MS_{REGRESSION}$	
population regression equation	MS_{ERROR}	
homoscedasticity	$\hat{\sigma}_Z^2$	
beta coefficient (beta weight)		
regression toward the mean	s_b	
correlation difference test	σ_b^2	
regression difference test		

PROBLEMS

General Problems

1. For the following data on 10 persons, construct a scatterplot showing the relationship between age and number of children, and describe the relationship in verbal terms.

Person (i)	Age (X_i)	Number of Children (Y_i)
1	42	5
2	26	2
3	38	2
4	23	1
5	21	0
6	19	0
7	79	6
8	25	2
9	75	4
10	67	3

2. Using data from 60 adults, a community sociologist wants to estimate an equation for the linear relationship between number of friends in the community (X) and community involvement (Y). He has the following statistics: $\bar{X} = 8$, $s_X^2 = 16$, $\bar{Y} = 19$, $s_Y^2 = 25$, $s_{XY} = 36$. Estimate the unstandardized regression equation. Give a substantive interpretation of the sociologist's findings.

3. The 1998 General Social Survey asked respondents to rate their political views on a scale from 1 ("extremely liberal") to 7 ("extremely conservative"). Regressing political views on age generates the following prediction equation: $\hat{Y}_i = 3.68 + 0.009X_i$. Using this equation,

   a. How conservative would you expect an 80-year-old to be?

   b. How conservative would you expect a 20-year-old to be?

4. Fill in the missing values in the table below:

SS_{TOTAL}	$SS_{REGRESSION}$	SS_{ERROR}
a.	4,050	16,200
b. 72.60		32.39
c. 1,427	471.30	
d. 411.62	59.78	

5. A sociologist studying work and organizations hypothesizes that part of the variance in employees' work satisfaction can be attributed to its linear regression on variety of work responsibilities. Data from 42 employees produced $SS_{ERROR} = 5,500$ and $s_Y^2 = 175$ for the dependent variable. Compute R^2 for this bivariate equation and test whether this value is statistically different from zero at $\alpha = .01$. Display your findings in an ANOVA-type format and state your decision.

6. If $b_{YX} = 1.1$, $s_X = 0.8$, and $s_Y = 0.9$, what do r_{XY} and R_{YX}^2 equal?

7. Suppose a social psychologist collects the following data from five subjects: their scores on a test measuring the extent to which they trust other people and the number of altruistic acts they performed in the last month. Create a bivariate regression equation for these variables, treating altruistic acts as the dependent variable.

Subject	Trust	Altruistic Acts
1	70	5
2	85	8
3	92	12
4	64	3
5	79	7

8. For the data in question 7, calculate the correlation coefficient, the coefficient of determination, and the coefficient of nondetermination. What can you conclude?

9. If $N = 31$, $b_{YX} = 1.4$, and $s_b = .60$, test the null hypothesis that $b = 0$ in the population, using a one-tailed test with $\alpha = .05$.

10. Find β^* for the following:

b_{YX}	s_Y	s_X
a. 3.00	5.65	0.25
b. −6.39	78	8
c. 0.48	4.70	7.69

Problems Requiring the 1998 General Social Survey

11. Are older people more likely to pray than younger people? Regress PRAYFREQ on AGE and report the equation. Change the "Don't Know," "No Answer," and "Not Applicable" responses to missing values. Test whether the b coefficient is significantly different from zero in the population at $\alpha = .05$, one-tailed.

12. Do mothers' and fathers' attendance at religious services explain variation in the rate of church attendance? Regress ATTEND on ATTENDMA and ATTEND on ATTENDPA, and report both R_{YX}^2 and the F ratios for the test that H_0: $\varrho_{YX} = 0$, at $\alpha = .01$. Change the "Can't Say or Can't Remember," "No Father-Mother Present," "No Answer," and "Not Applicable" responses to missing values.

13. Does the parent's age at first child's birth explain the number of children he or she has? Regress CHLDS on AGEKDBRN. Change the "Don't Know," "No Answer," and "Not Applicable" responses to missing values. Report the correlation coefficient, standardized regression equation, and the t-test for β^*_{YX}, and whether you can reject H_0: $\beta^*_{YX} = 0$ at $\alpha = .001$.

14. Does a person's educational level explain the educational level of his or her spouse? Regress SPEDUC on EDUC, and report the unstandardized regression equation, the F test for the multiple R-square, and whether the sample b differs significantly from zero in the population at $\alpha = .01$. Change the "Don't Know," "No Answer," and "Not Applicable" responses to missing values.

15. Does income explain giving to nonreligious charitable organizations? Regress GIVEOTH on RINCOM98. Change the "Don't Know," "No Answer," and "Not Applicable" responses to missing values. Report R_{YX}^2 and the F ratio, setting $\alpha = .01$.

IV. MULTIVARIATE MODELS

7

THE LOGIC OF MULTIVARIATE
CONTINGENCY ANALYSIS

In our examination of relationships between two variables, we have discussed measures of association and tests of significance for both discrete and continuous variables. We presented tools to help you determine whether two variables systematically covary and whether the sample relationship is likely to reflect the population from which the sample was drawn.

For some research purposes, establishing the fact that two variables significantly covary may be sufficient. In most instances the fact that, for example, men usually have higher earned incomes than women, even in the same occupation, hardly needs to be verified again with a new set of data. But the researcher may want to explore the income difference as a consequence of other social factors, such as amount of education, work experience, employment status (full- or part-time), and employer discrimination. In such cases the research problem changes from the examination of a two-variable relationship to a consideration of three or more variables, as their relationships bear upon some theoretical issue. In this chapter we present some basic procedures for conducting **multivariate contingency analysis**, or statistical analysis of data on three or more variables, using both discrete and continuous variables. A more advanced treatment appears in chapter 10.

multivariate contingency analysis—statistical techniques for analyzing relationships among three or more discrete variables

7.1 Controlling Additional Variables

covariation—joint
variation, or association,
between a pair of variables

A basic reason for bringing additional variables into the analysis of the relationship between an independent and a dependent variable is to clarify the true relationship between them. **Covariation** between two variables can arise because of the confounding effects of other factors. To establish the true amount of covariation between two variables, we need to remove the part that is due to other factors.

In laboratory-type experiments, researchers remove the effects of other factors by applying an experimental design. Some additional variables can literally be "held constant" by making sure they apply uniformly to all subjects under experimental and control conditions. For example, in studying the effects of different amounts of fertilizer on the productivity of seed crops, we hold constant the effects of soil, water, and sunlight by making sure that all experimental plots contain the same type of soil, receive the same amounts of water, and have the same exposure to sunlight. Then we can be fairly sure that any plant growth differences we find would not be due to differences in these rival factors, which are known to affect crop growth. In a social experiment we might hold constant our methods of presenting stimuli to subjects and recording their responses.

random assignment—
in an experiment, the
assignment of subjects
to treatment levels on
a chance basis

Variables that might disturb a bivariate relationship can be controlled in experiments by **random assignment** of subjects to the different experimental treatments. For example, to study the effects of exercise on weight loss, we must try to eliminate such possible confounding effects as diet and metabolism rate. Clearly, the results of the experiment would not be credible if all the subjects eating low-fat diets had been exposed to high levels of exercise and the subjects eating high-fat diets to low levels of exercise. Because of the difficulty in obtaining subjects who have identical diets and metabolism rates, the preferred solution is to assign persons at random to exercise at different levels for a specified period of time before measuring their weight (including a control group that would not exercise). Random assignment to a treatment group might be made by flipping coins or by consulting a table of random numbers. The purpose of this procedure is to ensure that no experimental group differs, *on average*, from any other group in diet and metabolism rate before subjects begin their exercise program.

The technique of random assignment of subjects to experimental treatment groups helps to eliminate the confounding effect of rival factors. Thus, it helps isolate the true impact of the independent variable on the dependent measure. Unfortunately, all social behavior cannot be studied experimentally. In naturally occurring data such as that collected through sample surveys, other techniques for eliminating rival factors must be used. These techniques consist of identifying the additional variables likely to affect a relationship, measuring these factors, and "holding constant" their effects through statistical manipulation of the data.

Statistical control of rival factors differs from experimental control in that the researcher has no direct physical ability to shape the attributes of the persons or objects studied. The methods for controlling additional variables statistically adjust the data in an attempt to render the respondents equivalent on the rival factors, thereby eliminating their impact on the bivariate relationship of interest. Statistical controls are less powerful than randomization in eliminating the confounding effects of other variables for two reasons:

1. Measurement error, which is always present to some degree, reduces the precision with which statistical adjustments can be made.
2. Identification or inclusion of all potential rival factors may be impossible.

The second of these limitations suggests the extreme importance of theory in guiding social research. The decision to select some variables to be controlled statistically and not to consider others among the many possible candidates depends on our understanding of the role such variables play in the theory under investigation. For example, in studying the impact of religiosity on teenage premarital sexual behavior, we would be guided by theory and past research to control such factors as degree of parental supervision, academic ability, participation in school sex education programs, and peer group attitudes. But we would not try to adjust for the effects of eye color or food preferences.

The basic purpose of statistical controls is to eliminate, or at least reduce, the effect of confounding factors on a bivariate relationship. It is possible to distinguish three special applications that provide various means to control spuriousness, explanation, and multiple causes.

7.1.1 Spuriousness

An important point to remember in controlling additional variables is that *establishing covariation between two variables is not equivalent to proving causation*. Even if the independent variable is shown to change in time prior to a change in the dependent variable, the conditions for inferring a causal relationship are not complete. Besides time order and covariation, a causal inference must eliminate the possibility of **spuriousness** in the

spuriousness—covariation between two variables due only to the effect of a third variable observed relationship. (See chapter 11 for a more-detailed discussion on causal inference.) Two variables are spuriously related when the only reason they correlate is that both are caused by one or more other variables.

A classic illustration of a spurious relationship is the observation that, in Holland, communities where many storks nest in chimneys have higher birth rates than communities where fewer storks nest. While covariation and (probably) temporal-order conditions can be reasonably met, we should not conclude that storks cause babies, even if we have no knowledge of human reproduction, because we have not ruled out the possibility that the observed pattern is a spurious consequence of one or more rival factors that simultaneously affect both the number of babies and the number of storks. Storks and babies are more prevalent in rural than in urban areas. Pollution and sanitation levels, community attitudes toward human and animal life, and historical patterns of selective migration may all combine to create a spurious correlation between these two variables.

Take another classic case: The number of fire trucks called to a fire and the subsequent amount of damage done to buildings covary together. Can you figure out what rival factor(s) makes this a spurious, non-causal relationship?

These examples present clear-cut cases of spurious relationships that disappear when the appropriate common cause of both variables is held constant (by techniques described later). Less obvious cases of spurious relationships may occur in social behavior.

> When a covariation results because two variables have a common cause but are causally unrelated themselves, statistically holding constant the common factor (also called *partialling out* the effects due to other variables) eliminates the covariation observed in the data. If successive statistical controls for alleged common causes fail to alter the observed covariation, there are much firmer grounds than existed in the simple bivariate relationship for asserting the establishment of a causal relationship.

The variables chosen to control in these cases, of course, must be realistic candidates as causes of spuriousness. Social theory and past empirical research are indispensable sources of information about appropriate factors to control when examining covariation for spuriousness.

explanation/interpretation of association—covariation between two variables due to an intervening third variable

7.1.2 Explanation

Another reason for bringing additional variables into the analysis of bivariate relationships is to attempt an **explanation** or **interpretation** of an observed **association**. Two variables may be causally related, but the process may be more complex than the simple correlation implies. Controlling the relationship for variables representing the *intervening process* connecting the independent and dependent variables can deepen our understanding of the bivariate relationship.

For example, an inverse relationship between age and liberalism in personal morality is widely known to exist. That is, older persons tend to adhere to less permissive attitudes concerning child-rearing, sexuality, drug usage, and the like. One possible explanation for this relationship might be the degree of religiosity. Traditional religious values are more often found among older persons, both because they were raised in an era when such beliefs were strongly socialized (a generational or period process) and because as people age they may become more concerned about ultimate values (an aging process). Traditional religious doctrines contain many injunctions and prescriptions for belief and behavior in nonreligious matters. Hence, one reason older people may support less permissive morality is their greater religiosity, compared to younger people. (This explanation is commonly accepted by both religious leaders and social scientists.) By holding constant the level of religiosity, we might expect to reduce some or all of the observed covariation between age and personal morality beliefs.

Such an outcome would not imply that the two variables are spuriously related, but rather that the explanation for their covariation can be interpreted—at least in part—by a process in which greater age induces greater religiosity, which in turn restricts permissiveness in other areas. In a statistical sense both spuriousness and explanation are similar in that holding constant other variables eliminates or reduces the original bivariate association. But in a substantive sense the spuriousness and the interpretive analyses are quite different.

> A *spurious relationship* exists when the two original variables have no causal connection but are dependent on a common cause. An *explanatory* or *interpretive relationship* exists when the two original variables have a causal connection and additional intervening variables elaborate the understanding of that connection.

Figure 7.1 illustrates the conceptual difference played by a third factor that completely accounts for the observed covariation between variables *A* and *B* according to the two types of effects, spuriousness and explanation. In the case of spuriousness, *C* is a common cause of both variables, while in the case of explanation, *C* is an intervening factor that

FIGURE 7.1
Two Roles Played by a Third Variable in the Analysis of Bivariate Covariation

A. Spuriousness   B. Explanation

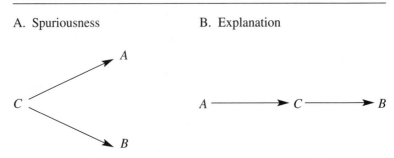

shows in greater detail how the causal effect of *A* is transmitted to *B*. An understanding of the role a third variable plays in explicating the covariation between two other variables is not revealed by the statistical pattern. *The proper understanding of whether spuriousness or explanation is implied by an analysis depends on the researcher's ability to draw on past research and theory to conceptualize the roles that third variables play.*

7.1.3 Multiple Causes

multiple causation—the view that social behavior is caused by more than one factor

Very few social theories, at least among those advanced since the nineteenth century, have posited that human behavior is due to a single factor. Instead, many suggest **multiple causation**; that is, they identify several variables as causally important in the explanation of the variation of some dependent variable. Some factors may carry important policy implications because their values may be subject to manipulation, such as through training programs or funding of services.

In this type of research the emphasis is not on the relationship between a single independent variable and the dependent measure, but on discovering the multiple, simultaneous relationships of several independent variables to the dependent measure(s) of interest. For example, in the study of social stratification, several researchers have developed and tested quite elaborate models of the status attainment process. An individual's earnings may be depicted as a consequence of the interplay of social background, education, occupation, industry, and other career variables. *By statistically controlling for several causal factors at the same time, the analyst can make some inferences about the relative importance of each factor for earnings, with spurious and explanatory relationships controlled.*

In this chapter we will lay the groundwork for analysis of multiple causes by investigating the basic techniques for statistically controlling a single, third variable in two-variable systems of categoric measures. The extension to more than three variables is straightforward, but we do not cover it in this chapter.

7.2 Controlling for a Third Variable in 2 × 2 Tables

As we noted in chapter 5, the simplest bivariate relationship can be examined by the crosstabulation of two dichotomous variables. Similarly, the basic principles of examining a bivariate relationship for the effects of other variables utilize a *three-variable crosstabulation*. To present these principles, we will describe the possible results of controlling for a third variable, illustrating different outcomes with purely hypothetical data.

7.2.1 A Hypothetical Example: Family Religiosity and Teenagers' Sexual Activity

To make the hypothetical example more meaningful, we will assume a relationship between family religiosity (X) and premarital sexual intercourse among teenagers (Y). The hypothetical data in Table 7.1 classify 192 responses by whether or not teenagers said they belonged to a "highly religious family" and whether or not they admitted to ever having sexual relations. Table 7.1 can be called a **zero-order table**, where *order* refers to the number of other variables held constant.

zero-order table— a crosstabulation of two variables in which no additional variables have been controlled

In this example, family religiosity is the independent variable and premarital sex is the dependent variable. For this reason we have percentagized the table on family religiosity; that is, the column percentages add up to 100. For these hypothetical data, nonreligious teenagers are considerably more likely to admit to premarital sex, at more than twice the rate of those who classify their families as religious. The correlation for this table is –0.26, indicating a moderate inverse relationship. To compute this and other correlations in this chapter, we have coded yes = 1 and no = 0. In addition, the formula used to calculate correlation coefficients

TABLE 7.1

Crosstabulation of Family Religiosity and Teenagers' Premarital Intercourse Variables, Hypothetical Data

		Family Highly Religious?		
		No	*Yes*	*Total*
Ever Premarital Sex?	*Yes*	42.9% (36)	16.0% (16)	27.1% (52)
	No	57.1% (56)	84.0% (84)	72.9% (140)
	Total	100.0% (92)	100.0% (100)	100.0% (192)

$$r_{XY} = -0.26$$

for 2×2 tables in this chapter is the formula for the phi coefficient (see section 5.3.2):

$$\varphi = \frac{bc - ad}{\sqrt{(a + b)(c + d)(a + c)(b + d)}}$$

We will consider whether this example's apparent causal relationship might be explained by the effects of other social processes that intervene between family religiosity and teenagers' premarital sexual experience. Suppose the provision of frequent opportunities to have sex is an important factor in determining whether a teenager actually has such an experience. Perhaps teenagers in more religiously oriented households are more likely to have their activities restricted by their parents. If this causal sequence exists, we would expect that when opportunity is statistically controlled, the relationship between religiosity and premarital sex might change.

Other possible outcomes could occur if the data in Table 7.1 were further crosstabulated by another dichotomy. In this hypothetical example, the control variable is whether or not the teenager has regular use of an automobile (*W*). Tables 7.2 to 7.5 illustrate four possible statistical patterns that might be found among these responses: no effect of a third variable, partial effect of a third variable, complete explanation by a third variable, and interaction effects of a third variable. Each result suggests a different interpretation about the original relationship (that interpretation

TABLE 7.2
Example of No Effect of a Third Variable, Hypothetical Data

		ACCESS TO A CAR?						
		No				*Yes*		
		Family Highly Religious?				*Family Highly Religious?*		
		No	*Yes*	*Total*		*No*	*Yes*	*Total*
	Yes	39.7% (25)	15.9% (11)	27.3% (36)	*Yes*	37.9% (11)	16.1% (5)	26.7% (16)
Ever Premarital Sex?	*No*	60.3% (38)	84.1% (58)	72.7% (96)	*No*	62.1% (18)	83.9% (26)	73.3% (44)
	Total	100.0% (63)	100.0% (69)	100.0% (132)	*Total*	100.0% (29)	100.0% (31)	100.0% (60)
			$r_{XY} = -0.27$				$r_{XY} = -0.25$	

will be discussed in sections 7.2.2 through 7.2.5). Each pair of these tables is called a **first-order table**, since the number of other variables held constant is one.

7.2.2 No Effect of a Third Variable

In Table 7.2 the original 2×2 table has been split into two *subtables*, each resembling the original table in general form but with different cell frequencies. We now have a $2 \times 2 \times 2$ table. Notice that the cell and marginal frequencies of the two subtables, when added pairwise, must exactly equal the frequencies in the original 2×2 table. As the total N's for both subtables show, about two-thirds of the teenager sample do not have regular use of an automobile. All respondents within the same subtable have the same level on the car access variable; that is, all 132 persons in the first subtable have no regular access and all 60 in the second subtable do have regular access. Thus, each subtable "holds constant" the variation in the third factor, permitting us to observe what happens to the covariation between the other two variables.

Note that in the example introduced with Table 7.1, the relationship between religiosity and sexual experience remains unchanged in Table 7.2. Both subtables of Table 7.2 show teens from highly religious fami-

first-order table— a subtable containing the crosstabulation or covariation between two variables, given a single outcome of a third, control variable

lies having sexual intercourse less than half as often as the other teenagers. The percentages are not noticeably different across the two subtables. Among teenagers without cars, $r_{XY} = -0.27$, and among teenagers with cars, $r_{XY} = -0.25$. These values are called **conditional correlation coefficients** because they refer to correlations under certain conditions of the third variable.

conditional correlation coefficients—correlation coefficients calculated between two crosstabulated variables within each category of a third variable

If both first-order relationships in the two subtables are of the same magnitude in the original zero-order relationship, we would conclude that opportunity—at least as operationalized by use of a car—has *no effect* on the original covariation. When such patterns are found, attention must be directed elsewhere for an explanation of why religiosity and premarital sex are related.

An alternative way to analyze the data is to compute odds ratios for the data in Tables 7.1 and 7.2. If access to a car has no effect on the relationship between premarital sex and religiosity, we would expect the odds ratios (see section 5.4) in the subtables of Table 7.2 to be approximately equal to the odds ratios for Table 7.1. The odds ratio for Table 7.1 is $(36)(84)/(16)(56) = 3.38$, while the odds ratio for the subtable associated with no access to a car in Table 7.2 is $(25)(58)/(11)(38) = 3.47$ and the odds ratio for those with access to a car is $(11)(26)/(5)(18) = 3.18$. For these hypothetical data, *regardless of access to a car*, teens who come from irreligious families are more than three times as likely to engage in premarital sex as those who come from highly religious families.

7.2.3 Partial Effect of a Third Variable

Table 7.3 demonstrates another possible result when a third variable is held constant. In this case we can see that the magnitude of the association between religiosity and premarital sexual experience is the same in both subtables, but it is somewhat weaker than in the original 2×2 table. The conditional correlation coefficients are -0.16 and -0.17, respectively, for no regular access and regular access to a car. We can conclude that opportunity, as measured by regular use of an automobile, partially accounts for the association observed originally between the other two variables.

To understand what this partial explanation means, consider the percentages within each subtable. Among persons who are *not* from highly religious families, those who are able to use a car regularly are twice as likely to have had sex as those without access to a car (53.3% to 25.5%). Similarly, among teenagers from highly religious homes, those with access to a car are more than twice as likely to have had sex as those lacking such access (33.3% to 12.9%). However, the opportunity to use a car does not eliminate all the differences in sexual experience between the

TABLE 7.3
Example of Partial Effect of a Third Variable, Hypothetical Data

		ACCESS TO A CAR?						
		No				*Yes*		
		Family Highly Religious?				*Family Highly Religious?*		
		No	*Yes*	*Total*		*No*	*Yes*	*Total*
	Yes	25.5%	12.9%	17.4%	*Yes*	53.3%	33.3%	48.3%
Ever		(12)	(11)	(23)		(24)	(5)	(29)
Premarital								
Sex?	*No*	74.5%	87.1%	82.6%	*No*	46.7%	66.7%	51.7%
		(35)	(74)	(109)		(21)	(10)	(31)
	Total	100.0%	100.0%	100.0%	*Total*	100.0%	100.0%	100.0%
		(47)	(85)	(109)		(29)	(31)	(31)

$$r_{XY} = -0.16 \qquad\qquad\qquad r_{XY} = -0.17$$

teens in religious and nonreligious families. Teens from nonreligious families are still more likely to have had sex than teens from religious families, regardless of access to a car, but the differences have been diminished somewhat from that found in Table 7.1, where opportunity was not held constant. Hence, if these results were found, we would conclude that opportunity explains *part* of the association between religiosity and premarital sex, but considerable covariation still remains to be accounted for by other factors not yet held constant.

7.2.4 Complete Explanation by a Third Variable

Table 7.4 shows what the data might look like when the third variable *completely accounts for the association* observed in the zero-order table. The correlations in both subtables (which you should check for yourself) are exactly zero, indicating that with each opportunity level held constant, no differences in sexual experience occur between the teens from highly religious and nonreligious families. Without regular access to a car, only 11.1% of the teenagers have had premarital intercourse, whereas among those with regular use of a car, two-thirds have had intercourse. The reason that the strong inverse relationship between family religiosity and sex

TABLE 7.4
Example of Complete Explanation by a Third Variable, Hypothetical Data

		ACCESS TO A CAR?							
		No				*Yes*			
		Family Highly Religious?				*Family Highly Religious?*			
		No	*Yes*	*Total*		*No*	*Yes*	*Total*
	Yes	11.1%	11.1%	11.1%	*Yes*	66.7%	66.7%	66.7%
Ever		(4)	(8)	(12)		(32)	(8)	(40)
Premarital								
Sex?	*No*	88.9%	88.9%	88.9%	*No*	33.3%	33.3%	33.3%
		(40)	(80)	(120)		(16)	(4)	(20)
	Total	100.0%	100.0%	100.0%	*Total*	100.0%	100.0%	100.0%
		(44)	(88)	(132)		(48)	(12)	(60)
		$r_{XY} = 0.00$				$r_{XY} = 0.00$		

appeared in the zero-order table is apparent from the marginal distributions in the two subtables: more than half of the nonreligious-background youths regularly use a car, but only one out of eight religious-background teenagers have regular access to a car. If we found such clear-cut patterns in real data, we would probably conclude that opportunity does explain the association. That is, a teenager's family religiosity determines the access he or she has to the family car (an opportunity process, in the sense that more religious parents are stricter about letting their children go on unchaperoned dates). In turn, the opportunity that use of a car permits is the major determinant of having premarital sexual intercourse.

As an alternative to computing the correlations in the subtables, one can easily compute the odds ratios (see section 5.4), which both equal 1.00, as they should, since access to a car explains the relationship between religiosity and premarital sex.

Why does holding access to automobiles constant explains the relationship of family religiosity to teenagers' premarital sex in Table 7.4 but not in Table 7.2? To find the answer, consider how access is related to the other two measures. As an exercise, form two tables, one showing the covariation between access and religiosity, the other showing the covariation between access and premarital sex. (Use the marginal totals in the columns and the rows of the subtables.) You will find that in the "no effects" situation (Table 7.2), access is virtually uncorrelated with both other variables. Holding access constant can do nothing to alter the relationship between religiosity and premarital sex. But in the "explanation" situation (Table 7.4), access (W) is strongly correlated with both variables, positively with premarital sex ($r_{WY} = 0.60$) and inversely with family religiosity ($r_{WX} = -0.43$).

Thus, by holding constant the level of automobile use, the inverse covariation between the other two variables is reduced to zero. This situation is of greatest importance in trying to find statistical explanations for observed associations among pairs of variables. *A third variable can produce an explanation for the covariation between two others only if it has nonzero relationships with both of the other variables.* If the original bivariate association is positive, the control variable must be positively associated with both the independent and dependent variables. If the original bivariate association is inverse, the control variable must be positively associated with one and inversely associated with the other, as in the example in Table 7.4.

Notice that the pattern in the first-order tables in Table 7.4 is the same as what we would find if the covariation of the original two variables were spurious. That is, in both explanation and spuriousness, when the rival factor is held constant, the first-order associations between the two variables fall to zero. Whether you should regard such statistical results as indicating an explanation of the original association or as revealing a spurious original association depends on your understanding of the causal role of the factor that is held constant. In the hypothetical example we regarded opportunity as an intervening process—that is, as a consequence of religiosity in the household and as a cause itself of premarital sexual experience. A different substantive variable that had a similar statistical effect of reducing the first-order correlations to zero might lead to an evaluation of the religiosity-sex association as spurious. For example, if we had achieved the same results as Table 7.4, where the variable held constant was family structure (such as whether the teenager lived in a two-parent family), we probably would be inclined to describe the relationship as spurious, if we reasoned that two-parent families would tend to be more strict in all kinds of personal behavior—religious, sexual, educational—than would single-parent families. Hence, the association of religiosity with premarital sex would reflect not a causal relationship but a more general pattern of morality stemming from the family condition.

Our discussion of the differences between explanation and spuriousness in bivariate associations controlled for the effects of third variables should alert you to the fact that the finding is not determined by the

TABLE 7.5
Example of Interaction Effect of a Third Variable, Hypothetical Data

		ACCESS TO A CAR?							
		No				Yes			
		Family Highly Religious?				*Family Highly Religious?*			
		No	*Yes*	*Total*		*No*	*Yes*	*Total*
Ever Premarital Sex?	*Yes*	50.0% (26)	11.8% (8)	28.3% (34)	*Yes*	25.0% (10)	25.0% (8)	25.0% (18)
	No	50.0% (26)	88.2% (60)	71.7% (86)	*No*	75.0% (30)	75.0% (24)	75.0% (54)
	Total	100.0% (52)	100.0% (68)	100.0% (120)	*Total*	100.0% (40)	100.0% (32)	100.0% (72)
		$r_{XY} = -0.42$				$r_{XY} = 0.00$		

statistical outcome. As with most situations, an understanding of social behavior requires thinking carefully about the meaning behind statistical relationships. A good grasp of basic social theory and previous empirical research, plus a little common sense, are helpful in this task.

7.2.5 Interaction Effect of a Third Variable

Table 7.5 shows another result from controlling a 2×2 table, which occurs with some frequency. The first-order associations differ substantially in the two subtables. In the example, the correlation between family religiosity and premarital sex for teens with access to a car is zero, but the correlation is –0.42 among those without access to a car. The use of odds ratios makes the interpretation of the interaction effect clear. For those who have access to a car, coming from a less than highly religious family has no effect on the likelihood of engaging in premarital sex; that is, the odds ratio equals 1.00, as it must whenever a correlation is zero. By contrast the odds ratio, if one does not have access to a car, is 7.5. That is, if one does not have access to a car and comes from a less than highly religious family, one is 7.5 times as likely to engage in premarital sex compared to someone who does not have access to a car and comes from a highly religious family. Holding constant the third variable reduces the association in one subtable but increases it in another. At times we can even find conditional correlations with opposite signs.

Whenever the relationships in subtables are not the same, an **interaction effect** is present. That is, *the association between two variables in each partial table differs when controlling for a third variable.* We cannot describe the effect of the third variable, as we did in the other three examples, by reference to a single type of outcome. Instead, we must specify which subtable we are referring to in describing the effect of the controlled variable.

The discovery of an interaction is often just the beginning for further analysis. It cries out for the researcher to provide an explanation of why the variables have different covariations for different levels of the third variable.

interaction effect—the association between two variables in each partial table differs when controlling for a third variable

7.2.6 Summary of Conditional Effects

Because graphing results often makes tabular results clearer, the results found in Tables 7.2 to 7.5 are diagrammed in Figure 7.2. Panel A, for example, shows clearly that having access to a car has no effect on the relationship between family religiosity and premarital sex—the lines are virtually identical for each category of access. Panel B, however, shows that *both* family religiosity and access to a car affect the rates of premarital sex. Both variables make independent contributions to explaining premarital sex. The large difference between the lines for access and no access indicates that availability of a car affects the percentage of teenagers ever having premarital sex. But the fact that each line still has a negative slope, across religious and nonreligious family membership, shows that religiosity has an independent effect on premarital sex; therefore, car access provides only a partial explanation. In Panel C the relationship between family religiosity and premarital sex is seen to be spurious, because, when car access is controlled, the slope of both lines is zero across family religiosity. An interaction effect is shown in Panel D; for those with car access, no relationship occurs between family religiosity and premarital sex. In contrast, for those without such access, there is a negative relationship between family religiosity and premarital sex.

One noteworthy point illustrated in Figure 7.2 is that *if there is no interaction effect, the relationship between the independent and dependent variables within categories of the control variables is the same.* Therefore, when the relationship is graphed, it is shown by parallel lines. The relationships in Panels A and C are shown by two parallel lines because

FIGURE 7.2
Examples of Conditional Effects, Hypothetical Data (Tables 7.2 to 7.5)

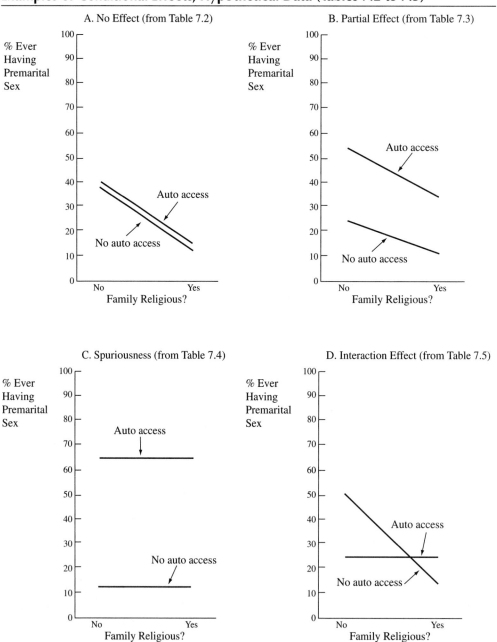

A. No Effect (from Table 7.2)

B. Partial Effect (from Table 7.3)

C. Spuriousness (from Table 7.4)

D. Interaction Effect (from Table 7.5)

there is no interaction between the independent and control variables. In contrast, the lines in Panel B are not quite parallel, indicating the partial effect, while the lines in Panel D are *not* parallel, indicating that an interaction effect does exist.

We deliberately chose the four examples above to give a clear-cut picture of different outcomes that might be found when a simple 2×2 relationship is controlled by a third variable. These illustrations were created to show ideal conditions. We cannot caution you too strongly that such exaggerated results are not likely to be found in most real data situations. In our personal experience we have almost never discovered a situation such as that shown in Table 7.4, in which a strong bivariate relationship completely disappeared when a single third variable was held constant. Partial effects (Table 7.3) or interaction effects (Table 7.5) are more likely to be found. Social behavior is seldom so simple that controlling for a single additional variable fully accounts for the observed two-variable relationship.

We did not compute significance tests on the zero-order relationships reported in this section, but had the data been real, we would have done so. We make such computations in the next section, where we show how statistical tests may be applied to three-variable crosstabulations, using examples from authentic GSS data.

7.3 The Partial Correlation Coefficient

Analyzing relationships of three variables together calls for computing the conditional correlation coefficients for each crosstabulation, as we did in section 7.2. When no interaction effects are present, a single coefficient that is a weighted average of the conditional correlation coefficients can be computed. This is called the **partial correlation coefficient**, given by

$$r_{XY \cdot W} = \frac{r_{XY} - r_{XW} r_{YW}}{\sqrt{1 - r_{XW}^2}\ \sqrt{1 - r_{YW}^2}}$$

Read the term $r_{XY \cdot W}$ as "the partial correlation between X and Y, controlling for (or in the presence of) W." Notice that the computation of $r_{XY \cdot W}$ requires first computing the three zero-order correlations, r_{XY}, r_{XW}, and r_{YW}.

A casual inspection of the formula for the partial correlation coefficient does not clearly reveal that it produces a correlation between two variables, controlling for a third. To clarify this measure of association we will use a visual presentation called the **Venn diagram**. In Figure 7.3 we have represented correlations of 0, 0.5, and 1.0 with three diagrams. In

partial correlation coefficient—a measure of association for continuous variables that shows the magnitude and direction of covariation between two variables that remains after the effects of a control variable have been held constant

Venn diagram—a type of graph that uses overlapping shaded circles to demonstrate relationships or covariation among a set of variables

FIGURE 7.3
Venn Diagrams Showing Correlation Between Two Variables

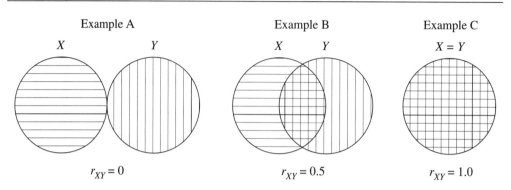

Panel A, where X and Y are uncorrelated, the two circles do not overlap at all. When the two are correlated so that $r_{XY} = 0.5$, as in Panel B, half the total area of Y overlaps with X. Perfect correlation is represented by the total overlap of X and Y in Panel C.

Now let us consider the interrelationship among three variables, W, X, and Y, using the Venn diagrams in Figure 7.4. Note that the three circles in Panel A are drawn to indicate that X and Y are correlated and so are X and W, but W and Y are *un*correlated. This diagram suggests clearly that controlling for W should not reduce the correlation between X and Y, since W does not intersect the $X - Y$ overlap. Now look at the numerator of the formula for the partial correlation coefficient. If Y and W are uncorrelated, as in Panel A, the numerator is $r_{XY} - (r_{XW})(0) = r_{XY}$. That is, the intuition drawn from the Venn diagram is correct: To reduce or "explain" the X, Y correlation, it is necessary for W to correlate with *both* X and Y.

Now consider Panel B in Figure 7.4. In this case the entire overlap between X and Y is also intersected by W. In correlational terms, this means that the entire correlation between X and Y can be explained by taking W into account. This situation occurs in partial correlation whenever $r_{XY} = (r_{XW})(r_{YW})$, since the numerator of the partial correlation coefficient equation, which is $r_{XY} = (r_{XW})(r_{YW})$, equals zero.

The typical situation is shown in Panel C in Figure 7.4. In this case one part of W intersects the X, Y crosshatch. Therefore, controlling for W does not entirely account for the correlation between X and Y. While the partial correlation $r_{XY \cdot W}$ will be smaller than the zero-order correlation r_{XY}, it will not be zero.

FIGURE 7.4
Venn Diagrams Showing Interpretation of $r_{XY \cdot W}$

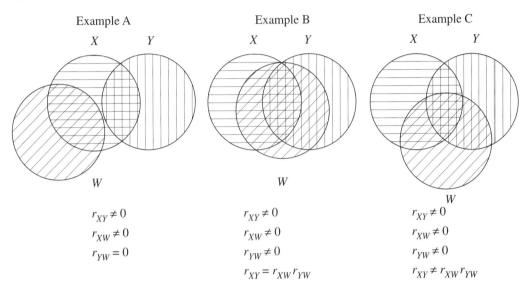

The squared partial correlation coefficient indicates the amount of variance in Y "explained" by X, controlling for W. If W is uncorrelated with either X or Y, r^2_{XY} and $r^2_{XY \cdot W}$ will be virtually the same. If, however, W is correlated with both X and Y, $r^2_{XY \cdot W}$ will usually be smaller than r^2_{XY}. That is, a lesser amount of variance in Y is explained by X, with W being taken into account.

7.3.1 An Example: Relationships Among Three Variables

To show how to use the partial correlation coefficient, we will consider the relationships between public drinking, premarital sexual attitudes, and gender from the 1998 GSS data set. Example A in Table 7.6 presents the zero-order relationship between visiting a public drinking place (X), such as a bar or tavern, and attitude toward premarital sexual intercourse (Y). The latter, originally a four-category response, has been collapsed into a dichotomy between those who think it is "always" or "almost always" wrong and those who are more tolerant.[1]

---

[1]We have collapsed this variable only to simplify our illustration. In an actual analysis of these data we would not have done so, since it will cause us to lose some valuable information.

Table 7.6
Zero-Order Relationships Between Public Drinking, Premarital Sex, and Gender

EXAMPLE A		Visit Bar (X)		
		Never	Yes	Total
Premarital Sex (Y)	Wrong	50.7% (443)	21.5% (198)	35.7% (641)
	Not Wrong	49.3% (431)	78.5% (724)	64.3% (1,155)
	Total	100.0% (874)	100.0% (922)	100.0% (1,796)

$$r_{XY} = 0.305$$

EXAMPLE B		Gender (W)		
		Male	Female	Total
Premarital Sex (Y)	Wrong	29.6% (232)	40.4% (409)	35.7% (641)
	Not Wrong	70.4% (552)	59.6% (603)	64.3% (1,155)
	Total	100.0% (784)	100.0% (1,012)	100.0% (1,796)

$$r_{YW} = 0.112$$

EXAMPLE C		Gender (W)		
		Male	Female	Total
Visit Bar (X)	Never	41.8% (328)	54.0% (546)	48.7% (874)
	Yes	58.2% (456)	46.0% (466)	51.3% (922)
	Total	100.0% (784)	100.0% (1,012)	100.0% (1,796)

$$r_{XW} = 0.120$$

Source: 1998 General Social Survey.

As Table 7.6 shows, these two variables are strongly related. Suppose we set $\alpha = .05$. The zero-order correlation coefficient is $r_{XY} = 0.305$, with $t = 13.55$. Therefore, we reject the null hypothesis that in the population $\varrho_{YX} = 0$ and conclude instead that those who claim never to drink in public places are considerably more likely to view premarital sex as wrong, but perhaps women are more likely than men to be intolerant of both public drinking and premarital sex.

To test for this possibility, we introduce gender (W) as a control variable. These zero-order tables are also shown in Table 7.6. In Example B the zero-order correlation of $r_{YW} = 0.112$ indicates that women are more likely than men to see premarital sex as wrong. Moreover, in Example C the zero-order correlation of $r_{XW} = 0.120$ suggests that women are less likely to visit a bar than men are. (Both of these zero-order correlations are significant at the $\alpha = .05$ level, with t values of 4.78 and 5.13.)

Now we can compute the partial correlation coefficient

$$r_{XY \cdot W} = \frac{0.305 - (0.120)(0.112)}{\sqrt{1 - (0.120)^2} \sqrt{1 - (0.112)^2}} = 0.296$$

That is, controlling for gender reduces the zero-order relationship between public drinking and attitudes toward premarital sex from 0.305 to 0.296—a very small amount. Hence, we would conclude that the relationship between public drinking and attitude toward premarital sex cannot be explained by gender.

7.3.2 Testing the Partial Correlation for Significance

We have computed a partial correlation coefficient, but we have not tested whether it is statistically significant. To do this we establish the null hypothesis, $H_0: \varrho_{XY \cdot W} \geq 0$, and the alternative hypothesis, $H_0: \varrho_{XY \cdot W} < 0$. Thus, we expect the relationship to be negative.

The test for the partial correlation is

$$F_{1, N-3} = \frac{r^2_{XY \cdot W}(N - 3)}{1 - r^2_{XY \cdot W}}$$

or, by taking the square root of the right side of the equation, the expression for a t test is

$$t_{N-3} = \frac{r_{XY \cdot W} \sqrt{N - 3}}{\sqrt{1 - r^2_{XY \cdot W}}}$$

Using the results from the example in section 7.3.1 and setting $\alpha = .05$, we find

$$F_{1,793} = \frac{(0.296)^2(1,796 - 3)}{1 - (0.296)^2} = 172.18$$

or

$$t_{793} = 13.12$$

Because the critical value for the *t* test is −1.65 for a one-tailed test, the null hypothesis can be confidently rejected. That is, we infer that in the population, visiting bars and premarital sexual attitude are correlated, even after holding gender constant.

Review of Key Concepts and Symbols

These key concepts and symbols are listed in the order of appearance in this chapter. Combined with the definitions in the margins, they will help you to review the material and can serve as a self-test for mastery of the concepts.

multivariate contingency analysis

covariation

random assignment

spuriousness

explanation (interpretation) of association

multiple causation

zero-order table

first-order table

conditional correlation coefficients

interaction effect

partial correlation coefficient

Venn diagram

$r_{XY \cdot W}$

PROBLEMS

General Problems

1. Consider the following two hypotheses. What type of causal relationship is expressed by these hypotheses? Diagram the relationship.

   a. Married partners who spend more time interacting with each other are more likely to respond to their partners' communication cues.

   b. Couples' satisfaction with their marital relationships increases with increased partner response to communication cues.

2. Suggest how a positive covariation between an employee's perceived job security and income could be spurious due to job seniority. Show this hypothesis as a causal diagram. What would you expect to happen to the correlation coefficient between perceived job security and income when seniority is held constant, if the spuriousness hypothesis is correct?

3. Suggest three interpretive relationships (by specifying potential intervening variables) for a causal connection between expensive political campaigns and candidates' success in winning elections. Use causal diagrams to illustrate the relationships you identify.

4. A three-way crosstabulation of gender, highest level of schooling, and attitude towards abortion yields the following partial frequency tables.

College Degree

		Men	Women
	Pro-Life	20	20
Attitude	*Pro-Choice*	25	30

High School Diploma

		Men	Women
	Pro-Life	40	30
	Pro-Choice	10	20

First, reconstruct the zero-order table for gender and abortion attitude. Then calculate the correlation coefficients and odds ratios for gender and abortion attitude for the zero-order relationship and for both partial tables. What kind of relationship is suggested by holding level of schooling constant?

5. A researcher hypothesizes that parents with school-aged children are more likely to vote in favor of a referendum increasing public school spending than adults without school-aged children, but wonders if this relationship holds for both Democrats and Republicans. Determine whether this hypothesis holds for the following data.

Democrats

		No Children	Children
	Yes	40	45
School Referendum	*No*	10	5

Republicans

		No Children	Children
	Yes	15	20
	No	35	30

Reconstruct the zero-order referendum attitude by parenting status table, and calculate the table's correlation coefficient. Then calculate the partial table correlations, and determine whether the hypothesis is correct.

6. Panel A is the zero-order table for the relationship of age to attitude towards forgiving the national debts of poor countries, and Panel B is the partial table of responses among highly religious persons.

| | | A. Zero-Order Table | | | B. Partial Table for Highly Religious | |
		Younger	Older		Younger	Older
Forgive Debts	Yes	40	30	Yes	25	20
	No	25	40	No	10	10

Calculate the zero-order correlation coefficient and the conditional correlation coefficients as well as the odds ratios. What kind of effect is observed when religiosity is held constant?

7. In the 1998 GSS, respondents were asked whether they had seen an X-rated movie in the last year and whether they believed that extramarital sex was wrong. The zero-order relationship for these variables is shown below.

| | | Seen X-rated film last year? | |
		No	Yes
Is extramarital sex wrong?	No	34	20
	Yes	590	187

Upon holding constant respondents' genders, the following partial tables are observed:

Seen X-rated film last year?

		Men				Women	
		No	*Yes*			*No*	*Yes*
Is	*No*	17	16		*No*	17	4
extramarital							
sex wrong?	*Yes*	235	120		*Yes*	355	67

Do these results support the hypothesis that the relationship between viewing X-rated films and attitude about extramarital sex can be completely explained by respondents' genders?

8. Calculate the partial correlation coefficients $r_{XY \cdot W}$ between X and Y after controlling for W.

	r_{XY}	r_{XW}	r_{YW}
a.	.20	.40	.60
b.	.10	.25	−.30
c.	.60	.35	.45
d.	.40	.70	.50

9. A researcher is interested in determining the partial correlation between age (X) and attitude towards interracial marriage (Y), controlling for place of residence (rural or urban) (W). The researcher finds the following correlations: $r_{XY} = 0.60$; $r_{XW} = 0.43$; $r_{YW} = 0.70$, for $N = 175$. Calculate the partial correlation coefficient and the t ratio. Set $\alpha = .05$. What should the researcher conclude?

10. A family social scientist surveys 100 adults and finds that the correlation between age at marriage (X) and subsequent divorce (Y) is $r_{XY} = -0.65$; that the correlation between age at marriage and socioeconomic status (SES) (W) is $r_{XW} = 0.75$; and that the correlation between divorce and SES is $r_{YW} = -0.17$. Calculate the partial correlation coefficient for the relationship between age at marriage and divorce, controlling for SES. Test the partial correlation coefficient for significance, setting $\alpha = .01$.

Problems Requiring the 1998 General Social Survey

11. Political analysts have noted that self-described liberals tend to be concentrated among the college educated, but this phenomenon may be a recent development. Test this hypothesis by dichotomizing POLVIEWS into conservative and nonconservative (moderate plus liberal) categories, EDUC into college graduates and nongraduates, and AGE into those 45 or younger versus older respondents. Change the "Don't Know," "No Answer," and "Not Applicable" responses to missing values. What happens to the POLVIEWS-EDUC correlation when AGE is held constant?

12. Attitudes toward abortion among single women (ABSINGLE) covary with religiosity (RELITEN), but is the strength of association the same for Catholics as for Protestants? Change the "Don't Know," "No Answer," and "Not Applicable" responses to missing values. (*Note:* Control for RELIG after excluding other categories.)

13. What is the correlation between subjective social class (CLASS) and attitude toward working if the financial reward would be unnecessary (RICHWORK)? Is the strength of this association the same when education is controlled? Dichotomize EDUC into college graduates (16 or more years) and nongraduates (less than 16 years). Change the "Don't Know," "No Answer," and "Not Applicable" responses to missing values.

14. What is the correlation between age (AGE) and attitude regarding whether aged adults should live with their children (AGED)? Dichotomize both AGE (18 through 59 = 1) (60 through 89 = 2) and FAMGEN (1, 2, 4, 5 = 1) (3, 6, 7 = 2). Recode the "Depends" response on AGED to missing values. Change the "Don't Know," "No Answer," and "Not Applicable" responses to missing values. How does this association change when FAMGEN, indicating whether an older third generation lives with the respondent, is controlled? State the zero-order correlation coefficient and the partial correlation coefficient.

15. Do people's attempts to transfer their religious beliefs to other aspects of their lives (RELLIFE) correlate with whether they favor or oppose sex education in the public schools (SEXEDUC)? What happens to this association when the number of children people have (CHILDS) is entered as a control variable? Dichotomize

these variables as follows: CHILDS (0 = 1) (1 through 8 = 2) and RELLIFE (1, 2 = 1) (3, 4 = 2). Change the "Don't Know," "No Answer," and "Not Applicable" responses to missing values. What are the zero-order and partial correlations between RELLIFE and SEXEDUC, with CHILDS held constant?

8

MULTIPLE REGRESSION ANALYSIS

Multiple regression analysis examines the joint relationship between a dependent variable and two or more independent, or predictor, variables. An extension of the bivariate methods introduced in chapter 6, it is the most widely applied version of the general linear model in contemporary social science. Therefore, the parameter estimation and significance testing procedures for the multiple regression model are the most important techniques described in this book, forming the foundation for more advanced methods described in later chapters.

Few social scientists today hypothesize that all the variation in some measure can be completely accounted for by its covariation with a single independent variable. Single-cause explanations, such as delinquency resulting from associating with deviant companions, have been largely replaced with complex accounts in which several unique sources of variation are posited. Thus, conflict between ethnic groups might be hypothesized to arise from competition for jobs, broad cultural, religious, and linguistic differences, income inequality, and exclusion from political power. Or, children's educational attainment may be a joint function of their parents' educational attainment, number of siblings, teacher encouragement, intellectual ability, personal aspirations, and peer pressures. The value of the multiple regression approach lies in its capacity to

multiple regression analysis—a statistical technique for estimating the relationship between a continuous dependent variable and two or more continuous or discrete independent, or predictor, variables

estimate the relative importance of several hypothesized predictors of the dependent variable of interest. Before presenting the regression model and the technical details involved in using it, we will describe a substantive problem for which regression techniques are appropriate.

8.1 An Example of a Three-Variable Regression Problem

High public confidence in the federal government is important for the continuing legitimization of political institutions in the United States. If citizens come to devalue and withdraw support from these constitutionally based structures, the government may have difficulty carrying out its mandated functions. Many types of beliefs, experiences, and events may promote or diminish confidence in governmental institutions. In this chapter, we examine the simultaneous impacts of two factors that influence citizens' confidence in the federal government. First, general ideological beliefs often affect orientations toward political institutions, with liberals more disposed to favor and conservatives more prone to oppose greater power for the national government. Therefore, the first proposition we will examine is

> P1: The more conservative the individual's political ideology, the lower the confidence in governmental institutions.

Because schooling typically provides the intellectual foundation for understanding and instilling support for democratic political principles, it should encourage citizens to value the core governmental institutions. The second proposition, therefore, is

> P2: The higher the individual's educational attainment, the greater the confidence in governmental institutions.

index—a variable that is a summed composite of other variables that are assumed to reflect some underlying construct

We will test these two hypotheses using the 1998 GSS data, in which confidence in governmental institutions is measured by a three-item index. An **index** is a variable that is a summed composite of other variables that are assumed to reflect some underlying construct. In this case the index is the sum of each individual's responses to three items, divided by three. The three items deal with attitudes toward the executive branch of the federal government, the U.S. Supreme Court, and the Congress. The 1998 GSS respondents were asked how much confidence they had in these three institutions (along with several others such as the press,

TABLE 8.1
Frequency Distributions for Three Items in Government Confidence Index

Code	Response	A. EXECUTIVE		B. JUDICIAL		C. LEGISLATIVE	
		N	%	N	%	N	%
1	Hardly any	671	36.4	267	14.8	571	31.0
2	Only some	909	49.3	950	52.5	1,071	58.1
3	A great deal	265	14.4	592	32.7	200	10.9
	Total	1,845	100.1*	1,809	100.0	1,842	100.0

*Does not sum to 100.0 due to rounding.
Source: 1998 General Social Survey.

business, and labor unions) and presented with three ordered response categories: "a great deal," "only some," and "hardly any." Table 8.1 shows the frequency and percentage distributions for the three governmental confidence items.

To construct an index, we must assume that the items composing it reflect some underlying latent, unobserved characteristic. In this case, we are assuming that people who have greater confidence in governmental institutions (the latent, unobserved factor) are more likely to say that they have a great deal of confidence in the executive, judicial, and legislative branches. In contrast, those persons who have little confidence in the federal government would be expected to indicate that they have hardly any confidence in these three branches. Figure 8.1 shows that we conceptualize the three observed GSS items as a function of a latent, unobserved theoretical **construct**—confidence in governmental institutions. Because

construct—unobserved concept used by social scientists to explain observations

FIGURE 8.1
Effects of Latent, Unobserved Variable on Covariation Among a Set of Observed Indicators

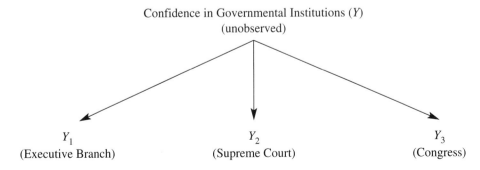

Confidence in Governmental Institutions (*Y*)
(unobserved)

Y_1
(Executive Branch)

Y_2
(Supreme Court)

Y_3
(Congress)

indicator—observable measure of an underlying unobservable theoretical construct

the three observed variables, or **indicators** as they are often called, are presumed to reflect a single underlying factor, we expect them to be positively correlated with each other. Indeed they are. In the 1998 GSS data, the correlations between confidence in the executive and judicial branches, the executive and legislative branches, and the judicial and legislative branches are 0.32, 0.40, and 0.39, respectively. These correlations provide some evidence that the three items can be used as a single index of confidence in governmental institutions. More details on index construction of this sort are given in Box 8.1, which also introduces the concept of **Cronbach's alpha**, a measure of internal reliability for multiple-item indices.

Cronbach's alpha— a measure of internal reliability for multi-item summed indexes

---

Box 8.1   An Introduction to Index Construction

Social scientists often use indexes constructed from other variables to reflect some underlying unobservable variable. Perhaps the most common example is the IQ test, with which you are familiar. Constructors of IQ tests assume that the responses to many individual items can be summed to a total score called IQ. Indices are often proxies for constructs, which social researchers find useful to explain observations. We do not really know if there is something called IQ, or religiosity, for example, but by positing such constructs we can account for observations in a succinct, logical, summary way.

When a set of indicators is posited to reflect an underlying construct, the items should be substantially correlated with one another. The higher the correlation among the items, the more confident we can be that the items are measuring the same construct. Furthermore, for a given level of correlation among the measures, the greater the number of indicators, the more confidence we can have in the index constructed from them. If five different people measure the length of an open field and the resulting five observations are averaged, we will be more confident about the true length of the field than we would if one person had made one measurement. For the same reason, our confidence in an index increases with the number of variables

(continued)

composing it. The important assumption, however, is that all the items do in fact reflect the same underlying construct. To summarize, *the quality of an index can be judged by the average intercorrelation among the indicators and by the number of indicators composing it.*

A statistic that summarizes the reliability of an index is Cronbach's alpha. It measures the internal consistency of a set of indicators, ranging from zero (no internal consistency) to unity (perfect internal consistency). The computing formula for Cronbach's alpha is

$$\alpha = \frac{k\bar{r}}{1 + (k - 1)\bar{r}}$$

where

k = The number of items in the index.
$\bar{r}$ = The average intercorrelation among the k items composing the index.

The formula reveals that increasing the number of items raises the scale's reliability and weaker interitem correlations decrease the reliability.

We demonstrate how to use alpha in the three-item example involving confidence in governmental institutions, discussed in the text. The $k = 3$ items intercorrelate 0.32, 0.39, and 0.40. Therefore, the average correlation is $\bar{r} = (0.32 + 0.39 + 0.40)/3 = 0.37$. And

$$\hat{\alpha} = \frac{3(0.37)}{1 + (3 - 1)(0.37)} = 0.64$$

where the caret (^) is used to indicate an estimate of the underlying population parameter.

Because this index is composed of only three items, an $\hat{\alpha}$ of 0.64 is barely acceptable. We strive for indices with alphas of 0.70 or higher. If we had six items with an average correlation of 0.40, we could use the formula to verify that $\hat{\alpha}$ would be 0.80. This computation demonstrates that the number of indicators, as well as their average intercorrelation, contributes to our confidence in an index.

Political ideology is measured by respondents' political views on a seven-point item ranging from extremely liberal (1) to moderate (4) to extremely conservative (7). Education is coded from 0, for no formal schooling, to 20, for eight years of college. The two hypotheses drawn from P1 and P2 to be tested are

H1: The more conservative the individual's political views, the lower the confidence in governmental institutions.

H2: The more the years of schooling, the greater the confidence in governmental institutions.

8.2 The Three-Variable Regression Model

As in the bivariate regression model introduced in section 6.1, the dependent variable in multiple regression is assumed to be linearly related to the independent variables. In the case of two independent variables, the three-variable *population regression equation* is

$$Y_i = \alpha + \beta_1 X_{1i} + \beta_2 X_{2i} + \varepsilon_i$$

where
α = The constant or intercept.
β_j = The regression coefficient showing the effect of independent variable X_j on dependent variable Y.
X_1 and X_2 = The two independent variables.
ε_i = The error or residual term for the ith case.

Then the population prediction equation is

$$\hat{Y}_i = \alpha + \beta_1 X_{1i} + \beta_2 X_{2i}$$

With two independent variables, the sample regression and prediction equations are given by

$$Y_i = a + b_1 X_{1i} + b_2 X_{2i} + e_i$$
$$\hat{Y}_i = a + b_1 X_{1i} + b_2 X_{2i}$$

ordinary least squares— a method for obtaining estimates of regression equation coefficients that minimize the error sum of squares

As in bivariate regression, we use **ordinary least squares** (OLS) methods to estimate values for α, β_1, and β_2, such that Σe_i^2 is a minimum.

We state without proof that the following sample values are unbiased estimates of the population parameters:

$$a = \bar{Y} - (b_1\bar{X}_1 + b_2\bar{X}_2)$$

$$b_1 = \left(\frac{s_Y}{s_{X_1}}\right)\frac{r_{YX_1} - r_{YX_2}r_{X_1X_2}}{1 - r^2_{X_1X_2}}$$

$$b_2 = \left(\frac{s_Y}{s_{X_2}}\right)\frac{r_{YX_2} - r_{YX_1}r_{X_1X_2}}{1 - r^2_{X_1X_2}}$$

Notice that the regression estimates can all be obtained if we simply know the sample means, standard deviations, and zero-order correlation coefficients for the three variables under investigation. Therefore, when performing a regression analysis, we must always compute and report these statistics in a summary table.

We have reported these values for the GSS confidence in governmental institutions example in Table 8.2. Notice that we have tabled only half the correlations, in the lower triangular portion of the matrix. Because $r_{XY} = r_{YX}$ for all X and Y, to show the upper triangle would be redundant. We also have tabled the sample data for political views and education. These data are used in examples later in this chapter.

In computing these and all other statistical estimates in the subsequent examples, we have used a **listwise deletion** procedure; that is, we have used an observation only if data on *all* variables being analyzed are present. The 1998 GSS has $N = 2,832$ cases. By using a listwise proce-

listwise deletion—in multiple regression analysis, the removal of all cases that have missing values on *any* of the variables

TABLE 8.2
Correlations, Means, and Standard Deviations Among Confidence in Governmental Institutions Index, Political Views, and Educational Attainment Variables

Variable		(Y)	(X_1)	(X_2)	Mean	Standard Deviation
Y	Confidence	1.000			1.927	0.491
X_1	Political Views	−0.075	1.000		4.150	1.370
X_2	Education	0.077	−0.048	1.000	13.340	2.770

Note: N = 1,700.
Source: 1998 General Social Survey.

pairwise deletion—in multiple regression analysis, the removal of a case from the calculation of a correlation coefficient only if it has missing values for one of the variables

dure we have lost 1,132 cases, resulting in $N = 1,700$ in Table 8.2. Most of these cases were lost because the GSS split-ballot questionnaire asked only half the respondents the three confidence items. The alternative to the listwise procedure is **pairwise deletion**. Because regression analysis depends on correlations for estimating regression coefficients, and because correlations are based on pairs of observations, we can use the available cases for each individual correlation coefficient.

Two potential problems arise with pairwise deletion. First, because the number of cases available varies from correlation to correlation, the N for any given problem is unclear. The N is crucial in computing tests of statistical significance. Second, the correlation matrix (table) generated by pairwise deletion in sample data is sometimes poorly conditioned, so the configuration of estimated correlations could not logically occur in the population. The technical details of this condition are beyond the scope of this text. Although an ill-conditioned correlation matrix is rarely generated when pairwise procedures are used, it can occur. When it does, the computer will be unable to obtain a solution for the regression estimates sought.

We recommend that pairwise deletion procedures only be used when a large loss of cases (roughly 5% or more) occurs when using a listwise procedure. The danger of using listwise deletion in such instances is the nonrandom loss of cases, which can produce biased estimates of population regression parameters. When a substantial missing data problem occurs for a variable, the researcher needs to show whether and how these missing cases might affect the analysis. The usual procedure is to show, using t tests, that the missing observations do not differ significantly from the observations that are present on major demographic characteristics such as gender, education, race, and so on. Showing that no significant differences exist for these variables is only partially reassuring, however, because we can never know for certain whether the missing data were generated by random or systematic processes. Can you think of some systematic ways that data losses might occur?

We can now apply the formulas presented previously to estimate the intercept and the two regression coefficients for political views and education, respectively, in the confidence in governmental institutions example. Because we need to know b_1 and b_2 to estimate the intercept, we estimate both regression coefficients, b_1 and b_2, prior to estimating a

$$b_1 = \left(\frac{0.491}{1.370}\right)\frac{-0.075 - (0.077)(-0.048)}{1 - (-0.048)^2} = -0.026$$

$$b_2 = \left(\frac{0.491}{2.770}\right)\frac{0.077 - (-0.075)(-0.048)}{1 - (-0.048)^2} = 0.013$$

$$a = 1.926 - [(-0.026)(4.15) + (0.013)(13.340)] = 1.860$$

Therefore, the prediction equation for this example is

$$\hat{Y}_i = 1.860 - 0.026X_1 + 0.013X_2$$

8.2.1 Interpretation of b_1 and b_2

The regression coefficients b_1 and b_2 have the following interpretation:

A **multiple regression coefficient** measures the amount of increase or decrease in the dependent variable for a one-unit difference in the independent variable, controlling for the other independent variable or variables in the equation.

multiple regression coefficient—a measure of association showing the amount of increase or decrease in a continuous dependent variable for a one-unit difference in the independent variable, controlling for the other independent variable(s)

In the confidence in governmental institutions example, the dependent variable ranges from 1 = "hardly any" to 3 = "a great deal." Thus, $b_1 = -0.026$ indicates that for a one-unit increase toward more conservative political views, a respondent's score on the confidence in governmental institutions index is expected to drop by -0.026 on average. And for each additional year of education, the respondent's confidence score is expected to increase by an average of 0.013, because $b_2 = 0.013$.

As we noted in describing the concept of control in chapter 7, if two independent variables are uncorrelated, controlling for one of them will not affect the relationship between the other independent variable and the dependent variable. This situation can be seen by noting that if $r_{X_1 X_2} = 0$, then

$$b_1 = \left(\frac{s_Y}{s_{X_1}}\right) \frac{r_{YX_1} - (r_{YX_2})(0)}{1 - 0^2}$$

$$= \left(\frac{s_Y}{s_{X_1}}\right) r_{YX_1}$$

This formula equals the bivariate regression coefficient, b, introduced in chapter 6. That is, when the two independent variables are uncorrelated, the relationship between one of them and the dependent variable is unchanged when controlling for the independent variable. In the confidence in governmental institutions example, $r_{X_1 X_2} = -0.048$, which is very close to zero. This value suggests that a bivariate regression coefficient relating an independent variable to the dependent variable should not differ much from its corresponding multiple regression coefficient. Only very small differences are indicated in the following table.

Independent Variable	Bivariate Coefficients	Multiple Regression Coefficients
Political Views	–0.027	–0.026
Education	0.016	0.013

8.2.2 Standardized Regression Coefficients (Beta Weights)

Because the measurement units of the dependent variable and political views are both arbitrary, the interpretation of the regression coefficients is less clear than might be desirable. For this reason we suggest that the standardized regression (beta) coefficients introduced in section 6.5 for the bivariate regression case be computed as well. We would obtain these *beta weights* if we converted the three variables to Z scores prior to estimating the regression equation.

Regardless of the number of independent variables, the following relationship exists between the metric coefficients and standardized regression coefficients (beta weights):

$$\beta^*_j = \left(\frac{s_{X_j}}{s_Y}\right) b_j$$

We simply multiply the metric regression coefficient by the ratio of the standard deviation of the independent variable X_j to the dependent variable Y. Hence, in the case of two independent variables, X_1 and X_2,

$$\beta^*_1 = \left(\frac{s_{X_1}}{s_Y}\right) b_1$$

$$\beta^*_2 = \left(\frac{s_{X_2}}{s_Y}\right) b_2$$

Using the data from the confidence in governmental institutions example, we have

$$\beta^*_1 = \left(\frac{1.370}{0.491}\right)(-0.026) = -0.073$$

$$\beta^*_2 = \left(\frac{2.770}{0.491}\right)(0.013) = 0.073$$

Because the means of Z-transformed variables are zero, the intercept for the standardized regression equation is zero. Hence,

$$\hat{Z}_Y = -0.073Z_1 + 0.073Z_2$$

The two independent variables are now in the same metric, so we can determine their relative ability to predict confidence in governmental institutions by examining which coefficient has the largest absolute value. In this example, the differences are zero, so we conclude that political views and education have equal impacts on confidence. For each standard deviation difference in political views, controlling for education, we can expect on average a –0.073-standard-deviation change in the confidence index. Similarly, for a one-standard-deviation difference in education, controlling for political views, the average confidence index score increases 0.073 standard deviation.

We still do not know how much of the variance in respondents' confidence in governmental institutions can be explained by these two independent variables. We also do not know yet whether either of these regression coefficients is statistically significant. In the following three sections we will consider these issues.

8.2.3 The Coefficient of Determination in the Three-Variable Case

We introduced the coefficient of determination $R^2_{Y \cdot X}$ in section 6.3.2 as the sum of squares due to regression ($SS_{REGRESSION}$) divided by the total sum of squares (SS_{TOTAL})

$$R^2_{Y \cdot X} = \frac{SS_{REGRESSION}}{SS_{TOTAL}}$$

We can use this same formulation to determine how much variance X_1 and X_2 can "explain" in the dependent variable Y.

An alternative formulation of the coefficient of determination is

$$R^2_{Y \cdot X} = \frac{\sum(Y_i - \bar{Y})^2 - \sum(Y_i - \hat{Y}_i)^2}{\sum(Y_i - \bar{Y})^2}$$

$$= \frac{SS_{TOTAL} - SS_{ERROR}}{SS_{TOTAL}}$$

because $SS_{TOTAL} = SS_{REGRESSION} + SS_{ERROR}$ and $SS_{REGRESSION} = SS_{TOTAL} - SS_{ERROR}$. In the bivariate case, $\hat{Y} = a + bX_i$, whereas in the case of two independent variables, $\hat{Y} = a + b_1 X_{1i} + b_2 X_{2i}$. This latter equation, therefore, must be substituted in the previous formula for $\hat{Y}_i$ in order to determine $SS_{REGRESSION}$.

Ordinarily the sum of squares due to regression will be larger in the multivariate case than in the bivariate case. It can *never* be smaller, because one reason for including additional independent variables is to explain additional variance in the dependent variable. Several computational formulas are available for $R^2_{Y \cdot X_1 X_2}$, four of which we present in this section. You should convince yourself that they all give identical numerical results.

The first two formulas for the coefficient of determination in the three-variable case are

$$R^2_{Y \cdot X_1 X_2} = \frac{r^2_{YX_1} + r^2_{YX_2} - 2r_{YX_1}r_{YX_2}r_{X_1X_2}}{1 - r^2_{X_1X_2}}$$

$$R^2_{Y \cdot X_1 X_2} = \beta^*_1 r_{YX_1} + \beta^*_2 r_{YX_2}$$

We have added subscripts to R^2 to clarify which independent variables are being used to predict the dependent variable. In the subscript, the predicted variable (Y) is on the left side of the dot and the predictor variables, X_1 and X_2, are on the right side of the dot.

We can use either of the preceding equations to compute the proportion of variance in confidence in governmental institutions that can be accounted for by political views and education. We will use the second formula because it involves fewer computations. Applying the GSS data in Table 8.2 and the beta weights calculated in the preceding section,

$$R^2_{Y \cdot X_1 X_2} = (-0.073)(-0.075) + (0.073)(0.077)$$

$$= 0.011$$

Thus, these two predictors account for just 1.1% of the variance in confidence. Given that almost 99% of the variance remains unexplained, a theoretical explanation that goes beyond these two simple propositions is obviously needed.

Two other formulations for the coefficient of determination are informative, not as computational formulas, but because they clarify the meaning of the coefficient. They are

$$R^2_{Y \cdot X_1 X_2} = r^2_{YX_1} + (r^2_{YX_2 \cdot X_1})(1 - r^2_{YX_1})$$

$$R^2_{Y \cdot X_1 X_2} = r^2_{YX_2} + (r^2_{YX_1 \cdot X_2})(1 - r^2_{YX_2})$$

These two equations indicate that with two independent variables, the coefficient of determination can be divided into two components. In the first equation the first component is the amount of variance in Y that X_1 alone can account for: $r^2_{YX_1}$. The second component is the additional

FIGURE 8.2
Venn Diagrams Showing Two Different but Equivalent Decompositions of $R^2_{Y \cdot X_1 X_2}$

A. $R^2_{Y \cdot X_1 X_2} = r^2_{YX_1} + (r^2_{YX_2 \cdot X_1})(1 - r^2_{YX_1})$

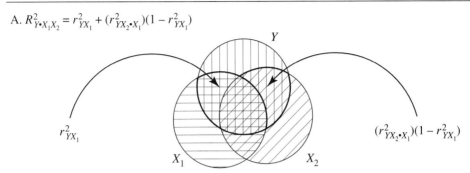

B. $R^2_{Y \cdot X_1 X_2} = r^2_{YX_2} + (r^2_{YX_1 \cdot X_2})(1 - r^2_{YX_2})$

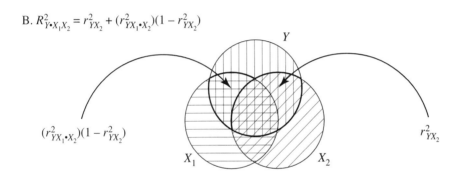

amount of variance in Y that X_2 alone can explain after controlling for X_1. This term, $(r^2_{YX_2 \cdot X_1})(1 - r^2_{YX_1})$, is the **part correlation** squared between Y and X_2, controlling for X_1. (Notice that the part correlation is the square of the partial correlation $(r_{YX_2 \cdot X_1})$, multiplied by the term $(1 - r^2_{YX_1})$. Hence, the part and partial correlations are intimately related.)

    Figure 8.2 uses Venn diagrams to examine how these two components relate to the coefficient of determination. Panel A, which diagrams the first equation, shows $(r^2_{YX_1})$ as the area of overlap between the Y and X_1 circles, including that portion of the Y and X_1 overlap that also overlaps X_2. And $(r^2_{YX_2 \cdot X_1})(1 - r^2_{YX_1})$ is shown as the overlap between Y and X_2, *excluding* that part of the Y and X_2 overlap that also overlaps X_1. In other words, we have first allocated to X_1 all the variance in Y that is *jointly contributed* by X_1 and X_2, and then we have added to it the variance in Y that is uniquely explained by X_2.

part correlation—
a measure of the proportion of variance in a dependent variable that an independent variable can explain, when squared, after controlling for the other independent variable in a multiple regression equation

An alternative but equivalent decomposition is shown in the second equation and in Panel B of Figure 8.2. This decomposition shows $r^2_{YX_2}$ as the overlap between the Y and X_2 circles, including that portion of the Y and X_2 overlap that also includes X_1. As in Panel A, the coefficient of determination also includes the amount of variance in Y that can be accounted for by X_1, controlling for X_2; that is, $(r^2_{YX_1 \cdot X_2})(1 - r^2_{YX_2})$.

These two alternative but equivalent formulas for $R^2_{Y \cdot X_1 X_2}$ make an important point

> When both X_1 and X_2 correlate with the dependent variable and are themselves intercorrelated, no unique way exists to partition the amount of variance in Y due to the two independent variables. However, when the two independent variables are uncorrelated, as they are in an experiment (or should be if the assignment of subjects to treatment conditions has indeed been random), we can uniquely partition the amount of variance in Y due to X_1 and X_2.

This difference in ability to partition variance is one reason that experimental research designs are preferable to nonexperimental procedures in social science research. When an experimental design is feasible and can be justified ethically, it provides a better method to determine the effects of independent variables on a dependent variable.

When X_1 and X_2 are uncorrelated, the total variance in Y can be uniquely partitioned into two segments, one due to X_1 and the other due to X_2. If, in the first formula for $R^2_{Y \cdot X_1 X_2}$, $r_{X_1 X_2} = 0$, then

$$R^2_{Y \cdot X_1 X_2} = \frac{r^2_{YX_1} + r^2_{YX_2} - 2r_{YX_1} r_{YX_2}(0)}{1 - 0^2}$$

$$= r^2_{YX_1} + r^2_{YX_2}$$

That is, if X_1 and X_2 are uncorrelated, the amount of variance each explains in Y is simply $r^2_{YX_1}$ and $r^2_{YX_2}$, respectively, and these two components sum to the coefficient of determination, $R^2_{Y \cdot X_1 X_2}$. This feature is shown with Venn diagrams in Figure 8.3.

The square root of the coefficient of determination is called the **multiple correlation coefficient**. Some researchers report $R_{Y \cdot X_1 X_2}$ in their articles, but because it has no clear meaning, the multiple correlation coefficient is less useful than $R^2_{Y \cdot X_1 X_2}$ as an interpretive statistic.

multiple correlation coefficient—the coefficient for a multiple regression equation, which, when squared, equals the ratio of the sum of squares due to regression to the total sum of squares

FIGURE 8.3
Venn Diagrams Showing the Decomposition of $R^2_{Y \cdot X_1 X_2}$ When X_1 and X_2 Are Uncorrelated

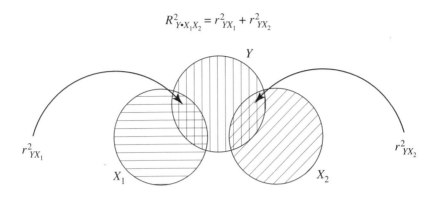

$$R^2_{Y \cdot X_1 X_2} = r^2_{YX_1} + r^2_{YX_2}$$

8.2.4 Testing the Significance of the Coefficient of Determination with Two Independent Variables

In section 6.4.1 for the bivariate regression, we tested $R^2_{Y \cdot X}$ for significance with an F test having 1 and $N - 2$ degrees of freedom. Where $\varrho^2_{Y \cdot X_1 X_2}$ is the coefficient of determination in the population with two independent variables, the null hypothesis is $H_0: \varrho^2_{Y \cdot X_1 X_2} = 0$. We will also test this hypothesis with an F test, although the degrees of freedom will differ from those in bivariate regression. The degrees of freedom associated with SS_{TOTAL} are $N - 1$, regardless of the number of independent variables. In the case of two independent variables, $SS_{REGRESSION}$ is estimated from the two regression coefficients and hence has 2 df associated with it. Because we know that, in general, $df_{TOTAL} = df_{REGRESSION} + df_{ERROR}$, by subtraction, $df_{ERROR} = N - 3$. You should be able to calculate this value for yourself.

We can compute the mean squares needed for the F test by dividing the sums of squares by the appropriate degrees of freedom. That is, with two independent variables,

$$MS_{REGRESSION} = \frac{SS_{REGRESSION}}{2}$$

$$MS_{ERROR} = \frac{SS_{ERROR}}{N - 3}$$

If the null hypothesis that $\varrho^2_{Y \cdot X_1 X_2} = 0$ in the population is true, both $MS_{\text{REGRESSION}}$ and MS_{ERROR} are unbiased estimates of the errors of prediction, σ^2_e. However, if $\varrho^2_{Y \cdot X_1 X_2}$ is greater than zero in the population, then $MS_{\text{REGRESSION}}$ is greater than MS_{ERROR} as well. If, in a given sample, the ratio of $MS_{\text{REGRESSION}}$ to MS_{ERROR} is larger than some predetermined critical value, we reject the null hypothesis that $\varrho^2_{Y \cdot X_1 X_2} = 0$ in the population.

Specifically, we choose an alpha level and calculate the following test statistic

$$F_{2, N-3} = \frac{MS_{\text{REGRESSION}}}{MS_{\text{ERROR}}}$$

We next look in Appendix E to determine the critical value for an F with 2 and $N - 3$ degrees of freedom at our chosen alpha level. If the test statistic is as large or larger than the critical value, we reject the null hypothesis that $\varrho^2_{Y \cdot X_1 X_2} = 0$ in the population; otherwise we do not reject it.

To calculate the mean squares for the F test statistic, we need to know the terms in the numerator and denominator, $MS_{\text{REGRESSION}}$ and MS_{ERROR}, respectively. We use the same logic that we followed in the bivariate case to estimate these sums of squares from sample data. Therefore,

$$SS_{\text{REGRESSION}} = R^2_{Y \cdot X_1 X_2} SS_{\text{TOTAL}}$$

and

$$SS_{\text{ERROR}} = SS_{\text{TOTAL}} - SS_{\text{REGRESSION}}$$

We can now ask whether the coefficient of determination observed in section 8.2.3, which was 0.011, is significantly different from zero in the population. We set $\alpha = .01$. An examination of Appendix E indicates that the critical value of F for 2 and 1,697 df is 4.61. To calculate the sums of squares, we note from Table 8.2 that $s_Y = 0.491$; therefore, the variance of the dependent variable Y in the sample is given by $s^2_Y = (0.491)^2 = 0.241$, with $N = 1,700$. Because, in general, $SS_{\text{TOTAL}} = s^2_Y(N - 1)$, it follows that

$$SS_{\text{TOTAL}} = (0.241)(1,700 - 1) = 409.46$$

$$SS_{\text{REGRESSION}} = (0.011)(409.46) = 4.50$$

$$SS_{\text{ERROR}} = 409.46 - 4.50 = 404.96$$

Next, we divide these estimates by their degrees of freedom to obtain the mean squares:

$$MS_{\text{REGRESSION}} = \frac{4.50}{2} = 2.25$$

$$MS_{\text{ERROR}} = \frac{404.96}{1,697} = 0.24$$

The test statistic is then

$$F_{2,1697} = \frac{2.25}{0.24} = 9.38$$

Because the estimated test statistic far exceeds the critical value, our decision is clear: reject the null hypothesis that the coefficient of determination is zero in the population from which the 1998 GSS sample was drawn. Although the linear effects of political views and education together account for only 1.1% of the variance in confidence in governmental institutions, we run a risk of just one chance in 100 that the population parameter $\varrho^2_{Y \cdot X_1 X_2} = 0$. The large survey sample N certainly helped us obtain a sufficiently robust R^2 to reject the null hypothesis. This example underscores the frequent observation that statistical significance does not always equal substantive importance.

8.2.5 Testing b_1 and b_2 for Significance

Two null hypotheses can be tested to decide whether the two regression coefficients are zero in the population. Both hypotheses assert that the population parameters are zero: $H_0: \beta_1 = 0$ and $H_0: \beta_2 = 0$. In this section we will first show how to test whether the estimated sample regression coefficient, b_1, is statistically significant and return later to the test of significance for b_2. However, the two tests are very similar.

To test whether the observed b_1 differs statistically from zero, we construct a t variable, just as we did in the bivariate regression case in chapter 6. In the three-variable case,

$$t = \frac{b_1 - 0}{s_{b_1}}$$

To obtain the t value, we need to estimate the standard error of the regression coefficient, s_{b_1}. If we assume that in the sample population the dependent variable, Y, is normally distributed for any joint outcome of X_1 and X_2, then the sampling distribution of b_1 (and of b_2 as well) is normally distributed as the sample N becomes larger. Furthermore, the mean of the sampling distribution of b_1 will equal β_1; that is, $E(b_1) = \beta_1$. The variance of the sampling distribution of b_1 is

$$\sigma^2_{b_1} = \frac{\sigma^2_e}{\Sigma(X_{1i} - \bar{X}_1)^2 (1 - \varrho^2_{X_1 \cdot X_2})}$$

As was true for the bivariate regression case, we can estimate the numerator, σ_e^2, with MS_{ERROR}. The term $\varrho_{X_1 \cdot X_2}^2$ is the correlation squared for predicting X_1 from X_2. It is estimated by the sample statistic $R_{X_1 \cdot X_2}^2$. Once we obtain both estimates of σ_e^2 and $\varrho_{X_1 \cdot X_2}^2$, we can calculate the sample estimate for $\sigma_{b_1}^2$. For the sample statistic,

$$s_{b_1}^2 = \frac{MS_{ERROR}}{\Sigma(X_{1i} - \bar{X}_1)^2 (1 - R_{X_1 \cdot X_2}^2)}$$

The square root of this value is used in the denominator of the t ratio. The t ratio has $N - 3$ degrees of freedom, because $N - 3$ df are associated with MS_{ERROR}. Hence, for b_1 we have

$$t_{N-3} = \frac{b_1}{s_{b_1}} = \frac{b_1}{\sqrt{\dfrac{MS_{ERROR}}{\Sigma(X_{1i} - \bar{X}_1)^2 (1 - R_{X_1 \cdot X_2}^2)}}}$$

In the preceding section we determined that MS_{ERROR} is 0.24 for the confidence example. Because $s_{X_1}^2 = \Sigma(X_{1i} - \bar{X}_1)^2/(N - 1)$, we also know that $\Sigma(X_{1i} - \bar{X}_1)^2 = s_{X_1}^2 (N - 1)$. And because Table 8.2 shows that $s_{X_1} = 1.370$, we can see that $s_{X_1}^2 = (1.370)^2 = 1.877$. With $N = 1,700$, it follows that $\Sigma(X_{1i} - \bar{X}_1)^2 = (1.877)(1,700 - 1) = 3,189.02$. And we see from Table 8.2 that $r_{X_1 X_2} = -0.048$. Hence, $R_{X_1 \cdot X_2}^2 = 0.0023$.

Now we set $\alpha = .01$ and calculate t_{1697}:

$$t_{1697} = \frac{-0.026}{\sqrt{\dfrac{0.24}{(3,189.02)(1 - 0.0023)}}}$$

$$= \frac{-0.026}{0.0087} = -2.99$$

For $\alpha = .01$ and $df = 1,697$ we see from Appendix D that the critical value for a two-tailed test is ± 2.576. Because the observed test statistic is larger than the critical value, we can reject the null hypothesis that β_1 equals zero in the population. Our conclusion is that more conservative political views decrease confidence in governmental institutions. But, what would have been our decision if we had chosen $\alpha = .001$?

The test of statistical significance for the b_2 coefficient is very similar to that for b_1. The calculation of t for this test is

$$t_{N-3} = \frac{b_2}{s_{b_2}} = \frac{b_2}{\sqrt{\dfrac{MS_{ERROR}}{\Sigma(X_{2i} - \bar{X}_2)^2 (1 - R_{X_2 \cdot X_1}^2)}}}$$

where

$$R^2_{X_2 \cdot X_1} = r^2_{X_2 X_1}$$

We already know that MS_{ERROR} is 0.24, and from Table 8.2 we can see that $s^2_{X_2} = (2.770)^2 = 7.6729$ and $r_{X_2 X_1} = -0.048$, with $N = 1,700$. Therefore, $\Sigma(X_{2i} - \bar{X}_2)^2 = s^2_{X_2}(N-1) = (7.6729)(1,699) = 13,036.26$. Furthermore, $R^2_{X_1 \cdot X_2} = (-0.048)^2 = 0.0023$. If we again set $\alpha = .01$, so that the critical value for a two-tailed test is ± 2.576, we can compute the test statistic

$$t_{1697} = \frac{0.013}{\sqrt{\dfrac{0.24}{(13,036.26)(1-0.0023)}}}$$

$$= \frac{0.013}{0.0043} = 3.02$$

Once again our decision is to reject the null hypothesis that β_2 equals zero in the population. Our conclusion is that more education increases confidence in governmental institutions. Would we have reached the same decision had we chosen $\alpha = .001$?

Table 8.3, which summarizes the results of testing the two hypotheses about confidence in governmental institutions, shows support for both propositions. That is, as conservative political ideology increases, confidence decreases, controlling for education. Similarly, as educational attainment rises, so does confidence, controlling for political ideology. Before accepting these propositions, however, we need to ascertain whether other variables, such as age and income, might account for these observed relationships. The multiple regression approach easily accom-

TABLE 8.3
Results of Regression of Confidence in Governmental Institutions Index on Political Views and Educational Attainment Variables

Independent Variable	b_j	B_j^*	s_{b_j}	t
Political Views	−0.026	−0.073	0.0087	−2.99*
Education	0.013	0.073	0.0043	3.02*
Intercept	1.859	—	0.0700	26.56*

*Significant at $\alpha = .01$.
Note: $N = 1,700$.

modates additional independent variables in an equation, as we show later in this chapter.

8.2.6 Confidence Intervals for b_1 and b_2

As in the case of bivariate regression, we can use the standard errors of b_1 and b_2 to construct confidence intervals around the sample point estimates of these multivariate regression parameters. If we pick $\alpha = .01$, the upper and lower limits for the 99% confidence interval for the population parameter, β_1, are $b_1 + s_{b_1}(2.576)$ and $b_1 - s_{b_1}(2.576)$. Since we saw in Table 8.3 that $s_{b_1} = 0.0087$ and $b_1 = -0.026$, we can calculate that $\text{UCL}_{99} = (-0.026) + (.0087)(2.576) = -0.0035$ and $\text{LCL}_{99} = (-0.026) - (.0087)(2.576) = -0.048$. Thus, the 99% confidence interval for β_1 is bounded between -0.0035 and -0.048.

The upper and lower limits for the 99% confidence interval for β_2 are calculated as $b_2 + s_{b_2}(2.576)$ and $b_2 - s_{b_2}(2.576)$, respectively. Convince yourself that, for the confidence in governmental institutions data, these limits are 0.024 and 0.002.

8.2.7 Partial Correlation in the Three-Variable Case

We introduced partial correlation methods in chapter 7. For three variables, Y, X_i, and X_j

$$r_{YX_j \cdot X_i} = \frac{r_{YX_j} - r_{YX_i} r_{X_i X_j}}{\sqrt{1 - r_{YX_i}^2}\ \sqrt{1 - r_{X_i X_j}^2}}$$

The partial correlation coefficient is an estimate of the relationship between a variable, Y, and a second variable, X_j, controlling for a third variable, X_i. The square of the partial correlation coefficient is the amount of variance in Y that can be accounted for by X_j, controlling for (or taking into account) X_i. As we showed in sections 8.2.2 and 8.2.3, the standardized regression coefficient (beta) is given by

$$\beta_j^* = \left(\frac{s_{X_j}}{s_Y}\right) b_j = \frac{r_{YX_j} - r_{YX_i} r_{X_i X_j}}{1 - r_{X_i X_j}^2}$$

partial regression coefficient—the effect of regressing a dependent variable on an independent variable, controlling for one or more other independent variables

Notice that the beta weights in this formula and the formula for the partial correlation coefficient have the same numerator. This equivalence means that both statistics will always have the same sign, and they usually are very similar in size. Their similarity leads some researchers and statisticians to refer to the standardized coefficients from multiple regression analysis as **partial regression coefficients**. We can illustrate the similarity between β_j^* and $r_{YX_j \cdot X_i}$ with the regression of confidence in governmental institutions on political views and education. As we found in section 8.2.2, $\beta_1^* = -0.73$ and

$$r_{YX_1 \cdot X_2} = \frac{-0.075 - (0.077)(-0.048)}{\sqrt{1 - (0.077)^2}\ \sqrt{1 - (-0.048)^2}} = -0.0716$$

Because the results from multiple regression and partial correlation analyses in the three-variable case are so similar, one of them is superfluous. Ordinarily the regression coefficients attract greater interest, so partial correlations are usually neither presented nor discussed in research reports. One interesting and important application of the partial correlation coefficient is a technique called *path analysis*, described in chapter 11.

> The tests of significance for the partial correlation coefficients are identical to those used in testing the regression coefficients. Therefore, if you test the regression coefficients for significance, you have also indirectly tested the partial correlation coefficients for significance.

8.3   Multiple Regression with *K* Independent Variables

If *K* independent variables are each hypothesized to affect a dependent continuous variable in a linear, additive manner, then the general **population regression model** for the *i*th observation is

$$Y_i = \alpha + \beta_1 X_{1i} + \beta_2 X_{2i} + \cdots + \beta_K X_{Ki} + \varepsilon_i$$

$$= \alpha + \sum_{j=1}^{K} \beta_j X_{ji} + \varepsilon_i$$

where
α = The constant or intercept.
β_j = The regression coefficient showing the effect of independent variable X_j on dependent variable *Y*.
ε_i = The error term, or residual, for the *i*th case.

To estimate the population regression parameters with sample data, we choose an estimator that provides the **best linear and unbiased estimate (BLUE)** having minimum variance. Box 8.2 summarizes the BLUE properties desired in a multiple regression equation. The **sample regression equation** and the **prediction equation** are

population regression model—a regression model for a population in which *K* independent variables are each hypothesized to affect a dependent, continuous variable in a linear, additive manner

best linear and unbiased estimate (BLUE)—an estimator for population regression parameters that assumes a linear relationship, no measurement error, and normally distributed error terms

sample regression equation—a regression model for a sample with *K* independent variables which includes the error term

prediction equation—a regression equation without the error term, useful for predicting the score on the dependent variable from the independent variable(s)

$$Y_i = a + b_1 X_{1i} + b_2 X_{2i} + \ldots + b_K X_{Ki} + e_i$$

$$\hat{Y}_i = a + b_1 X_{1i} + b_2 X_{2i} + \ldots + b_K X_{Ki}$$

In the case of K independent variables, a multiple regression coefficient, b_j, shows the amount of difference in the dependent variable that can be attributed to a one-unit difference in the jth independent variable, controlling (holding constant) the effects of the other $K - 1$ independent variables included in the equation. The intercept term shows the expected value of the dependent variable when all the independent measures equal zero.

Box 8.2   The BLUE Regression Criteria

Several properties constitute the best linear unbiased estimator (BLUE) characteristics traditionally sought in making inferences about population regression parameters (α and β) from estimates based on sample data (a and b). Among these assumptions are the following:

1. The relationship between the dependent variable and its predictors is linear, and no irrelevant variables are either omitted from or included in the equation.

2. All variables are measured without error.

3. The error term (e_i) for a single regression equation has the following properties:

   a. e_i is normally distributed.

   b. The expected value (mean) of the errors is zero: $\sum_{i=1}^{N} e_i = 0$.

   c. The errors are independently distributed with constant variances (homoscedasticity): $\dfrac{\sum e_i^2}{N} = \sigma_e^2$.

   d. Each predictor is uncorrelated with the equation's error term: $\varrho_{X_{ji} e_i} = 0$.

4. In systems of interrelated equations (see chapter 12), the error in one equation is assumed to be uncorrelated with the errors in the other equations: $\varrho_{e_i e_j} = 0$.

Violating the BLUE assumptions may result in ordinary least squares regression estimates that are biased or significance tests

(continued)

that are incorrect, although parameter estimates may be "robust" to some violations. Advanced methods for assessing how severely assumptions have been violated, such as examining residuals, are suggested in D. Belsley et al. (1980) *Regression Diagnostics* (New York: Wiley). Alternatives to OLS estimation methods, such as weighted least squares, can be substituted where appropriate.

Estimation of the population regression parameters, α and β_j, is done with ordinary least squares (OLS) techniques, thus assuring that the sum of the squared errors in the prediction ($\sum e_i^2$) is minimized. For those students familiar with calculus, Box 8.3 explains the principles behind OLS estimation. The basic inputs to computerized multiple regression programs are a matrix of correlations among K variables and vectors of their means and standard deviations. Table 8.4 illustrates such data for an example to be analyzed below. Only the lower triangular portion of the correlation matrix is reported. Because $r_{AB} = r_{BA}$ for all pairs A and B, showing the upper half of the matrix would be redundant.

To illustrate multiple regression with more than two independent variables, we analyze the eight variables in Table 8.4. We attempt to explain variation in a dependent variable reporting the respondent's

TABLE 8.4
Correlations, Means, and Standard Deviations for Sexual Frequency Regression Analysis

Variable	(1)	(2)	(3)	(4)	(5)	(6)	(7)	(8)	Mean	s
(1) Sexual Frequency	1.000								2.82	1.97
(2) Age	−0.437	1.000							44.41	16.34
(3) Marital Status	0.261	0.114	1.000						0.47	0.50
(4) Children	−0.057	0.431	0.263	1.000					1.74	1.61
(5) Church Attendance	−0.060	0.121	0.183	0.168	1.000				3.56	2.75
(6) Prayer	−0.098	0.171	0.066	0.201	0.546	1.000			4.20	1.53
(7) Education	0.130	−0.153	0.058	−0.232	0.061	−0.030	1.000		13.40	2.92
(8) Occupation	0.045	0.074	0.131	−0.069	0.099	0.052	0.521	1.000	43.52	13.46

Note: N = 1,086.
Source: 1998 General Social Survey.

Box 8.3   Deriving OLS Estimators of *a* and *b* for Regression Equations

The basic principle of ordinary least squares (OLS) estimation is to find values of a and b_k that make the sum of squared errors as small as possible. The situation is most easily illustrated with a two-predictor regression equation

$$Y_i = a + b_1 X_{1i} + b_2 X_{2i} + e_i$$

The error for observation i is just the difference between that case's observed score and its value predicted by the regression equation

$$e_i = (Y_i - \hat{Y}_i)$$

If $\hat{Y}_i$ is replaced by its regression equation estimate, squared, and summed across all N cases, the value that OLS seeks to minimize is the sum of the squared errors ($\sum e_i^2$), or

$$\sum (Y_i - \hat{Y}_i)^2 = \sum (Y_i - a - b_1 X_{1i} - b_2 X_{2i})^2$$

According to basic calculus, any quadratic equation attains a minimum at the point where the first derivative equals 0. Therefore, taking partial derivatives of the right-side expression above for each of the a and b_k estimates and setting them equal to zero give

$$-2\sum (Y_i - a - b_1 X_{1i} - b_2 X_{2i}) = 0$$
$$-2\sum X_{1i}(Y_i - a - b_1 X_{1i} - b_2 X_{2i}) = 0$$
$$-2\sum X_{2i}(Y_i - a - b_1 X_{1i} - b_2 X_{2i}) = 0$$

Simplifying and rearranging give the usual form of three so-called normal equations (which have nothing to do with the normal distribution) for a straight line

$$\sum Y_i = Na + b_1\sum X_{1i} + b_2\sum X_{2i}$$
$$\sum X_{1i}Y_i = a\sum X_{1i} + b_1\sum X^2_{1i} + b_2\sum X_{1i}X_{2i}$$
$$\sum X_{2i}Y_i = a\sum X_{2i} + b_1\sum X_{1i}X_{2i} + b_2\sum X^2_{2i}$$

(continued)

Three equations with three unknowns can be solved to give unique estimates of the unknowns. To obtain a, divide the first normal equation by N and rearrange

$$a = \bar{Y} - b_1\bar{X}_1 - b_2\bar{X}_2$$

This equation shows that the least squares regression line always passes through the point whose coordinates are the means of all variables, $\bar{Y}$, $\bar{X}_1$, and $\bar{X}_2$.

To find formulas for the b's, begin with the definition of the regression error as $e_i = Y_i - \hat{Y}_i$. Because $\hat{Y}_i = a + b_1 X_{1i} + b_2 X_{2i}$ and $a = \bar{Y} - b_1\bar{X}_1 - b_2\bar{X}_2$, we can substitute for a in the equation for the expected score

$$\hat{Y}_i = \bar{Y} + b_1(X_{1i} - \bar{X}_1) + b_2(X_{2i} - \bar{X}_2)$$

and then substitute into the equation for the error term

$$e_i = (Y_i - \hat{Y}_i) = Y_i - [\bar{Y} + b_1(X_{1i} - \bar{X}_1) + b_2(X_{2i} - \bar{X}_2)]$$
$$= (Y_i - \bar{Y}) - b_1(X_{1i} - \bar{X}_1) - b_2(X_{2i} - \bar{X}_2)$$

Because OLS estimators of the b's must minimize the sum of squared error terms, the next step is to form these sums of squares

$$\sum e_i^2 = \sum(Y_i - \hat{Y}_i)^2 = \sum[(Y_i - \bar{Y}) - b_1(X_{1i} - \bar{X}_1) - b_2(X_{2i} - \bar{X}_2)]^2$$

Finally, taking derivatives of the expression on the right with respect to each of the b's results in these estimators

$$b_1 = \frac{(\sum YX_{1i})(\sum X_{2i}^2) - (\sum YX_{2i})(\sum X_{1i}X_{2i})}{(\sum X_{1i}^2)(\sum X_{2i}^2) - (\sum X_{1i}X_{2i})}$$

$$b_2 = \frac{(\sum YX_{2i})(\sum X_1^2) - (\sum YX_{1i})(\sum X_{2i}X_{1i})}{(\sum X_{2i}^2)(\sum X_{1i}^2) - (\sum X_{2i}X_{1i})}$$

Similar procedures can be used to derive estimators of parameters for regression equations with more independent variables, but writing these becomes increasingly formidable as predictors are added to the equation. Consequently, solutions to multiple regression equations are compactly obtained through matrix algebra manipulations, which are performed by computer programs.

frequency of sexual activity (a seven-point ordinal scale from "never" to "four or more times per week") as a linear additive function of seven independent variables. Three predictors represent life-cycle stages (age, marital status, children), two measure religious activity (church attendance, frequency of praying), and two are indicators of social status (education, occupational prestige). We later compare the results of three **nested regression equations**, in which independent variables are successively added to an equation to observe changes in the predictors' relations to the dependent variable. (All analyses reported were performed by a computer, with calculations carried out to many decimal places; hence some results may differ due to rounding.)

nested regression equations—regression equations where independent variables are successively added to an equation to observe changes in the predictors' relationships to the dependent variable

Our first equation regresses sexual frequency on the three life-cycle indicators: X_1 = age in years; X_2 = marital status, currently married = 1, not married = 0; and X_3 = number of children ever born to the respondent. The estimated prediction equation for this equation is

$$\hat{Y}_i = 4.802 - 0.061X_{1i} + 1.171X_{2i} + 0.102X_{3i}$$

As discussed in section 8.2, each *metric regression coefficient* measures the amount of increase or decrease in the dependent variable for a one-unit difference in the independent variable, controlling for the other independent variables in the equation. In this example, the dependent variable measures sexual activity. Thus, $b_1 = -0.061$ means that, for each additional year of age, a respondent's expected sexual activity decreases on average by –0.061 points on the six-point scale. Thus, comparing a 20-year-old with a 60-year-old person yields an average estimated difference of $(-0.061)(40) = 2.44$ points, more than scale distance between "two or three times per month" and "two or three times per week." Married persons are more sexually active than unmarried persons by more than one point ($b_2 = 1.171$) on the dependent variable, and each additional child increases sexual activity by one-tenth of a point ($b_3 = 0.102$).

Recall from section 8.2.2 that standardized regression coefficients (or beta weights) are formed by multiplying the metric regression coefficients by the ratio of the standard deviation of the independent variable X_j to the standard deviation of the dependent variable Y. Hence, in the case of the three-predictor regression equation, the beta weights are

$$\beta^*_1 = \left(\frac{16.34}{1.967}\right)(-0.061) = -0.507$$

$$\beta^*_2 = \left(\frac{0.50}{1.967}\right)(1.171) = 0.298$$

$$\beta^*_3 = \left(\frac{1.61}{1.967}\right)(0.102) = 0.083$$

Because the means of Z-transformed variables are zero (see Box 2.4 in chapter 2), no intercept exists in a standardized regression equation. Therefore, the complete standardized multiple regression equation is

$$\hat{Z}_{Y_i} = -0.507Z_{X_{1i}} + 0.298Z_{X_{2i}} + 0.083Z_{X_{3i}}$$

All three independent variables now share the same scale (i.e., standard deviation units), so their relative impacts on sexual activity can be compared by examining which coefficients have the largest absolute values. Respondent's age clearly has the largest beta, with marital status next and number of children the smallest. Thus, we can conclude that, controlling for the other variables' effects, children are a less potent predictor of sexual behavior than are age and marital status. The -0.507 standardized coefficient for age means that a standard-deviation difference in respondents' ages reduces expected sexual frequency by one-half standard deviation. In contrast, a one-standard-deviation change in children, controlling for the other two variables, results in only a $+0.102$-standard-deviation increase in sexual frequency.

8.3.1 The Coefficient of Determination with K Independent Variables

A simple formula for the multiple regression coefficient of determination for an equation with K predictors is

$$R^2_{Y \cdot X_1 X_2 \dots X_K} = \beta^*_1 r_{YX_1} + \beta^*_2 r_{YX_2} + \cdots + \beta^*_K r_{YX_K}$$

$$= \sum_{j=1}^{K} \beta^*_j r_{YX_j}$$

The subscripts attached to R^2 clarify which independent variables predict the dependent variable. The predicted variable (Y) is on the left side of the centered dot, and all the predictor variables, X_1 through X_K, are listed to the right side of the dot. Note that the value of a multiple regression coefficient of determination just sums the products of each standardized regression coefficient and that predictor variable's correlation with the dependent measure. Whenever a β^*_j is smaller than its corresponding r_{YX_j}, meaning that the predictors are correlated, that X's net contribution to multiple R^2 is less than the full amount of its squared correlation with Y. In effect, the multiple R-squared summarizes the portion of each predictor's covariation with the dependent variable that remains after controlling for the effects jointly shared with the other predictors. For this reason, multiple regression coefficients are sometimes referred to as *partial regression coefficients*.

Using the standardized regression equation and the correlations in Table 8.4, the estimated value of R^2 for this example is

$$R^2_{Y \cdot X_1 X_2 X_3} = (-0.507)(-0.437) + (0.298)(0.261) + (0.083)(-0.057)$$
$$= 0.2946$$

The linear, additive combination of the three independent variables jointly accounts for 29.5% of the variation in sexual frequency.

Because 70.5% of the variation remains unexplained, capacity remains for additional predictors to be added to our initial regression equation to try to increase the amount of explained variance. However, the more predictors that we add to an equation, the greater the possibility that we will be unwittingly taking advantage of chance covariation to increase the R^2. Consequently, we cannot add predictors without penalty. An **adjusted coefficient of determination** (R^2_{adj}) takes into account the number of independent variables relative to the number of observations. In effect, any increase in explained variation must be paid for with the degrees of freedom required to include each predictor and the intercept a:

adjusted coefficient of determination—
a coefficient of determination that takes into account the number of independent variables relative to the number of observations

$$R^2_{adj} = R^2_{Y \cdot X_1 \dots X_K} - \left(\frac{(K)(1 - R^2_{Y \cdot X_1 \dots X_K})}{(N - K - 1)} \right)$$

For large samples such as the GSS data set, the adjustment may only slightly reduce the unadjusted R^2 value. In the equation with three predictors, the adjustment produces a 0.2% drop in explained variation:

$$R^2_{adj} = 0.2946 - \left(\frac{(3)(1 - 0.2946)}{(1,086 - 3 - 1)} \right) = 0.2926$$

In multiple regression, as in life, there is "no free lunch."

As in the three-variable multiple regression case, another approach to calculating multiple R-squared in the K-variable case is

$$R^2_{Y \cdot X_1 \dots X_K} = \frac{\Sigma(Y_i - \bar{Y})^2 - \Sigma(Y_i - \hat{Y}_i)^2}{\Sigma(Y_i - \bar{Y})^2}$$

$$= \frac{SS_{TOTAL} - SS_{ERROR}}{SS_{TOTAL}}$$

$$= \frac{SS_{REGRESSION}}{SS_{TOTAL}}$$

because $SS_{\text{TOTAL}} = SS_{\text{REGRESSION}} + SS_{\text{ERROR}}$ and, thus, $SS_{\text{REGRESSION}} = SS_{\text{TOTAL}} - SS_{\text{ERROR}}$. Every multiple regression computer program automatically computes these sums of squares and calculates the value of both R^2 and R^2_{adj}.

8.4   Significance Tests for Parameters

8.4.1   Testing Multiple R^2 with K Independent Variables

For the three-variable case in section 8.2.4, we tested the hypothesis that the population coefficient of determination (ϱ^2) differed significantly from zero, using an F test with 1 and $N - 3$ degrees of freedom. In parallel fashion, a sample multiple regression R^2 can also be used to test the null hypothesis H_0: $\varrho^2 = 0$ in the case of K independent variables. This null hypothesis is equivalent to a test that all K regression coefficients are zero; i.e., in the population H_0: $\beta_1 = \beta_2 = \ldots = \beta_K = 0$. The degrees of freedom associated with the SS_{TOTAL} in a regression equation are always $N - 1$, regardless of the number of independent variables. If an equation has K independent variables, $SS_{\text{REGRESSION}}$ has K df associated with it, one for each predictor variable. Because in general, $df_{\text{TOTAL}} = df_{\text{REGRESSION}} + df_{\text{ERROR}}$, by subtraction $df_{\text{ERROR}} = N - K - 1$.

To compute the mean squares required in the F test, divide each sum of squares by its associated degrees of freedom. That is, with K independent variables,

$$MS_{\text{REGRESSION}} = \frac{SS_{\text{REGRESSION}}}{K}$$

$$MS_{\text{ERROR}} = \frac{SS_{\text{ERROR}}}{N - K - 1}$$

When the null hypothesis that $\varrho^2 = 0$ in the population is true, both $MS_{\text{REGRESSION}}$ and MS_{ERROR} are unbiased estimates of the variance of the errors of prediction, σ^2_e. However, if $\varrho^2 > 0$ in the population, then $MS_{\text{REGRESSION}}$ will be greater than MS_{ERROR}. The F ratio test statistic is

$$F_{K, N - K - 1} = \frac{MS_{\text{REGRESSION}}}{MS_{\text{ERROR}}}$$

For given levels of α, use the appropriate table in Appendix E to find the critical value of F with K (column heading) and $N - K - 1$ (row heading) degrees of freedom necessary to reject the null hypothesis as probably untrue.

Calculating the mean squares for the F test requires computing both $SS_{\text{REGRESSION}}$ and SS_{ERROR} from the sample data. The procedures are identical to those followed in the bivariate regression (see section 6.4.1 of chapter 6) and three-variable regression (see section 8.2.4) cases:

$$SS_{\text{TOTAL}} = (s_Y^2)(N - 1)$$

$$SS_{\text{REGRESSION}} = (R^2_{Y \bullet X_1 \ldots X_K})(SS_{\text{TOTAL}})$$

$$SS_{\text{ERROR}} = SS_{\text{TOTAL}} - SS_{\text{REGRESSION}}$$

To determine whether the coefficient of determination is significantly different from zero in the population, we set $\alpha = .001$, which fixes the c.v. for $F = 5.42$ with $df = 3$ and $1,082$. The standard deviation of sexual frequency is $s_Y = 1.967$ (Table 8.3 reports a rounded value); therefore, the sample variance is 3.869. As a result,

$$SS_{\text{TOTAL}} = (3.869)(1,086 - 1) = 4,197.87$$

$$SS_{\text{REGRESSION}} = (0.2946)(4,197.87) = 1,236.69$$

$$SS_{\text{ERROR}} = 4,197.87 - 1,236.69 = 2,961.18$$

Next, divide these values by their degrees of freedom to find the mean squares:

$$MS_{\text{REGRESSION}} = \frac{1,236.69}{3} = 412.23$$

$$MS_{\text{ERROR}} = \frac{2,961.18}{1,082} = 2.74$$

Hence, the test statistic is

$$F_{3,\ 1082} = \frac{412.23}{2.74} = 150.45$$

Because the critical value at $\alpha = .001$ for F with $df = 3$ and $1,082$ is 5.42, we can reject with great confidence the null hypothesis that $\varrho^2 = 0$ in the population.

An even simpler alternative way to calculate F directly using the multiple R^2 is

$$F_{K,\ N-K-1} = \frac{MS_{\text{REGRESSION}}}{MS_{\text{ERROR}}}$$

$$= \frac{R^2_{Y \bullet X_1 \ldots X_K}/K}{(1 - R^2_{Y \bullet X_1 \ldots X_K})/(N - K - 1)}$$

Using the results from the sexual frequency example, we have

$$F_{3,\,1082} = \frac{0.2946/3}{(1 - 0.2946)/(1{,}086 - 3 - 1)} = 150.63$$

The small difference between this result and the preceding calculation of F is due to rounding. A variation of this latter formulation comes in very handy in comparing coefficients of determination from nested regression equations. Box 8.4 presents the derivation of this formula.

Box 8.4 Deriving the *F* Test for the Coefficient of Determination with Several Independent Variables

---

When the coefficient of determination is tested with two or more independent variables, $MS_{\text{REGRESSION}} = SS_{\text{REGRESSION}} / df_{\text{REGRESSION}}$ and $MS_{\text{ERROR}} = SS_{\text{ERROR}} / df_{\text{ERROR}}$. For K independent variables, K degrees of freedom are associated with $SS_{\text{REGRESSION}}$ and $N - K - 1$ df with SS_{ERROR}. Therefore,

$$F_{K,\,N-K-1} = \frac{SS_{\text{REGRESSION}}/K}{SS_{\text{ERROR}}/(N-K-1)}$$

As shown in section 6.4.1 of chapter 6,

$$SS_{\text{REGRESSION}} = (R^2_{Y\bullet X})\,(SS_{\text{TOTAL}})$$

$$1 = R^2_{Y\bullet X} + \frac{SS_{\text{ERROR}}}{SS_{\text{TOTAL}}}$$

From the latter, it follows that $SS_{\text{ERROR}} = (1 - R^2_{Y\bullet X})(SS_{\text{TOTAL}})$. Substituting these two results for the case of K independent variables into the equation for F yields

$$F_{K,\,N-K-1} = \frac{(R^2_{Y\bullet X_1 \ldots X_K})(SS_{\text{TOTAL}})/K}{(1 - R^2_{Y\bullet X_1 \ldots X_K})(SS_{\text{TOTAL}})/(N-K-1)}$$

$$= \frac{R^2_{Y\bullet X_1 \ldots X_K}/K}{(1 - R^2_{Y\bullet X_1 \ldots X_K})/(N-K-1)}$$

because SS_{TOTAL} cancels in both the numerator and the denominator.

8.4.2 Testing b_i

For the jth independent variable, X_j, the standard error of its estimated regression parameter, b_j, can be computed with

$$s_{b_j} = \sqrt{\frac{\sigma_e^2}{(s_{X_j}^2)(N-1)(1-R_{X_j \cdot X_1 \dots X_{K-1}}^2)}}$$

The term in the numerator, the standard error of estimate (σ_e), is simply the square root of the mean square error

$$\sigma_e^2 = MS_{ERROR} = \frac{SS_{ERROR}}{N-K-1}$$

In the sexual frequency equation with three predictors, $\sigma_e^2 = 2{,}961.18/(1{,}086 - 3 - 1) = 2.737$. For the first two terms in the denominator of the formula $((s_{X_j}^2)(N-1))$, the sexual frequency example gives the following results: for age, $(16.34)^2(1{,}085) = 289{,}690.23$; for marital status, $(0.50)^2(1{,}085) = 271.25$; and for children, $(1.61)^2(1{,}085) = 2{,}812.43$.

The third term in the denominator of the standard error formula is a bit more complicated. It involves regressing in turn the independent variable X_j on the remaining $K - 1$ predictors in the equation and then subtracting the resulting R^2 from 1. Thus, for the sexual activity example, three additional multiple regression equations are necessary, each of which regresses one of the X_j on the other two. For example, age (X_1) is regressed on marital status (X_2) and children (X_3). When these regressions are done, the following three R^2's result: for age, 0.186; for marital status, 0.069; and for children, 0.232. Therefore, the three estimated standard errors of the regression coefficients are

$$s_{b_1} = \sqrt{\frac{2.737}{(289{,}690.23)(1-0.186)}} = 0.003$$

$$s_{b_2} = \sqrt{\frac{2.737}{(271.25)(1-0.069)}} = 0.104$$

$$s_{b_3} = \sqrt{\frac{2.737}{(2{,}812.43)(1-0.232)}} = 0.036$$

These values are shown in parentheses in the first column of Table 8.5. In practice, of course, computer programs routinely calculate the standard errors for all multiple regression coefficients from the correlation matrix and the vector of standard errors.

TABLE 8.5
Nested Multiple Regression Equations for Sexual Frequency

Independent Variables	(1)	(2)	(3)
Intercept	4.802***	4.985***	4.345***
	(0.149)	(0.191)	(0.318)
Age	–0.061***	–0.060***	–0.061***
	(0.003)	(0.003)	(0.003)
Marital Status	1.171***	1.208***	1.167***
	(0.104)	(0.105)	(0.106)
Children	0.102**	0.113**	0.134***
	(0.036)	(0.036)	(0.037)
Church Attendance	—	–0.044*	–0.050*
		(0.022)	(0.022)
Prayer	—	–0.022	–0.020
		(0.040)	(0.040)
Education	—	—	0.003
			(0.021)
Occupational Prestige	—	—	0.005
			(0.004)
R^2	0.295***	0.300***	.304***
R^2_{adj}	0.293***	0.296***	.300***

Note: Numbers in parentheses are standard errors.
$N = 1,086$.
*$p < .05$ **$p < .01$ ***$p < .001$

The final step in testing a regression coefficient for statistical significance involves a t test of the null hypothesis that the population regression value is zero: $H_0: \beta_j = 0$. The alternative hypothesis may be either one-tailed, if the presumed direction of the effect is known: $H_1: \beta_j < 0$ or $H_1: \beta_j > 0$; or two-tailed, if no a priori information about the probable sign of the regression parameter can be stated: $H_0: \beta_j \neq 0$. Given a sample estimate of b_j from a multiple regression, the t test is identical to that for the bivariate regression case:

$$t_{N-K-1} = \frac{b_j - \beta_j}{s_{b_j}} = \frac{b_j - 0}{s_{b_j}} = \frac{b_j}{s_{b_j}}$$

To continue with the sexual activity example, the following t ratios are computed:

$$t_{1082} = \frac{b_1}{s_{b_1}} = \frac{-0.061}{0.003} = -20.33$$

$$t_{1082} = \frac{b_2}{s_{b_2}} = \frac{1.171}{0.104} = 11.26$$

$$t_{1082} = \frac{b_3}{s_{b_3}} = \frac{0.102}{0.036} = 2.83$$

Appendix D shows that the critical value required to reject a null hypothesis in favor of a two-tailed alternative when $df = \infty$ at $\alpha = .01$ is ± 2.576. Thus, we conclude that a respondent's frequency of sexual activity varies as a linear function of all three independent variables.

Two cautionary notes are in order here. First, unless the K independent variables have correlations equal to zero with one another, the K t ratios used for significance testing are not independent. Thus, reported probabilities of statistical significance may be slightly biased, although the biases will generally be too small to cause any practical concern. Second, and more importantly, extremely high correlations among the K predictors can seriously distort the estimates of the b_j standard errors. As can be seen from the formula presented above, a coefficient's standard error increases to the extent that it can be predicted by a linear combination of the remaining $K - 1$ predictors. Such a condition is called **multicollinearity**. Exact prediction of one predictor by the others (that is, perfect multicollinearity in which $R^2 = 1.00$) results in an inability to estimate the specified equation. Much more common is the situation in which a very large proportion of the variance in an independent variable is explained by the others. Although several tests for the presence of multicollinearity exist, they are beyond the scope of this text. However, researchers should always visually inspect the correlation matrix of the variables used in their equations (such as Table 8.1). If high correlations (e.g., 0.80 or higher) occur among the predictor variables, then regressions may risk multicollinearity that produces large standard errors. In such cases, one or more predictors can be eliminated from the regression and the equation re-estimated.

A significance test also exists for hypotheses about the multiple regression population intercept, α. Because of the rarity with which substantive problems in social research concern this term, we do not present formulas for calculating its standard error. Rather, computer programs will generate an estimate of s_a from the sample data that can be entered into a t test:

$$t_{N-K-1} = \frac{a - \alpha}{s_a}$$

multicollinearity— a condition of high or near perfect correlation among the independent variables in a multiple regression equation

The intercept standard error for the sexual frequency equation is 0.149; hence, the observed t ratio is $4.802/0.149 = 32.23$, sufficiently large to reject the null hypothesis that the population parameter is zero at $\alpha < .001$. That null hypothesis is not meaningful, however, because we had no reason to believe that sexual activity would be zero when the values of all three predictors were also zero.

The significance testing procedures described above apply only to regression coefficients in their metric form. No parallel tests are presented for the standardized regression coefficients (beta weights), because identical results would occur. Most computer programs calculate and print only the standard errors for the b_j estimates, not for the β^*_j values. But the t ratios that apply to the former also apply to the latter.

After all standard errors and t scores have been calculated for a multiple regression equation, the full set of sample descriptive and inferential statistics can be compactly displayed. Journal styles vary across the social science disciplines, but the format we find most informative consists of four lines: (1) the unstandardized regression coefficients, written in equation form, followed by the adjusted R^2; (2) the standardized regression parameters, also in equation form; (3) the standard errors in parentheses; and (4) the t ratios and F ratio in parentheses. Thus, for the sexual frequency equation,

$$\hat{Y}_i = 4.802 - 0.061\,X_1 + 1.171\,X_2 + 0.102\,X_3, \quad R^2_{\text{adj}} = .293$$
$$\hat{Z}_{Y_i} = -0.507\,Z_1 + 0.298\,Z_2 + 0.083\,Z_3$$
$$(0.149) \quad (0.003) \quad (0.104) \quad (0.036)$$
$$(32.23) \quad (-20.33) \quad (11.26) \quad (2.83) \quad (F_{3,1082} = 150.63)$$

When several equations must be reported, a tabular display offers a more suitable compact format, such as the presentation of nested multiple regression equations in Table 8.5.

8.4.3 Confidence Intervals for b_i

Using the regression coefficients' standard errors, we can construct confidence intervals around each b_j point estimate, as in the three-variable regression case in section 8.2.6. For example, setting $\alpha = .01$, the lower and upper limits for the 99% confidence interval for the age parameter, β_j, are $b_j \pm (s_b)(t_{\text{c.v.}})$. Given that $b_1 = -0.061$ and $s_b = 0.003$, the lower confidence limit is $-0.061 - (0.003)(2.576) = -0.069$ and the upper confidence limit is $-0.061 + (0.003)(2.576) = -0.053$. Hence, the 99% confidence interval for the age parameter is bounded by -0.069 and -0.053, which obviously does not include zero (recall that the preceding two-tailed significance test allowed us to reject the null hypothesis that the true population parameter is zero). Convince yourself that the 99% confidence limits for marital status are 0.90 and 1.44 and for children are 0.01 and 0.19.

8.5 Comparing Nested Equations

We mentioned that additional independent variables can be entered into a regression equation, resulting in a nested set. Table 8.5 shows the results of two expansions of the initial equation predicting frequency of sexual activity (which appears in column one). The equation in column two adds two measures of religious practice, church attendance and praying. Adding these predictors makes only small changes in the values of several estimated coefficients in the first equation. Only one of the two new variables is significant, church attendance (significant at $p < .05$). Note also that adding these variables marginally increases the adjusted R^2 (which is more meaningful than the unadjusted R^2) from 29.3% in the first equation to 29.6% in the second, with the loss of two degrees of freedom from adding the two new predictor variables. More frequent church attendance is associated with less frequent sexual activity. Finally, the equation in the third column adds education and occupational prestige variables, which are not statistically significant and which change the adjusted R^2 increases by less than one-half percent at the cost of two more degrees of freedom.

The independent variables in equation 1 are contained within the more inclusive set of variables in equation 2, which in turn is a subset of the predictors in equation 3. We can perform a test to determine whether the variables added to an equation result in a significant increase in the explained variance. Just as the test for whether R^2 is significantly greater than zero takes the *df* into account, so we must pay for the nested regression equation test with the difference in degrees of freedom used by each equation. The formula uses the *unadjusted* coefficients of determination (because an adjustment for *df*'s occurs during the computation):

$$F_{(K_2 - K_1), (N - K_2 - 1)} = \frac{(R^2_2 - R^2_1)/(K_2 - K_1)}{(1 - R^2_2)/(N - K_2 - 1)}$$

where the subscripts attached to R^2 and K indicate whether these values come from the first (less-inclusive) equation or from the second (more inclusive) equation. For the F ratio to be significant, the difference in

R-squares must be large relative to the number of independent variables added to the second equation.

To illustrate the procedure, calculate the test statistic to compare the first and second equations in Table 8.5:

$$F_{(5-3),(1086-5-1)} = \frac{(0.300 - 0.295)/(5-3)}{(1 - 0.300)/(1{,}086 - 5 - 1)} = \frac{0.005/2}{0.700/1{,}080} = 3.86$$

For 2 and 1,080 *df*, this *F* ratio is large enough to reject the null hypothesis $H_0: \varrho_2^2 - \varrho_1^2 = 0$ at $p < .05$, because the c.v. at $\alpha = .05$ is roughly 3.00. Can you determine whether the third equation significantly raises the explained variance over that obtained by the second equation, also setting $\alpha = .05$?

8.6   Dummy Variable Regression: ANCOVA with Interactions

8.6.1   The Analysis of Covariance

Up to this point, our discussion of multiple regression analysis has assumed that all variables are continuous measures. However, many important social variables are discrete or categoric in nature. In chapters 5, 7, and 10 we discuss how to analyze such dependent variables. In this section we will introduce methods for using discrete measures as independent variables in regressions involving continuous dependent variables. To illustrate the approach, consider a hypothesis that occupational prestige—a measure of a job's "goodness"—varies according to a person's gender–race category. Using the 1998 General Social Survey to test this hypothesis, we regressed the NORC occupational prestige scores (which range from 17 [equivalent to "miscellaneous food preparation occupations"] to 86 [equivalent to "physician"]) on four categories: 1 = white women, 2 = white men, 3 = black women, and 4 = black men (we dropped all cases of "other race"). Because these numbers are arbitrary, the gender–race variable cannot be entered directly into a regression equation. One way to create an interpretable classification is to use a set of *J* **dummy variables** as predictors. Each D_j is a separate variable that is coded 1 to indicate the presence of specific attributes for a case or 0 to indicate their absence. Thus, for the four gender–race combinations, the set of four dummy variables might be as follows:

dummy variable— a variable coded 1 to indicate the presence of an attribute and 0 its absence

$D_{WW} = 1$ if a respondent is a white woman, 0 if not.
$D_{WM} = 1$ if a respondent is a white man, 0 if not.
$D_{BW} = 1$ if a respondent is a black woman, 0 if not.
$D_{BM} = 1$ if a respondent is a black man, 0 if otherwise.

Any $J-1$ variables of a set of J dummy variables may be entered as predictors in a regression equation. Because information about all but one of the dummies determines the value of the last category, the Jth dummy predictor is not linearly independent of the others. For example, if a respondent is coded 0 on D_{WW}, 0 on D_{WM}, and 1 on D_{BW}, then we know that person must be 0 on D_{BM}, because the person is a black woman, and hence not a black man. Similarly, knowing that D_{WM}, D_{BW}, and D_{BM} are each scored 0 reveals a respondent to be a white woman (i.e., $D_{WW} = 1$). In general, if a discrete variable has J categories, then any $J - 1$ unique dummy variables created from it can be used in a regression equation. In particular, a dichotomous variable, such as teacher/student, is represented in regression analysis by a single 0–1 dummy variable.

Choosing "white man" as the omitted category, we regress occupational prestige scores of 2,496 GSS respondents on the white woman, black woman, and black man dummy variables, yielding the following equation (with t ratios in parentheses):

$$\hat{Y}_i = 45.26 - 0.61\,D_{WW} - 6.47\,D_{BM} - 4.07\,D_{BW}, \quad R^2_{adj} = 0.015$$
$$(105.05)\ (-1.03) \qquad (-5.29) \qquad (-4.12) \qquad (F_{3,2492} = 13.69)$$

The equation intercept indicates that, after controlling for gender and race, the mean prestige of respondents' occupations is 45.26, about that of insurance salespersons, plumbers, and dental assistants. All three dummy variable coefficients have negative signs, and two are significant at $p < .001$. Thus, relative to white men, the other three gender–race groups have lower average occupational prestige, although the coefficient for white women is not significant even at $p < .05$. Note that the adjusted R^2 of 0.015 is significant at the $\alpha = .001$ level, because the c.v. for F with 3 and 2,492 df is 5.42, as can be determined from Appendix E. However, the four race–gender combinations explain only 1.5% of the variation in occupational prestige.

Separate regression equations for the four gender–race categories can now be derived from the single equation, as follows. When $D_{WW} = 1$, the predicted occupational prestige for white women is

$$\hat{Y}_{WW} = 45.26 - 0.61(1) - 6.47(0) - 4.07(0)$$
$$= 44.65$$

Similarly, when $D_{BM} = 1$, the predicted occupational prestige for black men is

$$\hat{Y}_{BM} = 45.26 - 0.61(0) - 6.47(1) - 4.07(0)$$
$$= 38.79$$

And when $D_{BW} = 1$, the predicted value for black women is

$$\hat{Y}_{BW} = 45.26 - 0.61(0) - 6.47(0) - 4.07(1)$$
$$= 41.19$$

Because the dummy variable for white men was omitted from the equation, this category may appear to have no equation, but as the following calculation shows, the predicted value is just the intercept:

$$\hat{Y}_{WM} = 45.26 - 0.61(0) - 6.47(0) - 4.07(0)$$
$$= 45.26$$

That is, white men hold occupations with an average prestige score of 45.26, which is higher than the predicted scores of the other three gender–race groups.

The t test associated with a given dummy variable has a special interpretation—it is a test for the difference between two means. In particular, it tests the difference between the mean associated with a given category (e.g., white women) and an omitted category (e.g., white men in this example). Thus, the t ratio for D_{WW} indicates whether there is no significant difference in the population between the mean occupational prestige scores of white women (44.65) and white men (45.26). If we choose $\alpha = .05$, the t value is the ratio of the regression coefficient to its standard error: $-0.61/0.59 = -1.03$. The difference in means is not significant, because the c.v. is a t ratio of ± 1.96. The t values for the other two dummy variables, $D_{BM} = -5.29$ and $D_{BW} = -4.12$, indicate that the mean occupational prestige of black women and black men both differ significantly from the mean of white men.

Importantly, the value of R^2 and the predicted values of the dependent variable are invariant regardless of which of the $J - 1$ dummy variables are entered in the equation. However, the t tests for the coefficients will necessarily differ because the reference (omitted) category will differ. An important implication is that researchers should carefully choose a substantively or theoretically important group for the omitted category, so that meaningful statistical tests are performed. In the preceding example, we purposely chose the category with the highest mean score on the dependent variable to serve as the reference dummy.

When a multiple regression equation includes *both* a set of dummy variables and one or more continuous measures as predictors, the model is called an **analysis of covariance** (ANCOVA), reflecting this method's origins in experimental research. A continuous variable is called a **covariate**, and the dummy variables are referred to as **treatment levels**. The ANCOVA predictors each exert additive effects on the dependent variable, so that within each category of the treatment dummies, the effect of a covariate is identical. Suppose we choose education (years of formal schooling) as a covariate (X_1) and include it in the occupational prestige equation along with the three gender–race dummy predictors. The result is the following equation (*t* ratios in parentheses)

$$\hat{Y}_i = 13.88 \quad -0.41\, D_{WW} \quad -3.67\, D_{BM} \quad -1.93\, D_{BW} \quad +2.31\, X_1, \quad R^2_{adj} = 0.258$$

$$\quad (11.97)\; (-0.81) \qquad (-3.44) \qquad (-2.24) \qquad (28.58)\; (F_{4,2491} = 217.88)$$

The *t* ratio for education clearly reveals it to be a powerful predictor of occupational prestige. In effect, for each additional year of schooling completed, an average respondent gains almost two and a quarter points on the scale. Thus, college graduates (16 years of schooling) have more than a 9-point higher expected occupational prestige than high-school graduates (12 years); that is, $(2.31)(16 - 12) = 9.24$. When education is in the equation, the intercept and all three gender–race dummy variable coefficients are somewhat smaller. Although the coefficient for white women remains nonsignificant, both black women and black men continue to have significantly lower occupational standing than white men.

As mentioned above, education in the ANCOVA equation exerts an additive effect on occupational prestige. For example, the predicted prestige score for a black woman with 12 years of schooling is $\hat{Y}_i = 13.88 - (1.93)(1) + (2.31)(12) = 39.67$ prestige points. This is exactly a 2.31-point difference from a college-attending black woman (i.e., with 13 years of education): $\hat{Y}_i = 13.88 - (1.93)(1) + (2.31)(13) = 41.98$. Identical 2.31-point differences also occur between the members of *any* gender–race group who are exactly one year apart in education. That is, the effect of education on occupational prestige is *constant* within each dummy variable category.

Researchers may want to know whether a set of dummy variables contributes significantly to the variance of a dependent variable (occupational prestige in this case) beyond that explained by a covariate (e.g., education). To answer this question, we can use the *F* test for the difference between coefficients of determination, introduced in section 8.5. In our example, $R^2_2 = 0.255$ is the *unadjusted* coefficient of determination for the equation including both the gender–race dummies and the education covariate, while $R_1^2 = 0.255$ is the square of the correlation between education and prestige. (We used the unadjusted R-squares instead of the adjusted values because the F test takes the degrees of freedom into account.) A significant F test means that at least one group intercept probably differs from the other group intercepts in the population. We set $\alpha = .05$; reference to Appendix E indicates that the c.v. for 3 and 2,491 df is 2.60. The significance test results are

$$F_{(4-1),(2496-4-1)} = \frac{(0.259 - 0.255)/(4-1)}{(1-0.259)/(2,496-4-1)} = 4.48$$

Given an F of 4.48, we are confident that one or more group intercepts differs significantly from the other intercepts. Examination of the regression coefficients for the dummies reveals that the intercepts for both black women and black men are significantly lower than the white males' intercept.

8.6.2 ANOVA with Dummy Variables

By now you probably realize that multiple regression and analysis of variance are special versions of the general linear model. A regression performed with only a single set of dummy variables is identical to a one-way ANOVA. Rather than deriving this fact mathematically, we demonstrate it with an example that translates dummy regression coefficients into ANOVA effects. Table 8.6 displays the coefficients produced by ANOVA and by regression when GSS respondents' political views (ranging from 1 = extremely liberal to 7 = extremely conservative) are the dependent variable and the seven categories of political party identification shown in the table's rows form the independent variable. In general, the more strongly one identifies with the Republican category, the more conservative the political views. At first glance, the two sets of effects appear contradictory. More than half of the ANOVA effect coefficients (α_j) are negative, while none of the dummy regression coefficients (b_j) has a negative sign. Recall, however, that the reference points for each scale differ. For ANOVA, the effects are calculated as deviations of each treatment category mean from the grand mean of the sample (see section 4.1.2 in chapter 4). For dummy regression, the effects are deviations from the mean of the omitted category, the "strong Democrats" in this example (see section 8.6.1).

Transforming the values from one scale into the second scale simply requires aligning them by an adjustment factor. For one-way ANOVA and

TABLE 8.6
Effects of Party Identification on Political Views, ANOVA Compared to Dummy Variable Regression

Party Categories	ANOVA α_j	Regression b_j	Mean
Grand Mean	4.10	—	4.10
Intercept	—	3.48	—
Strong Democrat	–0.62	0.00[a]	3.48
Not Strong Democratic	–0.36	0.26	3.74
Independent, Leans Democratic	–0.44	0.18	3.66
Independent	–0.17	0.45	3.93
Independent, Leans Republican	0.42	1.04	4.52
Not Strong Republican	0.51	1.13	4.61
Strong Republican	1.31	1.93	5.41
	$\eta^2 = 0.169*$	$R^2 = 0.169*$	
	$F_{6,2615} = 88.51*$	$F_{6,2615} = 88.51*$	

Note: $N = 2{,}622$; Missing data = 210.
[a]Omitted category in dummy variable regression.
*$p < .001$
Source: 1998 General Social Survey.

regression with a comparable set of dummy variables, the adjustment factor involves the sample mean, $\bar{Y}$, and the sample estimate of the regression intercept, a. A dummy regression coefficient translates into an ANOVA effect: $\alpha_j = b_j + (a - \bar{Y})$. And, by rearrangement, an ANOVA effect translates into a dummy regression coefficient: $b_j = \alpha_j + (\bar{Y} - a)$.

For example, using the values in Table 8.6, the regression coefficient for Independents (+0.45) can be changed into the ANOVA effect (–0.17) by adding to it the difference between the intercept and the mean (3.48 – 4.10 = –0.62). Similarly, the ANOVA effect for strong Democrats (–0.62) becomes the regression value (0.00, because it is the omitted category), by adding the difference between mean and intercept (4.10 – 3.48 = +0.62). Convince yourself that all the remaining coefficients in one method can be transformed to their corresponding values in the other procedure. The means generated for the seven categories (see the last column in Table 8.6) are the same as the predicted means computed from the dummy variable analysis. That is, one can capture all of the information in an analysis of variance using dummy variable analysis. Thus, analysis of variance and multiple regression are fundamentally equivalent variations of a common underlying general linear model.

8.6.3 Regression Equations with Interaction Terms

Dummy variables are especially useful for estimating and testing **interaction effects**, which reflect differences in the relationship between two variables within categories of a third variable. Suppose we believe not only that gender–race affects occupational prestige, but also that those effects vary according to people's educational attainment. That is, highly educated members of one gender–race group may be more likely to achieve higher or lower occupational prestige than are highly educated members of another group. In other words, not only might the intercepts for the different gender–race groups vary, but so too might their regression slopes. To examine this hypothesis, we must enter the education variable (X_1) into the regression equation along with the dummy variables and also include three interaction terms created by multiplying each dummy category by the continuous measure: for example, $X_1 D_{WW}$. Consequently, each interaction term takes on values equal to the continuous measure for group members, but it is 0 for nongroup members. Thus, the interaction variable for education times the white woman dummy $(X_1 D_{WW})$ gives each white female respondent the same score that she has on the education variable, but it gives each black female and black male respondent a score of 0.

interaction effects— differences in the relationship between two variables within categories of a third variable

To test a set of interactions, the R_2^2 for the equation with the multiplicative interaction terms is compared to the R_1^2 for the equation that includes only the additive effects of the variables. The test statistic for the difference in the two equations' coefficients of determination is the same F ratio test used in section 8.5 to compare nested equations. Our null hypothesis is that H_0: $\varrho_2^2 - \varrho_1^2 = 0$ in the population. If this hypothesis can be rejected at a chosen α value, we conclude that significant interaction effects exist. For the equation with only education and the three gender–race dummies, $R^2 = 0.259$, while for the equation that also includes the three interaction terms, $R^2 = 0.263$. (Again, we use the two *unadjusted* coefficients of determination because the F ratio test statistic takes the degrees of freedom into account.) Therefore,

$$F_{(7-4),(2496-7-1)} = \frac{(0.263 - 0.259)/(7-4)}{(1-0.263)/(2{,}496-7-1)} = 4.50$$

We conclude that at least one significant interaction effect occurs in this example. The full regression equation is (with t ratios in parentheses)

$$\hat{Y}_i = 17.11 \;\; -7.33\, D_{WW} + 0.97\, D_{BM} - 5.35\, D_{BW} + 2.08\, X_1$$
$$\quad (9.94)\; (-3.07) \qquad (0.18) \qquad (-1.32) \qquad (16.77)$$

$$+\, 0.51\, X_1 D_{WW} - 0.40\, X_1 D_{BM} + 0.25\, X_1 D_{BW}, \qquad R_{adj}^2 = 0.263$$
$$\quad (2.87) \qquad\quad (-0.93) \qquad\quad (0.81) \qquad\qquad (F_{7,2488} = 126.54)$$

Although these relationships appear more complex than those in the ANCOVA equation estimated in section 8.6.1, they can be interpreted by calculating the effect of education for each specific gender–race category. The effect of education that is common to every group is +2.08 prestige points per year of schooling. The three education–dummy interaction effects apply only to that group whose dummy variable score is 1. Because there is no dummy variable for the omitted white men, their education effect is just the common coefficient, +2.08 prestige points per year of schooling. For white women, their significant +0.51 interaction coefficient must be added to the common education coefficient, producing an increase of 2.08 + 0.51 = +2.59 prestige points per year of schooling. Thus, in the population, an additional year of education yields a higher expected occupational prestige gain for white women than for white men. The black women's education effect is 2.08 + 0.25 = +2.33 prestige points per year. However, this interaction effect is not significantly different from zero, meaning that the prestige impact of an additional year of schooling for black women probably does not differ from that of white men. Similarly, the negative interaction coefficient for black men (–0.40) is not significant, indicating the effect of education on occupational prestige is probably identical for black and white men in the population.

8.7 Comparisons Across Populations

Standardizing the coefficients in a multiple regression has the advantage of allowing interpretations that do not depend on the units in which the variables are measured (e.g., years, days, or minutes). But suppose that we are interested in comparing the coefficients from regression equations estimated for samples drawn from two different populations. For example, we might be interested in comparing the multiple regressions obtained from different historical periods, from different nations, or from different subpopulations within the same society. We have no reason to expect that the standard deviations of variables (used to compute the β^*'s) will be equal across these populations. Indeed, we typically expect them to differ. For example, as years of education and annual incomes increased during the twentieth century, the variability among these measures also increased. Therefore, if we were to standardize the b's in each equation using either the population or sample estimates of the standard deviations, we might reach misleading conclusions about the relative importance of each predictor.

TABLE 8.7
Regressions of Annual Income (in Thousands of Dollars) for Samples of All Respondents, Men, and Women

Independent	All	Men	Women
Intercept	–33.55[a]	–37.06	–33.12
	—	—	—
	(3.12)[c]***	(4.96)***	(3.48)***
Occupational Prestige	0.43[a]	0.55	0.36
	0.24[b]	0.27	0.25
	(0.04)[c]***	(0.07)***	(0.05)***
Education	2.11	2.16	2.16
	0.23	0.22	0.28
	(0.22)***	(0.33)***	(0.25)***
Age	0.40	0.50	0.29
	0.20	0.23	0.19
	(0.04)***	(0.06)***	(0.04)***
Black	–4.81	–5.22	–2.27
	–0.07	–0.06	–0.04
	(1.46)***	(2.56)*	(1.49)
R^2_{adj}	0.230***	0.245***	0.268***
(N)	(1,839)	(875)	(964)

Missing data = 993.
[a]Unstandardized regression coefficient.
[b]Standardized regression coefficient.
[c]Standard error.
For t ratios: *$p < .05$ **$p < .01$ ***$p < .001$
Source: 1998 General Social Survey.

Table 8.7 illustrates a situation with three multiple regression equations of the 1998 GSS respondents' annual incomes (in thousands of dollars) on their occupational prestige scores, years of education, current age, and a dummy variable for race (black vs. other). The equation in column one applies to all 1,839 respondents without missing data. Columns two and three report the regression estimates for 875 men and 964 women, respectively. The effect of race on income is not significantly different from zero in the women's equation, while all other variables have significant effects. The education coefficients are identical for both genders (2.16), but the coefficients for both occupational prestige and age on income appear to be greater for men than for women. However, the size of these differences depends on which type of coefficient is examined. For example, although the unstandardized coefficients for education are the same for men and women (ratio = 2.16/2.16 = 1.00), the ratio of the standardized coefficients is about a quarter larger for women than for men (0.28/0.22 = 1.27). Similar divergences occur for the age effects (standardized ratio = 0.23/0.19 = 1.21, unstandardized ratio = 0.50/0.29 = 1.72) and the occupational prestige effects (standardized ratio = 0.27/0.25 = 1.08, unstandardized ratio = 0.55/0.36 = 1.53).

Given these different results, which set of coefficients should be emphasized? First, we urge researchers always to report both types of equations, just as we have done in Table 8.7, so that readers can compare them and draw their own conclusions. Second, we argue that each type of coefficient has a valuable but distinct use. The standardized β^*'s are useful in comparing the relative importance of predictors *within* equations. Thus, by squaring each β^* in the men's equation, we see that occupational prestige (0.073 of the variance in income) has somewhat larger net impact than either age (0.053) or education (0.048) in predicting annual incomes. For the women, the most important predictor is education (0.078), followed by occupation (0.063) and age (0.036).

When we seek to contrast the predictors *between* equations, the unstandardized coefficients are more meaningful. For example, the standardized coefficients for age are very similar for men and women (0.23 versus 0.19), which appears to indicate only a small difference in the two age effects on income. However, comparing the unstandardized coefficients reveals a substantial gender contrast: the expected difference in annual incomes for a man and a woman is (0.50 − 0.29) × $1,000 = $210 at each year of age. Thus, the gender gap in incomes steadily widens annually across working life, doubling from $6,300 at age 30 to $12,600 at age 60. The main reason for the large metric coefficient impacts lies in the substantial gender difference in income variation. Not only did men make higher mean annual incomes than did women ($36,120 versus $24,190), but the men's income standard deviation ($27,010) was more than a third larger than the women's standard deviation ($19,700). Consequently, standardizing the age coefficient in each equation resulted in a major shift in the relative ratios of the unstandardized regression coefficients.

The differences in the multiple regression coefficients estimated for a pair of identically specified equations can be tested for statistical significance using a t test for the difference in unstandardized regression coefficients. The null hypothesis is that a regression coefficient in the first population equals its corresponding regression coefficient in the second equation. That is, $H_0: \beta_{k_1} = \beta_{k_2}$ for the kth predictor. The formula for a t test with $N_1 + N_2 - k_1 - k_2 - 2$ degrees of freedom is

$$t_{N_1 + N_2 - k_1 - k_2 - 2} = \frac{b_{k1} - b_{k2}}{\sqrt{s^2_{e1} + s^2_{e2}}}$$

where
b_{k1} and b_{k2} = The estimated regression coefficients of variable k in each equation.
s^2_{e1} and s^2_{e2} = The squares of the coefficients' standard errors.

The t test for the age coefficients in Table 8.7 yields

$$t_{1829} = \frac{0.50 - 0.29}{\sqrt{(0.06)^2 + (0.04)^2}} = 2.91$$

which is significant at $p < .01$. Therefore, we conclude that the effect of age on annual income is probably greater for men than for women in the population. You should apply this test to demonstrate a gender difference in the effect of occupational prestige, but not education or race, on income.

Review of Key Concepts and Symbols

These key concepts and symbols are listed in the order of appearance in this chapter. Combined with the definitions in the margins, they will help you to review the material and can serve as a self-test for mastery of the concepts.

multiple regression analysis	population regression model
index	best linear and unbiased estimate (BLUE)
construct	sample regression equation
indicator	prediction equation
Cronbach's alpha	nested regression equations
ordinary least squares	adjusted coefficient of determination
listwise deletion	multicollinearity
pairwise deletion	dummy variable
multiple regression coefficient	analysis of covariance (ANCOVA)
part correlation	covariate
multiple correlation coefficient	treatment level
partial regression coefficient	interaction effect

α	$MS_{\text{REGRESSION}}$
β_j	MS_{ERROR}
a	$r_{YX_j \cdot X_i}$
b	$R^2_{Y \cdot X_1 X_2 \ldots X_K}$
β^*_j	R^2_{adj}
$R^2_{Y \cdot X_1 X_2}$	S_{b_j}
SS_{TOTAL}	σ^2_e
$SS_{\text{REGRESSION}}$	D
SS_{ERROR}	

PROBLEMS

General Problems

1. Using the following information, compute the a, b_1, and b_2 coefficients for the regression of Y on X_1 and X_2, and display the results as a prediction equation:

Variable	Mean	Standard Deviation	Correlations X_1	X_2	Y
X_1	5	3	1.00		
X_2	25	8	0.60	1.00	
Y	20	6	0.40	−0.30	1.00

2. Compute the beta weights for the data shown in Problem 1, writing out the regression prediction equation for standardized variables.

3. Using survey data from a sample of 123 respondents, a regression equation with four independent variables predicting attitudes toward the death penalty has a coefficient of determination of 0.035. Is the coefficient of determination significantly different from zero at $\alpha = .05$? If the sample size were 1,230, would the coefficient of determination differ significantly from zero at the same probability level?

4. A regression of attitude toward legalizing marijuana on age (X_1) and education (X_2) produced the following estimated coefficients and standard errors for a sample of 265 persons:

$b_1 = -6.24$ $\qquad\qquad\qquad s_{b_1} = 3.46$

$b_2 = +0.33$ $\qquad\qquad\qquad s_{b_2} = 0.12$

Test one-tailed alternatives to the null hypotheses that $\beta_1 < 0$ and $\beta_2 > 0$; use $\alpha = .01$.

5. If $N = 300$, $b_1 = -3.83$, $MS_{ERROR} = 12.75$, $\Sigma(X_{1i} - \bar{X}_1)^2 = 16.83$, and $R^2_{X_1 \cdot X_2} = 0.294$, is b_1 significant at $\alpha = .001$ for a two-tailed test?

6. Form the 95% and 99% confidence intervals around b_1 in Problem 5.

7. Write a substantive interpretation of the following unstandardized regression equation based on a sample of 743 city residents, where Y is a 10-point scale measuring the number of professional sporting events attended per year, X_1 is education, X_2 is annual income (divided by \$10,000), and X_3 is a dummy variable for gender (1= female, 0 = male). The t ratios appear in parentheses

$\hat{Y} = -8.73 - 0.59X_1 + 1.46X_2 - 5.40X_3$
$\quad\;\;(-3.76)\;(-1.42)\quad(2.14)\quad(-2.87)$

8. Construct dummy variable codes for favorite type of music, as measured by these categories: country, rock, rap, jazz, classical, none. Show your results in a matrix (row-and-column) format.

9. For a study of 634 companies in three industries, $D_M =$ manufacturing, $D_R =$ retail, and $D_T =$ transportation; X_1 measures annual sales; and Y is annual profit rate. Set up two multiple regression equations that would enable you to investigate whether the type of industry and sales interact in predic.ing a company's profit rate.

10. A regression analysis for a sample of 718 people predicts the number of hours per day spent watching televised sports (Y) by annual income (X) (in thousands of dollars) and a set of two dummy variables for occupation: $D_1 =$ white collar and $D_2 =$ blue collar. Three estimated regression equations are

$\hat{Y} = 2.76 - 0.64D_1,\ R^2_1 = 0.153$
$\hat{Y} = 2.84 - 0.57D_1 - 0.08X,\ R^2_2 = 0.197$
$\hat{Y} = 2.84 - 0.48D_1 - 0.06X + 0.07XD_1,\ R^2_3 = 0.214$

a. Is there a significant interaction between occupational category and watching sports on TV? Set $\alpha = .001$.

b. Using the interaction equation, calculate the predicted hours of TV sports-watching for a white-collar worker making $45,000 per year.

Problems Requiring the 1998 General Social Survey

11. Regress satisfaction with one's job (SATJOB) on EDUC and AGE.

   a. Present the regression coefficients with their tests of significance and beta weights.

   b. Present the adjusted coefficient of determination with its test of significance.

   c. Interpret the results.

   Note: Recode job satisfaction so that the most satisfied category has the highest value: RECODE satjob (1=4)(2=3)(3=2)(4=1). Set missing values for all variables. Use $\alpha = .001$ for t tests.

12. To the regression equation for job satisfaction in Problem 11, add four dummy variables for marital status (MARITAL). Create codes for married, widowed, divorced, and separated persons, and treat "never married" as the reference category.

   a. What are the effects of the four marital statuses on SATJOB relative to the reference category?

   b. Did the addition of the marital status dummies increase this equation's R^2 significantly, compared to the R^2 for the equation in Problem 11? Set $\alpha = .05$.

13. Regress respondent's education (EDUC) on father's education (PAEDUC) and occupational prestige (PAPRES80). Compare the standardized regression coefficients, and decide which independent variable has the strongest effect on the respondent's educational attainment. How much of the variation in the dependent variable is explained by the linear combination of the independent variables, adjusted for the degrees of freedom?

14. Does the effect of age on church attendance vary with religious affiliation? Using RELIG, create dummy variables for Protestant, Catholic, and Jewish (using Other/None as the omitted category), and form all three interaction terms with AGE.

   a. Test the R^2 for an ANCOVA equation with ATTEND predicted by age and the three religious dummy variables, setting $\alpha = .05$.

   b. Test the R^2 for the regression equation that includes the AGE–RELIG dummy variable interaction terms, with $\alpha = .05$.

   c. Test the difference in R^2 for the two equations above, setting $\alpha = .05$.

15. Use regression and analysis of variance to determine whether respondents' political views (POLVIEWS) differ significantly across the nine U.S. census regions (REGION).

   a. Report both the ANOVA effects and the dummy regression coefficients, using the Pacific region as the omitted category.

   b. What is the formula for translating each regression β_j into an ANOVA α_j?

   c. Present an ANOVA summary table for the results, and find the critical value at $p < .001$ to reject the null hypothesis.

9

NONLINEAR AND LOGISTIC REGRESSION

9.1 Nonlinear Regression
9.2 Dichotomous Dependent Variables
9.3 The Logistic Transformation and Its Properties

9.4 Estimating and Testing Logistic Regression Equations
9.5 The Multinomial-Logit Model

In the preceding chapter, all the variables used in multiple regression analyses were measured on scales having intervals of constant width. Consequently, a metric regression coefficient represents the net effect of an independent variable on a dependent variable that remains constant throughout that predictor's range. That is, an estimated β_j indicates that the dependent variable increases by equal β amounts per unit of the independent variable. For example, if each year of education is estimated to produce a $950 return in a person's annual income, the effect of an additional year of education is the same for those persons with 10 years as for those with 20 years of schooling. In this chapter we will consider situations in which the amount of change in the dependent variable *varies* according to the level of the independent variable. Although such relations cannot be accurately represented by a straight regression line, nonlinear relations can be converted to linear ones by transforming the variables' scales. Relationships among the transformed variables can then be estimated with techniques presented in previous chapters. In this chapter we will also examine logistic regression analysis, in which the dependent variable may be either a dichotomous or a multi-category discrete variable. We will discuss the techniques required to estimate these relationships.

9.1 Nonlinear Regression

9.1.1 Comparing Linear to Nonlinear Relations

In the absence of reasons for expecting that two continuous variables are related in a nonlinear fashion, researchers can test a hypothesis that only linearity is present. The procedure involves comparing proportions of the dependent variable's variance that can be attributed to its linear and nonlinear relationships with a predictor variable. To simplify the presentation, we examine only the bivariate case, although the procedure readily applies to multivariate equations. We seek to reject the following null hypothesis:

H_0: Y has only a linear relation to X.

The hypothesis testing procedure follows several familiar steps:

1. Collapse the independent variable into a set of ordered discrete categories that do not seriously distort the original distribution. In general, between six and 20 categories should suffice.

2. Perform a one-way analysis of variance (ANOVA; see chapter 4) on the dependent variable, using the collapsed categories created in step 1 as the independent variable.

3. Using the ANOVA sums of squares, compute η^2 (eta-squared; see section 4.4 in chapter 4). This statistic measures the proportion of variance in the dependent variable that is explained statistically *by both linear and nonlinear relationships* with the predictor's categories.

4. Regress the dependent variable on the same collapsed independent variable, treating it as a continuous predictor. Compute R^2 (R-square), which measures the proportion of variance in the dependent variable that is statistically explained by its *linear relationship* to the predictor.

5. Subtract R^2 from η^2 to remove the linear component of the relationship, leaving only the nonlinear component. Calculate an F ratio of this difference to test whether the nonlinearity differs from zero in the population at a chosen α level:

$$F_{K-2, N-K} = \frac{(\eta^2 - R^2_{Y \cdot X})/(K-2)}{(1 - \eta^2)/(N-K)}$$

where

K = The number of categories associated with ANOVA.
$(K-2)$ and $(N-K)$ = The degrees of freedom for the F ratio.

If F is significantly larger than the critical value, then we must reject the null hypothesis that the variables are linearly related in the population (i.e., that H_0: $\eta^2 = \varrho^2_{Y \bullet X}$) in favor of the alternative, H_1: $\eta^2 > \varrho^2_{Y \bullet X}$. That is, after linearity is taken into account, the nonlinear relationship is probably greater than zero in the population.

To illustrate, Figure 9.1 uses the 1998 GSS data to plot the mean number of children born to 1,596 women categorized into seven current age intervals, or cohorts. The means clearly do not fall on a straight line. Women aged 18–30 years have the fewest children (0.89), in part because many are still in their peak childbearing years. Women who were 61–70 years old in 1998 had borne the most children (mean of 3.17), while the two older cohorts on average had fewer offspring. This dynamic may be mainly historical, given that the cohort aged 61 to 70 years came of childbearing age during the Baby Boom era of the 1950s, while the older women had experienced the Depression era's "birth dearth."

The linear regression of children borne on women's ages in decades yields an estimated $R^2 = 0.159$, indicating that current age linearly ex-

FIGURE 9.1
Mean Number of Children Born to Women by Current Age

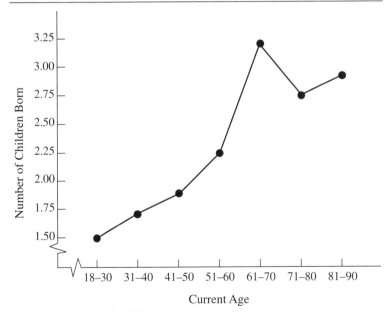

Source: 1998 General Social Survey.

plains 15.9% of the variance in number of children. However, a one-way ANOVA with these seven categories yields $\hat{\eta}^2 = 0.177$, showing that, allowing for nonlinearity, current age explains 17.7% of the childbearing variance. For $\alpha = .001$, Appendix E shows that the critical value is $F_{5,1589} = 4.10$. The test statistic's value is

$$F_{5,\ 1589} = \frac{(0.177 - 0.159)/(7 - 2)}{(1 - 0.177)/(1596 - 7)} = 6.95$$

Therefore, we can reject the null hypothesis in favor of the alternative that childbearing is nonlinearly related to women's current ages in the population from which the GSS sample came, with only a very small probability of Type I error.

9.1.2 Functional Forms of Nonlinear Equations

Once nonlinearity is detected, the next step is to determine its precise functional form. In mathematical notation, the expression $Y = f(X)$ simply means that the expected value of the dependent variable $\hat{Y}_i$ is some (unspecified) function of the independent variable value, X_i. Ordinary least squares (OLS) regression specifies that the relationship takes a linear and additive form: $\hat{Y}_i = \alpha + \beta X_i$. But many other functional forms express various types of nonlinear relations, as illustrated by the plots of some example equations in Figures 9.2A–D for positive values of X. In the quadratic (parabolic) function in diagram 9.2A, $\hat{Y}_i = \alpha + \beta X_i^2$, the intercept α indicates the point at which the curve crosses the Y-axis (i.e., where $X_i = 0$). At successive values on the X-axis, the amount of change in Y grows increasingly larger. If the β coefficient has a negative sign, then the parabola is inverted, indicating that successive values of X predict increasingly negative amounts of Y. In the reciprocal function in diagram 9.2B, $\hat{Y}_i = \alpha + \beta/X_i$, as larger values of X are divided into the constant parameter β, successively smaller decreases in the predicted value of Y slowly approach a limit (asymptote) at α on the Y-axis.

In the two natural logarithmic functions plotted in diagram 9.2C, $\hat{Y}_i = \alpha + \beta \log_e X_i$, successively larger values of X predict increasingly smaller changes in Y, although no ultimate limit is approached. The rapidity with which a logarithmic curve flattens out depends on the size of β (both equal 1 in the two examples), while the point at which the curve crosses the X-axis depends on the value of α (the line never intercepts the Y-axis, as the logarithm of a negative X value is not defined). Finally, the exponential function in diagram 9.2D, $\hat{Y}_i = e^{\alpha + \beta X_i}$, resembles the parabola, but the values of Y change much more rapidly as a function of changes

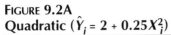

FIGURE 9.2A
Quadratic ($\hat{Y}_i = 2 + 0.25X_i^2$)

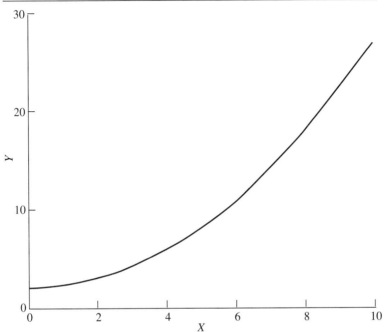

in X. (Calculate and compare X^2 to e^X for the same values of X.) The precise shape and location of an exponential curve depend on its parameters: if $\beta > 0$, the curve increases as X increases, as in Figure 9.2D, while if $\beta < 0$, the curve decreases as X increases. The term e is **Euler's constant**, an irrational number that is used as the base of natural logarithms (the natural log of X is symbolized by $\log_e X$ or by $\ln X$). Its approximate numerical value is 2.71828.

> **Euler's constant**—an irrational number that is used as the base of natural logarithms

These and other nonlinear functions can be brought into the conventional OLS estimation methods by transforming the predictor variables. The independent variable's values are changed to a new variable according to the desired functional form, and then this new variable is entered into an OLS regression equation. For example, if X_i has both a linear and a quadratic relation with Y_i, the equation in population notation is $\hat{Y}_i = \alpha + \beta_1 X_i + \beta_2 X_i^2$. If we create a second variable that consists of the squared values of X, the equation is linear in terms of the *parameters* while remaining nonlinear in terms of the *variables*. Both X and X^2 may be

FIGURE 9.2B
Reciprocal ($\hat{Y}_i = 2 + 8/X_i$)

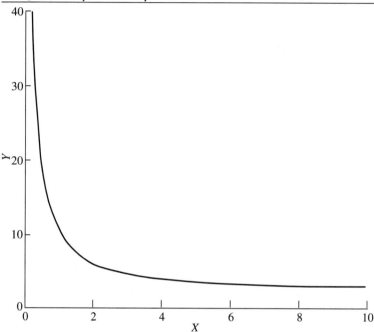

entered into the same regression equation if they are not severely multi-collinear (i.e., they do not have a high correlation; see section 8.2.2).

To illustrate this procedure, consider the relationship between people's annual incomes (Y) and their ages (X). Although we expect incomes to increase with age (in large measure through work experiences that increase older employees' value to employers), we also do not expect their incomes to rise throughout the entire 40-year range of prime working ages. Rather, after an initial rise, incomes will tend to level off and may even fall as people near retirement age. Hence, a quadratic specification in sample notation seems plausible: $\hat{Y}_i = \alpha + \beta_1 X_i - \beta_2 X_i^2$, where Y is annual income in hundreds of dollars, X is age in years, and X^2 is age-squared. While the β_1 has a positive sign, consistent with a hypothesized increase of income with age, the negative sign of the β_2 coefficient reflects our hypothesized decrease of income with the square of age. Using the 879 currently working men in the 1998 GSS and recoding respon-

FIGURE **9.2C**
Natural Logarithmic

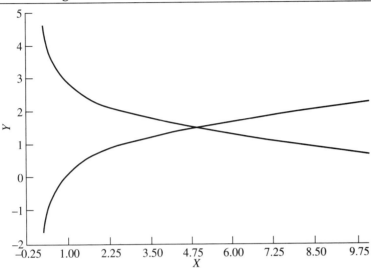

dents' income categories to midpoint values in thousands of dollars, the estimated OLS regression equation (with standard errors in parentheses) is

$$\hat{Y}_i = -49.970 + 3.758X_i - 0.037X_i^2$$
$$(8.05) \quad (0.381) \quad (0.004)$$
$$R^2_{adj} = 0.130$$

Both the linear and the quadratic coefficients differ significantly from zero at $\alpha = .05$. Each year of age increases a man's annual income by $3,758, but the quadratic term decreases his income by $37 per squared year of age. To find where the peak earning age occurs, elementary differential calculus can be applied to determine the point on the age scale where the slope of the curve equals zero. Take the first derivative of the estimated equation with respect to X:

$$\frac{\delta Y}{\delta X} = 3.758 - (2)(0.037)X$$

FIGURE 9.2D
Exponential ($\hat{Y}_i = e^{0.5 + 0.25X_i}$)

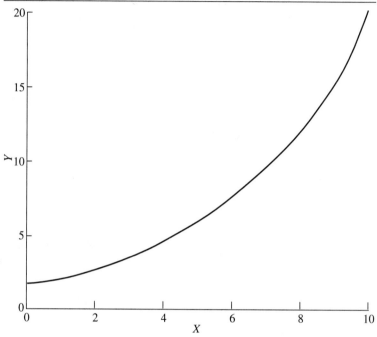

Set the equation equal to zero: $3.758 - 0.074X = 0$. Solving the equation gives $X = 50.8$ years.

The logarithmic function can also be estimated by transforming the predictor variable. Then an OLS regression using the transformed measure is linear in the estimated parameters while remaining logarithmic in terms of the variables. To illustrate, we specify a logarithmic function between the number of children born to a woman and her age at first childbirth. The younger the age at which a woman bears her first child, the more children she is likely to bear. We hypothesize that the total number of children ever born to a woman decreases in a negative logarithmic pattern the older a woman is at her first childbirth. Thus, an appropriate specification is $\hat{Y}_i = \alpha - \beta \log_e X_i$, where Y is the number of children ever born and $\log_e X$ is the natural logarithm (base e) of age in years at first marriage. The β coefficient is shown with a negative sign, consistent with our hypothesis that women who start bearing children later will ultimately have fewer children. Using the 1,199 women in the

1998 GSS, the OLS regression estimates (with standard errors in parentheses) are as follows:

$$\hat{Y}_i = 9.343 - 2.188 \log_e X_i$$
$$(0.610) \quad (0.197)$$
$$R^2_{adj} = 0.093$$

As any nonlinear function implies, the expected number of children is not constant across the (log-transformed) age variable. For example, the equation predicts that a woman having her first child at 17 years ($\log_e 17 = 2.833$) will have $9.343 - (2.188)(2.833) = 3.14$ children, while first childbirth at age 20 years ($\log_e = 2.996$) produces only $9.343 - (2.188)(2.996) = 2.79$ children, a difference of 0.35 children for the three-year delay. However, women married at ages 27 and 30 years are expected to bear 2.13 and 1.90 children, respectively—a difference of only 0.23 children for that three-year span. Clearly, a woman's childbirth history depends significantly on when she begins.

The exponential function shown in Figure 9.2D is just one of several alternative specifications. Another exponential form, often used to examine growth processes, is $\hat{Y}_i = \alpha X_i^\beta$. Here, the intercept is separated from the regression parameter, which is an exponent for the predictor variable. An appropriate transformation that preserves linearity in the parameters takes natural logarithms of *both* sides of the estimated equation

$$\hat{\log_e} \hat{Y}_i = \log_e \alpha + \beta \log_e X_i$$

Unbiased estimates of the β and $\log_e \alpha$ parameters can be obtained from an OLS regression of $\log_e Y$ on $\log_e X$. To recover the original α parameter value, take the antilog of the estimated $\log_e \alpha$. To illustrate, Figure 9.3A displays the population of the United States (in millions) at each decennial census from 1790 to 1990. The pattern clearly implies accelerating growth over the two centuries (with a notable disruption at the 1930–1940 Depression). But the plot in Figure 9.3B more closely approximates a straight-line relationship. The estimated double-logged OLS equation (with standard errors in parentheses) is

$$\hat{\log_e} \hat{Y}_i = -0.25 + 1.92(\log_e X_i)$$
$$(0.080) \quad (0.070)$$
$$R^2_{adj} = 0.972$$

where the values of X for time in decades were recoded from $1790 = 2$ to $1990 = 22$. The R-square value shows that almost all the variation in

FIGURE 9.3A
U.S. Population by Census Year

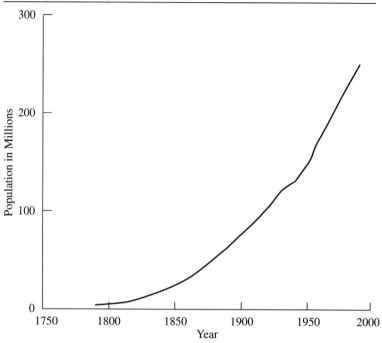

logged population is captured by this specification (the linear regression of nonlogged population on decade time produces an $R^2 = 0.920$). The antilog$_e$ of the estimated intercept (–0.25) is 0.78. Thus, the estimated equation for the U.S. population's exponential growth is $\hat{Y}_i = 0.78X_i^{1.92}$. The exponent (1.92) can be interpreted as the "elasticity" of the dependent variable with respect to the independent variable. That is, a 1% change in X is associated with an expected 1.92% change in the expected value of the dependent variable. Because 1% of two centuries under analysis is 2 years, the U.S. population grew on average by 1.92% every two years (i.e., 9.60% per decade). The derivative of the exponentiated double-log equation can also be used to calculate the expected value of the slope of the exponential growth line at any point X_i on the X-axis:

$$\frac{\delta Y}{\delta X} = \text{slope at } X_i = \alpha\beta X_i^{\beta - 1}$$
$$= (0.78)(1.92)X_i^{1.92 - 1}$$
$$= 1.50X_i^{0.92}$$

FIGURE 9.3B
U.S. Population (Log$_e$) by Census Year

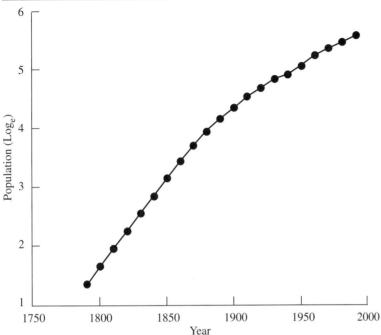

An exponential slope changes nonlinearly, becoming increasingly larger as time goes by. For example, at the 9th Census (1860), the equation estimates the U.S. population to be growing by $(1.50)(9)^{0.92} = 11.3$ million per decade, while by the 21st Census (1980) the expected slope value had more than doubled to $(1.50)(21)^{0.92} = 24.7$ million additional Americans. The actual population increases were 8.4 million and 26.5 million, respectively. When the logarithmic equation is used to forecast growth in the decade A.D. 2090–2100 (the 32nd Census observation), a predicted $(1.50)(32)^{0.92} = 36.4$ million new people would be added to the U.S. population during that decade. Whether such rapid growth can actually be sustained over the coming century remains to be seen.

9.2 Dichotomous Dependent Variables

Until now, we have estimated regressions only with continuous dependent variables because they most closely approximate the best linear unbiased estimator (BLUE) criteria discussed in Box 8.2 of chapter 8. Nothing technically prevents us from analyzing dichotomous (1–0) or dummy dependent variables within an OLS framework. For example, in the 1998 GSS, 923 respondents said they voted for Bill Clinton (coded 1) and 589 reported voting for Bob Dole (coded 0) for president in 1996. (For this illustration, we ignore the 215 respondents reporting that they voted for Ross Perot or some other candidate outside the two major parties.) The proportion voting for Clinton is 0.61. OLS regression of this dichotomy on four predictors yields the following unstandardized parameters (standard errors in parentheses):

$$\hat{Y}_i = 1.389 - 0.136X_{1i} - 0.054X_{2i} - 0.087X_{3i} - 0.008X_{4i} - 0.038X_{5i}$$
$$\quad\;\; (0.051)\;\; (0.005)\qquad (0.007)\qquad (0.024)\qquad (0.003)\qquad (0.019)$$
$$R^2_{adj} = 0.532$$

where $\hat{Y}$ is the expected vote for Clinton; X_1 is the respondent's party identification (coded from 0 = strong Democrat to 6 = strong Republican); X_2 signifies his or her political views (1 = extremely liberal to 7 = extremely conservative); X_3 is a dummy variable for race (1 = white, 0 = other); X_4 is education (0 to 20 years); and X_5 is region of residence (1 = South, 0 = other). Because the dependent variable's range is confined between two choices, the equation can be interpreted as a **linear probability model** of the vote for Clinton. For example, each point in the Republican direction on the party identification decreases the proportion a person voted for Clinton by –0.136; whites are –0.087 less likely than nonwhites to vote for Clinton; and so forth.

linear probability model—a linear regression model in which the dependent variable is confined between two choices

Two fundamental assumptions in regression analysis are violated by dichotomous dependent variables, making such linear probability models undesirable. First, the BLUE assumption that the error terms are normally distributed is not met. A regression error is the difference between an observed and a predicted score: $e_i = Y_i - \hat{Y}_i = Y_i - (\alpha + \Sigma\beta_{ji}X_{ji})$. However, because respondents can have observed scores of only 1 or 0, their error terms therefore can take only two values. For $Y_i = 1$, $e_i = 1 - \alpha - \Sigma\beta_{ji}X_{ji}$; while for $Y_i = 0$, $e_i = -\alpha - \Sigma\beta_{ji}X_{ji}$. Consequently, although the OLS parameter estimates of the β_j's are unbiased, they are not the most efficient estimates (i.e., with the smallest possible sampling variances; see section 3.10). Hypothesis tests using these estimated parameters and their standard errors can reach invalid conclusions, even for very large samples.

The second problem with dichotomous dependent variable regression is that some expected values may be nonsensical. Because the parameters depict multivariate linear relations of the predictors to the dependent measure, the expected scores for some extreme combinations may fall outside the range from 0 to 1. Such results are meaningless because negative probabilities and chances greater than 1.00 are undefined. To illustrate, consider the expected score of a voter with the extreme high values on all the independent variables predisposing him or her to vote for Clinton:

$$\hat{Y}_i = 1.389 - 0.136(6) - 0.054(7) - 0.087(1) - 0.008(20) - 0.038(1)$$
$$= -0.09$$

A probability of voting for Clinton that is –0.09 is impossible to comprehend. Similarly, persons with a contrasting configuration of independent values generate an expected Clinton vote:

$$\hat{Y}_i = 1.389 - 0.136(0) - 0.054(1) - 0.087(0) - 0.008(0) - 0.038(0)$$
$$= 1.34$$

This positive probability of voting for Clinton also cannot be imagined.

As these examples make clear, the linear probability version of OLS regression is unsatisfactory. We need an alternative approach that does not require unrealistic assumptions about probabilities that are linear functions of the predictor variables. Fortunately, such alternative nonlinear functional forms exist, for both dichotomous and nonordered discrete dependent variables, as discussed in the remainder of this chapter.

9.3 The Logistic Transformation and Its Properties

Percentages and proportions (p) are not the only ways to measure a dichotomous response variable. The **logistic transformation of p** is a useful alternative with some insightful properties. Using the natural logarithm (that is, with Euler's constant e as the base), the logistic probability unit, or **logit**, for the ith observation is computed by forming the odds of p_i to its reciprocal, $1 - p_i$, and taking the $\log_e$ of this ratio (i.e., the logit is the natural log of an odds):

logistic transformation of p—a natural logarithmic change in the odds of a probability

logit—logistic probability unit

$$L_i = \log_e\left(\frac{p_i}{1 - p_i}\right)$$

The logit is symmetrically distributed around a central value. When $p_i = 0.50$, its reciprocal value is also $1 - 0.50 = 0.50$. Hence, the natural log of this ratio is $L_i = \log_e (0.50/0.50) = \log_e 1 = 0$. As the dichotomy becomes more extreme in either direction, approaching 0 or 1, the logit values move farther apart, as shown by these calculations:

p_i:	0.10	0.20	0.30	0.40	0.50	0.60	0.70	0.80	0.90
$1 - p_i$:	0.90	0.80	0.70	0.60	0.50	0.40	0.30	0.20	0.10
logit:	−2.20	−1.39	−0.85	−0.41	0.00	0.41	0.85	1.39	2.20

Although these probabilities have constant 0.10 intervals, their corresponding logits have increasingly wider intervals the farther they are from $p_i = 0.50$. Also note that, although no upper or lower limit exists for the logit, when p_i exactly equals 1.00 or 0.00, the logit is undefined. Figure 9.4 plots the continuous transformation of probabilities into their logits. It shows the cumulative probability distribution for the probability that Y_i equals one (i.e., $p(Y_i) = 1$), where Y_i is a dichotomy, for values of the log

FIGURE 9.4
The Logistic Probability Form

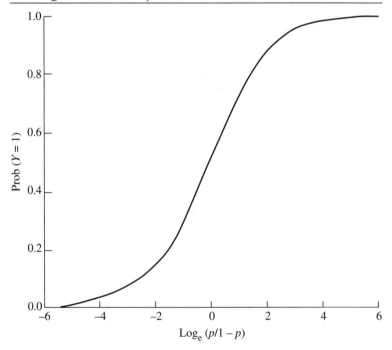

odds that range from negative infinity to positive infinity. This S-shaped curve closely resembles the plot of the cumulative probability for the standardized normal distribution (Z scores). The logistic transformation is nearly linear within the range from $p_i = 0.25$ to 0.75, and consequently the linear probability model gives results very similar to the logistic. However, as a dichotomy becomes more skewed in either direction, the nonlinearity of the logistic grows more pronounced. For very large L_i values in both the positive or negative direction, the probabilities for Y_i approach but never quite reach 1.00 and 0.00, respectively. Thus, even very extreme logit estimates can never be associated with expected probabilities that fall outside the meaningful 0–1 range. *This constraint on the expected values of the logistic transformation is its most important advantage over the linear probability form.*

Because they "stretch out" very high and low probabilities, logits are useful for making comparisons among proportions at differing levels. Table 9.1 shows the later school enrollments of four U.S. cohorts that entered the fifth grade at approximately four-year intervals between 1945 and 1960. The top panel displays the proportions of each cohort that entered the eighth grade, graduated from high school, and entered college. Over this period, the rates rose for each successive cohort at all three schooling levels, but comparisons are complicated by the different initial rates of the three schooling levels. For example, comparing 1945 to 1960 proportions, the eighth grade enrollments were only 0.109 higher, while high school graduate and college attendance rates appear to have changed by more than twice as much, increasing 0.265 and 0.218, respectively. But, we could also assert that, relative to their 1945 proportions, the college entry rate almost doubled, the high school rate was 50% higher, but eighth grade attendance was up by only one-eighth over the 15-year period. Both these interpretations of the proportions suggest that school attendance changed at different rates between 1945–1960 across the three schooling levels. Because proportions and percentages are constrained to the interval between 0.00 and 1.00 (or 0% and 100%), such comparisons fail to adjust for "floor" and "ceiling" effects. That is, a 1% change in a 50% rate is not the same as a 1% change in a 98% rate.

Because of its symmetrical nature, the logistic transformation of an odds $p_i/(1 - p_i)$ and an inverse odds $(1 - p_i)/p_i$ result in equal but oppositely signed logits. For example, the proportions 0.75 and 0.25 correspond to odds of $0.75/(1 - 0.75) = 3.000$ and inverse odds of $0.25/(1 - 0.25) = 0.333$. Taking natural logs, these ratios yield logits of $+1.0986$ and -1.0996, respectively, indicating their fundamental equivalence. The second and third panels of Table 9.1 transform the school enrollment proportions, first into odds, then into logits. Figure 9.5 plots these logits,

TABLE 9.1
Enrollments by Four Cohorts at Three Schooling Levels

Cohort Entering Fifth Grade in:	SUBSEQUENT SCHOOLING		
	Entered Eighth Grade	Graduated High School	Entered College
	Proportions		
1960	0.967	0.787	0.452
1955	0.948	0.642	0.343
1951	0.921	0.582	0.308
1945	0.858	0.522	0.234
	Odds		
1960	29.303	3.695	0.825
1955	18.231	1.793	0.522
1951	11.658	1.392	0.445
1945	6.042	1.092	0.305
	Logits		
1960	3.378	1.307	–0.193
1955	2.903	0.584	–0.650
1951	2.456	0.331	–0.809
1945	1.799	0.088	–1.186

Source: U.S. Census Bureau. 1975. *Historical Statistics of the United States: Colonial Times to 1970. Part 1.* Washington, DC: U.S. Government Printing Office. Series H587–597, p. 379.

revealing the four cohorts' enrollment trends for the three schooling levels during this 15-year period. Each trend is roughly linear in the $\log_e$ odds, with the major deviation being a noticeable spurt in high school graduation by the 1960 cohort. We may reasonably conclude that the mid-century U.S. cohorts' school attendance grew at approximately constant rates at all three schooling levels.

The logit provides a suitable basis for an alternative to the unsatisfactory linear probability model. We begin this derivation with the linear probability model, which expresses the probability that the ith observation has a score of 1 on the dependent variable as a linear, additive function of K predictor variables:

$$\text{Prob } (Y_i = 1) = p_i = \alpha + \sum_{j=1}^{K} \beta_j X_{ji}$$

FIGURE **9.5**
Logits of Enrollments by Four Cohorts at Three Schooling Levels

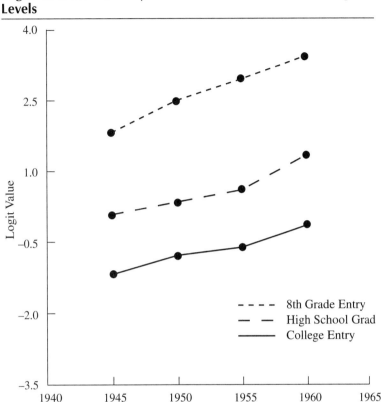

As noted in section 9.2, the problem with the linear probability model is that a probability p_i is constrained within the range of 0–1 but the expression $\alpha + \Sigma \beta_j X_{ji}$ is not so constrained. To avoid this conundrum, in the case of a dichotomous variable, we can eliminate the upper bound on probability by forming the ratio of the probabilities that a case has an observation value of 1 or 0. That is, in the odds formed by these two probabilities,

$$\frac{\text{Prob } (Y_i = 1)}{\text{Prob } (Y_i = 0)} = \frac{p_i}{1 - p_i}$$

the ratio must be positive because $0 \leq p_i \leq 1$, but the ratio has no upper limit as p_i gets closer and closer to 1. By taking the natural logarithm of the odds, $\log_e (p_i/1 - p_i)$, we eliminate the lower probability bound of zero, and the resulting values range across the real numbers from negative to positive infinity. Note that this logged ratio of probabilities was defined above as the logit (L_i). Now equate this transformed dependent variable to a linear function of the predictor variables:

$$\log_e \left(\frac{p_i}{1 - p_i} \right) = \alpha + \sum_{j=1}^{K} \beta_j X_{ji}$$

Simplify the right-side notation by setting $\alpha + \Sigma \beta_j X_{ji} = Z$:

$$\log_e \left(\frac{p_i}{1 - p_i} \right) = Z$$

To solve for p_i, we apply the antilogarithm or exponentiation function, $\exp X$ or e^X, to both sides of this equation. (The base for natural logarithms is Euler's irrational number $e \approx 2.71828$, where $\log_e (e^X) = X$ and the antilog of $X = e^X$.) Therefore, the solution for p_i is

$$\exp \log_e \left(\frac{p_i}{1 - p_i} \right) = \exp Z$$

$$\frac{p_i}{1 - p_i} = \exp Z$$

$$p_i = (1 - p_i) e^Z$$

$$p_i = e^Z - p_i e^Z$$

$$p_i + p_i e^Z = e^Z$$

$$p_i (1 + e^Z) = e^Z$$

$$p_i = \frac{e^Z}{(1 + e^Z)} = \frac{1}{(1 + e^{-Z})}$$

The two expressions on the right side in the final step are called the logistic function. By resubstituting the original expression for Z, we see that the probability that the ith case has a score of 1 on the dependent dichotomy is

$$p_i = \frac{1}{(1 + e^{-\alpha - \Sigma \beta_j X_{ji}})}$$

Because the logit (L_i) for the ith observation is defined as the natural logarithm of the odds, we can replace the probability p_i with the logistic function

$$L_i = \log_e \left(\frac{p_i}{1 - p_i} \right)$$

$$L_i = \log_e (e^{\alpha + \Sigma \beta_j X_{ji}})$$

$$L_i = \alpha + \Sigma \beta_j X_{ji}$$

Box 9.1 gives additional details of this derivation. In the presidential voting example, the odds of the probability of a vote for Clinton relative to the probability of a vote for Dole is $0.61/(1 - 0.61) = 0.61/0.39 = 1.56$. The natural log of this number is 0.445. Figure 9.6 illustrates the difference between hypothetical linear probability and logistic regression lines calculated using the same dichotomous sample data. The predicted linear probability is less than 0 and greater than 1 for extreme values of Z, but the logit never exceeds these limits for any value of Z.

Although the underlying probability is not a linear function of the predictors, the log-odds transformation makes the logit a linear additive function of the X_K independent variables. A dichotomous logit is directly interpretable as (the natural log of) the odds of the probability that $Y = 1$ to the probability that $Y = 0$. Given the symmetry of the logistic curve shown in Figure 9.4, when the probability that an observation has a score

---

Box 9.1   The Derivation of the Logit

First, to simplify notation, set $\alpha + \Sigma \beta_j X_{ji} = Z$. Given that the probability that the ith case has a score of 1 is

$$p_i = \frac{1}{1 + e^{-Z}}$$

its reciprocal must be

$$1 - p_i = 1 - \frac{1}{1 + e^{-Z}} = \frac{1 + e^{-Z} - 1}{1 + e^{-Z}} = \frac{e^{-Z}}{1 + e^{-Z}}$$

Take the ratio of these reciprocal terms and simplify:

$$\frac{p_i}{1 - p_i} = \frac{1/(1 + e^{-Z})}{e^{-Z}/(1 + e^{-Z})} = \frac{1}{e^{-Z}} = e^Z$$

Next, take natural logarithms of the ratio:

$$\log_e \left(\frac{p_i}{1 - p_i} \right) = \log_e \left(\frac{1}{e^{-Z}} \right) = \log_e (e^Z) = Z$$

Finally, substituting for Z and defining the result as the logit L for the ith case, we have

$$\log_e \left(\frac{p_i}{1 - p_i} \right) = L_i = \alpha + \Sigma \beta_j X_{ji}$$

FIGURE 9.6
Linear Probability Compared to Logistic Regression

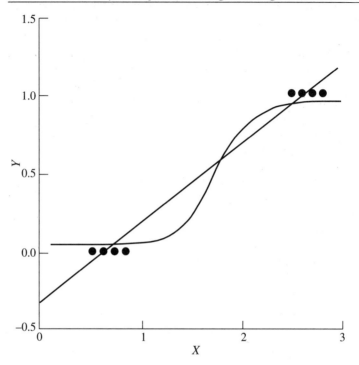

of 1 exactly equals 0.50, the logit equals 0 (i.e., $p_{Y=1}/p_{Y=0} = 0.50/0.50$ = 1.00 and thus $\log_e 1.00 = 0.0$). When the probability that $Y = 1$ is greater than the probability that $Y = 0$, the logit is greater than 0. Finally, when the probability that $Y = 1$ is less than the probability that $Y = 0$, the logit is smaller than 0. The logit is undefined in the situation where the probability that $Y = 0$ is exactly zero; division by zero in the denominator is mathematically impossible. However, as the probability that $Y = 1$ approaches certainty (i.e., $p_{Y=1} \rightarrow 1.00$) and thus the probability that $Y = 0$ drops toward zero (i.e., $p_{Y=0} \rightarrow 0$), the logit approaches positive infinity (see the right-hand side of Figure 9.4). In the opposite situation, where the probability that $Y = 0$ approaches certainty and hence the probability that $Y = 1$ drops toward zero, the logit approaches negative infinity (see the left-hand side of Figure 9.4). This property of the logit, the natural logarithm of the ratio of two probabilities in the dichotomous case, makes it a very useful functional form for multivariate analysis.

9.4 Estimating and Testing Logistic Regression Equations

9.4.1 Parameter Estimates

Logistic regression parallels multiple regression analysis, with the dependent variable as the log odds of a dichotomy rather than a continuous measure. Just as in multiple regression, the independent or predictor variables in a logistic regression may be continuous measures, dichotomies, multi-category dummy variables, or interaction terms. The basic **dichotomous logistic regression equation** for K independent variables is

$$\hat{L}_i = \alpha + \beta_1 X_{1i} + \beta_2 X_{2i} + \cdots + \beta_K X_{Ki}$$

dichotomous logistic regression equation—a regression of the logit for a dichotomous dependent variable that is a linear function of the independent variables

The expected natural log (logit) of the ratio of the two probabilities, $p_i/(1 - p_i)$, is a linear function of the K predictors. Taking antilogs of the preceding equation (i.e., applying the principles that $e(\log_e W) = W$ and $e(Z) = e^Z$), we can rewrite the basic dichotomous logistic regression equation to reveal how the independent variables affect the ratio of the probabilities:

$$e(\hat{L}_i) = e\left[(\log_e\left(\frac{p_{Y=1}}{p_{Y=0}}\right)\right]$$

$$\frac{p_{Y=1}}{p_{Y=0}} = e^{\alpha + \beta_1 X_1 + \beta_2 X_2 + \cdots + \beta_K X_K}$$

The logistic regression equation resembles a linear, additive multiple regression equation, in that a β_j coefficient indicates by how much the log of the dependent variable's odds changes when the corresponding predictor variable X_j changes by one unit.

Logistic regression parameters cannot be estimated using the OLS techniques that are suitable to multiple regression. Instead, logistic regression uses a method called **maximum likelihood estimation (MLE)**. Briefly, MLE attempts a series of successive approximations to the unknown true population parameter values, α and the β_i's. The goal is to use the sample data to estimate the parameters, a and b_j's, that maximize the likelihood of obtaining those observed sample values. In contrast to OLS regression, which uses a least-squares criterion (sum of squared differences) for judging the fit between observed and predicted values of Y, the MLE method calculates the probability of observing each sample Y_i if a given set of parameters is assumed to be true. The set that yields the highest probability comprises the maximum likelihood estimates.

maximum likelihood estimation—a method of estimating parameter values that chooses the set with the highest probability of generating the sample observations

Because MLE has no algebraic formulas similar to the normal equations used in OLS regression, its solution requires a computer program capable of examining many parameter sets until the best choice is identified. (Most computer programs use the Newton–Raphson method.) The procedure begins with an initial estimate (typically that all parameters equal 0). A series of *iterations*, or cycles, produces new estimates and compares them with the previous ones. The iterations continue until successive estimates differ from the preceding ones by less than a specified small amount. For large samples, MLE parameter estimates are unbiased, efficient, and normally distributed, and thus they allow significance tests using statistics we previously examined.

Recall the example in section 9.2, from the 1998 GSS, where we used five independent variables (party identification, liberal vs. conservative political views, white race, education, and Southern residence) to predict the expected vote for Clinton vs. Dole in the 1996 presidential election. We now use these same variables to estimate a logistic regression equation. The estimated equation (standard errors in parentheses) is

$$\hat{L}_i = 6.932 - 0.812X_{1i} - 0.459X_{2i} - 1.104X_{3i} - 0.072X_{4i} - 0.280X_{5i}$$
$$\;\;\;\;\;(0.571)\;\;(0.046)\;\;\;\;\;(0.066)\;\;\;\;\;(0.281)\;\;\;\;\;(0.028)\;\;\;\;\;(0.171)$$

The *t* ratios for the five predictor variables, which can be calculated by dividing the parameter estimates by their standard errors, are statistically significant, except region of residence, at $\alpha < .05$ or less.[1]

Directly interpreting each coefficient is problematic because it requires thinking in terms of log odds, hardly a conventional framework. However, a positive or negative sign indicates how a predictor linearly increases or decreases the log odds. Thus, a coefficient can be interpreted similarly to a linear regression parameter, as long as we remember that the dependent variable is *not* a probability, but rather a logarithm of the odds of two probabilities. In the above example, the positive coefficients mean that identifying as a Republican (i.e., a higher score on X_1), holding conservative political views (X_2), being white (X_3), having more years of education (X_4), and living in the South (X_5) decrease the log odds of voting for Clinton. Persons with lower scores on these predictors had higher log odds of voting to re-elect the president.

---

[1]The SPSS logistic regression routine produced the equation estimate. Its output reports the estimated β's and standard errors, but instead of *t* ratios, it calculates the "Wald statistic." This test statistic is distributed as a chi-square with one degree of freedom, and its value exactly equals the square of a *t* ratio. Hence, to stress the similarities between OLS regression and logistic regression, we calculate and discuss only the *t* values.

Calculating the confidence interval around a logistic regression coefficient point estimate resembles procedures used in OLS regression. For a large sample with a chosen level of α, the upper and lower confidence limits for the $(1 - \alpha)(100\%)$ interval around the estimate of b_j are given by

$$b_j \pm t_{\alpha/2} s_{b_j}$$

where

s_{b_j} is the standard error of the estimated b_j coefficient.

For example, the 95% confidence limits for the party identification (X_1) logistic coefficient are $-0.812 \pm (0.046)(1.96)$, or LCL $= -0.902$ and UCL $= -0.722$.

We showed in section 9.2 that extreme values of independent variables may lead to out-of-bounds predictions (i.e., predictions not falling within the 0.00 to 1.00 range of probability) if a dichotomous dependent variable is estimated using OLS regression. Applying the same extreme combinations for a pro-Clinton voter to the logistic regression equation yields

$$\hat{L}_i = 6.932 - 0.812(6) - 0.459(7) - 1.104(1) - 0.072(1) - 0.280(1)$$

$$= 6.932 - 4.872 - 3.213 - 1.104 - 0.072 - 0.280 = -2.609$$

To translate -2.609 back into a probability, we make use of the basic logistic function $F(Z) = e^Z/(1 + e^Z)$, where $Z = a + \Sigma b_j X_{ji}$. Thus, the expected probability of a Clinton vote by a person having those extreme anti-Clinton values on the five independent variables is

$$P(Y = 1) = \frac{e^{-2.609}}{1 + e^{-2.609}} = \frac{0.074}{1 + 0.074} = \frac{0.074}{1.074} = 0.069$$

In other words, such persons have a predicted probability of 0.069 to vote for Clinton, not the absurd -0.09 chance calculated with the OLS regression equation. Similarly, for voters with extreme pro-Clinton predictor values, the logistic regression equation yields $Z = 6.473$, which translates into an expected probability for a Clinton vote of 0.998. This result is more plausible than the linear probability model's meaningless probability estimate (1.34).

9.4.2 Exponentiating Parameters

In linear regression, a β_j parameter measures the effect on the dependent variable of a one-unit change or difference in an independent variable.

This regression effect is constant for all values of the independent variable. In logistic regression, the nonlinear relationship of the variables in their original scales makes interpretation difficult because the effects of an independent variable vary across levels of the independent variable. Consider a bivariate logistic regression of the 1996 presidential vote on education, which results in this estimated equation: $\hat{L}_i = 1.612 - 0.084X_i$. A literal interpretation of the β parameter estimate is that a one-year difference in schooling reduces the logarithm of the odds for a Clinton vote by -0.084. Because we never think in log-odds, this inference is not very revealing. However, by exponentiation (anti-logging), a logistic regression coefficient can be translated into a numerical value revealing the independent variable's effect on the unlogged odds.

By exponentiating both sides of the preceding logistic regression equation, we find the relationship between the odds of voting for Clinton relative to Dole for each year of education: $p_1/p_2 = e^{1.612 - 0.084X_1}$. Figure 9.7 shows how the predicted logits and their translation into voting odds both change across the range of education. The nonlinear shape of the latter relationship is easy to see: as education levels increase, the odds of a vote for Clinton fall, but at a decreasing rate. We can obtain a quantitative estimate for this changing relationship by subtracting 1 from the exponentiated value of the education parameter: $e^{-0.084} - 1 = 0.919 - 1.000$

FIGURE 9.7
Logistic Regression of Vote and Education

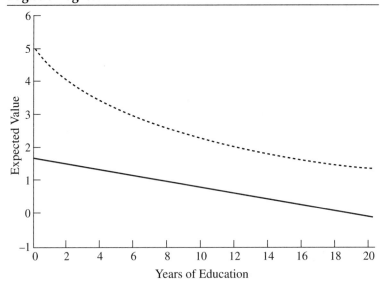

= –0.0805. Finally, by multiplying this proportion by 100%, we obtain the value –8.05%, which reveals that each one-year increment in education reduces the odds of voting for Clinton by more than 8%. This constant-proportional effect occurs at every value of the independent variable, although the magnitude of the decrease is greatest at lower education levels. Apply the parameter transformation formula $(e^\beta - 1)(100\%)$ to the multivariate logistic regression coefficients for party identification and political ideology in subsection 9.4.1, and interpret your calculations as percentage changes per unit of these two continuous independent variables.

For a dichotomous (0–1) independent variable, another simple transformation permits a direct *probability* interpretation of its effect on the dependent variable. Just multiply the estimated logistic regression parameter by the variance of the dependent dichotomy, which is $(p_1)(1 - p_1)$. The resulting product indicates the proportional effect of the predictor on the dependent variable's probability of occurring (evaluated at the sample mean), net of the other variables in the equation. In the presidential voting example, because the proportion voting for Clinton is 0.61, its variance is $(0.61)(1 - 0.61) = 0.238$. Therefore, the effect of being white on voting for Clinton is $(-1.104)(0.238) = -0.263$. That is, white race decreases the probability of voting for Clinton by 26.3% relative to being nonwhite. What effect does residing in the South have on the probability of voting for Clinton?

9.4.3 Measuring Equation Fit

Four procedures are available to assess the overall fit of a logistic regression equation to the data. The first, the **log likelihood ratio**, contrasts two nested logistic regression equations, where one equation is a restricted version of the other. If the less-restricted equation has K_1 independent variables and the more-restricted equation has K_0 independent variables, all of which also appear in the less-restricted equation, the null hypothesis states that none of the additional $K_1 - K_0$ logistic regression parameters differ significantly from zero in the population. That is, for all β_j where $j > K_0$, H$_0$: $\beta_{K_0 + 1} = \beta_{K_0 + 2} = \cdots \beta_{K_1} = 0$. The alternative hypothesis is that at least one of the β_j parameters is significantly different from zero.

L_1 is the maximized likelihood for the less-restricted equation that has K_1 independent variables. It has $N - K_1 - 1$ degrees of freedom. L_0 is the likelihood for the more restricted equation with K_0 predictors. It has $N - K_0 - 1$ *df*. The test statistic, G^2, which is usually labeled in computer programs as the *model chi-square*, compares the ratio of these two likelihoods. It is distributed as a chi-square variable with degrees of freedom

log likelihood ratio— a ratio that contrasts two nested logistic regression equations, where one equation is a restricted version of the other

equal to the difference in the number of predictors between the two equations, that is, $df = K_1 - K_0$. The formula for the test statistic is

$$G^2 = -2 \log_e\left(\frac{L_0}{L_1}\right) = (-2 \log_e L_0) - (-2 \log_e L_1)$$

The most common application of the log likelihood ratio test is that *all* the parameters in an equation equal zero, except the intercept α, whose value then equals the sample proportion coded 1 on the dependent variable. In the voting example, the equation with only the intercept (i.e., $K_0 = 0$) yields $-2L_0 = 1,011.9$.[2] The equation including all five predictors (i.e., $K_1 = 5$) has $-2L_1 = 1,948.1$. Hence, $G^2 = (-2 \log L_0) - (-2 \log L_1) = 1,948.1 - 1,011.9 = 936.2$, with $df = 5$. If we set $\alpha = .05$, Appendix B shows that the c.v. equals 9.49. Therefore, we reject the null hypothesis that all five predictors have zero coefficients in favor of the alternative hypothesis that at least one parameter is probably nonzero.

The individual β_j coefficients can also be tested using the log likelihood ratio. A set of K_1 more-restricted equations are estimated, each of which omits just one of the predictors. The differences between the log likelihood ratios for the full, less-restricted equation and each more-restricted equation are tested relative to the single degree-of-freedom difference (critical value of chi-square = 3.84 at $\alpha = .05$). For example, when education is dropped from the full five-predictor equation, $-2 \log L = 1,018.6$, so $G^2 = 1,018.6 - 1,011.9 = 6.7$, which is significant at $p < .01$ but not at $p < .001$. Given that $-2 \log L$ for the equation omitting party identification equals 1,454.8, for omitting political views, 1,062.5, for dropping race, 1,029.4, and for dropping region of residence, 1,014.6, convince yourself that every predictor except residence significantly improves the equation's fit to the data for $\alpha = .05$.

goodness-of-fit statistic— a test statistic that uses standardized residuals to compare the observed probabilities to those predicted by the equation

A second test statistic, the **goodness-of-fit statistic**, uses the standardized residuals to compare the observed probabilities to those predicted by the equation. The goodness-of-fit statistic is the sum of the squared ratio of a residual divided by its estimated standard deviation:

$$Z^2 = \sum_{i=1}^{N} \frac{(p_i - \hat{p}_i)^2}{(\hat{p}_i)(1 - \hat{p}_i)}$$

The closer each predicted probability comes to the observed probability, the better the fit and hence the smaller the Z^2 value. This statistic is distributed as chi-square with df approximately equal to $N - K_1 - 1$. In the five-predictor voting model, the goodness-of-fit value is 1,763.4 for

[2]This value is routinely calculated by standard logistic regression software packages.

df = 1,447, leading to the same conclusion we reached above. That is, at least one of the four logistic regression coefficients differs significantly from zero.[3]

A third procedure, **pseudo-R^2**, takes into account the fact that chi-square distributions are proportional to sample size. It adjusts the model chi-square for *N* and is a measure of the variance explained by the K_1 independent variables:

$$\text{pseudo-}R^2 = \frac{G^2}{N + G^2}$$

This measure equals zero when the predictor variables are all unrelated to the dependent variable (and hence $G^2 = 0$), but it can never reach a value of 1, even when the independent variables perfectly predict the dependent variable. The pseudo-R^2 formula also does not take into account the number of predictors in the equation; that is, its value is not adjusted for the degrees of freedom. Furthermore, the measure has no sampling distribution. Hence, a significance test for pseudo-R^2 does not exist, and it is only a descriptive measure that indicates roughly the proportion of observed variation accounted for by the K_1 predictors.

For the five-predictor voting model, pseudo-R^2 = (936.2) / (1,453 + 936.2) = 0.39, meaning that about two-fifths of the variation in voting choice is accounted for by these four independent variables.

Finally, a logistic regression equation can be used to classify each observation according to its most probable category on the dependent variable, given that observation's particular combination of values for its independent variables. These predicted values are then compared to the observed values for all *N* sample cases, and the percentage of accurate classifications is used to judge how well the equation accounts for the dichotomous outcomes. In the voting data, the five-predictor logistic equation correctly identified 777 of the 881 Clinton voters (88.2%) and 473 of the 572 Dole voters (82.7%), for an overall accuracy of 86.0% (1,250/1,453). This success rate is not as impressive as it seems; merely guessing that all GSS respondents voted for Clinton would prove correct 61% of the time (the sample proportion). However, the information on the voters' party identification, political views, race, education, and geographical region did reduce the errors of classification by nearly two-thirds (from 39% incorrect to 14% incorrect placements).

> **pseudo-R^2**—a descriptive measure for logistic regression that indicates roughly the proportion of variation in the dependent variable accounted for by the predictors

---

[3]The goodness-of-fit statistic is routinely calculated and printed out by logistic regression software packages such as SPSS.

9.5   The Multinomial-Logit Model

multinomial-logit model—a logistic regression equation whose dependent variable has three or more categories

Logistic regression analysis of dichotomies is a special instance of nonlinear regression involving a multicategory dependent variable, the **multinomial-logit model**. Natural dichotomies do not cover all measures of potential interest. For example, a worker's employment status may be classified as working full-time, working part-time, laid-off, unemployed, or not in the labor force. Artificially forcing all observations into an employed–unemployed dichotomy could be more concealing than revealing. Fortunately, the logistic regression estimation techniques discussed above can be extended to analyze M nonordered discrete categories. We illustrate by adding the 830 nonvoting GSS respondents to the 589 Dole voters and the 923 Clinton voters previously analyzed, creating a trichotomy ($M = 3$) among $N = 2,342$ cases in the GSS electorate sample (we continue to ignore respondents who voted for Perot and other third-party presidential candidates).

The probability that the ith observation occurs in the jth category of a multicategory dependent variable is designation p_{ij}. Thus, if the Dole voters, Clinton voters, and nonvoters are respectively labeled categories 0, 1, and 2, these probabilities are symbolized p_{i0}, p_{i1}, and p_{i2}. Probabilities are defined as relative frequencies, so their sum across the M categories must always equal unity:

$$\sum_{j=1}^{M} p_{ij} = 1$$

Thus, in our GSS electorate sample, $p_{i0} + p_{i1} + p_{i2} = .251 + .394 + .354 = 1.00$ (rounded).

In a logistic regression equation, the expected probabilities depend in nonlinear ways on the set of K independent variables that predict them. The relationship is given by a multivariate logistic distribution function

$$p_{ij} = \frac{e^{\Sigma \alpha + \beta_{kj} X_{kji}}}{\sum_{j=1}^{J} e^{\Sigma \alpha + \beta_{kj} X_{kji}}}$$

where

p_{ij} = The probability that the ith case is in the jth category of the dependent variable.

The triple subscripts indicate the ith observation on the kth predictor variable in the logistic equation for the jth category of the multicategory dependent variable. To solve these equations for unique parameter estimates, a linear constraint must be placed on the set of β's pertaining to the kth predictor. A conventional constraint is that they sum to zero

$$\sum_{j=1}^{M} \beta_{kj} = 0$$

Just as with dummy-variable predictors in a linear regression (see section 8.6), the M categories of a multi-category dependent variable have only $M-1$ degrees of freedom. In addition to requiring that the β's for the K predictors sum to 1.00, we can also specify that all coefficients in the Mth equation equal zero. Then, each estimated coefficient β_{kj} reveals the effect of the predictor X_k on the odds of respondent i being in the jth dependent variable category *relative to* the omitted category M. Which dependent variable category we designate as our reference, or baseline, group is arbitrary. For the dichotomous presidential voting example in section 9.4, we chose Dole voters as the omitted category; mirror-image results would have occurred if we had instead designated the Clinton voters as our baseline. For the multinomial-logit model, the nonlinear transformations cannot assure that the probabilities will add to 1.00. But, as Box 9.2 demonstrates, the natural logarithms of the ratios of the probabilities for each category relative to the baseline category must sum to 1.00, as required.

Box 9.2 Multicategory Probabilities Relative to a Baseline Category

For $M \geq 2$ discrete nonordered categories of a dependent variable and $K \geq 1$ predictor variables, let any arbitrarily chosen baseline or reference category M have the logit probability

$$p(Y_i = M) = \cfrac{1}{1 + \sum_{j=1}^{M-1} e^{Z_{im}}}$$

where Z_{im} represents

$$\alpha + \sum_{k=1}^{K} \beta_{jk} X_{jki}$$

for the $m = M - 1$ other categories of the dependent variable (the subscript i stands for the ith individual observation).

(continued)

Given an mth dependent variable category, its logit relative to the Mth baseline category is

$$\log_e\left(\frac{p(Y_i = m)}{p(Y_i = M)}\right) = Z_{im}$$

Exponentiate this expression and rearrange as follows:

$$\frac{p(Y_i = m)}{p(Y_i = M)} = e^{Z_{im}}$$

Therefore, $p(Y_i = m) = (p(Y_i = M))(e^{Z_{im}})$.

Now, substituting the first equation in this box into the equation immediately preceding this paragraph and then carrying out the multiplication, we obtain the following equation for the probability that the ith observation falls into the mth category of the dependent variable:

$$p(Y_i = m) = \left(\frac{1}{1 + \sum_{j=1}^{M-1} e^{Z_{im}}}\right)(e^{Z_{im}}) = \frac{e^{Z_{im}}}{1 + \sum_{j=1}^{M-1} e^{Z_{im}}}$$

Next, normalize the denominator of the preceding equation by setting α and all the β's in the Mth baseline equation equal to 0. In general, $e^0 = 1$, so $e^{Z_{im}} = 1$ when all the α and β parameters in the Mth equation are set to zero. Consequently, we can replace the 1 in the denominator with this exponential term:

$$p(Y_i = m) = \frac{e^{Z_{im}}}{1 + \sum_{j=1}^{M-1} e^{Z_{im}}} = \frac{e^{Z_{im}}}{e^{Z_{im}} + \sum_{j=1}^{M-1} e^{Z_{im}}} = \frac{e^{Z_{im}}}{\sum_{j=1}^{M} e^{Z_{im}}}$$

because the denominator now sums across all M equations. Thus, the probability that observation Y_i is in the mth category is expressed relative to the sum over all M categories.

Finally, also apply the probability formula to the Mth category where all parameters were set to zero:

$$p(Y_i = M) = \frac{e^0}{e^0 + \sum_{j=1}^{M-1} e^{Z_{im}}} = \frac{1}{1 + \sum_{j=1}^{M-1} e^{Z_{im}}} = \frac{1}{\sum_{j=1}^{M} e^{Z_{im}}}$$

(continued)

When the probabilities for all *M* categories are added, their sum equals 1.00. That is,

$$\sum_{j=1}^{M} p_i = \sum_{j=1}^{M-1} \left(\frac{e^{Z_{im}}}{\sum_{j=1}^{M} e^{Z_{im}}} \right) + \frac{1}{\sum_{j=1}^{M} e^{Z_{im}}}$$

$$= \frac{\sum_{j=1}^{M-1} e^{Z_{im}} + 1}{\sum_{j=1}^{M} e^{Z_{im}}}$$

$$= \frac{\sum_{j=1}^{M} e^{Z_{im}}}{\sum_{j=1}^{M} e^{Z_{im}}} = 1.00$$

Table 9.2 displays the parameter estimates for the trichotomous voting example, where nonvoters were the omitted baseline category. Whereas the dichotomous equation coefficients in section 9.4 indicate the chances of voting for Clinton relative to voting for Dole, the multinomial-logit coefficients in the upper panel of Table 9.2 indicate the effects of each predictor on voting for Dole relative to nonvoting, while the parameters in the lower panel indicate the effects of voting for Clinton relative to nonvoting. Logically enough, many of these coefficients have opposite signs. For example, the +0.513 party identification parameter for Dole voting means that Republican identifiers were more likely to vote for him than to stay home, while the –0.484 parameter for Clinton voting means Republicans were less likely to vote than to cast their ballots for the Democratic candidate. Similarly, political conservatives were more likely to vote for Dole (0.434), but less likely to support Clinton (–0.040), than not to vote. The positive signs for both sets of voters for race and education indicate that both whites and more educated respondents were more likely to vote than to stay at home, while the coefficient sizes were somewhat higher for Dole than for Clinton. In both equations,

TABLE 9.2
Additive Parameter Estimates for Multinomial-Logit Regression of the 1996 Presidential Election, Where Nonvoters Are the Omitted Reference Category

Independent Variables	Logistic Coefficients	Standard Errors	t Ratios
Dole Voters			
Intercept	−8.259	0.516	−16.00**
Party Identification	0.513	0.044	11.66**
Political Views	0.434	0.056	7.75**
Race	1.397	0.251	5.6**
Education	0.220	0.025	8.80**
Region	−0.100	0.139	−0.72
Clinton Voters			
Intercept	−0.434	0.324	−1.33
Party Identification	−0.484	0.036	−13.44**
Political Views	−0.040	0.043	−0.93**
Race	0.188	0.126	1.49
Education	0.132	0.019	6.95**
Region	−0.264	0.114	−2.32*

*$p < .05$
**$p < .001$
$N = 2,181$.
Missing data = 651.
Source: 1998 General Social Survey.

the negative coefficients for region of residence indicate that Southerners were less likely to vote for either candidate than to stay home on Election Day.

In the multinomial-logit model with K_1 = ten predictors (two equations with five independent variables), $-2 \log L_1 = 2,228.5$. For the equation that includes only the intercept ($K_0 = 0$ predictors), $-2 \log L_0 = 3,489.4$. Therefore, the improvement in fit is $G^2 = 3,489.4 - 2,228.5 = 1,260.9$ for $df = 10 - 0 = 10$, a highly statistically significant improvement, because at $\alpha = .001$ the c.v. for a chi-square with $df = 10$ is 29.6.

The rule for predicting outcomes using a multicategory logistic regression equation is to classify the ith case as belonging in the jth category if p_j for that case has the highest predicted probability. Using this rule to classify the 2,181 respondents into the three dependent variable categories and comparing these predictions to the observed values, we find correct classifications for only 65.0% of the sample. The success level varies across categories: 73.6% were correctly classified among the Dole voters, compared to 77.2% of the Clinton voters. However, only 43.5% of the nonvoters were correctly classified. Clearly, the five predictors are much more useful in placing the voters' choices than in distinguishing who did not vote. Further research should concentrate on including additional predictors that better explain voting turnout—for example, the respondents' levels of interest in political affairs.

Review of Key Concepts and Symbols

These key concepts and symbols are listed in the order of appearance in this chapter. Combined with the definitions in the margins, they will help you to review the material and can serve as a self-test for mastery of the concepts.

Euler's constant	$\log_{10}$
linear probability model	L_i
logistic transformation of p	
logit	$\text{Prob}(Y_i = 1)$
dichotomous logistic regression equation	e^Z
maximum likelihood estimation	
log likelihood ratio	MLE
goodness-of-fit statistic	K_0
pseudo-R^2	K_1
multinomial-logit model	
	G^2
e	
	Z^2
$\log_e$	

PROBLEMS

General Problems

1. A sample of employees were asked "How satisfied are you with your job?" A linear regression of 1,500 responses to this item on 20 income categories yielded an R^2 of 0.045, while a one-way analysis of variance for the same variables resulted in an $\hat{\eta}^2$ of 0.078. Is there a significant nonlinear relationship between work satisfaction and income at $\alpha = .001$?

2. The following pairs of numbers represent, respectively, the median education levels and tuberculosis infection rates per 1,000 for ten nations:

   (1, 6.0) (2, 5.8) (3, 5.8) (5, 5.5) (7, 5.0) (9, 4.2) (10, 4.0) (11, 3.5) (12, 3.0) (14, 2.0)

   Plot these pairs on graph paper, with tuberculosis rate on the Y-axis and education on the X-axis, and interpret their relationship based on the shape of the graph.

3. A regression of annual income (in thousands of dollars) for 1,846 respondents in the 1998 GSS on their education (X_i, measured in years) and the squared values of their education (X_i^2) produces the following equation (standard errors in parentheses):

$$\hat{Y}_i = 19.937 - 2.038X_i + 0.193X_i^2$$
$$(8.056)\ (1.166)\quad (0.042)$$

   a. What is the expected income of someone with 8 years of education?

   b. What is the expected income of someone with 12 years of education?

   c. What is the expected income of someone with 20 years of education?

   d. At what level of education does the minimum expected income occur, and what is that income?

4. Regressing the 1998 GSS respondents' annual incomes (in thousands of dollars) on the natural logarithm of their education yields the following equation (standard errors in parentheses):

$$\hat{Y}_i = -67.451 + 37.377(\log_e X_i)$$
$$\quad\quad (6.437) \quad (2.466)$$

a. What is the expected income of someone with 8 years of education?

b. What is the expected income of someone with 12 years of education?

c. What is the expected income of someone with 20 years of education?

5. In the 1998 GSS, 1,747 respondents were asked whether they thought it should be possible for a pregnant woman to obtain a legal abortion if "the woman wants it for any reason." A logistic regression of their dichotomous responses (1 = yes, 0 = no) on a nine-point church attendance scale (X_1) and a dichotomous Catholic–other religion variable (X_2) produced the following equation (standard errors in parentheses):

$$\hat{L}_i = \; 0.428 - 0.209X_{1i} - 0.276X_{2i}$$
$$\quad\quad (0.086) \;(0.019) \quad (0.120)$$

Is either predictor significantly related to support for abortion under any circumstances; if so, in which direction and at what probability level?

6. Construct the 95% confidence intervals around the logistic regression β's in Problem 5.

7. Adding education (X_3) to the logistic regression in Problem 5 yields the following equation (with standard errors in parentheses):

$$\hat{L}_i = -1.642 - 0.232X_{1i} - 0.238X_{2i} + 0.160X_{3i}$$
$$\quad\quad (0.261) \;(0.020) \quad (0.122) \quad (0.192)$$

Exponentiate the β parameters, and interpret their effects as proportional changes or differences in the odds of supporting abortion under any circumstances.

8. In the equation shown in Problem 7, what are the probabilities that a person supports abortion if he or she is (a) Catholic ($X_1 = 1$), attends church nearly every week ($X_2 = 6$), and has 12 years of education; and (b) other religion ($X_1 = 0$), never attends church ($X_2 = 0$), and has 20 years of education?

9. The logistic regression equation in Problem 7 has a –2 log likelihood of 2,148.36, while an equation that has only the intercept yields a –2 log likelihood of 2,361.79. Calculate G^2, and test whether the model in Problem 7 is a significant improvement, using $\alpha = .001$. What is the pseudo-R^2 given that $N = 1,747$?

10. Below are multinomial-logit equations (standard errors in parentheses) predicting the current marital status of 1,220 men in the 1998 GSS. The omitted category of the dependent variable is currently married men, the second category is never-married men, and the third category is previously married men (widowed, divorced, or separated). The independent variables are age (X_1), number of children ever born at any time (X_2), and education (X_3):

$$\hat{L}_{2i} = 3.844 - 0.066X_{1i} - 1.351X_{2i} - 0.043X_{3i}$$
$$(0.543)\ (0.008)\quad (0.110)\quad (0.032)$$

$$\hat{L}_{3i} = 0.166 + 0.008X_{1i} - 0.113X_{2i} - 0.086X_{3i}$$
$$(0.431)\ (0.005)\quad (0.047)\quad (0.024)$$

Test each coefficient for significance, report the lowest probability level at which the null hypothesis can be rejected, and give a substantive interpretation.

Problems Requiring the 1998 General Social Survey

11. Does the number of hours of daily television viewing (TVHOURS) have a linear or nonlinear relationship with education (EDUC), as measured by years of schooling, from 0 to 21? Test the difference between R^2 and $\hat{\eta}^2$, setting $\alpha = .05$.

12. Does occupational prestige (PRESTG80) vary significantly with both linear age (AGE) and with the square of age? Create an age-squared variable (compute AGESQ = AGE*AGE) and enter both predictors into a regression. Report all parameter estimates and standard errors, and calculate the 95% confidence intervals for the β coefficients. At what age is occupational prestige expected to reach its maximum value, and what is the expected prestige score?

13. Respondents were asked, "Tell me if you agree or disagree with this statement: 'Most men are better suited emotionally for politics than are most women'" (FEPOL). After recoding into a 1–0 "agree–disagree" dichotomy (eliminating the "not sure" responses), estimate a logistic regression equation with respondent's gender, age, and occupational prestige as independent variables. Report the sample N, parameter estimates, standard errors, and t ratios. Also give the –2 log likelihoods for this equation and for a logistic regression where only the intercept is specified. What are the percentages of correctly predicted respondents who agree and disagree with the statement?

14. Add a dichotomous independent variable for southern residence to the equation in Problem 13. Test whether the G^2 difference in the two equations' –2 log likelihoods is significant at $\alpha = .001$.

15. Create dichotomous variables for gun ownership (ROWNGUN), southern residence, and female gender. Regress gun ownership on the other two variables, report the exponentiated β's, and interpret the predictors' effects as percentage changes in the odds of owning a gun.

v. Advanced Topics

10

LOG-LINEAR ANALYSIS

10.1 Log-Linear Models for 2×2 Tables	**10.3** More Complex Models
10.2 Log-Linear Models for Three-Variable Tables	**10.4** Special Topics in Log-Linear Analysis

In the preceding chapters we have presented multivariate statistical techniques suitable for continuous variables. In this chapter, we offer some basic procedures for conducting **multivariate contingency table analysis**, that is, statistical analysis of data on three or more categorical variables. The technique for analyzing cross-classified data presented in this chapter is called **log-linear analysis**.

In examining the various aspects of the crosstabulation between two categorical variables in chapter 5, we discussed measures of association and tests of significance for both discrete and ordered variables. We presented methods that help to determine whether two variables systematically covary and whether the covariation observed in sample data is likely to reflect the population from which the sample was drawn. As we pointed out in chapter 5, establishing whether two variables, such as smoking and gender, significantly covary may be sufficient for some research purposes. But most researchers want to determine whether such bivariate relationships are affected by other factors (e.g., age, education, social class, and health attitudes). In such cases, the research problem changes from describing a two-variable relationship to considering three or more variables, as their relationships bear upon some theoretical issue.

multivariate contingency table analysis—the statistical analysis of data on three or more categorical variables

log-linear analysis—a technique for analyzing cross-classified data

10.1   Log-Linear Models for 2 × 2 Tables

To demonstrate log-linear analysis for tabular data, we analyze a specific substantive problem: white Americans' attitudes toward racial segregation. Despite the civil rights movement's success at tearing down formal *legal* subordination of minorities, a significant proportion of the white majority still favor restrictions on African-Americans' rights to live, work, attend school, and marry as they choose. In the 1998 GSS, respondents were asked the strength of their agreement or disagreement with the following statement:

> "African-Americans shouldn't push themselves where they are not wanted."

For the frequency and percentage crosstabs displayed in Table 10.1, we collapsed the "agree strongly" and "agree slightly" categories and also the "disagree strongly" and "disagree slightly" categories to form a dichotomy. The row marginals show that 56.9% of white respondents dis-

TABLE 10.1
Frequency and Percentage Crosstabulations of Racial Segregation Attitude by Education for Whites

Racial Segregation (S)	EDUCATION (E)		
	No Degree	*College Degree*	*Total*
Frequency Crosstabulation			
Agree	$f_{11} = 497$	$f_{12} = 108$	$f_{1\bullet} = 605$
Disagree	$f_{21} = 524$	$f_{22} = 273$	$f_{2\bullet} = 797$
Total	$f_{\bullet 1} = 1,021$	$f_{\bullet 2} = 381$	$f_{\bullet\bullet} = 1,402$
Percentage Crosstabulation			
Agree	48.7	28.3	43.2
Disagree	51.3	71.7	56.8
Total	100.0%	100.0%	100.0%
(*N*)	(1,021)	(381)	(1,402)

Missing data: 1,430 cases.
Source: 1998 General Social Survey.

FIGURE **10.1**
Schematic Showing Computation of Conditional Odds

agreed with this racial segregation item. As discussed in section 5.4, the odds of agreeing with the item (i.e., supporting segregation) are 605/797 = 0.76. However, as the conditional odds in the two columns of Table 10.1 reveal, disagreement with the item depends on level of education: Among the college-educated (persons with bachelor or graduate degrees), the odds are 108/273 = 0.396, but among nondegreed persons, the odds of supporting segregation are much greater, 497/524 = 0.948. The odds ratio formed by these two conditional odds, a ratio that indicates the association of education with attitudes toward racial segregation, is 0.948/0.396 = 2.394. In other words, the nondegreed are more than two and a third times more likely to support racial segregation than are the college-educated. Because the chi-square test of independence is 46.8 for $df = 1$, this association is statistically significant, since the critical value is 10.8 at $\alpha = .001$.

In the frequency crosstab of Figure 10.1, we denote the four cell frequencies by subscripts (f_{ij}), where the first subscript indexes the ith row and the second subscript indexes the jth column. In general, the odds ratio between two variables X and Y is the ratio of the two conditional odds:

$$OR^{YX} = (f_{11}/f_{21})/(f_{12}/f_{22})$$

Or, on rearrangement, the cross-product ratio for a 2×2 table of two variables X and Y is

$$OR^{YX} = (f_{11})(f_{22})/(f_{21})(f_{12})$$

The marginal frequencies for the row variable are designated by $f_{i\bullet}$ and those of the column variable by $f_{\bullet j}$ (see Figure 10.1).

10.1.1 Expected Frequencies as Functions of Effect Parameters

A log-linear model expresses the *expected value* of the frequency in the i,jth cell (labeled F_{ij}) as a function of a set of parameters that represent the categorical effects of the variables and their relationships. In the log-linear notational system that we use, the natural logarithm (ln or $\log_e$) of each expected cell frequency is the sum of four parameters:

$$\ln F_{ij} = \mu + \lambda_i^X + \lambda_j^Y + \lambda_{ij}^{XY}$$

saturated model—a log-linear model in which all possible effects among variables are present

and for the data in Table 10.1, $\ln F_{ij} = \mu + \lambda_i^S + \lambda_j^E + \lambda_{ij}^{SE}$. This particular model is called a **saturated model** because all possible effects among the variables are present (i.e., none are constrained a priori to equal zero). Because all possible effects are present, $F_{ij} = f_{ij}$ (i.e., the expected cell frequency equals the observed cell frequency). The format for these parameters makes clear that an expected logged cell frequency is a linear combination of the categorical effects of the variables, hence the name "log-linear analysis." Note the superficial resemblance of a log-linear equation to a multiple regression or logistic regression equation.

The μ (mu) is a constant that applies to every cell in the crosstab. Its presence is necessary to assure that the frequencies sum to the correct total. Although μ seems analogous to the intercept in a regression equation or to the grand mean in an ANOVA, in fact, it has no substantive interpretation. The λ (lambda) terms represent the effects of the cross-tabulated variables on the expected logs of the cell frequencies. Each category of a variable has a unique lambda parameter associated with it, as do all combinations of categories. Positive lambda values increase the size of an expected logged cell frequency, negative lambdas decrease their magnitudes, and a $\lambda = 0$ indicates that a variable category has no effect on the tabled frequency, leaving the expected logged frequency unchanged. The superscripts attached to each lambda indicate the variable or combination of variables to which the effects occur. The λ_i^S capture the effects (one for each of the i categories of S) of an unequal marginal distribution of racial segregation attitudes. Similarly, the λ_j^E (one for each of the j categories of E) capture the effects of unequal marginals for education. If the expected frequencies in both categories of a dichotomous variable are exactly equal, then the odds are $F_{1\bullet}/F_{2\bullet} = 1$ and its lambda parameter is 0 because the natural logarithm of 1 is zero (i.e., because $e^0 = 1$ and $\ln 1 = 0$). In general, lambda for a single variable departs from 0 to the extent that a category has either more or less than $1/K$th of the observations, where K is the number of categories for that variable.

The λ_{ij}^{SE} parameters (one for each of the i,j cells of the crosstab) reveal the extent to which variables S and E are associated. If its value is 0, the two variables are unrelated, while a positive value indicates both "high" categories are associated. A negative value means that the high category of one variable covaries with the low category of the other variable.

The nine log-linear parameters, associated with the 2×2 table frequencies in our example, appear in Table 10.2. For dichotomies such as segregation attitude and education, the two lambda effect parameters associated with a pair of categories are inverses:

$$\lambda_1^S = -\lambda_2^S = \lambda^S$$

$$\lambda_1^E = -\lambda_2^E = \lambda^E$$

Because the lambda effects for each pair of categories are inverses of one another, the effects for dichotomous variables are represented by nonsubscripted lambdas—in this case, by λ^S and λ^E. In general, for a variable with K categories, only $K - 1$ unique parameter values exist, with the Kth category's value determined by the others. Thus, both education and segregation attitudes have only one independently determined lambda parameter, with the second parameter having the same value but opposite sign of the first parameter.

In similar fashion, the four parameters representing the association between education and segregation attitude are not independent of one another:

$$\lambda_{11}^{SE} = \lambda_{22}^{SE} = -\lambda_{12}^{SE} = -\lambda_{21}^{SE} = \lambda^{SE}$$

Thus, instead of four unique values, any one joint parameter determines the values of the remaining three. In the saturated model for a 2×2 table,

TABLE 10.2
Expected Cell Frequencies for Saturated Model of Racial Segregation Attitude by Education for Whites

Racial Segregation (S)	EDUCATION (E)	
	No Degree	*College Degree*
Agree	$F_{11} = \mu + \lambda_1^S + \lambda_1^E + \lambda_{11}^{SE}$	$F_{12} = \mu + \lambda_1^S + \lambda_2^E + \lambda_{12}^{SE}$
Disagree	$F_{21} = \mu + \lambda_2^S + \lambda_1^E + \lambda_{21}^{SE}$	$F_{22} = \mu + \lambda_2^S + \lambda_2^E + \lambda_{22}^{SE}$

only four effect parameters are independent: one each for μ, S, E, and SE. These four values produce the four expected cell frequencies (the F_{ij}s in Table 10.2), which exactly equal the observed cell frequencies (the f_{ij}s in Table 10.1). Section 10.1.2 explains how the effect parameters are calculated for the saturated model for a 2×2 table and how their values combine to produce the expected cell frequencies. Other log-linear models that require fewer effect parameters to generate the expected cell frequencies thereby gain degrees of freedom for assessing the fit between these expected values and the observed cell frequencies. Section 10.2.2 discusses how to test the fit of log-linear models with the tabulated data.

10.1.2 Parameters as Functions of Expected Frequencies

Numerical values of the effect parameters for the saturated log-linear model applied to a 2×2 crosstab can be calculated as functions of the four expected frequencies. The estimate of the constant (μ) is the average of the natural logs of the four cells (recalling that observed and expected values are identical in the saturated model):

$$\hat{\mu} = \frac{\ln (F_{11} F_{12} F_{21} F_{22})}{4}$$

For the data in Table 10.1: $\hat{\mu} = [\ln(497) + \ln(108) + \ln(524) + \ln(273)]/4 = 5.690$ because the logarithm of a product equals the sum of the logarithms.

The λ_{ij}^{SE} effect parameters show the strength and direction of the association between the two variables. First, consider the SE relationship as an odds ratio of expected frequencies:

$$E(OR^{SE}) = \frac{F_{11} F_{22}}{F_{12} F_{21}}$$

which is 2.398 for the education-segregation example. Next, take the natural logarithm of the right-hand side and recall that the logarithm of a ratio is the difference of logarithms to yield:

$$\ln \left(\frac{F_{11} F_{22}}{F_{12} F_{21}} \right) = \ln F_{11} + \ln F_{22} - \ln F_{12} - \ln F_{21}$$

Now, replace each expected frequency with its equivalent equation (see Table 10.2):

$$\ln \left(\frac{F_{11} F_{22}}{F_{12} F_{21}} \right) = (\mu + \lambda_1^S + \lambda_1^E + \lambda_{11}^{SE}) + (\mu + \lambda_2^S + \lambda_2^E + \lambda_{22}^{SE})$$
$$- (\mu + \lambda_1^S + \lambda_2^E + \lambda_{12}^{SE}) - (\mu + \lambda_2^S + \lambda_1^E + \lambda_{21}^{SE})$$

After simplification of terms,

$$\ln\left(\frac{F_{11}F_{22}}{F_{12}F_{21}}\right) = \lambda_{11}^{SE} + \lambda_{22}^{SE} - \lambda_{12}^{SE} - \lambda_{21}^{SE}$$

Thus, the OR depends only on the size and direction of the association between S and E and not on the marginal effects of either variable. Because we previously showed that the four individual effect parameters for this association are opposites of one another, we can rewrite this logged OR as a single parameter without subscripts:

$$\ln\left(\frac{F_{11}F_{22}}{F_{12}F_{21}}\right) = 4\lambda^{SE}$$

Dividing both sides by 4 and rearranging terms, the estimated parameter of the association between two variables in a saturated log-linear model for dichotomies is

$$\hat{\lambda}^{SE} = \frac{\ln\,(F_{11}F_{22}/F_{12}F_{21})}{4}$$

Entering the numerical values from Table 10.1 (again recalling that the expected frequencies equal the observed frequencies in a saturated model), the estimated value of the λ^{SE} parameter is

$$\hat{\lambda}^{SE} = \frac{\ln\,[(497)(273)/(108)(524)]}{4} = 0.219$$

The positive parameter estimate indicates a tendency for the largest frequencies to occur in table cells where both variables have the same subscript value (i.e., nondegreed and agreement with racial segregation; degreed and disagreement).

The two single superscripted lambda parameters are derived for a saturated 2×2 log-linear model by similar procedures. For racial segregation (S), begin with the logarithm of the product of two conditional odds, the first for the nondegreed and the second for the degreed respondents:

$$\ln\left(\frac{F_{11}}{F_{21}}\right)\left(\frac{F_{12}}{F_{22}}\right) = (\mu + \lambda_1^S + \lambda_1^E + \lambda_{11}^{SE}) + (\mu + \lambda_1^S + \lambda_2^E + \lambda_{12}^{SE})$$
$$- (\mu + \lambda_2^S + \lambda_1^E + \lambda_{21}^{SE}) - (\mu + \lambda_2^S + \lambda_2^E + \lambda_{22}^{SE})$$

which simplifies to

$$\ln\left(\frac{F_{11}F_{12}}{F_{21}F_{22}}\right) = (\lambda_1^S + \lambda_1^S - \lambda_2^S - \lambda_2^S) = 4\lambda^S$$

Solving for λ^S, we find the estimate

$$\hat{\lambda}^S = \frac{\ln\left[(F_{11}F_{12})/(F_{21}F_{22})\right]}{4}$$

The estimated value for the racial segregation parameter, λ^S, in our example is

$$\hat{\lambda}^S = \frac{\ln\left[(497)(108)/(524)(273)\right]}{4} = -0.245$$

Similarly, the estimated effect parameter for education is a function of its two conditional odds, the first for respondents who agree with the racial segregation item and the second for those who disagree:

$$\hat{\lambda}^E = \frac{\ln\left[(F_{11}F_{21})/(F_{12}F_{22})\right]}{4}$$

which has the estimated numerical value

$$\hat{\lambda}^E = \frac{\ln\left[(497)(524)/(108)(273)\right]}{4} = 0.545$$

For dichotomous variables, these last two parameters indicate how the observations are distributed. The farther a lambda is from 0, the more unevenly are the cases divided. The negative segregation parameter simply means that more respondents disagreed than agreed with the segregation item. The positive education parameter reveals that a larger proportion of respondents fell into the nondegreed category than into the college-degreed category. These patterns are evident from the row and column marginal frequencies, respectively, in Table 10.1.

We can now combine the numerical estimates of the four effect parameters for a saturated model to calculate the logged values of the four expected cell frequencies in the 2×2 table:

$$\ln F_{11} = 5.690 - 0.245 + 0.545 + 0.219 = 6.209$$
$$\ln F_{12} = 5.690 - 0.245 - 0.545 - 0.219 = 4.681$$
$$\ln F_{21} = 5.690 + 0.245 + 0.545 - 0.219 = 6.261$$
$$\ln F_{22} = 5.690 + 0.245 - 0.545 + 0.219 = 5.609$$

When anti-logs of these values are computed, the results equal the frequencies in the four cells of Table 10.1, as they must in any saturated model. That is, exponentiate the values to transform the natural logarithms into frequencies that equal the cell entries in Table 10.1 (within rounding error):

$$\exp (\ln F_{11}) = \exp 6.209 = 497.20$$
$$\exp (\ln F_{12}) = \exp 4.681 = 107.88$$
$$\exp (\ln F_{21}) = \exp 6.261 = 523.74$$
$$\exp (\ln F_{22}) = \exp 5.609 = 272.87$$

Because the saturated model always fits the data perfectly, it is not a substantively interesting model. Instead, it is valuable as a model against which to compare alternative models with fewer parameters—that is, non-saturated models—a topic to which we turn in section 10.1.4.

10.1.3 Standard Errors for Parameters

The standard errors of the lambda effect parameters for a saturated log-linear model can be computed by the formula

$$\hat{s}_\lambda = \sqrt{\frac{\sum_{i}^{K_R} \sum_{j}^{K_C} (1/F_{ij})}{[(K_R)(K_C)]^2}}$$

where K_R is the number of categories in the row variable and K_C is the number of categories in the column variable. For large samples, if the null hypothesis is true that the population value of a lambda is zero, its significance can be assessed by a t test.

In our 2×2 example, the estimated standard error is

$$\hat{s}_\lambda = \sqrt{\frac{\frac{1}{497} + \frac{1}{108} + \frac{1}{524} + \frac{1}{273}}{[(2)(2)]^2}} = 0.032$$

Dividing each of the three parameter estimates calculated previously by this standard error yields t scores of -7.66 for racial segregation attitude, $+17.03$ for education, and $+6.84$ for the education-segregation association. All three ratios are significant at $\alpha = .001$ for a two-tailed test because the critical value is $+3.29$ for sample $N = 1,767$.

10.1.4 Nonsaturated Models

nonsaturated model—
a log-linear model in which one or more of the lambda parameters equals 0

As pointed out in section 10.1.2, the expected frequencies in a saturated model always equal the observed frequencies. A less complex, but more interesting and important, **nonsaturated model** can be specified by setting one or more lambda parameters equal to 0. Estimates of the remaining parameters then may result in expected cell frequencies that do not exactly reproduce the observed frequencies.

The most obvious nonsaturated model for a 2×2 table sets the two-variable association parameter (λ^{SE}) equal to zero:

$$\ln F_{ij} = \mu + \lambda_i^S + \lambda_j^E$$

This model asserts that the conditional odds for either variable are identical to the marginal odds. In other words, the two variables are independent. The four expected cell frequencies are simply the sum of the constant plus the two marginal effects. For the data in Table 10.1, the parameter estimates for this model, produced by a log-linear computer program, are

$$\mu = 5.733$$
$$\lambda^S = -0.139$$
$$\lambda^E = +0.493$$

Setting $\lambda^{SE} = 0$, the model for independence implies

$$F_{11} = \mu + \lambda_1^S + \lambda_1^E$$
$$F_{12} = \mu + \lambda_1^S + \lambda_2^E$$
$$F_{21} = \mu + \lambda_2^S + \lambda_1^E$$
$$F_{22} = \mu + \lambda_2^S + \lambda_2^E$$

For our data, the estimated values of $\ln F_{ij}$ are

$$\ln F_{11} = 5.733 - 0.139 + 0.493 = 6.087$$
$$\ln F_{12} = 5.733 - 0.139 - 0.493 = 5.101$$
$$\ln F_{21} = 5.733 + 0.139 + 0.493 = 6.365$$
$$\ln F_{22} = 5.733 + 0.139 - 0.493 = 5.379$$

Hence, taking anti-logs (exponentiating):

$$F_{11} = 440.1 \text{ compared with } f_{11} = 497,$$
$$F_{12} = 164.2 \text{ compared with } f_{12} = 108,$$
$$F_{21} = 581.1 \text{ compared with } f_{22} = 524$$
$$\text{and} \quad F_{22} = 216.8 \text{ compared with } f_{22} = 273.$$

If the independence model fits the data, the difference between the F_{ij} and the f_{ij} should be so small that these differences can be attributed to sampling error alone.

The expected frequencies F_{ij} for this log-linear independence model are the same values as the expected frequencies computed for the chi-square significance test in section 5.2. In fact, this log-linear model *is* equivalent to that independence hypothesis. The discrepancies between observed and expected frequencies can be tested for a statistically significant fit of the log-linear model to the data using procedures described in the next section.

10.2   Log-Linear Models for Three-Variable Tables

In this section we consider log-linear models for three-variable tables, such as Table 10.3, where the original racial segregation attitudes by education crosstab has been split into two subtables according to respondents' ages (A, where category 1 = persons aged 50 years and younger; category 2 = persons 51 years and older). The observed odds ratio of education and racial segregation attitude, OR^{SE}, was 2.394 in the original two-way table; but the **conditional odds ratios** are not identical in the two subtables created by controlling for age. The relationship between education and segregation attitude seems to be weaker among the younger group ($OR^{SE|A=1} = 1.995$) than among the older respondents ($OR^{SE|A=2} = 3.008$). Read the notation $OR^{SE|A=1}$ as "the odds ratio for segregation attitude by education, given that age equals 1" (i.e., for persons 50 or younger). How would you read $OR^{SE|A=2}$? The important question is whether this difference in the sample odds ratios reflects an interaction among the three variables in the population from which the 1998 GSS drew its sample. In other words, can we reject the null hypothesis that education and racial segregation attitude is the same within both age groups, with only a small probability of a Type I error? To answer this question,

conditional odds ratio— an odds ratio between two variables for a given category of a third variable

TABLE 10.3
Frequency Crosstabulation of Racial Segregation Attitude by Education by Age for Whites

AGE (A):	50 YEARS AND YOUNGER EDUCATION (E)			51 YEARS AND OLDER EDUCATION (E)		
Racial Segregation (S)	*No Degree*	*Degree*	*Total*	*No Degree*	*Degree*	*Total*
Agree	241	62	303	256	46	302
Disagree	376	193	569	148	80	228
Total	617	255	872	404	126	530

Missing data: 1,430 cases.
Source: 1998 General Social Survey.

we must specify a log-linear model consistent with the null hypothesis of no interaction among the three measures, compute the expected frequencies, and compare them to the observed frequencies.

The class of models used to examine hypotheses of this sort are called **hierarchical log-linear models** because whenever a complex multivariate relationship is present, less complex relationships are also included. For example, if a model specifies a two-variable effect parameter between variables X and Y (i.e., λ^{XY}), it also includes both the single-variable effect parameters (λ^X and λ^Y). Similarly, any hierarchical model that includes a three-way effect parameter must also include all possible two-way effects involved in that three-way interaction as well as the three single-variable effects. Thus, a hierarchical model that specifies λ^{XYZ} also must include six other parameters: λ^{XY}, λ^{XZ}, λ^{YZ}, λ^X, λ^Y, and λ^Z as well as the constant μ.

hierarchical log-linear model—a model in which the inclusion of multi-way effects also implies the inclusion of all less-complex effects

10.2.1 The Standard Notation

The nested nature of hierarchical log-linear models provides researchers with a compact standard notational system for designating the parameters of a log-linear equation. This standard notation encloses within curly braces—{ }—the combinations of capital letters representing variables whose relationships are hypothesized *not* to have zero lambdas. (The constant term is always present, even in a model with no other parameters.) All subsets of letters within braces are also understood to have nonzero-effect parameters in the equation. For example, the saturated model described in section 10.1.1 was written in full equation form as

$$\ln F_{ij} = \mu + \lambda_i^S + \lambda_j^E + \lambda_{ij}^{SE}$$

and more compactly as simply $\{SE\}$. Because both S and E are included within the same pair of braces, we know that a lambda parameter for the association between these two variables is specified, as well as both the single-variable parameters. However, if the standard notation designates these two variables in separate braces—$\{S\}\{E\}$—we know that only λ^S and λ^E are included in the equation. In other words, model $\{S\}\{E\}$ tells us that λ^{SE} is hypothesized to equal zero. (Note that model $\{S\}\{E\}$ is the independence model for a two-variable crosstab, in which the pair has no significant association.) Because the model $\{SE\}$ contains not only λ^{SE}, but also λ^S and λ^E, we can say that model $\{S\}\{E\}$ is *nested within* model $\{SE\}$. Thus, hierarchical log-linear models are also **nested models**. One model is nested within a second model if every parameter in the first also appears in the second.

> **nested models**—models in which every parameter included in one model also appears in another model

Consider some alternative hypothesized log-linear models for the three variables, S, E, and A. The model $\{SEA\}$ corresponds to the equation

$$\ln F_{ijk} = \mu + \lambda_i^S + \lambda_j^E + \lambda_k^A + \lambda_{ij}^{SE} + \lambda_{ik}^{SA} + \lambda_{jk}^{EA} + \lambda_{ijk}^{SEA}$$

Clearly, the curly-brace notation system allows for great economy of expression! What are the equations designated by models $\{SE\}\{A\}$ and $\{SA\}\{SE\}$? Convince yourself that the model $\{SE\}\{A\}$ corresponds to the equation

$$\ln F_{ijk} = \mu + \lambda_i^S + \lambda_j^E + \lambda_k^A + \lambda_{ij}^{SE}$$

What equation corresponds to the model $\{SA\}\{SE\}$?

In addition to concise communication, the standard notational system also reveals an important aspect of the log-linear estimation method. The combinations of V variables enclosed within curly braces constitute the set of **marginal subtables**—or simply "the marginals"—that are necessary and sufficient to generate the expected cell frequencies of the full V-way crosstab (where V is the number of variables) under the hypothesized model. That is, the expected frequencies generated by the model must exactly equal the observed frequencies of these marginal subtables. But any relationships involving combinations of variables that do *not* appear within curly braces are constrained to have expected odds ratios

> **marginal subtable**—a method to show the combinations of V variables that are necessary and sufficient to generate the expected cell frequencies of a full crosstab

exactly equal to one [and their lambda parameters thus equal zero, because ln(1) = 0]. Indeed, the discrepancies between the expected and observed frequencies among unspecified marginals become the basis for testing the statistical significance of a hypothesized model. Thus, the standard notation for a log-linear model is often referred to as the **fitted marginals** for that hypothesis. For example, we say that model $\{SA\}\{E\}$ "fits the marginals SA and E" (and we understand that marginals $\{A\}$ and $\{S\}$ are also fitted). This specification assures that expected odds ratios of the marginals $\{SE\}$, $\{EA\}$, and $\{SEA\}$ will equal exactly 1.00 (i.e., no association occurs among these combinations of variables), and hence $\lambda^{SE} = \lambda^{EA} = \lambda^{SEA} = 0.0$.

fitted marginal—the standard notation for a log-linear model

Details of the computer algorithms for generating the expected cell frequencies (F_{ijk}) from the fitted marginals are too complex to explain here. A two-variable crosstab (whether involving dichotomous or multiple-category variables) has simple formulas for directly estimating the expected frequencies for its nonsaturated models of the type used in section 10.1.2. For larger V-way tables, however, most log-linear programs use either **iterative proportional fitting** procedures or **Newton–Raphson algorithms** because simple analytic (algebraic) solutions do not exist.[1] These methods proceed by successively refining estimates of the fitted marginal subtables hypothesized by the standard notation, until it meets an arbitrarily small difference from one cycle to the next. The final expected cell frequencies are maximum likelihood estimates, which have such desirable statistical properties as consistency and efficiency. Once these F_{ijk}s have been produced, they are used to calculate the lambda effect parameters for the hypothesized model, as section 10.1.2 demonstrated.

iterative proportional fitting—a computer algorithm for successively approximating the expected frequencies in an unsaturated log-linear model

Newton–Raphson algorithm—an iterative proportional fitting procedure used in log-linear analysis

10.2.2 Testing Models for Statistical Significance

To determine whether the hypothesized relationships among variables in a population of interest are supported by observed relationships in the sample, we compare the observed cell frequencies to the frequencies generated by a log-linear equation for the hypothesized model. The fit between observed and expected frequencies can be assessed with the Pearson chi-square test statistic (χ^2), discussed in section 3.11. However, the preferred test statistic is the **likelihood ratio** (L^2), because it is mini-

likelihood ratio—the preferred test statistic for testing the fit between expected and observed frequencies in an unsaturated log-linear model

---

[1]For details, see pp. 82–102 in Yvonne M. M. Bishop, Stephen E. Fienberg, and Paul W. Holland. 1975. *Discrete Multivariate Analysis: Theory and Practice*. Cambridge, MA: MIT Press. Also see Shelby J. Haberman. 1978. *Analysis of Qualitative Data. Volume 1: Introductory Topics*. New York: Academic Press.

mized by the maximum likelihood estimates of the expected frequencies. Its formula is

$$L^2 = 2\sum_{i=1}^{K} f_i \ln\left(\frac{f_i}{F_i}\right)$$

where the summation occurs over the K cells of the crosstab.

The L^2 test statistic is distributed approximately as a chi-square variable with degrees of freedom equal to the number of unique lambda parameters that are set equal to zero. In general, if a variable X has C_X categories, then $C_X - 1$ of its parameters are free to vary. In our example crosstab, each dichotomous variable has $C = 2$ categories. Thus, the log-linear model specification $\{AE\}\{SE\}\{SA\}$ includes all parameters except the three-way interaction λ^{SEA}, which is hypothesized to equal zero. This model has $(C_S - 1)(C_E - 1)(C_A - 1) = (2 - 1)(2 - 1)(2 - 1) = 1$ df for the likelihood-ratio test. One degree of freedom makes sense because one unique parameter was set to zero, λ^{SEA}.

Another important advantage in using the likelihood-ratio test statistic is that it can be easily partitioned so that conditional independence tests can be carried out on multi-way crosstabs. As indicated in section 10.2.1, a pair of hierarchical log-linear models applied to the same table is nested if one model consists only of a subset of the effect parameters found in the second model. For example, every parameter in model $\{SE\}\{A\}$ is also included in model $\{AE\}\{SE\}\{SA\}$. The difference in L^2 values for these nested models, relative to the difference in the degrees of freedom of the two models, is a test of significance. Thus, if model 2 is more inclusive than model 1,

$$\Delta L^2 = L_1^2 - L_2^2 \quad \text{and} \quad \Delta df = df_1 - df_2$$

where Δ (delta) means *difference*.

Table 10.4 illustrates the application of these principles, showing the likelihood ratios, *df*s, and probabilities for seven nested hierarchical models estimated with the three-variable crosstab in Table 10.3. Model 1 is the least complex, fitting only the marginal distributions of the three variables. Because λ^{SA}, λ^{SE}, λ^{EA}, and λ^{SEA} have all been fixed to zero, model 1 has $df = 4$. With $L^2 = 117.6$ for $df = 4$, it also provides a terrible fit of the expected frequencies to the observed frequencies. Note that, in seeking to identify the "best-fitting model" for a given sample crosstab, we ultimately want to find a hypothesized log-linear specification that *cannot* be rejected on statistical grounds. Thus, our goal is to find a model with

TABLE 10.4
Hierarchical Log-Linear Models for the Data in Table 10.2

Model	L^2	df	p
1. {E}{A}{S}	117.6	4	< .0001
2. {EA}{S}	112.5	3	< .0001
3. {EA}{SE}	64.3	2	< .0001
4. {EA}{SA}	46.1	2	< .0001
5. {SA}{SE}	2.9	2	.231
6. {EA}{SA}{SE}	2.3	1	.128
7. {SEA}	.00	0	1.000

a low likelihood ratio relative to its *df*, which has a high probability of representing the relationships that exist in the population.

The *p*-values associated with a given model are to be interpreted as follows. "If Model A is true in the population, then the probability of observing this result is *p*." Thus, if Model 1 is the true model, we would expect the fit we observe to occur less than one time in ten thousand. If we set $\alpha = .05$, we require that the observed *p*-value be .05 *or greater* in order not to reject the hypothesis associated with the model. Hence, the *higher* the probability that the observed data could have been generated by a given model, the more plausible the model. Unlike the standard hypothesis testing where support is provided for the alternative hypothesis by observing small *p*-values, when you posit a specific log-linear model for the data, support for that model is provided by observing high *p*-values.

Model 2 adds the two-variable marginal {*EA*} to the three single-variable marginals in model 1, at the cost of 1 *df*; that is, model 2 has 3 *df*. This price is well worth paying, as $\Delta L^2 = L_1^2 - L_2^2 = 117.6 - 112.5 = 5.1$ is a significant improvement in fit at $\alpha = .05$ for $\Delta df = df_1 - df_2 = 4 - 3 = 1$. Note that when testing for the difference between two competing models (models 1 and 2 in this case), we are back to traditional hypothesis testing. In this case the null hypothesis is that H_0: $\Delta L^2 = 0$ and the alternative hypothesis is H_1: $\Delta L^2 > 0$. At $\alpha = .05$, the critical value for L^2 is 3.84 for $df = 1$. Because $\Delta L^2 = 5.1$, the probability is low that $\Delta L^2 = 0$ in the population, and thus we reject H_0, concluding that {*EA*} is necessary to fit the data. However, the overall fit of model 2 is still improbable because $p < .0001$, so we continue testing more-inclusive models. Model 2 is nested within both models 3 and 4 because each of the latter models fits one of the other two-variable relationships involving S. At $\alpha = .05$ both parameters significantly improve the fit between observed and expected frequencies ($L_2^2 - L_3^2 = 112.5 - 64.3 = 48.2$ and $L_2^2 - L_4^2 = 112.5 - 46.1 = 66.4$), each at the cost of just one df. Thus, we conclude that education and age probably have nonzero relationships with segregation attitudes in the population.

Next, considering model 6, which includes *both* $\{SE\}\{SA\}$ and $\{EA\}$, we find significant improvements in ΔL^2s compared to either model 3 or model 4. However, if we compare model 6 to model 5, which does not include the $\{EA\}$ relationship, we now find that this age-education association is no longer necessary to fit the three-way table. That is, $L_5^2 - L_6^2 = 2.9 - 2.3 = 0.6$ and $\Delta df = df_6 - df_5 = 2 - 1 = 1$, which falls below the critical value of 3.84 at $\alpha = .05$. Thus, unlike the earlier comparison of models 1 and 2, this test indicates that age and education are probably independent in the population when both the $\{SA\}$ and $\{SE\}$ associations are taken into account. Although both models 5 and 6 provide overall good fits to the observed crosstab (both p-levels are well above $p = .05$), model 5 is less complex than model 6. Thus, we prefer model 5 to model 6 because it offers a more parsimonious explanation of likely relationships among the three variables.

Finally, although the saturated model 7 designated by $\{SEA\}$, which specifies the three-variable interaction parameter, obviously reproduces the relationships perfectly (and its $p = 1.00$), importantly the saturated model is not a significant improvement over model 6 designated by $\{EA\}\{SA\}\{SE\}$. By using the one remaining degree of freedom to estimate λ^{SEA}, we decrease L^2 by only 2.3, which is not a significantly improved fit at $\alpha = .05$. Therefore, because model 6 also did not produce a better fit than model 5, we must conclude that model 5 offers the most likely representation of the relationships among the variables in the population from which the sample crosstabulation was drawn.

Importantly, just because model 5 fits the data better than the other models does not mean it is true. We can never uncover truth by hypothesis testing. The most we can say is that the observed relations in the sample data are consistent or conformable with model 5. But other models that include additional variables might fit the data just as well. Hence, our most reasonable conclusion should be that the data are conformable (or not conformable) with a given hypothesis (or model).

To aid in the substantive interpretation of model 5, Table 10.5 displays the expected cell frequencies, the actual observed frequencies, and the parameter estimates. Because model 5 constrained both λ^{SEA} and λ^{EA} parameters to equal zero, both the three-variable interaction and one two-variable association observed in the original crosstab (see Table 10.3) have not been preserved. For example, the two conditional odds in each age category have been constrained to equal one another (within rounding error):

$$OR^{(ES|A=1)} = \frac{(248.91)(194.90)}{(374.10)(54.09)} = 2.398$$

$$OR^{(ES|A=2)} = \frac{(248.09)(78.10)}{(149.90)(53.91)} = 2.398$$

Furthermore, as a direct consequence of setting $\lambda^{SEA} = 0$, the odds ratio formed by these two conditional odds ratios is constrained to equal 1.00; that is,

$$OR^{(SE|A)} = \frac{OR^{(SE|A=1)}}{OR^{(SE|A=2)}} = \frac{2.398}{2.398} = 1.00$$

Under this constraint, the relationship between education and racial segregation attitude is the same regardless of respondents' ages. The odds that nondegreed persons disagree with the racial segregation question are $(497/524) = 0.9485$, the odds that the college-degreed disagree with the segregation item are $(108/273) = 0.3956$, and their odds ratio is $(0.9485/0.3956) = 2.398$. Because model 5 fits the data so well, we conclude that age does not condition the effect of education on racial attitude. An equivalent substantive conclusion could be drawn that the effect of age on racial segregation attitude does not vary by education. (Use the expected frequencies in Table 10.5 to convince yourself that odds ratios for age and attitude are identical for both categories of respondent education.) However, we emphasize the former interpretation because our example began with the bivariate education-attitude relationship. The fact that both interpretations are consistent with the data underscores the point that a good statistical fit does not imply that a model is necessarily the true one.

The log-linear parameter estimates in the bottom half of Table 10.5 tell a similar story. The single-variable effects show that fewer respondents agree with the racial segregation item ($\hat{\lambda}^S = -0.195$), more are nondegreed ($\hat{\lambda}^E = 0.545$), and more are younger ($\hat{\lambda}^A = 0.229$) than those persons falling into the opposite categories. Younger respondents disagreed with segregation ($\hat{\lambda}^{SA} = -0.228$), and more of the nondegreed supported segregation ($\hat{\lambda}^{SE} = 0.219$) than the contrasting two-variable associations. Finally, note that most expected frequencies are very close to the observed frequencies, offering further evidence that model 5 provides a very good fit to the data.

We demonstrate how the lambda parameters estimated by the model-fitting marginals $\{SA\}\{SE\}$ generate the expected crosstab frequencies.

TABLE 10.5
Expected Frequencies and Effect Parameters for Model {SA}{SE} Fitted to Racial Segregation Attitude by Education by Age

AGE (A):	*50 YEARS AND YOUNGER* *EDUCATION (E)*		*51 YEARS AND OLDER* *EDUCATION (E)*	
Racial Segregation (S)	*No Degree*	*Degree*	*No Degree*	*Degree*
Expected Frequencies				
Agree	248.91	54.09	248.09	53.91
Disagree	374.10	194.90	149.90	78.10
Observed Frequencies				
Agree	241	62	256	46
Disagree	376	193	148	80

Effect Parameters

	Category	$\hat{\lambda}$	$\hat{s}_\lambda$	t
μ	Constant	4.947	—	—
λ_1^S	Agree	−0.195	0.034	−5.80***
λ_1^E	No Degree	0.545	0.032	16.79***
λ_1^A	Younger	0.229	0.028	8.13***
λ_{11}^{SA}	Agree—Younger	−0.228	0.028	−8.06***
λ_{11}^{SE}	Agree—No Degree	0.219	0.032	6.74***

***$p < .001$

The general equation for the expected log frequency in the crosstab cell identified by the first categories of the three variables is $\ln F_{111} = \mu + \lambda_1^S + \lambda_1^E + \lambda_1^A + \lambda_{11}^{SE} + \lambda_{11}^{SA}$. Although the constant (μ) is not calculated by the computer program, it can be estimated as the mean of the logged values of the expected cell frequencies. For this model, μ is 4.947. By summing the constant with the other estimated parameters, the expected $\ln F_{111} = 4.947 - 0.195 + 0.545 + 0.229 - 0.228 + 0.219 = 5.517$. The antilog of this value is 248.89, whose small difference from the expected frequency (248.91) in Table 10.5 is due to rounding. Can you use the six lambda parameters to compute the expected frequencies for the other seven cells of Table 10.5? (*Hint:* Remember to reverse parameter signs when a subscript changes value from 1 to 2.)

Before moving on to the next section, a review of model-fitting strategies might be useful. In the example developed in this section, we followed a systematic *forward-fitting strategy*. That is, we began by examining the simplest, most concise model that contained only the marginal distributions of the variables. We then added one of the two-variable associations to the three single-variable marginals to see if the fit could be improved. It did improve significantly, suggesting that this association should be retained in the model. If the fit had not improved, we would have dropped this term. Next, we tested three additional models, each having just two of the three two-variable associations, followed by a model that included all three two-variable effects. Only two of these two-way relations significantly improved the fit compared to both simpler and more complex models. This model, which excluded the two-variable association that we initially thought to be necessary, also provided a close fit to the data overall.

An alternative *backward-elimination strategy* could be to start with the complex model having all three two-variable associations (model 6) and then to drop these terms one at a time to see whether the fit of the model worsened (comparing model 6 in turn to models 3–5). Demonstrate to yourself that, for the example developed in this section, by following this backward-elimination strategy, you would have reached the same conclusion as the forward-fitting strategy about which model produced the best fit to the observed crosstabulation.

A third approach to testing log-linear models is first to hypothesize a specific model prior to examining the data. Next, fit the data to that model and ask whether the probability that the model could have generated the observed data is greater than or equal to some chosen value for α. This strategy presumes that a researcher has a strong theoretical argument that specifies in detail the expected relationships. Also, because the hypothesized model is not tested against more parsimonious alternatives, this strategy may accept a log-linear model that includes unnecessarily complex effects.

10.2.3 Testing Models for Large Data Sets

The likelihood ratio is a useful test statistic for finding discrepancies between models and data when samples are moderate in size, such as GSS data sets ranging up to 3,000 cases. With much larger samples, however, the L^2 is almost guaranteed to reject even a good model, because its value increases with the total sample size, N. A more appropriate test statistic

TABLE 10.6
Frequency Crosstabulation of Scientists' Sectors of Employment by Field, Gender, and Year (Hundreds of Scientists)

			SECTOR OF EMPLOYMENT (S)		
Year (Y)	*Gender (G)*	*Field (F)*	*Business*	*Education*	*Government*
1981	Men	Physical Science	1,085	504	171
1981	Men	Engineering	11,180	682	1,037
1981	Men	Social Science	457	635	189
1981	Women	Physical Science	135	80	24
1981	Women	Engineering	263	30	25
1981	Women	Social Science	79	177	100
1997	Men	Physical Science	1,228	631	371
1997	Men	Engineering	10,142	667	1,698
1997	Men	Social Science	637	799	242
1997	Women	Physical Science	330	169	116
1997	Women	Engineering	925	73	239
1997	Women	Social Science	854	771	186

Sources: National Science Foundation. 1982. *Science Indicators 1982.* Washington, DC: United States Government Printing Office. National Science Foundation. 2000. *Science Indicators 2000.* Washington, DC: United States Government Printing Office.

for assessing log-linear models fitted to large-sample crosstabulations is the BIC (Bayesian information criterion) statistic.[2] It is computationally approximated for a log-linear model by the equation

$$\text{BIC} = L^2 - (df)(\ln N)$$

where
$\ln N$ = the natural logarithm of sample size
df = the degrees of freedom for the model

The BIC for a saturated log-linear model must equal 0, because both L^2 and df equal zero. The saturated model is preferred whenever the BICs for alternative models are greater than zero. When BICs are less than zero, the model with the most negative value provides the better fit to the data.

To illustrate applications of the BIC statistic for finding a good fit to a large data set, consider Table 10.6. This four-variable crosstabulation

[2]Adrian E. Raftery. 1986. "Choosing Models for Cross-Classifications." *American Sociological Review 51:* 145–146. Adrian E. Raftery. 1995. "Bayesian Model Selection in Social Research." *Sociological Methodology 25:* 111–163.

TABLE 10.7
Some Log-Linear Models for the Data in Table 10.6

Model	L^2	df	BIC
1. {GFSY}	0.00	0	0.00
2. {FSY}{GFS}{GFY}{GSY}	57.0	4	14.9
3. {GFS}{GFY}{GSY}	167.8	8	83.7
4. {FSY}{GFY}{GSY}	83.8	8	−0.3
5. {FSY}{GFS}{GSY}	104.1	6	41.0
6. {FSY}{GFS}{GFY}	78.7	6	15.6
7. {FSY}{GFS}{GY}	124.4	8	40.3
8. {FSY}{GFY}{GS}	104.6	8	20.5
9. {GFS}{GFY}{SY}	217.5	8	133.4

displays the number (in hundreds) of U.S. scientists and engineers in three sectors of employment (business, education, and government), broken down by field (physical science, engineering, and social science), year (1981 and 1997), and gender (men and women). The table $N = 36,931$, more than three and half million cases. Table 10.7 reports a series of nested log-linear models fitted to the data. We follow a backward-elimination strategy by starting with the saturated model and dropping more complex terms. If we applied only the L^2 criterion to assess model fit, we would conclude that the saturated model, {GFSY}, is the best model. Model 1, which eliminates the four-way marginal table, produces $L^2 = 57.0$ for $df = 4$, which requires us to reject the model as an unacceptable fit to the four-way crosstab (at $\alpha = .05$ the critical value of L^2 is 9.49). The saturated model obviously does not yield a simplified explanation of the relationships observed in the crosstabulation. But by applying the BIC formula to the models in Table 10.7, we reach a different conclusion regarding the best-fitting model. The only negative BIC value occurs for model 3, which excludes both the four-way interaction and one of the three-variable relationships {GFS}. One substantive interpretation of model 3 is that gender differences among fields changed during the seventeen-year interval {GFY}, as did gender differences in sector of employment {GSY}. Although the field-sector composition also shifted over time {FSY}, the absence of the {GFS} marginal table indicates that the field-sector relationship did not differ between men and women.

10.3   More Complex Models

10.3.1   A Four-Variable Crosstabulation

To demonstrate the complexity of analyses for large-dimensioned tables, we added a fourth dichotomous variable—region (R), split between southerners and nonsoutherners—to the three used in the preceding racial segregation example. Table 10.8 displays the observed frequencies. The eight conditional odds of agreeing relative to disagreeing with the racial segregation item vary markedly across combinations of the other three variables. In particular, the younger, college-degreed respondents residing outside the South are the least likely to agree (odds = 0.245), while the older, nondegreed respondents residing in the South are the most likely to agree (odds = 2.386). The series of log-linear models in Table 10.9 all include the fitted marginal {ARE}. Our reason for always including {ARE} is that we assume these three variables are interrelated, and therefore we are not seeking to test any hypotheses about their two- or three-variable associations. In other words, we view any causal relationships among these predictor variables as arising outside our scope of substantive interest. Instead, we focus on estimating how these three antecedent variables relate to the racial segregation item, the variable we consider to be dependent in this log-linear model.

TABLE 10.8
Frequency Crosstabulations of Racial Segregation Attitude by Education, Age, and Region for Whites

			RACIAL SEGREGATION		
Region	*Education*	*Age*	*Agree*	*Disagree*	*Odds*
South	No Degree	Younger	98	104	0.942
South	No Degree	Older	105	44	2.386
South	Degree	Younger	26	46	0.565
South	Degree	Older	22	27	0.815
Nonsouth	No Degree	Younger	143	272	0.526
Nonsouth	No Degree	Older	151	104	1.452
Nonsouth	Degree	Younger	36	147	0.245
Nonsouth	Degree	Older	24	53	0.453

Missing data: 1,430 cases.
Source: 1998 General Social Survey.

TABLE 10.9
Some Log-Linear Models for the Data in Table 10.4

Model	L^2	df	p
1. {ARE} {S}	138.6	7	<.0001
2. {ARE} {SR}	109.5	6	<.0001
3. {ARE} {SE}	90.4	6	<.0001
4. {ARE} {SA}	72.1	6	<.0001
5. {ARE} {SR} {SE}	62.2	5	<.0001
6. {ARE} {SA} {SR}	47.0	5	<.0001
7. {ARE} {SA} {SE}	28.3	5	<.0001
8. {ARE} {SA} {SR} {SE}	3.7	4	.451
9. {ARE} {SER} {SA}	3.3	3	.345
10. {ARE} {SEA} {SR}	0.8	3	.846
11. {ARE} {SAR} {SE}	3.3	3	.343

In this example, we follow a forward-fitting strategy. Model 1 serves as our "baseline model" in the sense that it specifies that no predictor variable is related to racial segregation attitude. As expected, we reject this baseline model because $L^2 = 138.6$ for $df = 7$ (the critical value at $\alpha = .001$ is 24.32). Comparing the differences in L^2s between the baseline model with models 2, 3, and 4, we see that each of the three two-variable associations involving one predictor variable with the segregation item is statistically significant (at $\alpha = .001$, the critical value of $\Delta L^2 = 10.83$ for $\Delta df = 1$). However, none of these three models fit the data well, because in each case the overall model $p < .0001$. We reach similar conclusions after comparing models that have only one two-variable association to models including pairs of two-variable associations (that is, comparing models 2–4 with models 5–8). To test whether all three of the two-variable associations {SA}{SR}{SE} are necessary, we include these marginals in model 8. Its L^2 is then tested pairwise against the L^2s of the three models (5, 6, and 7) that contain only pairs of these two-variable associations. The null hypothesis is that $\Delta L^2 = 0$ for each of the three comparisons. First, $L^2_5 - L^2_8 = 62.2 - 3.7 = 58.5$, indicating that fitting the segregation-by-age marginal table {SA} significantly decreases the differences between the expected frequencies and observed frequencies. Similarly, $L^2_6 - L^2_8 = 47.0 - 3.7 = 43.3$, showing that the segregation-by-education association {SE} also significantly improves the fit. Finally, $L^2_7 - L^2_8 = 28.3 - 3.7 = 24.6$, which reveals that the segregation-by-region relation {*SR*} is also significant. Furthermore, model 8 produces an excellent overall fit, with $L^2 = 3.7$, $df = 4$, and $p = .451$.

As a final check to determine whether any three-way relationships involving racial segregation attitude should be included in the best-fitting model, we compare model 8 to models 9, 10, and 11. Because each of the three tests involves a difference of one degree of freedom, a significant difference in L^2s must exceed the critical value ($\Delta L^2 = 10.83$ at $\alpha = .001$). No difference exceeds this critical value, so we conclude that the expected frequencies produced by model 8—{*ARE*}{*SA*}{*SR*}{*SE*}—provide the best fit to the observed data. Table 10.10 reports the lambda parameters, standard errors, and t ratios for each effect. Three values tell the basic story. The $\lambda^{SE} = 0.214$ parameter means that nondegreed respondents are more likely than college-degreed persons to agree with the racial segregation item. The $\lambda^{SA} = -0.219$ parameter indicates that younger respondents are less likely than older respondents to agree. And the $\lambda^{SR} = 0.147$ parameter shows that persons living in the South are more prone than persons living outside that region to endorse racial segregation. Note that none of the four parameters involving the three independent variables are

TABLE 10.10
Effect Parameters for Model {*ARE*}{*SA*}{*SR*}{*SE*} Fitted to Racial Segregation Attitude by Education by Age by Region for Whites

	Category	λ	$\hat{s}_\lambda$	t
μ	Constant	4.192	—	—
λ_1^S	Agree	−0.149	0.035	4.25***
λ_1^E	No Degree	0.549	0.035	15.83***
λ_1^A	Younger	0.225	0.034	6.62***
λ_1^R	South	−0.310	0.033	−9.22***
λ_{11}^{AE}	Younger—No Degree	−0.014	0.034	−0.39
λ_{11}^{RE}	South—No Degree	−0.013	0.034	−0.38
λ_{11}^{AR}	Younger—South	−0.053	0.034	−1.57
λ_{11}^{SA}	Agree—Younger	−0.219	0.029	7.57***
λ_{11}^{SE}	Agree—No Degree	0.214	0.033	6.40***
λ_{11}^{SR}	Agree—South	0.147	0.030	4.95***
λ_{11}^{ARE}	Younger—No Degree—South	0.039	0.033	1.17

*** $p < .001$

statistically significant. As we noted, however, we necessarily included them in fitting the {ARE} marginal table in all models, even though we were not interested in determining whether any of these relations are probably different from zero in the population.

To summarize, we sought to find the simplest hierarchical log-linear model whose expected cell frequencies closely fit the observed frequencies in the four-variable crosstabulation. We again followed a forward incremental fitting strategy, moving from less-complex to more-complex models. Alternatives would have been either to use a backward stepwise strategy or to hypothesize a specific model and test its fit to the data.

10.3.2 The Logit Model

All the log-linear analyses to this point used a general specification, one that does not distinguish between independent and dependent variables in the calculation of effect parameters. When one dichotomous variable is considered to be dependent on the other variables, a special type of log-linear model, the **logit model**, is appropriate. A logit is simply the natural logarithm of an odds—that is, the ratio of two expected frequencies:

logit model—a log-linear model in which one dichotomous variable is considered to be dependent on the other variables

$$\text{logit}\left(\frac{F_1}{F_2}\right) = \ln\left(\frac{F_1}{F_2}\right) = \ln F_1 - \ln F_2$$

Thus, the parameters of a logit model are easily derived from a general log-linear model, as shown in Box 10.1. *Instead of predicting expected*

Box 10.1   Deriving Logit Effect Parameters from General Log-Linear Parameters

The logit specification in log-linear analysis is analogous to the logistic regression equations in chapter 9, except that the predictor variables are categoric rather than continuous measures. Assume that variable Y is a dichotomous dependent variable and variables X and Z are categoric predictors in a three-variable log-linear model $\{YX\}\{YZ\}\{XZ\}$, which yields the following equation for the expected frequency in the i,j,kth cell of the crosstab:

(continued)

$$\ln F_{ijk} = \mu + \lambda_i^Y + \lambda_j^X + \lambda_k^Z + \lambda_{ij}^{YX} + \lambda_{ik}^{YZ} + \lambda_{jk}^{XZ}$$

Because $\ln(A/B) = \ln A - \ln B$ in general, the logged ratio of expected frequencies for any pair of cells involving the dependent variable Y is

$$
\begin{aligned}
\ln\left(\frac{F_{1jk}}{F_{2jk}}\right) &= \ln F_{1jk} - \ln F_{2jk}\\
&= (\mu + \lambda_1^Y + \lambda_j^X + \lambda_k^Z + \lambda_{1j}^{YX} + \lambda_{1k}^{YZ} + \lambda_{jk}^{XZ})\\
&\quad - (\mu + \lambda_2^Y + \lambda_j^X + \lambda_k^Z + \lambda_{2j}^{YX} + \lambda_{2k}^{YZ} + \lambda_{jk}^{XZ})
\end{aligned}
$$

Collecting and canceling terms, we have

$$\ln\left(\frac{F_{1jk}}{F_{2jk}}\right) = \lambda_1^Y - \lambda_2^Y + \lambda_{1j}^{YX} - \lambda_{2j}^{YX} + \lambda_{1k}^{YZ} - \lambda_{2k}^{YZ}$$

For dichotomous variables $\lambda_1^Y = -\lambda_2^Y$, $\lambda_{1j}^{YX} = -\lambda_{2j}^{YX}$, and $\lambda_{1k}^{YZ} = -\lambda_{2k}^{YZ}$, the equation for the expected log odds of Y further simplifies to

$$\ln\left(\frac{F_{1jk}}{F_{2jk}}\right) = 2\lambda_1^Y + 2\lambda_{1j}^{YX} + 2\lambda_{1k}^{YZ}$$

To distinguish logit effect parameters from general log-linear parameters, we replace them in the preceding equation with appropriate subscripted and superscripted betas:

$$\ln\left(\frac{F_{1jk}}{F_{2jk}}\right) = \beta_1^Y + \beta_{1j}^{YX} + \beta_{1k}^{YZ}$$

where $\beta_1^Y = 2\lambda_1^Y$, $\beta_{1j}^{YX} = 2\lambda_{1j}^{YX}$, and $\beta_{1k}^{YZ} = 2\lambda_{1k}^{YZ}$. Thus, the effect parameters for a logit equation are twice the corresponding lambda parameters from the general log-linear equation.

individual cell frequencies, the logit model predicts the log odds of the dependent variable.

To illustrate the transformation, consider the logit equation for the log-odds of racial segregation disagreement from the three-variable analysis shown in Table 10.5 in section 10.2. This equation is

$$\ln\left(\frac{F_{1jk}}{F_{2jk}}\right) = \beta^S + \beta_j^{SA} + \beta_k^{SE}$$

The numerical values for these three coefficients are obtained by doubling the corresponding lambdas, that is, $\beta^X = 2\lambda^X$ and $\beta^{YX} = 2\lambda^{YX}$. Positive betas indicate that an independent variable increases the expected log-odds for the dependent variable, while negative betas reveal that an independent variable decreases the log-odds. Using the parameters in Table 10.5, $\beta^S = -0.390$, $\beta^{SA} = -0.456$, and $\beta^{SE} = +0.438$. Our substantive interpretations of these logit coefficients are identical to our conclusions about the log-linear parameters. Respondents were less likely to agree than to disagree with the racial segregation item; younger people were less likely to support segregation; and the nondegreed were more prone to agree with the segregation item.

By systematically changing the 1-2 subscripts of the two independent variables in the logit equation, and thus the alternating signs of the beta parameters, we can estimate the log-odds on segregation attitude for each of the four age-education combinations. The predicted log-odds of agreeing with racial segregation for respondents who are younger and nondegreed (where $A = 1$ and $E = 1$) is

$$\ln\left(\frac{F_{111}}{F_{211}}\right) = (2)(-0.195) + (2)(-0.228) + (2)(0.219)$$
$$= -0.390 - 0.456 + 0.438 = -0.408$$

The expected log-odds of approving of segregation for the older, nondegreed respondents ($A = 2$, $E = 1$) is

$$\ln\left(\frac{F_{121}}{F_{221}}\right) = -0.390 + 0.456 + 0.438 = +0.504$$

for the younger, college-degreed respondents the log-odds is

$$\ln\left(\frac{F_{112}}{F_{212}}\right) = -0.390 - 0.456 - 0.438 = -1.284$$

and for the older, nondegreed respondents the log-odds is

$$\ln\left(\frac{F_{122}}{F_{222}}\right) = -0.390 + 0.456 - 0.438 = -0.372$$

This exercise illustrates the additive impact of age and education on attitude. The respondents who agree most with racial segregation are older and nondegreed, while those people who agree least are younger and college-degreed. The attitudes of the other two age-education combinations fall between these extremes.

10.4   Special Topics in Log-Linear Analysis

Log-linear analysis is a powerful statistical method in the social researcher's tool kit, with applications to many substantive problems. Space limitations allow us to examine only a few special topics, whose comprehension requires a firm grasp of the fundamentals discussed in the preceding sections.

10.4.1   Zero Cells

The log-linear analysis is potentially applicable to tables of very large dimensions, both in numbers of variables and numbers of categories. However, as these dimensions expand, the number of cells in the table will increase relative to the number of observations, resulting in decreasing numbers of cases per cell. As a general rule, a practical limit on crosstabulation analysis can arise with as few as five variables having only three categories apiece. Completely crossing such measures yields $3^5 = 243$ cells, which results in an average cell frequency of barely five cases for a typical survey with only 1,500 respondents. Many cells will have zero observed frequencies, particularly when variables are highly skewed. Rare combinations of variables may go unrepresented in a particular sample (e.g., black female heads of major corporations). Because **random zeros** pose problems in defining odds-ratios, researchers who seek to analyze such tables are well-advised to add a small constant— typically 0.5—to *all* cell counts before fitting log-linear models. (Using 0.5 as the constant value concurs with the convention of rounding such fractional values arbitrarily up or down to the nearest integer.)

random zero— a combination of variables that is unrepresented in a sample

By contrast, **structural zeros** arise because certain combinations of variable categories cannot logically occur. Teenage grandparents or women with prostate cancer are conditions that are not just unlikely, but impossible. Such structural zeros cannot be adjusted by adding a small constant but must be treated as fixed-zero cells in log-linear analyses.

structural zero— a combination of variables that cannot logically occur

The top panel of Table 10.11 contains the observed frequencies for a crosstabulation for 1998 GSS respondents of five categories of their current marital status by previous widowhood. Because current widows were not asked this question, and because never-married respondents logically cannot have experienced widowhood, these two cells are structural zeros. However, the currently married, separated, and divorced respondents might have been widowed before their current marriages, and 77 respondents answered "yes" to this question. The second panel

TABLE 10.11
Observed and Expected Frequencies in Crosstabulation of Current Marital Status by Previous Widowhood

| Current Status | OBSERVED FREQUENCIES | | INDEPENDENCE MODEL | | QUASI-INDEPENDENCE MODEL | |
| | Previously Widowed | | Previously Widowed | | Previously Widowed | |
	No	Yes	No	Yes	No	Yes
Married	1,304	41	1,308.42	36.58	1,290.06	54.94
Widowed	283	0*	275.30	7.70	283.00	0*
Divorced	417	30	434.84	12.16	428.74	18.26
Separated	87	6	90.47	2.53	89.20	3.80
Never Married	663	0*	644.97	18.03	663.00	0*

*Structural zero.
Source: 1998 General Social Survey.

shows the expected cell frequencies when the independence model $\{M\}\{W\}$ is applied to the full 5×2 table. This hypothesis is strongly rejected at the $\alpha = .001$ level, whose c.v. is 18.5 for $df = 4$ since $L^2 = 75.5$. But this model is clearly absurd because it generates nonzero expected frequencies in both structural zero cells.

quasi-independence model—a model that ignores structural-zero cells and tests for independence only among the remaining entries

The relevant model for a table with one or more structural zeros is the **quasi-independence model**, which ignores the structural zero cells and tests for independence only among the remaining entries. Most log-linear analysis computer programs have an option that allows an analyst to designate which cell entries must be fixed to zero. The degrees of freedom for a quasi-independence model are adjusted by subtracting one *df* for each fixed-zero cell. Thus, for a two-variable crosstab having R rows, C columns, and Z structural zeros, the *df* for the quasi-independence model is $(R - 1)(C - 1) - Z$.

The third panel of Table 10.11 displays the expected frequencies for the quasi-independence model, which has a much better fit to the data ($L^2 = 11.8$, $df = [(5 - 1)(2 - 1) - 2] = 2$, $p = .003$). The expected odds of previous widowhood are 0.043 among the currently married, divorced, and separated respondents, or about one to 24. However, the saturated model fits the data even better because the quasi-independence model's probability level is less than .05. Using the observed frequencies in the first panel of Table 10.11, we can calculate that the odds of prior widowhood are lower for currently married persons (0.03) than for the currently separated (0.07) or the divorced (0.07). Therefore, in the population, current marital status is probably related to the dissolution of a previous marriage through a spouse's death.

10.4.2 Symmetry

Many research problems concern relationships within a square crosstabulation, where both variables have the same K categories in the same sequence. Such tables might be formed by re-measuring a variable for the same respondents at two time periods (so-called "turnover tables" produced by a panel survey with repeated questions). For example, a marketing researcher may ask consumers each month to report their current cereal purchases in order to investigate brand-name loyalty and defection. Square tables may also be constructed by jointly classifying two partners in a social interaction, using the same set of categories. For example, pairs of workers and supervisors may be asked how much satisfaction they find in their relationship.

The basic substantive hypotheses about a $K \times K$ square table are the patterns of stability and change over time (in panels) or agreement and difference (in interaction pairs). The **symmetry model** predicts exactly equal frequencies in the corresponding cells; that is, $f_{ij} = f_{ji}$ for all $i \neq j$. The observed frequency in the ith row, jth column equals the observed frequency in the jth row, ith column for all nondiagonal cells. A symmetrical pattern also implies **marginal homogeneity**; that is, the corresponding row and column marginal totals are equal (i.e., $f_{i\bullet} = f_{\bullet i}$). However, the converse is not true; homogenous marginals do *not* imply symmetry within the body of the square crosstab because identical row and column totals can be produced in many ways.

symmetry model— a model that predicts exactly equal frequencies in corresponding cells of a $K \times K$ crosstabulation

marginal homogeneity— corresponding row and column marginal totals are equal

Because the GSS is not a longitudinal survey, we illustrate symmetry with a cross-sectional assortative mating process. The top panel of Table 10.12 contains the observed frequency counts from the 1994 GSS for a crosstab classifying married respondents (R) and their spouses (S) by their religions at age 16, using five broad groupings. (To adjust for the four cells with random zeros, we added a constant 0.5 to all 25 cells, giving a total of 761.5 cases.) Clearly, we do not expect couples' religious affiliations to be independent, as the large majority of Americans are known to marry primarily within their own religious groups. Indeed, when the $\{R\}\{S\}$ independence model (i.e., $\ln F_{ij} = \mu + \lambda_i^R + \lambda_j^S$) is fitted to the bivariate table, it must be rejected at the $\alpha = .001$ level with 16 *df* (c.v. = 39.3) because $L^2 = 233.5$. As can be seen by summing the frequencies in the five cells of the main diagonal of Table 10.12, almost two-

TABLE 10.12

Observed and Expected Frequencies in Crosstabulation of Religious Affiliations of Respondents and Spouses at Age 16

Respondent's Religion	SPOUSE'S RELIGION					
	Protestant	Catholic	Jewish	No Religion	Other	Total
Observed Frequencies**						
Protestant	341.5	78.5	0.5	18.5	22.5	461.5
Catholic	79.5	128.5	3.5	10.5	3.5	225.5
Jewish	4.5	2.5	3.5	1.5	0.5	12.5
No Religion	12.5	7.5	1.5	10.5	1.5	33.5
Other	8.5	3.5	0.5	0.5	15.5	28.5
Total	446.5	220.5	9.5	41.5	43.5	761.5
Expected Frequencies in Symmetry Model						
Protestant	341.5*	79.0	2.5	15.5	15.5	454.0
Catholic	79.0	128.5*	3.0	9.0	3.5	223.0
Jewish	2.5	3.0	3.5*	1.5	0.5	11.0
No Religion	15.5	9.0	1.5	10.5*	1.0	37.5
Other	15.5	3.5	0.5	1.0	15.5*	36.0
Total	454.0	223.0	11.0	37.5	36.0	761.5

*Cell frequencies were fixed to structural zeros.

**A constant 0.5 was added to each cell frequency to correct for random zeros.

Missing data: 2,230 cases.

Source: 1994 General Social Survey.

thirds of respondents and their spouses were raised in the same religion (499.5/761.5 = 65.6%). Leaving aside this obvious clustering on the main diagonal, do interfaith marriages tend to occur more in one direction than the other? Such a pattern seems unlikely given that, for example, a person raised Catholic marrying a person raised Protestant seems no more likely than a person raised Protestant marrying a person raised Catholic. Furthermore, the corresponding row and column marginals are close for Protestants and Catholics, although somewhat different for the other three categories. Thus, we might hypothesize that a symmetrical model should fit the $(5 \times 5) - 5 = 20$ off-diagonal cells of the $R \times S$ crosstab in Table 10.12. That is, we seek to fit a log-linear model $\ln F_{ij} = \mu + \lambda_i^R + \lambda_j^S + \lambda_{ij}^{RS}$ that specifies symmetrical choices of respondents and their spouses.

To estimate the symmetry model's expected frequencies and test their fit to the observed frequencies, we create a three-variable crosstab in which the main diagonal cells (i.e., respondents and spouses both raised in the same religion) are treated as structural zeros. The off-diagonal cells can be viewed as two triangular arrays, one above and one below the main diagonal. Therefore, we can use the observed frequencies in Table 10.12 to construct a new dataset consisting of four variables for each of these 20 off-diagonal cells: Triangle (T) is coded 1 for the ten lower triangular cells and 2 for the ten upper triangular cells; respondent's religion (R) and spouse's religion (S) are coded from 1 to 5 to represent the five religion categories from Protestant to Other; and frequency (F) is the number of cases observed in each cell of the two triangular portions. The dataset for Table 10.12 looks like this:

T	R	S	F
1	2	1	79.50
1	3	1	4.50
1	4	1	12.50
1	5	1	8.50
1	3	2	2.50
1	4	2	7.50
1	5	2	3.50
1	4	3	1.50
1	5	3	0.50
1	5	4	0.50
2	2	1	78.50
2	3	1	0.50
2	4	1	18.50
2	5	1	22.50
2	3	2	3.50
2	4	2	10.50
2	5	2	3.50
2	4	3	1.50
2	5	3	0.50
2	5	4	1.50

We test the symmetry hypothesis by fitting the $\{RS\}$ marginal table to this three-variable crosstabulation, weighting the data by the (F) variable to generate the correct observed cell frequencies. The symmetry model forces the corresponding expected row and expected column marginals in the $R \times S$ crosstab to be equal; that is, $F_{i\bullet} = F_{\bullet i}$ even when the observed $f_{i\bullet} \neq f_{\bullet i}$. For example, the expected number of Protestant respondents and Protestant spouses is $(446.5 + 461.5)/2 = 454$. Further, the symmetry model's expected cell frequencies are computed as averages of the corresponding pairs of observed off-diagonal entries, i.e., $F_{ij} = F_{ji}$ = $(f_{ij} + f_{ji})/2$. For example, the expected number of Protestant-Catholic marriages is $(78.5 + 79.5)/2 = 79.0$. Because the five main diagonal frequencies are treated as structural zeros (and hence ignored in fitting the symmetry model to the three-way crosstab) and because the pairs of off-diagonal expected frequencies are symmetrized (i.e., $F_{ij} = F_{ji}$), the symmetry model's degrees of freedom are $(K^2 - K)/2$; for the five religious categories, $df = (5^2 - 5)/2 = 10$.

For this assortative religious mating example, the symmetry model produces an excellent fit: $L^2 = 12.6$, $df = 10$, $p > .50$. The bottom panel of Table 10.12 displays the expected frequencies for this model. Note that the expected frequencies in the corresponding pairs of cells across the two triangles are equal and most expected frequencies differ very little from the observed frequencies in the top panel. Because the symmetry model fits interfaith marriages among the five broad religious origins so well, we cannot reject the hypothesis that American marriages are basically a symmetrical process. People of various religions marry those of differing religious backgrounds in roughly the same proportions.

10.4.3 Quasi-Symmetry

The symmetry model described in the preceding subsection does not require that the row and column marginals for the expected frequencies equal the observed marginal frequencies. An alternative log-linear model that preserves these marginal frequencies is the **quasi-symmetry model**, which also produces equal corresponding odds ratios among the off-diagonal cells. To illustrate this approach, we analyze intergenerational mobility from father's (F) to offspring's (O) occupations, using the five broad categories shown in Table 10.13. (The convention in stratification and network research is to arrange the origin categories in the rows and the destination categories in the columns, ranging from highest status to lowest status. Thus, the upwardly mobile appear in the cells below the main diagonal, while the downwardly mobile are above the diagonal.) The now well-known historical shift in the American labor force is evident in the grossly unequal marginal distributions: the offspring generation has twice as many lower white-collar workers as their fathers' generation but only half as many upper blue-collar workers and far fewer farmers. Although the independence hypothesis $\{F\}\{O\}$ is clearly rejected at $\alpha = .001$ ($df = 16$, c.v. $= 39.3$) since $L^2 = 163.5$, the symmetry hypothesis $\{FO\}$ is also rejected ($L^2 = 595.8$, $df = 10$). The corresponding row and column totals differ too drastically to accommodate equivalent upward and downward intergenerational mobility flows.

quasi-symmetry model— a special type of symmetry that preserves the inequality of the corresponding row and column marginals but produces equal corresponding odds ratios among the off-diagonal cells

Because symmetry is rejected, we know that the corresponding cell frequencies are not equal ($f_{ij} \neq f_{ji}$) and the corresponding row and column marginals are not homogeneous (i.e., $F_{i\bullet} \neq F_{\bullet i}$). We could stop the analysis here and conclude only that symmetry is not present, but one option is to continue the analysis within the constraint of nonhomogeneous marginals to see if a special type of symmetry can be detected. The quasi-symmetry model preserves the inequality of the corresponding row and column marginals but allows us to test whether corresponding odds ratios among the off-diagonal cells are equal. For the occupational mobility example, the hypothesis is that movement across pairs of occupations has the same magnitude whether the direction of movement is upward or downward. That is, the fathers' and the offsprings' occupational distribu-

TABLE 10.13

Observed and Expected Frequencies in Crosstabulation of Father's and Respondent's Occupations

Father's Occupation	*RESPONDENT'S OCCUPATION*					
	Upper White Collar	*Lower White Collar*	*Upper Blue Collar*	*Lower Blue Collar*	*Farm*	*Total*
Observed Frequencies						
Upper White Collar	234*	141	25	97	3	500
Lower White Collar	108	102*	22	55	2	289
Upper Blue Collar	133	146	63*	148	8	498
Lower Blue Collar	136	191	53	193*	4	577
Farm	71	62	33	100	21*	287
Total	682	642	196	593	38	2,251
Expected Frequencies in Quasi-Symmetry Model						
Upper White Collar	234.0*	141.0	29.7	91.6	3.7	500
Lower White Collar	108.0	102.0*	17.3	60.0	1.6	289
Upper Blue Collar	128.3	150.7	63.0*	148.4	7.7	498
Lower Blue Collar	141.4	186.0	52.7	193.0*	4.0	577
Farm	70.3	62.4	33.4	100.0	21.0*	287
Total	682	642	196	593	38	2,251

*Cell frequencies were fixed with structural zeros.
Missing data: 670 cases.
Source: 1998 General Social Survey.

tions are allowed to equal the observed values, rather than constrained to be identical to a symmetry model. Only the paired off-diagonal frequencies are free to vary within these looser constraints.

As in the symmetry model (see section 10.4.2), we construct a new dataset consisting of four variables for the off-diagonal cells representing cross-category mobility: Triangle (T) is coded 1 for the lower triangular cells and 2 for the upper triangular cells; father's (P) and respondent's (R) occupations are coded from 1 to 5 to represent the five categories from upper white-collar to farm occupations; and frequency (F) is the number of cases observed in each cell of the two triangular portions. The dataset for Table 10.13 looks like this:

T	P	R	F
1	2	1	108
1	3	1	133
1	4	1	136
1	5	1	71
1	3	2	146
1	4	2	191
1	5	2	62
1	4	3	53
1	5	3	33
1	5	4	100
2	2	1	141
2	3	1	25
2	4	1	97
2	5	1	3
2	3	2	22
2	4	2	55
2	5	2	2
2	4	3	148
2	5	3	8
2	5	4	4

Note that this dataset is equivalent to that used in the symmetry model. However, the quasi-symmetry model is tested by fitting the three two-way marginal tables $\{PR\}\{PT\}\{RT\}$. For these data, the quasi-symmetry model yields an excellent fit to the mobility table: $L^2 = 3.6$, $df = 3$, $p > .50$. Furthermore, we can test a marginal homogeneity hypothesis by taking the difference in fits between the symmetry and quasi-symmetry models. In this example, marginal homogeneity is soundly rejected: $\Delta L^2 = L_S^2 - L_{QS}^2 = 595.8 - 3.6 = 592.2$ and $\Delta df = df_s - df_{QS} = 10 - 3 = 7$, $p < .001$.

As a comparison of upper and lower panels of Table 10.13 reveals, the corresponding pairs of observed and expected row and column marginals are equal. However, the corresponding pairs of cells in the upper and lower triangles are not constrained to equality. For example, the expected number of farm to upper-white-collar movers is almost 20 times greater than the reverse direction (70.3 versus 3.7). Instead, after fitting the nonhomogeneous marginals, the quasi-symmetry model requires symmetry in the intergenerational upward and downward mobility *across corresponding pairs of categories*. For example, among respondents whose fathers were farmers or lower-blue-collar workers, their odds of rising to upper- and lower-white-collar jobs is

$$\frac{(141.4)(62.4)}{(186.0)(70.3)} = 0.66$$

which is identical to the odds that the offspring of upper- and lower-white-collar fathers fell into the lower-blue-collar and farm categories:

$$\frac{(91.6)(1.6)}{(3.7)(60.0)} = 0.66$$

We hope these examples illustrate the fact that many useful applications of log-linear methods are available to social scientists. To benefit fully from these complex analysis tools, of course, much extended study is essential.

Review of Key Concepts and Symbols

These key concepts and symbols are listed in the order of appearance in this chapter. Combined with the definitions in the margins, they will help you to review the material and can serve as a self-test for mastery of the concepts.

multivariate contingency table analysis	OR
log-linear analysis	F_{ij}
saturated model	
nonsaturated model	$\ln F_{ij}$
conditional odds ratio	μ
hierarchical log-linear model	
nested models	λ_{ij}^{XY}
marginal subtables	$\hat{s}_\lambda$
fitted marginal	$OR^{XY|Z=1}$
iterative proportional fitting	
Newton–Raphson algorithm	$\{XY\}$
likelihood ratio	L^2
logit model	
random zero	ΔL^2
structural zero	Δdf
quasi-independence model	
symmetry model	BIC
marginal homogeneity	β^X
quasi-symmetry model	

PROBLEMS

General Problems

1. Here is a 2×2 crosstabulation of responses to the question "Please tell me whether or not *you* think it should be possible for a pregnant woman to obtain a *legal* abortion if the woman wants it for any reason" by respondent's gender in the 1998 GSS:

Support for Access to Abortion by Gender

	Gender	
Should a pregnant woman be able to obtain a legal abortion for any reason?	*Women*	*Men*
Yes	418	310
No	618	432

Missing data = 1,054.
Source: 1998 General Social Survey.

Calculate the odds in favor of abortion access for the table as a whole and the conditional odds in favor for each gender. Calculate the odds ratio for women compared to men. What is the relationship of gender to abortion support?

2. For the 1998 GSS, a saturated log-linear model fitted to a 2×2 crosstabulation of race (R, classified as white = 1 and black = 2) and responses to a question "Do you favor or oppose capital punishment for persons convicted of murder?" (C, with favor = 1 and oppose = 2), produced the following log-linear coefficient estimates:

$$\mu = 5.9688 \qquad \lambda_1^R = +0.7786$$
$$\lambda_1^C = +0.3188 \qquad \lambda_{11}^{CR} = +0.3216$$

Calculate the expected frequencies for the four cells of the table, rounding to the nearest whole integer.

3. For the 1998 GSS, a crosstabulation of responses to "How often do you pray?" (P, once a day or more often = 1, less often = 2) with responses to "Would you call yourself a strong (religious preference) or not very strong (religious preference)?" (R, strong = 1, not very strong or no religion = 2) produced the following observed frequencies:

Religious Intensity by Frequency of Praying

How often do you pray? (P)	Religious Intensity (R)	
	Strong	Not Strong
Daily	398	331
Less Often	93	528

Missing data = 1,482.
Source: 1998 General Social Survey.

Estimate the log-linear effect parameters for the saturated model:

$$\ln F_{ij} = \mu + \lambda_i^R + \lambda_j^P + \lambda_{ij}^{RP}$$

4. Estimate the standard error of the lambda effect parameters in Problem 3 and calculate the three t scores.

5. When the independence log-linear model $\{R\}\{P\}$ is fitted to the data in Problem 3, the following parameter estimates result: $\mu = 5.7798$; $\lambda_i^R = -0.2797$; $\lambda_j^P = +0.0802$.

   a. Calculate the four expected frequencies for the 2×2 table.

   b. Using these expected frequencies and the observed frequencies in Problem 3, calculate L^2 for the independence model, and test whether the null hypothesis can be rejected at $\alpha = .001$.

6. For the 1998 GSS, a crosstabulation of three questions: "Would you favor or oppose a law that would require a person to obtain a police permit before he or she could buy a gun?"(L); "Do you happen to have in your home any guns or revolvers?" (G); and "Are we spending too much money, too little money, or about the right amount on halting the rising crime rate?" (S); produced the following observed frequencies:

Spending to Halt Crime by Gun Laws and Gun Ownership

Own Gun (G)	Gun Law (L)	Spending to Halt Crime (S)		
		Too Much	About Right	Too Little
Yes	Favor	142	56	12
Yes	Oppose	44	23	14
No	Favor	339	142	35
No	Oppose	35	22	4

Missing data = 1,964.
Source: 1998 General Social Survey.

For each of the two gun ownership categories, calculate the conditional odds ratio of gun law attitude to the categories "too much" and "about right" and the conditional odds ratio of gun law attitude to the categories "too much" and "too little." What is your interpretation?

7. Five log-linear models were fitted to the three-variable crosstabulation in Problem 6, with the following likelihood ratios:

Model	L^2	df	p
1. $\{G\}\{L\}\{S\}$	52.6	7	<.0001
2. $\{GL\}\{GS\}$	11.4	4	.022
3. $\{GL\}\{LS\}$	4.5	4	.343
4. $\{GS\}\{LS\}$	43.1	4	.000
5. $\{GL\}\{GS\}\{LS\}$	3.9	2	.146

Does model 5 produce a better fit to the observed data, testing for differences in L^2s with each of the other four models with $\alpha = .05$?

8. For the 1998 GSS, a four-way crosstabulation was created using dichotomous 1996 presidential vote (V, Clinton = 1, Dole = 2) by dichotomous party identification (P, Democrat or Independent = 1, Republican = 2), liberal-conservative self-placement (C, liberal or moderate = 1, conservative = 2), and education (E, high school or less = 1, some college or more = 2). Log-linear models were fitted to the 1,452 cases in this table, producing the following likelihood ratios:

Model	L^2	df	p
1. $\{PCE\}\{V\}$	730.6	7	.000
2. $\{PCE\}\{EV\}$	719.4	6	.000
3. $\{PCE\}\{CV\}$	447.2	6	.000
4. $\{PCE\}\{PV\}$	80.0	6	.000
5. $\{PCE\}\{EV\}\{CV\}$	436.4	5	.000
6. $\{PCE\}\{EV\}\{PV\}$	74.8	5	.000
7. $\{PCE\}\{CV\}\{PV\}$	15.0	5	.010
8. $\{PCE\}\{CV\}\{EV\}\{PV\}$	9.0	4	.060

Calculate the BIC statistics for each model and decide which provides the best fit. Does your conclusion differ from that reached by testing for differences in model L^2s when $\alpha = .001$?

9. The effect parameters for model 7 in Problem 8 are as follows:

$$\mu = 3.986 \qquad \lambda_1^P = 0.396 \qquad \lambda_1^C = 0.136$$
$$\lambda_1^E = -0.210 \qquad \lambda_1^V = -0.092 \qquad \lambda_{11}^{PC} = 0.290$$
$$\lambda_{11}^{PE} = 0.071 \qquad \lambda_{11}^{VP} = 0.746 \qquad \lambda_{11}^{VC} = 0.304$$
$$\lambda_{11}^{CE} = 0.024 \qquad \lambda_{11}^{PCE} = -0.105$$

a. What is the expected frequency of cases having the first category on all four variables?

b. What is the expected frequency of cases having the first category on V and C and the second category on P and E?

10. Using the effect parameters in Problem 9, calculate the expected logits of voting for Clinton for respondents who are (a) liberal ($C = 1$) and Democratic or Independent ($P = 1$); (b) conservative ($C = 2$) and Republican ($P = 2$).

Problems Requiring the 1998 General Social Survey

11. Crosstabulate happiness (HAPPY) and relative financial well-being (FINRELA). Report L^2 and the expected frequencies from the independence model, which fits the $\{H\}\{F\}$ marginals. Can you reject this model at $\alpha = .001$?

12. Perform a log-linear analysis of the relationship between GRASS and gender (SEX). Report L^2 for the independence model, which fits the $\{G\}\{S\}$ marginals. Can you reject this model at $\alpha = .001$? Report the effect parameters for the saturated model $\{GS\}$.

13. Is the relationship between the number of children and the ideal number of children the same for men and women? Dichotomize CHILDS and CHLDIDEL into low (0–2) and high (3–8) categories, then fit a log-linear model having all two-way effects to the $2 \times 2 \times 2$ crosstabulation with SEX. Report the L^2 and the effect parameters, and state your conclusion.

14. Fit a log-linear model having all two-way effects to the $2 \times 2 \times 2$ crosstabulation of RELITEN (1 = 1)(2, 3 = 2), CONCHURH (1, 2 = 1)(3, 4, 5 = 2), and ATTEND (0 through 5 = 1)(6, 7, 8 = 2). Then, successively test a series of models each of which removes one of the two-variable effects. Report the L^2s and BIC statistics for each model and decide which provides the best fit.

15. Fit a log-linear model having all two-way effects to the $3 \times 2 \times 2$ crosstabulation of RELIG (Protestants, Catholics, and Jews only), AGE (dichotomized at 50 years and under vs. 51 years and older), and approval or disapproval of the Supreme Court's ruling that "no state or local government may *require* the reading of the Lord's Prayer or Bible verses in public school" (PRAYER). Can you reject this model at $\alpha = .05$? Report the model's effect parameters, and give an interpretation of how age and religion affect approval of the Court's prayer decision.

11

CAUSAL MODELS AND PATH ANALYSIS

11.1 Causal Assumptions   **11.3** Path Analysis
11.2 Causal Diagrams

Throughout this text we have stressed the idea that social research investigates two or more variables in an implicitly causal relationship. In this chapter we elaborate on the causal mode of thinking about social behavior, describing a basic technique—path analysis—for representing causal relations among quantitative variables. Causal reasoning dominates many areas of social research, but the foundations of these conceptualizations often are not carefully articulated. Considerable pseudo-philosophical mumbo-jumbo may accompany efforts to explain social phenomena in cause-and-effect terms. In the first section of this chapter we state the basic assumptions that must be met before causal explanations can be seriously entertained.

11.1 Causal Assumptions

Hypotheses of the form, "If A, then B," or "The higher the A, the higher (lower) the B," merely state an expectation that variables A and B are related. Such hypotheses are covariation statements that systematically relate differences or changes in one variable to differences or changes in a second variable. Often, the author of a research proposition clearly intends a causal effect to be present. For example, "The higher the level of test anxiety, the lower the performance on a final exam" quite obviously means that test anxiety precedes and is a cause of poor scores. However, "The greater the practice of irrigation, the more centralized the state authority in early civilizations," is unclear about which variable—technology or political structure—is the cause and which is the effect. A genuinely causal hypothesis should explicitly state the researcher's expectations. Statements of the format, "An increase in variable *A* causes an increase (decrease) in variable *B*," leave no doubt as to the author's intentions.

A proposition in causal form is more informative than one that is only covariational. Causation is typically (but not necessarily) asymmetrical, in the sense that a change in the cause creates a change in the effect, whereas the reverse is not true—changing the dependent variable should leave the independent variable unaltered. Consider a causal hypothesis from agricultural economics: "Greater rainfall causes higher crop yields" (everything else being equal, which it seldom is). Because extensive experimental and observational data have been collected, the covariation of moisture and productivity is well established. Knowledge of plant physiology provides a sound basis for inferring which variable is cause and which is effect. A student who asserted that sowing more seeds per acre would increase a locality's rainfall would soon be laughed out of agriculture school. This trite but true hypothesis, therefore, is unambiguously causal in its intent and consequences.

Many theoretical statements in social research are not so clear. Sometimes theorists and researchers are simply confused about the "chicken-and-egg" sequence of the phenomena they study. More often, social reality is so incredibly complex that disentangling a causal process is almost impossible. Rarely does any interesting social behavior have a single cause that can be easily isolated. Rather, human activity is governed by a variety of influences, not the least of which is intentionality (purpose). For example, crime rates in the United States may rise or fall through a complex interplay of poverty, school truancy, suburbanization, targets of opportunity, policing efforts—the list of potential causes is endless. To assert that a single variable has a discernible impact is a bold step that cannot be undertaken lightly.

As social research has matured, researchers have abandoned the simplistic, monocausal thinking of the nineteenth century for the contemporary emphasis on multicausal theories or models. An important statistical development—path analysis—provides one method for formulating hypotheses in explicit multicausal frameworks. Three basic conditions are necessary to establish causal priority among variables, none of which is sufficient by itself. These causality conditions are covariation, time order, and nonspuriousness.

For a causal relationship to be present between a pair of variables, **covariation** between the independent and dependent variables must exist. Systematic changes or differences in one variable must accompany systematic changes or differences in the other. Covariation can take several forms: positive or negative linear association or several kinds of nonlinear relationships (see chapter 9).

The **time order** condition of causality is a metatheoretical assumption shared almost unconsciously by most Western peoples. For causality to occur, the change in the purported independent variable must precede in time the change in the alleged dependent measure. Temporal order helps to establish the essential asymmetry in a causal relationship. Causal research on social mobility and socioeconomic attainment developed rapidly by applying knowledge about the time sequences among parents' status and their offsprings' occupations. Causal explanations of attitude structures, however, have been frustrated by an inability to determine temporal sequences among expressed attitudes recorded during a single interview. Researchers frequently assume that certain background characteristics of survey respondents—race, education, religion, or occupation, for example—were formed sufficiently prior to later behaviors—such as voting, drinking, marrying, or divorcing—and that these characteristics can safely be assumed to cause the behaviors.

Even if two variables covary and a temporal order can be determined, a third condition must be satisfied before a causal relationship can be seriously considered to exist: The pattern of association between variables Y and X must not arise from other, common causal factors. The classic observation is that Dutch communities that have many storks nesting in chimneys have higher birth rates than communities where fewer storks nest. While covariation and temporal-order conditions reasonably can be met in this example, various "rival factors" might affect both the number of nesting storks and the number of human babies. The predominance of rural areas, pollution and sanitation levels, community attitudes, and patterns of selective migration may all combine to produce a spurious correlation between the two variables.

Establishing **nonspuriousness** in a causal relationship is one of the most difficult problems to solve in social research. We cannot literally examine every possible alternative explanation for why two variables are related. Various research methods and statistical techniques have been developed that reduce much opportunity for spurious covariation to remain undetected. Controlled experiments represent the most effective way to control rival factors. When subjects are randomly assigned to various

covariation—joint variation, or association, between a pair of variables

time order—the necessary condition that changes in a purported independent variable must precede in time the change in the dependent measure, when a causal relationship between the two is assumed

nonspuriousness— covariation between two variables that is causal and not due to the effects of a third variable

experimental and control conditions, all factors except the manipulated independent variable can be expected to be held constant. Nonexperimental research, such as field studies or systematic interviews, provide fewer means to control potential common causes. Hence, the conclusions drawn from nonexperimental research about causal relationships among variables are far more tentative.

11.2   Causal Diagrams

The three basic assumptions described in the preceding section (covariation, time order, and nonspuriousness) must be satisfied before causality can be imputed among variables. They are embedded graphically in a **causal diagram** that reveals the hypothesized cause-and-effect relationships. The conventions for causal diagrams are indispensable aids in thinking through problems of causal reasoning, as well as communicating your ideas to other researchers.

causal diagram—a visual representation of the cause-and-effect relationships among variables, using keyword names and directed arrows

In a causal diagram, variables are represented by short names or letters. Annual household unit income might be labeled "Income" in a diagram. Scores on the Stanford-Binet intelligence test could be shortened to "IQ." Time order is conventionally organized from left to right, as in

---

Box 11.1   Rules for Constructing Causal Diagrams

1. Variable names are represented either by short keywords or letters.
2. Variables placed to the left in a diagram are assumed to be causally prior to those on the right.
3. Causal relationships between variables are represented by single-headed arrows.
4. Variables assumed to be correlated but not causally related are linked by a curved double-headed arrow.
5. Variables assumed to be correlated but not causally related should be at the same point on the horizontal axis of the causal diagram.
6. The causal effect presumed between two variables is indicated by placing + or − signs along the causal arrows to show how increases or decreases in one variable affect the other.

Western culture reading and writing. Therefore, variables placed to the left in a diagram are considered temporally antecedent to those located farther to the right. Variables placed at the leftmost side of the diagram are considered to be **exogenous variables**, or predetermined variables, because their causes remain unspecified, unanalyzed, and therefore outside the scope of the model. Each pair of predetermined variables is linked by a curved double-headed arrow, indicating that they are correlated but not causally connected within the diagram. Variables that are not exogenous are **endogenous variables**; that is, the causes of their variation are represented within the model. If a researcher posits a direct causal connection between two variables—either from a predetermined to an endogenous variable or between two endogenous variables—it is represented by a single-headed, straight arrow. The tail emerges from the causal variable and the arrowhead points at the effect variable. If two dependent variables are not hypothesized to have a direct causal connection, no arrow is drawn between the two. The direction of the causal effect between a pair of variables is indicated by placing signs along their arrow. A plus sign indicates positive causation: The higher the cause, the higher the effect. A negative sign indicates an inverse causal effect: The higher the cause, the lower the effect. Box 11.1 summarizes these rules.

Figure 11.1 displays some elementary types of causal diagrams using these diagrammatic conventions. Letters rather than substantive variable names are used. Figure 11.1A illustrates a bivariate pattern, showing a simple **direct effect**, or causal relationship, between *A* (the independent variable) and *B* (the dependent variable). By adding a third variable *C* in the temporal sequence, the simple causal chain in Figure 11.1B shows that increases in levels of *A* raise the value of *B*, and in turn, a higher level of *B*

exogenous variable— a predetermined variable whose causes remain unexplained, unanalyzed, and outside the scope of a model

endogenous variable— a variable whose cause(s) of variation are represented in a model

direct effect—a connecting path in a causal model between two variables without an intervening third variable

FIGURE **11.1**
Some Elementary Causal Diagrams

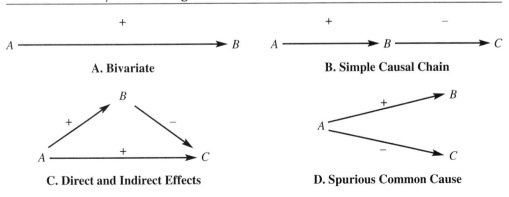

A. Bivariate

B. Simple Causal Chain

C. Direct and Indirect Effects

D. Spurious Common Cause

reduces the level of *C*. By inference, then, the higher the amount of *A*, the less the amount of *C*. The sign of this **indirect effect** of *A* on *C* via *B* can also be calculated by multiplying the signs of the two paths. A positive (+) times a negative (−) is a negative, so the indirect effect of *A* on *C* is negative.

Figure 11.1C, the direct-and-indirect-effects model, depicts *A* as having both types of impact on *C*, but the two effects are opposite in sign. The indirect effect through *B* is still negative, while the direct effect, holding constant the contributions of *B*, is for *A* to raise the level of *C*. This diagram does not give enough information to determine whether the negative indirect effect or the positive direct effect is stronger. Later, in discussing path analysis, we will show how to estimate actual values of each causal effect, in order to answer this question.

The spurious common cause model, Figure 11.1D, shows how an observed covariation between *B* and *C* might arise without any direct causal link between these two variables. Variable *A* is a common cause of both, raising the level of *B* while lowering the magnitude of *C*, thereby generating an inverse covariation between both dependent variables. If *B* is the number of trucks at a fire and *C* is the amount of undamaged property, what variable might *A* be?

You now should have enough information about causal thinking and diagramming to begin to put it to use in your own social research. We will work through one simple example to show you how all these pieces fit together. This is a model of the development of political democracy among nations. Four causal propositions capture the verbal essentials.

P1:   The greater a nation's economic wealth, the more likely it is to be a political democracy.

P2:   The more militarized a nation, the less likely it is to be a political democracy.

P3:   The more industrialized a nation, the greater its wealth.

P4:   The more militarized a nation, the greater its wealth.

Figure 11.2 displays the hypothesized causal relations among these four variables. The double-headed curved arrow between industrialization and militarization indicates that no causal assumptions are made about this exogenous pair. Figure 11.2 also introduces another convention of causal diagrams: arrows to each dependent variable from unmeasured variables (e.g., to Democracy from U). Such unobserved factors, called **residual variables**, represent the belief that the variation in Democ-

indirect effect—
a compound path connecting two variables in a causal model through an intervening third variable

residual variable—an unmeasured variable in a path model that is posited as causing the unexplained part of an observed variable

FIGURE 11.2
Causal Diagram for Model of Political Democracy

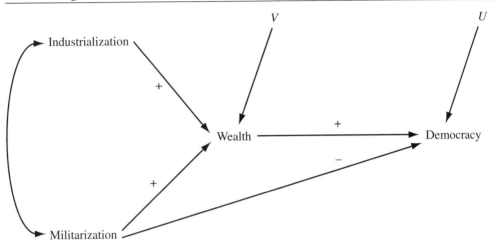

racy is not completely explained by the causal factors explicitly included in the model. Therefore, our model is **probabilistic**, or stochastic, rather than **deterministic**. Note also that a residual cause is shown as uncorrelated and not causally related to any independent or residual variables in the diagram.

The model in Figure 11.2 is also a **recursive** model. That is, all of the causal influences are assumed to be in one direction and one direction only. If *X* causes *Y*, then we do not allow for *Y* in return to cause *X*. Models that allow for bidirectional causality are said to be **nonrecursive** models. The estimation of nonrecursive models is complex, and our discussion is restricted to recursive models. The following section shows how the numerical values of the paths, as well as the values of the residual effects, are estimated.

11.3   Path Analysis

Path analysis is a statistical method for analyzing quantitative data that yields empirical estimates of the effects of variables in a hypothesized causal system. Originally developed by the geneticist Sewell Wright, path analysis and its structural equation model variants (see chapter 12) gained wide currency among social researchers. The technique requires all the

probabilistic—a causal relationship in which a change in one variable produces a change in another variable, with a certain probability of occurrence

deterministic—a causal relationship in which a change in one variable always produces a constant change in another variable

recursive model—a model in which all the causal influences are assumed to be asymmetric (one-way)

nonrecursive model—a model in which causal influences between dependent variables may occur in both directions

path analysis—a statistical method for analyzing quantitative data that yields empirical estimates of the effects of variables in a hypothesized causal system

causal assumptions discussed above, and it makes extensive use of diagrams to represent the cause-and-effect relationships among empirical variables. Moreover, before you can follow the discussion in this section, you must be familiar with standardized multiple regression equations, as described in section 8.2.2.

11.3.1 An Example: Approval of Abortion

The example we use to illustrate path analytic principles is a simple four-variable causal system representing some hypothesized causes of respondents' approval of abortion if an unmarried woman does not want children, as shown in Figure 11.3. The pluses (+) and minuses (–) indicate the direction of the hypothesized relationships. The intensity of respondents' religious beliefs and their educational attainments are both posited as predetermined variables and thus are placed to the left in the diagram. The curved double-headed arrow indicates we are not interested in explaining the causal relationship between these two measures. Higher self-reported religiosity (R) is hypothesized to decrease permissive attitudes toward premarital sexual relations (S), while more education (E) is expected to increase respondents' tolerance of premarital sex. Religiosity, education, and premarital sex attitude all are hypothesized to have direct causal impacts on approval of abortion for single

FIGURE 11.3
Causal Diagram for Abortion Attitude Model

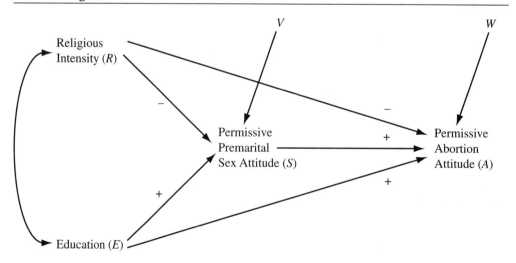

women (*A*). The direct effect of religiosity is posited to be negative, but the direct effects of education and premarital sex attitude are posited to be positive. Both dependent variables in the diagram have arrows drawn from uncorrelated residual factors (*V* and *W*) to indicate effects from unknown causes of abortion and premarital sex attitudes other than those shown. The operationalization of these variables is described in section 11.3.6, where we also discuss how to estimate the model's coefficients.

11.3.2 Structural Equations

Path analysis begins with a set of **structural equations** that represent the structure of interrelated hypotheses in a model. These equations bear a one-to-one relationship to a causal diagram such as Figure 11.3. Typically, the variables in a path analysis have been put in standardized, or *Z*-score, form.

    The four relations among the variables—religious intensity (*R*), education (*E*), approval of premarital sex relations (*S*), and approval of abortion for unmarried women (*A*)—can be represented by two structural equations for the causes of the two endogenous variables. The first equation captures the hypothesized effects of religiosity and education on premarital sex attitudes, under the assumption that the two predetermined variables are linearly related to the endogenous variable. In general, if p_{IJ} represents a **path coefficient** to variable *I* from variable *J*, the equation linking premarital sex attitude (*S*) to religious intensity (*R*) and education (*E*) is

$$S = p_{SR}R + p_{SE}E + p_{SV}V$$

structural equation— a mathematical equation representing the structure of hypothesized relationships among variables in a social theory

path coefficient— a numerical estimate of the causal relationships between two variables in a path analysis

The path coefficient linking each causal variable to the effect variable is multiplied by the causal variable. Also, a path coefficient (p_{SV}) represents the causal link between the unobservable residual term, *V*, and the effect variable, *S*. The second structural equation depicts two exogenous variables (religiosity, *R*, and education, *E*) and one endogenous variable (premarital sex attitude, *S*) as causes of the second endogenous variable (approval of abortion, *A*):

$$A = p_{AR}R + p_{AE}E + p_{AS}S + p_{AW}W$$

Again a path coefficient is present for each direct cause of abortion attitude, plus a residual path from variable *W*. Figure 11.4 is the causal diagram that incorporates the two equations.

FIGURE 11.4
Path Diagram with Coefficient Symbols for Abortion Attitude Model

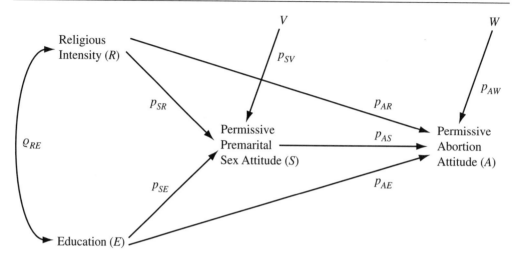

Path analysis has two major tasks.

1. Estimate numerical values of the path coefficients.
2. Show that the presumed causal population parameters account for the correlations between all pairs of variables in the system.

These problems are considered in the next two subsections.

11.3.3 Estimating Path Coefficients

To estimate numerical values of the path coefficients, we need only presume that the effect variables are linearly related to the causal variables in each equation. Then, one simply regresses each dependent variable on its predictors. Because all variables are in standardized form, the beta weights from the multiple regression are BLUE estimates of the path coefficients (see section 6.5 and Box 8.2). Thus, for the first structural equation

$$\hat{p}_{SR} = \beta^*_{SR}$$
$$\hat{p}_{SE} = \beta^*_{SE}$$

The first subscript of a path coefficient is always the dependent variable, followed by the independent variable, just as the subscripts for *R*-squared. The double subscripts *SR* and *SE* make clear which dependent variable is being predicted by religious intensity and education, because these two variables are also assumed to be causally linked to abortion attitude in the second equation. We state without proof that the residual path can be estimated by

$$\hat{p}_{SV} = \sqrt{1 - R^2_{S \bullet RE}}$$

That is, the path coefficient from a residual variable to a dependent variable is simply the square root of the coefficient of nondetermination. The carets (ˆ) above the path coefficients make clear that they are estimates of the population path coefficient parameters obtained from standardized regressions with sample data.

The estimated path coefficients for the second equation are similarly obtained by a multiple regression of abortion attitude on religiosity, education, and premarital sex attitude. Thus,

$$\hat{p}_{AR} = \beta^*_{AR}$$

$$\hat{p}_{AE} = \beta^*_{AE}$$

$$\hat{p}_{AS} = \beta^*_{AS}$$

$$\hat{p}_{AW} = \sqrt{1 - R^2_{A \bullet RES}}$$

11.3.4 Decomposing Implied Correlations into Causal Parameters

The solution to the second task, showing that the path coefficients imply or account for the correlations between pairs of variables, is less straightforward. It involves **decomposition**, or separation of a correlation coefficient into its components.

In this process, the correlation is re-expressed in terms of path coefficients. Some algebra with which you may not be familiar is required. The theorem you need to know is: $\Sigma aX = a\Sigma X$, where *a* is a constant and *X* is a variable. That is, the sum of *a* times *X* equals *a* times the sum of *X*. You also need to know that $\Sigma(X + Y) = \Sigma X + \Sigma Y$. That is, the sum of the variable *X* plus the variable *Y* equals the sum of *X* plus the sum of *Y*. The details of these theorems are given in Appendix A as rules 2 and 5.

decomposition—the division of a correlation coefficient into its component parts, involving direct effects, indirect effects, and dependence on common causes

Now consider the first equation given in section 11.3.2:

$$S = p_{SR}R + p_{SE}E + p_{SV}V$$

To find the correlation between religious intensity and premarital sex attitude, we first multiply both sides by R:

$$RS = R(p_{SR}R + p_{SE}E + p_{SV}V)$$

$$= p_{SR}R^2 + p_{SE}RE + p_{SV}RV$$

Then we take the sum of both sides:

$$\Sigma RS = \Sigma(p_{SR}R^2 + p_{SE}RE + p_{SV}RV)$$

$$= \Sigma p_{SR}R^2 + \Sigma p_{SE}RE + \Sigma p_{SV}RV$$

(This last step follows from Rule 5 in Appendix A.) Next, we divide both the left-hand and right-hand terms by N and bring the p's outside the summation signs (i.e., apply Rule 2):

$$\frac{\Sigma RS}{N} = p_{SR}\frac{\Sigma R^2}{N} + p_{SE}\frac{\Sigma RE}{N} + p_{SV}\frac{\Sigma RV}{N}$$

As we showed in section 6.3.4, however, the sum of the product of two Z scores divided by $N-1$ in the sample (or by N in the population, as here) just equals their correlation. That is,

$$\frac{\Sigma RS}{N} = \varrho_{RS}$$

$$\frac{\Sigma RE}{N} = \varrho_{RE}$$

$$\frac{\Sigma RV}{N} = \varrho_{RV}$$

These terms appear in the equation below. Further, $\Sigma(R^2/N) = \varrho_{RR}$. However, because the correlation of a variable with itself equals 1.0, $\varrho_{RR} = 1$. Substituting this information into the equation above yields

$$\varrho_{SR} = p_{SR} + p_{SE}\varrho_{RE} + p_{SV}\varrho_{RV}$$

In the correlation between religiosity and the residual term (ϱ_{RV}), the V is an unobservable variable, so it cannot be measured. Thus, we have no way directly to estimate ϱ_{RV}. Instead, consistent with the BLUE requirements (see Box 8.2), the correlations between the residual variable and the independent variables in a given equation are *assumed* to be zero. That is, in the first equation, we assume that $\varrho_{RV} = 0$.

Incorporating this assumption into the path equation above, we add a prime (') to make clear this correlation is implied by the model and not necessarily equal to the correlation observed in the sample data:

$$\varrho'_{SR} = p_{SR} + p_{SE}\,\varrho_{RE}$$

That is, the implied correlation between R and S, ϱ'_{SR}, is due to a direct path from religiosity to premarital sex attitude, p_{SR}, and the product of the path from education to premarital sex and the correlation between religiosity and education (i.e., $p_{SE}\,\varrho_{RE}$).

In the same way, we can also decompose the implied correlation between education and premarital sex attitude suggested by the causal model. We again begin with the first equation:

$$S = p_{SR}R + p_{SE}E + p_{SV}V$$

This time we multiply both sides by E (because we want to analyze ϱ_{SE}):

$$ES = E(p_{SR}R + p_{SE}E + p_{SV}V)$$

$$= p_{SR}ER + p_{SE}E^2 + p_{SV}EV$$

Now, sum both sides and divide by N:

$$\Sigma ES = \Sigma(p_{SR}ER + p_{SE}E^2 + p_{SV}EV)$$

$$\frac{\Sigma ES}{N} = \Sigma p_{SR}\frac{ER}{N} + \Sigma p_{SE}\frac{E^2}{N} + \Sigma p_{SV}\frac{EV}{N}$$

Then bring the path coefficients outside the summation signs:

$$\frac{\Sigma ES}{N} = p_{SR}\frac{\Sigma ER}{N} + p_{SE}\frac{\Sigma E^2}{N} + p_{SV}\frac{\Sigma EV}{N}$$

Now, $\Sigma ES/N = \varrho_{ES}$, $\Sigma ER/N = \varrho_{ER}$, $\Sigma E^2/N = \varrho_{EE}$, and $\Sigma EV/N = \varrho_{EV}$. Recall that the correlation between a variable and itself is 1.0, that is, $\varrho_{EE} = 1.0$. Furthermore, on the BLUE assumption that the independent variables in a given equation are uncorrelated with the residual variable, we assume $\varrho_{EV} = 0$. Substituting these results into the equation above and rearranging terms yields

$$\varrho'_{SE} = p_{SR}\varrho_{RE} + p_{SE}$$

$$= p_{SE} + p_{SR}\varrho_{RE}$$

In words, the implied correlation between education and premarital sex attitude is composed of a direct path from education to premarital sex (p_{SE}) plus the product of the path from religiosity to premarital sex and the correlation between education and religiosity $(p_{SR}\varrho_{RE})$.

The same procedures can decompose the bivariate correlations between the effect variable (A) and three causal variables (R, E, S) in the second equation, as implied by the hypothesized causal structure. In outline form, follow these steps for *each* causal variable.

1. Multiply the dependent variable by the causal variable, and multiply each independent variable on the right-hand side of the equation by the causal variable.

2. Take sums of both sides of the equation, distributing the sum across all terms on the right-hand side of the equation.

3. Divide both sides of the equation by N in order to form correlations between the independent variable and all other variables in the equation.

4. Simplify the result, taking into account two assumptions.

    a. A variable correlated with itself is 1.0.

    b. The correlation between an independent variable and the residual variable is zero.

5. Repeat steps 1–4 for each causal variable in the equation.

As an exercise, you should be able to prove the following results

fundamental theorem of path analysis—an equation stating that the bivariate correlation between variables i and j implied by the hypothesized causal model is the sum of the products consisting of the path from variable q to variable i and the correlation between variable q and variable j; the sum of these products is formed over all Q variables that have direct paths to variable i

$$\varrho'_{SA} = p_{AS} + p_{AR}\varrho_{SR} + p_{AE}\varrho_{SE}$$

$$\varrho'_{RA} = p_{AR} + p_{AS}\varrho_{SR} + p_{AE}\varrho_{RE}$$

$$\varrho'_{EA} = p_{AE} + p_{AS}\varrho_{SE} + p_{AR}\varrho_{RE}$$

The five implied correlations that we derived previously (two for the first structural equation and three for the second structural equation) are summarized in the **fundamental theorem of path analysis**:

$$\varrho'_{ij} = \sum_{q=1}^{Q} p_{iq}\varrho_{qj}$$

The fundamental theorem of path analysis states that the bivariate correlation between variables i and j implied by the hypothesized causal model is the sum of the products consisting of the path from variable q to variable i and the correlation between variable q and variable j. The sum of these products is formed over all Q variables that have direct paths to variable i. Convince yourself that the fundamental theorem of path analysis could have been used to decompose each of the five implied correlations.

The three implied correlations with A as the endogenous variable each contain one or more correlations involving S. These correlations were themselves previously decomposed into path components in analyzing the first structural equation with S as the endogenous variable. In particular, as we saw above,

$$\varrho'_{SR} = p_{SR} + p_{SE}\,\varrho_{RE}$$

$$\varrho'_{SE} = p_{SE} + p_{SR}\,\varrho_{RE}$$

If we substitute these two quantities for ϱ_{SR} and ϱ_{SE} into the equation for ϱ'_{SA}, we obtain

$$\varrho'_{SA} = p_{AS} + p_{AR}(p_{SR} + p_{SE}\,\varrho_{RE}) + p_{AE}(p_{SE} + p_{SR}\,\varrho_{RE})$$

$$= p_{AS} + p_{AR}p_{SR} + p_{AR}p_{SE}\,\varrho_{RE} + p_{AE}p_{SE} + p_{AE}p_{SR}\,\varrho_{RE}$$

Similarly,

$$\varrho'_{RA} = p_{AR} + p_{AS}(p_{SR} + p_{SE}\,\varrho_{RE}) + p_{AE}\,\varrho_{RE}$$

$$= p_{AR} + p_{AS}p_{SR} + p_{AS}p_{SE}\,\varrho_{RE} + p_{AE}\,\varrho_{RE}$$

and

$$\varrho'_{EA} = p_{AE} + p_{AS}(p_{SE} + p_{SR}\,\varrho_{RE}) + p_{AR}\,\varrho_{RE}$$

$$= p_{AE} + p_{AS}p_{SE} + p_{AS}p_{SR}\,\varrho_{RE} + p_{AR}\,\varrho_{RE}$$

We recognize that these results are somewhat complex. Bear in mind that we have expressed the implied correlations between the causal variables and the effect variables as a function of the hypothesized path coefficients. Notice, too, that the right side of each of the final versions of the equations contains only path coefficients and the correlation between the two exogenous variables, religiosity and education (ϱ_{RE}). As a general principle of the fundamental theorem, *the end result of decomposing an implied bivariate correlation contains only path coefficients and the correlations among the predetermined variables.*

11.3.5 Decomposing Implied Correlations by Tracing Paths

We can also obtain the decompositions for the five implied correlations by *tracing paths* in the diagram itself. In stating the following rules, which summarize how to trace paths to obtain decompositions, we assume that variable j is causally prior to variable i. The steps are as follows.

1. Beginning with a particular endogenous variable i, trace backward along the arrow that comes from variable j, if such a path exists. This is the simple *direct path coefficient, p_{ij}.* To its value should be added all the *compound paths* found by applying the following steps.

2. If other arrows come to variable i from third variables, q, trace all the connections between i and j that involve each q, multiplying the values of the path coefficients for these compound paths. In general, two kinds of compound linkages will occur.

    a. Variable q sends arrows to both i and j (either directly or through still other intervening variables). In this case, trace backward along the paths from i to q and then forward along the paths from q to j, multiplying coefficient values as you go. If more than one distinct compound pathway exists for a given q, treat each separately.

    b. Variable j sends an arrow to variable q, which in turn sends an arrow to variable i (either in two steps or through yet other intervening variables). In this case simply trace backward from i through q to j, multiplying path values as you go. If more than one distinct compound pathway back to j exists, treat each separately.

3. The following rules must be observed during tracing.

    a. You may trace backward along a series of arrows (from arrow head to arrow tail) for as many links as necessary to reach variable q. But once the direction has been changed in order to trace forward from q to j (from arrow tail to arrow head, as allowed in rule 2a), no subsequent reversals of direction are allowed.

b. A particular double-headed curved arrow (for the correlation between two predetermined variables) can be traversed only once during the tracing of a given compound path; and only one double-headed arrow can be traversed during any given compound linkage. Note that a traverse of a double-headed arrow always results in a change of direction, from backward to forward tracing. A traverse of a double-headed arrow results in a multiplication of the compound path by that correlation coefficient.

c. All the legitimate compound paths presented in the path diagram must be traced and their values multiplied to determine the magnitude and sign of the compound effects.

4. When all direct and compound path values have been calculated, add them together to obtain the correlation between i and j implied by the causal model (ϱ'_{ij}).

To illustrate the use of tracing procedures, we show how to decompose the correlation between abortion attitude (A) and education (E), ϱ_{AE}. Referring to Figure 11.4 we can see that, applying rule 1, the direct path between education (E) and abortion attitude (A) is

$$p_{AE}$$

Using rule 2, we see that there are two q variables, religious intensity (R) and premarital sex attitude (S), with direct paths to abortion attitude. Therefore, these variables must provide indirect links with education. Under rules 2a and 3b, we trace backward from abortion to religiosity (p_{AR}) and traverse the double-headed arrow to reach education (ϱ_{RE}). This compound path will be added to the equation for decomposing ϱ'_{AE} into direct and indirect effects:

$$p_{AR}\varrho_{RE}$$

Notice that we *cannot* trace a compound path via premarital sex, such as $p_{AR}\,p_{SR}\,p_{SE}$, because it violates rule 3a about changing directions more than once. However, a second compound path connecting abortion attitude to education through religiosity is permissible:

$$p_{AS}\,p_{SR}\,\varrho_{RE}$$

Because no other compound paths via religiosity occur, we next turn to the indirect connections involving premarital sex. One of these paths, also involving religiosity, has just been noted. The only remaining compound path allowed by rule 2b is

$$p_{AS}\,p_{SE}$$

Putting these four direct and indirect paths together and reordering terms, we arrive at the final dissection of the implied correlation between abortion attitude and education

$$\varrho'_{AE} = p_{AE} + p_{AS}p_{SE} + p_{AS}p_{SR}\varrho_{RE} + p_{AR}\varrho_{RE}$$

which is the same result obtained with algebraic methods at the end of section 11.3.4. Notice that the basic theorem did not permit any indirect pathways involving the paths from the residual factors, V and W. As stated above, one assumption of path analysis is that residual variables are uncorrelated with the independent variables in the model, and, hence, no compound paths involve these residuals.

Table 11.1 shows how the entire correlation matrix can be rewritten in terms of path equations. (The results have been rearranged slightly compared to those derived earlier.) As a check of your understanding of the basic path theorem, you should derive these decompositions yourself, using the tracing rules presented above, and compare them to the table. Because the results can be obtained using either algebra or the tracing method, the technique you choose is immaterial.

11.3.6 Estimating the Abortion Attitude Model

We now have all the tools necessary to estimate the model shown in Figure 11.4, using data from the 1998 GSS. Respondent's education is coded in number of years of schooling completed (from 0 to 20). Religious intensity is a follow-up question to respondent's affiliation (e.g., Catholic,

TABLE 11.1
Decomposition of Correlations in Path Model Shown in Figure 11.4

	Education (E)	Religious Intensity (R)	Premarital Sex Attitude (S)
Religious Intensity (R)	ϱ_{RE}		
Premarital Sex Attitude (S)	$p_{SE} + p_{SR}\varrho_{RE}$	$p_{SR} + p_{SE}\varrho_{RE}$	
Abortion Attitude (A)	$p_{AE} + p_{AS}p_{SE}$ $+ p_{AR}p_{RE}$ $+ p_{AS}\varrho_{SR}p_{RE}$	$p_{AR} + p_{AS}p_{SR}$ $+ p_{AE}\varrho_{RE}$ $+ p_{AS}p_{SE}\varrho_{RE}$	$p_{AS} + p_{AE}p_{SE}$ $+ p_{AR}p_{SR}$ $+ p_{AE}\varrho_{RE}p_{SR}$ $+ p_{AR}\varrho_{RE}p_{SE}$

Baptist, Lutheran, Jew, etc.): "Do you consider yourself a strong (preference named) or a not very strong (preference named)?" The three response categories are recoded "strong" = 3, "somewhat strong" = 2 (this was not one of the two choices offered by the interviewer, but some people volunteered this middle answer), and "not very strong" = 1. The premarital sex relations item asks: "If a man and woman have sex relations before marriage, do you think it is always wrong, almost always wrong, wrong only sometimes, or not wrong at all?" Responses were coded from "always wrong" = 1 to "not wrong at all" = 4. Finally, abortion attitude comes from responses to a battery of seven questions asking whether the respondent believes "it should be possible for a pregnant woman to obtain a *legal* abortion if…" a variety of conditions exist. In our analysis, we chose only the responses to the condition "…if she is not married and doesn't want to marry the man." A "yes" response was coded 1, and a "no" response coded 0. The matrix of observed correlations among these four variables, using pairwise deletion of cases with missing values, appears in Table 11.2. Only 666 of the 2,832 GSS respondents had complete data, because the two attitude items were restricted to a third of the sample, according to the GSS questionnaire design.

The results of the regression analysis appear in Table 11.3. Because path analysis uses only the standardized regression coefficients, the metric (unstandardized) coefficients are not tabled. For a recursive model, the estimated path coefficients are simply the beta weights, and a residual path is just the square root of the coefficient of nondetermination (1 minus the coefficient of determination; see section 11.3.3). The path coefficients for this example appear on the path diagram in Figure 11.5.

TABLE 11.2
Correlation Matrix of Variables in Abortion Attitude Path Analysis

	Religious Intensity	*Education*	*Premarital Sex Attitude*	*Abortion Attitude*
Religious Intensity (*R*)	1.00			
Education (*E*)	0.056	1.00		
Premarital Sex Attitude (*S*)	−0.358*	0.119*	1.00	
Abortion Attitude (*A*)	−0.192*	0.194*	0.385*	1.00

*$p < .01$
$N = 666$; missing data = 2,166.
Source: 1998 General Social Survey.

TABLE 11.3
Standardized Regression Coefficients (Beta Weights) for
Premarital Sex and Abortion Attitude Equations

Independent Variables	Premarital Sex Attitude	Abortion Attitude
Religious Intensity	–0.366**	–0.080*
Education	0.139**	0.158**
Premarital Sex Attitude	—	0.337**
Coefficient of Determination (R^2)	0.147**	0.176**

*$p < .05$
**$p < .001$
$N = 666$; missing data = 2,166.
Source: 1998 General Social Survey.

Because path coefficients are standardized values, the interpretation of causal effects must be made in terms of standard deviation (Z-score) units. For example, $\hat{p}_{AS} = 0.337$ means that one-standard-deviation increase in permissive premarital sex attitude leads to about a one-third-standard-deviation increase in approval of abortion for unmarried women.

FIGURE 11.5
Path Diagram with Numerical Estimates of Path Coefficients, Abortion Attitude Model

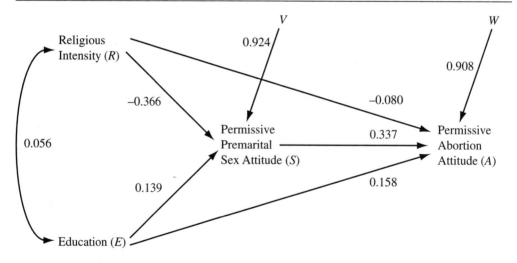

And because all path coefficients are standardized, comparison between the direct effects of causal variables is straightforward, as it is in multiple regression. Thus, we see that the direct causal impacts of religiosity and of education on a permissive abortion attitude are opposite in direction, with more-religious respondents less favorable to abortion ($\hat{p}_{AR}$ = –0.080), but more-educated people approving abortion for single women ($\hat{p}_{AE}$ = 0.158). We also find that both variables have much smaller effects on abortion attitude than does premarital sex attitude. The diagram also shows that more-religious persons hold less permissive premarital sex attitudes ($\hat{p}_{SR}$ = –0.366), while more-educated respondents express more permissive premarital sex attitudes ($\hat{p}_{SE}$ = +0.139).

Path coefficients also permit the calculation of **indirect causal effects** through the multiplication of path values of compound paths connecting two variables via intervening variables. As section 11.3.4 showed, the sample estimates are

indirect causal effect— a causal effect of one variable on another that occurs through one or more intervening variables

$$r'_{AR} = \hat{p}_{AR} + \hat{p}_{AS}\hat{p}_{SR} + \hat{p}_{AS}\hat{p}_{SE}r_{RE} + \hat{p}_{AE}r_{RE}$$

The first term on the right is, of course, the estimated direct effect ($\hat{p}_{AR}$ = –0.080). The second term, $\hat{p}_{AS}\hat{p}_{SR}$, is the estimated indirect causal effect, which shows the effect of religiosity on abortion attitude via premarital sex attitude. Note that the estimated indirect effect of religiosity lies in the same direction as the direct effect, $(0.337)(–0.366) = –0.123$, and it has a slightly higher numerical value.

By adding together the direct and indirect causal effects and comparing the sum to the observed correlation in Table 11.2, we can see how much of the covariation is due to the correlated effects involving education. Thus, the observed correlation between religious intensity and abortion attitude is –0.192; the direct effect is –0.080, and the indirect effect is –0.123, which leaves only 0.011 of the observed correlation due to their dependency on education. This effect is small because religiosity and education have a correlation very close to zero, as can be seen in the final two terms of the decomposition. Such effects are called **correlated effects**, because their values depend on the correlation between R and E: $\hat{p}_{AS}\hat{p}_{SE}r_{RE} + \hat{p}_{AE}r_{RE} = (0.337)(0.139)(0.056) + (0.158)(0.056) = 0.0114$. As an exercise, you should determine how much of the correlation between abortion attitude and education (r_{AE}) is due to a direct effect, to an indirect effect, and to the correlation of education with religious intensity.

correlated effect— a component in the decomposition of a correlation coefficient that is due to a correlation among predetermined variables

By squaring the path coefficients from the residual variables, we can discover how much of the variance in the endogenous variables remains unexplained by the hypothesized causal process. Both values are very large: 85.4% of the variance in premarital sex attitude and 82.4% of abortion attitude cannot be explained by the causal structure. Clearly, this simple example does not come close to containing all the important social and psychological causes of these two attitudes. If we were to pursue this research, we would want to specify more elaborate models, including additional possible sources of abortion attitude.

Fully recursive path models, in which all possible one-way arrows between variables are present, will always exactly reproduce the observed correlations when the basic path theorem is applied. Because the causal sequence among variables can be arbitrarily reordered, the empirical estimates of path coefficients generally provide no definitive answer to the question of whether a causal model is plausible or absurd. For example, if the locations of premarital sex attitude and abortion attitude were switched in Figure 11.3, we could still derive path coefficients for each arrow. Or, even more drastically, we could switch the places between the two predetermined variables and the two dependent measures and still generate path coefficients that would add up to the observed correlations. Clearly, the credibility of a path model cannot be based on statistical criteria alone.

A causal model must justify its specifications on nonstatistical grounds. In this text, we have stressed the importance of theoretical understanding of social behavior in guiding empirical research. In hypothesizing a causal model for path analysis, all the researcher's knowledge of social relationships, past empirical research, and logical deduction must be brought to bear. In specifying a causal sequence among variables, understanding their temporal order is often indispensable. For example, given that people's formal schooling is typically completed many years before the survey interview, we can plausibly treat this variable as temporally antecedent to the two current attitudes. Unless a causal analysis is firmly grounded in basic principles of social behavior, the resulting path model estimates can be no firmer than the foundation of a house built on sand.

11.3.7 A Chain Path Model Example

We stated above that fully recursive path models offer no statistical basis for their own rejection. Path models that are not fully recursive—that is, those in which some possible arrows are not present—do offer limited grounds for deciding whether a specific model fits the data. When some possible causal paths are hypothesized to be zero, the implied correlations (r'_{ij}) from the path model do not necessarily and often will not equal the observed correlations (r_{ij}). When such discrepancies occur, the analyst may conclude that the model was incorrectly specified as a representation of the causal process, unless the discrepancy is small enough to be caused by sampling fluctuation.

To illustrate, we use data from the National Longitudinal Survey of Youth (NLSY). Beginning in 1979, this sample of 6,111 young American women and men born between 1957 and 1964 was interviewed annually about family, school, work, and other behaviors and attitudes. In 1979, 1982, and 1987, the interviewers asked the respondents to report their disagreement–agreement on a four-category scale with a series of items about women's employment, including, "Women's place is in the home, not the office or shop." Among the simplest models of attitude causation through time is the chain model, in which responses at time $t + 1$ depend solely on responses at the immediately preceding time, t. (This property is called the **Markovian principle**, which maintains that history prior to time t has no causal impact on the present.)

In path diagrammatic terms, a **chain path model** for attitude toward women's employment is shown in Figure 11.6. We assume that Y_3, attitude toward women's employment in 1987, is caused by attitude in 1982 (Y_2) but not by attitude in 1979 (Y_1). And attitude in 1982 (Y_2) is assumed to be caused only by attitude in 1979. Figure 11.6 implies two structural equations:

$$Y_2 = p_{21}Y_1 + p_{2V}V$$

$$Y_3 = p_{32}Y_2 + p_{3U}U$$

Because these two equations are recursive, they can be estimated by the two beta coefficients obtained by regressing Y_2 on Y_1 and by regressing Y_3 on Y_2:

Markovian principle— variables measured prior to time t have no causal impact on variables measured at time $t + 1$

chain path model—a causal model in which variables measured on the same sample three or more times are depicted as the causes of their own subsequent values

FIGURE 11.6
Causal Diagram of Attitude Toward Women's Employment, 1979–1987, with Estimated Path Coefficients

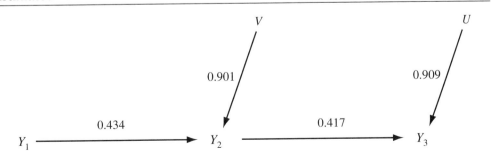

$$\hat{p}_{21} = \beta_{21}^*$$

$$\hat{p}_{2V} = \sqrt{1 - R_{2\cdot1}^2}$$

$$\hat{p}_{32} = \beta_{32}^*$$

$$\hat{p}_{3U} = \sqrt{1 - R_{3\cdot2}^2}$$

Table 11.4 shows the correlations among the three variables. Because beta weights are zero-order correlations in the case of a single independent variable, we have $\hat{p}_{21} = 0.434$, $\hat{p}_{2V} = 0.901$, $\hat{p}_{32} = 0.417$, and $\hat{p}_{3U} = 0.909$. Now we want to test whether the correlation implied between Y_1 and Y_3 equals the observed correlation (0.339). To determine the implied correlation, we follow the method used in section 11.3.4. We begin with

$$Y_3 = p_{32}Y_2 + p_{3U}U$$

Then we multiply this equation by Y_1, yielding

$$Y_1Y_3 = p_{32}Y_1Y_2 + p_{3U}Y_1U$$

We sum both sides, distribute the summation, and divide by N:

$$\frac{\Sigma Y_1 Y_3}{N} = \frac{p_{32}\Sigma Y_1 Y_2}{N} + \frac{p_{3U}\Sigma Y_1 U}{N}$$

Because we assume that $p_{Y_1U} = 0$, we have $\varrho'_{13} = p_{32}\varrho_{21} = p_{32}p_{21}$, because $p_{21} = \beta_{21}^* = \varrho_{21}$. That is, the correlation between Y_1 and Y_3 implied by the causal model equals the product of the two paths, p_{32} and p_{21}. Now convince yourself that you get the same results by tracing paths between Y_3 and Y_1.

TABLE 11.4
Correlation Matrix of Attitudes Toward Women's Employment, 1979–1987

	Y_1	Y_2	Y_3
Y_1: Attitude in 1979	1.000	0.434	0.339
Y_2: Attitude in 1982		1.000	0.417
Y_3: Attitude in 1987			1.000

Source: National Longitudinal Survey of Youth.

In the NLSY data,

$$r'_{13} = (0.434)(0.417) = 0.181$$

But, as seen in Table 11.4, the actual observed correlation is 0.339. Hence, the large discrepancy between observed and implied correlations, $r_{13} - r'_{13} = 0.158$, suggests a **misspecification** of the causal model.

misspecification— a condition in which a structural equation or path model includes incorrect variables or excludes correct variables

A plausible alternative model for these three variables is shown in Figure 11.7. Here we assume a **lagged causal effect** from 1987 attitude to 1979 attitude. (A lagged causal effect is also the same as a direct effect.) The two structural equations in this case are

lagged causal effect— direct effect of a variable measured prior to time t on a variable measured at time $t + 1$

$$Y_2 = p_{21}Y_1 + p_{2V}V$$

$$Y_3 = p_{31}Y_1 + p_{32}Y_2 + p_{3U}U$$

The estimates of the path coefficients are

$$\hat{p}_{21} = \beta^*_{21}$$
$$\hat{p}_{2V} = \sqrt{1 - R^2_{2\cdot 1}}$$
$$\hat{p}_{31} = \beta^*_{31}$$
$$\hat{p}_{32} = \beta^*_{32}$$
$$\hat{p}_{3U} = \sqrt{1 - R^2_{3\cdot 21}}$$

FIGURE 11.7
Causal Diagram of an Alternative Set of Relations Among Attitudes Toward Women's Employment, 1979–1987

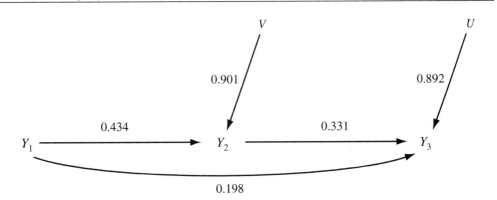

Using the data from Table 11.4, these estimates are shown in Figure 11.7. This model fits the observed correlations perfectly, because all three possible one-way paths are present. However, this alternative is only one of several possible causal models that might account for the pattern of correlations over time. Other models could include additional independent variables, with correlated residual variables and measurement errors. Some of these techniques are considered in chapter 12, but here we have demonstrated that the simple causal chain must be rejected as the explanation of the observed pattern of covariation.

This chapter introduced the bare essentials of path analysis. We hope we have convinced you that causal inferences can be drawn from non-experimental data if you have strong theoretical propositions. When you cannot conduct experiments, path models can be very useful for estimating presumed causal processes. As we suggested, however, to avoid nonsensical results you must pay close attention to meeting the assumptions of the model.

In chapter 12, we generalize the principles of path analysis to more complex structural equation models, introducing techniques that allow for evaluating the goodness-of-fit of hypothesized models to observed variances and covariances.

Review of Key Concepts and Symbols

These key concepts and symbols are listed in the order of appearance in this chapter. Combined with the definitions in the margins, they will help you to review the material and can serve as a self-test for mastery of the concepts.

covariation

time order

nonspuriousness

causal diagram

exogenous variable (predetermined variable)

endogenous variable

direct effect

indirect effect

residual variable

probabilistic (stochastic)

deterministic

recursive model

nonrecursive model

path analysis

structural equation

path coefficient

decomposition

fundamental theorem of path analysis

indirect casual effect

correlated effect

Markovian principle

chain path model

misspecification

lagged causal effect

p_{ij}

$\hat{p}_{ij}$

p'_{ij}

r'_{ij}

PROBLEMS

General Problems

1. Rewrite this statement as a causal proposition: "Whenever workers feel that the distribution of rewards between workers and managers in their company is unjust, they will attempt to organize a union in order to change this distribution."

2. Diagram the causal process implied by the following set of hypotheses.

   a. The better a student's school attendance, the higher that student's academic skills.

   b. The higher a student's academic skills, the greater that student's academic confidence.

   c. The higher a student's academic skills, the stronger that student's attachment to school norms.

   d. The greater a student's academic confidence, the more likely that student is to graduate.

   e. The stronger a student's attachment to school norms, the more likely that student is to graduate.

3. Based on the following path equations, derive the formula for the correlation between Q and T:

$$T = p_{TQ}Q + p_{TS}S$$

$$S = p_{SQ}Q + p_{SR}R$$

4. Consider the following path diagram, in which A is age at marriage, B is socioeconomic status (SES), C is number of children, and D is marital satisfaction.

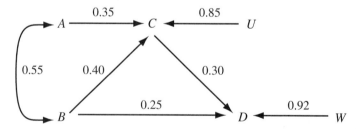

a. Does age at marriage or SES have a larger indirect causal effect on marital satisfaction?

b. How much variance in marital satisfaction is explained by age at marriage, SES, and number of children?

5. Consider the following path diagram.

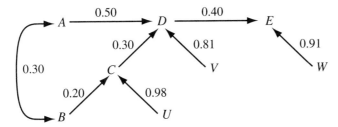

a. Does *A* or *B* have a larger indirect causal effect on *E*?
b. How much variance in *E* is explained by *A*, *B*, *C*, and *D*?

6. A researcher conducts a panel study in which respondents are interviewed annually three years in a row about their attitudes toward capital punishment. The researcher models the three years with the following chain path model. If the correlation between attitudes at times one and two is 0.85 and the correlation between attitudes at times two and three is 0.91, what is the estimated correlation between attitudes at times one and three?

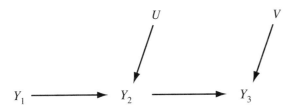

7. In the following causal diagram, A is the socioeconomic status of the neighborhood, B is the time lived in the neighborhood, C is the number of neighbors known, and D is satisfaction with the neighborhood. Write an equation in symbolic terms for the correlation between satisfaction with the neighborhood and time lived in the neighborhood. Identify which portion of the equation arises from causal connections and which portion is due to correlated effect.

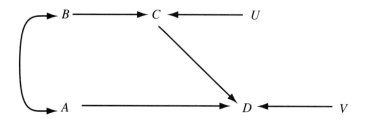

8. For the causal relations in Problem 7, what is the correlation between B and D if the following values occur: $r_{AB} = +0.30$; $p_{CB} = +0.70$; $p_{DC} = +0.50$; $p_{DA} = +0.70$? What is the correlation between A and D?

9. Consider the following causal diagram. Based on the given p_{ij} values, generate the matrix of correlations implied among the five variables.

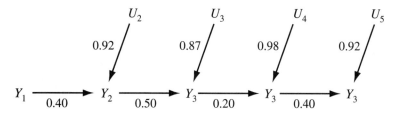

10. The following chain path model assumes a lagged causal effect from Y_1 to Y_3. Write the two structural equations that are implied by this model.

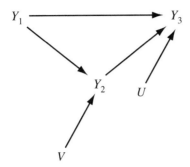

Problems Requiring the 1998 General Social Survey

11. Do parents' religious service attendance (ATTENDMA, ATTENDPA) affect their children's strength of religious affiliation (RELITEN) and religious service attendance (ATTEND)? To answer this question, estimate the following path model. Specify which path coefficients are statistically significant. Reverse code RELITEN $(4 = 1)(2 = 3)(3 = 2)(1 = 4)$, and change its value labels: $(1 = $ "No Religion," $2 = $ "Not Very Strong," $3 = $ "Somewhat Strong," $4 = $ "Strong"). For all variables, recode "Don't Know," "No Answer," "Not Applicable," "No Father–Mother Present," and "Can't Say or Can't Remember" responses to missing values.

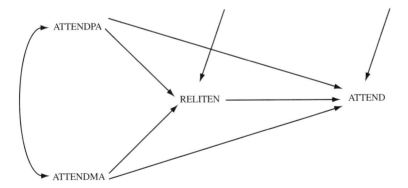

12. Estimate the following path model, which suggests that mother's occupational prestige (MAPRES80), father's occupational prestige (PAPRES80), and educational level (EDUC) may explain occupational prestige (PRESTG80). For all variables, recode "Don't Know," "No Answer," "Not Applicable," and "Disabled" responses to missing values. Which path coefficients are statistically significant?

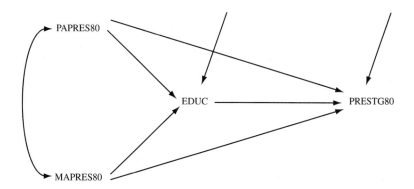

13. Do education (EDUC) and family income (INCOME98) influence charitable giving to nonreligious organizations (GIVEOTH)? Estimate the following path model to answer this question. For all variables, recode "Don't Know," "No Answer," "Not Applicable," and "Refused" responses to missing values. Indicate the statistically significant path coefficients.

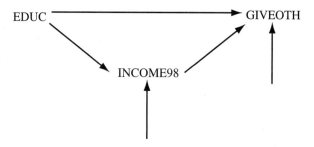

14. Some political sociologists have argued that lower social status produces greater rigidity and intolerance in political thought and behavior. Test this idea by using an index of intolerance (INTOL) towards those opposed to churches and religion, created by summing responses to SPKATH (should not be allowed to make speeches), COLATH (should not be allowed to teach in a college), and LIBATH (book written by an atheist should be removed from public library). Estimate the following path model. Recode "Don't Know," "No Answer," and "Not Applicable" responses to missing values. Specify which of the path coefficients are statistically significant. What can you conclude?

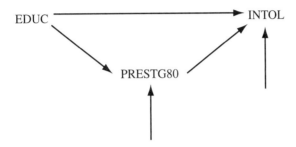

15. Do higher education and income lead to increased political conservatism? Estimate the following path model. Recode "Don't Know," "No Answer," "Not Applicable," "Refused," and "Other Party" responses to missing values.

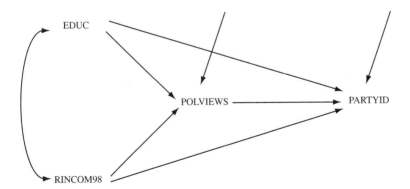

12

STRUCTURAL EQUATION MODELS

This chapter concludes our presentation of statistics for social data analysis with an introduction to **structural equation models** and estimation. The techniques for analyzing multivariate relationships among systems of equations build directly on the path analysis methods in chapter 11. However, they are far more comprehensive and flexible in their ability to link multiple observed indicators to unmeasured causes, to make quantitative estimates of model parameters and their standard errors, to assess the overall fit of a model to data, and even to determine the equivalences of model parameters across several samples. Although these methods can be applied to even more complex problems, such as nonrecursive models that estimate reciprocal causal effects, this book's space constraints allow us only to explore a basic set of applications.

> **structural equation model**—a causal model with latent variables and observable indicators

The particular structural equation method we examine is **LISREL** (**LI**near **S**tructural **REL**ations). It has been developed continuously since the 1960s by the Swedish statisticians Karl Jöreskog and Dag Sörbom and is currently available in both UNIX and interactive Windows versions.[1] Other structural equation analysis programs are available,

> **LISREL (LInear Structural RELations)**—a computer program for estimating structure equation and confirmatory factor analysis models

---

[1]LISREL, SIMPLIS, and PRELIS are distributed by Scientific Software International <http://www.ssicentral.com/lisrel/mainlis.htm>.

including Mplus, AMOS, EQS, and the CALIS in SAS.[2] Students and instructors may wish to read more detailed and advanced treatments of the topic.[3]

We will begin this chapter by reviewing correlation and covariance statistics and then move on to discuss measurement reliability and validity. We will use confirmatory factor analysis to model responses to multiple indicators of unobserved attitude constructs. Finally, we will investigate several path models with multiple indicators of unobserved constructs using structural equation methods. All our applications have been performed using the SIMPLIS command language on a UNIX machine; however, this chapter does not display the computer commands that estimated the examples.

12.1 Review of Correlation and Covariance

As discussed in chapter 6, the Pearson product-moment correlation coefficient for two continuous variables, Y and X, measures the amount of

---

[2]AMOS is distributed in the United States by SmallWaters and SPSS and in Europe by ProGamma <http://www.gamma.rug.nl>. EQS is distributed by Multivariate Software <http://www.mvsoft.com>. CALIS is part of the SAS package of statistical programs <http://www.sas.com>. MPLUS is distributed by Muthén & Muthén <http://www.statmodel.com>.

[3]The following is a partial list of books on this topic:

Bollen, Kenneth A. 1989. *Structural Equations with Latent Variables.* New York: Wiley.

Bollen, Kenneth A., and J. Scott Long. 1993. *Testing Structural Equation Models.* Thousand Oaks, CA: Sage.

Byrne, Barbara M. 1998. *Structural Equation Modeling with LISREL, PRELIS and SIMPLIS: Basic Concepts, Applications and Programming.* Mahwah, NJ: Erlbaum.

Hayduk, Leslie A. 1996. *LISREL: Issues, Debates and Strategies.* Baltimore, MD: Johns Hopkins Press.

Hoyle, Rick H. (Ed.) 1995. *Structural Equation Modeling: Concepts, Issues and Applications.* Thousand Oaks, CA: Sage Publications.

Kelloway, Kevin E. 1998. *Using LISREL for Structural Equation Modeling: A Researcher's Guide.* Thousand Oaks, CA: Sage Publications.

Loehlin, John C. 1992. *Latent Variable Models: An Introduction to Factor, Path and Structural Analysis.* Mahwah, NJ: Erlbaum.

Marcoulides, George A., and Randall E. Schumacker. (Eds.) 1996. *Advanced Structural Equation Modeling: Issues and Techniques.* Mahwah, NJ: Erlbaum.

Maruyama, Geoffrey M. 1998. *Basics of Structural Equation Modeling.* Thousand Oaks, CA: Sage Publications.

dispersion (spread) around a linear least-squares regression line. The correlation coefficient, r_{YX}, can be derived from the coefficient for the bivariate regression of Y on X, β_{YX}. The OLS estimator for the regression
slope in a population is

$$\beta_{YX} = \frac{\sum_{i=1}^{N}(Y_i - \overline{Y})(X_i - \overline{X})}{\sum_{i=1}^{N}(X_i - \overline{X})^2}$$

The numerator is the sum across the N observations of the cross-product
of deviations of both variables around their means. The denominator is
the sum of squared deviations of X around its means. Dividing both the
numerator and denominator by N gives

$$\beta_{YX} = \frac{\sum_{i=1}^{N}(Y_i - \overline{Y})(X_i - \overline{X})/N}{\sum_{i=1}^{N}(X_i - \overline{X})^2/N}$$

The numerator is now the covariance of Y and X and the denominator is
the variance of the independent variable. Thus, we can re-express the OLS
estimator of the bivariate regression coefficient as the ratio of those two
components:

$$\beta_{YX} = \frac{\sigma_{YX}}{\sigma_X^2}$$

Depending on the direction of the covariance of Y and X, a bivariate regression slope may have a positive or negative sign, indicating the direction of the relationship between Y and X.

In a bivariate regression, the population coefficient of determination,
ϱ^2, indicates the proportion of total variation in Y that can be accounted
for by its linear relationship with X. One of its formulas (see page 184 for
alternative formulas) involves the ratio of the squared covariance to the
product of both variances:

$$\varrho^2 = \frac{\sigma_{YX}^2}{\sigma_X^2 \sigma_Y^2}$$

Due to squaring, ϱ^2 must be nonnegative.

The correlation coefficient is defined as the square root of the coefficient of determination. It summarizes the linear relationship and takes
the same sign (plus or minus) as the regression slope because both share
σ_{YX} in the numerator in their formulas:

$$\varrho_{YX} = \sqrt{\varrho^2_{YX}} = \frac{\sigma_{YX}}{\sigma_Y \sigma_X}$$

Thus, the sample correlation coefficient can also be defined as the covariance of Y and X divided by the product of the standard deviations of both variables. It ranges between +1.00 and –1.00 and has a value of 0 when the two variables do not covary (i.e., are unrelated).

Covariances and correlations are symmetric statistics; that is, in the population, $\varrho_{YX} = \varrho_{XY}$ and $\sigma_{YX} = \sigma_{XY}$, which can be ascertained by noting that the order of cross-product multiplication is irrelevant in the regression slope formula above. One important relation between covariance and correlation is to observe what happens when both X and Y are standardized variables, that is, turned into Z scores by subtracting the mean and dividing by the standard deviation. Substituting Z scores for both variables into the formula above for ϱ_{YX} yields

$$\varrho_{Z_Y Z_X} = \frac{\sigma_{Z_Y Z_X}}{\sigma_{Z_Y} \sigma_{Z_X}} = \frac{\sigma_{Z_Y Z_X}}{(1)(1)} = \sigma_{Z_Y Z_X}$$

Because the standard deviation of a Z score is 1.00, the correlation coefficient for two standardized measures equals their covariance. Correlation coefficients are "scale-free" in that they are unaffected by whether the units of measurement are the original scales or their transformed Z scores. We will see that structural equation models can be estimated using either covariances or correlations (or both).

12.2   Reliability and Validity in Measurement Theory

A powerful advantage of structural equation models lies in their ability to combine observed measures with relations among unobserved constructs into a single integrated system. We conceptualize the connection between these measurement and structural levels of analysis as a version of neo-Platonism: the shadows that we see on the cave wall are obscure reflections of an underlying reality that we cannot fully understand through our intellectual reasoning. As Plato pointed out, a triangle drawn with pencil and paper is not synonymous with the abstract, eternal concept of "triangle" that exists beyond the realm of our senses. By analogy, social scientists can never directly observe people's attitudes (not even their behaviors) but can only infer existence of these concepts by examining error-filled measures, such as the respondents' answers to survey questions, which are presumably affected in part by their unobservable constructs (attitudes or behaviors).

12.2.1 Defining Reliability and Validity

Measurement theory concerns the relationships between empirical observations and unobserved constructs. It seeks to represent a latent (unobserved) construct with one or more observable indicators (operational measures or variables) that accurately capture this theoretically intended construct. As discussed in chapter 1, two desired properties of any empirical measure are high levels of validity and reliability.

- **Validity:** The degree to which a variable's operationalization accurately reflects the concept it is intended to measure.

- **Reliability:** The extent to which different operationalizations of the same concept produce consistent results.

Many validity issues concern how well or poorly an observable variable reflects its latent counterpart. Another central concern involves accurately depicting the (causal or covariational) relationships among several theoretical constructs, using information about the covariation among observed indicators. This latter interest lies at the heart of factor analysis and structural equation models examined in later sections of this chapter.

Reliability refers to the replication of measurement results under the same conditions. A perfectly reliable measure must generate the same scores when conditions are identical. A measure may be very reliable but not valid; that is, an instrument can precisely measure some phenomenon yet represent complete nonsense. For example, suppose your bathroom scale consistently gives identical readings when you step off and on, but it invalidly operationalizes your true weight because you moved the dial back five pounds.

To be valid, a measure or indicator must be reliable. In the extreme, if its reliability is zero, its validity is also zero. However, a given indicator may vary in the extent of its validity as a measure of different concepts. For example, education, measured as years of formal schooling, might be used both as an indicator of educational persistence and as an indicator of socioeconomic status (SES). Validity is clearly affected by the choice of one's indicator(s). For example, we can treat church attendance as a measure of Americans' religiosity, but this indicator might have only moderate validity because some highly religious persons don't attend services, and some people go to church more for social purposes than for religious ones. A more valid measure of religiosity not only would

validity—the degree to which a variable's operationalization accurately reflects the concept it is intended to measure

reliability—the extent to which different operationalizations of the same concept produce consistent results

consider attendance at religious services but also would query people about their religious beliefs (e.g., belief in the efficacy of prayer, the existence of an afterlife, and infallibility of scriptures).

Unfortunately, researchers never obtain perfect measurements in the real world; that is, all measures are subject to measurement errors, and hence they all are unreliable and are invalid to some degree. Measurement theory is therefore also a theory about how to estimate magnitudes and sources of errors in empirical observations.

As we deal with the concept here, reliability assumes random errors. When a measurement is repeated over numerous occasions under the same conditions, if **random error** occurs, then the resulting variations in scores form a normal distribution about the measure's true value. The standard error of that distribution represents the magnitude of the measurement error: the larger the standard error, the lower the measure's reliability. By definition, random errors are uncorrelated with any variable, including other random error variables. **Systematic error** (nonrandom error) implies a miscalibration of the measuring instrument that biases the scores by consistently over- or underestimating a latent construct (e.g., your miscalibrated bathroom scale). Such consistent biases don't alter the measure's reliability, but they clearly alter its validity because they prevent the indicator from accurately representing the theoretical concept.

The research methodology literature discusses several types of validity, but we lack space to examine all these conceptual distinctions (Box 12.1 defines a variety of validity concepts). For purposes of explicating structural equation models, we'll assume that the empirical observations we use have adequate content validity as indicators of the designated latent constructs. Therefore, we turn next to the quantification of reliability in classical test theory.

random error—errors of measurement that are unpredictable

systematic error—errors of measurement arising from miscalibrated instruments

12.2.2 Classical Test Theory

Classical test theory depicts the observed score (X) of respondent i on a measuring instrument, such as an aptitude test score or a survey item, as arising from two hypothetical unobservable sources: the respondent's "true score" and an error component:

$$\text{True}_i \longrightarrow X_i \longleftarrow \text{Error}_i$$

$$X_i = T_i + \varepsilon_i$$

A person's true score is the average that would be obtained across infinitely repeated measures of X. In the theoretical definition of random

---

Box 12.1 Varieties of Validity

Validity indicates the appropriateness of a measurement instrument, such as a battery of test items, for the concept it intends to measure. In other words, an instrument's validity denotes the extent to which it measures what it is supposed to measure. Validity can be established by experts knowledgeable about a substantive domain or by demonstrating a measure's consistency with the theoretical concepts it is designed to represent. Three traditional types of measurement validity are construct, criterion-related, and content validity. Brief definitions and examples of these various validity types are given below.

Construct validity: the extent to which a measure agrees with theoretical expectations; for example, IQ test items try to measure theoretically hypothesized dimensions of intelligence. Measures with high *convergent validity* and *discriminant validity* exhibit high agreement with theoretically similar measures but low correlations with dissimilar measures, respectively.

Criterion-related validity: the extent to which a measure accurately predicts performances on some subsequently observable activity (the criterion); for example, how highly a written driving-test score correlates with people's actual skills in operating an automobile. A measure's *concurrent validity* is assessed by its ability to discriminate between persons with and without the criterion. A measure's *predictive validity* is demonstrated by its accuracy in forecasting future behavior.

Content validity: the extent to which a measure adequately represents the defined domain of interest that it was designed to measure; for example, a mathematical ability test should cover the full range of students' mathematical knowledge.

---

error, the distribution of error forms a normal distribution around a mean value of zero. Because these error deviations around the true score cancel one another, the expected value (mean) of the errors is zero and the expected value of the observed scores equals the respondent i's true score:

$$E(X_i) = \mu_{T_i}$$

Further, the error term is assumed to be uncorrelated with its true score (which makes sense if the error is random). Both components make unique contributions to the variances of the observed scores in a population:

$$\sigma_X^2 = \sigma_T^2 + \sigma_\varepsilon^2$$

That is, the observed score variance is the sum of the true score and error variances. For good measures, the error variance will be small relative to the observed variance; the opposite will be true for poor measures.

The ratio of true score to observed score variances is defined as the reliability of X:

$$\varrho_X = \frac{\sigma_T^2}{\sigma_X^2} = 1 - \frac{\sigma_\varepsilon^2}{\sigma_X^2}$$

Note again how the reliability of X depends on the size of the error variance. This formula also demonstrates that reliability ranges between 0 and 1: if the entire observed variance is error, $\varrho_X = 0$; but if no random error exists, then $\varrho_X = 1$.

Rearranging the reliability formula above reveals that the true score variance equals the observed score variance times the reliability:

$$\sigma_T^2 = \varrho_X \sigma_X^2$$

Hence, we can estimate the unobserved true score variance from a measure's reliability and its observed variance. Note that when the reliability of a measure is zero, the variance of the true score is also zero.

12.2.3 Parallel Measures

parallel measures—
measures with equal
true scores

If we have a second measure of the same unobservable construct, T_i, differing from the first indicator only in the error (i.e., the true scores of both measures are equal), we have what are defined to be **parallel measures**, where

$$X_{1i} = T_i + \varepsilon_{1i}$$
$$X_{2i} = T_i + \varepsilon_{2i}$$

Assuming that the population variances of their error terms are equal, *reliability is the correlation between the parallel measures*. The proof appears in Box 12.2.

Box 12.2   Reliability of Parallel Forms

1. The correlation coefficient for two variables is defined as the ratio of the covariance to the product of standard deviations:

$$\varrho_{X_1 X_2} = \frac{\sigma_{X_1 X_2}}{\sigma_{X_1} \sigma_{X_2}}$$

2. In the numerator, substitute the two variables' true and error scores

$$\sigma_{X_1 X_2} = \sigma_{T + \varepsilon_1} \sigma_{T + \varepsilon_2}$$

$$= \sigma_T^2 + \sigma_{T\varepsilon_1} + \sigma_{T\varepsilon_2} + \sigma_{\varepsilon_1 \varepsilon_2}$$

$$= \sigma_T^2$$

because the error terms and true scores are assumed to be uncorrelated.

3. Because the standard deviations of parallel measures are assumed to be equal, the denominator simplifies to

$$\sigma_{X_1} \sigma_{X_2} = \sigma_X^2$$

4. Hence, by substituting step 3 into step 1, the correlation coefficient for parallel measures is

$$\varrho_{X_1 X_2} = \frac{\sigma_T^2}{\sigma_X^2}$$

5. The text shows that the right-side expression is defined as the reliability; thus,

$$\varrho_{X_1 X_2} = \varrho_X$$

An important consequence of this identity is that the true score's variance can be estimated as the product of just two empirical measures, the correlation coefficient and the variance. Rearranging step 4 in Box 12.2 gives

$$\sigma_T^2 = \varrho_{X_1 X_2} \sigma_X^2$$

Although not proven here, the correlation between the true score and an observed variable equals the square root of the reliability:

$$\varrho_{TX_1} = \sqrt{\varrho_X}$$

This equation shows that the correlation between an observable indicator and the unobservable true score it measures can be estimated by the square root of the reliability of indicator X. For example, the estimated correlation between a true score and an indicator with reliability 0.64 is 0.80. The measurement theory principles discussed in this section are encompassed within structural equation models, which we introduce next through the confirmatory factor analytic approach to modeling the relationships between observed indicators and latent constructs.

12.3   Factor Analysis

factor analysis—a method that represents relations among observed variables in terms of latent constructs

common factors—latent constructs that create covariation among observed variables

confirmatory factor analysis (CFA)— a structural equation model, with one or more unobserved variables having multiple indicators, in which the research specifies the pattern of indicator loadings

Factor analysis refers to a family of statistical methods that represent the relationships among a set of observed variables in terms of a hypothesized smaller number of latent constructs, or **common factors**. The common factors presumably generate the observed variables' covariations (or correlations, if all measures are standardized with zero means and unit variances). For example, respondents' observed scores on several ability tests result from unobserved common verbal and quantitative factors. Or covariations among numerous socioeconomic indicators of urban communities depend on latent industrialization, health, and welfare factors.

Of the two major classes of factor analysis, exploratory and confirmatory, we limit our discussion to the latter. In **confirmatory factor analysis (CFA)** a researcher posits an a priori theoretical measurement model to describe or explain the relationship between the underlying unobserved constructs ("factors") and the empirical measures. Then the analyst uses statistical fit criteria to assess the degree to which the sample data are consistent with the posited model, that is, to ask whether the results confirm the hypothesized model. In practice, however, researchers seldom conduct only one test of a confirmatory factor model. Rather, based on initial estimates, they typically alter some model specifications and re-analyze the new model, trying to improve its fit to the data. Hence, most applications of CFA to investigate latent factors involve successive modeling attempts. We apply this successive model-fitting strategy in estimating alternative models to explain the empirical relationships among a set of observed variables.

FIGURE 12.1
A Single-Factor Model with Four Indicator Variables

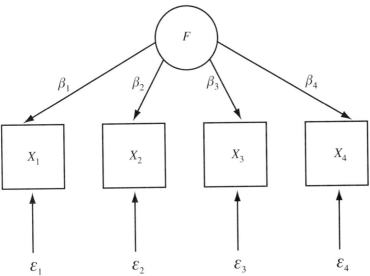

Researchers use confirmatory factor analysis to estimate the parameters of a measurement model. Consider the diagram in Figure 12.1. A single latent factor is measured by four empirical variables. The latent common factor is F; the four X_i's are observable variables (indicators); the four β_i's are the **factor loadings** of each observed variable on the common factor F; and the four ε_i's are the variables' error terms.[4] This diagram implies that only the latent construct is responsible for the variation and covariation among the observed variables. Each observed score is a linear combination of this common underlying factor plus its unique error term. We can also see these relationships by writing the four implied measurement equations in population notation:

factor loadings—
parameters showing how observed variables are related to latent constructs

$$X_1 = \beta_1 F + \varepsilon_1$$
$$X_2 = \beta_2 F + \varepsilon_2$$
$$X_3 = \beta_3 F + \varepsilon_3$$
$$X_4 = \beta_4 F + \varepsilon_4$$

[4]In the language of factor analysis, F is generally used to denote an unobserved latent construct rather than T to denote true score in classical test theory notation. However, you should think of the two symbols as identical.

Note the similarity of each factor analytic equation to classical test theory's representation of an observed score as a sum of a true score plus an error term.

Figure 12.1 shows that all error terms are uncorrelated with the factor and among themselves. Hence, the only sources of an indicator's variance are the common factor F and its unique error term

$$\sigma^2_{X_i} = \beta^2_i \sigma^2_F + \Theta^2_{\varepsilon_i}$$

where we use $\Theta^2_{\varepsilon_i}$ to signify the variance of the error in X_i. Because F is unobserved, its variance is unknown. And because it is unknown, we can assume it is a standardized variable, which means that its variance is 1.0. Therefore,

$$\sigma^2_{X_i} = \beta^2_i + \Theta^2_{\varepsilon_i}$$

Note that this formula closely resembles the classical test theory in which the variance of a measure equals the sum of two components—the true score variance plus the error variance. Next, note that if we standardize X_i, then the sum of these two components must equal 1.0. A CFA model has another similarity to the classical test theory. The reliability of indicator X_i is defined as the squared correlation between a factor and an indicator. This value is the proportion of variation in X_i that is statistically "explained" by the common factor (the "true score" in classical test theory) that it purports to measure:

$$\varrho_{X_1} = \varrho^2_{FX_i} = \beta^2_i$$

Finally, the covariance between two indicators in a single-factor model is the expected value of the product of their two factor loadings:

$$\sigma_{X_1 X_2} = E[(\beta_1 F + \varepsilon_1)(\beta_2 F + \varepsilon_2)]$$

which, because the error terms are uncorrelated with the factor and with each other, simplifies to

$$\sigma_{X_1 X_2} = \beta_1 \beta_2 \sigma^2_F = \beta_1 \beta_2$$

When all variances are standardized, this relationship further simplifies to

$$\sigma_{Z_1 Z_2} = \varrho_{Z_1 Z_2}$$

That is, the correlation of a pair of observed variables loading on a common factor is the product of their standardized factor loadings.

12.3.1 A One-Factor Model

To illustrate estimation of a confirmatory factor model, we use responses in the 1998 General Social Survey to the following seven statements about the effects of psychiatric medicines.

> Please tell me how much you agree or disagree with the following statements about medicines prescribed by doctors to help people who are having problems with their emotions, nerves or their mental health:

PSYCMED1: Psychiatric medicine is harmful to the body.

PSYCMED2: People should stop taking psychiatric medicine if their symptoms disappear.

PSYCMED3: Taking these medicines interferes with daily activities.

PSYCMED4: Psychiatric medicine helps people deal with day to day stresses.

PSYCMED5: Psychiatric medicine makes things easier in relations.

PSYCMED6: These medications help to control symptoms.

PSYCMED7: Psychiatric medicine helps people feel better about themselves.

GSS interviewers recorded the responses using a five-point Likert scale: 1 = Strongly Agree; 2 = Agree; 3 = Neither Agree nor Disagree; 4 = Disagree; 5 = Strongly Disagree. For the analyses reported here, we reversed these codes so that strongly agreeing with a statement received the highest numerical score. The data, which we ultimately analyzed using LISREL8, comprise a matrix of correlations or covariances among the indicators, treated as continuous variables. Table 12.1 shows these values for the seven psychiatric medicine items. The top panel displays the Pearson product-moment correlations in a lower-triangular format, along with the means and standard deviations, while the lower panel displays the covariances with the indicators' variances in the main diagonal. These sample values were calculated with a listwise case deletion procedure, using information only from the 1,070 GSS respondents who answered all seven items.

TABLE 12.1
Correlations and Covariances Among Psychiatric Medicine Variables (N = 1,070)

	PSYCMED1	PSYCMED2	PSYCMED3	PSYCMED4	PSYCMED5	PSYCMED6	PSYCMED7
Correlations							
PSYCMED1	1.000						
PSYCMED2	0.366	1.000					
PSYCMED3	0.431	0.416	1.000				
PSYCMED4	−0.270	−0.259	−0.226	1.000			
PSYCMED5	−0.294	−0.283	−0.297	0.576	1.000		
PSYCMED6	−0.261	−0.284	−0.243	0.559	0.563	1.000	
PSYCMED7	−0.261	−0.220	−0.222	0.412	0.498	0.435	1.000
Means	2.758	3.199	3.095	3.842	3.650	3.917	3.505
Standard Deviations	1.093	1.256	1.060	0.758	0.870	0.681	0.923
Covariances							
PSYCMED1	1.194						
PSYCMED2	0.502	1.578					
PSYCMED3	0.499	0.554	1.123				
PSYCMED4	−0.223	−0.247	−0.181	0.575			
PSYCMED5	−0.279	−0.310	−0.274	0.380	0.757		
PSYCMED6	−0.194	−0.243	−0.175	0.289	0.333	0.464	
PSYCMED7	−0.264	−0.256	−0.217	0.288	0.400	0.274	0.853

Missing data = 1,762 cases.
Source: 1998 General Social Survey.

reference variable—an observed variable in a confirmatory factor analysis with a fixed factor loading

A latent psychiatric medicine effects construct (F) is unobserved and hence has no definite scale; that is, its origin and unit of measurement are arbitrary. A researcher usually fixes the construct's origin by assuming it has a mean of zero. The latent construct's unit of measurement can be scaled one of two ways: (1) constraining the unobserved construct to have unit variance or (2) constraining or fixing the factor loading of one indicator (b_i) to take a specific value (typically to equal 1.00). This latter approach forces the unobserved construct's variance to be equal to the variance of the constrained indicator, called the **reference variable**. Researchers typically identify a reference variable after an initial CFA reveals which indicator has the highest loading on the construct, although this adjustment is by no means required.

We illustrate the second technique for setting the factor scale by constraining the factor loading of the PSYCMED5 indicator equal to 1.00 and estimating a single-factor model using the sample covariance matrix in Table 12.1. The researcher instructs the LISREL program to read the covariances and to treat some parameters as fixed (to 0, 1, or some other values), while other parameter values are to be estimated. LISREL has several estimation **algorithms**, or computer routines, available depending on various characteristics of the data and model to be estimated. The most commonly used algorithm is maximum likelihood estimation (MLE), which chapter 9 described for logistic regression. MLE assumes multivariate normality—that is, the *k*th parameter in the model has a normalized sampling distribution at all values of the other parameters. Taking the input covariance matrix, the MLE routine proceeds iteratively (i.e., through a series of successively improved approximations) to generate estimates for the free parameters that make the expected covariance matrix as close to the observed values as possible. When improvement on a successive step is smaller than a specified value (e.g., 0.001), the estimation routine stops and LISREL prints the resulting parameter estimates.

algorithm—computer routine

Figure 12.2 displays the LISREL estimates of the one-factor model. The first three indicators have negative factor loadings, and the remaining four indicators have positive loadings. This differentiation is not surprising, given the substantive wordings of the seven items, respectively emphasizing harmful or beneficial effects. Because respondents generally do not regard psychiatric medicines as simultaneously harmful and beneficial, an inverse covariance between these two indicator subsets occurs. This differentiation is evident in the pattern of plus and minus signs among the correlations and covariances in Table 12.1. Before deciding to accept the single-factor results, we examine some statistics used to assess the overall fit of the model to the covariance data.

Researchers might be tempted to assume that they can judge the relative "goodness" of items by comparing the sizes of their factor loadings. For example, an examination of Figure 12.2 suggests that after PM5, the second best item is PM7 because its loading has the next highest absolute value (0.82). Unfortunately, such a simple conclusion cannot be drawn unless the standard deviations of all items are roughly equal. An examination of Table 12.1 suggests that equality is unlikely, given the range of standard deviations from 0.681 to 1.256.

Given the difficulty in making such comparisons, analysts very often analyze correlation coefficients instead of covariances. Although analysis

FIGURE 12.2
LISREL Estimates for a Single-Factor Model with Seven Psychiatric Medicine Indicators

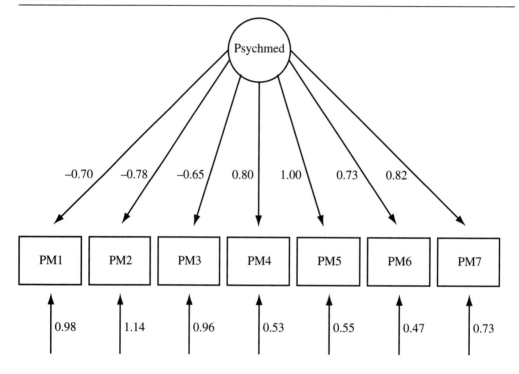

of correlations does allow for a comparison of factor loadings, regrettably, these coefficients are not simple linear transformations of the loadings based on the analysis of covariances. Because the resulting coefficients are in the metric of the measures used in the analysis, the analysis of covariances is the preferred method. Using the t test can help to describe the "goodness" of items in comparison to the reference item (i.e., the item whose loading is set to 1.0).

12.3.2 Model Fit Statistics

The entire confirmatory factor analysis or structural equation model's fit to the data can be assessed statistically. A specific model implies an expected covariance (or correlation) matrix for the K observed variables, $\Sigma(\theta)$, where θ is a vector of parameters to be estimated. The empirical data for a sample of *N* cases produces the sample covariance matrix, **S**, used to estimate the model parameters. LISREL fits a model to the data by minimizing a fit function *F* involving both the observed and implied matrices:

$$F[\mathbf{S},\Sigma(\theta)] = \ln |\Sigma| + \mathrm{tr}(\mathbf{S}\Sigma^{-1}) - \ln |\mathbf{S}| + t$$

where *t* is the number of independent parameters estimated and "tr" means "trace," the sum of the diagonal elements. The *F* function is non-negative and zero only if a perfect fit occurs, that is, if $\mathbf{S} = \Sigma$.

For a large sample *N*, multiplying $F[\mathbf{S}, \Sigma(\theta)]$ by $(N-1)$ yields a test statistic that is approximately distributed as a χ^2 with degrees of freedom equal to

$$d = [k(k+1)/2] - t$$

To use this minimum fit function as a chi-square test, a researcher chooses an α level of significance at which to reject the model, for example, by setting $\alpha = .05$. If the model χ^2 exceeds the $(1 - \alpha)$ percentile of the chi-square distribution with *d* degrees of freedom, then that model must be rejected as producing a poor fit to the observed variance–covariance matrix. For example, a model is a poor fit if $p < .05$; but if $p > .05$, then the model has an acceptable fit for a researcher setting the region of rejection at $\alpha = .05$.

In practice, a researcher who wants to find an acceptable latent structure model (i.e., not seeking to reject the model) hopes to obtain a *low* chi-square value relative to the degrees of freedom. Because the minimum fit function χ^2 test statistic increases proportional to sample size, $(N-1)$, obtaining low chi-square values with large samples often proves difficult. Many analysts come to regard chi-square as being more useful as an overall "goodness-of-fit" measure than as a test statistic. That is, χ^2 measures the distance (difference) between the sample covariance matrix and the expected covariance matrix, $(\mathbf{S} - \Sigma)$. Jöreskog and Sörbom half-jokingly refer to χ^2 as a "badness-of-fit" measure in the sense that large chi-square corresponds to a bad fit and low chi-square to a good fit. Zero χ^2 is a "perfect" fit.

LISREL prints several goodness-of-fit measures that are functions of chi-square. Two measures that do not depend explicitly on sample size measure how much better the specified model fits the data, compared to no model at all. Both indices range between 0 and 1, with values closer to 1 indicating a better fit of model to data. Most researchers seek values of 0.95 or higher. The **goodness-of-fit index (GFI)** is

$$\mathrm{GFI} = \frac{F[\mathbf{S},\Sigma(\theta)]}{F[\mathbf{S},\Sigma(0)]}$$

goodness-of-fit index (GFI)—the ratio between the minimum of the fitting function after the model is fitted to the fitting function before any model is fitted

adjusted goodness-of-fit index (AGFI)—the re-expression of the GFI in terms of the numbers of degrees of freedom used in fitting the model

where the numerator is the minimum of the fitted model's fit function and the denominator is the fit function for a model whose parameters all equal zero. The **adjusted goodness-of-fit index (AGFI)** takes into account the degrees of freedom used in estimating the parameters:

$$AGFI = 1 - \frac{k(k + 1)}{2d}(1 - GFI)$$

where k = the number of observed variables and d = the model df.

Using chi-square as a test statistic assumes that the model holds exactly in the population, an implausible assumption. Models that hold approximately in the population will be rejected for large samples. An alternative approach takes into account the errors of approximation in the population and the precision of the fit measure. The population discrepancy function (PDF) is defined as:

$$\hat{F}_0 = \text{Max } \{\hat{F} - (d/(N - 1)), 0\}$$

root mean square error of approximation (RMSEA)—a measure of model fit that adjusts the population discrepancy function for the number of degrees of freedom used in fitting the model

Because the PDF usually decreases when additional parameters are added to the model, the **root mean square error of approximation (RMSEA)** measures the discrepancy per degree of freedom:

$$\varepsilon = \sqrt{\hat{F}_0 - d}$$

An RMSEA value of $\varepsilon \le 0.05$ indicates a "close" fit, while values up to 0.08 indicate "reasonable" errors of approximation in the population. A 90% confidence interval for RMSEA indicates whether the sample point estimate falls into a range that also includes the 0.05 criterion.

For the single-construct confirmatory factor analysis of seven psychiatric medicine indicators, the four goodness-of-fit statistics are (1) χ^2 = 279.7, df = 14, p < .0001; (2) GFI = 0.92; (3) AGFI = 0.84; and (4) RMSEA = 0.14. None of these statistics suggests an acceptable fit of the single-factor model to the data. Given the split between positive and negative factor loadings, we estimated a respecified confirmatory factor model with two correlated latent constructs.

12.3.3 A Two-Factor Model

Figure 12.3 displays the LISREL estimates for a two-factor model where the three harmful and four beneficial aspects of psychiatric medicines are hypothesized to load on separate but correlated factors, labeled "Psychmed1" and "Psychmed2." This model produced a good fit to the covariance matrix: χ^2 = 24.1, df = 13, p = 0.03; GFI = 0.99; AGFI = 0.99; and

FIGURE 12.3
LISREL Estimates for a Two-Factor Model with Seven Psychiatric Medicine Indicators

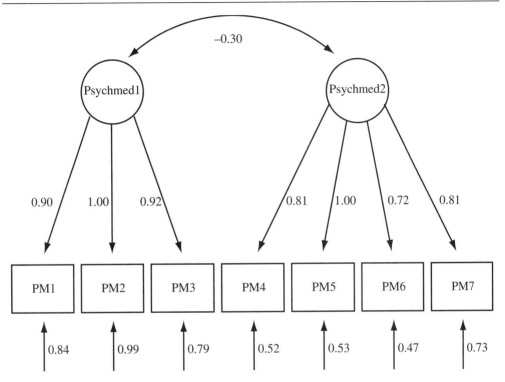

RMSEA = 0.029, with 90% confidence interval from 0.009 to 0.046, indicating a close fit between the model and the data.

Finding that a given set of data has an "acceptable fit" to a posited model does not imply that the model is "true" or correct. Instead, we are limited to the following conclusion: If a model is correct, then the fit of the data to it will be acceptable. The difference between these alternative statements may seem subtle. As we saw in chapter 3 on hypothesis testing, such tests can lead to the rejection of a hypothesized model, but never to its acceptance.

Because the two-factor model has an acceptable fit, we can now test the significance of and interpret the individual parameter estimates. The most useful test statistics are the individual parameters' standard errors, used to calculate the *t* ratios according to the formula presented in section 6.4.3. For a two-tailed null hypothesis that a causal parameter equals zero in the population, the critical values for a large sample are ±1.96 at $\alpha = .05$, ±2.58 at $\alpha = .01$, and ±3.29 at $\alpha = .001$. The negative covariance (–0.30) between the two latent constructs shows that high responses to one subset of items are inversely related to high responses on the other subset. The standard error of this estimated covariance is 0.03, producing a t ratio of –0.30/0.03 = –10.0. Hence, the null hypothesis that the two factors are unrelated in the population can be rejected, with the probability of a false rejection error (Type I error) far less than $p < .001$. Similarly, the tests of the individual factor loadings are all highly significant, as revealed by the following LISREL output, with standard errors in parentheses and the t ratios in the third lines:

	psych1	psych2
PSYCHMED1	0.90 (0.07) 13.45	—
PSYCHMED2	1.00	—
PSYCHMED3	0.92 (0.07) 13.62	—
PSYCHMED4	—	0.81 (0.04) 22.00
PSYCHMED5	—	1.00
PSYCHMED6	—	0.72 (0.03) 22.03
PSYCHMED7	—	0.81 (0.04) 18.34

These t values allow us to determine the relative goodness of PSYCHMED1 and PSYCHMED3 compared to the reference item PSYCHMED2. The confidence interval for PSYCHMED1 is 0.90 ± (1.96)(0.07); i.e., the lower and upper limits are 0.76 and 1.04, respectively. Across repeated samples, 95% of the confidence intervals will contain the true population parameter. Because the 1.0 value we fixed for PSYCHMED2 also lies in this interval, we cannot reject the hypothesis that the two item loadings are equal. Similarly, the estimated loading for PSYCHMED3 lies inside the 95% confidence interval bounded by 0.78 and 1.06, which again means that we cannot reject the hypothesis that it, too, is as good an indicator of the unobserved factor as PSYCHMED2. By contrast, convince yourself that neither PSYCHMED4, PSYCH-MED6, nor PSYCHMED7 are as good as PSYCHMED5 as indicators for the second factor.

The error variances all have high t ratios, meaning that, in the population, each psychiatric medicine item has a significant error variation apart from any common factors it shares with other indicators:[5]

PSYCHMED1	PSYCHMED2	PSYCHMED3	PSYCHMED4	PSYCHMED5	PSYCHMED6	PSYCHMED7
0.71	0.99	0.63	0.27	0.28	0.22	0.54
(0.04)	(0.06)	(0.04)	(0.02)	(0.02)	(0.01)	(0.03)
16.32	17.07	15.08	17.32	14.71	17.29	20.28

Consistent with the path model convention that all coefficients reflect the original units of measurement, Figure 12.3 displays the square roots of these error variances.

In our discussions of bivariate and multivariate regression (section 6.4 of chapter 6 and section 8.1 of chapter 8) and path analysis (section 11.3 of chapter 11), we pointed out that the relationships among variables could be measured in two forms: metric and standardized coefficients. LISREL solutions also can represent relationships in both unstandardized and standardized forms. Because a structural equation model consists of both structural and measurement levels of analysis, standardization may be done separately at each level: (1) the **standardized solution** scales the latent constructs to have standard deviations of one but leaves the observed variables in their original metrics; (2) the **completely standardized solution** transforms the standard deviations of *both* latent and observed variables to unity. Figure 12.4 displays the completely standardized solution for the two-factor psychiatric medicine model. The correlation between the two latent factors is –0.57, indicating that they share 32.5% of their variation ($r^2 = (-0.57)(-0.57) = 0.325$). Unlike the factor model in Figure 12.3, the

standardized solution— latent constructs have unit variances, while the indicators are still in their original metrics

completely standardized solution—all observed and unobserved variables are standardized, and parameters are expressed in standard deviation units

---

[5]Some portion that we term error variance could in fact be unique, reliable variance. With longitudinal data we can separate the unique variance from error, but with cross-sectional data we are forced to assume that all of the unexplained variance is error.

FIGURE 12.4
Completely Standardized Solution for a Two-Factor Model with Seven Psychiatric Medicine Indicators

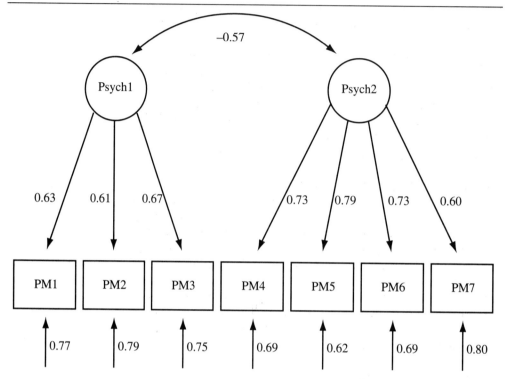

completely standardized solution does not constrain any of the indicators to have loadings equal to 1, so their magnitudes can be compared. Further, the sum of a squared factor loading and its square error term equals 1.00, showing that all the variation in an observed indicator is determined by these two sources. For example, the first indicator has a standardized factor loading of 0.63 and an error term of 0.77; the sum of their squared values is $(0.63)^2 + (0.77)^2 = 0.397 + 0.593 = 1.000$. You should verify that the other six pairs of squared coefficients likewise sum to one, within rounding.

12.4   Multiple-Indicator Causal Models

In this section we elaborate on the confirmatory factor analysis models to consider causal models where one or more latent variables are represented by several indicators. The parameter estimates at the measurement level show how well (or poorly) the observed variables serve as indicators of the unobserved theoretical concepts. Parameters at the structural level show the magnitudes and significance of the hypothesized causal effects among the latent concepts. And, again in common with factor analysis, the various goodness-of-fit statistics reveal how well the combined measurement and structural equation models reproduce the matrix of covariances among the indicators.

12.4.1 A MIMIC Model

Our first example of a structural equation model is a **MIMIC** or **Multiple Indicator–MultIple Cause model**. At the structural equation level, variation in a single dependent variable is assumed to be caused by several predetermined variables. At the measurement equation level, the dependent variable has several observed measures, while each exogenous or predetermined variable is represented by only one indicator, each of which is assumed to be perfectly measured. These predictors can be termed "directly observed variables." In effect, a MIMIC model is a form of multiple regression with an unobserved construct as the dependent variable. More complex structural equation models discussed in later subsections have multiple indicators for both independent and dependent constructs.

Our MIMIC example involves four indicators of attitudes towards the federal government's role in solving social problems, using the 1998 GSS. Each observed variable is measured on a five-point scale, where "I strongly agree with [the governmental involvement position]" = 1, "I strongly agree with [the individualist position]" = 5, and "I agree with both answers" = 3. The four item wordings:

> HELPPOOR: I'd like to talk with you about issues some people tell us are important. Please look at CARD AT. Some people think that the government in Washington should do everything possible to improve the standard of living of all poor Americans; they are at Point 1 on this card. Other people think it is not the government's responsibility, and that each person should take care of himself; they are at Point 5.

> HELPNOT: Some people think that the government in Washington is trying to do too many things that should be left to individuals and private businesses. Others disagree and think that the government should do even more to solve our

MIMIC model—multiple-indicator and multiple-cause model in which variation in a single dependent variable with two or more indicators is directly caused by several predetermined variables, each of which has only a single indicator

country's problems. Still others have opinions somewhere in between.

HELPSICK: In general, some people think that it is the responsibility of the government in Washington to see to it that people have help in paying for doctors and hospital bills. Others think that these matters are not the responsibility of the federal government and that people should take care of these things themselves.

HELPBLK: Some people think that (Blacks/Negroes/African-Americans) have been discriminated against for so long that the government has a special obligation to help improve their living standards. Others believe that the government should not be giving special treatment to (Blacks/Negroes/African-Americans).

The four single-indicator independent measures for the MIMIC model, all treated as continuous variables, are the respondent's age (AGE), liberal–conservative political views (POLVIEWS), Democratic–Republican political party identification (PARTYID), and frequency of church attendance (ATTEND). Listwise deletion produced a matrix of covariances among the eight observed variables for 1,592 cases.

Figure 12.5 displays the model and estimated parameters from the completely standardized solution. Arrows from the latent construct (Help) to the four indicators occur at the measurement level of analysis, while the arrows to Help coming directly from the four independent variables occur at the structural level. (To avoid clutter, the six correlations among the four exogenous variables are not shown.) This model produced a very good fit to the covariance matrix: $\chi^2 = 28.3$, $df = 14$, $p = .05$; GFI = 1.00; AGFI = 0.99; and RMSEA = 0.020, with a 90% confidence interval from 0.000 to 0.024. At the measurement level, the indicators of the latent Help construct all have highly significant factor loadings ($p < .001$) and roughly equal magnitudes. At the structural level, three of the four structural coefficients are highly significant ($p < .001$). The effect of church attendance (–0.06) differs from zero only at the $\alpha = .05$ level. POLVIEWS and PARTYID have much stronger standardized effects (0.25 and 0.32 standard deviations, respectively) than AGE (0.13) on the latent Help construct. As revealed by the residual arrow coming into Help, the four predictors jointly explain about 23% of the variation in Help ($R^2 = 1 - (0.88)^2 = 0.226$). High scores on the four social problem indicators mean that respondents prefer the individual or nongovernmental solutions to

FIGURE 12.5
Completely Standardized Solution for a MIMIC Model

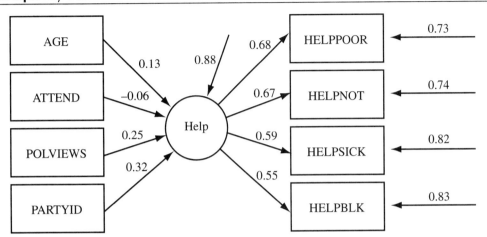

social problems. Therefore, the positive path coefficients suggest that conservatives, Republicans, and older respondents are more likely to endorse such policy positions. The negative coefficient for church attendance suggests that persons who attend church more frequently are less likely to choose individual or nongovernmental solutions to social problems.

As is true for path models, the results we get depend on the correct specification of the model. Therefore, researchers must always be careful in drawing conclusions from nonexperimental data.

12.4.2 A Single-Link Causal Chain

One widespread application of structural equation models involves two or more latent constructs with multiple indicators. A simple version is a **single-link causal chain**, in which one exogenous variable is assumed to cause variation in one endogenous variable, both of which have multiple indicators. Our example, shown in Figure 12.6, specifies two political measures (PARTYID and POLVIEWS) as indicators of a latent political ideology construct (Politics), which we assume affects the four-indicator Help construct. Again, the data come from the 1998 GSS.

The model has a very good fit: $\chi^2 = 15.7$, 8 *df*, $p = .052$; RMSEA = 0.024; GFI = 1.00; AGFI = 0.99. The measurement coefficients are all highly significant. The estimated structural parameter (0.63) means that a

single-link causal chain— a LISREL model in which one exogenous variable causes variation in one endogenous variable, both of which have multiple indicators

FIGURE 12.6
Completely Standardized Solution for a Single-Link Causal Chain Model

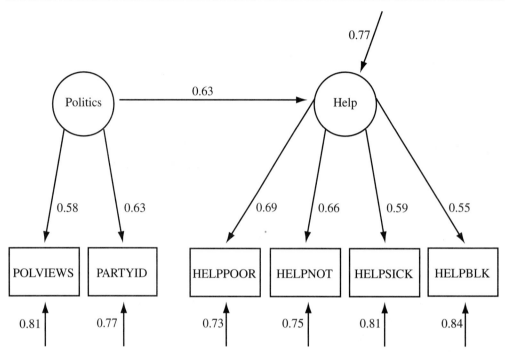

difference of one standard deviation in political ideology is associated with a difference of three-fifths standard deviation in attitude towards the federal government's role in solving social problems. Its positive sign means that more conservative respondents favor more individualistic solutions, consistent with what we expected.

These single-link causal chain model results suggest that the estimated parameters of the four indicators of the unobserved attitude towards the federal government's role in solving social problems (Help) are of roughly similar magnitudes (0.55 to 0.69). LISREL allows an explicit statistical test of the hypothesis that all four parameters equal one another in the population. Constraining a pair of parameters to be equal (rather than allowing them to be free to take on differing values) requires estimation of only one parameter instead of two. As a result, one degree

Table 12.2
Equality Constraints Among Help Indicators in Chain Model

Equality constraints	Model χ^2	Model df	χ^2/df
1. No equality constraints	15.7	8	1.96
2. HELPPOOR = HELPNOT	15.7	9	1.74
3. HELPPOOR = HELPSICK	18.6	9	2.07
4. HELPPOOR = HELPBLK	24.9	9	2.77
5. HELPPOOR = HELPSICK = HELPNOT	19.2	10	1.92

of freedom then becomes available to test whether the two models' chi-square goodness-of-fit statistics differ at a chosen alpha level. If no significant difference occurs in the model with free versus constrained pairs of parameters, then the more parsimonious version having equal parameters (i.e., the model with fewer free parameters) would be preferred.

Table 12.2 shows the chi-squares and degrees of freedom for comparisons of several alternative models constraining various combinations of parameters for the four Help indicators, along with the ratio of the chi-squares to their degrees of freedom. In comparison to the baseline model with no equality constraints (model 1), setting some parameters equal does not result in significantly worse fits to the data. For example, the difference in χ^2 for model 3 versus model 1 is 18.6 – 15.7 = 2.9 for 1 df. The critical value at $\alpha = .05$ is 3.84, so we cannot reject the null hypothesis that the parameters of HELPPOOR and HELPSICK are equal in the population. However, the hypothesized equality of HELPPOOR and HELPBLACK must be rejected (χ^2 difference in model 4 versus model 1 is 24.9 – 15.7 = 9.2 for 1 df). But model 5, which sets the first three parameters equal to one another, yields a fit that is not significantly worse than the baseline model of no constrained parameters (χ^2 difference of 19.2 – 15.7 = 3.5 for 2 df).

Figure 12.7 displays this constrained single-link causal chain model using the standardized solution parameters, which standardizes only the parameters among the latent constructs while leaving the parameters involving the observed variables in their original metrics. Note that the first three Help indicators have the same factor loading (0.76), while the fourth indicator has a lower parameter estimate (0.66).

FIGURE 12.7
**Standardized Solution for a Single-Link Causal Chain Model with Parameters
Constrained to Equality**

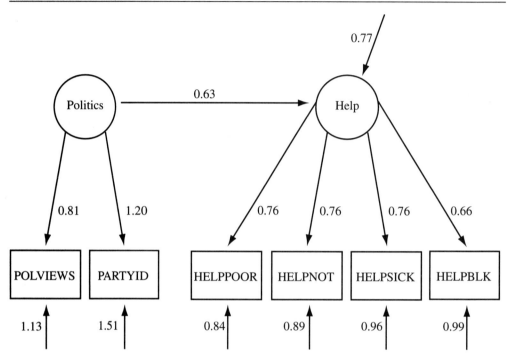

12.4.3 A Path Model with Multiple Indicators

This subsection extends the preceding MIMIC and single-link causal
chain examples to a causal model of the relationships among four unobservable constructs each having two or more observed variables. As
shown in Figure 12.8, the indicators for Politics and Help are the same
as in the preceding subsection. The two SES indicators are EDUC and
PRESTG80 (a measure of occupational prestige), and the two Religion
indicators are frequency of prayer and church attendance (PRAYFREQ
and ATTEND).

The model produced a good fit to the covariance matrix: $\chi^2 = 66.0$,
$df = 30$, $p = .0002$; GFI = 0.98; AGFI = 0.97; and RMSEA = 0.041, with
90% confidence interval bounded by 0.027 and 0.055. Note that the error
term for ATTEND has a value of zero. An initial analysis produced a neg-

FIGURE **12.8**
Completely Standardized Solution for a Path Model

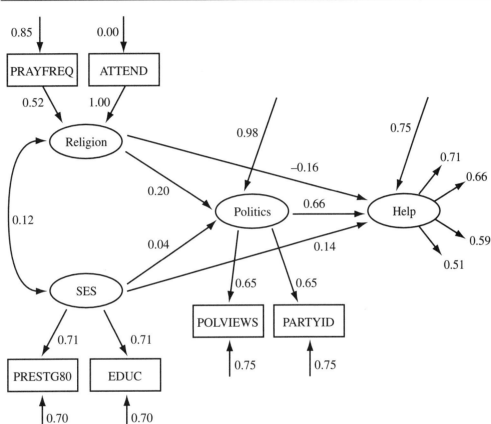

ative error variance estimate, which is, of course, illogical. Hence, we constrained that variable to be a perfect indicator of Religion, by setting its error variance to zero. The coefficients for the factor loadings are all highly significant, and the path values at the structural level of analysis are all significant at $p < .05$ or lower, except for a nonsignificant path from SES to Politics.

The largest estimated structural parameter, 0.66 from Politics to Help, means that a one-standard-deviation difference in conservative orientation is associated with a two-thirds standard deviation greater preference for individualistic solutions to social problems. The path coefficients for SES (0.14) and Religion (–0.16) indicate that small differences in individualistic preferences are associated with high SES and low religious activity, respectively. However, the positive indirect effect of Religion on Help by increasing political conservatism, $((0.20)(0.66) = 0.13)$, is almost as strong as its negative direct effect. Thus, these opposing effects almost cancel one another, yielding a net effect of religious activity on policy preference that is close to zero $(0.13 - 0.16 = -0.03)$.

12.5   Models with Ordered Indicators

If a structural equation analysis involves variables that are orderable discrete or dichotomous measures rather than continuous variables, computing a covariance or correlation matrix and applying maximum likelihood estimation may lead to distorted parameter estimates and inaccurate test statistics. Researchers need to consider each case on its own merits. For example, gender coded as "0" for males and "1" for females, where gender is an independent variable, makes sense in an OLS model, as do separate dichotomous (dummy) variables for region or religious affiliation. However, in other dichotomies, an observed variable with orderable categories may be viewed as a crude classification of an unobserved (latent) continuous variable z^* with a standard normal distribution. For example, a low–medium–high measure X could be trichotomized at three threshold values for z^*:

$$X \text{ is scored 1 if } z^* \leq \alpha_1$$
$$X \text{ is scored 2 if } \alpha_1 < z^* \leq \alpha_2$$
$$X \text{ is scored 3 if } \alpha_2 < z^*$$

A variety of correlation coefficients can be calculated when one or both observed variables are orderable measures.

- **Polychoric** correlation coefficient for two orderable discrete variables assumes their underlying continuous measures have a bivariate normal distribution.

- **Tetrachoric** correlation, a subtype of polychoric, is used for two dichotomies.

- **Polyserial** correlation involves estimating the relationship between an orderable variable and a continuous variable, assuming an underlying bivariate normal distribution.

- **Biserial** correlation, a subtype of polyserial, estimates the relationship between a dichotomy and a continuous variable, again assuming that the underlying bivariate distribution is normal.

To include orderable variables in a structural equation model, a LISREL preprocessor program (PRELIS) iteratively computes a matrix of Pearson, polychoric, and polyserial correlations among the observed indicators. LISREL then uses this matrix to compute estimated model parameters and to calculate fit statistics. Instead of maximum likelihood estimation (MLE), LISREL obtains correct large-sample standard errors and chi-square values using a **weighted least squares** (WLS) estimation method. A weight matrix required for WLS is the inverse of an estimated asymptotic covariance matrix (**W**) of polychoric and polyserial correlations. This inversion will be performed by LISREL, based on input of a **W** matrix generated by PRELIS and stored on the computer as a binary file.

weighted least squares (WLS)—an estimation method used to estimate correlations among ordered indicators

To illustrate, we analyze the latent factor structure for seven abortion attitude items in the 1998 GSS, where the answers by 1,578 respondents were coded only as dichotomies (yes = 1, no = 0).

> Please tell me whether or not you think it should be possible for a pregnant woman to obtain a legal abortion if:
>
> ABDEFECT: There is a strong chance of serious defect in the baby?
>
> ABNOMORE: She is married and does not want any more children?
>
> ABHLTH: The woman's own health is seriously endangered by the pregnancy?
>
> ABPOOR: The family has a very low income and cannot afford any more children?
>
> ABRAPE: She became pregnant as a result of rape?
>
> ABSINGLE: She is not married and does not want to marry the man?
>
> ABANY: The woman wants it for any reason?

Table 12.3 reports the matrix of estimated tetrachoric correlations among these indicators in the top panel. Their values are noticeably larger than the corresponding Pearson correlation coefficients computed for these dichotomies in the lower panel. That is, Pearson product-moment correlations underestimate the true relationships between the variables.

Our substantive research question is whether a single factor or multiple factors can best explain the relationships among these variables.

TABLE 12.3
Tetrachoric and Pearson Correlations Among Abortion Variables (N = 1,578)

	ABDEFECT	ABNOMORE	ABHLTH	ABPOOR	ABRAPE	ABSINGLE	ABANY
Tetrachoric Correlations							
ABDEFECT	1.000						
ABNOMORE	0.845	1.000					
ABHLTH	0.913	0.803	1.000				
ABPOOR	0.797	0.960	0.794	1.000			
ABRAPE	0.853	0.832	0.903	0.819	1.000		
ABSINGLE	0.830	0.969	0.803	0.964	0.833	1.000	
ABANY	0.795	0.968	0.794	0.948	0.842	0.966	1.000
Pearson Correlations							
ABDEFECT	1.000						
ABNOMORE	0.450	1.000					
ABHLTH	0.646	0.335	1.000				
ABPOOR	0.441	0.818	0.343	1.000			
ABRAPE	0.622	0.440	0.638	0.445	1.000		
ABSINGLE	0.445	0.841	0.336	0.828	0.441	1.000	
ABANY	0.422	0.837	0.326	0.789	0.434	0.832	1.000

Missing data = 1,254 cases.
Source: 1998 General Social Survey.

Although the single-factor model yields a high $\chi^2 = 110.7$ (14 *df*; $p <$ 0.0001), the other statistics indicate a better fit: GFI = 1.00; AGFI = 1.00; RMSEA = 0.066. However, a two-factor model, with ABDEFECT, ABHLTH, and ABRAPE all loading on a separate factor from the other five indicators, produced a much better fit for all statistical criteria: $\chi^2 =$ 25.4 for 13 *df*, $p = .02$; GFI = 1.00; AGFI = 1.00; and RMSEA = 0.025, with 90% confidence interval from 0.009 to 0.039. As shown in Figure 12.9, all seven factor loadings are very high, reflecting the large polychoric correlations on which they are based, as is very high positive correlation (0.88) between the two latent factors. As usual, the substantive meanings of latent constructs can be inferred by the contents of the specific indicators that load on them. What two dimensions of abortion attitudes do you conjecture, based on the content of the GSS questions?

FIGURE 12.9
Completely Standardized Solution to Two-Factor Model of Dichotomous Abortion Attitudes

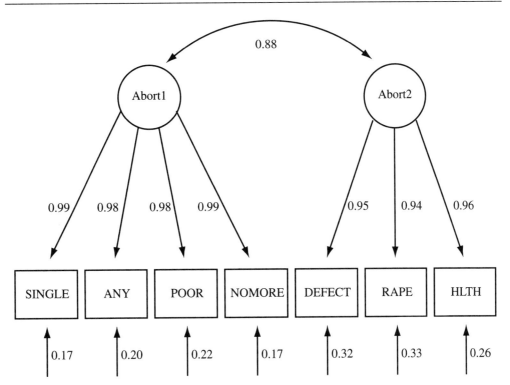

This chapter has provided only a brief introduction to structural equation modeling. More complex models, as well as details about their estimation methods, are covered in more advanced courses and texts (e.g., Bollen, 1989) that deal with structural equation models.

Review of Key Concepts and Symbols

These key concepts and symbols are listed in the order of appearance in this chapter. Combined with the definitions in the margins, they will help you to review the material and can serve as a self-test for mastery of the concepts.

structural equation model
LISREL
validity
reliability
random error
systematic error
parallel measures
factor analysis
common factors
confirmatory factor analysis
factor loadings
reference variable
algorithm
goodness-of-fit index (GFI)

adjusted goodness-of-fit index (AGFI)
root mean square error of approximation
    (RMSEA)
standardized solution
completely standardized solution
MIMIC model
single-link causal chain
weighted least squares

ϱ_X

σ_T^2

F

$F[\mathbf{S}, \Sigma(\theta)]$

PROBLEMS

General Problems

1. If the variance of an observed variable is 0.81 and the true score variance is 0.64, using classical measurement theory assumptions, what is the item's reliability?

2. The correlation of two parallel measures of X is 0.81. What is the reliability of these items?

3. Here is the completely standardized solution from a one-factor analysis for five indicators of confidence in U.S. institutions (business, churches, Congress, courts, schools). Give a substantive interpretation of this model, being sure to assess reliability. What is the estimated correlation between CONBIZ and CONSCHLS based on this model? Between CONCHURH and CONCOUR?

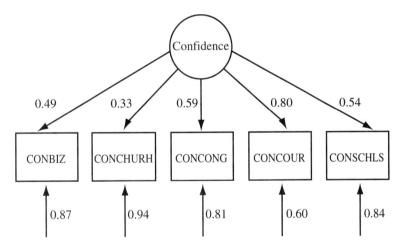

4. The goodness-of-fit statistics for the one-factor model in the previous problem are $\chi^2 = 19.6$, $df = 5$, $p = .0015$, GFI = 0.99, AGFI = 0.96, and RMSEA = 0.067, with 90% confidence interval between 0.038 and 0.099. Is this an acceptable fit of the model to the data? Explain your answer.

5. Here is the completely standardized solution from a two-factor analysis for five indicators of confidence in U.S. institutions.

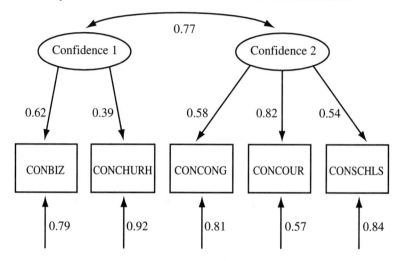

The goodness-of-fit statistics for this two-factor model are $\chi^2 = 11.7$, $df = 4$, $p = .02$, GFI = 0.99, AGFI = 0.97, and RMSEA = 0.054, with 90% confidence interval bounded by 0.019 and 0.091. Show whether this model has a significantly better fit to the data than the one-factor model. Give a substantive interpretation of the results.

6. Here are completely standardized solution estimates for a MIMIC model with three job values (importance of job security, high income, and promotion opportunities) that are assumed to be associated with the respondent's age, occupational prestige, and income. Only the coefficient for income is not significant. The model's goodness-of-fit statistics are $\chi^2 = 10.5$, $df = 6$, $p = .10$, GFI = 1.00, AGFI = 0.98, and RMSEA = 0.031, with 90% confidence interval bounded by 0.000 and 0.061. Discuss the acceptability of the model fit and give a substantive interpretation of the results.

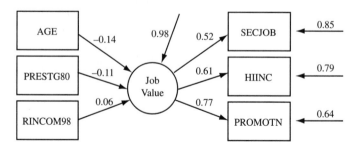

7. Here is a similar MIMIC model in which the dependent construct
   with the three job-value indicators in Problem 6 are predicted by
   directly observed measures of occupational prestige, education,
   and income. The coefficients for the latter two predictors are not
   significant. The goodness-of-fit statistics are $\chi^2 = 18.0$, $df = 6$,
   $p = .007$, GFI = 0.99, AGFI = 0.97, and RMSEA = 0.050, with
   90% confidence interval bounded by 0.024 and 0.077. Give a
   substantive interpretation of this model.

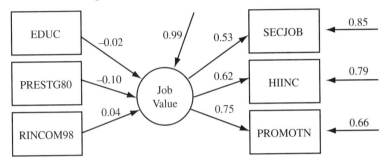

8. Here are completely standardized solution estimates for a single-
   link causal chain model where the dependent construct has the
   three job-values indicators in Problem 6 and the independent
   construct has three socioeconomic status indicators (education,
   occupational prestige, and income). All parameters are significant
   at $p < .05$ or lower. The model's goodness-of-fit statistics are $\chi^2 =$
   19.9, $df = 8$, $p = .011$, GFI = 0.99, AGFI = 0.98, and RMSEA =
   0.043, with a 90% confidence interval bounded by 0.019 and
   0.068. Discuss the model fit and give a substantive interpretation
   of the results.

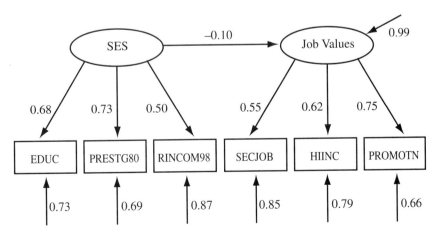

9. Here are estimates from a completely standardized solution to a single-link causal chain model where the dependent construct has three indicators of respondents' beliefs that the federal government is spending too much on social problems (drugs, crime, and cities) and the independent construct has three indicators of political conservatism (political views, party identification, and 1996 presidential vote for either conservative candidate, Dole or Perot). All parameters are significant at $p < .05$ or lower. The model's goodness-of-fit statistics are $\chi^2 = 18.3$, $df = 8$, $p = .019$, GFI = 0.99, AGFI = 0.97, and RMSEA = 0.053, with a 90% confidence interval ranging from 0.020 to 0.086. Discuss the adequacy of the fit and give a substantive interpretation of the results.

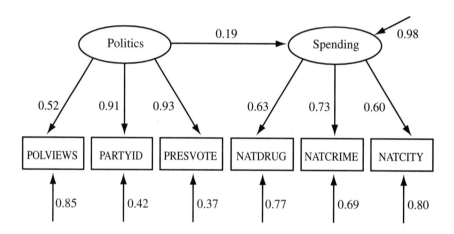

10. Here are estimates from a completely standardized solution to a path model where the dependent construct has three indicators of respondents' religious behavior (prayer, prayer frequency, and praying privately), one independent construct has four indicators of religious beliefs (in afterlife, heaven, hell, and miracles), and the other independent construct has three indicators of socioeconomic status (education, occupational prestige, and income). All parameters are significant at $p < .001$ or lower. The model's goodness-of-fit statistics are $\chi^2 = 122.9$, $df = 22$, $p < .001$, GFI = 0.96, AGFI = 0.93, and RMSEA = 0.070, with 90% confidence interval from 0.057 to 0.083. Give a substantive interpretation of this model.

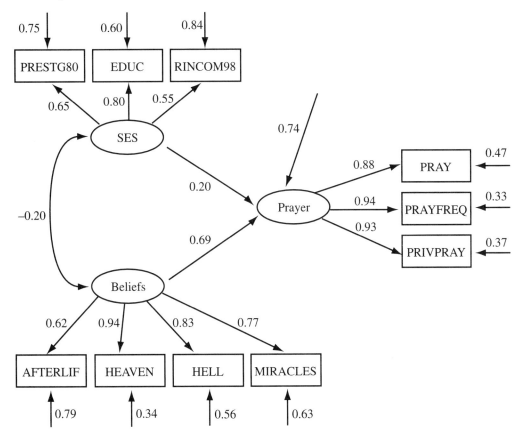

Problems Requiring the 1998 General Social Survey

11. Respondents were presented with four contrasting images of God and asked, "On a scale of 1 to 7, where would you place your image of God between the two contrasting images?" These pairs are MAPA (Mother–Father); MASTERSP (Master–Spouse); JUDGELUV (Judge–Lover); FRNDKING (Friend–King). Responses to the middle two images were reverse coded, resulting in this covariance matrix for 1,347 cases.

	MAPA	*MASTERSP	*JUDGELUV	FRNDKING
MAPA	1.00			
*MASTERSP	0.43	1.00		
*JUDGELUV	0.26	0.42	1.00	
FRNDKING	0.19	0.19	0.22	1.00

Perform a factor analysis with one factor, display the parameters from the completely standardized solution, and report the goodness-of-fit statistics. Provide a substantive interpretation.

12. Respondents were given a card with 20 statements about medical care and instructed, "As you read each of the following statements, please think about the medical care you are now receiving. If you have not received any medical care recently, circle the answer based on what you would expect if you had to seek care today. Even if you are not entirely certain about your answers, we want to remind you that your best guess is important for each statement." Responses of 1,129 persons were recorded on a five-point scale from "strongly agree" to "strongly disagree."

DOC12: I worry that my doctor is being prevented from telling me the full range of options for my treatment.

DOC13: I worry that I will be denied the treatment or services I need.

DOC14: I worry that my doctor will put cost considerations above the care I need.

DOC16: I trust my doctor's judgments about my medical care.

DOC18: I trust my doctor to put my medical needs above all other considerations when treating my medical problems.

DOC20: I trust my doctor to tell me if a mistake was made about my treatment.

Here is the covariance matrix for these six items.

	DOC12	DOC13	DOC14	DOC16	DOC18	DOC20
DOC12	1.00					
DOC13	0.57	1.06				
DOC14	0.58	0.64	1.06			
DOC16	−0.26	−0.25	−0.26	0.59		
DOC18	−0.28	−0.28	−0.29	0.32	0.65	
DOC20	−0.27	−0.30	−0.33	0.31	0.40	0.99

Perform a factor analysis first with a single factor and then with two correlated factors, using the first three indicators for the first construct and the last three indicators for the second construct; show a diagram with the parameters from the completely standardized solution for both models. Using a chi-square difference test and the goodness-of-fit statistics, decide which model you prefer. Give a substantive interpretation for your preferred model.

13. Using three of the items in Problem 12 (DOC16, DOC18, DOC20) as indicators of a doctor distrust construct, estimate a MIMIC model with three independent variables: the respondents' AGE, EDUC, and HEALTH ("Would you say your own health, in general, is excellent, good, fair, or poor?" recoded so that the highest score means excellent health). Here is the covariance matrix for 1,263 respondents.

	DOC16	DOC18	DOC20	AGE	EDUC	HEALTH
DOC16	0.57					
DOC18	0.30	0.64				
DOC20	0.30	0.40	1.00			
AGE	−1.63	−1.44	−1.50	289.04		
EDUC	−0.01	0.08	0.06	−7.78	19.58	
HEALTH	−0.03	0.00	−0.01	−3.42	0.60	0.62

Show a diagram with the parameters from the completely standardized solution, report the goodness-of-fit statistics, and give a substantive interpretation.

14. Another series of items instructed, "Before giving an individual a *secret* or *top secret* clearance, the government should have the right to ask him or her detailed, personal questions in the following areas." Use three of these indicators for an unobserved construct, where high scores indicate opposition to governmental inquiries into personal matters.

ASKCRIME: Criminal arrests and convictions

ASKDRUGS: Illegal drug use

ASKFINAN: Financial and credit history

Estimate a MIMIC model with three independent variables: the respondents' AGE, EDUC, and the dichotomized responses to this civil liberties question: "If some people in your community suggested that a book someone wrote against churches and religion should be taken out of your public library, would you favor removing this book, or not?" (LIBATH, recoded so that not favoring = 1, favoring = 0). Specify the LIBATH measure as dichotomous and the other indicators as continuous variables in the PRELIS2 analysis that creates a correlation matrix and asymptotic covariance matrix. Show a diagram with the parameters from the completely standardized solution, report the goodness-of-fit statistics, and give a substantive interpretation.

15. Estimate a causal path model in which an antecedent three-indicator SES construct (EDUC, PRESTG80, RINCOM98) is assumed to affect directly a three-indicator Low Self-Esteem construct (NOCHEER, EFFORT, WRTHLESS), and both these constructs are assumed to affect directly a three-indicator Happiness construct (HAPPY, HAPUNHAP, HAPMAR). Specify all non-SES variables as ordinal in the PRELIS2 analysis that creates a correlation matrix and asymptotic covariance matrix. Show a diagram with the parameters from the completely standardized solution, report the goodness-of-fit statistics, and give a substantive interpretation.

APPENDICES

A

THE USE OF SUMMATIONS

1. Variables and Subscripts

In this text we use the letters X, Y, and Z to stand for *variables*. Variables have outcomes that can be kept track of through the use of *subscripts*. If we have N individuals, then X_i denotes the particular value or outcome observed for individual i. For example, if we have four persons in a sample, then the four outcomes associated with them are represented by X_1, X_2, X_3, and X_4.

2. Sums

Many of the statistical techniques used in this text depend on the *sum* of observations across the N individuals in the sample. The summation sign, denoted by the Greek symbol sigma (Σ), is used to stand for the sum of the values that immediately follow the summation sign. An index value written under the Σ indicates the lowest value the subscript will take, and an index value written above Σ indicates the highest value the subscript will take in the summation. Therefore,

$$\sum_{i=1}^{N} X_i$$

is read as "the sum of the N outcomes of X_i from X_1 to X_N," or

$$\sum_{i=1}^{N} X_i = X_1 + X_2 + X_3 + \cdots + X_N$$

Suppose we observe four individuals (i.e., $N = 4$) and the four outcomes are $X_1 = 2$, $X_2 = 6$, $X_3 = 0$, $X_4 = 3$. Then,

$$\sum_{i=1}^{4} X_i = 2 + 6 + 0 + 3 = 11$$

The simplest use of the summation is in computing the *mean*, the average value of a set of observations. As you probably know, an average of this sort is computed by adding all the outcomes and then dividing the total by the number of observations. In summation notation, the mean is simply

$$\frac{\sum_{i=1}^{N} X_i}{N}$$

or, in the preceding example, the mean is

$$\frac{\sum_{i=1}^{4} X_i}{4} = \frac{11}{4} = 2.75$$

After you become familiar with the use of Σ and it becomes clear from the context that we are summing across all observations, we may use either $\sum_i X_i$ or $\sum X_i$, instead of the longer $\sum_{i=1}^{N} X_i$ notation.

Sometimes variables are represented by more than a single subscript. Multiple subscripts will be used for two situations. The first use is when we wish to represent not only an individual, i, but also a group, j, to which the person belongs (e.g., sex or religious identification). In this case the notation is X_{ij}. If the last observation in group j is notated by n_j, then the sum across the n_j individuals in group j is

$$\sum_{i=1}^{n_j} X_{ij}$$

Written out, this is

$$\sum_{i=1}^{n_j} X_{ij} = X_{1j} + X_{2j} + X_{3j} + \cdots + X_{n_j j}$$

If we wish to sum across all J groups of n_j individuals, this is symbolized by

$$\sum_{j=1}^{J} \sum_{i=1}^{n_j} X_{ij}$$

When written out, it is

$$\sum_{j=1}^{J} \sum_{i=1}^{n_j} X_{ij} = (X_{11} + X_{21} + \cdots + X_{n_1 1})$$
$$+ (X_{12} + X_{22} + \cdots + X_{n_2 2})$$
$$+ (X_{1J} + X_{2J} + \cdots + X_{n_J J})$$

As an example, suppose we have three political groups where 1 = Republican, 2 = Democrat, and 3 = Other, and there are four Republicans, three Democrats, and two Others in the groups. We observe the following nine outcomes:

$$i =$$

	1	2	3	4
$j =$ 1	3	4	2	3
2	2	0	1	
3	2	4		

Now if we want to sum the values of the Republicans (where $i = 1$), we have

$$\sum_{i=1}^{4} X_{i1} = 3 + 4 + 2 + 3 = 12$$

The sum of the others is

$$\sum_{i=1}^{2} X_{i3} = 2 + 4 = 6$$

Or, summing *all* observations across all groups,

$$\sum_{j=1}^{3} \sum_{i=1}^{n_j} X_{ij} = (3 + 4 + 2 + 3) + (2 + 0 + 1) + (2 + 4)$$
$$= 12 + 3 + 6 = 21$$

Where there is no ambiguity about the groups and individuals being summed across, we will also use $\sum_j \sum_i X_{ij}$ or $\sum\sum X_{ij}$, instead of the more cumbersome $\sum_{j=1}^{J} \sum_{i=1}^{n_j} X_{ij}$.

The second use of double subscripts is applied when we want to distinguish the same individual on two different variables. For example, we may have two variables, X_1 and X_2. In this case X_{1i} and X_{2i} symbolize the ith individual's outcomes on the two variables, and

$$\sum_{i=1}^{N} X_{1i} = X_{11} + X_{12} + \cdots + X_{1N}$$

3. Rules of Summation

There are a few simple rules of summation that you should learn. If you do so, you should have no difficulty with the few derivations presented in this book.

> **Rule 1:** The sum over a constant for N observations equals N times the constant. That is, if a is a constant, then

$$\sum_{i=1}^{N} a = Na$$

This may not seem intuitively obvious, but an example should make the rule clear. Suppose we have $N = 4$ observations, and each observation equals 5. Then $a = 5$ and

$$\sum_{i=1}^{4} a = (5 + 5 + 5 + 5) = (4)(5) = 20$$

We can also extend this rule, as follows.

> **Rule 2:** If each observation is multiplied times a constant, the sum of the constant times the observations equals the constant times the sum of the observations. That is,

$$\sum_{i=1}^{N} aX_i = a\sum_{i=1}^{N} X_i$$

For example, consider $a = 4$ and $X_1 = 2$, $X_2 = 6$, and $X_3 = 1$. Then,

$$\sum_{i=1}^{3} 4X_i = (4)(2) + (4)(6) + (4)(1)$$
$$= 4(2 + 6 + 1)$$
$$= 4\sum_{i=1}^{3} X_i = 36$$

This rule can also be applied to double sums. That is,

$$\sum_{j=1}^{J} \sum_{i=1}^{n_j} aX_{ij} = a\sum_{j=1}^{J} \sum_{i=1}^{n_j} X_{ij}$$

> **Rule 3:** If the only operation to be carried out before a summation is itself a sum, the summation can be distributed.

This rule sounds more complex than it is. Consider the following example:

$$\sum_{i=1}^{3}(X_i + 2) = (X_1 + 2) + (X_2 + 2) + (X_3 + 2)$$
$$= (X_1 + X_2 + X_3) + (2 + 2 + 2)$$
$$= \sum_{i=1}^{3}X_i + \sum_{i=1}^{3}2$$
$$= \sum_{i=1}^{3}X_i + (3)(2)$$
$$= \sum_{i=1}^{3}X_i + 6$$

A more general expression of this double summation rule is

$$\sum_{i=1}^{N}(X_i \pm a) = \sum_{i=1}^{N}X_i \pm \sum_{i=1}^{N}a = \sum_{i=1}^{N}X_i \pm Na$$

This last step, that $\sum_{i=1}^{N}a = Na$, follows from Rule 1. Note, however, that

$$\sum_{i=1}^{N}(X_i + a)^2 \neq \sum_{i=1}^{N}X_{i1}^2 + \sum a^2$$

We can only distribute the summation sign when the term within the parentheses is itself a simple sum or difference.

If we expand the term $(X_i + a)^2$, then we can distribute the sum. Now if follows from Rules 1 and 2 that we can simplify this expression even further as follows:

$$\sum(X_i + a)^2 = \sum(X_i^2 + 2aX_i + a^2)$$
$$= \sum X_i^2 + \sum 2aX_i + \sum a^2$$
$$= \sum X_i^2 + 2a\sum X_i + Na^2$$

4. Sums of Two or More Variables

Sometimes we will want to examine sums of two or more variables at once. Suppose we ask what is the sum of a product of two variables across N observations.

Rule 4: If each observation has a score on two variables, X_i and Y_i, then

$$\sum_{i=1}^{N} X_i Y_i = X_1 Y_1 + X_2 Y_2 + \cdots + X_N Y_N$$

Suppose we have observations on two variables, X and Y, for each of three persons. The observations are

	X_i	Y_i
1	2	1
$i =$ 2	4	-2
3	2	-3

Then

$$\sum_{i=1}^{3} X_i Y_i = (2)(1) + (4)(-2) + (2)(-3) = -12$$

Convince yourself, using this last example, that, in general,

$$\sum_{i=1}^{N} X_i Y_i \neq \sum X_i \sum Y_i$$

Thus, we *cannot* distribute a summation sign across products. But Rule 2 *does* apply to products. That is,

$$\sum a X_i Y_i = a \sum X_i Y_i$$

This relationship can be seen using the data from the previous example. If $a = 3$, then

$$\sum_{i=1}^{3} 3 X_i Y_i = 3(2)(1) + 3(4)(-2) + 3(2)(-3)$$

$$= 3[(2)(1) + (4)(-2) + (2)(-3)] = (3)(-12) = -36$$

$$= 3 \sum_{i=1}^{3} X_i Y_i$$

Rule 5: The sum of two or more variables equals the sum of the sums of the variables. That is,

$$\sum_{i} (X_{1i} + X_{2i} + \cdots + X_{ki})$$

$$= \sum_{i} X_{1i} + \sum_{i} X_{2i} + \cdots + \sum_{i} X_{ki}$$

where

$$X_1, X_2, \ldots, X_k = k \text{ different variables}$$

A special case of this rule is

$$\sum_i (X_i + Y_i) = \sum_i X_i + \sum_i Y_i$$

Again using the data from the preceding example, we can show this rule as

$$\sum_{i=1}^{3} (X_i + Y_i) = (2 + 1) + [4 + (-2)] + [2 + (-3)]$$
$$= (2 + 4 + 2) + [1 + (-2) + (-3)] = 4$$
$$= \sum_{i=1}^{3} X_i + \sum_{i=1}^{3} Y_i$$

Rule 6: For constants a and b,

$$\sum_i (aX_i + bY_i) = a\sum_i X_i + b\sum_i Y_i$$

Rule 6 is really a derivative from Rules 2 and 5. Rule 5 states that we can distribute the summation sign across sums of variables, and Rule 2 states that we can pull a constant out in front of a sum.

Again using the example data, let $a = 2$ and $b = 4$. Then

$$\sum_{i=1}^{3} (2X_i + 4Y_i) = [(2)(2) + (4)(1)] + [(2)(4) + (4)(-2)] + [(2)(2) + (4)(-3)]$$
$$= 2(2 + 4 + 2) + 4(1 - 2 - 3)$$
$$= 0$$
$$= 2\sum_{i=1}^{3} X_i + 4\sum_{i=1}^{3} Y_i$$

With this set of rules you should be able to follow the algebra used in this text. Our one piece of advice is not to be overwhelmed by sums. When in doubt about an equivalence, for example, try writing out the sums. They usually are not as complex as they seem.

B

CRITICAL VALUES OF CHI SQUARE

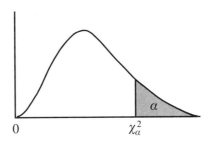

			LEVEL OF SIGNIFICANCE (α)			
df	*.100*	*.050*	*.025*	*.010*	*.005*	*.001*
1	2.7055	3.8414	5.0238	6.6349	7.8794	10.828
2	4.6051	5.9914	7.3777	9.2103	10.5966	13.816
3	6.2513	7.8147	9.3484	11.3449	12.8381	16.266
4	7.7794	9.4877	11.1433	13.2767	14.8602	18.467
5	9.2363	11.0705	12.8325	15.0863	16.7496	20.515
6	10.6446	12.5916	14.4494	16.8119	18.5476	22.458
7	12.0170	14.0671	16.0128	18.4753	20.2777	24.322
8	13.3616	15.5073	17.5346	20.0902	21.9550	26.125
9	14.6837	16.9190	19.0228	21.6660	23.5893	27.877
10	15.9871	18.3070	20.4831	23.2093	25.1882	29.588
11	17.2750	19.6751	21.9200	24.7250	26.7569	31.264
12	18.5494	21.0261	23.3367	26.2170	28.2995	32.909
13	19.8119	22.3621	24.7356	27.6883	29.8194	34.528
14	21.0642	23.6848	26.1190	29.1413	31.3193	36.123

(continued)

Source: Abridged from Table IV of Fisher and Yates: *Statistical Tables for Biological, Agricultural, and Medical Research,* 6th ed. (London: Longman Group Ltd., 1974). Previously published by Oliver & Boyd Ltd (Edinburgh) and used by permission of the authors and publishers.

df	LEVEL OF SIGNIFICANCE (α)					
	.100	.050	.025	.010	.005	.001
15	22.3072	24.9958	27.4884	30.5779	32.8013	37.697
16	23.5418	26.2962	28.8454	31.9999	34.2672	39.252
17	24.7690	27.5871	30.1910	33.4087	35.7185	40.790
18	25.9894	28.8693	31.5264	34.8058	37.1564	42.312
19	27.2036	30.1435	32.8523	36.1908	38.5822	43.820
20	28.4120	31.4104	34.1696	37.5662	39.9968	45.315
21	29.6151	32.6705	35.4789	38.9321	41.4010	46.797
22	30.8133	33.9244	36.7807	40.2894	42.7956	48.268
23	32.0069	35.1725	38.0757	41.6384	44.1813	49.728
24	33.1963	36.4151	39.3641	42.9798	45.5585	51.179
25	34.3816	37.6525	40.6465	44.3141	46.9278	52.620
26	35.5631	38.8852	41.9232	45.6417	48.2899	54.052
27	36.7412	40.1133	43.1944	46.9680	49.6449	55.476
28	37.9159	41.3372	44.4607	48.2782	50.9933	56.892
29	39.0875	42.5569	45.7222	49.5879	52.3356	58.302
30	40.2560	43.7729	46.9792	50.8922	53.6720	59.703
40	51.8050	55.7585	59.3417	63.6907	66.7659	73.402
50	63.1671	67.5048	71.4202	76.1539	79.4900	86.661
60	74.3970	79.0819	83.2976	88.3794	91.9517	99.607
70	85.5271	90.5312	95.0231	100.425	104.215	112.317
80	96.5782	101.879	106.629	112.329	116.321	124.839
90	107.565	113.145	118.136	124.116	128.299	137.208
100	118.498	124.342	129.561	135.807	140.169	149.449

C

AREAS UNDER THE NORMAL CURVE

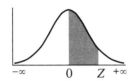

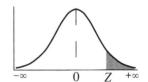

Z score	Area from 0 to Z	Area from Z to ∞	Z score	Area from 0 to Z	Area from Z to ∞
0.00	0.0000	0.5000	0.21	0.0832	0.4168
			0.22	0.0871	0.4129
0.01	0.0040	0.4960	0.23	0.0910	0.4090
0.02	0.0080	0.4920	0.24	0.0948	0.4052
0.03	0.0120	0.4880	0.25	0.0987	0.4013
0.04	0.0160	0.4840			
0.05	0.0199	0.4801	0.26	0.1026	0.3974
			0.27	0.1064	0.3936
0.06	0.0239	0.4761	0.28	0.1103	0.3897
0.07	0.0279	0.4721	0.29	0.1141	0.3859
0.08	0.0319	0.4681	0.30	0.1179	0.3821
0.09	0.0359	0.4641			
0.10	0.0398	0.4602	0.31	0.1217	0.3783
			0.32	0.1255	0.3745
0.11	0.0438	0.4562	0.33	0.1293	0.3707
0.12	0.0478	0.4522	0.34	0.1331	0.3669
0.13	0.0517	0.4483	0.35	0.1368	0.3632
0.14	0.0557	0.4443			
0.15	0.0596	0.4404	0.36	0.1406	0.3594
			0.37	0.1443	0.3557
0.16	0.0636	0.4364	0.38	0.1480	0.3520
0.17	0.0675	0.4325	0.39	0.1517	0.3483
0.18	0.0714	0.4286	0.40	0.1554	0.3446
0.19	0.0753	0.4247			
0.20	0.0793	0.4207			*(continued)*

Z score	Area from 0 to Z	Area from Z to ∞	Z score	Area from 0 to Z	Area from Z to ∞
0.41	0.1591	0.3409	0.71	0.2611	0.2389
0.42	0.1628	0.3372	0.72	0.2642	0.2358
0.43	0.1664	0.3336	0.73	0.2673	0.2327
0.44	0.1700	0.3300	0.74	0.2703	0.2297
0.45	0.1736	0.3264	0.75	0.2734	0.2266
0.46	0.1772	0.3228	0.76	0.2764	0.2236
0.47	0.1808	0.3192	0.77	0.2794	0.2206
0.48	0.1844	0.3156	0.78	0.2823	0.2177
0.49	0.1879	0.3121	0.79	0.2852	0.2148
0.50	0.1915	0.3085	0.80	0.2881	0.2119
0.51	0.1950	0.3050	0.81	0.2910	0.2090
0.52	0.1985	0.3015	0.82	0.2939	0.2061
0.53	0.2019	0.2981	0.83	0.2967	0.2033
0.54	0.2054	0.2946	0.84	0.2995	0.2005
0.55	0.2088	0.2912	0.85	0.3023	0.1977
0.56	0.2123	0.2877	0.86	0.3051	0.1949
0.57	0.2157	0.2843	0.87	0.3078	0.1922
0.58	0.2190	0.2810	0.88	0.3106	0.1894
0.59	0.2224	0.2776	0.89	0.3133	0.1867
0.60	0.2257	0.2743	0.90	0.3159	0.1841
0.61	0.2291	0.2709	0.91	0.3186	0.1814
0.62	0.2324	0.2676	0.92	0.3212	0.1788
0.63	0.2357	0.2643	0.93	0.3238	0.1762
0.64	0.2389	0.2611	0.94	0.3264	0.1736
0.65	0.2422	0.2578	0.95	0.3289	0.1711
0.66	0.2454	0.2546	0.96	0.3315	0.1685
0.67	0.2486	0.2514	0.97	0.3340	0.1660
0.68	0.2517	0.2483	0.98	0.3365	0.1635
0.69	0.2549	0.2451	0.99	0.3389	0.1611
0.70	0.2580	0.2420	1.00	0.3413	0.1587

Z score	*Area from 0 to Z*	*Area from Z to ∞*	*Z score*	*Area from 0 to Z*	*Area from Z to ∞*
1.01	0.3438	0.1562	1.31	0.4049	0.0951
1.02	0.3461	0.1539	1.32	0.4066	0.0934
1.03	0.3485	0.1515	1.33	0.4082	0.0918
1.04	0.3508	0.1492	1.34	0.4099	0.0901
1.05	0.3531	0.1469	1.35	0.4115	0.0885
1.06	0.3554	0.1446	1.36	0.4131	0.0869
1.07	0.3577	0.1423	1.37	0.4147	0.0853
1.08	0.3599	0.1401	1.38	0.4162	0.0838
1.09	0.3621	0.1379	1.39	0.4177	0.0823
1.10	0.3643	0.1357	1.40	0.4192	0.0808
1.11	0.3665	0.1335	1.41	0.4207	0.0793
1.12	0.3686	0.1314	1.42	0.4222	0.0778
1.13	0.3708	0.1292	1.43	0.4236	0.0764
1.14	0.3729	0.1271	1.44	0.4251	0.0749
1.15	0.3749	0.1251	1.45	0.4265	0.0735
1.16	0.3770	0.1230	1.46	0.4279	0.0721
1.17	0.3790	0.1210	1.47	0.4292	0.0708
1.18	0.3810	0.1190	1.48	0.4306	0.0694
1.19	0.3830	0.1170	1.49	0.4319	0.0681
1.20	0.3849	0.1151	1.50	0.4332	0.0668
1.21	0.3869	0.1131	1.51	0.4345	0.0655
1.22	0.3888	0.1112	1.52	0.4357	0.0643
1.23	0.3907	0.1093	1.53	0.4370	0.0630
1.24	0.3925	0.1075	1.54	0.4382	0.0618
1.25	0.3944	0.1056	1.55	0.4394	0.0606
1.26	0.3962	0.1038	1.56	0.4406	0.0594
1.27	0.3980	0.1020	1.57	0.4418	0.0582
1.28	0.3997	0.1003	1.58	0.4429	0.0571
1.29	0.4015	0.0985	1.59	0.4441	0.0559
1.30	0.4032	0.0968	1.60	0.4452	0.0548

(continued)

Z score	Area from 0 to Z	Area from Z to ∞	Z score	Area from 0 to Z	Area from Z to ∞
1.61	0.4463	0.0537	1.91	0.4719	0.0281
1.62	0.4474	0.0526	1.92	0.4726	0.0274
1.63	0.4484	0.0516	1.93	0.4732	0.0268
1.64	0.4495	0.0505	1.94	0.4738	0.0262
1.65	0.4505	0.0495	1.95	0.4744	0.0256
1.66	0.4515	0.0485	1.96	0.4750	0.0250
1.67	0.4525	0.0475	1.97	0.4756	0.0244
1.68	0.4535	0.0465	1.98	0.4761	0.0239
1.69	0.4545	0.0455	1.99	0.4767	0.0233
1.70	0.4554	0.0446	2.00	0.4772	0.0228
1.71	0.4564	0.0436	2.01	0.4778	0.0222
1.72	0.4573	0.0427	2.02	0.4783	0.0217
1.73	0.4582	0.0418	2.03	0.4788	0.0212
1.74	0.4591	0.0409	2.04	0.4793	0.0207
1.75	0.4599	0.0401	2.05	0.4798	0.0202
1.76	0.4608	0.0392	2.06	0.4803	0.0197
1.77	0.4616	0.0384	2.07	0.4808	0.0192
1.78	0.4625	0.0375	2.08	0.4812	0.0188
1.79	0.4633	0.0367	2.09	0.4817	0.0183
1.80	0.4641	0.0359	2.10	0.4821	0.0179
1.81	0.4649	0.0351	2.11	0.4826	0.0174
1.82	0.4656	0.0344	2.12	0.4830	0.0170
1.83	0.4664	0.0336	2.13	0.4834	0.0166
1.84	0.4671	0.0329	2.14	0.4838	0.0162
1.85	0.4678	0.0322	2.15	0.4842	0.0158
1.86	0.4686	0.0314	2.16	0.4846	0.0154
1.87	0.4693	0.0307	2.17	0.4850	0.0150
1.88	0.4699	0.0301	2.18	0.4854	0.0146
1.89	0.4706	0.0294	2.19	0.4857	0.0143
1.90	0.4713	0.0287	2.20	0.4861	0.0139

Z score	Area from 0 to Z	Area from Z to ∞	Z score	Area from 0 to Z	Area from Z to ∞
2.21	0.4864	0.0136	2.51	0.4940	0.0060
2.22	0.4868	0.0132	2.52	0.4941	0.0059
2.23	0.4871	0.0129	2.53	0.4943	0.0057
2.24	0.4875	0.0125	2.54	0.4945	0.0055
2.25	0.4878	0.0122	2.55	0.4946	0.0054
2.26	0.4881	0.0119	2.56	0.4948	0.0052
2.27	0.4884	0.0116	2.57	0.4949	0.0051
2.28	0.4887	0.0113	2.58	0.4951	0.0049
2.29	0.4890	0.0110	2.59	0.4952	0.0048
2.30	0.4893	0.0107	2.60	0.4953	0.0047
2.31	0.4896	0.0104	2.61	0.4955	0.0045
2.32	0.4898	0.0102	2.62	0.4956	0.0044
2.33	0.4901	0.0099	2.63	0.4957	0.0043
2.34	0.4904	0.0096	2.64	0.4959	0.0041
2.35	0.4906	0.0094	2.65	0.4960	0.0040
2.36	0.4909	0.0091	2.66	0.4961	0.0039
2.37	0.4911	0.0089	2.67	0.4962	0.0038
2.38	0.4913	0.0087	2.68	0.4963	0.0037
2.39	0.4916	0.0084	2.69	0.4964	0.0036
2.40	0.4918	0.0082	2.70	0.4965	0.0035
2.41	0.4920	0.0080	2.71	0.4966	0.0034
2.42	0.4922	0.0078	2.72	0.4967	0.0033
2.43	0.4925	0.0075	2.73	0.4968	0.0032
2.44	0.4927	0.0073	2.74	0.4969	0.0031
2.45	0.4929	0.0071	2.75	0.4970	0.0030
2.46	0.4931	0.0069	2.76	0.4971	0.0029
2.47	0.4932	0.0068	2.77	0.4972	0.0028
2.48	0.4934	0.0066	2.78	0.4973	0.0027
2.49	0.4936	0.0064	2.79	0.4974	0.0026
2.50	0.4938	0.0062	2.80	0.49744	0.00256

(continued)

Z score	Area from 0 to Z	Area from Z to ∞	Z score	Area from 0 to Z	Area from Z to ∞
2.81	0.49752	0.00248	3.05	0.49886	0.00114
2.82	0.49760	0.00240	3.10	0.49903	0.00097
2.83	0.49767	0.00233	3.15	0.49918	0.00082
2.84	0.49774	0.00226	3.20	0.49931	0.00069
2.85	0.49781	0.00219	3.25	0.49942	0.00058
			3.30	0.49952	0.00048
2.86	0.49788	0.00212	3.35	0.49960	0.00040
2.87	0.49795	0.00205	3.40	0.49966	0.00034
2.88	0.49801	0.00199	3.45	0.49972	0.00028
2.89	0.49807	0.00193	3.50	0.499767	0.000233
2.90	0.49813	0.00187			
			3.60	0.499841	0.000159
2.91	0.49819	0.00181	3.70	0.499892	0.000108
2.92	0.49825	0.00175	3.80	0.499928	0.000072
2.93	0.49831	0.00169	3.90	0.499952	0.000048
2.94	0.49836	0.00164	4.00	0.499968	0.000032
2.95	0.49841	0.00159			
			4.10	0.499979	0.000021
2.96	0.49846	0.00154	4.20	0.499987	0.000013
2.97	0.49851	0.00149	4.30	0.499991	0.000009
2.98	0.49856	0.00144	4.40	0.499995	0.000005
2.99	0.49861	0.00139	4.50	0.499997	0.000003
3.00	0.49865	0.00135			

D

STUDENT'S τ DISTRIBUTION

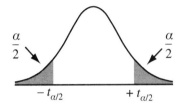

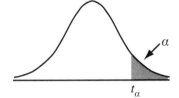

LEVEL OF SIGNIFICANCE FOR

| Two-Tailed Test | df | .20 | .10 | .05 | .02 | .01 | .001 |
One-Tailed Test		.10	.05	.025	.01	.005	.0005
	1	3.078	6.314	12.706	31.821	63.657	636.619
	2	1.886	2.920	4.303	6.965	9.925	31.598
	3	1.638	2.353	3.182	4.541	5.841	12.941
	4	1.533	2.132	2.776	3.747	4.604	8.610
	5	1.476	2.015	2.571	3.365	4.032	6.859
	6	1.440	1.943	2.447	3.143	3.707	5.959
	7	1.415	1.895	2.365	2.998	3.499	5.405
	8	1.397	1.860	2.306	2.896	3.355	5.041
	9	1.383	1.833	2.262	2.821	3.250	4.781
	10	1.372	1.812	2.228	2.764	3.169	4.587
	11	1.363	1.796	2.201	2.718	3.106	4.437
	12	1.356	1.782	2.179	2.681	3.055	4.318
	13	1.350	1.771	2.160	2.650	3.012	4.221
	14	1.345	1.761	2.145	2.624	2.977	4.140
	15	1.341	1.753	2.131	2.602	2.947	4.073
	16	1.337	1.746	2.120	2.583	2.921	4.015
	17	1.333	1.740	2.110	2.567	2.898	3.965
	18	1.330	1.734	2.101	2.552	2.878	3.922
	19	1.328	1.729	2.093	2.539	2.861	3.883
	20	1.325	1.725	2.086	2.528	2.845	3.850

(continued)

Source: Adapted from Table III of Fisher and Yates: *Statistical Tables for Biological, Agricultural, and Medical Research,* 6th ed. (London: Longman Group Ltd., 1974). Previously published by Oliver & Boyd Ltd (Edinburgh) and used by permission of the authors and publishers.

LEVEL OF SIGNIFICANCE FOR

| Two-Tailed Test | df | .20 | .10 | .05 | .02 | .01 | .001 |
One-Tailed Test		.10	.05	.025	.01	.005	.0005
	21	1.323	1.721	2.080	2.518	2.831	3.819
	22	1.321	1.717	2.074	2.508	2.819	3.792
	23	1.319	1.714	2.069	2.500	2.807	3.767
	24	1.318	1.711	2.064	2.492	2.797	3.745
	25	1.316	1.708	2.060	2.485	2.787	3.725
	26	1.315	1.706	2.056	2.479	2.779	3.707
	27	1.314	1.703	2.052	2.473	2.771	3.690
	28	1.313	1.701	2.048	2.467	2.763	3.674
	29	1.311	1.699	2.045	2.462	2.756	3.659
	30	1.310	1.697	2.042	2.457	2.750	3.646
	40	1.303	1.684	2.021	2.423	2.704	3.551
	60	1.296	1.671	2.000	2.390	2.660	3.460
	120	1.289	1.658	1.980	2.358	2.617	3.373
	∞	1.282	1.645	1.960	2.326	2.576	3.291

E

F **Distribution**

The *F* distribution table consists of three parts, for $\alpha = .05$, $\alpha = .01$, and $\alpha = .001$. These tables appear on the next three pages.

$\alpha = .05$

v_1/v_2	1	2	3	4	5	6	7	8	9	10	12	15	20	24	30	40	60	120	∞
1	161.4	199.5	215.7	224.6	230.2	234.0	236.8	238.9	240.5	241.9	243.9	245.9	248.0	249.1	250.1	251.1	252.2	253.3	254.3
2	18.51	19.00	19.16	19.25	19.30	19.33	19.35	19.37	19.38	19.40	19.41	19.43	19.45	19.45	19.46	19.47	19.48	19.49	19.50
3	10.13	9.55	9.28	9.12	9.01	8.94	8.89	8.85	8.81	8.79	8.74	8.70	8.66	8.64	8.62	8.59	8.57	8.55	8.53
4	7.71	6.94	6.59	6.39	6.26	6.16	6.09	6.04	6.00	5.96	5.91	5.86	5.80	5.77	5.75	5.72	5.69	5.66	5.63
5	6.61	5.79	5.41	5.19	5.05	4.95	4.88	4.82	4.77	4.74	4.68	4.62	4.56	4.53	4.50	4.46	4.43	4.40	4.36
6	5.99	5.14	4.76	4.53	4.39	4.28	4.21	4.15	4.10	4.06	4.00	3.94	3.87	3.84	3.81	3.77	3.74	3.70	3.67
7	5.59	4.74	4.35	4.12	3.97	3.87	3.79	3.73	3.68	3.64	3.57	3.51	3.44	3.41	3.38	3.34	3.30	3.27	3.23
8	5.32	4.46	4.07	3.84	3.69	3.58	3.50	3.44	3.39	3.35	3.28	3.22	3.15	3.12	3.08	3.04	3.01	2.97	2.93
9	5.12	4.26	3.86	3.63	3.48	3.37	3.29	3.23	3.18	3.14	3.07	3.01	2.94	2.90	2.86	2.83	2.79	2.75	2.71
10	4.96	4.10	3.71	3.48	3.33	3.22	3.14	3.07	3.02	2.98	2.91	2.85	2.77	2.74	2.70	2.66	2.62	2.58	2.54
11	4.84	3.98	3.59	3.36	3.20	3.09	3.01	2.95	2.90	2.85	2.79	2.72	2.65	2.61	2.57	2.53	2.49	2.45	2.40
12	4.75	3.89	3.49	3.26	3.11	3.00	2.91	2.85	2.80	2.75	2.69	2.62	2.54	2.51	2.47	2.43	2.38	2.34	2.30
13	4.67	3.81	3.41	3.18	3.03	2.92	2.83	2.77	2.71	2.67	2.60	2.53	2.46	2.42	2.38	2.34	2.30	2.25	2.21
14	4.60	3.74	3.34	3.11	2.96	2.85	2.76	2.70	2.65	2.60	2.53	2.46	2.39	2.35	2.31	2.27	2.22	2.18	2.13
15	4.54	3.68	3.29	3.06	2.90	2.79	2.71	2.64	2.59	2.54	2.48	2.40	2.33	2.29	2.25	2.20	2.16	2.11	2.07
16	4.49	3.63	3.24	3.01	2.85	2.74	2.66	2.59	2.54	2.49	2.42	2.35	2.28	2.24	2.19	2.15	2.11	2.06	2.01
17	4.45	3.59	3.20	2.96	2.81	2.70	2.61	2.55	2.49	2.45	2.38	2.31	2.23	2.19	2.15	2.10	2.06	2.01	1.96
18	4.41	3.55	3.16	2.93	2.77	2.66	2.58	2.51	2.46	2.41	2.34	2.27	2.19	2.15	2.11	2.06	2.02	1.97	1.92
19	4.38	3.52	3.13	2.90	2.74	2.63	2.54	2.48	2.42	2.38	2.31	2.23	2.16	2.11	2.07	2.03	1.98	1.93	1.88
20	4.35	3.49	3.10	2.87	2.71	2.60	2.51	2.45	2.39	2.35	2.28	2.20	2.12	2.08	2.04	1.99	1.95	1.90	1.84
21	4.32	3.47	3.07	2.84	2.68	2.57	2.49	2.42	2.37	2.32	2.25	2.18	2.10	2.05	2.01	1.96	1.92	1.87	1.81
22	4.30	3.44	3.05	2.82	2.66	2.55	2.46	2.40	2.34	2.30	2.23	2.15	2.07	2.03	1.98	1.94	1.89	1.84	1.78
23	4.28	3.42	3.03	2.80	2.64	2.53	2.44	2.37	2.32	2.27	2.20	2.13	2.05	2.01	1.96	1.91	1.86	1.81	1.76
24	4.26	3.40	3.01	2.78	2.62	2.51	2.42	2.36	2.30	2.25	2.18	2.11	2.03	1.98	1.94	1.89	1.84	1.79	1.73
25	4.24	3.39	2.99	2.76	2.60	2.49	2.40	2.34	2.28	2.24	2.16	2.09	2.01	1.96	1.92	1.87	1.82	1.77	1.71
26	4.23	3.37	2.98	2.74	2.59	2.47	2.39	2.32	2.27	2.22	2.15	2.07	1.99	1.95	1.90	1.85	1.80	1.75	1.69
27	4.21	3.35	2.96	2.73	2.57	2.46	2.37	2.31	2.25	2.20	2.13	2.06	1.97	1.93	1.88	1.84	1.79	1.73	1.67
28	4.20	3.34	2.95	2.71	2.56	2.45	2.36	2.29	2.24	2.19	2.12	2.04	1.96	1.91	1.87	1.82	1.77	1.71	1.65
29	4.18	3.33	2.93	2.70	2.55	2.43	2.35	2.28	2.22	2.18	2.10	2.03	1.94	1.90	1.85	1.81	1.75	1.70	1.64
30	4.17	3.32	2.92	2.69	2.53	2.42	2.33	2.27	2.21	2.16	2.09	2.01	1.93	1.89	1.84	1.79	1.74	1.68	1.62
40	4.08	3.23	2.84	2.61	2.45	2.34	2.25	2.18	2.12	2.08	2.00	1.92	1.84	1.79	1.74	1.69	1.64	1.58	1.51
60	4.00	3.15	2.76	2.53	2.37	2.25	2.17	2.10	2.04	1.99	1.92	1.84	1.75	1.70	1.65	1.59	1.53	1.47	1.39
120	3.92	3.07	2.68	2.45	2.29	2.17	2.09	2.02	1.96	1.91	1.83	1.75	1.66	1.61	1.55	1.50	1.43	1.35	1.25
∞	3.84	3.00	2.60	2.37	2.21	2.10	2.01	1.94	1.88	1.83	1.75	1.67	1.57	1.52	1.46	1.39	1.32	1.22	1.00

Source: Adapted from E. S. Pearson and H. O. Hartley: *Biometrika Tables for Statisticians*, 2nd ed. (Cambridge: Cambridge University Press, 1962).

$\alpha = .01$

v_1/v_2	1	2	3	4	5	6	7	8	9	10	12	15	20	24	30	40	60	120	∞
1	4052	4999.5	5403	5625	5764	5859	5928	5982	6022	6056	6106	6157	6209	6235	6261	6287	6313	6339	6366
2	98.50	99.00	99.17	99.25	99.30	99.33	99.36	99.37	99.39	99.40	99.42	99.43	99.45	99.46	99.47	99.47	99.48	99.49	99.50
3	34.12	30.82	29.46	28.71	28.24	27.91	27.67	27.49	27.35	27.23	27.05	26.87	26.69	26.60	26.50	26.41	26.32	26.22	26.13
4	21.20	18.00	16.69	15.98	15.52	15.21	14.98	14.80	14.66	14.55	14.37	14.20	14.02	13.93	13.84	13.75	13.65	13.56	13.46
5	16.26	13.27	12.06	11.39	10.97	10.67	10.46	10.29	10.16	10.05	9.89	9.72	9.55	9.47	9.38	9.29	9.20	9.11	9.02
6	13.75	10.92	9.78	9.15	8.75	8.47	8.26	8.10	7.98	7.87	7.72	7.56	7.40	7.31	7.23	7.14	7.06	6.97	6.88
7	12.25	9.55	8.45	7.85	7.46	7.19	6.99	6.84	6.72	6.62	6.47	6.31	6.16	6.07	5.99	5.91	5.82	5.74	5.65
8	11.26	8.65	7.59	7.01	6.63	6.37	6.18	6.03	5.91	5.81	5.67	5.52	5.36	5.28	5.20	5.12	5.03	4.95	4.86
9	10.56	8.02	6.99	6.42	6.06	5.80	5.61	5.47	5.35	5.26	5.11	4.96	4.81	4.73	4.65	4.57	4.48	4.40	4.31
10	10.04	7.56	6.55	5.99	5.64	5.39	5.20	5.06	4.94	4.85	4.71	4.56	4.41	4.33	4.25	4.17	4.08	4.00	3.91
11	9.65	7.21	6.22	5.67	5.32	5.07	4.89	4.74	4.63	4.54	4.40	4.25	4.10	4.02	3.94	3.86	3.78	3.69	3.60
12	9.33	6.93	5.95	5.41	5.06	4.82	4.64	4.50	4.39	4.30	4.16	4.01	3.86	3.78	3.70	3.62	3.54	3.45	3.36
13	9.07	6.70	5.74	5.21	4.86	4.62	4.44	4.30	4.19	4.10	3.96	3.82	3.66	3.59	3.51	3.43	3.34	3.25	3.17
14	8.86	6.51	5.56	5.04	4.69	4.46	4.28	4.14	4.03	3.94	3.80	3.66	3.51	3.43	3.35	3.27	3.18	3.09	3.00
15	8.68	6.36	5.42	4.89	4.56	4.32	4.14	4.00	3.89	3.80	3.67	3.52	3.37	3.29	3.21	3.13	3.05	2.96	2.87
16	8.53	6.23	5.29	4.77	4.44	4.20	4.03	3.89	3.78	3.69	3.55	3.41	3.26	3.18	3.10	3.02	2.93	2.84	2.75
17	8.40	6.11	5.18	4.67	4.34	4.10	3.93	3.79	3.68	3.59	3.46	3.31	3.16	3.08	3.00	2.92	2.83	2.75	2.65
18	8.29	6.01	5.09	4.58	4.25	4.01	3.84	3.71	3.60	3.51	3.37	3.23	3.08	3.00	2.92	2.84	2.75	2.66	2.57
19	8.18	5.93	5.01	4.50	4.17	3.94	3.77	3.63	3.52	3.43	3.30	3.15	3.00	2.92	2.84	2.76	2.67	2.58	2.49
20	8.10	5.85	4.94	4.43	4.10	3.87	3.70	3.56	3.46	3.37	3.23	3.09	2.94	2.86	2.78	2.69	2.61	2.52	2.42
21	8.02	5.78	4.87	4.37	4.04	3.81	3.64	3.51	3.40	3.31	3.17	3.03	2.88	2.80	2.72	2.64	2.55	2.46	2.36
22	7.95	5.72	4.82	4.31	3.99	3.76	3.59	3.45	3.35	3.26	3.12	2.98	2.83	2.75	2.67	2.58	2.50	2.40	2.31
23	7.88	5.66	4.76	4.26	3.94	3.71	3.54	3.41	3.30	3.21	3.07	2.93	2.78	2.70	2.62	2.54	2.45	2.35	2.26
24	7.82	5.61	4.72	4.22	3.90	3.67	3.50	3.36	3.26	3.17	3.03	2.89	2.74	2.66	2.58	2.49	2.40	2.31	2.21
25	7.77	5.57	4.68	4.18	3.85	3.63	3.46	3.32	3.22	3.13	2.99	2.85	2.70	2.62	2.54	2.45	2.36	2.27	2.17
26	7.72	5.53	4.64	4.14	3.82	3.59	3.42	3.29	3.18	3.09	2.96	2.81	2.66	2.58	2.50	2.42	2.33	2.23	2.13
27	7.68	5.49	4.60	4.11	3.78	3.56	3.39	3.26	3.15	3.06	2.93	2.78	2.63	2.55	2.47	2.38	2.29	2.20	2.10
28	7.64	5.45	4.57	4.07	3.75	3.53	3.36	3.23	3.12	3.03	2.90	2.75	2.60	2.52	2.44	2.35	2.26	2.17	2.06
29	7.60	5.42	4.54	4.04	3.73	3.50	3.33	3.20	3.09	3.00	2.87	2.73	2.57	2.49	2.41	2.33	2.23	2.14	2.03
30	7.56	5.39	4.51	4.02	3.70	3.47	3.30	3.17	3.07	2.98	2.84	2.70	2.55	2.47	2.39	2.30	2.21	2.11	2.01
40	7.31	5.18	4.31	3.83	3.51	3.29	3.12	2.99	2.89	2.80	2.66	2.52	2.37	2.29	2.20	2.11	2.02	1.92	1.80
60	7.08	4.98	4.13	3.65	3.34	3.12	2.95	2.82	2.72	2.63	2.50	2.35	2.20	2.12	2.03	1.94	1.84	1.73	1.60
120	6.85	4.79	3.95	3.48	3.17	2.96	2.79	2.66	2.56	2.47	2.34	2.19	2.03	1.95	1.86	1.76	1.66	1.53	1.38
∞	6.63	4.61	3.78	3.32	3.02	2.80	2.64	2.51	2.41	2.32	2.18	2.04	1.88	1.79	1.70	1.59	1.47	1.32	1.00

$\alpha = .001$

ν_1/ν_2	1	2	3	4	5	6	7	8	9	10	12	15	20	24	30	40	60	120	∞
1	4053*	5000*	5404*	5625*	5764*	5859*	5929*	5981*	6023*	6056*	6107*	6158*	6209*	6235*	6261*	6287*	6313*	6340*	6366*
2	998.5	999.0	999.2	999.2	999.3	999.3	999.4	999.4	999.4	999.4	999.4	999.4	999.4	999.5	999.5	999.5	999.5	999.5	999.5
3	167.0	148.5	141.1	137.1	134.6	132.8	131.6	130.6	129.9	129.2	128.3	127.4	126.4	125.9	125.4	125.0	124.5	124.0	123.5
4	74.14	61.25	56.18	53.44	51.71	50.53	49.66	49.00	48.47	48.05	47.41	46.76	46.10	45.77	45.43	45.09	44.75	44.40	44.05
5	47.18	37.12	33.20	31.09	29.75	28.84	28.16	27.64	27.24	26.92	26.42	25.91	25.39	25.14	24.87	24.60	24.33	24.06	23.79
6	35.51	27.00	23.70	21.92	20.81	20.03	19.46	19.03	18.69	18.41	17.99	17.56	17.12	16.89	16.67	16.44	16.21	15.99	15.75
7	29.25	21.69	18.77	17.19	16.21	15.52	15.02	14.63	14.33	14.08	13.71	13.32	12.93	12.73	12.53	12.33	12.12	11.91	11.70
8	25.42	18.49	15.83	14.39	13.49	12.86	12.40	12.04	11.77	11.54	11.19	10.84	10.48	10.30	10.11	9.92	9.73	9.53	9.33
9	22.86	16.39	13.90	12.56	11.71	11.13	10.70	10.37	10.11	9.89	9.57	9.24	8.90	8.72	8.55	8.37	8.19	8.00	7.81
10	21.04	14.91	12.55	11.28	10.48	9.92	9.52	9.20	8.96	8.75	8.45	8.13	7.80	7.64	7.47	7.30	7.12	6.94	6.76
11	19.69	13.81	11.56	10.35	9.58	9.05	8.66	8.35	8.12	7.92	7.63	7.32	7.01	6.85	6.68	6.52	6.35	6.17	6.00
12	18.64	12.97	10.80	9.63	8.89	8.38	8.00	7.71	7.48	7.29	7.00	6.71	6.40	6.25	6.09	5.93	5.76	5.59	5.42
13	17.81	12.31	10.21	9.07	8.35	7.86	7.49	7.21	6.98	6.80	6.52	6.23	5.93	5.78	5.63	5.47	5.30	5.14	4.97
14	17.14	11.78	9.73	8.62	7.92	7.43	7.08	6.80	6.58	6.40	6.13	5.85	5.56	5.41	5.25	5.10	4.94	4.77	4.60
15	16.59	11.34	9.34	8.25	7.57	7.09	6.74	6.47	6.26	6.08	5.81	5.54	5.25	5.10	4.95	4.80	4.64	4.47	4.31
16	16.12	10.97	9.00	7.94	7.27	6.81	6.46	6.19	5.98	5.81	5.55	5.27	4.99	4.85	4.70	4.54	4.39	4.23	4.06
17	15.72	10.66	8.73	7.68	7.02	6.56	6.22	5.96	5.75	5.58	5.32	5.05	4.78	4.63	4.48	4.33	4.18	4.02	3.85
18	15.38	10.39	8.49	7.46	6.81	6.35	6.02	5.76	5.56	5.39	5.13	4.87	4.59	4.45	4.30	4.15	4.00	3.84	3.67
19	15.08	10.16	8.28	7.26	6.62	6.18	5.85	5.59	5.39	5.22	4.97	4.70	4.43	4.29	4.14	3.99	3.84	3.68	3.51
20	14.82	9.95	8.10	7.10	6.46	6.02	5.69	5.44	5.24	5.08	4.82	4.56	4.29	4.15	4.00	3.86	3.70	3.54	3.38
21	14.59	9.77	7.94	6.95	6.32	5.88	5.56	5.31	5.11	4.95	4.70	4.44	4.17	4.03	3.88	3.74	3.58	3.42	3.26
22	14.38	9.61	7.80	6.81	6.19	5.76	5.44	5.19	4.99	4.83	4.58	4.33	4.06	3.92	3.78	3.63	3.48	3.32	3.15
23	14.19	9.47	7.67	6.69	6.08	5.65	5.33	5.09	4.89	4.73	4.48	4.23	3.96	3.82	3.68	3.53	3.38	3.22	3.05
24	14.03	9.34	7.55	6.59	5.98	5.55	5.23	4.99	4.80	4.64	4.39	4.14	3.87	3.74	3.59	3.45	3.29	3.14	2.97
25	13.88	9.22	7.45	6.49	5.88	5.46	5.15	4.91	4.71	4.56	4.31	4.06	3.79	3.66	3.52	3.37	3.22	3.06	2.89
26	13.74	9.12	7.36	6.41	5.80	5.38	5.07	4.83	4.64	4.48	4.24	3.99	3.72	3.59	3.44	3.30	3.15	2.99	2.82
27	13.61	9.02	7.27	6.33	5.73	5.31	5.00	4.76	4.57	4.41	4.17	3.92	3.66	3.52	3.38	3.23	3.08	2.92	2.75
28	13.50	8.93	7.19	6.25	5.66	5.24	4.93	4.69	4.50	4.35	4.11	3.86	3.60	3.46	3.32	3.18	3.02	2.86	2.69
29	13.39	8.85	7.12	6.19	5.59	5.18	4.87	4.64	4.45	4.29	4.05	3.80	3.54	3.41	3.27	3.12	2.97	2.81	2.64
30	13.29	8.77	7.05	6.12	5.53	5.12	4.82	4.58	4.39	4.24	4.00	3.75	3.49	3.36	3.22	3.07	2.92	2.76	2.59
40	12.61	8.25	6.60	5.70	5.13	4.73	4.44	4.21	4.02	3.87	3.64	3.40	3.15	3.01	2.87	2.73	2.57	2.41	2.23
60	11.97	7.76	6.17	5.31	4.76	4.37	4.09	3.87	3.69	3.54	3.31	3.08	2.83	2.69	2.55	2.41	2.25	2.08	1.89
120	11.38	7.32	5.79	4.95	4.42	4.04	3.77	3.55	3.38	3.24	3.02	2.78	2.53	2.40	2.26	2.11	1.95	1.76	1.54
∞	10.83	6.91	5.42	4.62	4.10	3.74	3.47	3.27	3.10	2.96	2.74	2.51	2.27	2.13	1.99	1.84	1.66	1.45	1.00

*Multiply these entries by 100.

F

FISHER'S *r*-to-Z Transformation

r	Z	r	Z	r	Z	r	Z	r	Z
.000	.000	.200	.203	.400	.424	.600	.693	.800	1.099
.005	.005	.205	.208	.405	.430	.605	.701	.805	1.113
.010	.010	.210	.213	.410	.436	.610	.709	.810	1.127
.015	.015	.215	.218	.415	.442	.615	.717	.815	1.142
.020	.020	.220	.224	.420	.448	.620	.725	.820	1.157
.025	.025	.225	.229	.425	.454	.625	.733	.825	1.172
.030	.030	.230	.234	.430	.460	.630	.741	.830	1.188
.035	.035	.235	.239	.435	.466	.635	.750	.835	1.204
.040	.040	.240	.245	.440	.472	.640	.758	.840	1.221
.045	.045	.245	.250	.445	.478	.645	.767	.845	1.238
.050	.050	.250	.255	.450	.485	.650	.775	.850	1.256
.055	.055	.255	.261	.455	.491	.655	.784	.855	1.274
.060	.060	.260	.266	.460	.497	.660	.793	.860	1.293
.065	.065	.265	.271	.465	.504	.665	.802	.865	1.313
.070	.070	.270	.277	.470	.510	.670	.811	.870	1.333
.075	.075	.275	.282	.475	.517	.675	.820	.875	1.354
.080	.080	.280	.288	.480	.523	.680	.829	.880	1.376
.085	.085	.285	.293	.485	530	.685	.838	.885	1.398
.090	.090	.290	.299	.490	.536	.690	.848	.890	1.422
.095	.095	.295	.304	.495	.543	.695	.858	.895	1.447
.100	.100	.300	.310	.500	.549	.700	.867	.900	1.472
.105	.105	.305	.315	.505	.556	.705	.877	.905	1.499
.110	.110	.310	.321	.510	.563	.710	.887	.910	1.528
.115	.116	.315	.326	.515	.570	.715	.897	.915	1.557
.120	.121	.320	.332	.520	.576	.720	.908	.920	1.589
.125	.126	.325	.337	.525	.583	.725	.918	.925	1.623
.130	.131	.330	.343	.530	.590	.730	.929	.930	1.658
.135	.136	.335	.348	.535	.597	.735	.940	.935	1.697
.140	.141	.340	.354	.540	.604	.740	.950	.940	1.738
.145	.146	.345	.360	.545	.611	.745	.962	.945	1.783
.150	.151	.350	.365	.550	.618	.750	.973	.950	1.832
.155	.156	.355	.371	.555	.626	.755	.984	.955	1.886
.160	.161	.360	.377	.560	.633	.760	.996	.960	1.946
.165	.167	.365	.383	.565	.640	.765	1.008	.965	2.014
.170	.172	.370	.388	.570	.648	.770	1.020	.970	2.092
.175	.177	.375	.394	.575	.655	.775	1.033	.975	2.185
.180	.182	.380	.400	.580	.662	.780	1.045	.980	2.298
.185	.187	.385	.406	.585	.670	.785	1.058	.985	2.443
.190	.192	.390	.412	.590	.678	.790	1.071	.990	2.647
.195	.198	.395	.418	.595	.685	.795	1.085	.995	2.994

GLOSSARY OF TERMS

adjusted coefficient of determination—a coefficient of determination that takes into account the number of independent variables relative to the number of observations

adjusted goodness-of-fit index (AGFI)—the re-expression of the GFI in terms of the numbers of degrees of freedom used in fitting the model

algorithm—computer routine

alpha area—the area in the tail of a normal distribution that is cut off by a given Z_α

alpha level—see **probability level**

alternative hypothesis—a secondary hypothesis about the value of a population parameter that often mirrors the research or operational hypothesis. Symbolized H_1

analysis of covariance (ANCOVA)—a multiple regression equation including one or more dummy variables, with a continuous independent variable and no interaction terms

analysis of variance—a statistical test of the difference of means for two or more groups

ANOVA summary table—a tabular display summarizing the results of an analysis of variance

applied research—research that attempts to explain social phenomena with immediate public policy implications

average absolute deviation—the mean of the absolute values of the difference between a set of continuous measures and their mean

bar chart—a type of diagram for discrete variables in which the numbers or percentages of cases in each outcome are displayed

basic research—research that examines the validity of general statements about relationships involving fundamental social processes

best linear and unbiased estimate (BLUE)—an estimator for population regression parameters that assumes a linear relationship, no measurement error, and normally distributed error terms

beta coefficient/beta weight—a standardized regression coefficient indicating the amount of net change, in standard deviation units, of the dependent variable for an independent variable change of one standard deviation

between sum of squares—a value obtained by subtracting the grand mean from each group mean, squaring these differences for all individuals, and summing them

bivariate crosstabulation/joint contingency table—a tabular display of the simultaneous outcomes of observations on two discrete variables

bivariate linear relationship/bivariate regression—a regression of Y on X

bivariate regression coefficient—a parameter estimate of a bivariate regression equation that measures the amount of increase or decrease in the dependent variable for a one-unit difference in the independent variable

boundary conditions—see **scope**

box-and-whisker/boxplot—a type of graph for discrete and continuous variables in which boxes and lines represent central tendency, variability, and shape of a distribution of observed data

causal diagram—a visual representation of the cause-and-effect relationships among variables, using keyword names and directed arrows

cell—the intersection of a row and a column in a crosstabulation of two or more variables. Numerical values contained within cells may be cell frequencies, cell proportions, or cell percentages

central limit theorem—if all possible random samples of N observations are drawn from any population with mean μ_Y and variance σ_Y^2, then as N grows larger, these sample means approach a normal distribution, with mean μ_Y and variance σ_Y^2/N

central tendency—average value of a set of scores

chain path model—a causal model in which variables measured on the same sample three or more times are depicted as the causes of their own subsequent values

Chebycheff's inequality theorem—the probability a variable differs absolutely from the mean by k or more standard deviations is *always* less than or equal to the ratio of 1 to k^2 (for all k greater than 1.0)

chi-square distribution—a family of distributions, each of which has different degrees of freedom, on which the chi-square test statistic is based

chi-square test—a test of statistical significance based on a comparison of the observed cell frequencies of a joint contingency table with frequencies that would be expected under the null hypothesis of no relationship

codebook—a complete record of all coding decisions

coefficient of determination—a PRE statistic for linear regression that expresses the amount of variation in the dependent variable explained or accounted for by the independent variable(s) in a regression equation

coefficient of nondetermination—a statistic that expresses the amount of variation in a dependent variable that is left *unex*plained by the independent variable(s) in a regression equation

column marginals—the frequency distribution of the variable shown down the columns of a crosstabulation

common factors—latent constructs that create covariation among observed variables

completely standardized solution—all observed and unobserved variables are standardized, and parameters are expressed in standard deviation units

computing formula for b—easy-to-use formula for calculating the bivariate regression coefficient

concept—a precisely defined object, behavior, perception (of self or others), or phenomenon that is relevant to the particular theoretical concerns at hand

concordant pair—in a crosstabulation of two orderable discrete variables, one observation has a higher rank on both variables than does the other member of the pair

conditional correlation coefficients—correlation coefficients calculated between two crosstabulated variables within each category of a third variable

conditional mean—the expected average score on the dependent variable, Y, for a given value of the independent variable, X

conditional odds—the chance of being in one category of a variable relative to the remaining categories of that variable, within a specific category of a second variable

conditional odds ratio—an odds ratio between two variables for a given category of a third variable

confidence interval—a range of values constructed around a point estimate that makes it possible to state the probability that an interval contains the population parameter between its upper and lower confidence limits

confidence interval for mean differences—an interval constructed around the point estimate of the difference between two means

confirmatory factor analysis (CFA)—a structural equation model, with one or more unobserved variables having multiple indicators, in which the research specifies the pattern of indicator loadings

consistent estimator—an estimator of a population parameter that approximates the parameter more closely as N gets larger

constant—a value that does not change

construct—unobserved concept used by social scientists to explain observations

continuous probability distribution—a probability distribution for a continuous variable, with no interruptions or spaces between the outcomes of the variable

continuous variable—a variable that, in theory, can take on all possible numerical values in a given interval

contrast—a set of weighted population means that sum to zero, used in making post hoc comparisons of treatment groups

correlated effect—a component in the decomposition of a correlation coefficient that is due to a correlation among predetermined variables

correlation coefficient—a measure of association between two continuous variables that estimates the direction and strength of linear relationship

correlation difference test—a statistical test to determine whether two correlation coefficients differ in the population

correlation ratio/eta-squared—a measure of nonlinear covariation between a discrete and a continuous variable, the ratio of $SS_{BETWEEN}$ to SS_{TOTAL}

covariance—the sum of the product of deviations of the X's and Y's about their respective means, divided by $N - 1$ in the sample and N in the population

covariate—a continuous variable in an analysis of covariance

covariation—joint variation, or association, between a pair of variables

critical value—the minimum value of Z necessary to designate an alpha area

Cronbach's alpha—a measure of internal reliability for multi-item summed indexes

cross-product ratio—see **odds ratio**

cumulative frequency—for a given score or outcome of a variable, the total number of cases in a distribution at or below that value

cumulative frequency distribution—a distribution of scores showing the number of cases at or below each outcome of the variable being displayed in the distribution

cumulative percentage—for a given score or outcome of a variable, the percentage of cases in a distribution at or below that value

cumulative percentage distribution—a distribution of scores showing the percentage of cases at or below each outcome of the variable being displayed in the distribution

data collection—the activity of constructing primary data records for a given sample or population of observations

data file—the entire set of numerical values for each variable for every case

deciles—the values of a number scale that divide a set of observations into 10 groups of equal size

decomposition—the division of a correlation coefficient into its component parts, involving direct effects, indirect effects, and dependence on common causes

degrees of freedom—the number of values free to vary when computing a statistic

dependent variable—a variable that has a consequent, or affected, role in relation to the independent variable

descriptive statistics—statistics concerned with summarizing the properties of a sample of observations

deterministic—a causal relationship in which a change in one variable always produces a constant change in another variable

diagram/graph—a visual representation of a set of data

dichotomous logistic regression equation— a regression of the logit for a dichotomous dependent variable that is a linear function of the independent variables

dichotomous variable—a discrete measure with two categories that may or may not be ordered

dichotomous variable/dichotomy—a variable having only two categories

direct effect—a connecting path in a causal model between two variables without an intervening third variable

discordant pair—in a crosstabulation of two orderable discrete variables, one member of a pair of observations ranks higher than the other member on one variable, but ranks lower on the second variable

discrete variable—a variable that classifies persons, objects, or events according to the kind or quality of their attributes

dummy variable—a variable coded 1 to indicate the presence of an attribute and 0 its absence

effect—the impact of the classification variable on the dependent variable

efficient estimator—the estimator of a population parameter among all possible estimators that has the smallest sampling variance

endogenous variable—a variable whose cause(s) of variation are represented in a model

epistemic relationship—the relationship between abstract, theoretical (unobserved) concepts and their corresponding operational (observed) measurements

error sum of squares—a numerical value obtained in linear regression by subtracting the regression sum of squares from the total sum of squares

error term—in ANOVA, that part of an observed score that cannot be attributed to either the common component or the group component. The difference between an observed score and a score predicted by the model

eta-squared—see **correlation ratio**

Euler's constant—an irrational number that is used as the base of natural logarithms

exhaustive—every case must receive a code for each variable, even if only a missing value can be assigned

exogenous variable—a predetermined variable whose causes remain unexplained, unanalyzed, and outside the scope of a model

expected frequency—in a chi-square test, the value that cell frequencies are expected to take, given the hypothesis under study (ordinarily, the null hypothesis)

expected value—the single number that best describes a probability distribution of discrete scores

explanation/interpretation of association—covariation between two variables due to an intervening third variable

exploratory data analysis—the methods for displaying distributions of continuous variables

F distribution—a theoretical probability distribution for one of a family of F ratios having v_1 and v_2 df in the numerator and denominator, respectively

factor analysis—a method that represents relations among observed variables in terms of latent constructs

factor loadings—parameters showing how observed variables are related to latent constructs

false acceptance error—see **Type II error**

false rejection error—see **Type I** error

first-order table—a subtable containing the crosstabulation or covariation between two variables, given a single outcome of a third, control variable

fitted marginal—the standard notation for a log-linear model

frequency distribution—a table of the outcomes, or response categories, of a variable and the number of times each outcome is observed

fundamental theorem of path analysis—an equation stating that the bivariate correlation between variables i and j implied by the hypothesized causal model is the sum of the products consisting of the path from variable q to variable i and the correlation between variable q and variable j; the sum of these products is formed over all Q variables that have direct paths to variable i

gamma—a symmetric measure of association suitable not only to crosstabs of two dichotomies, but also to tables whose variables are both ordered discrete measures with more than two categories

general linear model—a model that assumes the relationships among independent and dependent measures basically vary according to straight-line patterns

goodness-of-fit index (GFI)—the ratio between the minimum of the fitting function after the model is fitted to the fitting function before any model is fitted

goodness-of-fit statistic—a test statistic that uses standardized residuals to compare the observed probabilities to those predicted by the cquation

grand mean—in analysis of variance, the mean of all observations

graph—see **diagram**

grouped data—data that have been collapsed into a smaller number of categories

hierarchical log-linear model—a model in which the inclusion of multi-way effects also implies the inclusion of all less-complex effects

hinge spread/*H*-spread—the difference between the upper and lower hinges, i.e., $H_U - H_L$. Symbolized by HS

histogram—a type of diagram that uses bars to represent the frequency, proportion, or percentage of cases associated with each outcome or interval of outcomes of a variable

homoscedasticity—a condition in which the variances of the prediction errors are equal at every outcome of the predictor variable

homoscedasticity—a condition in which the variances of two or more population distributions are equal

independent variable—a variable that has an antecedent or causal role, usually appearing first in the hypothesis

index—a variable that is a summed composite of other variables that are assumed to reflect some underlying construct

index of diversity—measures whether two observations selected randomly from a population are likely to fall into the same or into different categories

index of qualitative variation—a measure of variation for discrete variables; a standardized version of the index of diversity

indicator—observable measure of an underlying unobservable theoretical construct

indirect causal effect—a causal effect of one variable on another that occurs through one or more intervening variables

indirect effect—a compound path connecting two variables in a causal model through an intervening third variable

inference—a generalization or conclusion about some attribute of a population based on the data in a sample. The process of making generalizations or drawing conclusions about the attributes of a population from evidence contained in a sample

inferential statistics—statistics that apply the mathematical theory of probability to make decisions about the likely properties of populations based on sample evidence

interaction effect—the association between two variables in each partial table differs when controlling for a third variable. Differences in the relationship between two variables within categories of a third variable

intercept— a constant value in a regression equation showing the point at which the regression line crosses the Y axis when values of X equal zero

iterative proportional fitting—a computer algorithm for successively approximating the expected frequencies in an unsaturated log-linear model

joint contingency table—see **bivariate crosstabulation**

lagged causal effect—direct effect of a variable measured prior to time t on a variable measured at time $t + 1$

latent variable—a variable that cannot be observed and can only be measured indirectly

likelihood ratio—the preferred test statistic for testing the fit between expected and observed frequencies in an unsaturated log-linear model

linear probability model—a linear regression model in which the dependent variable is confined between two choices

linear regression model—a model that takes into account deviations from the linear prediction by showing the linear relationship between a continuous dependent variable and one or more independent variables, plus an error term

linear relationship—covariation in which the value of the dependent variable is proportional to the value of the independent variable

linearity—the amount of change (increase or decrease) in one concept caused by a change in another concept is constant across its range

LISREL (LInear Structural RELations)—a computer program for estimating structure equation and confirmatory factor analysis models

listwise deletion—in multiple regression analysis, the removal of all cases that have missing values on *any* of the variables

log likelihood ratio—a ratio that contrasts two nested logistic regression equations, where one equation is a restricted version of the other

log-linear analysis—a technique for analyzing cross-classified data

logistic transformation of *p*—a natural logarithmic change in the odds of a probability

logit—logistic probability unit

logit model—a log-linear model in which one dichotomous variable is considered to be dependent on the other variables

lower confidence limit—the lowest value of a confidence interval

lower hinge—the value of the observation that divides the lower quartile from the upper three-quarters of an ordered distribution. Symbolized by H_L

lower inner fence—that part of an ordered distribution below which an observation is considered an outlier. Symbolized by LIF

manifest variable—a variable that can be observed

marginal distributions—the frequency distribution of each of two crosstabulated variables

marginal homogeneity—corresponding row and column marginal totals are equal

marginal subtable—a method to show the combinations of V variables that are necessary and sufficient to generate the expected cell frequencies of a full crosstab

Markovian principle—variables measured prior to time t have no causal impact on variables measured at time $t + 1$

maximum likelihood estimation—a method of estimating parameter values that chooses the set with the highest probability of generating the sample observations

mean—the arithmetic average of a set of data in which the values of all observations are added together and divided by the number of observations

mean of a probability distribution—the expected value of a population of scores

mean difference hypothesis test—a statistical test of a hypothesis about the difference between two population means

mean square—estimate of variance used in the analysis of variance. Estimate of variance in a linear regression

mean square between—a value in ANOVA obtained by dividing the between sum of squares by its degrees of freedom

mean square error—a value in linear regression obtained by dividing the error sum of squares by its degrees of freedom

mean square regression—a value in linear regression obtained by dividing the regression sum of squares by its degrees of freedom

mean square within—a value in ANOVA obtained by dividing the within sum of squares by its degrees of freedom

measurement—the process of assigning numbers to observations according to a set of rules

measurement interval/measurement class—a grouping of observations that is treated equally

measures of association—statistics that show the direction and/or magnitude of a relationship between pairs of discrete variables

measures of association—statistics that show the direction and/or magnitude of a relationship between variables

median—the outcome that divides an ordered distribution exactly into halves

midpoint—a number exactly halfway between the true upper and lower limits of a measurement class or interval, obtained by adding the upper to the lower limits and dividing by 2

MIMIC model—multiple-indicator and multiple-cause model in which variation in a single dependent variable with two or more indicators is directly caused by several predetermined variables, each of which has only a single indicator

missing data—no meaningful information for a given observation on a particular variable

misspecification—a condition in which a structural equation or path model includes incorrect variables or excludes correct variables

mode—the single category among the K categories in a distribution with the largest number (or highest percentage) of observations

multicollinearity—a condition of high or near perfect correlation among the independent variables in a multiple regression equation

multinomial-logit model—a logistic regression equation whose dependent variable has three or more categories

multiple causation—the view that social behavior is caused by more than one factor

multiple correlation coefficient—the coefficient for a multiple regression equation, which, when squared, equals the ratio of the sum of squares due to regression to the total sum of squares

multiple regression analysis—a statistical technique for estimating the relationship between a continuous dependent variable and two or more continuous or discrete independent, or predictor, variables

multiple regression coefficient—a measure of association showing the amount of increase or decrease in a continuous dependent variable for a one-unit difference in the independent variable, controlling for the other independent variable(s)

multivariate contingency analysis—statistical techniques for analyzing relationships among three or more discrete variables

multivariate contingency table analysis —the statistical analysis of data on three or more categorical variables

mutually exclusive—each observation must receive one and only one code on a given variable

negative skew—the tail of a skewed distribution is to the left of the median (median greater than mean)

nested models—models in which every parameter included in one model also appears in another model

nested regression equations—regression equations where independent variables are successively added to an equation to observe changes in the predictors' relationships to the dependent variable

Newton–Raphson algorithm—an iterative proportional fitting procedure used in log-linear analysis

nonorderable discrete variable—a discrete measure in which the sequence of categories cannot be meaningfully ordered

nonrecursive model—a model in which causal influences between dependent variables may occur in both directions

nonsaturated model—a log-linear model in which one or more of the lambda parameters equals 0

nonspuriousness—covariation between two variables that is causal and not due to the effects of a third variable

normal distribution—a smooth, bell-shaped theoretical probability distribution for continuous variables that can be generated from a formula

null hypothesis—a statistical hypothesis that one usually expects to reject. Symbolized H_0

odds—the frequency of being in one category relative to the frequency of not being in that category

odds ratio/cross-product ratio—the ratio formed by dividing one conditional odds by another conditional odds

one-tailed hypothesis test—a hypothesis test in which the alternative is stated in such a way that the probability of making a Type I error is entirely in one tail of a probability distribution

operational hypothesis—a proposition restated with observable, concrete referents or terms replacing abstract concepts

orderable discrete variable—a discrete measure that can be meaningfully arranged into an ascending or descending sequence

ordinary least squares—a method for obtaining estimates of regression equation coefficients that minimizes the error sum of squares

outcome—a response category of a variable

outlier—an observed value that is so extreme (either large or small) that it seems to stand apart from the rest of the distribution

pairwise deletion—in multiple regression analysis, the removal of a case from the calculation of a correlation coefficient only if it has missing values for one of the variables

parallel measures—measures with equal true scores

part correlation—a measure of the proportion of variance in a dependent variable that an independent variable can explain, when squared, after controlling for the other independent variable in a multiple regression equation

partial correlation coefficient—a measure of association for continuous variables that shows the magnitude and direction of covariation between two variables that remains after the effects of a control variable have been held constant

partial regression coefficient—the effect of regressing a dependent variable on an independent variable, controlling for one or more other independent variables

path analysis—a statistical method for analyzing quantitative data that yields empirical estimates of the effects of variables in a hypothesized causal system

path coefficient—a numerical estimate of the causal relationships between two variables in a path analysis

percentage—a number created by multiplying a proportion by 100

percentage distribution—a distribution of relative frequencies or proportions in which each entry has been multiplied by 100

percentile—the outcome or score below which a given percentage of the observations in a distribution falls

phi—a symmetric measure of association for 2×2 crosstabulations

phi adjusted—a symmetric measure of association for a 2×2 crosstabulation in which phi is divided by phi maximum to take into account the largest covariation possible, given the marginals

phi maximum—the largest value that phi can attain for a given 2×2 crosstabulation; used in adjusting phi for its marginals

planned comparison—hypothesis test of differences between and among population means carried out before doing an analysis of variance

point estimate—a sample statistic used to estimate a population parameter

point estimate for mean differences—the difference between the sample means used to estimate the difference between two population means

polygon—a diagram constructed by connecting the midpoints of a histogram with a straight line

population—the entire set of persons, objects, or events that has at least one common characteristic of interest to a researcher

population parameter—a descriptive characteristic of a population, such as a mean, standard deviation, or variance. Symbolized by θ

population regression equation—a regression equation for a population rather than a sample

population regression model—a regression model for a population in which K independent variables are each hypothesized to affect a dependent, continuous variable in a linear, additive manner

positive skew—the tail of a skewed distribution is to the right of the median (mean greater than median)

post hoc comparison—hypothesis test of the differences among population means carried out following an analysis of variance

power of the test—the probability of correctly rejecting H_0 when H_0 is false

prediction equation—a regression equation without the error term, useful for predicting the score on the dependent variable from the independent variable(s)

predictor variable—independent variable in a regression analysis

probabilistic—a causal relationship in which a change in one variable produces a change in another variable, with a certain probability of occurrence

probability distribution—a set of outcomes, each of which has an associated probability of occurrence

probability/alpha level—the probability selected for rejection of a null hypothesis, which is the likelihood of making a Type I error

proportion—see **relative frequency**

proposition—a statement about the relationship between abstract concepts

pseudo-R^2—a descriptive measure for logistic regression that indicates roughly the proportion of variation in the dependent variable accounted for by the predictors

quantile—a division of observations into groups with known proportions in each group

quartiles—the values of a number scale that divide a set of observations into four groups of equal size

quasi-independence model—a model that ignores structural-zero cells and tests for independence only among the remaining entries

quasi-symmetry model—a special type of symmetry that preserves the inequality of the corresponding row and column marginals but produces equal corresponding odds ratios among the off-diagonal cells

quintiles—the values of a number scale that divide a set of observations into five groups of equal size

r-to-Z transformation—a natural logarithm transformation in the value of the correlation coefficient to a Z score, to test the probability of observing r under the null hypothesis

random assignment—in an experiment, the assignment of subjects to treatment levels on a chance basis

random error—errors of measurement that are unpredictable

random sample—a sample whose cases or elements are selected at random from a population

random sampling—a procedure for selecting a set of representative observations from a population, in which each observation has an equal chance of being selected for the sample

random zero—a combination of variables that is unrepresented in a sample

range—the difference between the largest and smallest scores in a distribution

recode—the process of changing the codes established for a variable

recoding—the process of grouping continuous variables from many initial values into fewer categories

recursive model—a model in which all the causal influences are assumed to be asymmetric (one-way)

reference variable—an observed variable in a confirmatory factor analysis with a fixed factor loading

regression difference test—a statistical test to determine whether two regression coefficients differ in the population

regression line—a line that is the best fit to the points in a scatterplot, computed by ordinary least squares regression

regression sum of squares—a number obtained in linear regression by subtracting the mean of a set of scores from the value predicted by linear regression, squaring, and summing these values

regression toward the mean—a condition demonstrated when the predicted scores on the dependent variable show less variability about the mean than the observed scores do, due to the imperfect correlation between two variables

relative frequency/proportion—the number of cases in an outcome divided by the total number of cases

relative frequency distribution—a distribution of outcomes of a variable in which the number of times each outcome is observed has been divided by the total number of cases

reliability—the extent to which different operationalizations of the same concept produce consistent results

representativeness—the selection of units of analysis whose characteristics accurately stand for the larger population from which the sample was drawn

research hypothesis—a substantive hypothesis that one usually does not expect to reject

residual—the amount that remains after subtracting the prediction equation from the linear regression model

residual variable—an unmeasured variable in a path model that is posited as causing the unexplained part of an observed variable

robust—methods used in which violating assumptions will seldom produce wrong conclusions

root mean square error of approximation (RMSEA)—a measure of model fit that adjusts the population discrepancy function for the number of degrees of freedom used in fitting the model

rounding—expressing digits in more convenient and interpretable units, such as tens, hundreds, or thousands, by applying an explicit rule

row marginals—the frequency distribution of the variable shown across the rows of a crosstabulation

sample—a subset of cases or elements selected from a population

sample regression equation—a regression model for a sample with K independent variables which includes the error term

sampling distribution of sample means—a distribution consisting of the means of all samples of size N that could be formed from a given population

saturated model—a log-linear model in which all possible effects among variables are present

scale construction—the creation of new variables from multiple items

scatterplot—a type of diagram that displays the covariation of two continuous variables as a set of points on a Cartesian coordinate system

Scheffé test—one form of post hoc comparison of differences in group means

scientific research—the effort to reduce uncertainty about some aspect of the world by systematically examining the relationships among its parts

scope/boundary conditions—the times, places, or activities under which the propositions of a social theory are expected to be valid

significance testing with proportions—using statistical tests to determine whether the observed difference between sample proportions could occur by chance in the populations from which the samples were selected

single-link causal chain—a LISREL model in which one exogenous variable causes variation in one endogenous variable, both of which have multiple indicators

skewed distribution—a distribution that is nonsymmetric about its median value, having many categories with small frequencies at one end

social theory—a set of two or more propositions in which concepts referring to certain social phenomena are assumed to be causally related

Somers's d_{yx}—an asymmetric PRE measure of association for discrete ordered variables that counts not only the number of concordant and discordant unified pairs, but also the number of tied pairs of a certain type

spuriousness—covariation between two variables due only to the effect of a third variable

standard deviation—the positive square root of the variance

standard error—the standard deviation of a sampling distribution

standardized solution—latent constructs have unit variances, while the indicators are still in their original metrics

statistical significance test—a test of inference that conclusions based on a sample of observations also hold true for the population from which the sample was selected

statistical table—a numerical display that either summarizes data or presents the results of a data analysis

statistically independent—a condition of no relationship between variables in a population

status variable—a variable whose outcomes cannot be manipulated

stem-and-leaf diagram—a type of graph that displays the observed values and frequency counts of a frequency distribution

structural equation—a mathematical equation representing the structure of hypothesized relationships among variables in a social theory

structural equation model—a causal model with latent variables and observable indicators

structural zero—a combination of variables that cannot logically occur

sufficient estimator—an estimator of a population parameter that cannot be improved by adding information

suspending judgment—a position taken by a researcher when the results of a statistical test permit neither clear rejection nor clear acceptance of the null hypothesis or alternative hypothesis

symmetry model—a model that predicts exactly equal frequencies in corresponding cells of a $K \times K$ crosstabulation

system file—a data file created by a computer software statistics package

systematic error—errors of measurement arising from miscalibrated instruments

systematic sampling interval—the number of cases between sample elements in a list used for a systematic random sample

t **distribution**—one of a family of test statistics used with small samples selected from a normally distributed population or, for large samples, drawn from a population with any shape

t **test**—a test of significance for continuous variables where the population variance is unknown and the sample is assumed to have been drawn from a normally distributed population

t **variable/*t* score**—a transformation of the scores of a continuous frequency distribution derived by subtracting the mean and dividing by the estimated standard error

tally—a count of the frequency of outcomes observed for a variable or the frequency of joint outcomes of several variables

tau *c*—a non-PRE-type measure of association that uses information about the number of concordant and discordant unified pairs in a crosstab of two discrete ordered variables

tied pair—a pair in which both cases have the same value on at least one of the variables

time order—the necessary condition that changes in a purported independent variable must precede in time the change in the dependent measure, when a causal relationship between the two is assumed

total sum of squares—a number obtained by subtracting the scores of a distribution from their mean, squaring, and summing these values. The total of regression and error sums of squares

treatment level—a term in experimental research to indicate the experimental group to which a subject has been assigned

true limits—the exact lower and upper bounds of numerical values that could be rounded into the category

2 × 2 table—a crosstabulation of a pair of dichotomies

two-tailed hypothesis test—a hypothesis test in which the region of rejection falls equally within both tails of the sampling distribution

Type I error/false rejection error—a statistical decision error that occurs when a true null hypothesis is rejected; its probability is alpha

Type II error/false acceptance error—a statistical decision error that occurs when a false null hypothesis is not rejected; its probability is beta

unbiased estimator—an estimator of a population parameter whose expected value equals the parameter

unit of analysis—an object for observation

untied pair—one in which both cases have different values on two variables

upper confidence limit—the highest value of a confidence interval

upper hinge—the value of the observation that divides the upper quartile from the lower three-quarters of an ordered distribution. Symbolized by H_U

upper inner fence—that part of an ordered distribution above which an observation is considered to be an outlier. Symbolized by UIF

validity—the degree to which a variable's operationalization accurately reflects the concept it is intended to measure

variable—any characteristic or attribute of persons, objects, or events that can take on different numerical values

variance—the mean squared deviation of a continuous distribution

variance of a probability distribution—the expected spread or dispersion of a population of scores

variation—the spread or dispersion of a set of scores around some central value

Venn diagram—a type of graph that uses overlapping shaded circles to demonstrate relationships or covariation among a set of variables

weighted least squares (WLS)—an estimation method used to estimate correlations among ordered indicators

within sum of squares—a value obtained by subtracting each subgroup mean from each observed score, squaring, and summing

Yule's Q—a symmetric measure of association for 2×2 crosstabulations

Z scores—a transformation of the scores of a continuous frequency distribution by subtracting the mean from each outcome and dividing by the standard deviation

zero-order table—a crosstabulation of two variables in which no additional variables have been controlled

LIST OF MATHEMATICAL AND STATISTICAL SYMBOLS

AAD   Average absolute deviation.

AGFI   Adjusted goodness-of-fit index.

a 1. The point at which a line intercepts the Y-axis ($X = 0$).
2. Intercept term in a regression equation for sample data.

α 1. Greek lowercase letter *alpha*.
2. Alpha area.
3. Probability level of committing a Type I error.
4. Population regression intercept.

α_j The effect of the jth group.

$\alpha/2$ Alpha area of only one tail of a distribution.

BIC   A test statistic for assessing log-linear models fitted to large-scale crosstabulations.

b Bivariate regression coefficient for a sample.

β 1. Greek lowercase letter *beta*.
2. Probability of committing a Type II error.
3. Population regression coefficient.

B   Greek uppercase letter *beta*.

β_j Regression coefficient for the jth predictor.

β_j^* Standardized regression coefficient for the jth predictor.

β^X Logit effect parameters for variable X.

β_{YX}	Population parameter for the regression of Y on X.
β^*_{YX}	1. Beta coefficient.
	2. Standardized regression coefficient for a population.
b_{YX}	Regression coefficient of Y on X in a sample.
cf	Cumulative frequency distribution.
c_j	Weights under the constraint that $c_1 + c_2 + \cdots + c_j = 0$.
$c\%$	Cumulative percentage.
D	1. Index of diversity.
	2. Dummy variable.
δ	Greek lowercase letter *delta*.
df	Degrees of freedom.
Δdf	Change in degres of freedom.
df_{ERROR}	Error degrees of freedom.
$df_{\mathrm{REGRESSION}}$	Regression degrees of freedom.
df_{TOTAL}	Total degrees of freedom.
D_i	Score of the ith decile.
d_i	Deviation (distance) of a score from the mean.
d_{yx}	Somers's d_{yx}, a measure of association.
e	1. Euler's constant.
	2. Base for natural logarithm.
$E(Y)$	Expected value of a probability distribution.
e_i	Error term for the ith observation.
e_{ij}	The error score unique to the ith case in the jth group.
ε	Greek lowercase letter *epsilon*.
η	Greek lowercase letter *eta*.
η^2	Correlation ratio for a population.
$\hat{\eta}^2$	Sample estimate of the correlation ratio.
F	1. Population discrepancy function.
	2. F distribution.
$f(Y)$	A function of Y.
F_{ij}	The expected value of the frequency in the (i,j)th cell.
$\ln F_{ij}$	Natural logarithm of the expected cell frequency.
f_{ij}	The observed frequency in the (i,j)th cell.

$\mathbf{F[S, \Sigma(0)]}$	Fit function.
$\mathrm{F(\mathbf{S}, \boldsymbol{\Sigma})}$	Fitting function for determining the fit closeness between $\mathbf{S}$ and $\boldsymbol{\Sigma}$.
f_i	Frequency associated with the ith outcome category of a variable.
G	Gamma, a measure of association.
G^2	Test statistic that compares the ratio of two likelihoods.
GFI	Goodness-of-fit index.
γ	1. Greek lowercase letter *gamma*. 2. Population parameter that G estimates.
Γ	Greek uppercase letter *gamma*.
$g(Y)$	A function of Y.
H_0	Null hypothesis.
H_1	Alternate hypothesis.
H_L	Lower hinge.
HS	*H*-spread.
H_U	Upper hinge.
$\mathbf{I}$	Identity matrix.
IQV	Index of qualitative variation.
K_i	Score of the ith quintile.
K_0	More-restricted equation.
K_1	Less-restricted equation.
λ_{ij}^{XY}	The effect of association between variables on the expected logs of crosstabulated cell frequencies.
L_i	1. Logit. 2. Natural log of an odds.
L^2	Likelihood ratio.
ΔL^2	The difference in L^2 values in nested models.
LIF	Lower inner fence.
$\log_e$	Natural logarithm.
$\log_{10}$	Base 10 logarithm.
m	The smaller of R rows and C columns.
Mdn	Median.
MLE	Maximum likelihood estimation.

MS_{BETWEEN}	Mean square between.
MS_{ERROR}	Mean square error.
$MS_{\text{REGRESSION}}$	Mean square regression.
MS_{WITHIN}	Mean square within.
μ	1. Greek lowercase letter *mu*.
	2. Constant applied to every cell of a crosstab in log-linear analysis.
μ_Y	Mean of a population.
$\mu_{\bar{Y}}$	Mean of the sampling distribution of means for variable Y.
$\mu_{(\bar{Y}_1 - \bar{Y}_2)}$	Mean difference between the means of variables Y_1 and Y_2 in two populations.
N	Total sample size.
n_d	Number of discordant pairs.
n_s	Number of concordant pairs.
ν	1. Greek lowercase letter *nu*.
	2. Degrees of freedom in a t distribution.
ν_1, ν_2	Number of degrees of freedom in an F distribution.
OR^{XY}	The odds ratio of variables X and Y.
$\text{OR}^{(XY|Z=1)}$	Conditional odds ratio.
$1 - \beta$	Power of the test.
φ	1. Greek lowercase letter *phi*.
	2. A measure of association.
Φ	Greek uppercase letter *phi*.
φ_{adj}	Phi adjusted.
φ_{max}	Phi maximum.
P_i	Score of the ith percentile.
p_i	Proportion of cases in the ith outcome of a variable.
p_{ij}	Path coefficient to variable i from variable j.
$\hat{p}_{ij}$	Estimate of population path coefficient parameter.
ψ	1. Greek lowercase letter *psi*.
	2. Contrast between population means.
Ψ	Greek uppercase letter *psi*.
PRE	Proportionate reduction in error.

$\text{Prob}(Y_i = 1)$	Probability that the ith observation of variable Y has a score of 1.
$p(Y_i)$	Probability of the ith outcome of variable Y.
Q	Yule's Q, a measure of association.
Q_i	Score of the ith quartile.
ϱ_X	Reliability of variable x.
ϱ_{YX}	Correlation of variables X and Y in a population.
$\varrho^2_{Y \cdot X}$	Coefficient of determination in a population.
r'_{ij}	Estimated correlation of variables i and j.
$\mathbf{R}$	Residual matrix.
R^2_{adj}	Adjusted coefficient of determination.
R^2_{YX}	1. R-square. 2. Coefficient of determination in a sample.
$R^2_{Y \cdot X}$	Coefficient of determination in a sample.
$R^2_{Y \cdot X_1 X_2 \ldots X_K}$	Multiple regression coefficient of determination for an equation with K predictors.
$r_{XY \cdot W}$	The partial correlation between X and Y, controlling for (or in the presence of) W.
$r_{YX_j \cdot X_i}$	Partial correlation coefficient.
r_{YX}	Correlation coefficient in a sample.
$r_{Z_X Z_Y}$	Correlation of two Z scores in a sample.
$\mathbf{S}$	1. Variance–covariance matrix. 2. Matrix of observed covariances among observable indicators.
$\hat{s}_\lambda$	The standard error of a lambda effect paramter in a saturated log-linear model.
s_b	Standard error of a regression coefficient in a sample.
s_{b_j}	Standard error of a regression coefficient for the jth predictor in a sample.
$s_{b_1 - b_2}$	Standard error of the difference in regression coefficients in a sample.
Σ	Greek uppercase letter *sigma*.
$\mathbf{\Sigma}$	Matrix of expected covariances among observable indicators.
σ^2_T	Variance of true score.

$\hat{\sigma}^2_\psi$	Estimated variance of a contrast.
$\hat{\sigma}^2_Z$	Estimated variance of a standardized variable.
σ^2_e	1. Standard error of estimate in a population.
	2. Variance of regression prediction errors.
σ_Y	Standard deviation of variable Y in a population.
$\hat{\sigma}_{\bar{Y}}$	Estimated standard error for a population.
σ^2_Y	Variance of variable Y in a population.
σ^2_b	Squared standard error of a regression coefficient in a population.
$\sigma_{(\bar{Y}_1 - \bar{Y}_2)}$	Standard error of the sampling distribution for the difference between the means of variables Y_1 and Y_2 in two populations.
$\hat{\sigma}_{(\bar{Y}_1 - \bar{Y}_2)}$	Estimated standard error of the sampling distribution for the difference between the means of variables Y_2 and Y_1 in two populations.
$\hat{\sigma}_{\tau_c}$	Standard error of the sampling distribution for tau c.
$\hat{\sigma}_{d_{yx}}$	Standard error of the sampling distribution for Somers's d_{yx}.
s_p	Standard error of a sampling distribution of proportions in a sample.
s^2	Variance of a sample.
$s^2_{Z_Y}$	Variance of estimated Z scores for variable Y.
s_{YX}	Covariance of variables X and Y in a sample.
s^2_Y	Variance of variable Y in a sample.
SS_{BETWEEN}	Between sum of squares.
SS_{ERROR}	Error sum of squares.
$SS_{\text{REGRESSION}}$	Regression sum of squares.
SS_{TOTAL}	Total sum of squares.
SS_{WITHIN}	Within sum of squares.
t	1. t variable.
	2. t score.
t_α	Critical value of t for a one-tailed test.
$t_{\alpha/2}$	Critical value of t for a two-tailed test.
τ_c	Tau c, a measure of association.

θ 1. Greek lowercase letter *theta*.
        2. Population parameter.

Θ Greek uppercase letter *theta*.

T True score of a variable.

T_r The number of ties associated with the row variable.

UIF   Upper inner fence.

$\{XY\}$ Fitted marginal table for variables X and Y in a log-linear analysis.

$\bar{Y}$ Mean of variable Y in a sample.

$\hat{Y}_i$ Predicted or expected value of variable Y for the ith observation.

χ^2 Chi-square distribution.

Z^2 Goodness-of-fit statistic.

Z_α Critical value of Z for a one-tailed test.

$Z_{\alpha/2}$ Critical value of Z for a two-tailed test.

Z_i Standardized score for the ith observation.

$\hat{Z}_Y$ Estimated Z score for variable Y.

Answers to Problems

Chapter 1

1. For example, *age strata* are divisions by age of people and roles within a society or group.

2. P1: The more time spent viewing television, the lower the school achievement. P2: The lower the parental supervision, the greater the incidence of delinquent behavior.

3. The theory probably applies to nonindustrial societies of the twentieth century with central government family planning programs.

4. Husbands and wives are more likely to share household chores when both spouses agree that men and women should have equal opportunities and responsibilities.

5. (a) Race is independent, and hourly wage is dependent.
   (b) Vulnerability to overseas competition is independent, and strategic alliance formation is dependent.
   (c) Psychological insecurity is independent, and cult popularity is dependent.

6. (a) Constant
   (b) Variable
   (c) Variable
   (d) Constant
   (e) Variable
   (f) Constant

7. Using a systematic sample of $k = 14$ will yield 312 employees to be interviewed.

8. (a) These six categories are neither mutually exclusive nor exhaustive.
   (b) For national origins, present a list of about 100 countries, excluding cities and continents, and allow respondents to volunteer responses not offered on the list.

9. (a) Continuous
   (b) Orderable discrete
   (c) Continuous
   (d) Continuous
   (e) Dichotomous
   (f) Nonorderable discrete
   (g) Orderable discrete
   (h) Continuous

10. (a) Social theory
    (b) Basic researchers
    (c) Reliable
    (d) Dependent, independent
    (e) Data collection
    (f) Population
    (g) Missing data

Chapter 2

1.

Score	Tally	f
5	I	1
6	IIII	4
7	IIIII	5
8	III	3
9	II	2
10	I	1
11	I	1
12	I	1
Total		18

2.

State	f	p	%
M	7	.368	36.8
W	4	.211	21.1
I	3	.158	15.8
N	2	.105	10.5
S	3	.158	15.8
Total	19	1.000	100.0%

3.

Prices	cf	c%
$999 and under	2	22.2
$1,000–1,499	4	44.4
$1,500–1,999	8	88.9
$2,000 and over	9	100.0
Total	9	100.0

4. (a) 9
   (b) 3
   (c) 6
   (d) 13
   (e) 19
   (f) 4

5. Graphs not shown.

6. (a) 6
   (b) 1.68
   (c) 5.30
   (d) 2.30

7. (a) 65.8
   (b) 63
   (c) 63

8. (a) 362.3 million
   (b) none
   (c) 163 million
   (d) 176,806.0
   (e) 420.5

9. 0.2496

10. (a) +2.43
    (b) −3.29
    (c) −1.86

11. The range is 30 brothers and sisters. The modal frequency is two siblings (19.8% of the sample), while the mean is 3.98 and the median is 3.00. The variance is 12.85, the standard deviation is 3.59, and the skewness is 2.39.

12. (a) 2
    (b) 2.00
    (c) 7 children
    (d) 2.44
    (e) 0.84
    (f) 0.91
    (g) 1.29
    (h) $Z = +1.71$

13. (a) 0
    (b) 3.00
    (c) 6
    (d) 2.81
    (e) 3.84
    (f) 1.96
    (g) −0.17
    (h) $Z = -0.92$

14. The modal category for ABSINGLE is "No," but the mode for ABHLTH is "Yes."

15. Percent expressing confidence in American institutions:

Amount of Confidence	Press	Medicine
A great deal	9.5	45.0
Some	47.2	46.1
Hardly any	43.4	8.9
Total	100.0%	100.0%
(N)	(1,862)	(1,875)

Confidence in the press and in medicine have almost inverse distributions, with respective means of 2.34 and 1.64 and identical standard deviations of 0.64.

Chapter 3

1. (a) 16.75
   (b) 13.5

2. At least .75.

3. (a) 30
   (b) 25
   (c) 10

4. (a) 1.64
   (b) 1.28
   (c) 2.33
   (d) ±1.96
   (e) ±1.75
   (f) ±1.44

5. (a) $\mu_{\bar{Y}} = 10.5, \sigma_{\bar{Y}} = 1.41$
   (b) $\mu_{\bar{Y}} = 50, \sigma_{\bar{Y}} = 1.00$
   (c) $\mu_{\bar{Y}} = 25, \sigma_{\bar{Y}} = .55$
   (d) $\mu_{\bar{Y}} = 12, \sigma_{\bar{Y}} = 1.41$
   (e) $\mu_{\bar{Y}} = 100, \sigma_{\bar{Y}} = .71$

6. (a) 1.711
   (b) ± 2.797

7. (a) LCL = 14.80, UCL = 21.20
   (b) LCL = 13.58, UCL = 22.42

8. (a) 2.492
   (b) 24
   (c) 3.00
   (d) Reject the null hypothesis.

9. (a) ± 3.646
   (b) 35
   (c) −1.25
   (d) Do not reject the null hypothesis.

10. With $df = 49$, the critical value for t at $\alpha = .01$, one-tailed, is 2.423.
    The observed value of $t_{49} = 5.304$, so reject the null hypothesis.

The senator's approval rating is above the minimum level for continuing her current agenda.

11. The empirical probability of being 28 or older when the first child is born is 0.2171, which is less than the probability of being 21 or younger.

12. $t_{1861} = 13.29$, so reject the null hypothesis that the mean on SOCOMMUN is equal to or less than 4.00.

13. $t_{682} = 27.51$, so reject the null hypothesis that females' mean on FAMSUFFR = 2.00.

14. $t_{381} = -7.52$, so reject the null hypothesis that full-time working men volunteered for a charitable organization one or more times in the last 12 months.

15. $t_{82} = 5.42$, so do not reject the null hypothesis that the mean response to MODPAINT is greater than 2.00.

Chapter 4

1. $H_0: \mu_D = \mu_I = \mu_R; H_1: \mu_D > \mu_I > \mu_R$

2. $\alpha_{65+} = +7.5; \alpha_{55-64} = +0.6; \alpha_{45-54} = -8.1$

3. $\alpha_{eng} = +8.8; \alpha_{tech} = +0.3; \alpha_{admin} = -8.1$

4. (a) $F_{2,17} = 3.59$
   (b) $F_{1,123} = 6.8$
   (c) $F_{5,30} = 5.53$
   (d) $F_{24,40} = 3.01$

5. (a) $F_{1,25} = 4.24$
   (b) $F_{2,40} = 5.18$
   (c) $F_{2,17} = 10.66$
   (d) $F_{3,60} = 6.17$

6. 41 years

7. $MS_{\text{BETWEEN}} = 15.56$

8. $\hat{\eta}^2 = 0.13$; $F_{3,120} = 5.90$, which is greater than the critical value of 2.68, so reject H_0 at $\alpha < .05$ and conclude that the four county means do differ.

9. $\alpha_{\text{adult}} = +0.67$; $\alpha_{\text{student}} = +0.07$; $\alpha_{\text{classmate}} = -0.73$

Source	SS	df	MS	F
Between	4.93	2	2.47	1.12
Within	26.40	12	2.20	
Total	31.33	14		

Because the critical value = 3.89 for $\alpha = .05$, do not reject the null hypothesis. We find $\hat{\eta}^2 = 0.157$; that is, only 15.7% of the variation in quiz scores can be explained by the type of reading group.

10. $\hat{\psi} = .50$; $\hat{\sigma}^2_\psi = 0.165$; $t = 1.23$; because the critical value = 2.79, do not reject H_0.

11. $F_{8,1380} = 4.28$, $p < .001$, $\hat{\eta}^2 = 0.024$. Approval of professional athletes thanking God is highest in the East South Central, South Atlantic, West South Central, and West North Central states, lowest in the other regions, but less than 3% of the variation in GODSPORT is explained by REGION.

12. $F_{5,\,1736} = 6.88$, $p < .001$, $\hat{\eta}^2 = 0.019$. Attitude towards divorce law is linear, increasing from 2.16 for people younger than 30 years old to 2.51 for those aged 60–69 years and 2.51 for those aged 70 or older. Age explains 2% of the variation in attitude towards divorce law.

13. $F_{2,1818} = 50.62$, $p < .001$, $\hat{\eta}^2 = 0.053$. Whites and "Others" are more likely than Blacks to believe that Blacks can work their way up and overcome prejudice without favors. Race explains 5.3% of the variation in attitude towards overcoming prejudice.

14. $t = -9.19$, $p < .001$. People who approve of the Supreme Court's ruling against reading the Lord's Prayer or Bible verses in public schools consider themselves to be somewhat less conservative than those who disapprove of the Court's decision.

15. $F_{5,1794} = 24.91, p < .001$. Attitude towards premarital sex is linear, decreasing from 3.07 for adults under 30 to 2.09 for adults aged 70 or older. Younger people are less likely to believe that premarital sex is wrong.

Chapter 5

1.

		Gender		
		Male	*Female*	*Total*
Smoking	Yes	8	4	12
	No	5	8	13
	Total	13	12	25

2. $\chi^2 = 14.83$, $df = 1$, $p < .001$; Yule's $Q = 0.20$; this indicates a very weak—almost nonexistent—relationship, with women more likely than men to vote for Clinton.

3. $\varphi = -0.42$

4. $\varphi_{adj} = -0.48$; this adjustment indicates a slightly stronger inverse relationship than suggested in the observed data.

5. Gamma = +0.66; there is a moderate positive relationship between political attitudes and views towards public funding of private schools.

6. $\tau_c = +0.48$ and $\hat{\sigma}_{\tau_c} = 0.11$; because $Z = 4.36$ and the c.v. at $\alpha = .01$ for $df = 59$ is 2.66, so we reject the null hypothesis that political attitudes and views on public funding for private schools are unrelated.

7. Somers's $d_{yx} = +0.49$ and $\hat{\sigma}_{d_{yx}} = 0.11$; because $Z = 4.45$, the c.v. at $\alpha = .01$ for $df = 59$ is 2.66, so we reject the null hypothesis that political attitudes and views on public funding for private schools are unrelated.

8. The odds in favor for men = 4.10; the odds in favor for women = 2.51; the odds ratio = 1.63, indicating that men are about 1.63 times more favorable than women towards allowing an atheist to speak.

9. The odds in favor for the more educated = 6.33; the odds in favor for the less educated = 2.33; the odds ratio = 2.72, indicating that the more educated are more than twice as likely to favor allowing an atheist to speak in public.

10. Gamma = +0.04; TV watching and confidence in the press are very weakly related.

11. $\chi^2 = 9.60$, $df = 1$, $p < .01$; phi = 0.08; whites are more willing than blacks to allow a racist to speak in public.

12. $\chi^2 = 142.47$, $df = 2$, $p < .001$; gamma = –0.52; tau $c = -0.27$; Somers's $d_{yx} = -0.23$, with SPKCOM dependent. People with more education are more willing to allow a communist to speak in public than are people with less education.

13. $\chi^2 = 40.55$, $df = 2$, $p < .001$; gamma = –0.27; tau $c = -0.15$; Somers's $d_{yx} = -0.13$, with SPKRAC dependent. People with more education are more willing to allow a racist to speak in public than are people with less education.

14. $\chi^2 = 90.89$, $df = 3$, $p < .001$; Somers's $d_{yx} = +0.33$, with PREMARSX dependent. People with more conservative sex role attitudes are more likely to believe that premarital sex is wrong.

15. $\chi^2 = 100.48$, $df = 12$, $p < .001$; Somers's $d_{yx} = 0.18$, with HOMOSEX dependent. Better-educated people tend to be more tolerant of homosexuality.

Chapter 6

1. Scatterplot not shown. Increased age is associated with a greater number of children.

2. $\hat{Y}_i = 1.0 + 2.25X_i$. Each increase of one friend in the community increases community involvement by 2.25.

3. (a) 4.40
   (b) 3.86

4. (a) 20,250
   (b) 40.21
   (c) 955.70
   (d) 351.84

5. $R^2_{YX} = 0.23$; reject the null hypothesis of no relationship between employees' work satisfaction and variety of responsibilities at $\alpha = .01$.

Source	SS	df	MS	F
Regression	1,675	1	1,675	12.18
Error	5,500	40	137.5	
Total	7,175	41		

6. $r_{YX} = 0.98$; $R^2_{YX} = 0.96$

7. $\hat{Y}_i = -15.62 + 0.29X_i$; a one-point increase on the trust scale increases the number of altruistic acts by almost one third.

8. $r_{YX} = 0.97$; $R^2_{YX} = 0.95$; $1 - R^2_{YX} = 0.05$; trust in other people is strongly related to the number of altruistic acts performed. Ninety-five percent of the variation in altruistic acts is "explained" by trust in other people. Five percent of the variation is not explained.

9. $t_{29} = 2.33$; reject H_0 at $\alpha = .05$.

10. (a) 0.13
    (b) −0.66
    (c) 0.79

11. $\hat{Y}_i = 6.16 + 0.03X_i$; $t_{1,1242} = 5.07$, meaning that older people are more likely to pray than younger people.

12. For mother's attendance: $R^2_{YX} = 0.05$; $F_{1,1098} = 62.19$; so reject H_0. For father's attendance: $R^2_{YX} = 0.06$; $F_{1,1030} = 59.53$; so reject H_0. Mother's and father's church attendance explains 5.0% and 6.0%, respectively, of the variation in religious service attendance.

13. $r_{YX} = -0.30$; $\hat{Z}_{Y_i} = -0.30Z_i$; $t_{1997} = -13.97$; meaning that the younger the parent's age at first birth, the more children ever born.

14. $\hat{Y}_i = 5.51 + 0.59X_i$; $F_{1,1304} = 707.95$, $p < .01$; so reject H_0. For each additional year of schooling, spouse's educational attainment increases by 1 year.

15. $R^2_{YX} = 0.004$; $F_{1,868} = 3.91$; $p > .01$; there is no relationship between income and giving to non-religious charitable organizations.

Chapter 7

1. These hypotheses suggest a causal sequence in which response to communication cues interprets the relationship between amount of interaction and marital satisfaction. Diagram is not shown.

2. Workers with more seniority likely perceive their jobs as more secure than workers with less seniority. Similarly, a significant portion of salary increases might be due to seniority in an organization. If these assumptions are correct, holding seniority constant would cause the correlation between perceived job security and income to fall to zero. Diagram is not shown.

3. Examples of such relationships include the following: (a) Higher campaign budgets allow candidates to develop higher-profile advertising campaigns, giving them greater visibility and increasing their chances of being elected. (b) Higher campaign budgets give candidates an ability to travel more extensively and meet more voters, increasing their chances of being elected. (c) Higher campaign budgets provide candidates with easier access to powerful social networks, raising their stature in the eyes of voters and increasing their chances of being elected. Diagrams are not shown.

4. The correlation in the zero-order table is $r_{XY} = -0.13$, with women holding more pro-choice attitudes. Controlling for highest level of schooling provides a partial explanation for this relationship, since it is reduced to –0.04 for college degrees, but increases to –0.22 for high school diplomas. The odds ratios show the same pattern. In the zero-order table the odds ratio is 0.58, whereas it is 0.83 for college degrees and 0.38 for high school diplomas. These results thus suggest an interaction effect: the relationship between gender

and abortion attitude is stronger among high school graduates than among college graduates.

5. The correlation for the zero-order table is $r_{XY} = 0.10$, with parents of school-aged children slightly more likely to vote for the referendum. Controlling for political party yields partial correlations of $r_{XY} = 0.14$ for Democrats and $r_{XY} = 0.10$ for Republicans, suggesting only minimal impact of political party.

6. For the age and attitude zero-order table, $r_{XY} = -0.19$; for the highly religious subtable $r_{XY} = -0.05$; and for the not highly religious subtable $r_{XY} = -0.26$. Similarly, the odds ratio for the zero-order table is 0.47, while the odds ratio is 0.80 for the highly religious subtable and 0.33 for the not highly religious subtable. This interaction effect shows that the relationship is strongest among persons who are not highly religious.

7. The zero-order $r_{XY} = 0.07$ does not completely disappear in the subtables, as it would if gender explained the entire relationship between viewing X-rated films and attitude about extramarital sex. Instead, an interaction effect occurs. For women, the correlation between the two variables is nearly zero ($r_{XY} = 0.02$); while the correlation is slightly stronger ($r_{XY} = 0.09$) for men.

8. (a) −0.05
   (b) 0.19
   (c) 0.53
   (d) 0.08

9. $r_{XY \cdot W} = 0.47$; $t_{172} = 7.0$; reject H_0: $\varrho_{XY \cdot W} = 0$.

10. $r_{XY \cdot W} = -0.80$; $t_{97} = -13.13$; reject H_0: $\varrho_{XY \cdot W} = 0$.

11. More highly educated people are slightly more conservative (36.9%) than those who are less educated (33.8%), $r_{XY} = -0.03$. Holding age constant, the POLVIEWS-EDUC correlation is virtually the same among the younger ($r_{XY} = -0.03$) and among the older ($r_{XY} = -0.04$) respondents. Note that these findings are not statistically significant.

12. Zero-order $r_{XY} = -0.26$; Protestant $r_{XY} = -0.14$; Catholic $r_{XY} = -0.17$. The correlation of religious intensity and attitude toward abortion for a single woman is slightly stronger among Catholics than among Protestants.

13. Zero-order $r_{XY} = -0.06$. The correlations are nearly the same in the two subtables (–0.04 and –0.03), but these two subtable correlations are not statistically significant.

14. $r_{XY} = 0.25$; $r_{XY \cdot W} = 0.25$

15. Zero-order $r_{XY} = -0.07$ (significant at $\alpha = .05$); partial, controlling for number of children, $r_{XY} = -0.06$ (not statistically significant).

Chapter 8

1. $\hat{Y} = 26.76 + 1.81X_1 - 0.63X_2$

2. $\hat{Z}_Y = 0.91Z_1 - 0.84Z_2$

3. For a sample $N = 123$, $F_{4,118} = 1.07$; the critical value is 2.45 at $\alpha = .05$, so do not reject the null hypothesis that the population coefficient of determination is zero. But for sample $N = 1,230$, $F_{4,1225} = 11.11$; the critical value is 2.37 at $\alpha = .05$, so reject the null hypothesis.

4. $t_{b_1} = -1.80$, $df = 263$; c.v. for $\alpha = .01$ one-tailed is 2.326, so do not reject H_0; $t_{b_2} = 2.75$, $df = 263$, so do reject H_0.

5. $t_{b_1} = -3.70$, $df = 297$; c.v. for $\alpha = .001$ is ± 3.29, meaning that b_1 is significantly different from 0 at $\alpha = .001$ for a two-tailed test.

6. $LCL_{95} = -5.86$, $UCL_{95} = -1.80$; $UCL_{99} = -6.50$; $UCL_{99} = -1.16$

7. Education has no significant effect on attendance; each $10,000 of annual income increases annual attendance by almost one and a half events; and women attend 5.40 fewer events per year than men.

8.

Music Category	D_1	D_2	D_3	D_4	D_5	D_6
Country	1	0	0	0	0	0
Rock	0	1	0	0	0	0
Rap	0	0	1	0	0	0
Classical	0	0	0	1	0	0
Jazz	0	0	0	0	1	0
None	0	0	0	0	0	1

9. Eq. 1: $\hat{Y} = a + b_M D_M + b_R D_R + b_X X$

   Eq. 2: $\hat{Y} = a + b_M D_M + b_R D_R + b_X X + b_1 D_M X + b_2 D_R X$

10. (a) $F_{1,714} = 15.44$; c.v. = 10.83, so reject H_0.
    (b) $\hat{Y} = 2.84 - 0.48\ (1) - 0.06\ (45) + 0.07\ (45) = 2.81$ hours per day.

11. (a)

Variable	b_j	t_j	β_j^*
Education	0.022	3.61*	0.076
Age	0.008	6.09*	0.128
Intercept	2.702	26.98*	

*Significant beyond $p < .01$, given critical value 2.58 for two-tailed test.

(b) $R_{adj}^2 = 0.021$; $F_{2,2204} = 23.99$. Because the critical value = 6.91 at $\alpha = .001$, reject H_0.

(c) The higher one's education (net of age), the greater the satisfaction with one's job. The older one is, the greater the satisfaction. The standardized effect of age is larger than the standardized education effect.

12. (a) Separated = −0.004; Divorced = +0.093; Widowed = +0.296; Married = +0.219.
    (b) Difference in $R^2 = 0.035 - 0.021 = 0.014$; $F_{4,2200} = 7.98$; c.v. = 4.62, so reject H_0 that marital status does not increase the coefficient of determination.

13. Because the standardized coefficient (beta weight) for father's education (0.427) is many times larger than the beta for father's occupation (0.070), it is much more important as a predictor of the respondent's own educational attainment. The linear combination of these two independent variables accounts for 21.8% of the variance in respondent's education.

14. (a) $R^2 = 0.137$; $F_{4,2561} = 101.35$; c.v. $= 2.60$, so reject H_0.
    (b) $R^2 = 0.140$; $F_{7,2558} = 59.53$; c.v. $= 2.60$, so reject H_0.
    (c) Difference in $R^2 = 0.140 - 0.137 = 0.003$; $F_{3,2558} = 26.77$; c.v. $= 2.60$, so reject H_0 that age-religious denomination interaction terms do not increase the coefficient of determination.

15. (a)

Region	μ_j	β_j
New England	0.035	0.221
Middle Atlantic	−0.195	−0.009
East North Central	−0.039	0.147
West North Central	0.120	0.306
South Atlantic	0.157	0.343
East South Central	0.134	0.320
West South Central	0.160	0.346
Mountain	−0.111	0.075
Pacific	−0.186	—
Mean/Intercept	4.100	3.914

(b) $\beta_j - 0.186 = \alpha_j$

(c)

Source	SS	df	MS	F
Between	55.88	8	6.984	3.65*
Within	5139.42	2682	1.916	
Total	5195.30	2690		

* Significant beyond $p < .001$, given critical value 3.27.

Chapter 9

1. Because $F_{18,1480} = 2.94$ and c.v. = 2.27 for $\alpha = .001$, reject the null hypothesis. Job satisfaction deviates significantly from a linear relationship with income.

2. Graph not shown. The plotted values show a quadratic relationship in which tuberculosis infection rate falls as median education rises.

3. (a) $15,985
   (b) $23,273
   (c) $56,377
   (d) 5.28 years of education; $14,557 annual income.

4. (a) $10,272
   (b) $25,427
   (c) $44,520

5. More frequent church attendance reduces support for abortion ($p < .001$) and being Catholic also decreases the log odds of abortion support ($p < .05$).

6. For church attendance, $LCL_{95} = -0.246$ and $UCL_{95} = -0.172$; for Catholic religion, $LCL_{95} = -0.511$ and $UCL_{95} = -0.041$.

7. For church attendance, $\exp \beta = .793$; for Catholic religion, $\exp \beta = .788$; for education, $\exp \beta = 1.174$. The odds of supporting abortion decrease by -20.7% with each increase in the church attendance scale; are -21.2% lower for Catholics than for persons of other religions; and increase by $+17.4\%$ with each additional year of schooling.

8. (a) $p = .201$
   (b) $p = .826$

9. $G^2 = 213.43$, $df = 3$. Because c.v. = 16.266 at $\alpha = .001$, reject the null hypothesis. At least one coefficient is significantly different from zero. Pseudo $R^2 = 0.552$.

10. For never-married men, a: $t = 7.08$, $p < .001$; X_1: $t = -8.25$, $p < .001$; X_2: $t = -12.28$, $p < .001$; X_3: $t = -1.34$, $p > .05$.

   For previously married men, a: $t = 0.39$, $p > .05$; X_1: $t = 1.60$, $p > .05$; X_2: $t = -2.40$, $p < .05$; X_3: $t = -3.58$, $p < .001$.

   Relative to currently married men, never-married men are likely to be younger and to have had fewer children. Relative to currently married men, previously married men are likely to have had fewer children and less education.

11. The significance test of the difference between $R^2 = 0.068$ and $\hat{\eta}^2 = 0.079$ produces $F_{19,2306} = 1.45$. At $\alpha = .05$, c.v. $= 1.57$; therefore, we do not reject the null hypothesis that education and television viewing are only linearly related.

12. $\hat{L}_i = 28.524 + 0.671X_i - 0.0064X_i^2$ $R^2_{adj} = 0.021$

   s.e. $= (2.053)$ (0.088) (0.001)

   For age: $UCL_{95} = 0.843$; $LCL_{95} = 0.500$.

   For age squared: $UCL_{95} = -0.005$; $LCL_{95} = -0.008$.

   At 52.42 years, occupational prestige reaches its expected maximum value of 46.11 prestige points.

13. $\hat{L}_i = -1.484 + 0.058X_1 + 0.019X_2 - 0.013X_3$

   s.e. $= (0.260)$ (0.120) (0.003) (0.004)

   $t = $ (-5.71) (-0.48) (6.33) (-3.25)

   Sample $N = 1,667$; equation -2 log likelihood $= 1,751.0$; constant only -2 log likelihood $= 1,787.2$; $G^2 = 36.2$, $df = 3$, $p < .001$. Correct predictions: 100% disagree, 0% agree.

14. Difference in $G^2 = 1,751.0 - 1,731.6 = 19.4$; $df = 1$; $p < .001$.

15. For females, $\exp \beta = .045$; for southern residence, $\exp \beta = 1.432$. Women are 95.5% less likely than men to own a gun, and southerners are 43.2% more likely to own a gun than are persons living in other regions.

Chapter 10

1. Odds in favor for entire table = 0.693; odds for women = 0.676; odds for men = 0.718; odds ratio = 0.943. Women are only slightly less likely than men to support abortion for any reason.

2.

<table>
<tr><td colspan="3">Capital Punishment by Race</td></tr>
<tr><td></td><td colspan="2">Race</td></tr>
<tr><td>Do you favor or oppose capital punishment
for persons convicted of murder?</td><td>White</td><td>Black</td></tr>
<tr><td>Favor</td><td>1,616</td><td>179</td></tr>
<tr><td>Oppose</td><td>449</td><td>180</td></tr>
</table>

3. $\mu = 5.648$; $\lambda_1^R = 0.247$; $\lambda_1^P = -0.388$; $\lambda_{11}^{RP} = 0.480$

4. $\hat{s}_\lambda = 0.034$; $t_{\lambda^P} = 7.26$; $t_{\lambda^R} = -11.41$; $t_{\lambda^{PR}} = 14.12$

5. (a) $F_{11} = 265.2$; $F_{12} = 463.9$; $F_{21} = 225.9$; $F_{22} = 392.9$
   (b) $L^2 = 241.0$; reject null hypothesis because c.v. = 10.8, $df = 1$, for $\alpha = .05$.

6. The conditional odds ratio for gun law opinion and too much spending versus about right is +1.33 for gun owners and +1.50 for non-owners. The conditional odds ratio for gun law opinion and too much spending versus too little is +3.77 for owners and +1.11 for non-owners. Both gun owners and non-owners about equally favor a gun law, if they think too much is being spent to halt crime, relative to about the right amount of spending. However, gun owners more strongly favor a gun law than do non-owners, if they think too much is being spent to halt crime, relative to too little spending.

7. Model 5 fits the data better than models 1, 2, and 4, but model 5 does not fit better than model 3 because $L_3^2 - L_5^2 = 4.5 - 3.9 = 0.6$ for $df_3 - df_5 = 4 - 2 = 2$, while c.v. = 5.99 at $\alpha = .05$.

8. The two smallest BIC statistics are for model 7 (BIC = −21.4) and model 8 (BIC = −20.1). Testing the differences in model L^2s,

model 7 fits significantly better than model 8 ($L_7^2 - L_8^2 = 15.0 - 9.0 = 6.00$; $df_7 - df_8 = 5 - 4 = 1$; c.v. = 10.8 at $\alpha = .001$). Hence, both the $\{CV\}$ and $\{PV\}$ effects seem essential to fit the data, but the $\{EV\}$ parameter is not necessary.

9. (a) 258.6
    (b) 21.2

10. (a) 1.916
    (b) −2.284

11. For the independence model $L^2 = 164.7$, $df = 6$; reject the null hypothesis because c.v. = 22.5 at $\alpha = .001$.

12. For the independence model $L^2 = 31.3$, $df = 1$; reject the null hypothesis because c.v. = 26.1 at $\alpha = .001$. For the saturated model $\{GS\}$, the parameters are

$\mu = 5.998$; $\lambda_1^G = -0.435$; $\lambda_1^S = -0.039$; $\lambda_{11}^{GS} = 0.146$.

13. Because the L^2 for the model $\{CI\}\{CS\}\{IS\}$ is 0.4, $df = 1$, $p > .50$, no significant difference occurs between men and women. The effect parameters, where C = CHILDS, I = CHLDIDEL, and S = SEX, are

$\mu = 5.265$; $\lambda^C = 0.441$; $\lambda^I = 0.100$; $\lambda^S = -0.159$; $\lambda^{CI} = 0.246$;
$\lambda^{CS} = 0.070$; $\lambda^{IS} = -0.028$

The actual number of children and ideal number strongly covary, and although men report having fewer children than women, the ideal number does not differ significantly across gender.

14. The model statistics, where R = RELITEN, C = CONCHURH, A = ATTEND, and $N = 975$, are shown below:

Model	L^2	df	BIC
1. $\{CR\}\{CA\}\{RA\}$	0.4	1	−6.5
2. $\{CR\}\{CA\}$	230.9	2	217.1
3. $\{CR\}\{RA\}$	20.1	2	6.3
4. $\{CA\}\{RA\}$	24.1	2	10.4

Both L^2 and BIC identify model 1 as the best fit.

15. The model containing all two-variable effects is the best fit because it has $L^2 = 5.7$, $df = 2$, $p = .06$, and no model that deletes one of the two-variable effects has ΔL^2 that is not significant at $\alpha = .05$. The effect parameters, where A = AGE, P = PRAYER, R = RELIG, are

$\mu = 3.867$; $\lambda_1^P = 0.224$; $\lambda_1^A = 0.175$; $\lambda_1^R = 1.577$;
$\lambda_2^R = 0.742$; $\lambda_{11}^{PA} = 0.143$; $\lambda_{11}^{PR} = -0.542$; $\lambda_{12}^{PR} = -0.385$;
$\lambda_{11}^{RA} = 0.057$; $\lambda_{11}^{CE} = 0.234$

Younger persons are more likely than older people to approve the Court's prayer decision. Protestants are the least likely to approve, followed by Catholics, then Jews. The absence of a significant three-variable effect means that the effect of age is the same for each denomination, or that the denomination effect is the same within both age groups.

Chapter 11

1. A sample answer: The greater the perceived gap in corporate resource distribution, the greater the likelihood of union organizing.

2.

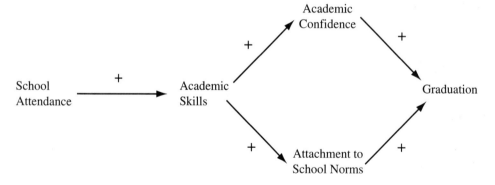

3. $r'_{QT} = p_{TQ} + p_{TS}p_{SQ} + p_{TS}p_{SR}r_{RQ}$

4. (a) SES has a larger indirect causal effect on satisfaction (0.12) than age at marriage (0.105).
   (b) 15% of the variance in marital satisfaction is explained.

5. (a) *A* has a larger indirect causal effect on *E* (0.20) than does *B* (0.024).
   (b) 17% of the variance in *E* is explained by *A*, *B*, *C*, and *D*.

6. $r'_{13} = 0.77$

7. $r'_{BD} = p_{DB} + p_{DC}p_{CB} + p_{DC}p_{CA}r_{AB}$; the first two terms are causal and the third is a correlated effect.

8. (a) $r'_{BD} = 0.56$
   (b) $r'_{AD} = 0.81$

9.

	Y_1	Y_2	Y_3	Y_4	Y_5
Y_1	1.00	0.40	0.20	0.04	0.02
Y_2		1.00	0.50	0.10	0.04
Y_3			1.00	0.20	0.08
Y_4				1.00	0.40
Y_5					1.00

10. $Y_2 = p_{21}Y_1 + p_{2V}V$; $Y_3 = p_{31}Y_1 + p_{32}Y_2 + p_{3U}U$

11. Both mother's and father's religious attendance affect respondent's attendance, directly and indirectly through religious intensity. Religious intensity has the strongest direct effect on respondent's attendance.

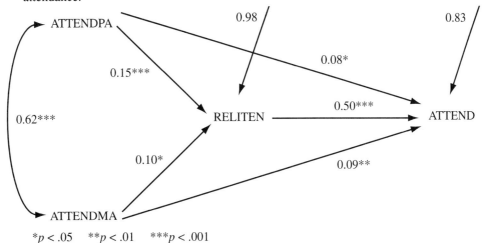

*p < .05 **p < .01 ***p < .001

12. Mother's and father's occupational prestige both influence respondent's educational level, which then affects respondent's occupational prestige.

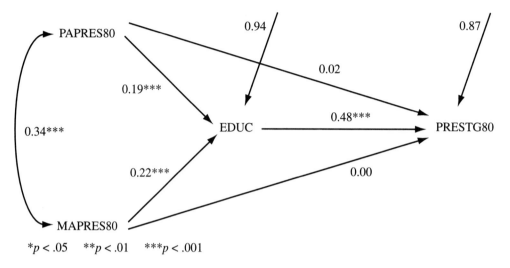

*p < .05   **p < .01   ***p < .001

13. Education does not directly affect charitable giving, but has an indirect effect through family income.

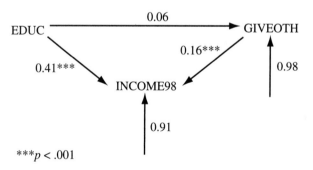

***p < .001

14. Higher education leads to lower intolerance and to higher occupational prestige, but education does not affect intolerance indirectly through occupational prestige.

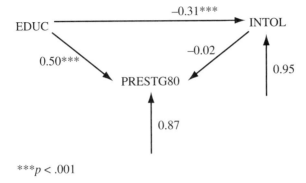

***p < .001

15. Higher education leads to less conservative political views, while more income results in greater conservatism. Neither education nor income directly affects political party affiliation, but more conservative respondents are more likely to identify with the Republican party.

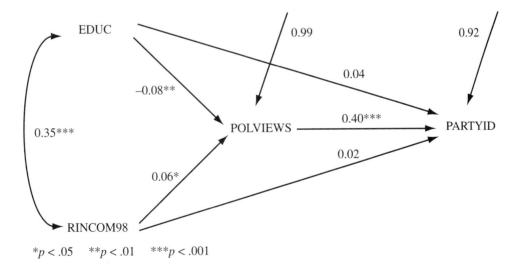

*p < .05   **p < .01   ***p < .001

Chapter 12

1. $\varrho_X = \dfrac{\sigma_T^2}{\sigma_X^2} = \dfrac{0.64}{0.81} = 0.79$

2. Reliability = 0.81

3. Confidence in the courts has the highest factor loading, and confidence in churches has the lowest, with the others intermediate. Reliabilities range from 0.64 for courts to 0.11 for churches. The estimated correlation between CONBIZ and CONSCHLS is 0.26; between CONCHURH and CONCOUR is 0.26.

4. The RMSEA and GFI indicate a reasonable fit, but the p-level suggests some room for improvement.

5. The difference in model $\chi^2 = 19.6 - 11.7 = 7.9$ for 1 df shows a significant improvement in fit at $p < .01$. The first factor consists of private-sector institutions, the second factor of public-sector institutions. The high correlation between the two factors shows that people who express confidence in one type of institution tend to express the same level of confidence in the other type.

6. All measures of fit indicate that the model has a close fit to the data. The three job values have high factor loadings, with promotion being the most reliable indicator. Older persons and those with high-prestige occupations feel that these job values are less important, but income level has no impact.

7. The model falls between a close and a reasonable fit to the data. The three job values have high factor loadings, with promotion again the most reliable indicator. Persons in high-prestige occupations feel that these job values are less important, but neither education nor income level have significant impacts.

8. The RMSEA shows a close fit of the model to the data, but chi-square with $p = .011$, which suggests room for improvement. High-SES respondents are less likely to report these job values are important. From the results of the preceding problem, the SES effect seems to reflect primarily respondent occupational prestige.

9. The RMSEA shows a reasonable fit of the model to the data. Although GFI and AGFI are high, chi-square with $p = .019$ suggests room for improvement. More conservative respondents say the federal government is spending too much on these social problems.

10. RMSEA shows a reasonable fit of the model to the data, but GFI, AGFI, and chi-square with $p < .001$ all indicate some room for improvement. Higher-SES persons and those expressing stronger religious beliefs are more likely to pray often.

11.

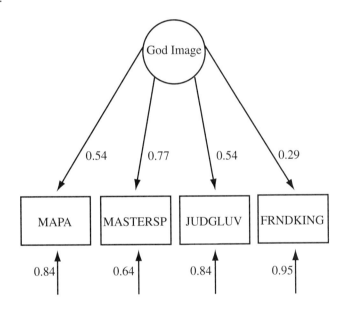

The goodness-of-fit statistics are $\chi^2 = 17.7$, $df = 2$, $p = .0001$; GFI = 0.99; AGFI = 0.97; and RMSEA = 0.075, with 90% confidence interval from 0.045 to 0.110. Although the RMSEA indicates a reasonable fit for a one-factor solution, the fourth indicator has an especially low factor loading, suggesting that response to the Friend-King image does not strongly covary with the Mother-Spouse-Lover versus Father-Master-Judge patterns.

12.

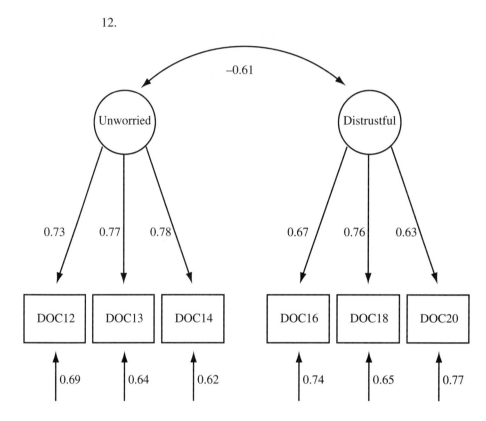

The two-factor model is preferred. Its goodness-of-fit statistics are $\chi^2 = 12.3$, $df = 8$, $p = .14$; GFI = 1.00; AGFI = 0.99; and RMSEA = 0.022, with 90% confidence interval from 0.000 to 0.045. The RMSEA indicates a close fit for this two-factor solution. High scores on the indicators of the first factor express an absence of worry about medical mistreatment; high scores on the second factor's indicators express distrust in doctors. The negative correlation between the two factors means that persons who agree with the first factor tend to disagree with the second.

13.

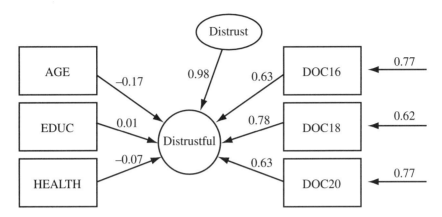

The goodness-of-fit statistics are $\chi^2 = 9.4$, $df = 6$, $p = .150$; GFI = 1.00; AGFI = 0.99; and RMSEA = 0.021, with 90% confidence interval from 0.000 to 0.046. The RMSEA indicates a close fit for this MIMIC model. The coefficient for age is significant at $p < .001$; for health at $p < .05$; but not significant for education. Healthier and older persons express less distrust in their physicians.

14.

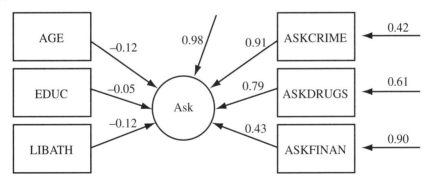

The goodness-of-fit statistics, based on a sample of 825 cases, are $\chi^2 = 18.4$, $df = 6$, $p = .005$; GFI = 1.00; AGFI = 0.99; and RMSEA = 0.050, with 90% confidence interval from 0.025 to 0.077. The RMSEA indicates a reasonable fit for this MIMIC model. The coefficients for AGE and EDUC are significant at $p < .05$, but the effect of LIBATH is not significant. Older and better-educated respondents are less opposed to governmental inquiries into personal matters, but civil libertarian views are unrelated to preferences about governmental inquiries.

15.

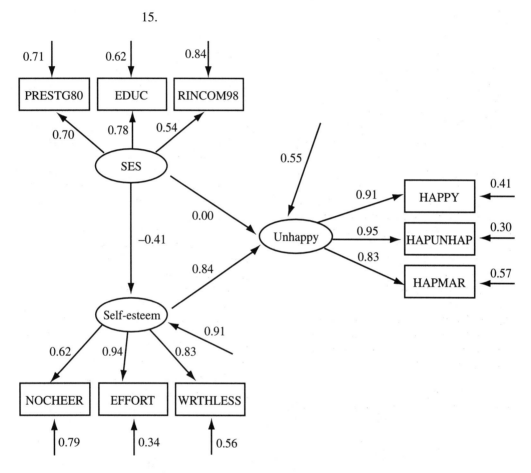

The goodness-of-fit statistics, based on a sample of 384 cases, are $\chi^2 = 50.2$, $df = 24$, $p = .001$; GFI = 0.99; AGFI = 0.99; and RMSEA = 0.053, with 90% confidence interval from 0.032 to 0.074. The RMSEA indicates a reasonable fit for this causal path model. All parameters are significant at $p < .001$, except the nonsignificant path from SES to Unhappy. People with low self-esteem have higher levels of unhappiness. Higher socioeconomic status indirectly decreases unhappiness by reducing low self-esteem: $(-0.41)(0.84) = -0.34$.

INDEX

STATISTICS FOR SOCIAL DATA ANALYSIS
Fourth Edition
Edited by Janet Tilden
Production supervision by Kim Vander Steen
Designed by Jeanne Calabrese Design, River Forest, Illinois
Paper, Finch Opaque
Typeface, Times
Printed and bound by Quebecor World, Fairfield, Pennsylvania